Practicing Financial Planning
for Professionals

SID MITTRA
with
TOM POTTS
and
LEON LABRECQUE

RH

RH Publishing
Rochester, Michigan 48307

Library of Congress Cataloging-in-Publication Data

Mittra, Sid *with* Potts, Tom *and* LaBrecque, Leon
  Practicing Financial Planning for Professionals
  Sid Mittra, *with* Tom Potts *and* Leon LaBrecque

   p. cm.
  Includes bibliographical references.
  1. Finance, Personal.. 2. Investments. I. Title.
HG179.M55 1990
332.024 ' 0622--dc20   89-48294
                CIP

RH
RH Publishing

© 2005 by RH Publishing, Ninth Edition
Rochester, Michigan 48307

The publisher offers discounts on this book when ordered
in bulk quantities. For more information write:
 RH Publishing
 1595 Pebble Creek Drive
 Rochester, Michigan 48307
 Tel. (734) 502-5611
 E-Mail: bob.crane@publishnow.net
 Web Site: www.publishnow.net

Printed in the United States of America

ISBN 1-881995-01-1

Foreword

by
Harold Evensky
John Henry McDonald
Stacy L. Schaus

Harold Evensky, CFP

I've been in the practice of financial planning for a long time. Even better, I was lucky enough to enter the profession during its relative infancy. My propitious timing has afforded me the privilege of meeting and working with a number of the pioneers who helped financial planning evolve from a concept to an internationally recognized profession. Sid Mittra stands in the front rank of those pioneers.

Having said that, I hate to begin my foreword by critiquing such a fine author, but I must. In his Preface, Sid refers to *Practicing Financial Planning for Professionals* as an "introductory financial planning text." I beg to differ. It may be, among many other things, an introductory text, but limiting the description to that narrow definition is akin to calling a Bentley a car. Let me explain.

The publication in 1990 of the first edition of *Practicing Financial Planning, A Complete Guide for Professionals* was a seminal event in our profession. Prior to its publication, the primary texts in our field were either quasi-academic publications, focused on single elements of the planning process or simplistic "how to" guides designed to package financial planning as a product instead of a professional process. Sid, a practitioner with impeccable academic credentials, by publishing *Practicing Financial Planning (PFP)*, provided financial planners with a critical missing element in the move towards professionalism. *PFP* provided (and like the Energizer bunny, with every new edition, continues to provide), practitioners, both new and old, an academically sound and practitioner friendly . . . .

See how hard it is to describe this book, I can't even finish my own sentence, as I can't think of a single word to accurately describe Sid's work. It's simply too multifaceted. Even a summary description requires its own paragraph.

For aspiring planners, *Practicing Financial Planning* serves as a comprehensive and effective educational program. For new planners, it is a daily reference guide to fill in areas of technical weakness and a practical guide providing experientially based guidance for those occasions when the planner's limited experience comes up short. For experienced planners, it's an invaluable educational reference when facing an issue only infrequently encountered and a handy technical reference when the little gray cells simply refuse to recall that last bit of detail necessary to finalize a recommendation. Finally, the innumerable and elegantly presented tables, graphs and flow charts are powerful tools when used in conjunction with clients' continuing education.

And, if that wasn't enough, there's more. My partner, Deena Katz, developed her original practice by specializing in working with "women in transition," i.e., widows and divorcees. She says she soon discovered that many of her clients, although well educated, had never been provided the opportunity to learn about even the fundamentals of basic financial management. Deena's solution was to offer "Up To Speed" courses; short, targeted but substantive courses on important areas of financial management. In many ways, in addition, to all of the benefits already noted, *PFP* is also a handsomely bound, easily portable collection of "Up To Speed" courses on all of the diverse issues faced by a financial planner in today's complex world.

In this process, you're treated as a professional, for one of the unique and most valuable attributes of *PFP* is, you'll not just learn the facts regarding issues but you'll learn the "why." For example, if your background is primarily tax or insurance, the investment section will not only bring you "up to speed" on index fund investing, it will also explain the "why" regarding some of the less known risks of index funds (e.g., skewed weighting systems and index tracking error). It will not just introduce you to ETFs and their tax advantages, it will also explain the "exchange in kind" basis for the tax advantage. There's even the likelihood that readers will improve their knowledge in areas of their own current specialty. I'm prepared to wager that many investment oriented practitioners' advice to clients will be improved after reading the warnings about the potential misuse of Alphas and Betas. Almost all will learn from the discussion regarding the use of the Sharpe's selection ratio in lieu of his Sharpe Ratio.

Now in its Ninth edition, *PFP* is not only a publication, it has become an institution. Publications tend to be static, *PFP* is anything but. That's good news for a profession with "planning" in its name. As my partner, Deena, so often reminds me, our job is to be our clients' futurist; hence those providing books for our profession need to be our futurist. Sid continues to deliver. Each edition has contributed to moving our profession forward and offered practitioners new and unique benefits. However this edition, the Ninth, by incorporating the complementary multi-author expertise of other recognized professionals, it enables the end product to more than meet Sid's goal of elevating "the book to a much higher professional and practical level, vastly expanding its coverage, improving its clarity, and adding new dimensions particularly suited to address the special financial problems of our time."

This metamorphous didn't happen by accident. It's a combined result of Sid's extensive academic knowledge and practical experience, his careful selection of his co-authors and his creativity. In this edition, his creativity includes a wonderful weaving of theory with reality and an emphasis on planning versus facts. The book would be worth having for the case studies alone.

Having personally, over the years, used Sid's efforts for all of these reasons, I speak from experience. *PFP* sits in easy arm reach behind my desk. It's more than a reference tool on my desk; it's a convenient second opinion, a handy reminder of technical issues I've forgotten and a quick education on issues I never learned. For example, not long ago I had a new client with a significant investment in a single premium whole life policy. Although I'd not had occasion to review such a policy in many years, I was proud of myself that I at least remembered its basic structure. I also remembered that there had been an earlier tax act that significantly altered the tax status of withdrawals. Unfortunately, I didn't remember the Act or the specifics of the impact. A quick reference to *PFP* led me to the details of TAMRA 1988 and enabled me to make an effective and professional recommendation.

In a field as dynamic as financial planning potential, entrants, new practitioners and experienced professional all need the very best and most timely information available. No one delivers this better than Sid, his co-authors and *PFP*.

> Harold Evensky, CFP
> Inductee, Movers & Shakers Hall of Fame
> Former Chairman, Certified Financial Planner,
> Board of Standards

John Henry McDonald , CFP, ChFC, CLU

In the last 35 years or so, a profession has been born. In my opinion, the profession is still in its infancy. Academia is far ahead. As the task of managing one's financial affairs has gotten increasingly complex, academics have compiled sources of information that aid the professional in defining and applying huge bodies of information that the public can consume. This is no easy task. Sid Mittra with Tom Potts and Leon LaBrecque has handled this task readily. The book, *"Practicing Financial Planning for Professionals"* starts with the basics and takes the practitioner on a journey that ends with completing a *comprehensive* financial plan. Nothing is missing.

As seasoned financial professionals know, financial planning is a process, a process that can be recognized and defined. The authors begin the book with an elegant explanation of the financial planning process. This is indeed where any book entitled *"Practicing Financial Planning for Professionals"* should begin. Also emphasized is the role of the client, the responsibility of communication, and the emphasis upon the CFP credentials as a sign of a competent and ethical planner. Congratulations to the authors for this stance.

This book starts with the building blocks of a comprehensive financial plan and develops each of the sections completely. *Each section stands alone*, and can be used as a source of reference. Part 2, entitled **Key Financial Planning Areas: S-E-C-U-R-I-T-Y** starts with the theory of risk transfer, takes us through the basic types of life insurance policies and guides our understanding of all types of life insurance before the discussion moves to life insurance planning. Basic primer? Sure. Substantial and complete? Absolutely!

Health-insurance, homeowners' insurance, automotive insurance, liability insurance-- all are nicely covered. No stones are unturned. This is the substance that all financial planning professionals must have at their fingertips to provide a comprehensive overview of risk management.

Cash management, educational planning, basic and complex estate planning, retirement needs and qualified plan design--all are handled evenly and thoroughly in this book. I looked hard for areas that fall short and couldn't find any. The authors even address such specialized topics as practice management and the sale of a financial planning firm. Nuts to bolts, beginning to end, the Alpha and the Omega of financial planning, are right here on my desk. Thank you gentlemen for this book.

No one who holds himself out as a financial planner should be without it.

John Henry McDonald , CFP, ChFC, CLU
President CEO
Austin Asset Management Company

Stacy L. Schaus, CFP®, MBA

Financial planning is more important today than ever before and will only continue to escalate in prevalence and significance in the coming years. We're in a changing world, from global competition, to employer trends from Defined Benefit to Defined Contribution, to a crisis in Retiree health care, to an uncertain tax code. Now more than ever, our clients need our help in this ever changing complex world.

I've worked in the investment and consulting field serving corporations for nearly 25 years now. Never has the interest in financial education and planning been greater than it is today. Employers are interested in offering support to their workforces, and they need it. Less than 10% of American workers have a financial plan, while arguably 100% need one. One in four workers is experiencing financial distress that negatively impacts their work productivity. The cost to corporations of this stress can equal 2% of payroll each year. Based on US gross payroll, the cost to US employers in productivity alone is as much as $40 billion a year. In addition there are the billions spent on employee benefit communications: 401(k), pension, health care, life insurance, and so on. Yet, in my years, I have yet to see instructions on the biggest benefit an employee gets: their paycheck. Employers turn to us, the financial planning profession to help in this matter: we have the means to reduce employee stress, increase employee awareness, promote financial security and increase the productivity of their workforce.

Whether we like it or not, we're all required to be financial planners at some level as we manage our own budgets, invest for our retirements and save for other important life goals. Yet, some of us are better skilled at financial planning than others. In *Practicing Financial Planning for Professionals*, you'll learn from some of our country's finest experts in the financial planning field. Authors Sid Mittra, Tom Potts and Leon LaBrecque together have nearly a century of experience in financial planning, covering the expanse of risk management, education planning, tax strategies, investment management, estate planning and more. You'll find the authors present the breadth of financial planning topics and issues with both insight and clarity.

Regardless of where you are in your development as a financial professional, you'll find this book invaluable. For beginners, it provides the basic concepts and applications such as calculating the time value of money. For more experienced planners, the book summarizes key topics as an introduction or reminder of what you perhaps once learned. For the most advanced, it provides a vital reference for facts and figures that no single mind could possibly retain or at least keep up to date. When faced with a new financial planning topic, or one that is a bit rusty or perhaps you know well but just one to check the facts – *Practicing Financial Planning for Professionals* is the book you'll reach for first. This is a 'must have' book for all of us.

Stacy L. Schaus, CFP®, MBA
Principal,
Hewitt Associates

Contents

Foreword, v
Preface to the Ninth Edition, xxiii
A Personal Message - 1990, xxvii
About the Authors, xxxi
Acknowledgments, xxxv

PART I   The General Setting

CHAPTER 1
The Emerging Role of the Financial Planner, 1-1

Demands of the Financial Future, 1-1
The Emerging Trends, 1-1
  Changing Family Patterns, 1-1
  The Reality of the American Dream, 1-2
  The Realities of Retirement, 1-2
  A Summary View, 1-2
Concept of Personal Financial Planning, 1-3
Key Areas of Financial Planning, 1-3
The Client, 1-4
  The Emerging Client, 1-4
  The Common Denominators, 1-5
Communication, 1-8
  The Potential Client, 1-8
  The Planning Client, 1-8
Coordination, 1-12
  Attorney, 1-13
  Accountant, 1-13
  Portfolio Manager, 1-14
  Insurance Counselor, 1-14

  Other Professionals, 1-14
  Summing Up, 1-14
Competence, 1-15
  Academic Degrees, 1-15
  The Credentials, 1-15
  The Experience, 1-16
  Continuing Education, 1-16
  Summing Up, 1-16
Commitment to Ethics, 1-17

CHAPTER 2
The Personal Financial Planning Process, 2-1

Introduction, 2-1
Financial Planning Process, 2-2
Subject Areas of Personal Financial
  Planning, 2-2
Qualifying a Potential Client, 2-3
  Case 1, 2-3
  Case 2, 2-5
  Case 3, 2-6
Signing of a Formal Contract, 2-6
Gathering the Data, 2-7
  Quantitative Data, 2-28
  Qualitative Data, 2-29
Processing and Analyzing Financial Data, 2-29
  Preliminary Analysis, 2-29
  Establish Client Objectives, 2-30
  Data Refinement, 2-30
  Analysis of Client Information, 2-31

Recommendations for Action, 2-32
  Basic Recommendations, 2-32
  Plan Presentation, 2-32
Implementation, 2-33
Monitoring and Reviewing, 2-33

CHAPTER 3
Time Value of Money: The Universal Tool, 3-1

THE BASIC CONCEPT, 3-1
Introduction, 3-1
Simple Interest, 3-1
Future Value: Fixed Sum, 3-2
  Multiple Year Annual Compounding, 3-2
  Rule of 72, 3-5
  Multiple Compound Periods Per Year, 3-6
Present Value: Fixed Sum, 3-7
Future Value: Annuity, 3-12
Present Value: Annuity, 3-15
Annuity Due: A Refinement, 3-16
  Annuity Due: Future Value, 3-17
  Annuity Due: Present Value, 3-17
Present Value of a Perpetuity, 3-17
Present Value of an Uneven Payment Series, 3-18
Nominal Versus Effective Interest Rate, 3-20
Role of Inflation in Financial Calculations, 3-20
Internal Rate of Return, 3-21
Problem Solving with the HP-12C Calculator, 3-23
Safety through Risk Management Planning, 3-23
  Problem I, 3-23
  Solution I, 3-23
  Problem II, 3-24
  Solution II, 3-24
Educational Planning, 3-24
  Problem III, 3-24
  Solution III, 3-25
Cash Management, Savings, Credit, and Debt Planning, 3-26
  Problem IV, 3-26
  Solution IV, 3-27
  Problem V, 3-27
  Solution V, 3-27
  Problem VI, 3-28
  Solution VI, 3-28
  Problem VII, 3-29
  Solution VII, 3-30

Ultimate Disposition through Estate Planning, 3-30
  Problem VIII, 3-30
  Solution VIII, 3-31
Retirement Planning, 3-31
  Problem IX, 3-31
  Solution IX, 3-31
Investment Planning, 3-32
  Problem X, 3-32
  Solution X, 3-32
  Problem XI, 3-33
  Solution XI, 3-33
Tax Planning, 3-33
  Problem XII, 3-33
  Solution XII, 3-33
Yearning for Financial Independence Planning, 3-35
  Problem XIII, 3-35
  Solution XIII, 3-35

PART II Key Financial Planning Areas: S-E-C-U-R-I-T-Y

SECTION I *S*: Safety through Risk Management Planning, 4-1

CHAPTER 4
Life Insurance: Structure, Concepts, and Planning Strategies, 4-1

SECTION I
LIFE INSURANCE: AN OVERVIEW, 4-1
Introduction, 4-1
Theory of Risk Transfer: Handling Risk, 4-2
  Risk Avoidance, 4-2
  Risk Retention, 4-3
  Risk Reduction, 4-3
  Risk Sharing, 4-3
  Risk Transfer, 4-3
Basic Types of Life Insurance Policies, 4-4
  Term Insurance, 4-7
  Cash Value Insurance, 4-12
  TAMRA of 1988, 4-17
  The Penalty Tax, 4-18
  Additional Advantages, 4-18
Universal Life, 4-18
Blended Insurance Policy, 4-21
Variable Life, 4-22
Variable Universal Life, 4-22
Interest-Sensitive Whole Life, 4-23
Adjustable Life Insurance, 4-23

Survivorship Life (Second-to-Die) Policy, 4-24
  First-to-Die Policies, 4-24
  Second-to-Die Policies, 4-25
Survivorship Variable Life, 4-27
Life Insurance for Individual Family Members, 4-27
  Spousal Insurance, 4-27
  Insurance for Children, 4-27
Group Life Insurance, 4-28
Cafeteria Plans, 4-29
  Insurance Premium - IRS Code Section 106, 4-30
  Unreimbursed Medical Expenses - IRS Code Section 105, 4-30
  Child or Dependent Care Assistance - IRS Code Section 129, 4-30
  Advantages of Cafeteria Plans, 4-30
Taxation of Life Insurance, 4-31
  Distribution upon Death, 4-31
  Distribution during Life, 4-32
Life Insurance and Estate Taxes, 4-33
Switching of Policies, 4-33
Ratings of Insurance Companies, 4-35
  An Overview, 4-35
  Role of Guaranteed Funds, 4-35
  Rating Agencies, 4-35

SECTION II
LIFE INSURANCE PLANNING, 4-38
Determination of Life Insurance Needs, 4-38
  Capital Needs Analysis, 4-39
Cost of Life Insurance, 4-40
  Basic Considerations, 4-40
  The Net-Cost Method, 4-41
  Interest-Adjusted Cost Index, 4-42
  Benchmark Method, 4-43
Loans from a Life Insurance Policy, 4-44
Life Insurance Settlement Options, 4-45
  Basic Considerations, 4-45
  Lump-Sum Payment: Tax-Free, 4-46
  Fixed Annuity: Partially Taxable, 4-46
  Variable Annuity Option, 4-47
  Indexed Annuity, 4-48
  Other Options, 4-48
  Funds Left with Insurance Company, 4-48
  Life Insurance in Irrevocable Trust, 4-49
Additional Life Insurance Planning Techniques, 4-50
  Buy-Sell Agreement, 4-50
  Section 419 Plan, 4-51
  Insurance in Qualified Plans, 4-51
  Key Man Insurance, 4-52
  Deferred Compensation, 4-52

Split-Dollar Life Insurance, 4-53
Ownership Methods, 4-55
Conclusion, 4-55
Insurance for the Professional, 4-55

SECTION III
LIFE INSURANCE NEEDS: A REAL WORLD EXAMPLE, 4-56

SECTION IV
MISCELLANEOUS LIFE INSURANCE ISSUES, 4-60
Capital Maximization Strategy (CMS), 4-60
  Introduction, 4-60
  The Basic Framework, 4-60
  Who Should Consider A CMS Plan?, 4-61
  How the Loan Works, 4-61
Life Settlement Options, 4-61
  Appraisal, 4-62
  Providers, 4-62
  Taxes, 4-63
Living Benefit Provision (Guaranteed Minimum Income Benefit), 4-63
  Managing Transfer Assets in a "B Trust", 4-64
New Allure For Defined Benefit Plans, 4-64
  New Split Dollar Regulations, 4-65
No – Lapse Guaranteed Option, 4-67

CHAPTER 5
Health, Homeowner's, Automobile, and Liability Insurance: Structure, Concepts, and Planning, 5-1

GENERAL PRINCIPLES, 5-1
Introduction, 5-1
Insurance Against Significant Risks, 5-2
Shopping for Insurance, 5-2
Loss Control through Preventive Measures, 5-3
Organization of Personal Records, 5-3

SECTION I
HEALTH INSURANCE, 5-4
Introduction, 5-4
Need for Health Insurance, 5-4
Types of Health Insurance, 5-5
  Hospital Insurance, 5-5
  Surgical Insurance, 5-5
  Medical Expense Insurance, 5-6
  Major Medical Expense Insurance, 5-6

Comprjehensive Health Insurance, 5-6
Dental Expense Insurance, 5-7
Eye Care Insurance, 5-7
Supplemental Health Insurance, 5-8
Disability Income Insurance, 5-8
    The Basic Need, 5-8
    Types of Disability Insurance, 5-8
    Waiting Period, 5-8
    Definition of Disability, 5-9
    Integration with Social Security, 5-9
    Determining the Income Need, 5-10
    Features of a Good Policy, 5-10
    Cost of a Disability Policy, 5-11
    Coordination of Benefits, 5-12
Disability-To-LTC "Conversion" Policies,
5-12
Filling Disability Benefit Gaps, 5-13
Group Health Insurance, 5-13
    An Overview, 5-13
    Important Developments, 5-15
Sources of Health Insurance, 5-15
    Blue Cross and Blue Shield, 5-16
    Health Maintenance Organizations
        (HMOs), 5-16
    Preferred Provider Organizations (PPOs),
        5-17
    Self-Funded Employee Health Benefits, 5-18
    Commercial Insurance Companies, 5-18
    Government Health Care Insurance, 5-18
    Gaps in Medicare, 5-19
Recent Improvements in Medicare, 5-23
Medicare Act Creates Healthy Savings Ac-
counts, 5-24
Medicare Prescription Drug Improvement &
Modernization Act of 2003, 5-26
    Medicare Supplement Policies, 5-27
    Long-Term Health Care, 5-27
    Private Long-Term Care Coverage, 5-30
The Ideal Health Insurance Company, 5-31
The Ideal Health Insurance Plan, 5-32
A Planning Strategy, 5-33
    Self-Analysis, 5-33

SECTION II
THE HOMEOWNER'S POLICY, 5-33
Introduction, 5-33
The Policy Forms, 5-34
Major Provisions, 5-40
    The Home, 5-40
    Unscheduled Personal Property, 5-40
    The Cost Issue, 5-41
    Special Insurance, 5-42
    Miscellaneous Considerations, 5-42
The Planning Strategy, 5-45

    Self-Analysis, 5-45
    Annual Check-up, 5-45

SECTION III
AUTOMOBILE INSURANCE POLICY, 5-47
Introduction, 5-47
Basic Coverages of Personal Auto Policy,
    5-49
Liability Coverage (Part A), 5-49
    Medical Payments (Part B), 5-50
    Uninsured Motorists (Part C), 5-50
    Coverage for Damage to Insured's Auto
        (Part D), 5-50
Duties after Accident or Loss (Part E),
    5-51
    General Provisions (Part F), 5-51
    Factors that Affect Premiums, 5-51
    Miscellaneous Considerations, 5-52
No-Fault Insurance, 5-53
    A Summary, 5-53
The Planning Strategy, 5-54
    Self-Analysis, 5-54
    Annual Check-up, 5-54

SECTION IV
**MISCELLANEOUS INSURANCE
    COVERAGE, 5-56**
Umbrella Liability Insurance, 5-56
Director's Liability Insurance, 5-57
Professional Liability Insurance, 5-57
The Planning Strategy, 5-58
    Self-Analysis, 5-58
    Annual Check-up, 5-58

**APPENDIX TO CHAPTER 5:
    ADDITIONAL SOURCES OF
    INSURANCE INFORMATION, 5-59**

**SECTION II   *E*: Educational
    Planning, 6-1**

**CHAPTER 6
Educational Planning, 6-1**

Introduction, 6-1
College Costs, 6-1
The Magic of Compounding, 6-2
Saving for College Cost, 6-4
College Savings Plans, 6-4
    UGMA and UTMA, 6-4
    Education IRAs, 6-5
    Section 529 Plans, 6-7

Tax Relief Reconciliation Act of 2001, 6-10
  Employer-Provided Educational Assis-
    tance, 6-10
  Student Loan Interest Deduction, 6-10
  Deduction for Higher Education Expenses,
    6-10
Instruments of Educational Investment
  Alternatives, 6-11
  The Zero Coupon Option, 6-11
  Savings Bonds for Education, 6-11
  Treasury Inflation Indexed Securities,
    6-12
  Low-load Insurance, 6-12
  CollegeSure CD, 6-13
  Section 2503(c) Minor's Trust, 6-13
Asset Allocation Strategy, 6-14
Financial Assistance, 6-14
  Grants and Scholarships, 6-14
  Student Loans, 6-15
  Work Study Programs, 6-16
Family's Expected Contribution, 6-17
Repayment of Student Loans, 6-17
  Deferment, 6-17
  Forbearance, 6-18
  Graduated Payment, 6-18
  Consolidation, 6-18
Reduction of College Debts, 6-18
  Financial Aid, 6-18
  Tuition at Freshman Rate, 6-18
  Lower Tuition Rate, 6-19
  Teaching Position, 6-19
Educational Planning: A Real World
  Example, 6-19

SECTION III C: Cash Management, Savings, Credit, and Debt Planning, 7-1

CHAPTER 7
Cash Management, Savings, Credit, and Debt Planning, 7-1

Introduction, 7-1

**NET WORTH AND CASH MANAGE-
MENT PLANNING, 7-2**
Net Worth Planning, 7-2
  The Basic Concept, 7-2
  Calculation of Net Worth, 7-2
  The Planning Strategy, 7-3
Cash Management Planning, 7-3
  The Basic Concept, 7-3
  Budgeting, 7-6

Cash Flow Analysis, 7-6
Steps in Cash Flow Analysis, 7-7
Cash Flow Planning, 7-9

**SYSTEMATIC SAVINGS PLANNING,
7-11**
Introduction, 7-11
The Starting Point, 7-11
Goal Setting, 7-11
  Adequate Savings Scenario, 7-13
  Inadequate Savings Scenario, 7-13
Effective Savings Strategies, 7-16
  Goal Setting, 7-16
  Self-Rewarding Plan, 7-16
  Savings-First Approach, 7-16
  Automatic Savings Plans, 7-16
Emergency Funding Strategies, 7-17
Criteria for Savings Media Selection, 7-17
  Safety, 7-17
  Liquidity, 7-18
  Return on Savings, 7-18
  Simplicity and Minimum Balance
    Requirements, 7-21
  Special Service Features, 7-21
  Tax Considerations, 7-21
  Summing Up, 7-21
  Record Keeping, 7-22

CREDIT AND DEBT PLANNING, 7-22
Introduction, 7-22
A Debt or a Credit?, 7-23
Sources of Consumer Credit, 7-24
  Commercial Banks, 7-24
  Consumer Finance Companies, 7-24
  Credit Unions, 7-24
  Savings and Loan Associations, 7-24
  Life Insurance Companies, 7-24
  Auto Dealers, 7-25
  Summing Up, 7-25
Credit History, 7-25
  Its Importance, 7-25
  Factors Influencing Credit History, 7-25
  Protection of Credit History, 7-26
Types of Credit, 7-26
  The Basic Issue, 7-26
  Categories of Credit, 7-26
Effective Interest Rate, 7-29
The Burden of Debt, 7-29
  An Overview, 7-29
  Guidance from the Business World, 7-29
  The Rule of Thumb Approach, 7-30
Bankruptcy, 7-30
  The Modern Interpretation, 7-30
  Avoiding Bankruptcy, 7-31

APPENDIX TO CHAPTER 7:
  ROAD TO A SECURE FINANCIAL
  FUTURE, 7-34

SECTION IV   U: Ultimate Disposition through Estate Planning, 8-1

CHAPTER 8
Basic Structure of Estate Planning, 8-1

Introduction, 8-1
Unauthorized Practice of Law, 8-1
History of Estate Taxes, 8-2
Dealing with Death: Psychological
  Implications, 8-3

**AN OVERVIEW OF ESTATE PLANNING,
  8-4**
Estate Planning: Objectives and Tools, 8-4
  The Common Misconceptions, 8-4
  Objectives of Estate Planning, 8-4
  Tools of Estate Planning, 8-4
The Will, 8-5
  Importance of a Will, 8-5
  Absence of a Will, 8-5
  Drafting a Will, 8-7
  Basic Structure of a Will, 8-8
  Codicil, 8-8
  Letter of Last Instructions (Memorandum),
    8-9
The Personal Representative, 8-10
  Power of Attorney, 8-10
  Durable Power of Attorney, 8-10
  Guardian for Minor Children, 8-12
  Probate, 8-12
Joint Ownership, 8-13
  Introduction, 8-13
  Community Property States, 8-13
  Common Law States, 8-13
  Community Property and the Transitory
    Couple, 8-14
Trusts, 8-14
  An Overview, 8-14
  Purpose of a Trust, 8-18
  Selection of a Trustee, 8-18
Lifetime Gifts, 8-19

COMPUTATION OF ESTATE TAX, 8-19
Federal Estate Taxes, 8-19
  An Overview, 8-19
  Economic Growth and Tax Relief
    Reconciliation Act of 2001, 8-20
  Estate Tax Calculation, 8-21
  Gross Estate, 8-22

  Deductions, 8-23
  Estate Tax Calculation, 8-23
State Inheritance Tax, 8-26

CHAPTER 9
**Estate Planning: Concepts and Strategies,
  9-1**

Introduction, 9-1

**ESTATE TAX REDUCTION STRATEGIES,
  9-2**
Introduction, 9-2
Marital Deduction, 9-2
Joint Ownership, 9-3
  Key Advantages, 9-3
  Key Disadvantages, 9-4
  Planning Strategies, 9-5
Lifetime Gifts, 9-6
  An Overview, 9-6
  Gift Tax Calculation, 9-7
  Planning Ideas Involving Gifts, 9-7
  Disadvantages of Gifts, 9-8
  Estate with and without Lifetime Gifts,
    9-9
  Conclusion, 9-10
Trusts, 9-10
  Estate Taxes and Trusts, 9-10
  Irrevocable Gift Trust, 9-20

**SOPHISTICATED ESTATE TAX REDUCTION
  STRATEGIES, 9-21**
Family Limited Partnerships, 9-21
Wealth Replacement Trust, 9-23
  Replacing Gifted Assets, 9-24
  Covering Estate Taxes, 9-24
Sprinkling Trusts, 9-24
The Crummey Trust, 9-25
Generation Skipping Transfer Tax, 9-26
Dynasty Trusts Leveraging the GSTT
  Exemption, 9-28
Split Dollar Arrangement, 9-28
Disclaimer, 9-29
Grantor Retained Annuity Trust (GRAT)
  and Grantor Retained Unitrust (GRUT),
  9-29
  An Overview, 9-29
  Key Advantages, 9-30
Installment Sales and SCINS, 9-31
  An Overview, 9-31
  Advantages, 9-31
Powers of Appointment, 9-32
Qualified Personal Residence Trust
  (QPRT), 9-33

Recapitalization, 9-35
Sale/Gift Leaseback, 9-35
Section 303 Stock Redemption, 9-36
Special Use Valuation, 9-36
Private Annuity, 9-36

**ESTATE PRESERVATION AND DISTRI-
BUTION STRATEGIES, 9-37**
The Will, 9-37
Probate, 9-38
  Advantages of Bypassing Probate, 9-38
  Disadvantages of Bypassing Probate,
    9-38
Revocable Living Trust, 9-38
Standby or Convertible Trust, 9-40
Minor's Trust (Power in Trust), 9-40

**MISCELLANEOUS ESTATE PLANNING
ISSUES, 9-40**
Estate Liquidity, 9-40
Federal Income Tax Considerations, 9-41
Stepped-Up Basis Rules, 9-41
Survivorship Life Insurance, 9-42
Estate Planning for Business Owners, 9-42
  Installment Sale, 9-42
  Private Annuity, 9-42
  Business Purchase Agreement, 9-43
Preparing the Family, 9-43
  The Basic Needs, 9-43
  Preparing the Wife, 9-44
  Paying the Bills, 9-45
  Locating Important Papers, 9-45
  The Survivors, 9-45
  Advanced Strategies, 9-45

A REAL WORLD ESTATE PLAN, 9-47
An Overview, 9-47
Traditional Estate Planning Strategies, 9-47

**SECTION V *R*: Retirement Planning,
10-1**

**CHAPTER 10
Basic Structure of Retirement Income,
10-1**

Introduction, 10-1

GOVERNMENT SPONSORED PLANS, 10-4
Social Security, 10-4
  General Remarks, 10-4
  The Eligibility Issue, 10-5
  Types of Benefits, 10-6

Medicare, 10-8
Taxation of Social Security Benefits, 10-8
Social Security Income Estimate, 10-9

CORPORATE RETIREMENT PLANS, 10-9
General Discussion, 10-9
Specific Requirements, 10-11
Participation Requirements, 10-11
Coverage Requirements, 10-11
  Ratio Percentage Test, 10-11
  The Average Benefits Test, 10-11
  Minimum Participation Test, 10-11
Vesting Requirements, 10-14
Funding Requirements, 10-14
Plan Investment Rules, 10-14
Types of Plans, 10-15
  Defined Contribution Plans, 10-15
  Defined Benefit Plans, 10-23
Age-Weighted Profit Sharing Plans, 10-26
  An Illustration, 10-27
  The Distribution Rules, 10-28
  Direct Rollovers, 10-28
  Mandatory Withholding Rules, 10-28
  Target Benefit Plans, 10-29
  Tax-Sheltered Annuity, 10-30

PERSONAL RETIREMENT PLANS, 10-31
Individual Retirement Account (IRA), 10-31
  An Overview, 10-31
  Long-Term Accumulation, 10-35
  Deductible versus Nondeductible
    Contributions, 10-35
  Types of IRAs, 10-36
  Rollover versus Transfer, 10-37
Keogh Plan, 10-39
  Introduction, 10-39
  Types of Keogh Plans, 10-39

**CHAPTER 11
Retirement Planning: Concepts and
Strategies, 11-1**

Introduction, 11-1

**RETIREMENT INCOME NEEDS ANALYSIS,
11-3**
Retirement Budget, 11-3
  Retirement Expenditure Analysis, 11-3
  Retirement Income, 11-3
  The Potential Shortfall, 11-4
  The Potential Surplus, 11-8

**DISTRIBUTION FROM QUALIFIED
PLANS, 11-8**

Introduction, 11-8
Pension Plans, 11-8
Profit Sharing Plans, 11-8
Other Qualified Plans, 11-8
Required Distributions, 11-9
  Minimum Distribution Rules, 11-9
Taxation of Plan Benefits, 11-11
  Lump Sum Distribution, 11-11
  Annuity Distribution, 11-12
  Rollovers, 11-12
Taxation of IRAs, 11-12
Taxation of Keogh Plans, 11-12
Other Tax Considerations, 11-13
  Premature Distributions, 11-13
  Excess Contributions, 11-13
  Insufficient Distributions, 11-14

RETIREMENT INCOME: THE ULTIMATE
DECISION, 11-14
Introduction, 11-14
  Company Sponsored Qualified Plan and
    Keogh Plan, 11-14
  Annuity, 11-14
  Tax Treatment of Annuity Payments, 11-17
  Lump Sum Distribution, 11-18
  IRA Rollover, 11-19
Lump Sum versus IRA: A Taxing Decision,
  11-19
IRA Distribution, 11-21
  Systematic Withdrawal: Personal
    Investment, 11-21
  Systematic Withdrawal: Insurance Plan,
    11-22
Social Security Benefits, 11-22

RETIREMENT PLANNING STRATEGIES,
11-22
Loans from Qualified Plans, 11-22
Pension Enhancement Strategy, 11-23
Social Security Taxes, 11-25
Early Retirement, 11-25
  Pensions, 11-25
  Health Insurance, 11-25
  Life Insurance, 11-26
Special Spousal Benefit, 11-26
Nonqualified Deferred Compensation Plan,
  11-26
Planning for Retirement: Additional
  Considerations, 11-27
  Early Planning Needed, 11-27
  Minimum Distribution Rules, 11-27
Combo Strategy, 11-28
  Basic Structure, 11-28
  Concluding Remarks, 11-29

APPENDIX TO CHAPTER 11: CURRENT
RULE REGARDING NOTICE OF BLACK-
OUT PERIODS, 11-30

SECTION VI *I*: Investment Planning,
12-1

CHAPTER 12
Investment Products and Markets: An
  Introduction, 12-1

Introduction, 12-1

FIXED-INCOME INVESTMENTS, PRE-
FERRED STOCKS, AND COMMON
STOCK INVESTMENTS, 12-1

Fixed-Income Investments, 12-1
  Savings Accounts, 12-1
  Certificates of Deposit, 12-2
  Marketable Government Issues, 12-2
  Non-marketable Government Issues, 12-3
  Treasury Inflation-Protection Securities,
    12-3
  Municipal Bonds, 12-4
  Corporate Bonds, 12-4
  Bond Ratings, 12-5
  Warrants and Rights, 12-6
Preferred Stock, 12-6
Common Stock, 12-7
  Key Features, 12-7
  Types of Stock, 12-7

MUTUAL FUNDS, 12-8
Introduction, 12-8
Closed-end versus Open-end Funds, 12-8
Advantages of Fund Investment, 12-9
  Diversification, 12-9
  Professional Portfolio Management, 12-9
  Liquidity, 12-9
Types of Funds, 12-9
  Aggressive Growth Funds, 12-9
  Growth Funds, 12-10
  International/Global Funds, 12-10
  Growth and Income Funds, 12-10
  Fixed Income Funds, 12-10
  Balanced/Equity Income Funds, 12-10
  Specialty/Sector Funds, 12-10
  Asset Allocation Funds, 12-11
  Money Market Funds, 12-11
  Index Funds, 12-11
Mutual Fund Fees and Expenses, 12-11

Load or Sales Charges, 12-11
Management Fees and Operating
    Expenses, 12-12
12b-1 Fee, 12-12
Redemption Fees, 12-12
Trustee Fees, 12-13
Supermarket Charges, 12-13
Expense Ratio, 12-13
Fee Reduction Strategies, 12-13
    Select the Right Asset Class, 12-13
    Take Advantage of the Fund Break, 12-14
    Sign a Letter of Intent, 12-14
    Carefully Time the Liquidation, 12-14
    Invest Fund Distributions, 12-14
    Consolidate Investments, 12-14
    Utilize Group Discounts, 12-14
    Find a Seller, 12-15
Mutual Fund Alphabet, 12-15
Reading a Mutual Fund Prospectus, 12-15
    Investment Objectives and Policies, 12-15
    Risk Factors, 12-16
    Investment Restrictions, 12-16
    Past Performance, 12-16
    Fund Information, 12-17
    Costs and Fees, 12-18
    Miscellaneous Information, 12-18
Mutual Fund Rating Services, 12-18
    Morningstar, 12-18
    Lipper, 12-18
    Standard & Poor's, 12-19
    Thomson Financial, 12-19

TRADITIONAL INDEX FUNDS, 12-19
An Overview, 12-19
Fewer Capital Gains, 12-20
    Keeping Pace with S&P, 12-20
    Painless Strategy, 12-20
Lower Cost, 12-20
Pitfalls of Index Funds, 12-21
    Downside Risk, 12-21
    Skewed Weighting Systems, 12-21
    Divergence Between Index Funds, 12-21
    Tax Ramifications, 12-21
    A Narrow Focus, 12-21
    Value Added by Money Managers, 12-21
    Increased Volatility, 12-22

NEW HORIZON IN INDEX FUNDS, 12-22
iShares, 12-22
Standard & Poor's Depositary Receipts,
    12-23
International Index Investing with iShares
    MSCI Funds, 12-23
Exchange-Traded Index Funds, 12-23

**VARIABLE ANNUITY AND LIFE
INVESTMENT PRODUCTS, 12-24**
Deferred Variable Annuity, 12-24
    Benefits of a VA Investment, 12-25
    Drawbacks of VAs, 12-25
    Key Check Points, 12-26
    New Features, 12-26
Variable Immediate Annuity, 12-26
Equity-Indexed Annuity, 12-27
Variable Life Insurance, 12-28
Variable Universal Life, 12-29

**SOPHISTICATED INVESTMENT
PRODUCTS, 12-29**
Real Estate Investment Trusts (REITs),
    12-29
Investment Derivatives, 12-30
Short Selling, 12-31
RunMoney, FOLIOfn, Etc., 12-31
Exchange-Traded Index Investing, 12-35
Exchange-Traded Funds Compared To
Closed-End Funds, 12-37
Exchange-Traded Index Funds, 12-38
Cyclical Nature of Index Performance, 12-46

**APPENDIX TO CHAPTER 12: MARKET
BENCHMARKS, 12-33**

**CHAPTER 13
Investment Management: Concepts and
Strategies, 13-1**

Introduction, 13-1

FIXED-INCOME SECURITIES, 13-2
Fixed-Income Security Return, 13-2
Fixed-Income Security Risk, 13-2
    Key Fixed-Income Risks, 13-2
    Risk Reduction Strategies, 13-4
    Buying a Bond, 13-5
    Selling a Bond, 13-6

EQUITY SECURITIES, 13-6
Equity Return, 13-6
Equity Risk, 13-9
    Key Measures, 13-9
    Morningstar Risk-Adjusted Rating, 13-14
Trading in Equities, 13-15
    Buying a Stock, 13-15
    Selling a Stock, 13-16
Limiting the Risk, 13-17
    Dollar Cost Averaging, 13-17
    Constant Ratio Plan, 13-19

Variable Installment Plan, 13-20
Strategy of Covered Calls, 13-20
Call Option with Stock Sale, 13-21
Mutual Fund Returns, 13-21
Sale of Mutual Funds, 13-21
    The Basic Issue, 13-21
    Change of Investment Objective, 13-21
    Consistent Poor Performance, 13-22
    Size of the Fund, 13-22
    Miscellaneous Changes, 13-23
Mutual Funds and Taxes, 13-24
    Fund Distributions, 13-24
    Calculating Capital Gains or Losses on
        Fund Sales, 13-24

**THEORY OF PORTFOLIO CONSTRUC-
TION, 13-25**
Introduction, 13-25
Theory of Efficient Portfolio, 13-26
Capital Asset Pricing Model, 13-27
Power of Diversification, 13-27
    Basic Observations, 13-27
    Global Diversification, 13-28
The Efficient Frontier, 13-29
Asset Allocation Model, 13-30
    The Risk-Reward Connection, 13-31
    An Essential Tool, 13-33
    Asset Allocation Model Steps, 13-34
    Risk Tolerance Guidelines, 13-34
    Summary, 13-36
Sizing Up a Mutual Fund Portfolio, 13-37
    Rebalancing a Portfolio, 13-39
    Rebalancing in Practice, 13-40
Portfolio Management and Monetary
    Policy, 13-40
**APPENDIX TO CHAPTER 13: FUNDA-
MENTAL AND TECHNICAL ANALYSIS,
13-42**
Fundamental Analysis, 13-42
    An Overview, 13-42
    Forecasting Earnings, 13-42
Technical Analysis, 13-45
    An Overview, 13-45
    Charting, 13-45
Understanding Tax Reform, 13-52

**CHAPTER 14
Investment Planning Strategies, 14-1**

Introduction, 14-1

INVESTMENT PLANNING PROCESS, 14-1
Introduction, 14-1
Goal Setting, 14-2

An Overview, 14-2
Life Cycle, 14-3
Basic Investment Objectives, 14-3
Diversification and Asset Allocation
    Model (AAM), 14-4
Tax Considerations, 14-6
Time Horizon, 14-6
Investment Return, 14-6
Prioritizing of Goals, 14-7
Summing Up, 14-7
Risk Tolerance Level, 14-8
    Risk versus Return, 14-8
    Risk Tolerance Level, 14-8
    Summing Up, 14-9
Investor Preference, 14-11
The Investment Portfolio, 14-12
    Cash Reserves and Emergency Funds, 14-14
    Income Flow, 14-14
    Growth, 14-15
    Long-Term Growth and Tax Advantages,
        14-16
    Target Investment Portfolio (TIP), 14-16
Portfolio Reorganization, 14-17
    The Basic Steps, 14-17
    The Strategy, 14-17

**A REAL WORLD INVESTMENT PLAN,
14-18**
Introduction, 14-18
Portfolio Presentation to the Kleins, 14-18
Goal Setting, 14-19
Risk Tolerance Level, 14-19
Target Investment Portfolio, 14-19
The Golden Retirement Years, 14-22
    The 15-Year Record, 14-22
    Investment Vehicles, 14-22
    Retirement Plan, 14-22
Final Thoughts, 14-23

**APPENDIX TO CHAPTER 14: THE
IMPACT OF TERRORISM ON THE
ECONOMY AND FINANCIAL MAR-
KETS, 14-26**
Nature of the Problem, 14-26
    911, 14-26
Financial and Psychological Impact, 14-26
    Financial Impact, 14-27
    Psychological Impact, 14-27
Conclusion, 14-29

SECTION VII   *T*: Tax Planning, 15-1

CHAPTER 15
The Basic Federal Income Tax Structure, 15-1
THE BASIC TAX STRUCTURE, 15-1
Introduction, 15-1
Computation of Federal Taxable Income, 15-3
  Calculation of Gross Income, 15-3
Adjustments to Gross Income, 15-10
  Maximum IRA Contributions, 15-11
  Elective Deferrals as Roth Contributions, 15-11
  Catch-Up IRA Contributions, 15-12
  Deemed IRAs under Employer Plans, 15-12
  Limits on Contributions to 401(k) and Other Plans, 15-12
  Increase in Plan Contribution and Benefit Limits, 15-12
  Deductions, 15-13
  Exemptions, 15-18
  Number of Dependents, 15-18

EDUCATION PROVISIONS, 15-18
  Modification of Education IRAs, 15-18
  Qualified Tuition Programs, 15-19
  Employer-Provided Educational Assistance, 15-20
  Student Loan Interest Deduction, 15-20
  Deduction for Higher Education Expenses, 15-20

COMPUTATION OF INCOME TAX, 15-21
Tax Computation, 15-21
  Basic Computation, 15-21
  Marginal Tax Rate, 15-21
  Tax Credits, 15-22
2005 Income Tax Table, 15-24
  Social Security Payroll Tax, 15-25
  Medicare Part A Payroll Tax, 15-25
  Personal Exemption, 15-25
  Standard Deduction, 15-26
  Capital Gains and Dividends, 15-26
  Alternative Minimum Tax, 15-27
  Itemized Deductions, 15-27
  Credits, 15-29
  Alternative Minimum Tax, 15-30
Taxation of Corporations, 15-31
  C Corporations, 15-31
  S Corporations, 15-31

APPENDIX TO CHAPTER 15: JOBS AND GROWTH TAX RELIEF RECON-CILIATION ACT OF 2003, 5-33

CHAPTER 16
Tax Planning: Concepts and Strategies, 16-1

Introduction, 16-1

THE INDIVIDUAL TAXPAYER, 16-1
Deduction, 16-2
  The Forgotten Deductions, 16-2
  Flexible Spending Arrangement, 16-3
  Moving Expenses, 16-3
  Tax-Deductible Interest, 16-4
  Prepayment Strategy, 16-4
  Marriage Penalty, 16-5
  Other Deductions, 16-5
Diversion, 16-6
  Home Ownership, 16-6
  Municipal Bonds, 16-7
  Matching Incomes and Losses, 16-7
  Tax Shelters, 16-7
  Limited Partnerships, 16-8
  Master Limited Partnerships (MLPs) and Publicly Traded Partnerships (PTPs), 16-8
  Personal Exemption, 16-8
  Like-Kind Exchanges, 16-8
  Charitable Donations, 16-9
  Tax-Free Social Security Benefits, 16-9
Deferral, 16-10
  Deferral with Pre-Tax Dollars, 16-10
  Deferral with After-Tax Dollars, 16-12
Deflection, 16-12
  Kiddie Tax, 16-12
  Gifts, 16-13
  Child Employment, 16-13
Diminution, 16-13
  Income Deferral, 16-14
  Income Acceleration, 16-14
  Itemized Deductions to Accelerate or Defer Income, 16-14
  State Income Tax, 16-14
  Charitable Contributions, 16-15
  Contributions of Appreciated Property, 16-15
  Medical Expenses, 16-15
  Accelerating Interest Deductions, 16-15
  Personal and Qualified Residence Interest, 16-16
  Investment Interest, 16-16
  Employee Business Expenses, 16-17
  Income Shifting, 16-18
  Expense Shifting, 16-19
  Second Home, 16-19
  Alternative Minimum Tax, 16-19

Social Security Benefits, 16-19
Splitting Business Income, 16-19
Mutual Fund Sales, 16-19
Early Withdrawal Penalty, 16-20
S Corporation Strategy, 16-20

REAL WORLD FEDERAL INCOME TAX CALCULATIONS, 16-21
Roger and Carol Kurt, 16-21
Sam and Betty Mason, 16-22

THE BUSINESS ORGANIZATION, 16-23
Introduction, 16-23
Sole Proprietors, 16-24
Executives, 16-24
Professionals, 16-24
S Corporations, 16-25
Limited Liability Companies, 16-25
Amendment of Tax Return, 16-26
Tax Audit, 16-26

SECTION VIII *Y*: Yearning for Financial Independence Planning, 17-1

CHAPTER 17
Financial Independence Planning, 17-1

Introduction, 17-1
Stay Ahead of the Shrinking Dollar, 17-1
The Case for Stocks, 17-2
Six Keys to Success, 17-2
  Live within Means, 17-2
  Build Up an Emergency Fund, 17-2
  Start Saving Early, 17-2
  Pay Yourself First, 17-3
  Reach for Higher Returns—Even at
    Some Risk, 17-3
  Know the Limits of Your Knowledge, 17-3

CHAPTER 18
A Comprehensive Financial Plan, 18-1

Introduction, 18-1
Confidential Financial Analysis, 18-2

WHAT IS FINANCIAL PLANNING?, 18-4
Net Worth/Balance Sheet, 18-5
Net Worth Statement, 18-6
Income and Expense Budget, 18-7
Budget Summary, 18-8

COLLEGE PLANNING - THREE CRITICAL ISSUES, 18-9
Education Funding Analysis, 18-11
Education Funding Summary, 18-12
Annual Education Fund Schedule, 18-13
Education Fund Analysis, 18-14

THE IMPORTANCE OF INSURANCE, 18-15
Insurance Needs Analysis, 18-16

MONTHLY DISABILITY ANALYSIS, 18-20
Disability Needs Calculator, 18-21
Disability Needs Analysis Summary, 18-22

ASSET ALLOCATION - HOW AND WHY, 18-24
ALTERNATIVE MINIMUM TAX, 18-27
Hypothetical Portofolio, 18-29
Asset Allocation Model, 18-30
Asset Diversification Analysis -Input Data, 18-31
Asset Diversification Analysis, 18-32
Target Portfolio Allocation, 18-33
2004 Federal Tax Analysis, 18-34
2004 Federal Income Tax, 18-35
2004 Federal Income Tax Analysis, 18-36
2004 Net Income Comparison, 18-38
Retirement Required Savings, 18-39
Retirement Savings Analysis Summary, 18-40
Retirement Required Saving Schedule, 18-41
Retirement Alternatives, 18-43
Retirement Matrix, 18-44
Review of Current Portfolio, 18-45
Review of Current Portfolio Summary, 18-46
Current Portfolio Detail Allocation, 18-47

MODERN ESTATE PLANNING, 18-48

UNDERSTANDING THE FEDERAL ESTATE TAX, 18-50

COMPUTING THE TRANSFER TAX, 18-52
Estate Analysis, 18-53
Estate Analysis Assumptions, 18-54
Assets Input Sheet, 18-55
Current Asset Inventory, 18-56
Estate Flow Chart, 18-57
Basic Estate Tax Calculation, 18-58
Estate Liquidity Analysis, 18-59
Estate Analysis Executive Summary, 18-60

Estate Distribution, 18-61
Estate Ownership, 18-62

PART III   Special Topics in Financial Planning

CHAPTER 19
Life After Divorce, 19-1

Role of Financial Advisor, 19-1
Property Valuations and Settlement, 19-2
  Property Valuation, 19-2
  Division of Property, 19-3
  Equal versus Equitable Concept, 19-4
Career Assets, 19-5
  The Family Business, 19-5
  Valuing the Business, 19-6
  Dividing the Business, 19-6
Dividing the House, 19-7
  Three Basic Options, 19-7
  Tax Issues for Sale of a Residence, 19-8
Pension Plans, 19-8
  Method of Dividing Plans, 19-8
  Defined Contribution Plan, 19-9
  Defined Benefit Plan, 19-10
  Public Employees Pension Plan, 19-13
Maintenance, 19-13
  Issues Relating to Maintenance, 19-13
  Rehabilitative Maintenance, 19-13
  Modifiable versus Non-modifiable
    Maintenance, 19-14
  Guaranteed Maintenance, 19-14
Child Support, 19-14
  Modifying Child Support, 19-15
Income Tax Considerations, 19-15
  Child Care Credit, 19-16
  Head of Household, 19-16

CHAPTER 20
Planning for Widows, 20-1

Introduction, 20-1
Differences Among Widows, 20-1
  Levels of Differences, 20-1
  The Age Issue, 20-2
  Cause of Husband's Death, 20-2
  Responsibilities for Dependents, 20-2
  Amount of Financial Knowledge, 20-2
  Amount of Financial Resources, 20-3

Similarities Among Widows, 20-3
Winning Widows Among Clients, 20-4
  Attorneys, 20-4
  Accountants, 20-4
  Estate Planning Council, 20-4
  Emotional/Spiritual Advisors, 20-4
  Funeral Directors, 20-5
  Widow Support Groups, 20-5
  Other Widows, 20-5
Working with Widows, 20-5
  Widows of Clients, 20-5
  Initial Office Visit, 20-5
  Avoiding Irrevocable Decisions, 20-6
  Follow-Up Meetings, 20-6
Explaining the Financial Planning
  Approach, 20-7
The Financial Plan, 20-9
Educating the Widow, 20-9
Beyond Implementation, 20-10
Non-Financial Advice, 20-10
Special Areas of Concern, 20-10
Conclusion, 20-11

CHAPTER 21
Managing a Financial Planning Practice, 21-1

Introduction, 21-1

SECTION I
CONCEPTUAL FRAMEWORK FOR PRACTICE MANAGEMENT, 21-2
Getting Started, 21-2
External Environment, 21-3
  Economics of Planning Business, 21-3
  Marketplace Analysis, 21-4
  Scope of the Target Market, 21-4
  Regulatory and Social Environment, 21-5
Corporate Structure, 21-5
  Company Organization, 21-5
  Administrative Management Functions, 21-8
  Marketing Strategies, 21-9

SECTION II
DEENA KATZ ON PRACTICE MANAGEMENT, 21-14
People Make It Happen, 21-14
  Hiring, Mentoring, and Internships, 21-15
  Taking Care of Your Most Valuable
    Asset: Your Staff, 21-16
  Money Plus, 21-16

Compensation, 21-18
Bonuses, 21-18
Empowerment, 21-19
Titles and Business Cards, 21-21
Realizing Potential, 21-21
Food, Comfort, and Other Care, 21-23
Owning Up to Mistakes, 21-23
Appreciation, 21-24
Employee Reviews, 21-25
Little Things, 21-25
If It Ain't Fixable, Break It Off, ASAP,
    21-26
People Management Is the Key, 21-27
Consistency and Succession, 21-27
Crisis Planning for Death, 21-27
Disability Crisis, 21-28
An Action Plan for Now, 21-29
During a Crisis, 21-30
After the Crisis, 21-30
Business Succession, 21-31
Outright Sale, 21-31
Valuation, 21-32
Don't Wait—Plan Now, 21-33

SECTION III
SALE OF PRACTICE, 21-34
Introduction, 21-34
Best Time to Sell a Practice, 21-34
The Process of Sale, 21-35
Valuation of Practice, 21-35
Conceptual Framework, 21-36
Estimating Cash Flow, 21-36
The Discount/Capitalization Rate, 21-37
A Real World Case Study, 21-37
Assets Generating Highest Fees, 21-37
Assets from Affluent Clients, 21-37
Assets in Qualified Plans, 21-37
Other Income, 21-39
Total Income, 21-39
Discounted Cash Flow Analysis, 21-39
Transaction Structure, 21-39
Structural Example, 21-41
True Net Cash Flow, 21-41
Concluding Remarks, 21-43

CONCLUSION, 21-43

APPENDIX, A-1

INDEX, I-1

Preface
to the
Ninth Edition

Dear Reader,

In 1990, the first edition of *Practicing Financial Planning, A Complete Guide for Professionals* was published. At that time, we dreamed that, when we enter the 21st century, *the financial planning profession would be perceived as venerable as the medical profession* (see "A Personal Message" of the first edition reproduced following this preface). We can say with great confidence that our dream has come a long way toward being fulfilled.

We strongly believe that any financial planning text must have the depth, the breadth, and the technical sophistication necessary to prepare financial planning professionals for meeting the difficult challenges of the 21st century. In preparing for the publication of the ninth edition we quickly realized that no one person, no matter how competent, could satisfactorily deliver such a service. Consequently, we embarked upon a journey, which can best be described as highly non-traditional. The ninth edition is truly a *multi-authored book*. In fact, in a real sense, all of the professionals who graciously participated in this exciting venture, individually and collectively, elevated the book to a much higher professional and practical level, vastly expanding its coverage, improving its clarity, and adding new dimensions particularly suited to address the special financial problems of our time.

It is easy to infer from the above discussion that the ninth edition is significantly different from the previous ones. Here are the highlights of the new features added to the current edition:

- In all of the key planning areas, new sections have been added which apply the theories and concepts to real world case studies.

- Numerous changes in tax and other laws have been incorporated into the discussions of the respective planning issues.
- The landscape of life insurance is ever changing. New developments and new insurance products have been identified and incorporated into the life insurance planning discussion.
- Educational planning chapter has been completely redesigned, incorporating in it all the new and significantly improved investment choices now available.
- Estate planning chapters have been vastly expanded, incorporating in the general discussion numerous technical estate planning tools generally overlooked by planners.
- All of the many changes in the rules and laws pertaining to retirement have been incorporated and weaved into the discussions on retirement planning.
- Investment planning chapters have been raised to a higher level of sophistication by expanding the discussion on investment theories and bringing into sharper focus sophisticated investment planning techniques.
- The focus of tax planning chapters has shifted from presentation of tax facts to the use of these facts in developing tax planning strategies.
- Chapter 19 on planning for divorce has been updated, and now reflects all of the latest developments which have occurred since this chapter was first published.
- The chapter on practice management has been completely redesigned. This chapter now covers issues relating to establishing a financial planning practice, managing it, and selling the practice.

We are especially pleased that several professionals with special expertise and unique insights produced a number of chapters or sections included in this edition. Alexandra Armstrong wrote the chapter on Planning for Widows, while Carol Wilson produced the chapter on Life after Divorce. Jack DiFranco developed a technical piece on the sale of a Financial Planning Practice. Joseph Champagne created a very thoughtful piece which summarizes his views on the long-term impact of the September 11, 2001 disaster on investment and the investing public. Charles Dharte shared his thoughts on the time-tested ways of accumulating net worth for the long term. Deena Katz transformed the practice management information into an *inspirational* piece. Finally, Salvatore LaMendola helped put together an advanced estate planning case study, which could only be produced by an astute and practicing estate planner.

We live in a dynamic world in which tax laws, availability of financial products, and financial rules and regulations continually change. Since these changes do not come to a screeching halt the day the book goes to press, we have devised a strategy for keeping the text users abreast of all the latest developments. Modern technology allows us to periodically update our website whenever important changes take place in the financial world.

There is yet another area in which we have introduced important changes. Practicing Financial Planning for Professionals is widely used in colleges, universities and other institutions across the country. It is our objective to make ancillary materials available to the instructors to enhance their pedagogical effectiveness. We have therefore created an Instructor's Manual especially designed to accomplish that objective. In addition, by frequently updating our website we intend to keep our instructors abreast of all the latest developments so their teaching material would always reflect the state of the art.

At this point, we would like to express our gratitude to Mr. Harold Evensky. He is an inductee to the Movers & Shakers Hall of Fame, and through his numerous professional contributions and public exposure, he has played a highly significant role in bringing financial planning closer to becoming a bona fide profession. We are grateful to him for writing a foreword to this book.

We would like to conclude with a philosophical expression of hope. The issue of whether financial planning is merely a career or truly a bona fide profession has come a long way toward resolution in favor of the latter definition. If the ninth edition of *Practicing Financial Planning for Professionals* helps us continue that venerable journey, then we will have achieved our objective.

January 1, 2005   Sid Mittra
                                                   Tom Potts
                                                   Leon LaBrecque

"It is one of the most beautiful compensations of this life that no man can sincerely try to help another without helping himself."

Ralph W. Emerson

A Personal Message - 1990

Dear Reader:

The millennium is almost here. As we embark upon the decade of the 1990s, incredible events unfold, inviting reflection, warning, hope, fear, and both optimistic and ominous predictions. Observed and analyzed ceaselessly, the current events provide compelling reasons to believe that the new decade will be *different* from the one before.

Americans are evolving into a different people: older, more diverse, insecure due to foreign domination, and worried about living too long with inadequate financial support. We are also realizing that, in the 1990s, most baby boomers will approach their 40s. For the first time in history, three-quarters of all Americans will be of prime working age—24 to 55. And as the median age rises to 36 for the first time, reassessments and creations at a rapid pace will become the order of the day.

Of all the different types of revolutions we are likely to experience in the 1990s, perhaps none is of greater interest to Americans than the financial and economic revolution. Even more importantly, economic prospects for the 1990s remain highly controversial at best, and totally confusing at worst. At one extreme is the view that America is fast becoming a third-rate world power and is doomed to permanently become a mediocre nation. We owe the world $600 billion—and the amount keeps rising. The rate of growth of productivity is down to 1 percent, which ensures a stagnant gross national product. Superimpose on this bleak situation a massive budgetary problem, inadequate domestic savings, a decaying infrastructure, a failing educational system, a turbulent financial market, and a strained economic system, and we have a picture of doom and gloom.

At the other extreme are the optimists who reject the doomsayer's analysis. According to this group, by the year 2000, America's debt of $1 trillion will be less than ten percent of the country's GNP of $12 trillion. The budget deficit, which in 1986 accounted for 5.2 percent of GNP, is likely to fall to less than 1 percent. A global *perestroika* and technological advancement will boost America's exports,

This section has been reproduced from the first edition published in 1990.

thereby wiping out massive deficits in her balance of payments. The baby-boom generation, highly educated, sensitive to the global economic challenges, and with two decades of work experience, will reach peak productivity, which will help push the nation's productivity growth to the 3 percent level. In short, the next ten years will bring unparalleled prosperity for the U.S.

And that brings us to the main point: The massive confusion in the backdrop against which all Americans must make decisions regarding their financial future. Even without this confusing state of affairs, establishing and reaching a variety of financial goals is at best an onerous task. With so much uncertainty looming on the horizon, the majority of the Americans believe they need external help and guidance in articulating and achieving their financial goals. However, because of the complex world in which we live, and also because of the multi-faceted needs of the American people, only the highly trained and experienced financial planners, who are committed to serve the public with dedication while maintaining the highest level of ethics and professionalism, can serve the financial planning needs of a changing nation.

This, then, is the backdrop against which *Practicing Financial Planning: A Complete Guide for Professionals* has been developed. It is not merely a collection of facts or a collage of practice-related ideas. Rather, my objective in writing this book is to educate the aspirants so they make take the *first* important step toward becoming a professional financial planner. Throughout the book important financial planning theories and concepts have been interwoven with practically-oriented planning strategies to emphasize the practice of comprehensive financial planning in a real world. I have also taken great care to ensure that the book encompasses the currently prevailing tax laws, theoretical developments, and state-of-the-art financial planning practices.

I should hasten to add that a book of this complexity and magnitude in an ever-changing financial world could not have been developed without the generous help of many practicing professionals associated with the financial planning industry. The names and contributions of those who have given their time so generously are presented on the following page. However, I would be remiss if I did not single out four persons for special recognition. The best way I can describe my deep gratitude to Dr. Lionel Goldstein, Ph.D., CPA, CFP, and Ms. Cynthia Forman, MA, MBA, CFP, is to state categorically that they could not have made a more valuable contribution, if they were co-authors of this book. In addition, thoughtful criticisms of Mr. Art Albin, CPA, MBA, CFP, and Dr. Dale Johnson, Ph.D., CFP, were responsible for both extensive revisions and a major expansion of the scope of the book. In fact, in a real sense, all are responsible for raising the book to a much higher professional and practical level, improving its clarity, expanding its coverage, and helping remove inaccuracies that slipped into the first draft.

Incidentally, publishing a book of this complexity can be a harrowing experience. Fortunately, that was not true in my case. The credit goes to John Willig, the Executive Editor at Prentice Hall. The frequent assurance by John that this book was "developing to be a winner" provided me with the impetus to do my best to live up to his expectations. My special thanks go to Jacqueline Jeglinski, Production Editor at prentice Hall, who should get most of the credit for the outstanding "production quality" of this book.

I would like to conclude with a personal note. On October 14, 1989, I attended the Parents & Partners Program at the University of Pennsylvania Medical School in Philadelphia where my son, Robert, is a second year medical student. In his opening remark to the attending parents of medical students, Dean Frederic D. Burg, M.D. challenged every potential medical professional to embrace the following philosophy:

> This is not a time of mediocrity
> It is a time of greatness
> This is not a time for timidness
> It is a time for courage
> This is not a time for dullness
> It is a time for imagination
> This is not a time for greed
> It is a time for charity
> This is not a time for followers
> It is a time for leaders . . .

For a long time it has been my dream to help raise the level of the financial planning profession so one day it would be perceived as venerable as the medical profession. I do believe that in the foreseeable future we will achieve that goal and financial planners will be able to embrace Dr. Burg's philosophy meant for the medical professional. And, if *Practicing Financial Planning* helps you become a more sophisticated, better educated, and prepared financial planner, thereby moving us a little closer to the goal of achieving a universally-accepted true profession, I will have achieved my objective.

Sid Mittra,
Oakland University

About the Authors

DR. SID MITTRA

Dr. Sid Mittra is the owner of the financial consulting firm, Mittra Associates. In this capacity, Dr. Mittra offers his services to individuals, foundations, associations, and corporations. The services include virtually all areas of financial planning, including: risk management, tax, investment, retirement, estate planning and financial independence planning.

Dr. Mittra is an active member of the Investment Management Team of Mittra & Associates. He participated in the creation of a proprietary mathematical model, called Dynamic One©, which the firm uses to provide investment management services for its individual and institutional clients.

Dr. Mittra uniquely combines conceptual and theoretical knowledge in financial management with communicative skills. He frequently speaks on financial economics, money and financial management. He also advises corporations, partnerships and closely-held corporations.

In developing comprehensive financial plans, Dr. Mittra is supported by a group of highly trained and experienced planners and financial consultants, including CPAs and attorneys. He also makes generic and specific recommendations for achieving stated financial goals in the most efficient manner.

Dr. Mittra holds the title of Emeritus Professor of Finance at Oakland University. He was a board member of the International Board of Standards and Practices of Certified Financial Planners. He has been regularly invited to offer seminars at the World Congress of the IAFP, including those in Japan and Australia.

Dr. Mittra is in several prestigious listings, including: International Authors' Who's Who, American Men of Science, and Who's Who in Finance and Industry.

Also, he has published 16 books, including, *Practicing Financial Planning: A Complete Guide for Professionals*, which enjoys wide acceptance among top universities and trade associations.

The City Council of Detroit has awarded Dr. Mittra the Spirit of Detroit Award in recognition of his long and distinguished service to the city. Dr. Mittra is also widely quoted in *Money Magazine, Kiplinger's Personal Finance Magazine* and various newspapers. His professional articles have appeared in *Journal of Accountancy, Financial Planning, Journal of Financial Planning, Personal Financial Planning, and American Economic Review.*

Dr. Mittra publishes one of Michigan's longest running, popular weekly financial columns in the *Oakland Press.*

Academic Degrees
Ph.D. in Economics and Finance
M.B.A. in Accounting and Finance
Associate of the Accounting Institute
   (London)
Associate of the Institute of Bankers

Article Publications
Personal Financial Planning
Financial Planning Magazine
Journal of Financial Planning
American Economic Review
Kyklos
Journal of Accountancy

Planning Certification
Certified Financial Planner
Registry of Financial Planning Practitioners

Professional Positions: Past & Present
Owner, Mittra & Associates
President, Coordinated Financial Planning
Professor of Finance, Oakland University
Chairman, Dept. of Economics, OU
Consultant, United Nations
Joint Advisor, Planning Commission,
   Government of Venezuela

Board: Past & Present
Editorial Review Board, Journal of the ICFP
Board of Examiners, CFP Board

Licenses and Registrations
Registered Investment Advisor
Life, Accident and Health Insurance License
Variable Annuity License
Series 24 and 7, NASD

International Planning Seminars
Japan, Australia, Spain, India

Book Publications
Sixteen books, including the following:
Practicing Financial Planning
   for Professionals, 9th Edition,
   RH Publishing
Personal Finance: Management by Objectives,
   Harper & Row
Investment Analysis and Portfolio Management,
   Harcourt Brace
Inside Wall Street, Dow-Jones Irwin
Money and Banking: Theory, Analysis, Policy,
   Random House

Biographical Listings
International Authors' and Writers' Who's Who
American Men of Science
World Who's Who of Authors
Dictionary of International Biography
Who's Who in North America
Who's Who in Finance and Industry
Who's Who in American Education

Honors and Awards
National Science Foundation Fellowship
Ford Foundation Fellowship
Federal Reserve Bank Study Grant
Spirit of Detroit Award, City Council of Detroit
Phi Kappa Phi

Organization Affiliations: Past & Present
American Economic Association
American Management Association
American Finance Association
Rotary International
ICFP, IAFP, and CFP

DR. TOM POTTS, Ph.D., CFP®

Dr. Tom L. Potts is a professor of finance and director of the Financial Services and Planning program in the Hankamer School of Business at Baylor University.

Professor Potts holds a B.B.A. and M.S. in Economics from Baylor University and a Ph.D. in Finance with a minor in Economics from the University of Illinois.

Dr. Potts has been very active in both the academic and professional environments of personal financial planning. He is past president of the Academy of Financial Services. He has served as a member of the International Association of Financial Planning's Academic Resources Council, the editorial review board of the *Journal of Financial Planning*, reviewer for the *Financial Services Review* and as a member of the Academic Review Board for the *Journal of Certified Financial Planners*. He has researched, taught and published in the financial planning field. In addition, he has worked as a financial consultant for individual clients and corporations. He was recently selected as an honorary director of the Japanese Academic Financial Planning Association.

His professional involvement includes: President and chairman of the Board of Governors of the Certified Financial Planner Board of Standards, and Chairman of the International CFP Council. He is currently serving the Financial Planning Association as chairman of the Global Advisory Council and as a member of the Career Development Strategic Team. He has served the International Association of Financial Planning as vice-chairman of the IAFP Registry Committee and is presently serving as a member of the Academic Resources Committee for the National Association of Personal Financial Advisors.

Dr. Potts has given research and professional papers around the world including France, Australia, Japan, Canada, United Kingdom and South Africa. He has been interviewed by the *Wall Street Journal*, *Money* magazine, Kiplinger's *Changing Times*, *USA Today*, *New York Times*, *Financial Planning*, *Boston Globe*, *Black Enterprise*, *The Gold Coast Bulletin* in Australia and the *Nikkei Newspaper* in Japan.

MR. LEON LABRECQUE, JD, CPA, CFP®, CFA

For over 27 years, Leon LaBrecque has been providing financial education, advice and counseling to millions of Americans. From a start in the accounting profession (including Arthur Andersen), to law, to the academic world (where he created the first Masters program in Financial Planning), Leon has truly been changing the face of American finance.

Leon received his Bachelor of Science in Accounting from the University of Detroit (magna cum laude) in 1977, and his Juris Doctor (magna cum laude) from the University of Detroit School of Law in 1981. He received his Chartered Financial Analyst Charter in 1989 and his CFP designation in 1990.

Among other accomplishments, Leon has written and provided financial education programs to employees of Ford Motor Company, General Motors, BellSouth, General Dynamics, Consolidated Edison, CalPERS, AT&T, Lucent Technologies, Avaya, SBC, Aerospace Corporation, Daimler-Chrysler, the State of Washington, the State of Idaho, the State of Montana, and many others. He has created multi-media programs in finance and retirement planning, including the well-known and critically acclaimed program "Personal Finance Matters" http://www.hewittPFC.com).

Leon LaBrecque brings a unique practitioner's eye to ***Practicing Financial Planning for Professionals.*** He has authored over 17 proprietary programs on a wide range of topics, from retirement and financial planning to real estate and college funding. He is currently the managing member of LJPR, LLC in Troy, Michigan, a fee-only financial planning and asset management firm that currently manages over $250 million for its clients.

As well as being a CEO, media personality and acclaimed planning professional, Leon is the father of 4. He enjoys running marathons and triathlons, and sea kayaks in the Great Lakes.

Acknowledgments

The authors hereby express their gratitude to the following outstanding professionals (presented in alphabetical order) who helped raise the book to a new horizon.

Ms. Alexandra Armstrong is Chairman, Armstrong, MacIntyre & Severns, Inc in Washington, D.C. She was Chairman, Foundation for Financial Planning, and serves on the boards of Reading is Fundamental and Boy Scouts of America National Capital Area Council. She is a member of Cosmos Club, D.C., Estate Planning Council, Economic Club of Washington, D.C. and New York, Washington Board of Trade, Financial Planning Association Junior League of Washington, D.C., National Association of Women Business Owners, and Planned Giving Study Group of Greater Washington, D.C. Ms. Armstrong was Chairman of IAFP and has served on CFP Board of Standards as well as Financial Service Corporation.

Ms. Armstrong is the co-author of "On Your Own: A Widow's Passage to Emotional and Financial Well-Being," a highly popular book, which has already gone through its third edition. She writes a monthly financial planning column in Better Investing Magazine published by the National Association of Investment Clubs.

Ms. Armstrong has appeared on such prestigious shows as Wall Street Week, CBS This Morning, Good Morning America, CNN, Fox News and CNBC.

Dr. Joseph E. Champagne, Ph.D., is widely recognized as an outstanding citizen of both the academic and the business community. Currently, he serves as Chairman of the Board of Ross Controls, a multi-national research, engineering and manufacturing corporation. He also serves on the Board of Directors of the Munder Funds, a multi-billion-dollar mutual group fund, and on the Board of Trustees of Lawrence Technological University.

Dr. Champagne is under contract to Macomb College as Vice President for Advanced Studies and Dean of its University Center. In addition, he is a Corporate and Executive Consultant to Business, Government and Higher Education, as well as a licensed Industrial/Organizational Psychologist.

Dr. Champagne is active in civic and professional affairs, having served on numerous committees, councils, advisory groups, and over 25 boards of directors. Professionally, he has served as professor of Management at the University of Houston and Oakland University. He was Vice President for Academic Affairs of the University of Houston system, President of the Houston Community College system and Oakland University and Chancellor of the Lamar University system. Dr. Champagne serves as an honorary member of the Board of Advisors of Mittra & Associates.

Mr. Charles G. Dharte, Jr. retired as Chairman of the Board and CEO of Huntington Bank of Michigan. He serves as a director or a board member of several organizations, including the following: St. Joseph Mercy Hospital-Macomb and chairperson of the Finance Committee; a trustee of Madonna University and Chair Person of the Finance Committee, P.I.M.E. Missionaries.

Mr. Dharte served as a director and chairperson of the Clinton Township Economic Development Corporation and was a director and chairperson of the City of Mount Clemens Downtown Development Authority. He also served on the advisory board of Walsh College in Troy. Mr. Dharte was also a director of Saratoga Hospital in Detroit, Michigan, and was also Board Chairman of the Boys and Girls Club of Southeastern Michigan. He serves as an honorary member of the Board of Advisors of Mittra & Associates.

Mr. Jack DiFranco is Managing Director, Corporate Finance at Stout Risius Ross. The firm provides corporate finance advisory services, including mergers, acquisitions and divestitures. He is responsible for project execution, business development and the overall management of the Corporate Finance Group.

Mr. DiFranco has had an impressive professional career. Prior to joining SRR, he was Vice President, Corporate Finance at First of Michigan Corporation, Member, NYSE. In that capacity, he provided investment banking transaction service to public and private companies. In addition, he offered a full range of corporate finance advisory services including mergers and acquisitions, public offerings, private placements of debt and equity and valuation services.

Mr. DiFranco was the president and founder of Varis Corporation, a provider of value-added information and consulting services. As president he provided finance and marketing related information services to the real estate industry, and was responsible for business development, client services and financial management. Mr. DiFranco has also served Earnst & Young as a Senior Consultant and Manager. He serves as an honorary member of the Board of Advisors of Mittra & Associates.

Mr. Harold Evensky is partner, Evensky, Brown & Katz. One of the best known and highly sought after financial planners in the U.S., Mr. Evensky was recently recognized as one of the most powerful people in the mutual fund industry. He was awarded the Dow Jones Investment Advisor Portfolio Management Award for lifetime achievement, and the Financial Planning Magazine inducted him into the "Movers & Shakers Hall of Fame," recognizing him as one of The Most Influential People in the Financial Planning Profession.

Mr. Evensky has published several books and numerous articles, and he continues to lecture widely on investment related topics. He was Chair of CFP Board of Standards, Chair of International CFP Council and a National Board Member of the International Association for Financial Planning. He belongs to the Financial Planning Association, the Association for Investment and Management, Academy of Financial Services, and is an Associate Member of American Bar Association.

Mr. David C. Fillo is Vice President of Great Lakes Pension Administrators, Inc. He holds the designations of Chartered Financial Consultant (ChFC), Chartered Life Underwriter (CLU), Certified Employee Benefit Specialist (CEBS), Qualified Pension Administrator (QPA) and Qualified 401(k) Administrator.

Mr. Fillo is a pension professional specializing in the design, installation and administration of all types of qualified retirement plans. After receiving his undergraduate degree in Business Administration (Finance), David entered the pension profession in 1986. He has extensive knowledge in all areas of qualified plan compliance and reporting.

Mr. Julius H. Giarmarco, Esq. is a partner of Cox, Hodgman & Giarmarco, P.C., where he heads up the firm's estate planning division. Mr. Giarmarco received his law degree (J.D.) from Wayne State University in 1975, and his masters of laws (LL.M.) from New York University in 1976. His primary practice areas include estate planning, business succession planning and wealth transfer. Mr. Giarmarco lectures frequently on a national basis on estate planning issues. He has authored a number of articles on estate planning appearing in financial planning magazines, and is the author of the nationally acclaimed brochure, *The Five Levels of Estate Planning.* He is also the co-author of a new book, *Estate Planning with Insurance* and was selected by the Michigan Institute of Continuing Legal Education to author the chapter on succession planning in the recently published book, *Advising Closely Held Businesses in Michigan.* He can be contacted at jhg@disinherit-irs.com and at www.disinherit-irs.com. Mr. Giarmarco serves as an honorary member of the Board of Advisors of Mittra & Associates.

Ms. Deena Katz, CFP, is President and Partner of Evensky, Brown and Katz. Ms. Katz has offered financial advice on such television programs as Good Morning America and CBS This Morning. She is a sought-after speaker for national and international legal and financial organizations and was the authority selected by Consumer Reports to evaluate the work of other financial planners. Fortune magazine's "1999 Investor's Guide" issue named her and her husband-partner, Harold Evensky, innovative "gurus" and described them as the most respected members of their profession.

Ms. Katz is the editor-in-chief of the Journal of Retirement Planning and has published extensively in other magazines such as Financial Planning and Investment Advisor. In January 2001 issue of Financial Planning, she was named by her peers as one of the five most influential people in the planning profession. She was also inducted into the "Movers & Shakers Hall of Fame."

Mr. Salvatore J. LaMendola, J.D., C.P.A., received his B.B.A. degree with highest honors and his J.D. degree from Notre Dame Law School. He practices solely in the estate planning field with a focus on charitable planning and wealth transfer planning. His wealth transfer planning subspecialty includes the design and drafting of family LLCs, buy-sell agreements, QPRTs, GRATs, and grantor trusts to assist clients in achieving their wealth and business succession goals while minimizing estate and gift taxes.

Mr. LaMendola has lectured before The Michigan Association of CPAs, the Michigan Institute of CFPs, the Society of Financial Services Professionals, and the National Association of Insurance of Insurance and Financial Advisors.

Mr. LaMendola has been admitted to the Michigan Bar Association, the Maryland State Board of Public Accountancy, the U.S. Tax Court and the U.S. District Court. He is a member of the Michigan Association of CPAs, National Association of Philanthropic Planners, National Committee on Planning Giving, and The Planning Giving Roundtable of Southeast Michigan.

Mr. LaMendola has authored a number of articles on estate and charitable planning, and is the author of The Five Levels of Charitable Planning.

Mr. Rick Laidler has been in the insurance business since 1971 starting out with Transamerica Insurance Company as an auditor/engineer. In 1975, he joined Community Insurance Center, which offers a wide variety of services relating to insurance. He obtained his Certified Insurance Counselor designation in 1986 and has continued his education in insurance. He is also licensed with the State of Michigan as an Insurance Counselor.

Mr. Laidler is currently with Community Insurance Center specializing in Commercial Insurance, including life and health. He has taught insurance at various levels and has lectured other agents required to earn their continuing education credits for the State of Michigan.

Mr. Robert Skubic is the owner of Robert J. Skubic, C.P.A., P.C. Mr. Skubic has been a Certified Public Accountant since 1977, and an owner of CPA firms since 1981. In this capacity, he offers services to corporations, limited liability companies, partnerships, individuals, not for profit organizations, and retirement plans. His services include: compilation and review of financial statements, monthly accounting, payroll returns and write-up services, tax preparation and audits, computer software installation and support, bank loan and SBA applications, financial projections and budgets, personal financial statements, and business planning.

Mr. Skubic is supported by a group of highly trained and experienced CPAs and staff. Such an arrangement enables him to offer a comprehensive range of quality taxation, accounting, computer and other financial services. He is a member of the Michigan Association of Certified Public Accountants.

Mr. Anton T. Vanek earned his Master of Business Administration with a concentration in Finance from the University of Wisconsin, Madison. Mr. Vanek received his Chartered Life Underwriters (CLU) and Chartered Financial Consultants (ChFC) designations in 1984 and Certified Financial Planner (CFP) in 1987. He is an instructor in Oakland University's Personal Financial Planning Program.

Mr. Vanek provides both insurance and investment services to individuals and businesses. He is a member of the Alpha chapter of Beta Gamma Sigma at the University of Wisconsin. He worked as Assistant Vice President in Commercial Lending at Bank One and currently works as a registered representative for AXA Advisors, LLC.

Ms. Carol Ann Wilson, CFP, CDP is President and Owner, Quantum Financial Inc., a pre-divorce financial consulting firm. She is also the founder of the Institute for Certified Divorce Planners.

Ms. Wilson is a leading authority on financial planning for divorced people, and in that capacity has been an expert witness in numerous court cases. She has published several books dealing with this challenging subject. Her latest book, *The Financial Guide to Divorce Settlement,* published by Marketplace Books, is now considered to be the leading text on the subject of divorce.

Ms. Wilson is a member of the Financial Planning Association, a member of the Institute for Certified Divorce Planners, and serves on the Board of Directors of the American Institute of Collaborative Professionals.

Ms. Wilson has presented numerous seminars and workshops and has been an instructor at the Continuing Legal Education Services. She has developed DIVORCE PLAN software for professionals, which is used in determining financial results in divorce settlements. She has also jointly produced a video tape, "How to be an Expert Witness in Court."

OUR SPECIAL THANKS

The spirit of cooperation and joint collaboration, which has been the hallmark of the production of this book, was clearly evident in the publication of the ninth edition.

Robert Crane acted as the Managing Editor of the text. In that role, he coordinated with remarkable finesse all aspects of the production process, including overseeing the support services and the final publication of the book. The authors are grateful to him for his valuable contribution, his professionalism, and his willingness to assume the many responsibilities associated with the publication of the ninth edition.

Lisa Sullivan was the production manager of this massive project, which frequently presented her with impossible challenges. Lisa coordinated numerous production activities with great efficiency. The authors are thankful to Lisa for her valuable contribution, her cheerful disposition, and her dedication to this project.

WEB SITE

In today's technological society, we have designed a web page to better serve our readers. Our site is: www.publishnow.net

This site includes:

- Updates for each of the chapters, as they become available
- Ability to e-mail questions and feedback directly to the authors
- Special section devoted to Professors and Teachers

- Information about future publications

It is our goal to make this publication an industry standard for all planners. With your help we will succeed.

A SPECIAL REQUEST

Financial Planning is a challenging discipline, and it is even more challenging to keep up with continuous changes that take place within the discipline. In this edition we have made a heroic effort to capture all the major changes through the year 2005. However, we are also realistic enough to recognize that this edition will be marred by both errors and omissions.

We therefore urge you, the reader, to bring to our attention any errors you detect so we may remove these inaccuracies before it goes into the next printing.

You may reach us via e-mail at: bob.crane@publishnow.net

Thank you,

Sid Mittra
Tom Potts
Leon LaBrecque

PART I

The General Setting

"An era can be said to end," observed playwright Arthur Miller, "when its basic illusions are exhausted." By that criterion, the era of casual or substandard personal financial planning is over. Some time ago, we began the new era of professional financial planning. The overriding consideration of this new era is to ensure that financial planners maintain the highest level of professionalism in every phase of the planning process. In short, personal financial planning has already passed the adolescent stage and is now a mature profession.

Before approaching financial planning in a systematic manner, a thorough understanding is needed of the respective roles financial planners and financially concerned Americans must play to assure success in the 21st century. The purpose of Part I is to provide the general setting necessary before undertaking a comprehensive analysis of financial planning concepts and practice.

Part I consists of three chapters. Chapter 1 describes the emerging role of the professional financial planner in an uncertain and highly complex economic and financial environment. Chapter 2 discusses how the financial planner begins the planning process by selecting and interacting with the client. Chapter 3 demonstrates how financial planners can use the universal tool of time value of money to solve myriads of financial problems.

CHAPTER 1

The Emerging Role of the Financial Planner

DEMANDS OF THE FINANCIAL FUTURE

Many goals were achieved in the twentieth century that were once thought impossible. The past century also gave us a vision of the awesome and astonishing possibilities of the future: technological marvels, sophisticated communications, artificial intelligence, walking on the moon, travel to planets, and most amazing of all, cloning life itself. But at the beginning of the 21st century, people also continued to paint a far different scenario: fear of living too long, agony of suffering from catastrophic illness, another major depression leading to a collapse of the world economy, widespread poverty after retirement, bankruptcy of the Social Security and the Medicare system, and the dethroning of the U.S. as the dominant economic power.

In conjunction with the bleak picture just painted, Americans also realize that they are enjoying a better quality of life than previous generations: longer life spans, better health, more leisure time, and more varied choices about lifestyles. But they also recognize that in order to take full advantage of these benefits they need financial security and thus must surmount complicated financial hurdles. In short, both unprecedented opportunities and difficult challenges have become the order of the day.

THE EMERGING TRENDS

Changing Family Patterns

Recent U.S. census figures suggest that in 2004 less than 25 percent of all U.S. households consisted of married couples with children—a monumental decline from the 70 percent that made this unit typical in 1950. Single-person households, on the other hand, have risen from 11 percent in 1950 to an amazing level of well over 25 percent of American families.

Where traditional families do continue, they are progressively becoming less able to financially assist their aging parents and their children. The implications are clear. In contrast to a society that traditionally buttressed each individual with a network of family support, the twenty-first century is marked by an increasing need for individuals to take responsibility for meeting their own financial goals.

The Reality of the American Dream

The cost of achieving the lifetime goals once taken for granted continues to mount. Mortgage payments on a home eat up 45 percent of the average 30-year-old's salary today, compared to just 14 percent in 1949. The expenses associated with having a family are escalating as well. In 1980, it cost less than $80,000 to raise a child to age 18; in 2004, it cost more than $400,000 to accomplish the same objective. With education costs in some states rising at more than seven percent per year—faster than wages or inflation—the pressures put on tomorrow's parents to save for raising and educating their children can only increase.

The Realities of Retirement

Based on current trends, in the future an average American is expected to enjoy a longer retirement period. One reason is that in this country the average life span is lengthening. Biotechnological advances are expected to stretch life expectancy even more in the future. As a result, the grandchildren of the current generation could live to be 100 or even older.

Concurrently, Americans are retiring earlier. Several U.S. Department of Labor studies have shown that early retirement is increasingly popular today, with over 60 percent of all private sector employees now retiring *before* the age of 65. But does the lengthening of retirement years guarantee that these will be *the golden years*? For many individuals, the answer is, *not necessarily.*

The Bureau of Labor Statistics estimates that 70 to 75 percent of preretirement income is needed to continue a comparable lifestyle during retirement. Where will this money come from? The Social Security system currently (2005) provides a maximum annual benefit of around $21,900 for a 65-year old—no matter how high the preretirement earnings. In short, the gap between retirement dreams and reality can be bridged only by personal savings and investments. The combination of a shorter working life (perhaps just 30 years) and a longer retirement (possibly more than 30 years) makes this goal progressively more difficult to reach.

A Summary View

Current trends suggest that the future will offer Americans unparallel opportunities in all areas of life. Yet, it is also clear that in order to enjoy them, individuals will have to assume increasing responsibility for their own financial well-being rather than rely on traditional sources of assistance. The process of making the most of one's money is an arduous and long-term endeavor. Therefore, it could be argued that the future, however distant it may seem, is *now.* Fortunately, Americans do not have to face the challenges alone. Professional financial planners, who only three decades ago were unknown even to most financial institutions, are now recognized by the general public as invaluable partners in planning for their financial future. In short, personal financial planning has finally come of age.

CONCEPT OF PERSONAL FINANCIAL PLANNING

The term *personal financial planning* has been loosely and broadly applied to a wide range of advisory services and financial products sales efforts. Several financial planning professional organizations have attempted to define the term in order to foster a unified financial planning profession.

The most comprehensive definition of financial planning has been developed by the Certified Financial Planner Board of Standards in its Code of Ethics and Professional Responsibility. The definition reads as follows:

> Personal financial planning, or financial planning, denotes the process of determining whether and how an individual can meet life goals through the proper management of financial resources. The management of financial resources can be seen as the technical side of the process; and in today's fast-changing financial world, this side of the process demands a willingness to stay abreast of new financial strategies and instruments. The other side of the process requires that all the planner's knowledge of financial strategies and instruments be brought to the surface of the client's *goals*. Perhaps the most distinctive skill a financial planner [needs] is that of helping clients to articulate their life goals so that together . . . [they] can begin to determine, first of all, whether these goals are achievable through financial resources, and then how. Working with clients in this state of the financial process requires sensitivity because . . . [financial planners] discuss issues that may be difficult for many people to address . . . [financial planners] may find that the planning process itself brings deeper values and unrealized conflicts to the surface, and from time to time it may be appropriate to refer clients to other counselors to resolve these conflicts before they can proceed with a financial plan.[1]

Financial planning is a *process* and not a *product*. It may lead to the recommendation of an investment or an insurance product. However, a financial planner should never act as an order taker, attempting to use life insurance or mutual fund investment as a panacea for all problems. Instead, financial planning should be thought of as a process for helping people achieve their financial goals either through the development of comprehensive plans or through the use of a segmented approach for solving specific problems. Thus, it is the skillful use of the process that converts an individual into a professional financial planner.

KEY AREAS OF FINANCIAL PLANNING

Financial planners should be informed in all aspects affecting their clients' lifetime financial decisions, and especially in the following key planning areas:

---

[1] *Financial Planning: A Career Profile*, Certified Financial Planner Board of Standards.

S: Safety through Risk Management Planning
E: Educational Planning
C: Cash Management, Savings, Credit, and Debt Planning
U: Ultimate Disposition through Estate Planning
R: Retirement Planning
I: Investment Planning
T: Tax Planning
Y: Yearning for Financial Independence Planning

The eight key planning areas are presented in Figure 1-1. Financial planners may be experts in only a few of these areas. But they must have a clear understanding of all of these areas so they could work with other professionals while servicing their clients. In order to provide valuable services as a true professional, a financial planner must recognize the importance of five Cs of financial planning:

*C*lient:	Client interests must always come first.
*C*ommunication:	Communication is the key to motivating clients to implement plan recommendations.
*C*oordination:	Coordination among various professionals provides the highest quality of overall planning service.
*C*ompetence:	Competence firmly based on both education and experience is essential for professional performance.
*C*ommitment to Ethics:	Commitment to ethics and professionalism is the basis for providing quality service.

THE CLIENT

Barbara Streisand recorded a very popular song about people who need people and how they are the luckiest people in the world. A similar theme applies to financial planning. People need financial planners, who are committed to fulfilling the needs of these people—or clients—with competence, care and professionalism.

The Emerging Client

From the end of World War II until the beginning of the 1970s, financial planning was simple and straightforward. Starting in the mid-1970's, with the advent of a double digit inflation, stagflation, high unemployment, massive budget and trade deficits, and constant tax law changes, financial planning became more complicated. As a result, a new breed of consumers emerged who started to demand from financial planners a far more complex set of services than they had routinely provided in the past.

At the turn of the 21st century, Americans have begun to stay single a lot longer. If two wage earners marry, often their financial plans do not include children. And even where children are included in the plan, each parent may have a prenuptial agreement, thereby making financial planning more complicated. Finally, even average families following the recommendations of their financial planners often find their lives disrupted as aging—and often ailing—parents move in with them. It is little wonder that today the *average client* of the 1970s is practically nonexistent, and there is not one comprehensive financial plan that fits all situations.

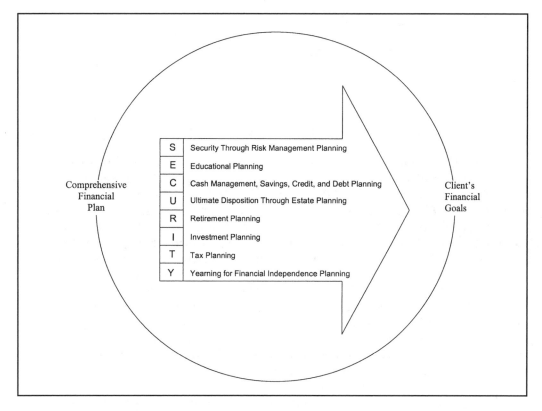

FIGURE 1-1 Overview of a comprehensive financial plan

The trend toward an endlessly diverse individual and family configuration is clear from the following expression: "The evolving icons of pop culture tell it all: The Cleavers' solid certitude has yielded prime time to the Huxtables' dual income dilemmas. The Bumsteads now share the comics with Cathy, a perennial single. Ad *infinitum.* 'People look at modern families and think they are seeing departures from the norm . . . in fact, departures *now* are the norm,' says Peter A. Morrison, director of Rand Corporation's Population Research Center."[2]

Notwithstanding the major changes that are taking place in the lifestyles of the American consumers, certain basic financial needs of these consumers remain intact. Identification of these needs can provide the basic foundation on which the financial planning process can be built.

The Common Denominators

Some people dread heights, others fear crowded rooms. But in the financial arena Americans have three distinct fears: the fear of living out old age with a vastly reduced income, dying too young, or becoming disabled during their professionally active years. Each fear is distinct and requires elaboration.

---

[2] Author, "The New Gospel of Financial Planning," *Money*, March 1989, p. 55.

Living too long. Many Americans have pension phobia: the fear of not having enough money to retire in peace and dignity. The reasons are not hard to find. The average life expectancy for men and woman have already reached 77 and 82 respectively, and these ages are expected to rise over time. The potential bankruptcy of the Social Security system distinctly looms on the horizon. Catastrophic health care costs threaten to cripple the Medicare system. Housing costs continue to skyrocket. Finally, the fear of double-digit inflation and the possibility of the collapse of the world economic system can turn the retirement dream into a nightmare.

There is a trend that is lengthening the period of retirement. More and more Americans are retiring well before age 65. According to the Social Security Administration, more than half of Social Security-eligible workers begin collecting Social Security at age 62—the earliest they can begin collecting benefits. These days many Americans declare their independence in their 50s and even in their 40s. For some, this might mean starting volunteer work at social service agencies, taking hobbies seriously, traveling around the world, or simply running part-time businesses. For the vast majority, however, early retirement still remains a fantasy.

Nearly everyone looks forward to retirement—be it early retirement or retirement at the "normal" age of 65—as a time of doing exactly as one pleases. Whatever lifestyle a person envisions, the best way to ensure that the retirement goal will be met is to plan early. The primary duty of financial planners is to (1) impress upon their clients that the choices they make at a young age largely determine how well they will reach their retirement goals, and (2) articulate the steps clients need to take to effectively plan for retirement.

Broadly defined, retirement planning encompasses a variety of financial planning areas. The first step in planning for the future is to determine retirement goals. How one wants to live after retirement is the basis for estimating how much money is needed to achieve the retirement goals.

The second step in this process is to determine the current financial status, measured by net worth. This is calculated by adding up all the assets and subtracting from that total the outstanding liabilities. Once it is determined how much income is needed after retirement and the amount of net worth available to generate that income, planning for the future can begin to take shape.

Savings planning constitutes the third step of retirement planning. It begins by estimating the annual expenses during retirement. Next, this amount is used to estimate the annual savings necessary during the working years to maintain the desired lifestyle after retirement. In this context, financial planners can help their clients recognize that (1) both the desired lifestyle and the amount of savings they wish to generate reflect their personal preferences, and (2) there is a trade-off between the sacrifice of present income that is necessary to increase current savings and future income.

Investment planning constitutes the fourth step of retirement planning. Here, the main objective is to channel the savings into various investment products. The selection criteria are formulated on the basis of answers to the following questions: (1) How much should the investment earn? (2) How much risk can be assumed? (3) How long is one willing to wait before the investment is likely to pay off? (4) Can the investment be easily liquidated? (5) What are the tax ramifications of investing in these products?

Integration of the investment plan with tax planning constitutes the fifth step of retirement planning. Tax-advantaged investments completely avoid or defer tax payments. Over time, this can result in substantial savings, thereby significantly contributing to the growth of net worth. Of course, as an integral part of tax planning, the attendant risks and lower investment returns of tax-advantaged investments must be weighed against the benefit of tax savings.

An ever-present desire of Americans is to accumulate a large estate that could be passed on to the beneficiaries. Known as estate planning, this constitutes the sixth step of retirement planning. Investment techniques designed to accumulate a large estate can be significantly different from those that are necessary for achieving educational, retirement, and other living goals. In addition, a sophisticated estate plan tends to eliminate, or significantly reduce, the federal estate and state inheritance taxes that must be paid before the estate can be distributed to the beneficiaries.

Dying too young. We live in a turbulent society in which the threat of an early death is ever-present. An untimely death of the breadwinner can be catastrophic, and the surviving family may never be able to financially recover from it. Risk management planning involves the transfer of the risk of untimely death to an insurance company by buying adequate life insurance. Such an action presents a major challenge for financial planners for two reasons. First, calculating what constitutes an adequate amount of life insurance coverage is not an exact science, since the quantification of several related variables requires making value judgments. For instance, if a wife with small children is willing and able to join the labor force at an adequate salary level immediately after her husband's death, the husband would need far less life insurance coverage than the husband whose wife wants to stay home until the children have completed their high school education. Second, because life insurance is frequently pushed on unwilling buyers, many people refuse to buy it, and that makes it difficult for them to appreciate the value of life insurance as a powerful tool for managing risk. Despite these difficulties, however, risk management planning remains one of the major challenges of every financial planner.

Becoming disabled. One of the major challenges faced by financial planners is to convince their clients that they should have an effective disability plan. Several reasons account for the universal apathy consumers have toward buying a comprehensive disability policy. First, most people do not recognize that long-term disability poses a real threat in their lives. Second, few people understand that unlike death, where all expenses related to the deceased cease, a long-term disability places a continuing financial burden on the family. Third, many people shy away from purchasing disability insurance because it *appears to be* far more expensive than a life insurance policy. For instance, a $5,000 annual premium may buy a $500,000 life insurance policy for a 55-year-old male, but the same premium would buy *only* a $4,000 a month disability income policy for the same individual. Clearly, many people fail to recognize that while the disability policy *appears* to be more expensive, that is not necessarily the case. The correct way to compare the true cost of these two policies is to calculate the present value of the two income benefits, a task better performed by a competent financial planner.

Summing up. Most Americans have the fears of living to a poverty-stricken old age, dying too early, or becoming disabled. It is the duty of financial planners to help their clients attain financial security. This can be achieved only if the clients are treated with understanding, care, and professionalism. That is, financial planners can achieve great success by developing comprehensive financial plans designed to help their clients achieve their short- and long-term objectives.

COMMUNICATION

Even the best-laid financial plan falls by the wayside if the advantages of implementing the recommendations contained in the plan are not effectively communicated to the client. For this reason, financial planners are expected to be professional communicators.

Over the years a great deal has been written on the development of communication skills by financial planners. Some of these publications deal with general, scientific techniques of communication, while others tailor their discussions to communicating specifically with financial planning clients. We will approach the subject from the perspective of communicating with both the potential clients and the planning clients at different levels of the planning process.

The Potential Client

It is widely believed that a prospective client sizing up a financial planner says: "I don't care how much you know until I know how much you care." It is also frequently asserted that people don't care to learn about doing financial planning themselves. They just want to dump their financial problems on the lap of a trusted person. This is the mindset of the client to which a financial planner must respond.

A financial planner needs a unique set of communicative skills to interact with a potential client. The financial planner first needs to convince the individual that he or she is:

A   Accountable for all planning-related actions.
B   Both caring and committed for the long term.
C   Competent, both academically and experientially.

This is achieved only when the planner explicitly recognizes the potential client's needs and fears, articulates the short- and long-term objectives, and develops a broad program for meeting these objectives. Additionally, the potential client should be made aware of the fact that financial planning is not an exact science and that quick fixes or unrealistic expectations will likely fail. Thus, through proper communication, the potential client would learn that financial planning is a long-term process, and continuous monitoring by the planner and total cooperation between the two parties are essential for the achievement of the client's short- and long-term objectives.

The Planning Client

Once the individual has formally engaged the financial planner, the planning process can be initiated. This process initially involves the translation of personal objectives into specific plans, and subsequently converting these plans into implementation strategies. The information used to develop the plans must be accurate, complete, up-to-date, relevant to the client's goals, and well organized. If that is not the case, then the financial plan will be deficient and ineffective.

Returning to the main theme, once the planning process has been initiated, the technique of communicating with the client dramatically changes. To appreciate this change in technique, it is important to identify the six key stages in financial planning, known as EGPRIM: (1) *E*stablishing client objectives; (2) *G*athering quantitative and qualitative data; (3) *P*rocessing and analyzing the planning data; (4) *R*ecommending specific actions for clients by producing a written comprehensive financial plan; (5) *I*mplementing the plan; and (6) *M*onitoring progress and conducting periodic reviews.

Establishing client objectives. As professional communicators, financial planners face their greatest challenge in this area for two reasons. First, most clients are not only unsure of their objectives but frequently are unable to articulate what they need. Second, since establishing client objectives is critical for creating an effective financial plan, planners must develop both nonverbal and verbal forms of communication skills to effectively perform this function. The former may take the form of supplying reading materials that emphasize the importance of articulating short- and long-term objectives. For the latter, a financial planner might use a variety of skills such as probing, restating, paraphrasing, and summarizing clients' views. This latter function can be performed effectively by using a special communication model, which we will call the goals and objectives interview. The salient features of this model are described next.

The process begins by asking the client to fill out a Financial Planning Questionnaire, which covers the eight financial planning areas; namely, risk management, educational planning, budget management, estate planning, retirement planning, investment planning, tax planning, and financial independence planning. After an in-depth analysis of the answers provided in the questionnaire, the financial planner would conduct an in-depth goals and objectives interview by covering each of the eight planning areas. In addition, the interview may cover other matters of importance to the client. At the conclusion of the interview, the planner can summarize for the client the results of the interview. If the client believes that the summary contains all of the important elements of the interview, then it would be committed to paper and transmitted to the client for future reference. This is the most effective way of getting the client to commit to a set of well-defined goals and objectives, and laying the foundation for providing a valuable planning service to the client.

Incidentally, it is the objectives, and not goals, that are at the heart of developing a financial plan. Goals are open-ended statements. For instance, "I want to be rich" is an example of a client's goal. In contrast, objectives are ***quantifiable targets*** that can be measured in accomplishing the stated goal. For instance, "I wish to retire at age 55 with an annual income of $150,000" is an objective statement. Of course, over time objectives can change due to a change in age, income prospects, marital status, or death in the family. A financial plan should be sufficiently flexible to accommodate changes in the client's objectives.

After meeting with the client, the planner should send minutes of the meeting to the client confirming all the items discussed, the proposed plan of action, and the persons responsible for providing information to the planner. This step enables the planner and the client to proceed toward accomplishing the stated objectives.

Gathering data. The planner's primary responsibility is to gather complete information that is relevant both to the client's problems and the type of plan is needed to solve them. Data gathering is a mechanical process. It is tedious, time-consuming, laborious, and, above all, onerous. Yet, it is a vital function, since the data gathered here is used exclusively to develop the client's comprehensive financial plan, which will only be as good as the quality of data used to produce it.

At first it might appear that the only task of the financial planner is to supply the client the Financial Planning Questionnaire, and to collect it after its completion. That is simply not true. The planner must not only convince the client that the data gathering is of utmost importance but also provide assistance in completing the questionnaire. This is especially true for answering such loaded questions as those dealing with the desired age of financial independence, future expected inflation rate, expected investment return, and desired retirement income. Even more important, the planner should: (1) assist the client in accurately completing the questionnaire; (2) win the client's confidence during an initial interview; and (3) use advanced technology to systematize all responses and effectively interpret all quantitative information.

A significant portion of the information gathered by a planner is quantitative in nature. This information provides the basis for a variety of financial analyses performed for plan development. Specific examples of quantitative information include: (1) general family profile; (2) names, addresses, and phone numbers of various advisors; (3) the value of assets and liabilities; (4) degree of cash inflows and outflows; (5) insurance policy information; (6) employee benefit and pension plan information; (7) tax returns for last three years; (8) details on current investments; (9) list of retirement benefits; (10) client-owned business information; (11) provisions contained in wills and trusts; (12) lifetime gifting programs; (13) contingency plans; (14) financial and economic assumptions; and (15) arrangement for distribution of client's estate at death.

Once the relevant quantitative information has been gathered, the financial planner can begin the collection of qualitative data which provides general information concerning the client's objectives, life style, health status, risk tolerance level and other pertinent details. Naturally, care should be exercised in collecting qualitative data, because it is the skillful use of this data that would bring the financial plan to life. For instance, the client's desire to relocate upon early retirement, fund only a portion of the child's college education, and start an expensive hobby prior to retirement—all of these represent important qualitative information which can be lost if not divulged by the client during the data gathering stage. Additional examples of qualitative information include: (1) insurability of the client and family members, since it might not be possible to use life insurance as a legitimate strategy if they are non-insurable; (2) interests and hobbies; (3) expectations about employment; (4) risk tolerance level; (5) anticipated changes in current or future lifestyle; (6) life values; (7) attitudes, fears and preferences; and (8) life's priorities.

One final point: the client should recognize that the process of data gathering can be time consuming, and that the planner would be exposed to a great deal of highly confidential and sensitive information pertaining to the client.

Processing and Analyzing Financial Data. This operation centers around putting the information just gathered into understandable financial format like balance sheet and income statement. The primary objective for generating these statements is to help the planner assess the current financial status of the client.

Clearly, this phase requires very little communication with the client. In fact, contact with the client can be virtually limited to clarifying unclear data and setting up the parameters for some key planning variables, such as expected inflation, desired investment returns, and so on.

Recommendations for action. A critical step in the communication process is the transmission of a comprehensive financial plan to the client. While the level of technical analysis, length of explanation, and the style of presentation may vary—sometimes considerably—among financial planners, the success of the comprehensive plan is assured only if the planner is able to effectively communicate to the client the recommendations contained in the plan and set the stage for their timely implementation.

Implementation. A successful financial planner is able to motivate the client to carry out the actions articulated in the *Action Plan* section of the comprehensive financial plan. While both parties explicitly recognize that the client is under no obligation to implement the recommendations through the planner who developed the plan, the client must realize that to derive full benefits the plan recommendations must be implemented in a timely fashion. Naturally, the financial planner has both the moral and professional obligation to assist the client in implementing the plan. In addition, if the client purchases insurance and investment products from the financial planner, the planner must also take the following steps: (1) Clearly specify that any commissions generated by these sales are in addition to, and not in lieu of, the planning fees already collected. (2) Provide in writing to the client the advantages, limitations and risks associated with each product. (3) Ensure that the client understands these products and is comfortable with them.

Incidentally, if the planner operates the practice on a fee-only basis, the planner should provide the client with a list of referrals to expedite the implementation process. These referrals should be trustworthy professionals who share the same common beliefs on how best the client can achieve his or her objectives.

Monitoring and Review. Personal financial planning is a never-ending process. Over time, a client's personal situation, financial conditions, economic framework, and tax environment—all of these can and do change. Consequently, the client's progress vis-à-vis the short- and long-range goals set in the plan should be monitored on a continual basis and the client should be apprised of the factors which could affect the plan's progress. In addition, a periodic review and revision of the plan's recommendations are essential if the planner wishes to participate in the planning process on a long-term basis. There is, of course, no universal definition of how frequently this periodic review should be conducted. A typical time cycle is an annual update with provision for a more frequent review whenever personal, financial, or economic conditions change.

Ideally, a comprehensive financial plan should contain the following distinct elements:

Results of the Goals and Objectives Interview. This section articulates the client's short- and long-term goals and objectives and establishes the basis for the planner's recommendations.

Basic Observations. Frequently, the body of the comprehensive financial plan is voluminous, and the client may find it burdensome to go through the entire plan. To obviate such a problem, a special section entitled "Basic Observations" can be added to the plan. This section summarizes the plan's key elements and presents in a capsule form the highlights of each of the eight major areas (S-E-C-U-R-I-T-Y).

Key Recommendations. This section presents all the recommendations in minute detail. The recommendations are first presented in a generic form. Specific investment, insurance, and legal products are then selected to supplement the generic recommendations.

Trip Tick. This section sets out in order of priority specific steps the client should take to implement the plan's recommendations.

Comprehensive Plan. The last section should contain the financial plan supported by a detailed analysis of the financial data pertaining to each of the major planning areas.

Plan transmission constitutes the biggest test of the financial planner as a professional communicator. Plan recommendations are likely to be accepted and quickly acted upon if the planner is able to convince the client that by implementing these recommendations the majority of the stated objectives would be achieved. This is a tall order, and it may be necessary to use both verbal and nonverbal forms of communication to achieve this goal. Of course, in the final analysis, action on the plan recommendations is assured only when the planner is able to meet the client in his or her comfort zone. This can be achieved by developing an implementation checklist which specifies: (1) what actions need to be taken, (2) who is responsible for taking these actions, and (3) the date of completion of each task. This will ensure that the plan will be implemented in an organized fashion.

COORDINATION

The discipline of financial planning is relatively new, and it has developed as a way of dealing with our modern complex society. Even as late as in the 1960s, there was little demand for financial planners. Most people were content with dealing with their traditional advisors, such as attorneys, accountants, bankers, insurance agents, and stockbrokers. However, as we entered the 1970s, our society grew more complex, especially after the 1973-74 period brought in the most severe recession since the 1930s. For the first time we experienced the oil embargo, double-digit inflation, an unacceptable level of unemployment, and the infamous bracket creep in personal and corporate taxes. Clearly, no profession was equipped to handle all of the myriad financial planning needs of American families. The idea of the financial planner, as we know today, was thus born to deal with this complex situation.

As is generally the case with the birth of a new discipline, initially most people believed that the financial planner could be *all things to all people*. That dream, however, was short-lived. It was quickly recognized that consumers' interests would be truly served only if the financial planners acted as a quarter-back or an orchestra leader and coordinated other traditional advisors for support in planning for the client. For instance, if a client needed a sophisticated estate plan, an attorney would be needed to fulfill that need. A complex tax return could be prepared by a CPA. Life insurance could be purchased from an insurance professional. Similarly, the investment portfolio could be reorganized with the help of a portfolio manager or a professional investment counselor.

Let there be no misunderstanding, however. To suggest that a financial planner should closely work with other professionals does not imply that the planner cannot—or should not—perform one or more of the tasks just listed. In fact, frequently financial planners are licensed members of one or more of these professions and hence can successfully perform the related tasks. For instance, most practicing financial planners are registered investment advisors and many are also licensed to sell securities and insurance products. In addition, some planners are CPAs, while others as JDs are licensed to practice law. Nevertheless, most sophisticated financial planners recognize that while it is desirable to be knowledgeable about the key areas of planning, when circumstances warrant, it is best to seek the professional services of other advisors. The following is a brief description of the approach taken by each type of professional and the importance of including such a person on the planning team.

Attorney

In recent years, a great deal has been written on the client-attorney relationship and on the legal community's indifferent behavior toward the financial planning community. These writings generally suggest that at least some of the dissension appears to stem from turf battles. The thinking behind such behavior is not only misplaced, but if allowed to continue, can be counterproductive and ultimately damaging to the client's best interests.

In the context of financial planning, an attorney's key function is to certify the legality of a proposal developed by a financial planner and to prepare the associated legal documents. For instance, if charitable giving is desired and a charitable trust is recommended, the attorney would be asked to either confirm the planner's choice of the legal instrument or suggest a better instrument to accomplish the client's objective. The attorney would then prepare the appropriate legal document to implement the recommendation. The same approach would be used for recommendations relating to education, life insurance, joint ownership, and other types of trust and estate planning issues. Clearly, in the scenario just described, there is no room for turf battles and acrimonious debates, for in this role the attorney operates not as an adversary but an integral part of the team of professionals.

Accountant

Traditionally, accountants and CPAs have performed two principal functions: maintenance of financial records and preparation of taxes. In addition, occasionally these professionals also perform certain financial planning functions. Whatever the role, traditionally CPAs have commanded the public's respect and admiration primarily because they were not permitted to receive commission on product sales. Today, however, commission rules are governed by individual state boards of accountancy, and many CPAs receive commission on the sale of investment and insurance products.

With the financial world becoming more complex and financial planners clearly establishing themselves as chief coordinators of the professional team, the role of accountants has significantly changed. Today, CPAs and accountants still perform financial record-keeping and compliance services like audit and tax preparation. But as team players they also play a major role in analyzing the overall tax consequences of buying an investment product or transacting an investment business. In addition, CPAs also provide invaluable assistance to the financial planners by (1) interpreting and evaluating the ever-changing tax laws, (2) recommending ways of taking advantage of these changes in the law, and (3) occasionally computing and monitoring investment results by acting as investment advisors.

Portfolio Manager

The two most important components of financial planning are the creation and preservation of a client's estate. While the attorney and the CPA help preserve the estate, the portfolio manager helps create or build it. This constitutes a two-step process. First, a financial planner creates a target investment portfolio that would help achieve the client's short- and long-term objectives. Second, a portfolio manager helps the planner identify the appropriate investment vehicles—stocks, bonds, mutual funds, annuities, limited partnerships, real assets, and so on—thereby helping the planner complete the investment planning process.

Insurance Counselor

An important dimension of asset protection is the purchase of life, disability, property, casualty, professional liability, long-term health care, and other forms of insurance. Also, in the event of an untimely death, a life insurance policy provides the liquidity for paying taxes and administrative expenses without imposing undue financial hardship on the surviving family. The financial planner is responsible for developing a coordinated risk management plan covering various types of insurance. The task of the insurance counselor is to select from a wide variety of those insurance products that are particularly suited for the client.

Other Professionals

The financial planner works with other professionals as well, depending upon the client's special needs and unique circumstances. These include trust officers, real estate brokers, investment bankers, and estate planners specializing in charitable giving and sophisticated planning strategies. In each instance, the planner's objective is to seek external assistance in order to enhance the overall value of the financial plan.

Summing Up

By establishing harmonious and productive relationships with traditional advisors, financial planners can provide valuable service for the client. If the activities of these advisors are coordinated well, it is possible to create a productive working environment that would ultimately benefit all parties: the client, the financial planner, and all the traditional advisors.

In an effort to promote a healthy cooperation between the financial planner and the traditional advisors, the financial planner should establish rapport with the client and the existing advisors. This can be achieved only if the planner makes a firm commitment to the client and coordinates the activities of the traditional advisors to serve the client with distinction.

COMPETENCE

Financial planning continues to be an emerging profession. Consequently, what constitutes a well-qualified, objective financial planner is often debated. In this section we will discuss this issue in terms of academic degrees, required credentials, and professional experience.

Academic Degrees

The most significant step in establishing financial planners' minimum standards of competence took place in June 1986 when the International Board for Standards and Practices of Certified Financial Planners (IBCFP) was formed. On February 1, 1994, the IBCFP changed its name to Certified Financial Planner Board of Standards (CFP Board). It may be some time before the CFP Board succeeds in firmly establishing universally acceptable model curriculum guidelines for financial planning degree-granting institutions. Nevertheless, it is worth reviewing the current status of the model curriculum developed by the CFP Board and published in the CFP Board's General Information Book.

The CFP Board recognizes that in the practice of personal financial planning, the professional planner helps achieve the client's short- and long-range goals. To assume these responsibilities, the planner should have a broad understanding of human experience, cultural values in the American society, business and finance, planning techniques, counseling issues and skills, and fiduciary obligations. Educational institutions should provide the necessary education to develop financial planners' understanding of such matters.

In order to guide educational institutions in their efforts to develop degree and certificate programs in financial planning, the CFP Board has developed the model curriculum guidelines. These guidelines are broad; they include studies in economics, finance, accounting, communication skills, business ethics, legal environment of business, taxation, investments, computer sciences, and financial analysis. Subject matter and required competencies derive from a study of the practice of financial planners.[3] At present, completion of this, or a similar, curriculum leads to a granting of an undergraduate or a graduate degree in financial planning. Any person seriously considering financial planning as a career would be well advised to obtain a degree in financial planning. These guidelines, which gave way to job knowledge requirements of the Certified Financial Planner, were revised in June 1996.

The Credentials

In 1986, when the CFP Board was formed, the CFP certification mark was transferred to the CFP Board from the Denver-based College for Financial Planning which since the 1970s had owned and granted the CFP certification marks. Initially the

---

[3] L. Skurnik, *Job Analysis of the Professional Requirements of the Certified Financial Planner* (Denver: College of Financial Planning, 1987).

CFP Board endorsed the passing of the six-part examination as a prerequisite to granting the CFP certification. The CFP Board has since replaced it with a single comprehensive examination comparable to the bar and CPA examinations.

CFP is not the only valid certification mark for practicing financial planning. There are several credentials, all of which ensure that whoever possesses any one of them can perform financial planning services. In fact, in addition to CFP (Certified Financial Planner), ChFC (Chartered Financial Consultant), PFS (Personal Financial Specialist), and RFP (Registered Financial Planner), other financial services credentials include CLU (Chartered Life Underwriter), CPA (Certified Public Accountant), and JD (Doctor of Jurisprudence).

The Experience

The CFP Board imposes various experience requirements, depending on the planner's level of education. A candidate with a baccalaureate degree from an accredited college or university must have three years of financial planning-related experience. However, those candidates who do not hold such a degree must complete five years of work experience to fulfill the requirement. The experience requirement can be completed either before or after meeting the examination requirement. A complete listing of experience requirements can be found in the CFP Board of Standard's *General Information Booklet*.

For purposes of this requirement, experience is defined as full-time (or equivalent part-time) employment in situations in which the candidate actively uses the knowledge, skills, and abilities required for the certification examination. Under this definition, experience gained in corporate settings (such as those associated with an accountant, attorney, banker, stockbroker, financial planner, insurance salesman, tax preparer, and so on) are accepted.

Continuing Education

The CFP Board of Standard's Licensee Manual specifies that each CFP licensee is required to fulfill 30 hours of continuing education (CE) every two years by completing programs that meet the specified requirements in two areas: (1) Two credit hours in ethics as required by the CFP Board's Code of Ethics and Professional Responsibility. (2) The remaining 28 hours of continuing education in one or more of the following areas: Fundamentals of Financial Planning; Estate Planning; Investments; Retirement Planning; Employee Benefit Planning; Tax Planning; and Knowledge of the CFP Board's Code of Ethics and Professional Responsibility. Credits must be earned after a licensee's certification date, and in the current two-year reporting period. Credits in excess of 30 hours required for the reporting period may not be carried over to subsequent reporting periods.

All CFP registrants are required to report continuing education credits to the CFP Board. The CFP Board has established 30 hours of continuing education every two years as one of the standards for continued use of the certification marks, CFP and Certified Financial Planner. A specific set of rules has now been developed that automatically qualifies continuing education seminars. The CFP Board has established that the standards of continuing education must be (1) consistent with the standards for certification and marks usages (that is, quality controlled); (2) meaningful and not financially burdensome or discriminatory; (3) protective of the public interest; and (4) effective as a means of helping ensure continued competency as a financial planner.

Summing Up

A qualified practicing financial planner should: (1) earn an appropriate academic degree in financial planning; (2) possess the appropriate professional certification; and (3) meet continuing education requirements. Of course, these are necessary, but not sufficient, conditions for becoming a professional financial planner. Also, depending upon the activities performed, the planner is required to possess the necessary securities, insurance, and registered investment advisor licenses.

In the final analysis, competent financial planners are entrusted with detailed knowledge of their clients' finances and assets as well as their personal financial goals and values. Ideally the financial planner is far more sophisticated and informed about financial, tax, economic, and legal considerations than the client; thus the client is almost always very dependent on the skills, judgment and guidance of the planner. Only a competent financial planner deserves to earn a client's complete trust.

COMMITMENT TO ETHICS

A *standard* definition of ethics is not very useful in defining the ethical standards by which financial planning professionals should conduct business. The reason is that there are well over 400 national associations, including medicine, law, and public accounting, all of which have published written codes. To this, one would have to add countless numbers of ethics codes among individual business firms, government bodies, and labor organizations in order to obtain a complete list of ethical standards from which to choose those for financial planners.

Let there be no misunderstanding, however. To say that financial planners must maintain the highest levels of ethical standards is not to deny the fact that they are also entrepreneurs engaged in a business to make a profit. So the key point is this: A less-than-ethical financial planner concentrates on making money by engaging in activities that could harm the client, whereas an ethical financial planner always serves the client's interests and his or her income is generated as a by-product of that service.

We have observed earlier that financial planning is an emerging profession. As the profession matures, a great deal continues to be written about financial planners' unethical practices, conflicts of interest, and self-serving activities. The water is muddied even further by the prevailing practices among many financial planners of both offering planning services and selling investment and insurance products. The establishment of the Board of Ethics as an integral part of the CFP Board of Standards is in response to the deep concerns our society has towards unethical practices. However, it is also argued that guarding the sanctity of the CFP marks and policing the ethical conduct of those who hold the marks are not sufficient to protect the consumer.

Some years ago the most comprehensive ethical code in the financial planning profession was developed by the CFP Board of Standards. The *Code of Ethics and Professional Responsibility* was designed to provide principles and rules of conduct for all CFP licensees. It contains principles which express the profession's recognition of its responsibilities to the public, clients, colleagues, and employers. These principles apply to all CFP designees and provide ethical and professional guidance and ideals for them in the performance of their professional services. The meaning of each principle is further explained in the following paragraph.

The Rules provide practical guidelines derived from the tenets embodied in the principles. These Rules set forth the standards of ethical and professional conduct expected to be followed in particular situations. In addition, it is emphasized that due to the nature of a CFP designee's particular field of endeavor, certain rules may not be applicable. The Code is structured so as to make parallel presentation of the Rules and the Principles.[4]

It is obvious that the task of policing unethical, self-designated, financial planners is complicated and should be left in the hands of regulatory agencies. However, we firmly believe that professional financial planners should be:

E   Efficient
T   Trustworthy
H   Honest
I   Ingenious
C   Caring
S   Sincere

That is, if financial planners make a firm commitment to be efficient, trustworthy, honest, ingenious, completely loyal to their clients, and sincere, then they will automatically maintain the highest levels of ethical standards, and financial planning will be universally recognized as a venerable profession.

In this chapter we discussed general financial planning issues. The financial planning process will be presented in the next chapter.

---

[4] Principles and Rules were extracted from the CFP Board's *Code of Ethics and Professional Responsibility*. A copy might be obtained by calling the CFP Board at (303) 830-7500.

To dream anything that you want to dream. That is the beauty of the human mind. To do anything that you want to do. That is the strength of the human will. To trust yourself to test your limits. That is the courage to succeed.

Bernard Edmonds

CHAPTER 2

The Personal Financial Planning Process

INTRODUCTION

Financial planning as a discipline endured rapid growth in the early 1980s. Virtually unknown in the 1970s, by 2005, it became a profession of almost 300,000 people. In its heyday, the lure of spectacular financial opportunities attracted into the industry both competent financial experts and those who nurtured individual get-rich-quick schemes.

Time has shown that beyond glamour and mystery this valuable financial service is urgently needed by Americans in the 21st century. Financial planning has already become a necessity—not only for the financial security but also for the general peace of mind it affords. In the face of today's ever-changing economy along with individual changeable circumstances, careful financial planning is essential.

In a very real sense, the process of financial planning begins when an individual recognizes a very simple fact: Every person or family is in a unique financial position. Therefore, any course of financial action designed to serve the specific goals and objectives of each family must also be unique. Obviously, what is right for one person with a given set of circumstances may not be right for another with a different set of circumstances.

Recognition of the need for appropriate action for a family, of course, does not automatically answer the question: What *is* the best course of action for that family? Furthermore, when we consider that an average American family is expected to make over $1 million before retirement, and some will make substantially more than that, designing unique strategies for American families becomes both daunting and challenging. To put it succinctly, only when people understand their (1) current financial position, (2) financial goals for the future, and (3) actions which affect their financial situation, can they begin to appreciate what strategies are appropriate for them. However, since many people are hard pressed to comprehend these difficult—and often confusing—issues, a financial planner can maximize their welfare by helping them achieve their goals in the most efficient manner.

In this chapter we will discuss in detail how the financial planning process is initiated, what constitutes the intermediate steps in this process, and how the process is successfully completed. In our discussion we will cover issues that arise before engaging the services of a financial planner. More specifically, the following sequence will be used to describe the personal financial planning process: (a) the initial interview; (b) signing of a formal contract; (c) gathering the data; (d) preliminary analysis; (e) goals, objectives, and strategy refinements; (f) data refinement; (g) analysis of client information; (h) plan presentation with recommended solutions; (i) plan implementation; and (j) plan monitoring and review.

FINANCIAL PLANNING PROCESS

There is no standardized process for performing personal financial planning activities. Even the six-step process that was once developed by the now-defunct Registry of the International Association for Financial Planning (IAFP) and widely adopted by the profession, was not as comprehensive as one would like. In fact, a comprehensive process adds several steps to the Registry's process for qualifying a client and defining the scope of engagement.

An important caveat should be added here. While every financial plan should complete the steps described by the acronym, EGPRIM (see pp. 1-9 to 1-12), not all plans have to achieve that level of comprehensiveness or sophistication. In fact, in the real world financial planners offer more than one level of service in order to accommodate clients with different needs and goals. A variety of terms has been applied to the many levels of services that currently exist. For instance, the American Institute of Certified Public Accountants (AICPA) has identified the following three levels of service: consultant engagements; segment planning engagements; and comprehensive personal financial engagements. A consultation is an informal or unstructured financial planning arrangement which explores the nature and the depth of the financial problem by requiring the prospective client to fill out an initial financial profile (or pre-data gathering) form. The consultation process generally ends with determining whether the client needs a more formal type of engagement, and it is communicated in the form of an oral or written report. Individual planners across the country refer to various levels and types of service by such names as retirement planning, investment planning, tax planning, and comprehensive financial planning. Regardless of the level or type of service performed, however, there is no substitute for a sophisticated, professional approach to financial planning.

SUBJECT AREAS OF PERSONAL FINANCIAL PLANNING

In practice, the comprehensive financial planning process, and the resulting comprehensive financial plan developed for a client, should address eight elements of the client's financial situation. These elements, and their respective chapter references, are presented here. Of course, a comprehensive plan should also have as an integral part a list of specific recommendations, an action plan, and a timetable to follow to complete the planning process.

Elements	Chapters
S	Safety through Risk Management Planning	4 and 5
E	Educational Planning	6
C	Cash Management, Savings, Credit, and Debt Planning	7
U	Ultimate Disposition through Estate Planning	8 and 9
R	Retirement Planning	10 and 11
I	Investment Planning	12, 13, and 14
T	Tax Planning	15 and 16
Y	Yearning for Financial Independence Planning	17

Against the backdrop of an overview of the financial planning process just presented, we will now elaborate on the essential steps associated with this process, a synopsis of which is presented in Figure 2-1.

QUALIFYING A POTENTIAL CLIENT

Every relationship between a financial planner and the client has a built-in life span. Unless great care is taken to nurture it, some relationships are destined to die prematurely, or last only a few years, while a few are likely to ripen to old age. Long-term success depends on those client relationships that stand the test of time.

Clearly, the most important factor contributing to a lasting relationship is a carefully-orchestrated all-important initial interview. During this interview the financial planner sizes up a potential client by determining if there is a firm basis for establishing a long-term relationship with the individual or the family.

To be sure, the initial interview is not an end in itself. It is designed to help the financial planner recognize the potential client's true desires and determine if the chemistry is right for establishing a long-lasting relationship. Sometimes the former element will not surface quickly, and the planner may have to probe *behind the scenes* in order to discover these desires. Here are three real-life examples that demonstrate the complexity of the task at hand.

Case 1

Bob Smith and his fiancee Jane Coy have engaged Karl Dixon to develop a comprehensive financial plan for them. Bob was a registered pharmacist in Cleveland for 20 years but has recently been forced to move to Arizona for health reasons. He sold his pharmaceutical business in Cleveland and is contemplating buying a suitable business in Arizona. Jane is a tenured school teacher in Cleveland and earns an annual salary of $48,000. She participates in the school's retirement benefit plan and enjoys the usual (health, disability, eye care, and so on) fringe benefits. Bob and Jane are planning to get married in a few months and settle down in Arizona. This is a second marriage for both, and there appears to be a great deal of understanding, open communication, and flexibility on the part of both. Karl Dixon's responsibility is to develop a comprehensive financial plan by assuming that Bob and Jane are already married, even though they will not be officially married for several months.

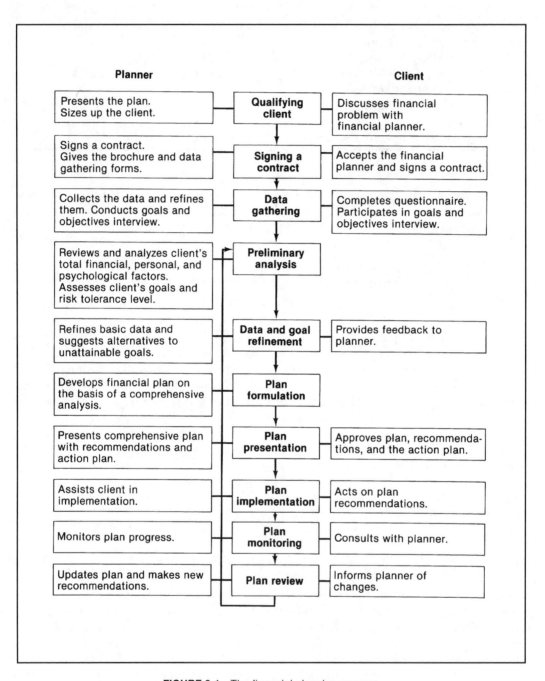

FIGURE 2-1   The financial planning process

Bob and Jane's situation is straightforward, or so it seems on the surface. But after the initial interview, planner Karl Dixon discovered that his responsibility goes far beyond developing a comprehensive financial plan for the couple. Bob Smith loves Jane and has no problem accepting the fact that Jane will quit her teaching job, lose her $48,000 teaching salary plus the associated fringe benefits, and be content with playing the role of an unemployed housewife. In contrast, Jane Coy is unwilling to take such a situation lightly. She fears that after marriage *she will lose* (1) an annual salary of $48,000 plus future increments, (2) her school's retirement contribution, (3) her fringe benefits, (4) her financial independence, (5) money because of the forced sale of her home, and (6) her option to retire at age 59 with full retirement benefits, currently offered by her school system to all employees with at least 25 years of service. She also agonizes over the fact that her daughter has been admitted to an Ivy League school, but Bob is totally opposed to financing such an expensive education. Given all of these concerns, Jane wants Bob to pay her $400,000 before marriage as compensation for the losses she would suffer, but Bob is willing to take the financial responsibility for her only after marriage, and is totally opposed to making any cash payments to Jane. Karl Dixon's task is much more complicated than he was initially led to believe, and he may not wish to handle this case loaded with psychological problems. This case illustrates the importance of the use of qualitative data in financial planning.

Case 2

Robert Powers, 52, and Janet Powers, 49, are a happily married couple. They have three children, ages 28, 25, and 23. Robert feels that their financial situation is in shambles, and he needs a financial planner to bring order to this chaotic situation. Janet feels the same way and is willing to pay a handsome planning fee ($4,000) to a financial planner. The Powers have just engaged Bill Kifer to develop a financial plan for them. Before making his final decision to engage Bill Kifer, however, Robert made the unusual request that his mother's net worth (in excess of $2 million) be included in their plan. A quick review of the Powers' initial data suggests that, with the exception of Bob's unusual request, the Powers' case is straightforward.

During the initial interview Bill Kifer discovered some very interesting facts. Robert, now 52, is currently unemployed and has no intentions of going back to work. He is the only child and will inherit his mother's estate of over $2 million. Furthermore, the mother is 85 years old and Robert argues that since he would have all of her money *very soon* it makes no sense for him to work. This is a source of great friction between Janet and Robert. Janet strongly believes that Robert should not count on this money at all because his mother could still live for a long time and could lose most of her wealth either through bad investments or because of her escalating medical expenses. That creates a special problem: Robert wants Bill Kifer to include his mother's net worth in their plan, whereas Janet wants Kifer to ignore the mother's estate altogether.

There is another family matter that is creating enormous friction between Robert and Janet. All three of their children are adults and should be firmly established in life. Unfortunately, that is not the case. None of them has more than a high school education, a job, or any means of support. The oldest one has a serious health problem, but physically the other two are normal. All the children live at home and are totally dependent on their parents for full financial support. Robert is very upset about the current situation and believes that the only way to resolve this problem is *to throw the children out of the house and force them to become responsible human beings.* Janet, however, feels that since it is the parents who have failed, they should set up separate trusts and adequately fund them to take care of the children for the rest of their lives.

Finally, there is an emotional problem. Since Janet is compelled to earn a livelihood because Robert refuses to work, Janet wants her salary to be spent solely on herself and does not want to support the family. Robert disagrees with that approach, since in his judgment family finances should never be split in that fashion. Here again, given the complexity of this case, Bill Kifer must decide if he is comfortable accepting the Powers as his clients.

Case 3

John and Nancy Well are an affluent couple. The Wells live in the exclusive suburb of Bloomfield Hills in Oakland County of Michigan. John owns two businesses and has an annual income of $400,000. The Wells have two children, both of whom are well settled in life. The Wells have had the benefit of counsel and professional help from a CPA, an attorney, an insurance counselor, a banker, a casualty/property insurance agent, and a retirement benefit specialist. However, John firmly believes that a financial planner would be able to *put it all together* and develop an exclusive road map for the family to follow.

The case of John and Nancy Well is not too different from the cases financial planner Cindy Rawlins routinely handles. Consequently, she is delighted to consider the Wells as valued potential clients. However, the initial interview raised great doubts in her mind about the advisability of accepting this case.

The facts discovered by Cindy Rawlins are as follows. Despite their apparent affluence, both John and Nancy feel that taxes and inflation are going to eventually *kill them.* Yet, they insist on maintaining an extravagant lifestyle which puts enormous strains on their spendable income. This leads the Wells to insist on earning unreasonably high rates of return on their investable funds. However, what really complicates the matter is the fact that both John and Nancy are risk averse investors and could not tolerate the loss of their principal. So, Cindy Rawlins wonders if there is any true benefit to developing a comprehensive financial plan unless the Wells are willing to reorient their investment expectations and their lifestyle.

On the basis of the three cases just presented, it is possible to make some general observations. Regardless of their orientation and expectations, what clients really need is an *objective* rather than a *subjective* perspective of their personal finances. True, a financial planner should be well versed with the mechanics of plan development and implementation. But, the planner should also be able to blend mechanical expertise with human understanding in developing acceptable solutions that will best serve the clients. Consequently, the success of a planning process is assured only when the financial planner succeeds in establishing a professional relationship with the *right type of clients.*

SIGNING A FORMAL CONTRACT

After the financial planner and the prospective client have agreed to establish a professional relationship, a formal contract or agreement—also called an engagement letter—must be signed. This contract should specify: (1) the range of services to be performed by the planner; (2) the method of compensation; and (3) the client's responsibility in the planning process. Also, the contract should specify that: (1) the client agrees to participate in the planning process on a voluntary basis; (2) the financial planner is not authorized to perform any legal functions; and (3) the client is responsible for compensating other professionals (for instance, CPA or attorney) if they are consulted by the financial planner on behalf of the client. Of course, to help achieve the third objective, the client should be asked to sign an Authorization for Information form.

As part of the contract signing ritual, if licensed as a registered investment advisor with the Securities and Exchange Commission (SEC), the financial planner is obliged to provide the client with a planning brochure in compliance with SEC Rule 204-3, commonly known as the *Brochure Rule*. The brochure must describe the financial planning services offered by the financial planner. Furthermore, the brochure should also specify that if the client implements through the planner any of the plan recommendations that generate commissions, then the planner will earn these commissions in addition to the planning fee (conflict of interest rule). This rule can also be satisfied by providing the client with ADV (Part II) of the registered investment advisor.

Finally, the contract should include a provision permitting the client to cancel it within five business days and have the advance planning fee, if any, fully refunded. This provision makes it possible for the client to go over the contract and the brochure carefully and, if desired, have them reviewed by an attorney. Such a provision also helps to emphasize that, by signing the contract, both parties agree to establish a long and fruitful relationship.

GATHERING THE DATA

In Chapter 1 we introduced EGPRIM, which covered the six important stages of planning. We will now elaborate on these stages.

It is often said that, irrespective of its complexity, a plan is only as good as the quality of data and assumptions on which it is based. There is a great deal of truth in that statement. Unless the data are accurate and reflective of the client's goals, aspirations, and fears, no matter how comprehensive and sophisticated, the plan will not have much value for the client. Consequently, a standard rule of thumb is that the data must be sufficiently comprehensive to enable the planner to: (1) evaluate the client's financial condition; (2) determine the client's personality, dreams, and fears; (3) articulate the client's short- and long-range goals; and (4) formulate a set of strategies for helping the client achieve these goals. For these reasons, the financial planner must collect both quantitative and qualitative data as the basis for developing a comprehensive plan.

At this point it is necessary to add an important caveat. Before starting the data collection process the financial planner should make the client comfortable by explaining why such a detailed personal, financial, and psychological set of data is needed to develop the plan. This is because few people appreciate the complexity of the planning process. Consequently, an informed and enlightened client might be expected to supply a far more complete and accurate set of data than an uninformed client who might find such an exercise overpowering and stressful.

Personal Financial Planning
Questionnaire

Personal Information _____

Client

First Name _____ Middle _____ Last _____

Birth Date (mm/dd/yyyy) _____ /_____ / _____   Gender: ___ Male ___ Female

  Address _____

  _____

  City _____ State _____ Zip _____

Phone (Day) _____ Phone (Eve) _____

Best Time To Call _____ ___am ___pm   E-mail Address _____

Spouse

First Name _____ Middle _____ Last _____

Birth Date (mm/dd/yyyy) _____ /_____ / _____   Gender: ___ Male ___ Female

Phone (Day) _____ Phone (Eve) _____

Best Time To Call _____ ___am ___pm   E-mail Address _____

Dependents

First Name	Middle Name	Last Name	Birth Date (mm/dd/yyyy)	Gender (M/F)
_____	_____	_____	_____	_____
_____	_____	_____	_____	_____
_____	_____	_____	_____	_____
_____	_____	_____	_____	_____
_____	_____	_____	_____	_____

•1

Risk Tolerance _____

Indicate your level of agreement with the following statements by checking the most appropriate box for each statement.

	Strongly Disagree				Strongly Agree	Don't Know
1. **Expected Return.** Given historical returns on different kinds of investments, my desired level of investment return is above average and I am willing to bear an above-average level of investment risk (volatility).	❑	❑	❑	❑	❑	❑
2. **Holding Period.** I am willing to maintain investment positions over a reasonably long period of time (generally considered at least 5 years or more).	❑	❑	❑	❑	❑	❑
3. **Ease of Management.** I want to be very actively involved in the monitoring and decision-making required to manage my investments.	❑	❑	❑	❑	❑	❑
4. **Dependents.** There are none or few dependents that rely on my income and my investment portfolio for support.	❑	❑	❑	❑	❑	❑
5. **Income Source.** My major source of income is adequate, predictable and steadily growing.	❑	❑	❑	❑	❑	❑
6. **Investment Experience.** I have prior investment experience with stocks, bonds, and other investments. I understand the concept of investment risk.	❑	❑	❑	❑	❑	❑
7. **Debt/Credit.** My debt level is low and my credit history is excellent.	❑	❑	❑	❑	❑	❑

• 2

8. Use the following table to answer the next two questions.

	Potential Average Return	Odds Of Losing Money In Any One Year	Worst Year Of 75 Years	Worst Year Of 30 Years
Portfolio A	12.5%	1 in 3	-46%	-24%
Portfolio B	12.0%	1 in 4	-41%	-21%
Portfolio C	11.3%	1 in 5	-37%	-18%
Portfolio D	10.0%	1 in 6	-28%	-12%
Portfolio E	9.0%	1 in 7	-22%	-8%
Portfolio F	7.8%	1 in 8	-15%	-3%

a.) Assuming you would prefer to avoid unnecessary investment risk if possible, choose the portfolio that best fits your ideal tolerance for risk:

Portfolio _____

b.) Sometime your ideal portfolio may be too conservative to produce returns that would enable you to meet your most important financial goals. If necessary, to meet financial goals you feel are critical, which portfolio has the most risk you could possibly tolerate?

Portfolio With The Most Risk You Could Tolerate _____

Assets

Provide the requested information about your assets.

Cash Assets

	Asset 1	Asset 2	Asset 3	Asset 4
Description	_____	_____	_____	_____
Owner: (check one)	__ Client __ Spouse __ JTWROS __ Community __ Tenants in Common	__ Client __ Spouse __ JTWROS __ Community __ Tenants in Common	__ Client __ Spouse __ JTWROS __ Community __ Tenants in Common	__ Client __ Spouse __ JTWROS __ Community __ Tenants in Common
Current Value	$ _____	$ _____	$ _____	$ _____
Yield Rate	_____ %	_____ %	_____ %	_____ %
Annual Contribution	$ _____	$ _____	$ _____	$ _____

Investment Assets (Non-Retirement)

	Asset 1	Asset 2	Asset 3	Asset 4
Description	_____	_____	_____	_____
Owner: (check one)	__ Client __ Spouse __ JTWROS __ Other	__ Client __ Spouse __ JTWROS __ Other	__ Client __ Spouse __ JTWROS __ Other	__ Client __ Spouse __ JTWROS __ Other
Current Value	$ _____	$ _____	$ _____	$ _____
Cost Basis	$ _____	$ _____	$ _____	$ _____
Tax Treatment: (check one)	__ Taxed __ Tax-Free __ Tax-Deferred	__ Taxed __ Tax-Free __ Tax-Deferred	__ Taxed __ Tax-Free __ Tax-Deferred	__ Taxed __ Tax-Free __ Tax-Deferred
Annual Contribution	$ _____	$ _____	$ _____	$ _____

Business/Real Estate

	Asset 1	Asset 2	Asset 3	Asset 4
Description	_____	_____	_____	_____
Type	_____	_____	_____	_____
(Rental, S Corp, LLC, etc.)				
Owner: (check one)	__ Client __ Spouse __ JTWROS __ Other	__ Client __ Spouse __ JTWROS __ Other	__ Client __ Spouse __ JTWROS __ Other	__ Client __ Spouse __ JTWROS __ Other
Current Value	$ _____	$ _____	$ _____	$ _____
Cost Basis	$ _____	$ _____	$ _____	$ _____

Personal Assets

	Asset 1	Asset 2	Asset 3	Asset 4
Description	_____	_____	_____	_____
Type	_____	_____	_____	_____
(Residence, Auto, Boat, etc.)				
Owner: (check one)	__ Client __ Spouse __ JTWROS __ Other	__ Client __ Spouse __ JTWROS __ Other	__ Client __ Spouse __ JTWROS __ Other	__ Client __ Spouse __ JTWROS __ Other
Current Value	$ _____	$ _____	$ _____	$ _____
Cost Basis	$ _____	$ _____	$ _____	$ _____

Retirement Assets

	Asset 1	Asset 2	Asset 3	Asset 4
Description	_____	_____	_____	_____
Type	_____	_____	_____	_____
Owner: (check one)	__ Client __ Spouse	__ Client __ Spouse	__ Client __ Spouse	__ Client __ Spouse
Current Value	$ _____	$ _____	$ _____	$ _____
Cost Basis	$ _____	$ _____	$ _____	$ _____
Tax Treatment: (check one)	__ Tax Def (Pre-Tax) __ Tax-Def (After-Tax) __ Tax-Free __ Taxable	__ Tax Def (Pre-Tax) __ Tax-Def (After-Tax) __ Tax-Free __ Taxable	__ Tax Def (Pre-Tax) __ Tax-Def (After-Tax) __ Tax-Free __ Taxable	__ Tax Def (Pre-Tax) __ Tax-Def (After-Tax) __ Tax-Free __ Taxable
Annual Contribution	$ _____	$ _____	$ _____	$ _____
Employer Match:	__ Yes __ No	__ Yes __ No	__ Yes __ No	__ Yes __ No
Employer-Only Annual Contribution	$ _____	$ _____	$ _____	$ _____

Stock Options

	Asset 1	Asset 2	Asset 3	Asset 4
Description	_____	_____	_____	_____
Type: (check one)	__ Incentive Stock Option __ Non-Qualified Stock Option	__ Incentive Stock Option __ Non-Qualified Stock Option	__ Incentive Stock Option __ Non-Qualified Stock Option	__ Incentive Stock Option __ Non-Qualified Stock Option
Owner: (check one)	__ Client __ Spouse __ Community	__ Client __ Spouse __ Community	__ Client __ Spouse __ Community	__ Client __ Spouse __ Community

Stock Options - Continued

	Asset 1	Asset 2	Asset 3	Asset 4
Number of Shares Granted	_____	_____	_____	_____
Current Stock Price	$ _____	$ _____	$ _____	$ _____
Strike Price	$ _____	$ _____	$ _____	$ _____
Date Vested (mm/dd/yyyy)	___ / ___ / ___	___ / ___ / ___	___ / ___ / ___	___ / ___ / ___
Year of Exercise	_____	_____	_____	_____

Deferred Compensation & Deferred Annuities

	Source 1	Source 2	Source 3	Source 4
Description	_____	_____	_____	_____
Type: (check one)	__ Def. Comp. __ Def. Annuity	__ Def. Comp. __ Def. Annuity	__ Def. Comp. __ Def. Annuity	__ Def. Comp. __ Def. Annuity
Owner: (check one)	__ Client __ Spouse	__ Client __ Spouse	__ Client __ Spouse	__ Client __ Spouse
Current Value	$ _____	$ _____	$ _____	$ _____

Deferred Compensation & Deferred Annuities - Continued

	(Asset 1)	(Asset 2)	(Asset 3)	(Asset 4)
Annual Deferral	$ _____	$ _____	$ _____	$ _____
Number of Yrs Deferrals Continue	_____	_____	_____	_____
Deferral Increase Rate	_____ %	_____ %	_____ %	_____ %
Year Payments Begin (yyyy)	_____	_____	_____	_____
Number of Yrs of Income	_____	_____	_____	_____
Remainder Value at Second Death	_____	_____	_____	_____

Liabilities

Provide the requested information about your liabilities.

	Liability 1	Liability 2	Liability 3	Liability 4
Description	_____	_____	_____	_____
Type: (Auto, consumer, mortgage, etc.)	_____	_____	_____	_____
Tax Deductible	__ Yes __ No	__ Yes __ No	__ Yes __ No	__ Yes __ No
Responsible Party: (check one)	__ Client __ Spouse __ Joint	__ Client __ Spouse __ Joint	__ Client __ Spouse __ Joint	__ Client __ Spouse __ Joint
Original Balance	$ _____	$ _____	$ _____	$ _____

• 8

Current
Balance $ _____ $ _____ $ _____ $ _____

Periodic
Payment $ _____ $ _____ $ _____ $ _____

Payment: __ Semi-Monthly   __ Client   __ Client   __ Client
Frequency: __ Monthly   __ Spouse   __ Spouse   __ Spouse
(check one)   __ Quarterly   __ Community   __ Community   __ Community
                 __ Semi-Annual   __ Semi-Annual   __ Semi-Annual   __ Semi-Annual
                 __ Annual   __ Annual   __ Annual   __ Annual

Interest Rate   _____ %   _____ %   _____ %   _____ %

Year of
Maturity (yyyy) _____   _____   _____   _____

Insurance _____

Life Insurance

	Policy 1	**Policy 2**	**Policy 3**	**Policy 4**
Description	_____	_____	_____	_____
Insured Party: (check one)	__ Client __ Spouse __ Irrev. Trust __ Community	__ Client __ Spouse __ Irrev. Trust __ Community	__ Client __ Spouse __ Irrev. Trust __ Community	__ Client __ Spouse __ Irrev. Trust __ Community
Beneficiary: (check one)	__ Client __ Spouse __ Irrev. Trust __ Third Party	__ Client __ Spouse __ Irrev. Trust __ Third Party	__ Client __ Spouse __ Irrev. Trust __ Third Party	__ Client __ Spouse __ Irrev. Trust __ Third Party
Annual Premium	$ _____	$ _____	$ _____	$ _____
Face Amount	$ _____	$ _____	$ _____	$ _____
Current Cash Value	$ _____	$ _____	$ _____	$ _____

Estimated Cash
Value at $ _____ $ _____ $ _____ $ _____
Retirement

Percent of Cash
Value Available _____ %   _____ %   _____ %   _____ %
To Fund Goals

Disability Insurance

	Policy 1	**Policy 2**	**Policy 3**	**Policy 4**
Description	_____	_____	_____	_____
Type: (check one)	__ Group __ Individual	__ Group __ Individual	__ Group __ Individual	__ Group __ Individual
Insured Party: (check one)	__ Client __ Spouse	__ Client __ Spouse	__ Client __ Spouse	__ Client __ Spouse
Annual Premium	$ _____	$ _____	$ _____	$ _____
Monthly Benefit	$ _____	$ _____	$ _____	$ _____
Waiting Period (Days)	_____	_____	_____	_____
Length of Benefit (Yrs)	_____	_____	_____	_____
Cost of Living Adjustment	_____ %	_____ %	_____ %	_____ %

• 10

Income

Provide the requested information about the sources of income available to you both now and in the future.

Earnings

	Client	Spouse
Salary	$ _____	$ _____
Self-Employment Earnings	$ _____	$ _____
Earnings Not Subject to FICA	$ _____	$ _____
Other	$ _____	$ _____

Defined Benefit Pensions

	Client	Spouse
Expected Years of Participation to be Completed by Retirement	_____	_____
Year Benefit Begins (yyyy)	_____	_____
Annual Benefit Amount	$ _____	$ _____
Have Us Estimate an Annual Benefit Amount?	__ Yes __ No	__ Yes __ No
Number of Years Benefit Continues	_____	_____
Increase Rate Before Benefit Begins	_____ %	_____ %
Increase Rate After Benefit Begins	_____ %	_____ %
Survivor Benefit	_____ %	_____ %
Current Value	$ _____	$ _____
Remainder Value at Second Death	$ _____	$ _____

• 11

Social Security Retirement Benefit

Covered by Social Security?	__ Yes __ No	__ Yes __ No
Begin Age	_____	_____
Portion Subject to Tax	__ 0% __ 50% __ 85%	
Annual Benefit Amount	$ _____	$ _____
Have LJPR Estimate an Annual Benefit Amount?	__ Yes __ No	__ Yes __ No

Miscellaneous Income

	Source 1	Source 2	Source 3	Source 4
Description	_____	_____	_____	_____
Type: (check one)	__ Ordinary __ Dividend __ Investment	__ Ordinary __ Dividend __ Investment	__ Ordinary __ Dividend __ Investment	__ Ordinary __ Dividend __ Investment
Cash/ Non Cash: (check one)	__ Cash __ Non Cash	__ Cash __ Non Cash	__ Cash __ Non Cash	__ Cash __ Non Cash
Active/ Passive: (check one)	__ Active __ Passive	__ Active __ Passive	__ Active __ Passive	__ Active __ Passive
Annual Income Amount	$ _____	$ _____	$ _____	$ _____
Year Income Begins (yyyy)	_____	_____	_____	_____
Number of Years Income Continues	_____	_____	_____	_____

• 12

Living Expenses

Provide the requested information about your living expenses. Do not include debt payments. Enter all debt payments in the Liabilities section.

Lifestyle Expenses

Description	Current Monthly Amount	Desired Retirement Monthly Amount (Today's Dollars)
_____	$ _____	$ _____
_____	$ _____	$ _____
_____	$ _____	$ _____
_____	$ _____	$ _____
_____	$ _____	$ _____
_____	$ _____	$ _____
_____	$ _____	$ _____
_____	$ _____	$ _____
_____	$ _____	$ _____
_____	$ _____	$ _____
_____	$ _____	$ _____
_____	$ _____	$ _____
_____	$ _____	$ _____
_____	$ _____	$ _____
_____	$ _____	$ _____
_____	$ _____	$ _____
_____	$ _____	$ _____

• 13

Description	Current Monthly Amount	Desired Retirement Monthly Amount (Today's Dollars)
_____	$ _____	$ _____
_____	$ _____	$ _____
_____	$ _____	$ _____
_____	$ _____	$ _____
_____	$ _____	$ _____
_____	$ _____	$ _____
_____	$ _____	$ _____
_____	$ _____	$ _____
_____	$ _____	$ _____
_____	$ _____	$ _____
_____	$ _____	$ _____
_____	$ _____	$ _____
_____	$ _____	$ _____
_____	$ _____	$ _____
_____	$ _____	$ _____
_____	$ _____	$ _____
_____	$ _____	$ _____
_____	$ _____	$ _____
_____	$ _____	$ _____
_____	$ _____	$ _____

• 14

Financial Goals

Provide the requested information about your long-term spending goals.

Education Goals

	Student 1	Student 2	Student 3	Student 4
Description	_____	_____	_____	_____
Years Until Need	_____	_____	_____	_____
Year Of Need	_____	_____	_____	_____
Annual Amount (Today's Dollars)	$ _____	$ _____	$ _____	$ _____
Portion to Fund	_____ %	_____ %	_____ %	_____ %

Other Accumulation Goals

	Goal 1	Goal 2	Goal 3	Goal 4
Description	_____	_____	_____	_____
Years Until Need	_____	_____	_____	_____
Year of Need	_____	_____	_____	_____
Number of Years Needed	_____	_____	_____	_____
Amount (Today's Dollars)	$ _____	$ _____	$ _____	$ _____

• 15

Other Retirement Goals

1. **Optional** - I/We have other specific goals we will need money for and would like to include these expenditures in our plan. (**Do not** include basic retirement income or estate goals.) They are as follows:

	Goal 1	Goal 2	Goal 3	Goal 4
Description	_____	_____	_____	_____
Begin Year (yyyy)	_____	_____	_____	_____
Year of Need	_____	_____	_____	_____
Number of Years Needed	_____	_____	_____	_____
Annual Amount	$ _____	$ _____	$ _____	$ _____

2. Ideally, I would like to retire at age _____, but if needed to meet other more important financial goals, would be willing to work to age _____. *(Input "now" if already retired)*

3. My spouse will retire at the same time as I do: ____ Yes or ____ No. If No, my spouse would ideally like to retire at age _____, but if needed to meet other more important financial goals, would be willing to work to age _____. *(Input "now" if already retired)*

4. If possible, I would like to leave an estate worth at least $ _____, but would be willing to leave as little as $ _____ if necessary to meet other more important goals.

5.   How would you like us to estimate your retirement income needs? (check one)

_____   I'd like you to estimate my retirement income needs based on my current
         income and your estimates of what would be needed to maintain my lifestyle
         *(do not select this option if already retired, input your annual spending needs
         below).* OR...

_____   I/We would ideally retire on an annual retirement spending budget of
         $ _____, BUT in no case less than $ _____.

6.   Please tell us which best describes your attitude about Social Security: (check one)

_____   I/We would prefer to not be dependent on Social Security in retirement.

_____   I/We would like to include estimated Social Security benefits in our
         Wealthcare Plan.

Please enter any additional information you would like us to consider which is not
already included in this questionnaire.

_____

_____

_____

_____

_____

_____

_____

_____

Priorities _____

Your plan will be designed to help you have a high confidence level that your most important financial goals will be achieved. To design the optimal set of the hundreds of potential choices, we need to prioritize your goals to identify those alternatives that make the most sense for what you want to accomplish. Please complete the following:

1.   Investment risk (volatility or the risk of losing money) is something we all wish to avoid if possible. We can often take less than our maximum tolerance for risk by making relatively minor modifications to our other goals. Please answer the following question:

I would be willing to do the following to design a plan that takes less risk than my maximum risk tolerance indicates (check all that apply):

    a. ____ Save $ _____ more a year than I'm currently saving
    b. ____ Retire later than my ideal retirement age
    c. ____ Leave a smaller estate than my ideal estate
    d. ____ Lower my retirement income to more modest levels
    e. ____ I'm comfortable with taking investment risk (based on my maximum tolerance) and I'd prefer to accept that level of investment risk rather ` than modify any of these other goals.

2.   Saving money is usually necessary to achieve your financial goals. However, it may also mean you are making sacrifices in your current lifestyle to achieve future goals. Please answer the following question:

If possible, I would like to reduce my current annual savings by $ _____ a year so I can improve my current lifestyle. To meet this goal I would be willing to modify the following goals (check all that apply):

    a. ____ Take more risk than my maximum risk tolerance indicates
    b. ____ Retire later than my ideal retirement age
    c. ____ Leave a smaller estate than my ideal estate
    d. ____ Lower my retirement income to more modest levels
    e. ____ I'm comfortable with saving more than my ideal annual savings amount rather than modify any of these other goals.

3.   When you plan to retire can have a significant impact on the probability of achieving your financial goals, because it is the age when you stop saving and begin withdrawals from investments. Please complete the following question:

To retire at my ideal retirement age, I would be willing to modify the following goals (check all that apply):

a. ____   Take more risk than my maximum risk tolerance indicates
b. ____   Save $ _____ more a year than I'm currently saving
c. ____   Leave a smaller estate than my ideal estate
d. ____   Lower my retirement income to more modest levels
e. ____   Retiring at my ideal retirement age isn't as important as these other goals, so I'm comfortable delaying retirement to later age to avoid modifying these other goals.

4.   Many people have charitable desires or wish to pass wealth on to their family to provide financial security. Doing so can mean compromising other goals. Please answer the following question:

To achieve my ideal estate or charitable goals, I would be willing to modify the following goals (check all that apply):

a. ____   Take more risk than my maximum risk tolerance indicates
b. ____   Retire later than my ideal retirement age
c. ____   Save $ _____ more a year than I'm currently saving
d. ____   Lower my retirement income to more modest levels
e. ____   While I'd like to achieve my estate goals, doing so isn't as important as these other objectives, so I'd be willing to reduce my estate goal to avoid modifying these other goals.

5.   Your lifestyle in retirement is dependent both on the resources you have available and your personal preferences. Most people would like to have a comfortable retirement income and lifestyle. Please answer the following question:

To maximize my retirement income, I would be willing to modify the following goals (check all that apply):

a. ____   Take more risk than my maximum risk tolerance indicates
b. ____   Retire later than my ideal retirement age
c. ____   Save more money than my ideal savings amount
d. ____   Leave a smaller estate than my ideal estate
e. ____   I'd like to have a very comfortable retirement, but I would be willing to live a more modest lifestyle in retirement rather than changing these other goals.

• 19

Estate Planning _____

Provide the requested information about your estate plan.

	Client	Spouse
Will	__ Yes __ No	__ Yes __ No
Trust Document	__ Yes __ No	__ Yes __ No

Estate Planning Assumptions

	Client	Spouse
Death Age (for estate plan)	_____	_____
Estimated Funeral Expenses	_____	_____

Select which assumption you would like to use for estate taxes after the year 2010.

____ Assume the sunset provision is not repealed and estate tax rates and exemption amounts apply as in 2001.

____ Assume the sunset provision is repealed and legislation is passed to abolish estate taxes as planned for 2010.

____ Assume new legislation is passed implementing a reduced estate tax as planned for 2009.

Notes/Comments _____

_____

_____

_____

_____

_____

_____

_____

_____

_____

_____

_____

• 20

Quantitative Data

Clearly, the magnitude of data collection depends upon the sophistication of the financial plan desired by the client. For instance, for a simple investment plan, data can be collected on a simple investment statement. In contrast, a comprehensive plan requires a far more sophisticated set of investment data, which can be obtained by completing the relevant portion of the accompanying Personal Financial Planning Questionnaire. In any event, most comprehensive plans require the collection of at least the following information:

- Personal Profile
- Checking, Savings, and Money Market
- Notes and Loans
- Mortgages
- Stocks, Bonds, and Mutual Funds
- Real Estate/Oil and Gas/Other Limited Partnerships
- Income Data
- Employee Benefits
- Insurance Coverage
- Educational Funding
- Tax-related Data
- Wills/Trusts/Estate-related Data

In addition, key documents are also required for obtaining additional quantitative data. A list of several important business and personal documents is presented below:

Personal documents
Wills: Clients and Spouse
Trust Agreements
Deeds or Contracts
Tax Returns
Divorce Decree
Nuptial Agreements
Separation Agreements
Children's Assets
Insurance Policies:
    Life
    Health
    Property/Casualty
    Liability

Business documents
Corporation or Partnership Papers
Income Tax Returns
Financial Statements
Stock Purchase Agreements
Employment Agreements
Employee Benefit Programs

Pension/Profit Sharing Plans
Leases

The most efficient method of collecting quantitative data is to use a fact finding questionnaire accompanied by an explanation sheet that elaborates on various questions which might be difficult to answer. The questionnaire could be relatively simple, or it could be designed as a comprehensive document if the complexity of the client's financial life so warrants.

Qualitative Data

The sophistication of a comprehensive plan also depends upon the nature of the qualitative data. A practical yet effective means of collecting this type of data is to conduct a *goals and objectives interview*. Examples of qualitative data include: (1) priorities of various objectives; (2) risk tolerance level; (3) good and bad experiences with investment products; (4) feelings toward life insurance; (5) budgetary problems; (6) financial independence goals; (7) educational goals for children; and (8) general feeling toward money management. As a general rule, open-ended questions are used to obtain qualitative data.

PROCESSING AND ANALYZING FINANCIAL DATA

Preliminary Analysis

The primary use of financial information in personal financial planning is in the analysis, planning, and control of ongoing personal financial decisions directed by the financial planner. It is difficult, if not impossible, to identify financial objectives and formulate strategies for their achievement without knowing a client's current financial situation and resources.

Following the gathering of quantitative and qualitative data, a preliminary analysis can be performed with three objectives in mind: (1) identifying gaps, inconsistencies, and inaccuracies in the data; (2) developing highlights of the client's current financial condition; and (3) identifying those goals that appear to be unrealistic. These objectives are achieved through the preparation of a number of specialized statements, a partial list of which follows:

- life insurance needs analysis
- budget analysis
- tax analysis
- investment analysis
- retirement analysis

Each statement should be carefully analyzed with the specific objective of generating a list of open questions or issues that still need to be addressed by the client.

Establish Client Objectives

An important step is to refine and articulate goals and objectives of every client, and identify detailed strategies for achieving them. There are two reasons for taking this step. First, many people casually use goals, objectives, and strategies as though they are synonymous terms, when in fact they are not. Second, even in those cases where a distinction is made between goals and strategies, people are generally vague about how these strategies can be implemented to reach specific goals.

Let us begin by distinguishing between goals and objectives. *Goals* are broad-based, relatively open-ended, projections of the client's aspirations. For instance, one client's goal might be to remain affluent both during working years and in retirement. By contrast, another client's goal might be to remain frugal during working years so as to maximize the size of the estate that can be passed on to the beneficiaries.

In contrast, *objectives* are quantifiable means of achieving the goals over a specified time period. For instance, becoming affluent is an expression of a goal, whereas saving $1,000,000 by age 55 is an objective. Similarly, living modestly during one's lifetime in order to maximize the estate is a goal. But living on a monthly budget of $4,000 and passing on a $1,000,000 estate to the beneficiaries is an objective, because the latter is quantifiable and is associated with a specific time frame.

Next, we turn our attention to strategies which are developed to achieve the defined objectives. A strategy refers to a detailed program that is carefully crafted to achieve a set of predefined objectives. For instance, accumulating $1 million by age 55 is a predetermined objective, whereas the steps that must be taken to achieve that objective constitute the strategy.

To recapitulate, defining goals, objectives, and strategies, and differentiating between them constitute an integral part of the planning process. Such an exercise: (1) forces the client to think clearly; (2) minimizes the risk of overlooking important objectives; (3) allows the client to appreciate the importance of key objectives; (4) establishes a rational basis for charting a course of action; (5) helps quantify the goals to be achieved within a given time frame; (6) makes it necessary for the client to prioritize his or her objectives; and (7) brings together the objectives and available resources when realistic strategies are formulated.

Data Refinement

This step begins with the presentation to the client of a list of questions generated by the completion of the preliminary analysis. The client should be encouraged to provide the missing data and clarify some of the information that is subject to misinterpretation. For instance, if the purchase price and dividend distribution record of ABC stock are missing, it would be impossible to accurately calculate the tax liability resulting from the sale of this stock. Another example of incomplete data relates to the pension plan balance which does not differentiate between fully vested and nonvested contributions. A third example of confusing data is a single premium deferred annuity (SPDA) investment purchased five years ago for which the surrender charge table is not available. If this SPDA does not impose surrender charges after four years, then it could now be sold without incurring these charges. If, on the other hand, the company imposes a six-year surrender charge, then the financial planner would have to take this factor into account if the liquidation of this investment is contemplated.

The modification of unrealistic goals constitutes an even bigger challenge for the financial planner. This is because complicated psychological, emotional and social factors may have to be handled to solve this type of problem. In general, an attempt can be made to solve the unrealistic goals problems by suggesting a variety of more realistic alternatives, examples of which now follow.

Analysis of Client Information

After the data have been refined and perfected, the strengths and weaknesses of the collected data can be identified by undertaking an analysis in two stages. First, the data can be analyzed by using a financial planning software program. The selection of a software program would of course depend upon the degree of sophistication desired. Some software programs are basic, while others are complex and require substantial technical knowledge on the part of the paraplanner.

An efficient way of undertaking this task is to conduct it at three different levels.

Level 1   Analysis of client's strengths and weaknesses revealed by a close examination of the statement of financial position, statement of inflows and outflows, and the key financial ratios calculated from these statements.

Level 2   Evaluation of economic and financial conditions as they impact upon the client's present and future resources.

Level 3   Re-prioritization of the client's objectives based on the above analysis.

Unattainable goal	*Alternative suggestions*
Become financially independent at a given age	1. Increase the time frame 2. Reduce the financial independence income 3. Increase investment return by assuming more risk 4. Reduce expenditures
Saving goal of a specified amount	1. Reduce flexible expenses 2. Reduce fixed expenses 3. Increase income (e.g., unemployed spouse may seek employment) 4. Employ forced savings techniques
Finance a college education involving a specified amount	1. Apply for a student loan 2. Seek employment for the child 3. Participate in an educational trust offered by the State

Once this analytical phase is completed, the financial planner can run *what if* simulations in order to determine the most efficient ways of addressing the client's concerns and achieving the desired objectives. This type of analysis brings the plan to life and makes the planning process truly meaningful.

RECOMMENDATIONS FOR ACTION

Basic Recommendations

An important feature of the comprehensive plan is the recommendations designed to help the client achieve the predetermined objectives. Of course, one of the unpleasant, albeit necessary, tasks of a financial planner is to modify those objectives that are unrealistic.

Assuming that all of the objectives are, or have been made, realistic, plan recommendations should be directed towards helping the client achieve the stated objectives in each of the eight major areas: namely, risk management, education, cash management, estate planning, retirement, investments, taxes, and financial independence. Initially, these recommendations should be made in general terms. For instance, the planner may suggest that the client purchase $500,000 of additional life insurance, invest $50,000 in a single premium deferred annuity, reduce taxes by investing in a tax shelter, and create an irrevocable trust. Subsequently, the planner should recommend specific steps that must be taken to implement these recommendations. For instance, the planner may recommend that the client purchase $500,000 universal life insurance from ABC Company and invest $50,000 in XYZ Insurance Company which markets one of the best single premium deferred annuity products. The planner should also assist the client in implementing these recommendations, if such assistance is desired.

Plan Presentation

The highlight of the financial planning process is the presentation of a comprehensive financial plan to the client. Ideally, the plan should be subdivided into the following sections:

Section	*Contents*
Goals and Objectives Interview	A summary of the initial interview with the client during which short- and long-term goals were articulated, and the client's fears, dreams, and major concerns were recognized.
Basic Observations	Highlights of the major components of the comprehensive financial plan.
Key Recommendations	Recommendations for achieving the specified objectives in each of the eight planning areas covered by S-E-C-U-R-I-T-Y.
Action Plan	"Trip tick," specifying the actions required on the part of the client, and the priorities of these action plans.

Naturally, the plan should contain not only a set of recommendations, but also the means to press them into action.

In presenting the financial plan to the client, the planner should emphasize the following points:

1. Plan recommendations are tentative and can be finalized only after they have been fully explored, and if necessary, modified.
2. Wherever necessary, these recommendations were developed in collaboration with the appropriate specialists.
3. The client should appreciate the nature of these recommendations so their chances of acceptance would be greatly enhanced.

In addition to the written comprehensive financial plan, if financially and administratively feasible, the financial planner may also provide the client with a video and an audio cassette as supplements to the written plan. These ancillary products could go a long way toward motivating the client to study the plan and implement its recommendations.

During the plan presentation session, the planner should impress upon the client that the value of the plan cannot be realized until its recommendations are fully implemented within a reasonable timeframe.

IMPLEMENTATION

An effective financial planner motivates the client to closely follow the action plan section of the comprehensive financial plan. While both parties explicitly recognize that the client is under no obligation to implement the recommendations through the developer of the plan, the client must realize that to derive full benefits the plan recommendations must be implemented in a timely fashion. The financial planner of course has a moral and professional obligation to assist the client in implementing the plan. In addition, if the client purchases insurance and investment products from the financial planner, the planner must (1) specify that commissions generated by these sales are in addition to, and not in lieu of, the planning fees already collected, (2) provide in writing the advantages, disadvantages and costs associated with each product, and (3) make sure that the client clearly understands their attendant risks and is comfortable with them.

The ultimate success of a financial plan depends on the speed and the efficiency with which the recommendations are implemented. Consequently, it behooves the planner to (1) set up a timetable for action, (2) assist the client in following the action plan, and (3) work closely with other professionals to ensure the speedy implementation of plan recommendations.

MONITORING AND REVIEW

Personal financial planning is a never-ending process. Over time, a client's personal situation, financial conditions, economic and tax environment—all of these can and do change. Consequently, the client's progress toward achieving the short- and long-range objectives set in the plan should be monitored on a continual basis, and the client should be kept abreast of the changes in those factors that could affect the plan's progress. In addition, a periodic review and revision of the plan's recommendations are essential if the financial planner wishes to participate in the finan-

cial planning process on a long-term basis. There is, of course, no universal definition of how frequently this periodic review should be conducted. A typical time
cycle is comprised of an annual update with provision for a more frequent review
whenever changes in personal, financial, or economic conditions warrant such a
review.

To conclude, the planner should periodically review a plan and determine if
changes in one or more of the following factors impacted upon the original plan:
tax laws, economic conditions, investment products and techniques, family situation (like birth, death, divorce, etc.), physical condition of family members (e.g.
disability), and employment. In addition, the planner should reevaluate the original objectives in order to determine if they have changed from their original form.
Clearly, the objective of these periodic reviews should be to ensure that the plan
remains current and viable.

In this chapter we have presented an overview of the personal financial planning process. Next, we will undertake a detailed analysis of the universal tool known
as the *time value of money*. A real-world comprehensive financial plan using the
financial planning process developed here will be presented in Chapter 18.

---

*No one ever attains very eminent success by simply doing what is re-
quired of him; it is the amount and excellence of what is over and above
the required, that determines the greatness of ultimate distinction.*
                                        Charles Kendall Adams

CHAPTER 3

Time Value of Money: The Universal Tool

THE BASIC CONCEPT

INTRODUCTION

We have observed that the planner's primary goal is to maximize the client's financial welfare by analyzing at least the following eight areas:

S: Safety through Risk Management Planning
E: Educational Planning
C: Cash Management, Savings, Credit, and Debt Planning
U: Ultimate Disposition through Estate Planning
R: Retirement Planning
I: Investment Planning
T: Tax Planning
Y: Yearning for Financial Independence Planning

A common theme permeating these eight planning areas is the calculation of cash flow values over various time periods. In fact, of all the techniques used in financial planning, none is more important than the calculation of the value of money over time, known as the time value of money (TVM) concept. In this chapter we will discuss in detail the conceptual framework of the TVM and its myriad applications.

SIMPLE INTEREST

Simple interest is the dollar return from investing, or dollar cost of borrowing money. Always stated on an annual basis, this interest is calculated by

$$I = P \times R \times N \qquad \text{Eq. 3-1}$$

where

I = Simple Interest
P = Principal
R = Rate of Interest
N = Time period for which the principal is invested or lent

Thus, the simple interest on $1,000.00 for 35 days at 11 percent is $10.55:

$$I = [\$1,000.00 \times .11] \times 35/365$$
$$= \$10.55$$

FUTURE VALUE: FIXED SUM

Multiple Year Annual Compounding

A dollar invested today would earn interest, and next year it would be worth more than one dollar. During the second year, the original dollar will earn interest, *and* the interest earned during the first year will also earn interest. To illustrate this process, called *compounding*, assume Marcia Simon deposited $1,000 in a bank certificate of deposit that paid ten percent interest, compounded annually. How much money would she have at the end of two years?

The future value of a fixed sum is calculated by:

$$FV = PV(1 + r)^n \qquad \text{Eq. 3-2}$$

where

FV = Future value of the investment at the end of n years
PV = Value of the investment today, or present value
r = Interest rate during each compounding period
n = Number of years, or compounding periods

We can use Eq. 3-2 to determine the value of $1,000 at the end of two years, compounded annually at ten percent:

$$FV = \$1,000 (1 + .10)^2$$
$$= \$1,000 \times 1.21$$
$$= \$1,210.00$$

If the CD had a maturity of ten years, the original investment of $1,000 would grow to $2,593,74:

$$FV = \$1,000 (1 + .10)^{10}$$
$$= \$1,000 \times 2.59374$$
$$= \$2,593.74$$

Fortunately, future value interest tables present the future values of interest in the form of future value of fixed sum factor (FVFF). Consequently, Eq. 3-2 can be rewritten as:

$$FV = PV \times FVFF \qquad \text{Eq. 3-2A}$$

where

$FVFF$ = Future value fixed sum factor

For instance, Table 3-1 shows that the future value fixed sum factor (FVFF) for $1, invested at ten percent for ten years, is 2.5937. Multiplying $1,000 by FVFF of 2.5937 produces the following result:

$$\$1{,}000 \ \times \ 2.5937$$
$$= \ \$2{,}593.70$$

This is approximately the same result we obtained by using the long method.

Figure 3-1 shows how a fixed sum of money grows over time at various interest rates. As expected, the higher the interest rate or the longer the compounding period, the larger the future value of a fixed sum at the end of the investment period.

At this point let us introduce the use of the HP-12C calculator which can be used to answer many questions in personal finance. Among them: How much must one save for future goals, such as college costs and retirement? How big a mortgage can one afford? How would interest rate changes affect monthly payment on an adjustable loan? Should one buy or lease a car? Should tax-exempt investment be preferable to taxable investment?

The keyboard of the HP-12C calculator is reproduced in Figure 3-2. The calculator keyboard shows (though not in this figure) three colors: white, gold, and blue. Two keys, one labeled "f" (gold) and the other "g" (blue), match the colors of the keyboard. These keys, shown above the key or the face of a key in the appropriate

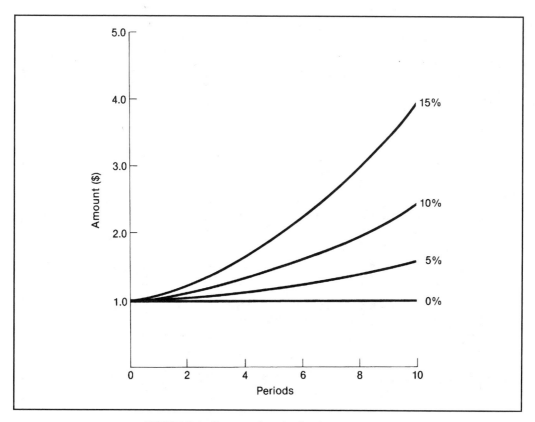

FIGURE 3-1   Future value of a fixed sum over time

TABLE 3-1 Future Value Fixed Sum Factor: FVFF

Period	1%	2%	3%	4%	5%	6%	7%	8%	9%	10%	12%	14%	15%	16%	18%	20%	24%	28%	32%	36%
1	1.0100	1.0200	1.0300	1.0400	1.0500	1.0600	1.0700	1.0800	1.0900	1.1000	1.1200	1.1400	1.1500	1.1600	1.1800	1.2000	1.2400	1.2800	1.3200	1.3600
2	1.0201	1.0404	1.0609	1.0816	1.1025	1.1236	1.1449	1.1664	1.1881	1.2100	1.2544	1.2996	1.3225	1.3456	1.3924	1.4400	1.5376	1.6384	1.7424	1.8496
3	1.0303	1.0612	1.0927	1.1249	1.1576	1.1910	1.2250	1.2597	1.2950	1.3310	1.4049	1.4815	1.5209	1.5609	1.6430	1.7280	1.9066	2.0972	2.3000	2.5155
4	1.0406	1.0824	1.1255	1.1699	1.2155	1.2625	1.3108	1.3605	1.4116	1.4641	1.5735	1.6890	1.7490	1.8106	1.9388	2.0736	2.3642	2.6844	3.0360	3.4210
5	1.0510	1.1041	1.1593	1.2167	1.2763	1.3382	1.4026	1.4693	1.5386	1.6105	1.7623	1.9254	2.0114	2.1003	2.2878	2.4883	2.9316	3.4360	4.0075	4.6526
6	1.0615	1.1262	1.1941	1.2653	1.3401	1.4185	1.5007	1.5869	1.6771	1.7716	1.9738	2.1950	2.3131	2.4364	2.6996	2.9860	3.6352	4.3980	5.2899	6.3275
7	1.0721	1.1487	1.2299	1.3159	1.4071	1.5036	1.6058	1.7138	1.8280	1.9487	2.2107	2.5023	2.6600	2.8262	3.1855	3.5832	4.5077	5.6295	6.9826	8.6054
8	1.0829	1.1717	1.2668	1.3686	1.4775	1.5938	1.7182	1.8509	1.9926	2.1436	2.4760	2.8526	3.0590	3.2784	3.7589	4.2998	5.5895	7.2058	9.2170	11.703
9	1.0937	1.1951	1.3048	1.4233	1.5513	1.6895	1.8385	1.9990	2.1719	2.3579	2.7731	3.2519	3.5179	3.8030	4.4355	5.1598	6.9310	9.2234	12.166	15.916
10	1.1046	1.2190	1.3439	1.4802	1.6289	1.7908	1.9672	2.1589	2.3674	2.5937	3.1058	3.7072	4.0456	4.4114	5.2338	6.1917	8.5944	11.805	16.059	21.646
11	1.1157	1.2434	1.3842	1.5395	1.7103	1.8983	2.1049	2.3316	2.5804	2.8531	3.4785	4.2262	4.6524	5.1173	6.1759	7.4301	10.657	15.111	21.198	29.439
12	1.1268	1.2682	1.4258	1.6010	1.7959	2.0122	2.2522	2.5182	2.8127	3.1384	3.8960	4.8179	5.3502	5.9360	7.2876	8.9161	13.214	19.342	27.982	40.037
13	1.1381	1.2936	1.4685	1.6651	1.8856	2.1329	2.4098	2.7196	3.0658	3.4523	4.3635	5.4924	6.1528	6.8858	8.5994	10.699	16.386	24.758	36.937	54.451
14	1.1495	1.3195	1.5126	1.7317	1.9799	2.2609	2.5785	2.9372	3.3417	3.7975	4.8871	6.2613	7.0757	7.9875	10.147	12.839	20.319	31.691	48.756	74.053
15	1.1610	1.3459	1.5580	1.8009	2.0789	2.3966	2.7590	3.1722	3.6425	4.1772	5.4736	7.1379	8.1371	9.2655	11.973	15.407	25.195	40.564	64.358	100.71
16	1.1726	1.3728	1.6047	1.8730	2.1829	2.5404	2.9522	3.4259	3.9703	4.5950	6.1304	8.1372	9.3576	10.748	14.129	18.488	31.242	51.923	84.953	136.96
17	1.1843	1.4002	1.6528	1.9479	2.2920	2.6928	3.1588	3.7000	4.3276	5.0545	6.8660	9.2765	10.761	12.467	16.672	22.186	38.740	66.461	112.13	186.27
18	1.1961	1.4282	1.7024	2.0258	2.4066	2.8543	3.3799	3.9960	4.7171	5.5599	7.6900	10.575	12.375	14.462	19.673	26.623	48.038	85.070	148.02	253.33
19	1.2081	1.4568	1.7535	2.1068	2.5270	3.0256	3.6165	4.3157	5.1417	6.1159	8.6128	12.055	14.231	16.776	23.214	31.948	59.567	108.89	195.39	344.53
20	1.2202	1.4859	1.8061	2.1911	2.6533	3.2071	3.8697	4.6610	5.6044	6.7275	9.6463	13.743	16.366	19.460	27.393	38.337	73.864	139.37	257.91	468.57
21	1.2324	1.5157	1.8603	2.2788	2.7860	3.3996	4.1406	5.0338	6.1088	7.4002	10.803	15.667	18.821	22.574	32.323	46.005	91.591	178.40	340.44	637.26
22	1.2447	1.5460	1.9161	2.3699	2.9253	3.6035	4.4304	5.4365	6.6586	8.1403	12.100	17.861	21.644	26.186	38.142	55.206	113.57	228.35	449.39	866.67
23	1.2572	1.5769	1.9736	2.4647	3.0715	3.8197	4.7405	5.8715	7.2579	8.9543	13.552	20.361	24.891	30.376	45.007	66.247	140.83	292.30	593.19	1178.6
24	1.2697	1.6084	2.0328	2.5633	3.2251	4.0489	5.0724	6.3412	7.9111	9.8497	15.178	23.212	28.625	35.236	53.108	79.496	174.63	374.14	783.02	1602.9
25	1.2824	1.6406	2.0938	2.6658	3.3864	4.2919	5.4274	6.8485	8.6231	10.834	17.000	26.461	32.918	40.874	62.668	95.396	216.54	478.90	1033.5	2180.0
26	1.2953	1.6734	2.1566	2.7725	3.5557	4.5494	5.8074	7.3964	9.3992	11.918	19.040	30.166	37.856	47.414	73.948	114.47	268.51	612.99	1364.3	2964.9
27	1.3082	1.7069	2.2213	2.8834	3.7335	4.8223	6.2139	7.9881	10.245	13.110	21.324	34.389	43.535	55.000	87.259	137.37	332.95	784.63	1800.9	4032.2
28	1.3213	1.7410	2.2879	2.9987	3.9201	5.1117	6.6488	8.6271	11.167	14.421	23.883	39.204	50.065	63.800	102.96	164.84	412.86	1004.3	2377.2	5483.8
29	1.3345	1.7758	2.3566	3.1187	4.1161	5.4184	7.1143	9.3173	12.172	15.863	26.749	44.693	57.575	74.008	121.50	197.81	511.95	1285.5	3137.9	7458.0
30	1.3478	1.8114	2.4273	3.2434	4.3219	5.7435	7.6123	10.062	13.267	17.449	29.959	50.950	66.211	85.849	143.37	237.37	634.81	1645.5	4142.0	10143.
40	1.4889	2.2080	3.2620	4.8010	7.0400	10.285	14.974	21.724	31.409	45.259	93.050	188.88	267.86	378.72	750.37	1469.7	5455.9	19426.	66520.	*
50	1.6446	2.6916	4.3839	7.1067	11.467	18.420	29.457	46.901	74.357	117.39	289.00	700.23	1083.6	1670.7	3927.3	9100.4	46890.	*	*	*
60	1.8167	3.2810	5.8916	10.519	18.679	32.987	57.946	101.25	176.03	304.48	897.59	2595.9	4383.9	7370.1	20555.	56347.	*	*	*	*

*FVIF > 99,999

HP–12C CALCULATOR

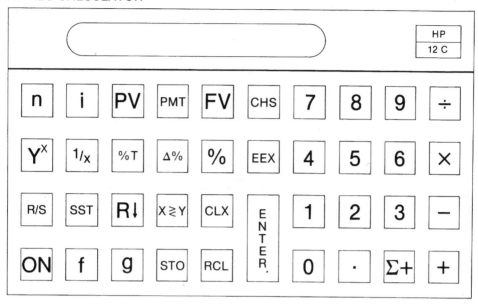

FIGURE 3-2 HP-12C calculator

color code, access specific operation modes of the calculator. The power key is labeled "ON." When the [ON] key is pressed, several zeros and a decimal point (0.00) appear on the window. The calculator can be cleared by pressing [f] followed by [CLX]. The gold lettering above CLX reads REG. Above this a gold bar appears with the word CLEAR. Knowing that the gold [f] accesses the gold operation mode, it is possible to tell that [f] [CLX] *clears the register (display).*

To set the number of decimal places one should press [f] and the number of decimal places desired. For example, [f] [4] results in 0.0000.

The value of a $1,000 CD earning ten percent and maturing in ten years can be calculated by using the HP-12C calculator. The use of the calculator in solving this problem is demonstrated in Table 3-2.

In a present/future value problem, four variables are involved; namely, (1) present value, (2) future value, (3) interest, and (4) number of years (period). If any three variables are known, the value of the fourth variable can be easily calculated.

Rule of 72

The *Rule of 72* provides a speedy method for determining the time or the interest rate required for an investment (or any index) to double in value. This *rule*, which is an estimate, is explained next.

In order to determine the number of years for an investment to double in value, 72 is divided by the annual interest rate. For example, if the annual interest rate is eight percent, the time required for an investment to double in value is 72/8, or nine years.

TABLE 3-2

Step 1:	Identify known variables:	
	Present value:	$1,000
	Interest:	10%
	Number of periods:	10 years
Step 2:	Clear calculator [f] [CLX]	
Step 3:	Enter data	
	Press [1] [0] [0] [0] [CHS] [PV]	
	[10] [i]	
	[10] [n]	
	[FV]	
	Answer: $2,593.74	

Note: [CHS] key is used when money is paid out. It is *not* used when money is received.

Looking at it another way, the interest rate required for an investment to double in value over a specified number of years is determined by dividing 72 by the number of years. For instance, if Betty Johnson wishes to double her investment in ten years, she must invest the principal to earn over that period an interest rate of 7.2 percent (72/10), compounded annually.

Multiple Compound Periods Per Year

The preceding section presented the case of annual compounding, where each year consisted of one compound period. Often, financial institutions use more frequent compounding periods. For example, semiannually compounding means there are two compound periods per year; monthly compounding means 12 compound periods per year; and daily compounding indicates there are 365 compound periods per year.

Equation 3-2 can be modified to calculate the compound value of $1,000 after n years if invested at r percent, and the amount is compounded over multiple periods per year:

$$FV = PV (1 + r_{nom/m})^{mn}$$ Eq. 3-3

where

$$r_{nom} = \text{Declared interest rate, or nominal interest rate}$$
$$m = \text{Number of compounding periods per year}$$
$$n = \text{Total number of years}$$

Using Eq. 3-3 we can calculate the *FV* for $1,000 after two years, which is invested at ten percent and is compounded quarterly:

$$FV = \$1,000 (1 + .10/4)^{4 \times 2}$$
$$= \$1,218.40$$

The same answer could be obtained by using the HP-12C calculator, as demonstrated in Table 3-3.

TABLE 3-3

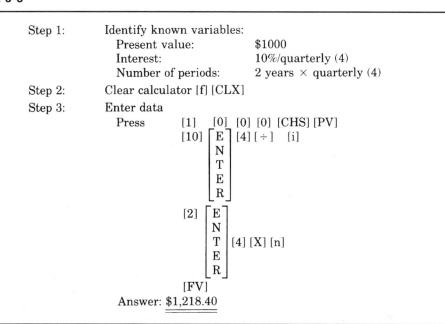

Step 1:   Identify known variables:
            Present value: $1000
            Interest: 10%/quarterly (4)
            Number of periods: 2 years × quarterly (4)

Step 2:   Clear calculator [f] [CLX]

Step 3:   Enter data
            Press   [1] [0] [0] [0] [CHS] [PV]
                                [10] [ENTER] [4] [÷] [i]

                                [2] [ENTER] [4] [X] [n]

                                [FV]
                   Answer: $1,218.40

Incidentally, note that the *quarterly* compounding resulted in a higher value of $1,218.40, as compared to the *annual* compounding value of $1,210.00. Values of other compounding periods ($PV = \$1,000$, $r = 10$ percent, $n = 2$ years) are given next:

Type of compounding	Future value
Annual	$1,210.00
Semiannual	1,215.51
Quarterly	1,218.40
Daily	1,221.37

These relationships are illustrated in Figure 3-3. Clearly, the more frequent the compounding period, the larger the final compound amount, because interest is earned on interest more often.

PRESENT VALUE: FIXED SUM

A dollar in hand today would be worth more than a dollar to be received next year because, if gainfully invested, the dollar would earn interest, and next year would be worth more than one dollar. For instance, if $100 is invested at five percent for one year, the amount will grow to $105. Put differently, the *present value* of $105

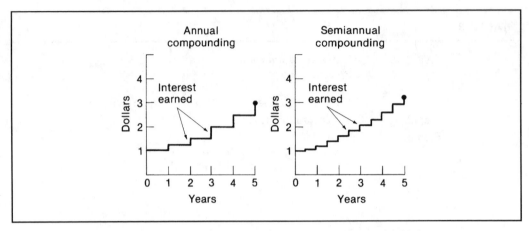

FIGURE 3-3 Future value of a fixed sum using multiple compound periods per year

expected to be received next year, *discounted* for one year at five percent, is $100. In general, the present value of a sum due n periods in the future is the amount which, if it were on hand today, would grow to equal the future sum. The concept of discounting a future value to arrive at the present value of a fixed sum is presented in Figure 3-4.

Finding the present value—or *discounting*, as it is generally known—is merely the reverse of compounding. For instance, the future value equation is:

$$FV = PV (1 + r)^n \qquad \text{(Eq. 3-2 restated)}$$

Solving for PV we obtain

$$PV = FV/(1 + r)^n$$
$$= FV (1 + r)^{-n}$$
$$= FV [1/(1 + r)^n]$$

where

PV = Value of the investment today, or present value

FV = Future value of amount expected to be received in n time periods

r = Interest rate with which the amount is discounted

n = Number of periods over which discounting is performed

For instance, an investor expects to receive $10,000 from a limited partnership seven years from today. Using a discount rate of ten percent, the present value of this investment is $5,132:

$$PV = \$10,000 [1/(1 + .10)^7]$$
$$= 10,000 \times .5132$$
$$= \$5,132$$

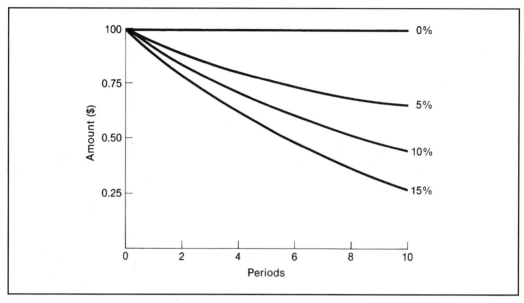

FIGURE 3-4 Present value of a fixed sum over time

As expected, by using the calculator we obtain the same result, as can be seen from Table 3-4. The PV concept is also useful in determining how much must be invested today at, say, eight percent in order to accumulate $15,000 five years from today to fund a child's education:

$$PV = \$15,000 \, [1/(1 \, + \, .08)^5]$$
$$= \, 15,000 \, \times \, .6806$$
$$= \, \$10,209$$

The present value (PV) table reproduces values of fixed sum factors (PVFF), which can be directly used to calculate present values. For instance, Table 3-6 shows

---

TABLE 3-4

Step 1:	Identify known variables:
	Future value: $10,000
	Interest: 10%
	Number of periods: 7 years
Step 2:	Clear calculator [f] [CLX]
Step 3:	Enter data
	Press [1] [0] [0] [0] [0] [FV]
	[1] [0] [i]
	[7] [n]
	[PV]
	Answer: $5,131.58

Note: [CHS] key is *not* used when money is being received.

that the PVFF for eight percent for five years is .6806. Therefore, using the previous example, an investor requiring $15,000 in five years from today at eight percent would invest $10,209:

$$PV = \$15{,}000 \times PVFF$$
$$= 15{,}000 \times .6806$$
$$= \$10{,}209$$

This is the same value we arrived at in our long calculation.

Since PV is a mirror reflection of FV, $10,209 invested at eight percent should grow to $15,000 in five years:

$$FV = \$10{,}209 \, (1 + .08)^5$$
$$= 10{,}209 \times 1.4693$$
$$= \$15{,}000$$

Interestingly, if interest were compounded *quarterly* and the investor wanted to find out how much must be invested today at eight percent to accumulate $15,000 five years from today, the PV calculation would be as follows:

$$PV = \$15{,}000 \, [1/(1 + .08/4)^{5 \times 4}]$$
$$= 15{,}000 \times .6729713$$
$$= \$10{,}094.57$$

The same calculation performed on a calculator is shown in Table 3-5. As expected, since more frequent compounding produces a larger terminal value, the investor

---

TABLE 3-5

Step 1:	Identify known variables:		
	Future value:	$15,000	
	Interest:	8%/quarterly (4)	
	Number of periods:	5 years × quarterly (4)	
Step 2:	Clear calculator [f] [CLX]		
Step 3:	Enter data		
	Press	[1] [5] [0] [0] [0] [FV]	
		[8] $\begin{bmatrix} E \\ N \\ T \\ E \\ R \end{bmatrix}$ [4] [÷] [i]	
		[5] $\begin{bmatrix} E \\ N \\ T \\ E \\ R \end{bmatrix}$ [4] [X] [n]	
		[PV]	
		Answer: $10,094.57	

TABLE 3-6 Present Value Fixed Sum Factor: PVFF

Period	1%	2%	3%	4%	5%	6%	7%	8%	9%	10%	12%	14%	15%	16%	18%	20%	24%	28%	32%	36%
1	.9901	.9804	.9709	.9615	.9524	.9434	.9346	.9259	.9174	.9091	.8929	.8772	.8696	.8621	.8475	.8333	.8065	.7813	.7576	.7353
2	.9803	.9612	.9426	.9246	.9070	.8900	.8734	.8573	.8417	.8264	.7972	.7695	.7561	.7432	.7182	.6944	.6504	.6104	.5739	.5407
3	.9706	.9423	.9151	.8890	.8638	.8396	.8163	.7938	.7722	.7513	.7118	.6750	.6575	.6407	.6086	.5787	.5245	.4768	.4348	.3975
4	.9610	.9238	.8885	.8548	.8227	.7921	.7629	.7350	.7084	.6830	.6355	.5921	.5718	.5523	.5158	.4823	.4230	.3725	.3294	.2923
5	.9515	.9057	.8626	.8219	.7835	.7473	.7130	.6806	.6499	.6209	.5674	.5194	.4972	.4761	.4371	.4019	.3411	.2910	.2495	.2149
6	.9420	.8880	.8375	.7903	.7462	.7050	.6663	.6302	.5963	.5645	.5066	.4556	.4323	.4104	.3704	.3349	.2751	.2274	.1890	.1580
7	.9327	.8706	.8131	.7599	.7107	.6651	.6227	.5835	.5470	.5132	.4523	.3996	.3759	.3538	.3139	.2791	.2218	.1776	.1432	.1162
8	.9235	.8535	.7894	.7307	.6768	.6274	.5820	.5403	.5019	.4665	.4039	.3506	.3269	.3050	.2660	.2326	.1789	.1388	.1085	.0854
9	.9143	.8368	.7664	.7026	.6446	.5919	.5439	.5002	.4604	.4241	.3606	.3075	.2843	.2630	.2255	.1938	.1443	.1084	.0822	.0628
10	.9053	.8203	.7441	.6756	.6139	.5584	.5083	.4632	.4224	.3855	.3220	.2697	.2472	.2267	.1911	.1615	.1164	.0847	.0623	.0462
11	.8963	.8043	.7224	.6496	.5847	.5268	.4751	.4289	.3875	.3505	.2875	.2366	.2149	.1954	.1619	.1346	.0938	.0662	.0472	.0340
12	.8874	.7885	.7014	.6246	.5568	.4970	.4440	.3971	.3555	.3186	.2567	.2076	.1869	.1685	.1372	.1122	.0757	.0517	.0357	.0250
13	.8787	.7730	.6810	.6006	.5303	.4688	.4150	.3677	.3262	.2897	.2292	.1821	.1625	.1452	.1163	.0935	.0610	.0404	.0271	.0184
14	.8700	.7579	.6611	.5775	.5051	.4423	.3878	.3405	.2992	.2633	.2046	.1597	.1413	.1252	.0985	.0779	.0492	.0316	.0205	.0135
15	.8613	.7430	.6419	.5553	.4810	.4173	.3624	.3152	.2745	.2394	.1827	.1401	.1229	.1079	.0835	.0649	.0397	.0247	.0155	.0099
16	.8528	.7284	.6232	.5339	.4581	.3936	.3387	.2919	.2519	.2176	.1631	.1229	.1069	.0930	.0708	.0541	.0320	.0193	.0118	.0073
17	.8444	.7142	.6050	.5134	.4363	.3714	.3166	.2703	.2311	.1978	.1456	.1078	.0929	.0802	.0600	.0451	.0258	.0150	.0089	.0054
18	.8360	.7002	.5874	.4936	.4155	.3503	.2959	.2502	.2120	.1799	.1300	.0946	.0808	.0691	.0508	.0376	.0208	.0118	.0068	.0039
19	.8277	.6864	.5703	.4746	.3957	.3305	.2765	.2317	.1945	.1635	.1161	.0829	.0703	.0596	.0431	.0313	.0168	.0092	.0051	.0029
20	.8195	.6730	.5537	.4564	.3769	.3118	.2584	.2145	.1784	.1486	.1037	.0728	.0611	.0514	.0365	.0261	.0135	.0072	.0039	.0021
21	.8114	.6598	.5375	.4388	.3589	.2942	.2415	.1987	.1637	.1351	.0926	.0638	.0531	.0443	.0309	.0217	.0109	.0056	.0029	.0016
22	.8034	.6468	.5219	.4220	.3418	.2775	.2257	.1839	.1502	.1228	.0826	.0560	.0462	.0382	.0262	.0181	.0088	.0044	.0022	.0012
23	.7954	.6342	.5067	.4057	.3256	.2618	.2109	.1703	.1378	.1117	.0738	.0491	.0402	.0329	.0222	.0151	.0071	.0034	.0017	.0008
24	.7876	.6217	.4919	.3901	.3101	.2470	.1971	.1577	.1264	.1015	.0659	.0431	.0349	.0284	.0188	.0126	.0057	.0027	.0013	.0006
25	.7798	.6095	.4776	.3751	.2953	.2330	.1842	.1460	.1160	.0923	.0588	.0378	.0304	.0245	.0160	.0105	.0046	.0021	.0010	.0005
26	.7720	.5976	.4637	.3607	.2812	.2198	.1722	.1352	.1064	.0839	.0525	.0331	.0264	.0211	.0135	.0087	.0037	.0016	.0007	.0003
27	.7644	.5859	.4502	.3468	.2678	.2074	.1609	.1252	.0976	.0763	.0469	.0291	.0230	.0182	.0115	.0073	.0030	.0013	.0006	.0002
28	.7568	.5744	.4371	.3335	.2551	.1956	.1504	.1159	.0895	.0693	.0419	.0255	.0200	.0157	.0097	.0061	.0024	.0010	.0004	.0002
29	.7493	.5631	.4243	.3207	.2429	.1846	.1406	.1073	.0822	.0630	.0374	.0224	.0174	.0135	.0082	.0051	.0020	.0008	.0003	.0001
30	.7419	.5521	.4120	.3083	.2314	.1741	.1314	.0994	.0754	.0573	.0334	.0196	.0151	.0116	.0070	.0042	.0016	.0006	.0002	.0001
35	.7059	.5000	.3554	.2534	.1813	.1301	.0937	.0676	.0490	.0356	.0189	.0102	.0075	.0055	.0030	.0017	.0005	.0002	.0001	*
40	.6717	.4529	.3066	.2083	.1420	.0972	.0668	.0460	.0318	.0221	.0107	.0053	.0037	.0026	.0013	.0007	.0002	.0001	*	*
45	.6391	.4102	.2644	.1712	.1113	.0727	.0476	.0313	.0207	.0137	.0061	.0027	.0019	.0013	.0006	.0003	.0001	*	*	*
50	.6080	.3715	.2281	.1407	.0872	.0543	.0339	.0213	.0134	.0085	.0035	.0014	.0009	.0006	.0003	.0001	*	*	*	*
55	.5785	.3365	.1968	.1157	.0683	.0406	.0242	.0145	.0087	.0053	.0020	.0007	.0005	.0003	.0001	*	*	*	*	*

*The factor is zero to four decimal places.

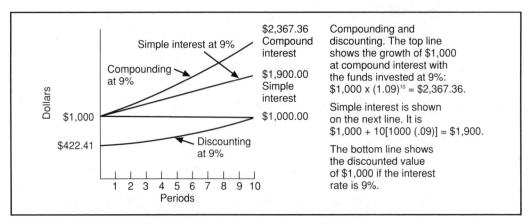

FIGURE 3-5   Relationship between simple interest, compounding, and discounting

needs to invest a smaller amount ($10,094.57) when quarterly compounding is involved as compared with annual compounding ($10,209).

The relationship between simple interest, FV, and PV is presented in Figure 3-5. An understanding of these relationships is essential for their effective use as financial planning tools.

FUTURE VALUE: ANNUITY

Frequently, individuals accumulate funds on an *annual* basis. For instance, for five years, at the end of each year a person may invest $2,000 into an IRA, and then wish to determine the total accumulated value of this IRA at the end of that period. In this case, since the same amount ($2,000) is invested for more than one year (in this case five years) this investment is called an *annuity*. As revealed by Figure 3-6, if the investment earns ten percent per year, this annuity would grow to $12,210.20. The future value of an annuity can be calculated by:

$$FVA = PMT \sum_{n=1}^{N} (1 + r)^{N-n} \qquad \text{Eq. 3-4}$$

where

$$
\begin{aligned}
FVA &= \text{Future value of an annuity} \\
PMT &= \text{Payment per compound period} \\
n &= \text{Number of compound periods} \\
N &= \text{Total number of years}
\end{aligned}
$$

Equation 3-4 can be used to calculate the value of the:

$$
\begin{aligned}
FVA &= \$2,000\,(1 + .10)^{5-1} + \$2,000\,(1 + .10)^{5-2} \\
&\quad + \$2,000\,(1 + .10)^{5-3} + \$2,000\,(1 + .10)^{5-4} \\
&\quad + \$2,000\,(1 + .10)^{5-5} \\
&= \$2,000\,(1.4641) + \$2,000\,(1.331) \\
&\quad + \$2,000\,(1.21) + \$2,000\,(1.10) + \$2,000\,(1) \\
&\quad + \$2,928.20 + \$2,662.00 + \$2,420.00 + \$2,200.00 + \$2,000.00 \\
&= \$12\,210.20
\end{aligned}
$$

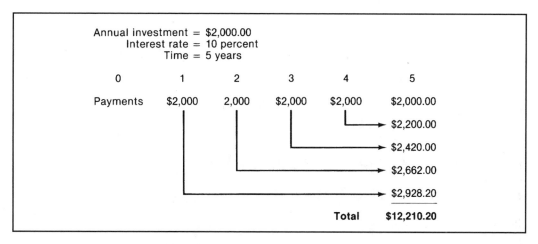

Annual investment = $2,000.00
Interest rate = 10 percent
Time = 5 years

FIGURE 3-6   Future value of an ordinary annuity

As in previous cases, future values of annuity factor are conveniently available for making future value *annuity* calculations. Symbolically:

$$FVA = PMT \times FVAF$$ Eq. 3-4A

where

$$FVAF = \text{Future value annuity factor}$$

For the previous problem, from Table 3-8 we see that the FVAF for ten percent for five years is 6.1051. Thus

$$FVA = \$2,000 \ (6.1051)$$
$$= \$12,210.20$$

As expected, the use of a calculator yields the same result, as revealed by Table 3-7.

TABLE 3-7

Step 1:   Identify known variables:
           Payment: $2000
           Interest: 10%
           Number of periods: 5 years
Step 2:   Clear calculator [f] [CLX]
Step 3:   Enter data
           Press [2]   [0] [0] [0] [CHS] [PMT]
                 [1]   [0] [i]
                 [5]   [n]
                 [FV]
           Answer: $12,210.20

TABLE 3-8 Future Value Annuity Factor: FVAF

Periods	1%	2%	3%	4%	5%	6%	7%	8%	9%	10%	12%	14%	15%	16%	18%	20%	24%	28%	32%	36%
1	1.0000	1.0000	1.0000	1.0000	1.0000	1.0000	1.0000	1.0000	1.0000	1.0000	1.0000	1.0000	1.0000	1.0000	1.0000	1.0000	1.0000	1.0000	1.0000	1.0000
2	2.0100	2.0200	2.0300	2.0400	2.0500	2.0600	2.0700	2.0800	2.0900	2.1000	2.1200	2.1400	2.1500	2.1600	2.1800	2.2000	2.2400	2.2800	2.3200	2.3600
3	3.0301	3.0604	3.0909	3.1216	3.1525	3.1836	3.2149	3.2464	3.2781	3.3100	3.3744	3.4396	3.4725	3.5056	3.5724	3.6400	3.7776	3.9184	4.0624	4.2096
4	4.0604	4.1216	4.1836	4.2465	4.3101	4.3746	4.4399	4.5061	4.5731	4.6410	4.7793	4.9211	4.9934	5.0665	5.2154	5.3680	5.6842	6.0156	6.3624	6.7251
5	5.1010	5.2040	5.3091	5.4163	5.5256	5.6371	5.7507	5.8666	5.9847	6.1051	6.3528	6.6101	6.7424	6.8771	7.1542	7.4416	8.0484	8.6999	9.3983	10.146
6	6.1520	6.3081	6.4684	6.6330	6.8019	6.9753	7.1533	7.3359	7.5233	7.7156	8.1152	8.5355	8.7537	8.9775	9.4420	9.9299	10.980	12.135	13.405	14.798
7	7.2135	7.4343	7.6625	7.8983	8.1420	8.3938	8.6540	8.9228	9.2004	9.4872	10.089	10.730	11.066	11.413	12.141	12.915	14.615	16.533	18.695	21.126
8	8.2857	8.5830	8.8923	9.2142	9.5491	9.8975	10.259	10.636	11.028	11.435	12.299	13.232	13.726	14.240	15.327	16.499	19.122	22.163	25.678	29.731
9	9.3685	9.7546	10.159	10.582	11.026	11.491	11.978	12.487	13.021	13.579	14.775	16.085	16.785	17.518	19.085	20.798	24.712	29.369	34.895	41.435
10	10.462	10.949	11.463	12.006	12.577	13.180	13.816	14.486	15.192	15.937	17.548	19.337	20.303	21.321	23.521	25.958	31.643	38.592	47.061	57.351
11	11.566	12.168	12.807	13.486	14.206	14.971	15.783	16.645	17.560	18.531	20.654	23.044	24.349	25.732	28.755	32.150	40.237	50.398	63.121	78.998
12	12.682	13.412	14.192	15.025	15.917	16.869	17.888	18.977	20.140	21.384	24.133	27.270	29.001	30.850	34.931	39.580	50.894	65.510	84.320	108.43
13	13.809	14.680	15.617	16.626	17.713	18.882	20.140	21.495	22.953	24.522	28.029	32.088	34.351	36.786	42.218	48.496	64.109	84.852	112.30	148.47
14	14.947	15.973	17.086	18.291	19.598	21.015	22.550	24.214	26.019	27.975	32.392	37.581	40.504	43.672	50.818	59.195	80.496	109.61	149.23	202.92
15	16.096	17.293	18.598	20.023	21.578	23.276	25.129	27.152	29.360	31.772	37.279	43.842	47.580	51.659	60.965	72.035	100.81	141.30	197.99	276.97
16	17.257	18.639	20.156	21.824	23.657	25.672	27.888	30.324	33.003	35.949	42.753	50.980	55.717	60.925	72.939	87.442	126.01	181.86	262.35	377.69
17	18.430	20.012	21.761	23.697	25.840	28.212	30.840	33.750	36.973	40.544	48.883	59.117	65.075	71.673	87.068	105.93	157.25	233.79	347.30	514.66
18	19.614	21.412	23.414	25.645	28.132	30.905	33.999	37.450	41.301	45.599	55.749	68.394	75.836	84.140	103.74	128.11	195.99	300.25	459.44	700.93
19	20.810	22.840	25.116	27.671	30.539	33.760	37.379	41.446	46.018	51.159	63.439	78.969	88.211	98.603	123.41	154.74	244.03	385.32	607.47	954.27
20	22.019	24.297	26.870	29.778	33.066	36.785	40.995	45.762	51.160	57.275	72.052	91.024	102.44	115.37	146.62	186.68	303.60	494.21	802.86	1298.8
21	23.239	25.783	28.676	31.969	35.719	39.992	44.865	50.422	56.764	64.002	81.698	104.76	118.81	134.84	174.02	225.02	377.46	633.59	1060.7	1767.3
22	24.471	27.299	30.536	34.248	38.505	43.392	49.005	55.456	62.873	71.402	92.502	120.43	137.63	157.41	206.34	271.03	469.05	811.99	1401.2	2404.6
23	25.716	28.845	32.452	36.617	41.430	46.995	53.436	60.893	69.531	79.543	104.60	138.29	159.27	183.60	244.48	326.23	582.62	1040.3	1850.6	3271.3
24	26.973	30.421	34.426	39.082	44.502	50.815	58.176	66.764	76.789	88.497	118.15	158.65	184.16	213.97	289.49	392.48	723.46	1332.6	2443.8	4449.9
25	28.243	32.030	36.459	41.645	47.727	54.864	63.249	73.105	84.700	98.347	133.33	181.87	212.79	249.21	342.60	471.98	898.09	1706.8	3226.8	6052.9
26	29.525	33.670	38.553	44.311	51.113	59.156	68.676	79.954	93.323	109.18	150.33	208.33	245.71	290.08	405.27	567.37	1114.6	2185.7	4260.4	8233.0
27	30.820	35.344	40.709	47.084	54.669	63.705	74.483	87.350	102.72	121.09	169.37	238.49	283.56	337.50	479.22	681.85	1383.1	2798.7	5624.7	11197.9
28	32.129	37.051	42.930	49.967	58.402	68.528	80.697	95.338	112.96	134.20	190.69	272.88	327.10	392.50	566.48	819.22	1716.0	3583.3	7425.6	15230.2
29	33.450	38.792	45.218	52.966	62.322	73.639	87.346	103.96	124.13	148.63	214.58	312.09	377.16	456.30	669.44	984.06	2128.9	4587.6	9802.9	20714.1
30	34.784	40.568	47.575	56.084	66.438	79.058	94.460	113.28	136.30	164.49	241.33	356.78	434.74	530.31	790.94	1181.8	2640.9	5873.2	12940.	28172.2
40	48.886	60.402	75.401	95.025	120.79	154.76	199.63	259.05	337.88	442.59	767.09	1342.0	1779.0	2360.7	4163.2	7343.8	22728.	69377.	*	*
50	64.463	84.579	112.79	152.66	209.34	290.33	406.52	573.76	815.08	1163.9	2400.0	4994.5	7217.7	10435.	21813.	45497.	*	*	*	*
60	81.669	114.05	163.05	237.99	353.58	533.12	813.52	1253.2	1944.7	3034.8	7471.6	18535.	29219.	46057.	*	*	*	*	*	*

PRESENT VALUE: ANNUITY

An important financial tool is the concept of *present value of an annuity* (PVA). Identification of an undervalued stock, evaluation of an income-producing limited partnership, or a lump sum versus a pension for life retirement settlement—all of these problems can be solved by using the PVA concept.

Here is an interesting problem that requires the use of the PVA concept. A valued client has just won a lottery. He is offered the following alternatives: (1) a four-year annuity with payments of $1,000 at the end of each year, or (2) a lump sum payment of $3,170 today. Which one should he choose? At first blush, either the four-year payment or the lump sum *may* appear to be more attractive. However, as revealed by Figure 3-7, if the money is expected to earn ten percent per year, *both alternatives are of equal value.* The algebraic equation for calculating the PVA is:

$$PVA = PMT \sum_{n=1}^{N} [1/(1 + r)]^n \qquad \text{Eq. 3-5}$$

In the preceding example, PVA equals

$$
\begin{aligned}
PVA &= \$1,000 \, [1/(1 + .10)]^1 + \$1,000 \, [1/(1 + .10)]^2 \\
&\quad + \$1,000 \, [1/(1 + .10)]^3 + \$1,000 \, [1/(1 + .10)]^4 \\
&= \$1,000 \times .90909 + \$1,000 \times .82644 \\
&\quad + \$1,000 \times .75131 + \$1,000 \times .68301 \\
&= \$909.09 + \$826.44 + \$751.31 + \$683.01 \\
&= \$3,169.85
\end{aligned}
$$

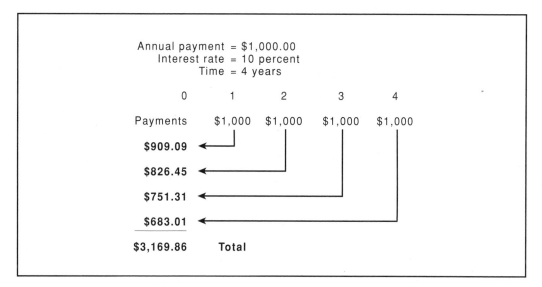

FIGURE 3-7   Present value of an ordinary annuity

The present value annuity factor (PVAF) table can be directly used to arrive at the present value. Consequently, Equation 3-5 can be modified as

$$PVA = PMT \times PVAF$$ Eq. 3-5A

where

$$PVAF = \text{Present value annuity factor}$$

Using Equation 3-5A, the PVA of $1,000 a year for four years, discounted at ten percent is $3,169.90:

$$PVA = PMT \times PVAF$$
$$= \$1,000 \times 3.1699$$
$$= \$3,169.90$$

By using the calculator, we obtain the same result as shown by Table 3-9.

ANNUITY DUE: A REFINEMENT

In our previous discussions we assumed that all payments were either received or made *at the end of the year*. That is not always the case. For instance, all insurance

---

TABLE 3-9

Step 1:	Identify known variables:
	Payment: $1,000
	Interest: 10%
	Number of periods: 4 years
Step 2:	Clear calculator [f] [CLX]
Step 3:	Enter data
	Press [1] [0] [0] [0] [PMT]
	[1] [0] [i]
	[4] [n]
	[PV]
	Answer: $3,169.87

Note: If the payments were received at the beginning of each period, step 3 would have been modified as follows:

Press [g]   [7]
      [1]   [0] [0] [0] [PMT]
      [1]   [0] [i]
      [4]   [n]
      [PV]
Answer: $3,486.85

Note:
1. [CHS] is *not* used since this is money being received, not paid out.
2. [g] [7] is pressed to initiate the "beginning" mode.

premiums are paid at the *beginning* of the period; the same is true of lease payments. The former type of payments, received at the end of the period, are called *ordinary* annuities. Payments due or made at the beginning of the period are called *annuity due*.

Annuity Due: Future Value

Let us revert to the IRA problem where the individual has invested $2,000 at the end of each year for five years. The *ordinary* annuity value was calculated as $12,210.20. Now let us assume that the money was invested at the beginning of each year. Equation 3-6 can be developed to accommodate this change:

$$FVA \text{ (Annuity Due)} = PMT \ (FVAF)(1 + r) \qquad \text{Eq. 3-6}$$
$$\$2,000 \ (6.10514)(1.10)$$
$$= \$13,431.22$$

Clearly, since the payments are made earlier, the annuity due ($13,431.22) has higher value than the ordinary annuity ($12,210.20).

Annuity Due: Present Value

The present value of an annuity due can be calculated by:

$$PVA \text{ (Annuity Due)} = PMT \ (PVAF)(1 + r) \qquad \text{Eq. 3-7}$$

Referring to the lottery example, had the $1,000 annual payments been received at the *beginning* of each year, the present value of the annuity due would have been $3,486.99:

$$PVA \text{ (Annuity Due)} = \$1,000 \times 3.1699 \times (1 + .10)$$

$$= \$3,486.89$$

As revealed in Table 3-9, this was also the result we obtained by using the calculator.

PRESENT VALUE OF A PERPETUITY

What is the present value of a preferred stock which has no maturity and makes annuity (dividend) payments indefinitely? Here the payments resemble an infinite series, which is defined as a *perpetuity*. The present value of a perpetuity is given by:

$$PV \text{ (Perpetuity)} = PMT/r \qquad \text{Eq. 3-8}$$

Let us assume that IBM Preferred pays an annual dividend of $5.00. If the rate of discount is eight percent, the present value of the IBM Preferred is $62.50:

$$PV \text{ (Perpetuity)} = \$5.00/.08$$
$$= \$62.50$$

PRESENT VALUE OF AN UNEVEN PAYMENT SERIES

In our previous discussions we assumed that the periodic payments were even. This would not be a valid assumption for a common stock, which can be expected to declare dividends on an uneven basis. What, then, is the present value of ABC Common Stock which declares uneven dividend payments?

The present value calculation of ABC Common is demonstrated in Figure 3-8. An arbitrary discount rate of eight percent is selected for this calculation. Two observations are apropos here. First, the PV of an uneven stream of expected future dividends is merely the sum of the PVs of the individual components of the stream. The PV of each individual dividend payment can be calculated by referring to Table 3-5. Second, if within the series dividend payments for two or more years remain constant, as is the case here during years 3 through 7, the Present Value Annuity Factor (Table 3-10) can be used to calculate the present value of the dividend payments for these years. Assuming that the ABC Common is sold for $70 in the tenth year and the future expected dividend payments and the sale price of ABC are discounted by an eight percent discount rate, the PV of ABC Common works out to $69.64.

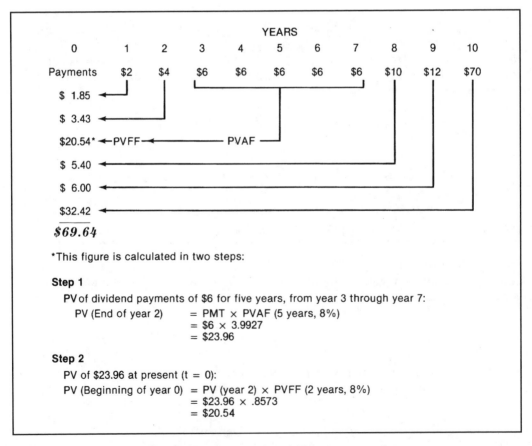

*This figure is calculated in two steps:

Step 1

PV of dividend payments of $6 for five years, from year 3 through year 7:

$$\begin{aligned} \text{PV (End of year 2)} &= \text{PMT} \times \text{PVAF (5 years, 8\%)} \\ &= \$6 \times 3.9927 \\ &= \$23.96 \end{aligned}$$

Step 2

PV of $23.96 at present (t = 0):

$$\begin{aligned} \text{PV (Beginning of year 0)} &= \text{PV (year 2)} \times \text{PVFF (2 years, 8\%)} \\ &= \$23.96 \times .8573 \\ &= \$20.54 \end{aligned}$$

FIGURE 3-8   Present value of ABC common stock

TABLE 3-10 Present Value Annuity Factor: PVAF

Number of Payments	1%	2%	3%	4%	5%	6%	7%	8%	9%	10%	12%	14%	15%	16%	18%	20%	24%	28%	32%
1	0.9901	0.9804	0.9709	0.9615	0.9524	0.9434	0.9346	0.9259	0.9174	0.9091	0.8929	0.8772	0.8696	0.8621	0.8475	0.8333	0.8065	0.7813	0.7576
2	1.9704	1.9416	1.9135	1.8861	1.8594	1.8334	1.8080	1.7833	1.7591	1.7355	1.6901	1.6467	1.6257	1.6052	1.5656	1.5278	1.4568	1.3916	1.3315
3	2.9410	2.8839	2.8286	2.7751	2.7232	2.6730	2.6243	2.5771	2.5313	2.4869	2.4018	2.3216	2.2832	2.2459	2.1743	2.1065	1.9813	1.8684	1.7663
4	3.9020	3.8077	3.7171	3.6299	3.5460	3.4651	3.3872	3.3121	3.2397	3.1699	3.0373	2.9137	2.8550	2.7982	2.6901	2.5887	2.4043	2.2410	2.0957
5	4.8534	4.7135	4.5797	4.4518	4.3295	4.2124	4.1002	3.9927	3.8897	3.7908	3.6048	3.4331	3.3522	3.2743	3.1272	2.9906	2.7454	2.5320	2.3452
6	5.7955	5.6014	5.4172	5.2421	5.0757	4.9173	4.7665	4.6229	4.4859	4.3553	4.1114	3.8887	3.7845	3.6847	3.4976	3.3255	3.0205	2.7594	2.5342
7	6.7282	6.4720	6.2303	6.0021	5.7864	5.5824	5.3893	5.2064	5.0330	4.8684	4.5638	4.2883	4.1604	4.0386	3.8115	3.6046	3.2423	2.9370	2.6775
8	7.6517	7.3255	7.0197	6.7327	6.4632	6.2098	5.9713	5.7466	5.5348	5.3349	4.9676	4.6389	4.4873	4.3436	4.0776	3.8372	3.4212	3.0758	2.7860
9	8.5660	8.1622	7.7861	7.4353	7.1078	6.8017	6.5152	6.2469	5.9952	5.7590	5.3282	4.9464	4.7716	4.6065	4.3030	4.0310	3.5655	3.1842	2.8681
10	9.4713	8.9826	8.5302	8.1109	7.7217	7.3601	7.0236	6.7101	6.4177	6.1446	5.6502	5.2161	5.0188	4.8332	4.4941	4.1925	3.6819	3.2689	2.9304
11	10.3676	9.7868	9.2526	8.7605	8.3064	7.8869	7.4987	7.1390	6.8052	6.4951	5.9377	5.4527	5.2337	5.0286	4.6560	4.3271	3.7757	3.3351	2.9776
12	11.2551	10.5753	9.9540	9.3851	8.8633	8.3838	7.9427	7.5361	7.1607	6.8137	6.1944	5.6603	5.4206	5.1971	4.7932	4.4392	3.8514	3.3868	3.0133
13	12.1337	11.3484	10.6350	9.9856	9.3936	8.8527	8.3577	7.9038	7.4869	7.1034	6.4235	5.8424	5.5831	5.3423	4.9095	4.5327	3.9124	3.4272	3.0404
14	13.0037	12.1062	11.2961	10.5631	9.8986	9.2950	8.7455	8.2442	7.7862	7.3667	6.6282	6.0021	5.7245	5.4675	5.0081	4.6106	3.9616	3.4587	3.0609
15	13.8651	12.8493	11.9379	11.1184	10.3797	9.7122	9.1079	8.5595	8.0607	7.6061	6.8109	6.1422	5.8474	5.5755	5.0916	4.6755	4.0013	3.4834	3.0764
16	14.7179	13.5777	12.5611	11.6523	10.8378	10.1059	9.4466	8.8514	8.3126	7.8237	6.9740	6.2651	5.9542	5.6685	5.1624	4.7296	4.0333	3.5026	3.0882
17	15.5623	14.2919	13.1661	12.1657	11.2741	10.4773	9.7632	9.1216	8.5436	8.0216	7.1196	6.3729	6.0472	5.7487	5.2223	4.7746	4.0591	3.5177	3.0971
18	16.3983	14.9920	13.7535	12.6593	11.6896	10.8276	10.0591	9.3719	8.7556	8.2014	7.2497	6.4674	6.1280	5.8178	5.2732	4.8122	4.0799	3.5294	3.1039
19	17.2260	15.6785	14.3238	13.1339	12.0853	11.1581	10.3356	9.6036	8.9501	8.3649	7.3658	6.5504	6.1982	5.8775	5.3162	4.8435	4.0967	3.5386	3.1090
20	18.0456	16.3514	14.8775	13.5903	12.4622	11.4699	10.5940	9.8181	9.1285	8.5136	7.4694	6.6231	6.2593	5.9288	5.3527	4.8696	4.1103	3.5458	3.1129
21	18.8570	17.0112	15.4150	14.0292	12.8212	11.7641	10.8355	10.0168	9.2922	8.6487	7.5620	6.6870	6.3125	5.9731	5.3837	4.8913	4.1212	3.5514	3.1158
22	19.6604	17.6580	15.9369	14.4511	13.1630	12.0416	11.0612	10.2007	9.4424	8.7715	7.6446	6.7429	6.3587	6.0113	5.4099	4.9094	4.1300	3.5558	3.1180
23	20.4558	18.2922	16.4436	14.8568	13.4886	12.3034	11.2722	10.3711	9.5802	8.8832	7.7184	6.7921	6.3988	6.0442	5.4321	4.9245	4.1371	3.5592	3.1197
24	21.2434	18.9139	16.9355	15.2470	13.7986	12.5504	11.4693	10.5288	9.7066	8.9847	7.7843	6.8351	6.4338	6.0726	5.4510	4.9371	4.1428	3.5619	3.1210
25	22.0232	19.5235	17.4131	15.6221	14.0939	12.7834	11.6536	10.6748	9.8226	9.0770	7.8431	6.8729	6.4642	6.0971	5.4669	4.9476	4.1474	3.5640	3.1220
26	22.7952	20.1210	17.8768	15.9828	14.3752	13.0032	11.8258	10.8100	9.9290	9.1609	7.8957	6.9061	6.4906	6.1182	5.4804	4.9563	4.1511	3.5656	3.1227
27	23.5596	20.7069	18.3270	16.3296	14.6430	13.2105	11.9867	10.9352	10.0266	9.2372	7.9426	6.9352	6.5135	6.1364	5.4919	4.9636	4.1542	3.5669	3.1233
28	24.3164	21.2813	18.7641	16.6631	14.8981	13.4062	12.1371	11.0511	10.1161	9.3066	7.9844	6.9607	6.5335	6.1520	5.5016	4.9697	4.1566	3.5679	3.1237
29	25.0658	21.8444	19.1885	16.9837	15.1411	13.5907	12.2777	11.1584	10.1983	9.3696	8.0218	6.9830	6.5509	6.1656	5.5098	4.9747	4.1585	3.5687	3.1240
30	25.8077	22.3965	19.6004	17.2920	15.3725	13.7648	12.4090	11.2578	10.2737	9.4269	8.0552	7.0027	6.5660	6.1772	5.5168	4.9789	4.1601	3.5693	3.1242
35	29.4086	24.9986	21.4872	18.6646	16.3742	14.4982	12.9477	11.6546	10.5668	9.6442	8.1755	7.0700	6.6166	6.2153	5.5386	4.9915	4.1644	3.5708	3.1248
40	32.8347	27.3555	23.1148	19.7928	17.1591	15.0463	13.3317	11.9246	10.7574	9.7791	8.2438	7.1050	6.6418	6.2335	5.5482	4.9966	4.1659	3.5712	3.1250
45	36.0945	29.4902	24.5187	20.7200	17.7741	15.4558	13.6055	12.1084	10.8812	9.8628	8.2825	7.1232	6.6543	6.2421	5.5523	4.9986	4.1664	3.5714	3.1250
50	39.1961	31.4236	25.7298	21.4822	18.2559	15.7619	13.8007	12.2335	10.9617	9.9148	8.3045	7.1327	6.6605	6.2463	5.5541	4.9995	4.1666	3.5714	3.1250
55	42.1472	33.1748	26.7744	22.1086	18.6335	15.9905	13.9399	12.3186	11.0140	9.9471	8.3170	7.1376	6.6636	6.2482	5.5549	4.9998	4.1666	3.5714	3.1250

NOMINAL VERSUS EFFECTIVE INTEREST RATE

Not all payments are received and compounded annually. For instance, bonds make interest payments semiannually, stock dividends are paid quarterly, and banks charge loan interest on a daily basis. As previously demonstrated, quarterly versus annual compounding produces the following results:

	Annual compounding	*Quarterly compounding*
Amount	$1,000.00	$1,000.00
Interest Rate	10%	10%
Number of Years	2	2
Compound Value	$1,210.00	$1,218.40

Since the future values are higher for more frequent compounding, it is appropriate to differentiate between the two by contrasting the *nominal*, or stated, interest rate with the *effective* annual rate (EAR). The EAR can be determined by:

$$EAR = (1 + inom/m)^m - 1.0 \qquad\qquad \text{Eq. 3-9}$$

where

$$EAR = \text{Effective annual rate}$$
$$inom = \text{Nominal, or stated, interest rate}$$
$$m = \text{Number of compounding periods per year}$$

Using the preceding example,

$$EAR = (1 + .10/4)^4 - 1.0$$
$$= (1.025)^4 - 1.0$$
$$= 1.1038 - 1.0$$
$$= .1038 = 10.38\%$$

In this case, the *nominal* interest rate is ten percent. However, if the amount is compounded quarterly, the *effective* annual rate, or the rate actually being earned, is 10.38 percent. The solution to this problem with the use of a calculator is presented in Table 3-11.

ROLE OF INFLATION IN FINANCIAL CALCULATIONS

It is important to take into consideration the effect of inflation in making decisions about future income needs. For instance, suppose Bob Smith wishes to receive $36,000 a year ($3,000 a month) in today's dollars at the beginning of each year for the next five years. Bob assumes that the rate of inflation over this period will be five percent a year and that he will be able to generate an after-tax return of eight percent on his investments. He wants to know from his financial planner how much money he should invest *now* to meet his objective.

TABLE 3-11

Step 1:	Clear calculator [f] [CLX]
Step 2:	[f] [5]
Step 3:	Effective annual rate

PRESS

$$[.]\,[1]\,[0]\begin{bmatrix} E \\ N \\ T \\ E \\ R \end{bmatrix}\,[4]\,\div\begin{bmatrix} E \\ N \\ T \\ E \\ R \end{bmatrix}$$

$[1] + [4]\,[Y^x]$
$[1] -$

Answer: .10380 or 10.38%

Note: [f] [5] will change the key function to 0.00000

Bob Smith's problem is graphically presented in Figure 3-9. The financial planner feeds this data into a HP-12C calculator and determines that Bob needs to invest $170,273.94 today in order to meet his objective. This calculation is presented in Table 3-12.

INTERNAL RATE OF RETURN

One of the most frequent questions raised by financial planners relates to the internal rate of return on an investment. For instance, suppose Judy Kelly wishes to invest $2,500 to purchase 10, ten-year zero-coupon bonds for $250 each. Upon maturity, each bond will pay her $1,000, or a total of $10,000. She wants to know what interest rate her $2,500 investment would earn. In technical jargon, she is asking what would be the internal rate of return (IRR) on this investment, assuming that the tax consequences and cost of this investment are ignored.

The calculation of the IRR on this investment, presented in Table 3-13, shows that Judy Kelly will receive an annual return of 14.35 percent.

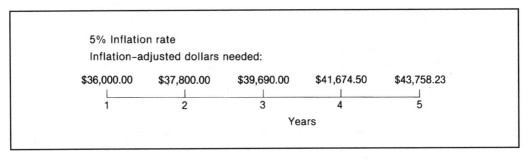

FIGURE 3-9   Impact of inflation on future income needs

TABLE 3-12

Step 1:	Identify key variables:	
	Payment:	$36,000
	Interest:	8% after-tax return
	Number of period:	5 years
	Inflation rate (r):	5%
Step 2:	Clear calculator [f] [CLX]	
Step 3:	Enter data	

Press [g]   [7]

           [3]   [6]   [0]   [0]   [0] [PMT]

Note* [1]   [.]   [0]   [8] $\begin{bmatrix} E \\ N \\ T \\ E \\ R \end{bmatrix}$ [1] [.] [0] [5] [÷]

           [1]   [-]   [1] [0] [0] [X] [i]

           [5]   [n]

           [PV]

Answer: $170,273.94

Note: The following equation is used:

$$d = \left[\frac{1 + i}{1 + r} - 1\right] \times 100$$

where d = inflation-adjusted interest rate
     i = after-tax interest rate
     r = inflation rate

TABLE 3-13

Step 1:	Identify known variables:	
	Present value:	$250 × 10 = $2,500
	Future value:	$1,000 × 10 = $10,000
	Number of periods:	10 years × semiannual (2)
Step 2:	Clear calculator [f] [CLX]	
Step 3:	Enter data	

Press [2] [5] [0] [0] [CHS] [PV]

      [1] [0] [0] [0] [0] [FV]

      [2] [0] [n]

      [i] [2] [x]

Answer: 14.35%

PROBLEM SOLVING WITH THE HP-12C CALCULATOR

In this section we will demonstrate the use of a HP-12C calculator in solving different types of financial problems. For convenience, we will select problems from each of the eight key areas of financial planning:

- *S:* Safety through Risk Management Planning
- *E:* Educational Planning
- *C:* Cash Management, Savings, Credit, and Debt Planning
- *U:* Ultimate Disposition through Estate Planning
- *R:* Retirement Planning
- *I:* Investment Planning
- *T:* Tax Planning
- *Y:* Yearning for Financial Independence Planning

SAFETY THROUGH RISK MANAGEMENT PLANNING

Problem I

John and Betty Storer came to you for risk management planning. An analysis of their finances produced the following result:

John Storer	
Amount of Current Life Insurance	$150,000

At John's Death	
Betty's Earned Income Per Month Available	$ 800
Income Per Month if Insurance Proceeds ($150,000) are invested at 8%	+$ 1,000
Total Dollars Per Month Available to Betty	$ 1,800
Monthly Income Betty Needs After John's Death	−$ 2,500
Monthly Shortfall for Betty	−$ 700

Betty is 55 years old and her life expectancy is 80. She wishes to ignore her Social Security payments. How much additional life insurance does John Storer need to provide Betty an additional $700 of monthly income if he were to die today?

Solution I

The problem should be stated as follows: What is the present value of an ordinary annuity (at the end of each month) which invested at, say, eight percent after taxes, will produce a monthly income of $700 for 25 years (Betty's life expectancy of 80 less her current age of 55)?

$$PVA = PMT \times PVAF$$
$$= \$700 \times 129.56453$$
$$= \$90,695.17$$

Thus, to achieve his objective John should purchase $91,000 (rounded off to nearest $1,000) worth of additional life insurance.

The solution to this problem by the use of a HP-12C calculator is presented in Table 3-14.

Problem II

You have recommended your client to purchase a $3,500 a month disability insurance policy, which costs $3,000 per year. The client, Rita Harris, who is 45 years old, is shocked to learn that a $3,500 policy would cost her $3,000 per year, and has summarily rejected your recommendation. Your task is to explain to Rita the *true* value of the policy you have recommended for purchase.

Solution II

The problem should be stated as follows: What is the present value of an annuity which, invested at, say, seven percent, will produce a monthly income of $3,500 for 20 years? You should explain to Rita that (1) the disability income is paid monthly, while the premium is paid annually; (2) if disabled today, the company will make *monthly* payments for 20 years until Rita reaches age 65; and (3) disability payments are completely tax-free. The present value of the disability policy is $451,438.77 as shown by Table 3-15. You can now point out that, by paying $3,500 today, Rita would purchase a *potential* value of $451,438.77. This is because all disability premium payments would stop, and monthly disability payments would begin (that would last for 20 years) if she were to become disabled today.

EDUCATIONAL PLANNING

Problem III

One of the commonly asked questions of financial planners relates to educational planning. Let us assume that Linda Garrison's son just turned five today.

TABLE 3-14

Step 1:	Identify known variables:	
	Payment:	$700/monthly
	Interest:	8%
	Number of periods:	25 years
Step 2:	Clear calculator [f] [CLX]	
Step 3:	Enter data	
	Press [7] [0] [0] [PMT]	
	[8] [.] [g] [i]	
	[2] [5] [g] [n]	
	[PV]	
	Answer: $90,695.17	

Note: [g] [i] makes adjustment for monthly interest calculations.
      [g] [n] makes adjustment for number of periods (not number of years) calculations.

TABLE 3-15

Step 1: Identify known variables:
Payment: $3,500/monthly
Interest: 7%
Number of payments: 20 years

Step 2: Clear calculator [f] [CLX]

Step 3: Enter data
Press [3] [5] [0] [0]   [PMT]
[7]   [.]   [g] [i]
[2]   [0] [g] [n]
[PV]
Answer: $451,438.77

She plans to save for his college education by making equal semiannual deposits in an investment account paying 9.1 percent compounded semiannually. Linda expects to provide $24,000 per year for four years after he turns 18. She wants to know how much money she should deposit twice a year from now until her son is 18 (13 years, or 26 deposits) to reach her stated goal.

Solution III

26 semiannual
deposits   4 annual withdrawals

PMT PMT $24,000 $24,000 $24,000 $24,000

Age   5   6   18   19   20   21

This problem can be solved in three steps.

Step 1. The effective rate is:
$$EAR = (1 + .091/2)^2 - 1$$

$$= 9.31\% \text{ is rounded off from } 9.307025\%$$

Step 2. At age 18, the present value of four withdrawals at 9.31 percent is:
$$= PMT \times PVAF$$
$$PV = \$24,000 \times 3.2178$$
$$= \$77,227.14$$

Step 3. To achieve the educational funding goal, the future value of the deposits at age 18 must equal $77,227.14. Therefore, the semiannual deposits required are:
$$= PMT \times FVAF$$
$$FV = PMT \times 47.911816$$
$$\frac{\$77,227.14}{PMT} = \$1,611.86$$

TABLE 3-16

Step 1:	Clear calculator [f] [CLX]
Step 2:	Enter data

Press   [·]   [0]   [9]   [1]   [ENTER]   [2]   [÷]

[1]   [+]

[1]   [·]   [0]   [4]   [5]   [5]   [X]

[1]   [−]

Answer: 9.31%

Step 3:   Enter data

Press   [2]   [4]   [0]   [0]   [0]   [CHS]   [PMT]

[9]   [·]   [3]   [1]   [i]

[4]   [n]

[PV]

Answer: $77,227.14

Step 4:   Enter data

Press

[7]   [7]   [2]   [2]   [7]   [·]   [1]   [4]   [FV]

[9]   [·]   [1]   [ENTER]   [2]   [÷]   [i]

[1]   [3]   [ENTER]   [2]   [X]   [n]

[PMT]

Answer: $1,611.86

Note: Since semiannual deposits are made, 9.1%/2 is used rather than the effective annual rate of 9.31%.

In this case, if Linda makes 26 semiannual deposits of $1,611.86 each earning 9.1 percent interest, she would be able to provide $24,000 per year for four years to finance her son's education when he turns 18.

The calculator-generated solution is presented in Table 3-16.

CASH MANAGEMENT, SAVINGS, CREDIT, AND DEBT PLANNING

Problem IV

John Jones has approached you with a budgetary problem. He is financing the purchase of a new car with a three-year loan at 10.5 percent annual interest, compounded monthly. The purchase price of the car is $7,250. His down payment is $1,500. How much does he have to pay at the end of every month?

Solution IV

It is best to set this problem up in the following manner:

PV = \$7,250 − \$1,500 = \$5,750

$$
\begin{array}{ccccc}
1 & 2 & \cdots & 35 & 36 \\
FV = 0 & i = 10.5\% & P/YR = 12 & & PMT = ?
\end{array}
$$

Using Eq. 3-5A we have

$$PVA = PMT \times PVAF$$
$$\text{or } PMT = PVA/PVAF$$
$$= \$5,750/30.767$$
$$= \$186.89$$

The use of the calculator in solving this problem is demonstrated in Table 3-17.

Problem V

Let us assume that in Problem IV John Jones informs you that he cannot pay more than \$177 per month. What is the highest interest rate he can afford to pay if he wishes to purchase this car?

Solution V

You could ask John Jones to shop around for a specific interest rate which would reduce his monthly payment to, say, \$176.89 (i.e., \$10 less than the current monthly payment).

Using Eq. 3-5A,

$$PVA = PMT \times PVAF$$
$$\$5,750 = \$176.89 \times PVAF$$
$$PVAF = 32.51$$

TABLE 3-17

Step 1:	Identify known variables:	
	Present value:	\$5,750
	Interest:	10.5%
	Number of periods:	3 years
Step 2:	Clear calculator [f] [CLX]	
Step 3:	Enter data	
	Press [5] [7] [5] [0] [CHS] [PV]	
	[1] [0] [.] [5] [g] [i]	
	[3] [g] [n]	
	[PMT]	
	Answer: \$186.89	

TABLE 3-18

Step 1:	Identify known variables
	Present value: $5,750
	Future value: $0
	Payments: $176.89/month
	Number of periods: 3 years
Step 2:	Clear calculator [f] [CLX]
Step 3:	Enter data
	[5] [7] [5] [0] [PV]
	[1] [7] [6] [.] [8] [9] [CHS] [PMT]
	[3] [g] [n]
	[i]
	$\begin{bmatrix} E \\ N \\ T \\ E \\ R \end{bmatrix}$ [12] [x]
	Answer: 6.75%

The interest rate associated with the PVAF of 32.51 is 6.75 percent. Therefore, John can purchase this car for $7,250 provided he can find a bank which offers him an interest rate of 6.75 percent. Of course, if such a low interest rate cannot be found, John would have to find a cheaper car or make a larger down payment.

The solution to this problem with the use of a HP-12C calculator is presented in Table 3-18.

Problem VI

Dick Shaft has just joined the brokerage firm of A. M. Merrill. They have offered Dick two different salary arrangements. He can have $50,000 per year for the next three years, or $25,000 per year for the next three years, along with a $50,000 initial bonus today. Dick wants to know which alternative is best for him. He wants to use an interest rate of 16 percent, compounded quarterly.

Solution VI

Step 1. First, we need to calculate the effective annual rate so the rate will be on the same basis as the payments. The effective annual rate is 16.986 percent:

$$EAR$$

$$= (1 + r_{nom/m})^m - 1.0$$

$$= (1 + .16/4)^4 - 1.0 \qquad \text{Eq. 3-10 restated}$$

$$= .1\ 6986 = 16.986\%$$

Step 2. The *PV* of $50,000 for three years with r = 16.986 percent is $110,504.31.

$$PVA$$
$$= PMT \times PVAF$$
$$= \$50{,}000 \times 2.2100862$$
$$= \$110{,}504.31$$

Step 3. The *PV* of \$25,000 for three years is \$55,252.16.

Step 4. The total value of option 2, which includes an immediate bonus of \$50,000, is only \$105,252.16 (\$55,252.16 + \$50,000.00). Consequently, the first option of \$50,000 per year for three years is more desirable.

The solution to this problem with the use of a HP-12C calculator is presented in Table 3-19.

Problem VII

Sam Johnson, your valued client, wants to purchase a home. He can make a down payment of \$12,000 and can afford a monthly payment of \$630. The interest rate on a 30-year fixed mortgage is 11.5 percent. How much mortgage can Sam afford to pay on this house?

TABLE 3-19

Step 1:   Clear calculator [f] [CLX]

Step 2:   [f] [5]

Step 3:   Effective annual rate

Press [.] [1] [6] $\begin{bmatrix} E \\ N \\ T \\ E \\ R \end{bmatrix}$ [4] [÷] $\begin{bmatrix} E \\ N \\ T \\ E \\ R \end{bmatrix}$

[1] + [4] [Yˣ]

[1] −

Answer = <u>.16986 or 16.986%</u>

Step 4:   Press [5]   [0] [0] [0] [0] [PMT]
          [1]   [6] [.] [9] [8] [6] [i]
          [3]   [n]
          [PV]
Answer: <u>\$110,504.31</u>

Step 5:   Press [2] [5] [0] [0] [0] [PMT]
          [1] [6] [.] [9] [8] [6] [i]
          [3] [n]
          [PV]
          [5] [0] [0] [0] [0] [−]
Answer: <u>\$105,252.16</u>

Step 6:   Option I (Step 4)   = \$110,504.32
          Option II (Step 5) = \$105,252.16
          Option I is better.

Note: [f] [5] will change the key function to 0.00000

Solution VII

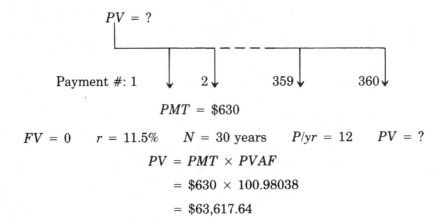

$$PMT = \$630$$

$$FV = 0 \quad r = 11.5\% \quad N = 30 \text{ years} \quad P/yr = 12 \quad PV = ?$$

$$PV = PMT \times PVAF$$

$$= \$630 \times 100.98038$$

$$= \$63,617.64$$

Clearly, a monthly payment of $630 for 30 years will be sufficient to purchase a home valued at $63,617.64. However, since Sam can make a down payment of $12,000, he can afford a home valued at $75,617.64 ($63,617.64 + $12,000.00).

The solution to this problem with the use of the calculator is presented in Table 3-20.

ULTIMATE DISPOSITION THROUGH ESTATE PLANNING

Problem VIII

Your client, Shirley Jones, is 40 years old and is in excellent health. Her husband, Jim, is also 40 and is paralyzed for life. Shirley holds a good position and believes that she will be able to take care of Jim until she retires at age 70. However, she fears that she might die soon thereafter and no one else would look after Jim.

TABLE 3-20

Step 1:	Identify known variables	
	Payment:	$630/monthly
	Interest:	11.5%
	Number of payments:	30 years
Step 2:	Clear calculator [f] [CLX]	
Step 3:	Enter data	
	Press	
	[6] [3] [0] [CHS] [PMT]	
	[1] [1] [.] [5] [g] [i]	
	[3] [0] [g] [n]	
	[PV]	
	[Add $12,000 down payment] [1] [2] [0] [0] [0] [+]	
	Answer: $75,617.64	

TABLE 3-21

Step 1:	Identify known variables		
	Future value:	$1,000,000	
	Interest rate:	8%	
	Number of periods:	30 years	
Step 2:	Clear calculator [f] [CLX]		
Step 3:	Enter data		
	Press	[g]	[7]
		[1]	[0][0][0][0][0][0] [FV]
		[8]	[g] [i]
		[3]	[0][g][n]
		[PMT]	
	Answer:	$666.54/month	

Shirley wants to create a revocable trust for the benefit of Jim. She will start putting money into this trust right away and hopes that it will have a value of $1 million when she reaches age 70. Upon her death, the entire amount will be transferred to Jim, and because of a marital deduction, no estate taxes will be due on this transfer. Shirley believes that she can obtain a compounded annual return of eight percent (after-tax) and wants to know how much she should invest at the beginning of each month to achieve her objective.

Solution VIII

The solution to this problem is presented in Table 3-21. Shirley should invest $666.54 at the beginning of each month for 30 years to accomplish her goal.

RETIREMENT PLANNING

Problem IX

John VanZandt, one of your valued clients, has been asked by his company to choose between a retirement payout of $500,000 and a lifetime annuity of $5,000 a month. He is impressed by the half-a-million-dollar lump sum payment, but his wife wants him to go for the annuity offer. John trusts you completely, and will accept your recommendation. What is your advice?

Solution IX

John should understand that the solution to this problem can be found only if certain specific assumptions are made. After much discussion, you make the following assumptions:

1. John's life expectancy is 82. That is, since he is 65 years old, you will assume that the annuity will pay him for 17 years, or a total payment for 204 (17 x 12) months.

TABLE 3-22

Step 1:		Clear calculator [f] [CLX]
Step 2:	Press	[g] [8]
		[5] [0] [0] [0] [PMT]
		[8] [g] [i]
		[1] [7] [g] [n]
		[PV]
	Answer:	$556,633.67

Step 3: The present value of the annuity payments exceeds the lump sum distribution by:

$$\begin{aligned}&\$556,633.67 \\ -&\$500,000.00 \\ \hline &\$\ 56,633.67\end{aligned}$$

2. If John receives a lump sum, he will be able to obtain a compounded annual return of eight percent, which translates into a monthly return of 0.6667 percent (8/12).

3. You will ignore the tax consequences of these payments.

The solution to this problem is presented in Table 3-22. Based on your findings, you recommend that John choose the lifetime annuity payment option.

Of course, you should emphasize to John that the outcome could be different if a different set of assumptions is made.

INVESTMENT PLANNING

Problem X

Sheldon Blair learned from his broker that the AAA-rated, XYZ bond, which has a coupon of ten percent and a ten-year maturity, is completely risk free. However, he became totally confused when he attended one of your seminars in which you pointed out that even AAA bonds are subject to interest rate risks. Sheldon is visiting with you and is anxious to find out if you are correct in your assertion.

Solution X

First, you should assure Sheldon that the interest rate risk is different from the possibility that the company would miss a coupon payment or would not pay the face value upon maturity. Next, you present the information given in Table 3-23. In this table, you demonstrate that if the market interest rate immediately rises to 12 percent, the price of the AAA-bond would drop to $885.30—a loss of $114.70. That is, if the interest rate rises to 12 percent today and Sheldon is forced to sell the bond, assuming the bond market to be efficient, he would incur a loss of $114.70 despite the fact that the bond represents a safe investment.

TABLE 3-23

Step 1:	Identify known variables	
	Future value:	$1,000
	Payment:	$100/year
	Interest:	12 percent × semiannual (0.5)
	Number of periods:	10 years × semiannual (2)
Step 2:	Clear calculator [f] [CLX]	
Step 3:	Enter data	
	Press [1] [0] [0] [0] [FV]	
	[5] [0] [PMT]	
	[6] [i]	
	[2] [0] [n]	
	[PV]	
	Answer: $885.30	

Problem XI

Bob Sweet is ecstatic about an investment he bought three years ago for $5,000. Since he claims that in this short period his gain is almost 100 percent, Bob wants to buy more of this investment. As a financial planner, your task is to point out the *true* annual return on this investment, given the fact that the current market value of this investment is $8,000.

Solution XI

The compounded annual return of this investment can be calculated by

$$FV = PV \times FVFF$$
$$\$8,000 = 5,000 \times 1.6$$

The interest rate associated with the future value of fixed sum factor of 1.6 for three years is 16.96 percent. The calculator-generated solution is presented in Table 3-24.

TAX PLANNING

Problem XII

Joan Pace, one of your valued clients in the 28 percent tax bracket, is excited about investing $100,000 in a tax shelter. Basically, she is a risk averse person; however she wants to purchase this tax shelter because of the 90 percent write-off she will receive from it for the next five years. She has asked you to calculate how much money she will have accumulated at the end of five years as a result of these writeoffs, assuming that she would expect to realize a nine percent annual interest.

Solution XII

Assuming that Betty is correct in her assumption about the write-off, the key facts are listed here:

TABLE 3-24

Step 1:   Identify known variables
            Present value: $5,000
            Future value: $8,000
            Number of periods: 3 years
Step 2:   Clear calculator [f] [CLX]
Step 3:   Enter data
            [5]   [0]   [0]   [0] [CHS]   [PV]
            [8]   [0]   [0]   [0] [FV]
            [3]   [n]
            [i]
            Answer: 16.96%

Total investment: $100,000
Write-off (90%): $90,000/year for 5 years

At her marginal tax bracket of 28 percent, Betty's tax savings are $25,200 at the end of each year (28% of $90,000) for five years. So the question is this: What is the future value of a $25,200 annuity for five years? Let us assume the interest rate to be used in this case is nine percent:

$$FV = PMT \times FVAF$$
$$= \$25,200 \times 5.9847107$$
$$= \$150,814.71$$

The solution is also presented in Table 3-25. Incidentally, as her financial planner you should explain to Joan that the tax writeoffs are not guaranteed and that these tax savings are merely deferred taxes which become due when the tax shelter is liquidated.

TABLE 3-25

Step 1:   Identify known variables
            Payment: $25,200/year
            Interest: 9%
            Number of periods: 5 years
Step 2:   Clear calculator [f] [CLX]
Step 3:   Enter data
            Press [2] [5] [2] [0] [0] [PMT]
                  [9] [i]
                  [5] [n]
                  [FV]
            Answer: $150,814.71

YEARNING FOR FINANCIAL INDEPENDENCE PLANNING

Problem XIII

Recently you were requested by a young executive named Sam Dunn to develop for him a financial independence plan. He wants to invest $5,000 per year at an effective annual rate of return (EAR) of nine percent for the next 30 years, with the first deposit beginning on his thirtieth birthday. Beginning at age 60 he will tour around the world for five years and will need a large sum each year to accomplish that objective. After Sam completes this tour, he would like to receive an annual income of $30,000 per year for the next 15 years. Assuming an EAR of nine percent for the entire time period what is the maximum amount of capital Sam can spend on his world tour?

Solution XIII

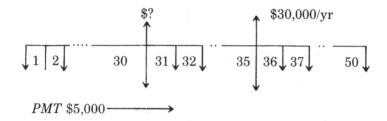

This problem should be broken down into four steps.

Step 1. Value of annual investments at age 60:

$$
\begin{aligned}
FVA &= PMT \times FVAF \\
&= \$5,000 \times 136.3075 \\
&= \$681,537.69
\end{aligned}
$$

Sam will have accumulated $681,537.69 by age 60.

Step 2. The PV of $30,000 in annual payments for 15 years, starting with year 36 (age 65) is:

$$
\begin{aligned}
PVA &= PMT \times PVAF \\
&= \$30,000 \times 8.0606883 \\
&= \$241,820.65
\end{aligned}
$$

Step 3. The PV of $241,820.65 at age 60, discounted for five years at nine percent, is:

$$
\begin{aligned}
PV &= FV \times PVAF \\
&= \$241,820.65 \times .6499313 \\
&= \$157,166.83
\end{aligned}
$$

Step 4. Therefore, Sam should be able to spend the difference between what he would have at age 60 and the amount he would need to generate current income starting at age 65. Specifically,

Amount accumulated by age 60 = $681,537.69

Amount needed to generate income at age 65 = $157,166.83

Amount available for world trip = $524,370.86

The calculator-based solution is presented in Table 3-26.

TABLE 3-26

Step 1:	Clear calculator [f] [CLX]
Step 2: Press	[5] [0] [0] [0] [CHS] [PMT]
	[9] [i]
	[3] [0] [n]
	[FV]
Answer:	$681,537.69
Step 3:	[0] [FV]
Step 4: Press	[3] [0] [0] [0] [0] [PMT]
	[9] [i]
	[1] [5] [n]
	[PV]
Answer:	$241,820.65
Step 5: Press	[2] [4] [1] [8] [2] [0] [·] [6] [5] [FV]
	[9] [i]
	[5] [n]
	[PV]
Answer:	$157,166.83
Step 6:	Sam should be able to spend
	$681,537.69
	−$157,166.83
	$524,370.86

In this chapter we have demonstrated the use of the concept of the time value of money and the HP-12C financial calculator in solving different types of financial problems. In the next chapter we will undertake a comprehensive analysis of the issues involving risk management planning.

One machine can do the work of fifty ordinary men. No machine can do the work of one extraordinary man.

Elbert Hubbard

PART II

Key Financial Planning Areas: S-E-C-U-R-I-T-Y

Part II is devoted to eight key financial planning areas. These areas are best described by the acronym, S-E-C-U-R-I-T-Y:

S: Safety through Risk Management Planning
E: Educational Planning
C: Cash Management, Savings, Credit, and Debt Planning
U: Ultimate Disposition through Estate Planning
R: Retirement Planning
I: Investment Planning
T: Tax Planning
Y: Yearning for Financial Independence Planning

In the following pages, we will undertake a detailed discussion of each of the eight planning areas. In each case, (except financial independence planning), we will present the basic structure of the area followed by the key planning strategies applicable to that area. Also, wherever appropriate, we will present case studies to demonstrate the application of theories and concepts to real life situations.

CHAPTER 4

Life Insurance: Structure, Concepts, and Planning Strategies

SECTION I
LIFE INSURANCE: AN OVERVIEW

INTRODUCTION

No one ever knows for sure when, where, and how our lives, and thus our ability to generate income, will end. The primary objective of purchasing life insurance is to convert the uncertainty that a person may not be able to meet all financial obligations in the event of a possible misfortune into the certainty that these financial obligations will be fulfilled.

The financial obligations may include the following short- and long-term financial needs during life and upon death:

1. Provide for spouse, children, and other financial dependents during pre- and post-retirement.
2. Pay off final expenses, estate taxes, state inheritance taxes, and administration costs.
3. Pay off all debts and mortgages.
4. Provide funds for education.
5. Pass on assets to heirs.

This chapter was critically reviewed for technical accuracy and enhancements by Mr. Anton T. Vanek Jr., CLU, ChFC, CFP, President, Anton T. Vanek Associates, 5435 Corporate Drive, Suite 230, Troy, Michigan 48098. Telephone: 800-753-7078. The review was completed in 2004. However, the authors are solely responsible for the contents.

6. Transfer ownership of a business or protect a business against the loss of a key employee.
7. Maintain an adequate emergency fund.
8. Provide insurance for an ex-spouse who is dependent upon the primary breadwinner's alimony, maintenance or child support payments.
9. Provide funds for charity to a church, synagogue, university or hospital.
10. Create an opportunity for recruiting, retaining, retiring, or rewarding employees through salary continuation plan, and financing the company's obligations under that plan to the dependents of a deceased key employee.

In purchasing life insurance the primary objective should be to determine how much insurance needs to be purchased. This amount, in turn, would depend upon how much income is needed to: (1) assure that the desired standard of living of the family would not be affected as a result of the untimely death of the breadwinner; and (2) meet other financial obligations just listed.

A secondary objective of buying life insurance is to treat it as a form of savings. Life insurance can offer a plan that forces a person to save, allowing the savings to grow tax-deferred. If life insurance is used for this purpose, the objective should be to insure that, after taking into consideration income tax and forced savings features, investment in a life insurance company does provide the policyholder with an opportunity for accumulating long-term savings. Of course, since money spent on insurance premiums is diverted from other investments, it is rarely desirable to buy as much insurance as one can afford. Also, in buying insurance, no one should get carried away by emotion.

Clearly, before purchasing life insurance as a form of investment, expected return on life insurance investment should be compared with returns expected from other investment opportunities. Furthermore, in calculating the net policy return, charges for mortality and operating expenses should be subtracted. Finally, since investments inside a life insurance policy grow tax-deferred, life insurance investment return should be compared with other investment returns on an after-tax, or preferably, on a tax-deferred basis.

THEORY OF RISK TRANSFER: HANDLING RISK

Risk is a way of life. There are five distinct ways of handling risk. These are: risk avoidance, risk reduction, risk retention, risk sharing, and risk transfer. Management of risk involves a three-step operation. First, the nature and cause of risk should be identified. Second, determination should be made of how much risk a person is willing to assume. Finally, the best method for handling the remaining degree of risk should be identified. Purchasing life insurance constitutes one of the most effective methods of handling risk. A brief discussion of each of the five ways of handling risk now follows.

Risk Avoidance

Certain types of risk can be totally avoided. Here are some examples. A physician may choose not to practice as an obstetrician to avoid the risk of being sued.

An individual afraid of getting injured may choose to avoid high-risk recreational activities like mountain climbing or skiing. An investor may avoid the risk of losing the principal by not investing in stocks. However, in the real world, it may not be practical to totally avoid these types of risk.

Risk Retention

An alternative to risk avoidance is to personally assume the risk. Naturally, this can be a viable alternative only where it does not pose a substantial financial or non-financial threat to the risk taker. Risk can be retained on either a voluntary or an involuntary basis. Generally, people assume risk voluntarily because they have sufficient resources to handle such risk. For instance, an individual may decide against purchasing life insurance because he is independently wealthy and his family would be able to maintain the current life style in the event of his untimely death. In contrast, involuntary risk assumption occurs when the risk-taker fails to transfer the risk to an organization. An example of involuntary risk assumption is when a home owner is unable to obtain an earthquake or a flood insurance.

Risk Reduction

Another way of handling risk is to take two distinct steps to reduce risk. The first step is taken through loss prevention and control. Examples of this approach include installation of smoke detectors and burglar alarms in a home or a theft alarm in a car. The second step is to take advantage of the law of large numbers. Life insurance provides the best illustration of this strategy. By insuring the lives of millions of people, insurance companies dramatically reduce their risk exposure because they know that statistically only a small percentage of insureds will die during any given time period.

Risk Sharing

A relatively safe method of handling risk is to assume a limited degree of manageable risk and transfer the balance of risk to one or more organizations. Examples of risk sharing include paying a deductible in health insurance, or participating in a self-insurance fund. In these situations, risk takers assume only a *manageable* degree of risk.

Risk Transfer

The last method of handling risk is to transfer it completely to a third party, most commonly an insurance company. The most popular type of risk transfer is insurance. Other examples of risk transfer include hedging, which refers to the simultaneous buying and selling of a contract, a surety arrangement where an individual is bonded against loss, and a hold harmless agreement in which one person assumes the potential loss of another person.

A summary of the above discussion on risk handling is presented in Figure 4-1. As this figure reveals, risk sharing and risk transfer are strategies that lead to the selection of appropriate insurance companies.

Examples of risks and risk management strategies are presented in Table 4-1. Clearly, transferring risk to an insurance company is only one of many ways of handling risk. For instance, personal savings, security plans, and health-enhancing behavior—all are methods of avoiding or reducing risk. However, not all risks can

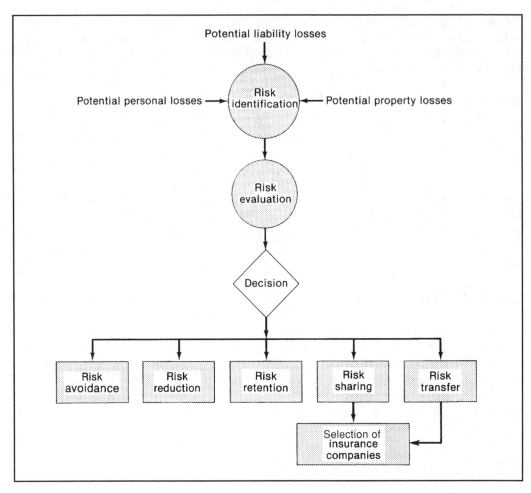

FIGURE 4-1   Personal risk management: an overview

be avoided or reduced to manageable levels through the use of personal resources. Consequently, transferring risk by purchasing life insurance is an integral part of risk management strategy. Various ways of handling risk are summarized in Table 4-2. Also, types of insurance available for covering various forms of risk are illustrated in Figure 4-2. In this chapter, because of its importance and significance in financial planning, we will only discuss risk management planning through the purchase of life insurance. Casualty, property, disability, and liability insurance plans will be discussed in the next chapter.

BASIC TYPES OF LIFE INSURANCE POLICIES

An overview of various types of life insurance policies, their relative advantages and disadvantages, and their appropriateness for different groups of people are presented in Table 4-3. In this section we will elaborate on each type of life insurance policy. Naturally, life insurance is a management tool, and the type of insurance policy selected must be designed to solve the problem at hand.

TABLE 4-1   Risks and Risk Management Strategies

Risks		Strategies for reducing financial impact		
Personal events	Financial impact	Personal resources	Private sector	Public sector
Disability	Loss of one income Loss of services Increased expenses Other losses	Savings, investments Family observing safety precautions Other resources	Disability insurance Other strategies Worker's compensation	Disability insurance Social Security Second Injury Funds
Illness	Loss of one income Catastrophic hospital expenses Other losses	Health-enhancing behavior Saving and Investing Nursing home care	Health insurance Health maintenance organizations Other strategies	Military health Medicare, Medicaid
Death	Loss of one income Loss of services Final expenses Other expenses	Estate planning Risk reduction Other resources	Life insurance Other strategies Long-term care insurance	Veteran's life insurance Social Security survivor's benefits
Retirement	Decreased income Other expenses	Savings Investments Hobbies, skills Other resources	Retirement and/ or pensions Other strategies	Social Security Pension plan for government employees
Property loss	Catastrophic storm damage to property Repair or replacement cost of theft	Property repair and upkeep Security plans Other resources	Automobile insurance Homeowners insurance Flood insurance (joint program with government)	Flood insurance (joint program with business) Federal Disaster Relief
Liability	Claims and settlement costs Lawsuits and legal expenses Loss of personal assets and income Other expenses	Observing safety precautions Maintaining property Other resources	Homeowners insurance Automobile insurance Malpractice insurance Other strategies	

Source: Adapted from *Personal and Family Financial Planning: A Staff Development Workshop for Secondary School Trainers and Teachers* (Washington, D.C.: American Council of Life Insurance, 1983, p. vi/13d.

TABLE 4-2 Various ways of handling risk

	High Frequency	Low Frequency
High Severity	Avoidance	Transfer/Sharing
Low Severity	Reduction	Retention/Sharing

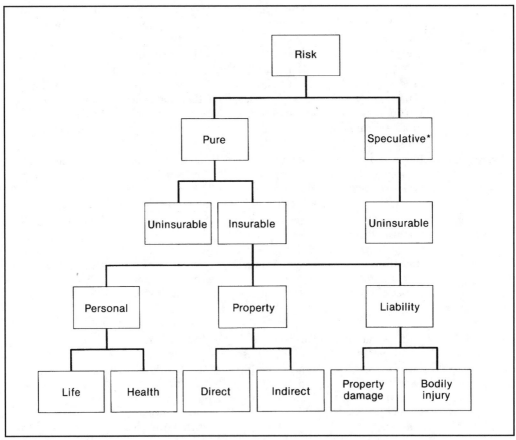

*A speculative risk is one in which there is a chance of either loss or gain. Starting a business and gambling are examples of speculative risk.

FIGURE 4-2 Types of insurance available for certain risks. Adapted from David L. Bickelhanpt, *General Insurance,* 11th ed. (Homewood, Ill.: Richard D. Irwin, 1979), p. 11, copyright 1983, Richard D. Irwin, Inc.

Term Insurance

The essential features. A term policy is one that is *rented* for a specified time, the time period typically varying from one to 30 years, but it can extend even up to age 100. At the end of the term, if the policy is renewable, the insured can renew the protection generally by paying a higher premium. These policies can be purchased in blocks of $1,000 or more, and for larger amounts a blood test and a medical examination may be required to establish the insurability of the buyer. As compared to other types of insurance policies, term insurance premiums are lower in a person's early years, but they increase dramatically in later years, and at age 70 can become prohibitively expensive.

For a specified time period, term insurance provides protection against financial losses resulting from death. This implies that the insured must die before any payments can be made to the beneficiary. So, if the insured survives the specified term, a term policy expires with no value. For this reason, term insurance policy is often characterized as providing *pure protection* because it pays only death benefits and does not accumulate cash value. This is why it provides the most protection per premium dollar and hence is most suitable for younger families with lower levels of income and/or high levels of debt.

The best way to appreciate the importance of term insurance is to ask why a family is likely to buy such insurance. The lifestyle of a family is almost always dependent upon the family's income. Since the possibility always exists that the flow of income would be greatly diminished or even eliminated by the death of a breadwinner, it is highly desirable to ensure that a significant percentage of the income would continue to flow in the event of the death of the income earner. For a price—a premium—an insurance company will guarantee to pay a specified amount, either as a lump sum, or in the form of monthly income, to the beneficiaries named in the policy, should the policyholder die during the period the contract is in force. However, as already mentioned, if the person outlives the term of the policy, the family does not receive any money from the insurance company in return for the premium dollars previously paid.

In a real sense, term life insurance is very similar to automobile or home insurance: The insurance company pays only when there is damage to *property*. There are, however, two important differences between term life insurance and property (automobile or home) insurance. First, in the former case one's life is insured, whereas in the latter case only the physical property is involved. Second, in the case of term insurance the beneficiaries of the policy receive the money, whereas in the latter case, the person carrying the insurance receives the benefits.

As is true of a cash value policy (discussed in the next section), a term policy can be either *participating* or *nonparticipating*. In a par (short for participating) policy, the insurance company initially charges a higher premium rate than would be necessary to provide the coverage. Later it returns the over- collection of premiums in the form of *dividends*, unless it has grossly miscalculated its expenses and income. Consequently, in a par policy, dividends are never guaranteed, and the insured must estimate future dividend payments on the basis of the company's history of dividend payments. In contrast, in a nonpar (short for nonparticipating) policy, the company fixes the premium at a level necessary to meet the insurer's expenses. For this reason, premium rates in a nonpar policy are generally lower than a par policy, but these policies pay no dividends. If a company has a good history of dividend payments, however, it is possible that dividends will bring the

TABLE 4-3 Overview of Life Insurance Policies

Type	General description	Investment products	Flexibility of investment	Safety of Cash Value	Potential rate of return	Death benefit
Term: Annual Renewable and Convertible	Quality Term. After-tax life insurance. Pure life insurance with no cash value element.	None	N/A	N/A	N/A	Fixed, Level or Decreasing
Whole Life	Basic Coverage. Dividends add flexibility. Guarantees	Long-term bonds and mortgages.	None Alternative is to borrow from policy and invest.	High	Low to Moderate	Fixed, Level
Interest Sensitive Whole Life	Combination of universal life and whole life.	Interest-sensitive investments.	Same as universal life.	High	Moderate	Fixed, Level
Adjustable Life	Similar to whole life, except may adjust death benefit and premiums	Interest-sensitive investments.	Same as universal life.	High	Moderate	Adjustable
Universal Life	Flexible Premium Payments.	Interest-sensitive investments.	None Insured may borrow from cash value or withdraw capital.	High	Moderate	Adjustable
Variable Life	Investment selected by insured.	Stocks, bonds, mutual funds, zero coupons, money market, instruments, etc.	Excellent Insured directs movement of funds.	Low to Moderate	High	Usually guaranteed minimum. Can increase with investment performance.
Universal Variable Life	Combination of universal and variable life.	Combination of universal and variable life.	High Insured directs movement of funds.	Low to Moderate	High	Adjustable Can increase with investment performance.
Survivorship/ Whole Life	Payment upon second death.	Long-term bonds and mortgates.	None	High	Low	Fixed, Level

Note: Survivorship life may be funded with variable, universal, or variable universal life.

TABLE 4-3   *(continued)*

Flexibility of premium	Alteration of death benefit	Advantages	Disadvantages	Appropriate buyer
None Increases periodically.	None	Lower initial cost. Dollars can be invested elsewhere. Pure death protection.	No savings element. Expires after specified period. Cost increases.	Young couples who need a large amount of insurance. People who do not want to invest in an insurance vehicle. People whose insurance needs will decrease over time. People who have temporary needs.
None Premium fixed, Dividends can lower or eliminate payments. Loans available.	None	Lifetime coverage. Savings element. Loan privileges. Variety of premium payment plans.	Higher cost of death protection. Low rate of return. Lack of flexibility. May not keep pace with inflation.	People who need forced savings, lifetime coverage, estate liquidity.
None May change based on insurer's experience.	Same as universal life.	Level fixed premiums between each redetermination period, forced savings element.	Policyholders bear more risk of adverse trends in mortality and expenses. Considerable loss if surrendered during first several years.	People who need forced savings for a period of time and who want the potential for better investment results than those quaranteed in traditional policies.
High	Same as universal life.	Flexibility with premium face amount.	Direct recognition method used to calculate dividends.	People who want flexibility and forced savings.
High Maximum: Allowed by law. Minimum: To cover mortality and expenses.	Excellent. Amount can be increased or decreased as desired.	Flexibility Potentially higher rate of return. Full disclosure of fees, loads, proportion invested.	No forced savings. Potential drop in rate of return. Not the most competitive investment vehicle.	People who want choice and flexibility. People who want a cash value fund with a higher rate of return.
None	None	Potentially high rate of return. Control of investments. Full disclosure required by law. Cash values are held in separate accounts which are segregated from the insurer's general investment portfolio.	No guaranteed cash value. Element of risk borne by policyholder. Need for familiarity with investments. Generally high expense ratio.	People who are investment-oriented and want a higher rate of return and/or want flexibility.
Flexible at option of policy owner.	Same as universal life.	Cash values are held in separate accounts which are segregated from the insurer's general investment portfolio.	No guaranteed cash value. Element of risk borne by policyholder. Need for familiarity with investments. Generally high expense ratio.	People who are investment-oriented and want a higher rate of return and/or want flexibility.
None	None	Lower insurance cost than insurance on each insured.	Low return. Lack of flexibility. Long period before death benefit becomes due.	People seeking funds for paying estate taxes upon second death.

Source: Adapted from Don Johnson and Cheryl Toman-Cubbage, "Have Your Cake...," *Financial Planning,* January 1986, p. 191.

true cost of a par policy below that of a nonpar policy if the policy is held for an extended period of time.

Types of term insurance. Several term insurance alternatives have gained considerable popularity. These are discussed next.

Level Term. Persons who dislike paying progressively higher annual premiums can buy level term policies. In this type of policy, the premium and the protection level remain fixed for the life of the policy, which typically covers 5-, 10-, 20-, or 30-year periods. During early years, the policyholder pays the insurance company more than is necessary to meet the claims, with the understanding that less than the cost of insurance would be needed in later years. These policies are generally not purchased at advanced ages because of prohibitive mortality cost.

Renewable Term. This type of policy includes a contractual provision guaranteeing the renewal of the policy for a limited number of additional periods, each usually of the same length as the original term period. For example, someone who purchases a 10-year term policy at age 25 and survives this period, will have the option of renewing the policy at age 35 for an additional 10 years without having to prove insurability. The level premium for this 10-year period would be higher than that for the previous 10 years, because of the insured's more advanced age and adverse seletion. The insured may renew the policy at age 45 and perhaps also at age 55. However, most insurance companies impose an age limit beyond which an automatic renewal is not permitted. A limited number of companies offer term policies that are renewable to age 100.

Convertible Term. The conversion provision grants the insured the option to exchange the term contract for some type of permanent life insurance contract without having to provide evidence of insurability. The option to renew regardless of health status provide the insured with complete protection against loss of insurability. The conversion is usually granted at the policyholder's attained age.

Variations In Renewal and Conversion Privileges. Renewal and conversion provisions and the premium structure in term policies may be combined in a variety of ways, creating a myriad of different contracts. Many term policies permit renewal for another period at a level premium. Some term policies that start off with a level premium for 5, 10, 20 or 30 years are converted into annually increasing premium policies after that initial period. Still other policies have a re-entry provision that allows the insured to re-qualify for a new level premium period at a reasonable rate. In this case, a new underwriting is required.

Decreasing Term. This policy requires the payment of a level premium during the term of the policy, but the face value of the policy declines progressively to zero at the expiration of the policy period. Decreasing term insurance is used in cases where protection is temporarily desired to meet a specific liability for a limited time.

A variation of the decreasing term policy is known as a mortgage redemption policy. It refers to a policy designed to provide protection in some amount, sufficient to pay off the mortgage at any given time. Since the mortgage is constantly decreasing, a policy designed to pay off the mortgage in the event of the death of the breadwinner may also decrease the face amount over its life. This policy is written on a decreasing term basis for the term of the mortgage. If the policyholder lives to pay off the mortgage, the policy expires without value at the same time the need for protection has disappeared. This policy may also be available on a joint (first to die) basis.

Family income policy. The family income policy also utilizes the concept of decreasing term insurance to fit a need for a decreasing amount of insurance. It is a combination of some form of permanent insurance plan (for example, whole life) with decreasing term insurance. The term insurance makes provision for the payment of some prespecified amount per month upon the date of the insured's death until some specified date in the future. The sum payable per month is typically one percent of the amount of permanent insurance, although many companies offer other options as well.

Term policies can differ significantly from one another, partly because they come with different options and features. While all options are not always attractive, in purchasing a term policy the following options should always be considered.

Convertibility. As mentioned, this feature gives policyholders the right to convert term policies into cash-value policies without having to provide an evidence of medical insurability. Anyone opting for this feature should ensure that the insurer will permit a conversion over a long period, ideally until the policyholder reaches age 65. Also, the quality of the cash-value should be examined. Low-load term polices should be convertible to low-load cash-value policies that charge reduced commissions. Finally, if the policyholder eventually expects to convert the term policy into a cash value building policy, then the insured may wish to ensure that the insurance company offers the desired cash value policy as well.

Flexibility. Many insurers let policyholders reduce their coverage and premium without having to apply for a new policy or pay additional fees. This may be helpful if the policyholder anticipates that the insurance needs will continually shrink until they finally disappear. As the needs decline, it might be prudent for the policyholder to reduce the coverage, thereby reducing the premium payments. Of course, in reducing the coverage, a decline in the value of the dollar due to inflation should be taken into account.

Shopping for Term Policies. The marketplace is so inundated with different types of term policies that the task of selecting the right policy has become extremely difficult. The quickest way to narrow the search is to contact: (1) Quotesmith (800-556-9393), a free service that provides price-comparison reports of 150 term life policies sold by agents and brokers. (2) Wholesale Insurance Network (800-808-5810), which provides quotes for low-load policies. (3) Select Quote (800-343-1985), which provides quotes for a wide variety of policies.

Finally, in selecting a term policy, wherever possible, it is desirable to assume the worst-case scenario. For instance, if a person is considering a ten-year level premium term policy but expects the need to continue for an additional 5-10 years, cost estimates should be based on the assumption that, for medical reasons, upon renewals the policyholder would have to pay a higher level of premium. In the final analysis, all else being equal, the best strategy is to purchase the term policy that is marketed by a quality company, is expected to be inexpensive over the long term, and offers most attractive options.

Cash Value Insurance

The essential features

Death Protection. Cash value insurance provides income protection for the family in the case of the breadwinner's premature death. As mentioned earlier, this is one of the primary reasons for buying life insurance today.

Permanence. Cash value insurance keeps the coverage in force until the insured dies or stops paying the premium and cancels the policy. Also, the level of premium paid by the insured remains fixed even after the cost of insurance goes up significantly due to advancing age.

Cash Value. In addition to providing death protection, cash value life insurance policies accumulate a savings element called *cash value*. When all the premiums required by the contract have been paid, that is, when the policy is *paid up*, the insurance company provides an option to the insured to withdraw the accumulated cash value either as a lump sum or in installments.

The role played by cash value is clearly demonstrated in Figure 4-3. This figure shows that a reducing term (net amount of risk) plus the increasing savings (cash value) add up to the face amount of the policy. Note that only the reducing-term portion, and not the face value, truly represents the liability of the insurance company. That is why every cash value insurance policy is presumed to be term plus a long-range savings plan called cash value.

Flexibility. Cash value life insurance accumulates a cash value against which a loan may be made. For instance, if the policyholder wishes to tap the cash value to make a premium payment, the insurance company can advance a premium loan to continue the protection, and the loan can be repaid at a later date. If the policyholder wishes to discontinue paying premiums on the policy but wants the policy to remain in force, the accumulated cash value, known as nonforfeitures value, may be used to convert the existing policy either into an extended term policy or a paid-up insurance policy with reduced face value. In the former case, the insured would continue to be covered for the original face value, but only for a reduced time period. In contrast, the reduced paid-up insurance calls for a reduction in the face value of the insurance (which becomes permanent and is explained later in this chapter), but no further premium payments are due on that policy.

Equal-Payment Plan (Level Premiums). The premium rate on a given policy is determined by the life expectancy of the insured. And since life expectancy

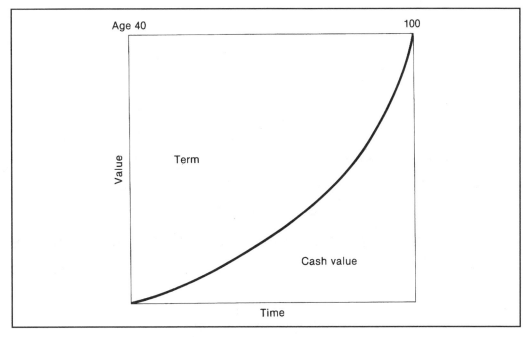

FIGURE 4-3   Cash value insurance

declines with age, premium rates are lower in earlier years but progressively increase in later years. This arrangement does not suit most people buying permanent life insurance. They would rather pay a little more in earlier years to avoid the burden of higher premium rates in later years. Consequently, insurance companies have devised a level premium system which permits an insured to pay higher premiums so in later years they would have to pay premiums that would be less than that required to cover the cost of protection at those ages. That is, the additional money paid in the earlier years helps to equalize the greater cost of life insurance protection in later years, so the company is not required to increase premium payments at that time. In Figure 4-4, a level premium policy, which remains fixed for life, is compared with a step-rate premium policy, which increases with age.

Dividend Option. Cash value insurance policies can be purchased on a *participating* (par) or *nonparticipating* (nonpar) basis. In a nonpar policy the company fixes the premium at a rate sufficient to cover the cost of death protection and promised cash value savings. Consequently, there is no provision in these policies to return in the form of dividends the *overcollection* of premiums. By contrast, in the case of a par policy, the insurance company initially charges a higher premium rate, but hopes to return the overpayment of premiums in the form of dividends. The policyholder of a par policy may elect to use these payments in one of five ways: (1) receive dividends in cash; (2) invest dividends with the insurance company at a specified interest rate; (3) purchase additional paid-up insurance; (4) reduce future premiums; or (5) buy additional one-year term insurance (known as fifth dividend option).

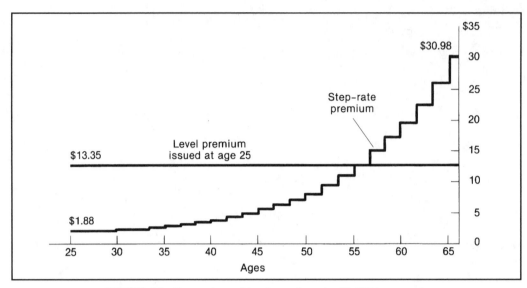

FIGURE 4-4 Comparison of level premiums for $1,000 insurance

Emergency Fund. Conventional wisdom suggests that an emergency fund should cover three to six months' living expenses for a family, and it should be used for emergencies only. Consequently, these funds should be placed in liquid accounts so the family could access them quickly without the loss of principal. The cash value accumulated inside an insurance policy may be tapped for a financial emergency when there is a shortfall in the traditional emergency fund. For instance, after 20 years the cash value of a $50,000 whole life policy issued at age 45 would be about $25,000. From the insurance company the policyholder may take a loan against this cash value at a low rate of interest. However, the policyholder should be mindful of the fact that the face amount of the policy would be reduced by the amount of the outstanding loan.

Lifetime (permanent) protection. A lifetime policy provides permanent insurance protection; that is, it is kept in force as long as the policyholder makes the premium payments. Subsequently, upon the death of the insured, the face value of the policy is paid to the beneficiary. In buying a permanent policy, the insured can make premium payments (1) for a lifetime, (2) for a predetermined number of years, (3) up to a certain age, or (4) in the beginning as a lump sum. The choice of the premium payment plan should be based upon the current financial condition and the tax situation of the insured. There are two major types of permanent life insurance policies, as described next.

Whole Life. Whole life insurance was originally devised as an alternative to the increasing level of premium payments associated with term insurance. The level premium in a whole life policy is the result of the spreading out of the increasing annual insurance costs over the life of the insured. A whole life policy, which is also known as straight life or ordinary life policy, has the lowest premium rate of any lifetime policy because it involves the payment of premiums over the longest period of time. It is one of the most widely purchased types of permanent policy because, to most families, it offers a fine balance between protection and cash accumulation.

LIFE INSURANCE CONTRACT

Title	*Explanation*
Incontestability Clause	The company cannot dispute the validity of a life insurance contract if the policy has been in effect for a period of time, generally for two years, even if there were material misstatements in the application.
Grace Period	Automatic extension for premium payment, usually to 31 days after due date.
Extended Insurance Coverage	Upon expiration of a permanent policy due to nonpayment of premium, if specified in the policy, the policy is continued as term insurance until cash value is exhausted. This is also called a non-forfeiture option.
Cash Values	The policy contains a table showing the cash value available to the policyholder.
Loan Values	Cash value policies permit borrowing on the policy up to a specified percentage of cash value, usually at guaranteed interest rates.
Reduced Paid-Up Insurance	Insurance which can be purchased with policy cash value. This is another nonforfeiture option that ensures the cash value is not lost upon nonpayment of premiums.
Dividend Option	Participating policies return excess premium as dividend in various forms: cash, reduced premium, paid-up additions, accumulations at a specified interest, and additional one-year term.
Beneficiary Provision	The insured can name first, second, third, or more beneficiaries and arrange distribution of death benefit through settlement options. Beneficiary can be an individual, a business entity, or a trust.
Ownership Clause	This clause names the person who owns the policy. The policy proceeds are generally included in the owner's estate. Change of policy ownership is permitted by all insurance companies (subject to acceptance by individual companies).
Policy Change	This clause describes the options the owner has in converting the existing policy into other types of policies.
Offer and Acceptance	If a person makes the first premium payment along with the application, the company generally agrees to insure the applicant if the applicant meets the insurability requirements. If a policy other than that applied for is issued, then the new policy becomes a counter-offer and the applicant accepts it by paying the first premium.
Consideration	The consideration given by the insurance company comprises its promises as defined in the contract. The consideration given by the insured comprises his or her statements made in the application and payment of the first premium.

Settlement Option Upon Death	Besides lump-sum, cash payment settlement options include the following: (1) Interest only: The policy proceeds are left on deposit with the insurance company for which the company makes interest payments. (2) Payments for stated period: The face amount of the policy together with earned interest is fully distributed over a fixed number of years. (3) Payment of stated amount: Fixed amount is distributed until the face amount and the interest are fully liquidated. (4) Life Income: The insurer guarantees a fixed amount for life of the insured or for joint life of both spouses.
Nonforfeiture Clause	Cash value policies offer three nonforfeiture options: (1) Withdraw the cash value (called cash surrender value) of the policy. (2) Trade the policy's cash surrender value for a fully paid-up policy of the same duration as the old policy, but with a reduced face amount. (3) Trade the policy's cash surrender value for a term policy with the same face amount, but with a shorter duration than the previous policy.
Spendthrift Clause	Some states have laws that automatically exempt proceeds of insurance from the claims of the beneficiary's creditors. Many states also allow the insured to add a "spendthrift clause" to the policy to protect the proceeds. These clauses, which state that proceeds are not assignable and are exempt from claims of creditors, are applicable only in cases of installment settlement options.
Simultaneous Death Clause	If the insured and the beneficiary die simultaneously, it will be presumed that the beneficiary died first. The proceeds will then be paid to the secondary beneficiary or to the estate of the insured, if no secondary beneficiary has been named.

In a whole life insurance policy, the insured does not control the investment vehicle. Instead, the premiums are invested in long-term bonds and mortgages and held in the company's general account. Because of regulatory pressures to play it safe, insurance companies generally limit their portfolio holdings to bonds of shorter maturity and high quality mortgages. As a result, these portfolios produce relatively modest investment returns. There is another important aspect of a whole life policy that deserves special mention. While this type of policy calls for premium payments for as long as the insured lives, after a stipulated period of time the policyholder can discontinue making premium payments and choose from the following nonforfeiture options: (1) leave the cash value with the insurance company for a reduced protection; (2) cancel the policy and take a cash settlement; (3) buy an extended term insurance; or (4) discontinue the policy and receive an income from the accrued cash value for life, or for a selected time period.

Limited-Payment Life. This type of policy differs from a whole life policy in three respects. First, although it provides lifetime protection, premium payments cease after a period of ten, 20, or 30 years, or at a certain age (usually 60 or 65), depending upon the insurance contract selected. Second, since the premium-paying period is limited, the premium rate is higher than for a whole life policy. Third, the policy builds up cash values faster than in a whole life policy because of the higher premium rate and the shorter payment period.

The limited-payment life policy is generally preferred by persons who anticipate enjoying high earnings over the early periods of their lives and therefore wish to build a nest egg faster should their earnings drop in later life, as in retirement.

Single-Premium Whole Life. Single-Premium Whole Life (SPWL) is a whole life insurance policy for which the life time premium is paid upfront as a lump sum. However, the difference between a traditional whole life and a SPWL is more than that implied by the method of premium payment. The compelling reason for buying a SPWL originates from the desire to use a life insurance policy as a tax-deferred investment. Consequently, SPWL increased in popularity after the passage of the Tax Reform Act of 1986 which severely limitedthe tax benefits associated with many other types of tax-privileged investments. However, the Technical And Miscellaneous Revenue Act (TAMRA) of 1988 made drastic reductions in the favorable tax treatment of SPWL policies. As a result, its popularity rapidly diminished following the passage of TAMRA.

A creative use of SPWL as well as Single Premium Variable Life (SPVL) is placing of this policy in a by-pass, or "B" trust. Typically, people place mutual funds in a "B" trust because, upon death, mutual funds receive a step-up in cost basis. The same objective can be achieved by placing an insurance policy in the trust, because the tax-free face value received upon death compares favorably with the step-up in basis advantage associated with stock and bond investments. It should also be noted that because a SPWL policy is created with a lump sum payment, frequently it becomes classified as a MEC policy. That should not concern people placing a SPWL in a by-pass trust. This is because generally they have no intentions of withdrawing money, or taking a loan, from this policy and therefore taxability of loans and withdrawals is rarely a problem.

TAMRA of 1988

The TAMRA of 1988 made several important changes in the method of taxation of life insurance contracts. The legislation did not end the treatment of Single Premium Whole Life (SPWL) insurance as a life insurance contract for federal income tax purposes, but it did change the treatment of distributions from a new class of contracts called Modified Endowment Contracts (MECs). Distributions include partial withdrawals, all policy loans, including those to pay premiums, loans or loan interest, and partial surrenders. If a contract is considered an MEC, distributions, including loans, received from it are treated first as taxable income and then as a nontaxable return of principal. In addition, if a distribution is taken prior to age 59-1/2, an additional ten percent penalty tax is imposed by the IRS. The income and estate taxation of death benefits, whether the plan is a traditional life or an MEC, remained unchanged under TAMRA of 1988.

All policies issued after June 20, 1988 are affected by TAMRA. In order to *avoid* being considered MEC, policies issued after this date must meet certain criteria, as described next.

Seven-pay test. If the cumulative premium paid into a contract during the first seven years exceeds a specified rate per thousand as determined by the Internal Revenue Service, then the policy will be considered an MEC. This test is applied each year to all premium payments. Each insurance contract may have different limits because the calculation is based on the individual contract's guaranteed interest rate and the applicable Commissioner's Standard Ordinary (CSO) Mortality Table. For instance, contracts that are unisex will have different maximum allowable premiums than those that distinguish between male and female or smoker and nonsmoker.

Material changes test. The second test to determine if a policy would be classified as MEC relates to the material changes instituted in the contract. Such changes include any increase in the future benefits provided under a life insurance contract. A material change also includes the exchange of one life insurance contract for another and the conversion of a term policy to a whole life policy.

The Penalty Tax

The 1988 legislation also provides that any payment received from a life insurance company and declared as taxable income is subject to a ten percent penalty tax. There are three exceptions to this penalty tax: (1) Distributions made on or after the taxpayer attains age 59-1/2. (2) Distributions attributable to the taxpayer becoming disabled. (3) Substantially equal distributions made for the life of the taxpayer or joint lives of the taxpayer and the beneficiary.

Additional Advantages

The SPWL policy provides three additional advantages in addition to its being a vehicle for tax-advantaged investment.

1. Unlike a corporate bond or a savings account where interest must be declared as ordinary income whether or not it is actually received, cash value left in SPWL policy continues to accumulate tax deferred.
2. Under the present tax law, tax-free municipal bond interest is added to other taxable income for determining the taxability of Social Security income. In contrast, interest earned on SPWL policy is not added to other taxable incomes for this purpose.
3. When a policyholder is ready to receive distribution from SPWL policy, the insurance company generally offers a variety of distribution choices to suit the special income needs of the policyholder.

UNIVERSAL LIFE

Universal life (UL) is a flexible insurance policy which permits a policyholder of an existing policy to increase the death benefit coverage with satisfactory evidence of insurability, or decrease coverage. A UL policy also allows the policyholder to increase or decrease the amount or frequency of premium payments as long as the accumulated cash value is sufficient to cover the cost of continuing the policy.

In the case of a UL policy, a percentage of the premium payment is used to cover the insurance company's operating expenses and mortality charges, based upon the mortality risks assumed by the company. The balance of the premium payment is credited to the policy's cash value. For this reason, a UL policy is considered to be transparent, since operating expenses, mortality charges, and cash value build-ups are unbundled and clearly identified. This makes it easier for insurance professionals to determine the true performance of a UL policy. Figure 4-5 demonstrates how a UL policy works.

A UL policy differs significantly from a whole life policy. In the case of the former policy: (1) the premium payments are flexible; (2) the death benefit is adjustable; and (3) the investment and mortality risks are shifted from the insurance company to the policyholder. This permits UL policyholders to tailor the policies to their changing financial situations, a privilege the whole life policyholders never enjoy.

In the case of a nonpar UL policy, essentially the insured buys a renewable term policy, the cost of which rises with the age of the insured. One part of the premium covers the cost of insurance. The other part flows into a cash accumulation fund. However, unlike a whole life policy, interest payments in excess of the guaranteed four percent level are deposited into the cash accumulation fund. In effect, the insured invests the funds with the insurance company which, in turn, invests them in fixed rate short-term debt instruments paying competitive interest rates. Each policy has an account value and a cash surrender value. The difference between the two values is a deferred sales charge, which could last anywhere from ten to 20 years.

In a UL policy the death benefit can be changed by the policyholder. Initially, the insured can select a face value. Subsequently, on an annual basis, with medical evidence required, this face value could be raised. Of course, the value could also be lowered, in which case no medical evidence would be required. Typically, insurance companies require that the insured choose between two options: (1) Option A or Option 1, which offers constant face value with an increasing cash value. In this case, upon death the beneficiary receives *only* the face value. (2) Option B or Option 2, which offers face value and cash value. In this option, upon death the beneficiary receives both the face value *and* the accumulated cash value. An added feature of this option is that a variable (higher or lower) premium or a fixed premium is paid at regular intervals, and if desired, occasionally the insured can even skip premium payments.

Option A or 1, which pays only the face value to the beneficiary, is more appropriate for older individuals because premiums are based only on the face value and not on the combination of the face value and the cash value. In contrast, Option B or 2 is particularly suited for younger people because their mortality charges are relatively low and hence both the face value and the cash value can be provided for a reasonable amount of premium payments made over a longer time.

As in the case of SPWL, a UL policy permits loans against accumulated cash value, although there is an interest cost associated with such borrowing. In addition, UL policies also permit the withdrawal of up to 90 percent of the cash value, although such an action could use up most of the cash value required to continue the policy. Another potential problem could arise if a UL policy is classified as a Modified Endowment Contract (MEC); in that case all loans and withdrawals representing gains in the contract are treated as taxable distributions from the contract. Of course, before taking out a loan, care should be exercised to ensure that the remaining cash value is sufficient to cover the monthly mortality costs and policy expenses.

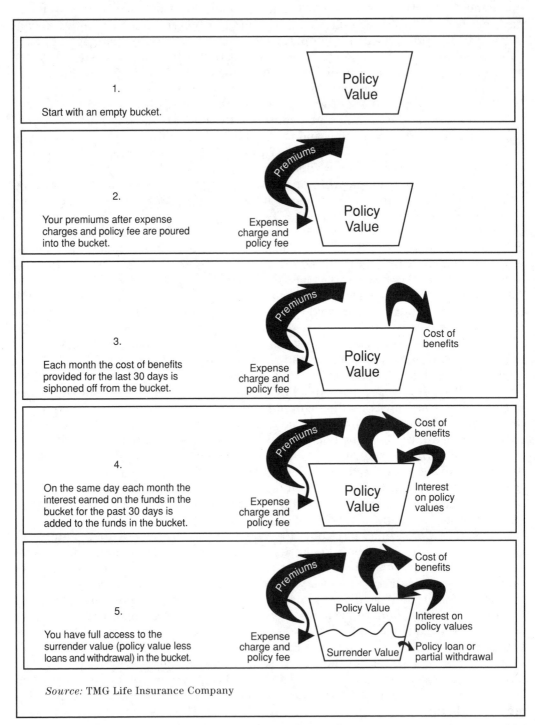

FIGURE 4-5   How universal life insurance works

Finally, because of its built-in flexibility, a variety of UL policies are used to meet business insurance needs. These include: split-dollar plans, non-qualified deferred compensation plans, key person insurance, insured qualified retirement plans, and buy-sell agreements.

UL policies issued before June 20, 1988 are not subject to the TAMRA rules, and therefore, they permit tax-free loans and withdrawals. For policies issued after that date, the usual MEC restrictions discussed earlier apply.

BLENDED INSURANCE POLICY

Term life provides only basic life insurance coverage and does not have any savings component associated with it. Naturally, chances of death increase significantly with age. That is why the premiums on a term policy are lower at younger ages, but they rise significantly as people get older. For instance, a man in his early 50's might pay less than $1,000 a year for a $250,000 term policy. However, for the same coverage the premium could rise to over $20,000 yearly for an 85-year old.

It is therefore understandable that sooner or later people who buy term policies at young ages wish to change them into level premium policies. This can be achieved by converting a term policy into a whole life policy. For instance, for a 50-year old, in contrast to a term policy, a level whole-life policy for $250,000 might cost $7,700 a year, but this premium will not increase with age, and will build up cash value.

People who do not like either of these two alternatives presented above still have a third choice. But it is somewhat complicated, because it uniquely blends term and whole life policies to suit individual needs. Here is how it works.

Suppose a 53-year old male wishes to buy $250,000 coverage. He blends a $100,000 whole life policy with a $150,000 term life policy. On the whole-life part of a blend, he pays a level premium for life. That guarantee is possible because the premium is much higher than is needed to cover him in the early years; the excess goes into a side fund that is used to cover the substantially higher mortality costs later in life.

This sounds like a terrific idea, but there is a catch. *Annual premiums are not guaranteed for life.* The more term life there is in the mix, the lower the annual premium in the earlier stages—and the greater the risk of premium escalation at a later stage. So the term-whole life blend becomes impractical unless it is combined with the third ingredient of dividends. Whole life policies typically pay annual dividends which can be used to purchase additional whole life insurance. In the blended policy, as the proportion of whole life increases, the proportion of term life gradually declines. So in a likely scenario, by using future dividends, in about 20 years a 50-year old male is able to transform a blended policy into a 100 percent whole life policy, thereby insuring a level premium for the rest of his life.

The blended approach described above works reasonably well only if all the underlying assumptions prove to be correct. But that may not necessarily be the case. For instance, over time interest rates might fall, causing the company to lower its future dividends. Similarly, increased expenses could force the insurer to raise its term rates or drop the dividends. In situations like these, a blended insurance policy may prove to be undesirable or unworkable.

VARIABLE LIFE

Variable life policy is a type of a whole life insurance policy in which death benefits and accumulated cash values vary with the value of equity and fixed income securities set up in "separate accounts" of the insurance companies. A variable life policy shifts the investment risk to the insured and lets the insured direct some or all of the policy's cash value into the securities markets, primarily through mutual fund-like investments. This permits the insured to enjoy the benefits of long-term growth in the equity market. When the cash value is invested in the market, the face amount of the policy—known as death benefit—and the cash value will rise and fall, depending upon the performance of the investment portfolio. However, in almost all instances, the insurance company guarantees that death benefit will never be less than the face amount of the policy as long as scheduled premiums are paid. So, in a real sense, what fluctuates in a variable life is the cash value. Because the insured is required to pay a level premium on a regular basis, the cash value continues to increase. But the rate of the increase may be adversely affected by the poor performance of the investment portfolio. As Indiana University insurance professor Joseph Belth has observed: "If you invest in a variable life policy, your beneficiary's best hope is that you will die on an uptick."

An interesting variant of variable life is single-premium variable life. This policy is suitable for someone who prefers a tax-deferred investment and is willing to use life insurance as a vehicle for earning a highly competitive tax-deferred rate of return.

Variable life policies issued before June 20, 1988 are not subject to the TAMRA rules and therefore permit tax-free loans which need not be repaid. However, outstanding loans are deducted from the face value upon death. For policies issued after that date, the usual restrictions discussed in the previous section apply.

VARIABLE UNIVERSAL LIFE

Variable universal life, also known as flexible-premium variable life and Universal Life II, permits both the premium payment and the death benefit to be variable. The initial death benefit can be made flexible, depending upon the family's needs and the performance of the portfolio in which the cash value is invested. Also, as in the case of traditional universal life policies, the cash value can be paid to a beneficiary federal income tax-free, in addition to, or as a part of, the death benefit. Another important option of this policy is that an insured may purchase a death benefit guaranty rider. Under this option, if a specified premium is paid, then for a predetermined period the company will guarantee that even when there are no funds available to cover the mortality charges, the death benefit would be paid.

Essentially, a variable universal life policy, which is similar to a tax-deferred mutual fund charging management and administration fees, permits a variety of investment choices. These include stocks, bonds, mutual funds, fixed income products and money market instruments. After the initial investment process is completed, switching between these products is permitted. The advantages of variable universal life are flexible family protection as well as premium and investment flexibility. However, the insured should be a knowledgeable investor in order to control the investment risk associated with such a policy.

INTEREST-SENSITIVE WHOLE LIFE

Interest-Sensitive Whole Life (ISWL), also known as Current Assumption Whole Life, is a type of policy that is offered by several life insurance companies. Typically, an ISWL policy combines the attractive features of both whole life and universal life insurance policies. In an ISWL policy, after an initial guarantee period, each year—referred to as redetermination period—the insurance company is permitted to use modified assumptions relating to mortality costs and interest rates. Any changes resulting from using these modified assumptions are reflected only in the accumulation of the cash value, while the original premium payments and death benefit remain unchanged. The interest rate used to calculate the cash value build-up is tied to a pre-specified rate, although policyholders are assured of a minimum interest rate guarantee. However, like other insurance policies, for an extended period, ISWL policies do impose back-end surrender charges if they are prematurely cancelled.

ADJUSTABLE LIFE INSURANCE

When people think of low-cost protection and strong guarantees, they probably think of term insurance. But when they want premium flexibility and the ability to accumulate cash value, they prefer universal life policies. Adjustable Life Insurance (ALI) policies offer the best of both policies.

The ALI policy is marketed by a group of the largest insurance companies under such titles as Max Term Achiever, Life Term Achiever, and Flexible Policy, each with a slightly different set of features. The following discussion underscores the difference between three types of ALI policies.

The first type of ALI policy provides the maximum death benefit protection per dollar of any UL policy, when measured on a current protection basis. Competitive with many term plans, it has a low first year premium, which must be paid in the first year. Thereafter, premiums become variable as long as there is enough policy value to meet the mortality cost associated with the insurance and any riders. In addition to the minimum premium, there exists a separate, higher target premium that is called the *safety net premium*. If during the safety net protection period total premiums paid, less any loans or withdrawals, are at least equal to the accumulated monthly safety net premiums, the policy will remain in force even if the policy value becomes insufficient to cover the monthly deductions necessary to pay for insurance costs.

The second type of ALI policy provides guaranteed coverage for a low annual premium. If a 35-year-old man buys this policy and continues to pay the annual insurance premium, the death benefit will be guaranteed to remain in force until age 97, even if the policy value is insufficient to cover monthly deductions.

The third type of ALI policy is similar to a traditional whole life policy in that *initially* both the level of premium and death benefit remain fixed. However, at certain pre-specified intervals known as adjustment periods, the policyholder is permitted to change premium payments, face amounts, protection period, and premium payment periods. Except for the changes during the adjustment periods, this type of ALI policy acts like a traditional whole life policy.

An important feature of an ALI policy is that the policyholders enjoy both the flexibility of coverage and the opportunity to accumulate tax-deferred cash value through forced savings. Also, the cash values are not exposed to significant market adjustments. However, on the negative side, in this type of contract the cash values of individual policies are not segregated, which makes it harder to determine how well the cash values have grown on an annual basis. One possible solution to this problem is to use a *direct recognition method* that can determine how favorable investment, mortality, and expense experiences affected the dividend picture over time. Another negative feature of ALI is that changes allowed during an adjustment period could possibly make it a Modified Endowment Contract (MEC) with adverse tax consequences.

In passing it should be mentioned that, because of the flexibility of universal life, adjustable life policies have significantly declined in popularity. However, they are still available and are issued when someone specifically requests it.

SURVIVORSHIP LIFE (SECOND-TO-DIE) POLICY

A Survivorship Life (SL) policy is a variation of Whole Life, Universal Life, and Variable Universal Life Policy in that the SL policy covers more than one life and pays the death benefit only upon the death of the last survivor. The premiums, cash values, and dividends are based on the joint-equal concept. That is, premium payments are required to be made until the death of both parties. Life insurance proceeds are received by the beneficiaries upon the second death.

The SL policy has gained in popularity as a result of the existence of unlimited marital deduction, which permits married couples with large estates to defer their estate tax liabilities until the second death. That is, a SL policy makes income-tax free funds available to the beneficiaries which they can use to pay estate taxes due upon the second death. Naturally, SL policies are most appropriate for married couples with sizeable taxable estates.

In the case of a SL policy, since an insurer has to set aside reserves for only one death-benefit payment, rather than for two separate payments, the premium costs are substantially lower than what two individuals would pay to purchase the same amount of Whole Life or Universal Life coverage. The amount of savings varies based on a variety of factors, including the ages of the insured and their risk status, and in certain instances premiums can vary by as much as 100 percent to 125 percent. For instance, one can easily obtain comparative quotes for a Second-do-Die policy and a universal life policy. These quotes will clearly demonstrate that Second-to-Die policies cost a lot less than universal life policies for individuals for the same amount of coverage. This is because the projected joint life expectancy is much longer than a single life expectancy; consequently, the insurance company's risk for the former type of policy is much lower than the latter policy. Another advantage is that a SL policy could cover individuals who are substandard risks, including those who may be uninsurable on their own.

A SL policy can be either a First-to-Die or a Second-to-Die policy. Following is a description of each type of policy.

First-to-Die Policies

Most of us wish to believe that we are immortal. That is why we have the tendency to put off dealing with death and its impact on our own families and business partners. This is especially true with persons who have entrepreneurial talents. Most business people, young and old, are extremely conscious, and they tend to focus on business plans, cash flow forecasting, bottom line profits, and other business related issues. But the same people do not pay adequate attention to the issues surrounding the death of business partners. First-to-Die policies and the appropriate riders are an excellent means of dealing with this eventuality.

Second-to-Die Policies

An Overview. Upon the death of a married person, the entire estate passes from one spouse to the other spouse totally free of federal estate taxes. However, upon the death of the surviving spouse, estates over $1.5 million (2005) become taxable. And since federal estate tax brackets start at 37 percent and rapidly reach the 48 percent level (2005), these tax payments could become onerous. Furthermore, estate taxes are generally due within nine months of the death of the estate owner, and hence there is only a limited time available for the beneficiaries to raise the required funds to meet their obligation. Second-to-Die insurance eliminates the liquidity problem altogether. This is because upon the death of both spouses such a policy makes federal income tax-free cash available to the beneficiaries with which they can make estate tax payments.

Ownership Options. The following are the three most popular ownership options available to the purchasers of Second-to-Die policies.

Irrevocable Trust. When an irrevocable trust is the policy's owner, the insured makes periodic payments to the trust which are then used to pay the premiums. The trust is also the policy's beneficiary, and the trust instrument specifies how the policy's benefits are to be designated. If the trust is created after the policy is issued, and the policy is subsequently transferred to this trust, then the insurance proceeds are added back to the estate if death occurs within three years after the transfer.

Charity. The client can designate a charity as the policy's owner and beneficiary. Each year a tax-deductible gift to the charity pays the policy's premium. Upon the second insured's death, the charity receives the policy's benefit. Another option is to set up a charitable trust and to fund the policy's premiums with an appreciated asset, which can then be sold inside the trust without the insured or their estate becoming liable for any tax liability generated by the sale of the appreciated assets. In that case an irrevocable trust can be set up outside the charitable trust to replace the assets going to the charity.

Children. The insured can make the children the policy's beneficiaries and owners. When the second parent dies, the adult children receive the face value free of income taxes. Parents can pay premiums utilizing gift tax rules. Currently, both parents can make a $22,000 annual gift to each beneficiary without triggering a gift tax.

Accelerated Death Benefits. Some insurance companies offer policyholders up to 50 percent of their death benefit if they are suffering from a terminal illness. While this may be an appealing option, there may also be some risks associated with it. For one thing, the benefit received by the policyholder could be treated by the IRS as taxable income. For another, if this option is exercised, a policyholder may be disqualified from a variety of government-subsidized programs available to terminally ill patients.

Living Death Benefits. All of us expect to lead long and healthy lives. But if a terminal illness or other life-limiting condition strikes, the emotional and financial hardship can devastate us. In order to ease this burden, many insurance companies allow policyholders to use a portion of their death benefit if the insured person is medically diagnosed with a condition limiting life expectancy to six months or less.

Generally, the insured can receive any amount between $5,000 and 75 percent of the proceeds that would be payable at death, up to a maximum (usually $500,000) specified amount. Insurance companies do not impose restrictions on how these funds can be used by the insured.

Living benefits paid to the insured act as a lien against the policy. It reduces the death benefit payable to the beneficiaries. It also reduces the amount of money available for loans as well as the cash value of the policy. The following is an illustration of how the concept of living benefits works.

Joe is 55 years old and has been diagnosed with cancer. He is not expected to live longer than six months. He decides to submit a claim for Living Benefits offered by the $200,000 Equitable whole life policy he purchased at age 45. The current cash value in his policy, which also equals its loan value, is $50,000. Joe contacts his Equitable agent and finds that the maximum Living Benefits available to him is $150,000 (75 percent of $200,000). He requests half of this amount on his claim and receives a lump sum payment of $75,000. Joe dies six months after filing his claim. His wife, as the beneficiary of his policy, receives $122,000. This amount is calculated as follows:

Before Payment of "Living Benefits"	
Death Benefit	$200,000
Cash Value and Loan Value	$ 50,000
"Living Benefits" Payment	
Maximum available	
[75 percent x $200,000]	$150,000
Amount requested ["Lien"]	$ 75,000
After Payment of "Living Benefits"	
Death Benefit	
[$200,000 - $75,000]	$125,000
Six Months Later	
Lien	$ 75,000
Interest on Lien*	$ 3,000
Lien plus interest	$ 78,000
Death Benefit	
[$200,000 - $78,000]	$122,000
Interest at eight percent for six months.	

Source: The Equitable Life Assurance Society.

SURVIVORSHIP VARIABLE LIFE

Survivorship Variable Life combines Variable Universal Life with Survivorship, or Second-to-Die, policies. This policy covers two people, pays out after death of the second insured, and enjoys all the advantages of a Second-to-Die policy. In addition, the variable universal life part of the policy allows policyholders to manage the cash value as their personal investment portfolio, choosing among professionally managed subaccounts similar to stock and bond mutual funds and money market instruments. Traditional survivorship life policies accumulate cash value only within the insurer's general account, normally consisting of a conservative bond-based mix guaranteed to grow at a rate of three or four percent. With a variable insurance feature added to the survivorship policy, policyholders can invest the cash value in the stock market in the hopes of earning a higher return over the long term.

It is important to add a caveat here. In a Survivorship Variable Life Policy the cash value is not guaranteed and it fluctuates with the performance of the portfolio. An increase in the cash value provides the funds to pay for the lifetime protection. However, a disappointing portfolio performance could exhaust the cash value, thereby threatening the viability of the policy.

In order to avoid such a contingency, insurance companies routinely add various guarantees as riders to these policies. A typical rider may provide that if a certain amount of premium is paid over a specified time period, then the insurance company will guarantee the payment of the face value for 30 years or until age 100 even if the cash value was not available to continue the policy.

LIFE INSURANCE FOR INDIVIDUAL FAMILY MEMBERS

Some life insurance agents are profit maximizers. Hence, it is reasonable to expect that at times some unprofessional, uninformed and short-sighted agents might sell policies that are not in their customers' best interests. Two important conclusions can be drawn from this observation. First, sometimes people are sold a more expensive policy when they really need a cheaper one. Second, overzealous agents might sell policies to family members who do not need insurance protection. It is therefore appropriate to ask: Who in the family *really* needs life insurance?

Spousal Insurance

If the wife is the family's sole breadwinner, the insurance rules applying to a husband breadwinner apply to her as well. Additionally, it is often argued that the economic value of a homemaker, particularly when she is also the caretaker of small children, is extremely high. To replace this person with maids, day care services, baby sitters, or other persons to provide even the minimum of essential services would cost a staggering sum. In this case, the strategy for spousal insurance should be to buy an annual renewable term or a level term policy in order to financially help the family in the event of a sudden death of the caretaker of minor children.

Insurance for Children

Popularly known as juvenile policies, insurance for children represents a huge business for the insurance industry. Each year, one of four cash value insurance policies sold covers the lives of children under age 18. But the decision to insure a child's life is at best a controversial one. If life insurance is designed for protecting one's dependents, why would a parent want insurance coverage on a child?

As a rebuttal, for a number of reasons, insurance companies strongly recommend the purchase of juvenile policies. First, children's policies cost less than comparable coverage on adults. Second, getting coverage for children guarantees that they will always have some life insurance, even if they later become uninsurable. Third, all cash value policies have an investment component. With a typical variable life policy, for example, a portion of the paid premium is invested in a separate tax-deferred account consisting of stocks, bonds, and money markets instruments. A child can borrow part of the policy's cash value, often at a low interest rate, and use it to pay for college tuition bills or other big ticket items.

There exist equally strong arguments against purchasing a juvenile policy. First, because the liability of insurance companies is extremely limited, juvenile policies can be considered to be very expensive. Second, besides life insurance, other less expensive products are available to achieve the same end-results. For instance, a variable life policy purchased for a one-year old child could amass a cash value of $13,200 by the time the infant reaches age 18. In this case, annual premiums are assumed to be $500 and the policy's investment accounts are predicted to earn an average of ten percent after expenses. But a parent investing $500 a year in a typical S&P 500 index fund earning ten percent a year would accumulate $20,000 over the same period after paying a 20 percent capital gain taxes on the earnings. Third, it can be safely assumed that parents who can set aside the funds necessary to pay the policy premiums should not need the financial protection offered by a juvenile insurance policy.

A careful consideration of the above arguments reveals that each side takes an extreme position. People should not reject the idea of buying a juvenile policy merely because they feel that it adds no value. Likewise, they should not buy this type of policy simply because it appears inexpensive. In the final analysis, in this case, as elsewhere, the philosophy of buying insurance remains the same: One should purchase children's insurance if the benefits of such a policy exceed its cost, and only after the insurance needs for breadwinner(s) and other adults are satisfied. While the cost of a juvenile policy can be easily handled, only a parent can decide if the net benefits of such a policy exceed its associated cost.

GROUP LIFE INSURANCE

Group life insurance provides a means for insuring a group of people under one policy. Generally, such a group is made up of employees or members of an organization. Without medical examination, or with simplified medical requirements, these employees are insured under a master contract issued to the organization. Each insured employee receives a certificate stating the amount of insurance coverage, the name of the beneficiary selected, and a summary of the rights and benefits. Typically, the amount of insurance is anywhere between one to two times the employee's annual salary or earnings.

Group life insurance is usually issued as a term life insurance policy. That is, the premium collected for the entire group buys protection only on a one-year basis, and permanent protection is not offered. In some cases, the employer and the

LIFE INSURANCE RIDERS	
Title	*Explanation*
Multiple Indemnity	This clause provides a doubling or tripling of the face amount if death results from certain specified causes, such as an accident.
Waiver of Premium Benefit	If the policyholder becomes totally or permanently disabled, the insurance will remain in force without further premium payments. There is usually a six month waiting or elimination period before this benefit becomes applicable. In a permanent policy, the cash value grows just as if the premiums are still being paid, and the insured is allowed to borrow against the cash value in the policy. Furthermore, in the case of a universal life policy, only the mortality costs are covered.
Guaranteed Insurability Rider	This rider guarantees that, up to the specified age, additional life insurance can be bought on certain "option dates" without proving insurability.
Accidental Death and Dismemberment	This rider provides benefits for loss of limb, eye, or death by accident.
Disability Income Rider	This rider provides a monthly income to the insured upon becoming disabled.

employees may wish to share the cost of group insurance. In other cases, the employer may choose to bear the entire cost of the insurance. In the former case, the employees' portion may be deducted (with their consent) from their salaries or wages, with the balance of the premium being paid by the employer. In the latter case, the employer may pay the entire premium cost, although the cost of coverage for amounts over $50,000 is taxable to the employee on the basis of what is known as Table I costs. However, the entire premium (even over $50,000) is deductible to the corporation. Coverage of this type of policy expires or drops substantially when the employee has reached an advanced age.

If an employee leaves the employer, the group insurance coverage is lost; but the employee may buy an individual permanent policy for the same coverage, even though he or she may be uninsurable at that time. This conversion privilege is required to be exercised within one month of the termination of employment.

A large portion of a person's life insurance coverage is likely to be group life protection. That is why the financial planner must watch out for clients who are likely to lose their group insurance after quitting their job. If possible, these people should be encouraged to start building individual insurance protection to guard against losing their group life insurance protection.

CAFETERIA PLANS

A cafeteria plan is a generic name for a plan that saves payroll taxes for a company and its employees. It has three important features, as described next.

Insurance Premium - IRS Code Section 106

Premium payments by an employee for covering individual and/or dependent family medical costs can be made with pretax salary dollars. Other medical insurance premiums—such as dental insurance—can also be paid with pretax dollars.

Unreimbursed Medical Expenses - IRS Code Section 105

Unreimbursed medical expenses paid under a Cafeteria Plan with pretax dollars may include:

- Group, medical and dental insurance plan deductibles.
- Out-of-pocket expenses not covered by the major medical insurance plan. These include, but are not limited to, birth control pills, braces, chiropractors, crutches, dental fees, prescription drugs, eye glasses (including examination fees), insulin, routine physicals, wheelchairs and x-rays. Form M-0888-2-92 documents additional expenses that qualify under IRS code Section 213.

Child or Dependent Care Assistance - IRS Code Section 129

A Cafeteria Plan may also reimburse employees for certain dependent care expenses for eligible children and other eligible dependents. The expenses must be incurred to allow the employee and the spouse to work, unless the spouse is a full-time student or incapable of self-care.

Dependent care expenses are covered if the dependent is under age 13 or is physically or mentally incapable of self-care. An incapacitated dependent who is over 13 must regularly spend at least eight hours a day in the employee's household to qualify.

Eligible child care can be provided inside or outside the employee's home. However, the service cannot be provided by a person claimed as a dependent. If the services are provided by a day care facility with more than six children, it must comply with applicable state and local requirements and laws. Preschool costs for a child may also qualify for reimbursement. Also, housekeeping expenses are reimbursable if provided by a full-time, live-in, housekeeper caring for dependent children.

Per calendar year, the amount of child or dependent care expenses reimbursed cannot exceed the lower of $5,000 and the employee's (or spouse's) annual income. Also, dependent care expenses reimbursed cannot be applied toward the federal income tax credit for dependent care.

Employees have three potential tax advantages for dependent care expenses: Dependent Care Flexibile Spending Arrangement (FSA), Federal Tax credit, and the supplemental young child tax credit. Employers should encourage their employees to review their options carefully for determining the best option.

Advantages of Cafeteria Plans

For the Employee. Each employee is given the opportunity to assemble a package of benefits that is most meaningful for the employee's personal situation. The use of pretax dollars to pay for these benefits results in tax savings, with a corresponding increase in the employee's take-home pay. Simultaneously, the benefit package increases the benefits for the entire family.

For the Employer. Since employee payroll taxes are reduced by the cost of the benefit package selected, the employer's taxable payroll is also reduced. This can result in substantial savings in the form of reduced FICA and FUTA taxes, and depending upon State regulations, further savings may result on other premiums that are part of employer's payroll. It has been estimated that under the Cafeteria Plan, total savings to an employer could approximate eight percent of the total dollar amount that is expended on a pretax basis.

TAXATION OF LIFE INSURANCE

Life insurance has always provided an important source of income protection for the loved ones in the event of an untimely death of the insured. Insurance proceeds can also be used to pay estate taxes and fund deferred compensation agreements, and if not used up, can create wealth for the family. The type of life insurance purchased depends on such factors as need, duration of need, and cost. Income tax considerations are also important and should be carefully evaluated in any life insurance transaction.

Life insurance has three distinct tax attributes: (1) The increase in a policy's cash value is not taxable. (2) Transfers between separate accounts are not taxable. (3) Proceeds paid by reason of the insured's death is generally excluded from taxable income. There are exceptions where these tax attributes are lost, especially when an active policy is changed or surrendered. These exceptions, in addition to other important tax considerations, are based primarily upon the tax basis of a policy. The *basis* is the total premiums paid, including dividends used to purchase additional insurance, less nontaxable distributions received (e.g., dividends and tax-free withdrawals).

A recent change in the taxability of split dollar policies should be noted. Equity growth in such a policy between employer and an employee may now be taxed as a loan. If it is not treated as a loan, then any additional beneficial interest in the policy's cash surrender value transferred to the employee may be taxed as a compensation. This change negatively impacts the sale of equity split dollar policies, because these policies can no longer be illustrated without possible tax considerations.

Distribution upon Death

Table 4-4 reveals that all death benefit distributions are exempt from federal income tax and, with few exceptions, from state inheritance taxes. In addition, whether a policy's death benefit is subject to federal estate taxes depends on the ownership of the policy. Life insurance proceeds are included in the gross estate of the insured if the insured is also the policy owner. If another person, or an irrevocable life insurance trust, owns the policy, the insurance proceeds are not included in the gross estate of the insured for purposes of figuring federal estate taxes. An exception to this rule applies when an insurance policy is transferred to an irrevocable life insurance trust within three years of death, in which case the insurance proceeds are included in the gross estate of the owner before the transfer. Of course, if the insurance is part of an irrevocable life insurance trust which owns the policy outright, then the three-year rule does not apply, since the life insurance was never *transferred* to the trust.

As mentioned, the death benefit is generally free of federal income taxes. However, there is an important exception that applies if the policy is sold to someone

TABLE 4-4   Taxability of Life Insurance Proceeds

Type of insurance	Policy owner	Upon death			During life		
		Federal income tax	State inheritance tax[1]	Estate tax	Loan Income tax	Annuity distribution Income tax	Total surrender Income tax
Term	Insured	None	Yes	Yes			
	Other than insured	None	None	None			
	Irrevocable life insurance trust	None	None	None			
Cash value	Insured	None	Yes	Yes	Taxed[2]	Tax on gain	On excess of cash over premium
	Other than insured	None	None	None	Taxed[2]	Tax on gain	On excess of cash over premium
	Life insurance trust	None	None	None	Taxed[2]	Tax on gain	On excess of cash over premium
Deferred annuity	Insured	Tax on gain	Yes	Yes		Only on interest	On excess of cash over premium
	Other than insured	Tax on gain	No	No		Only on interest	On excess of cash over premium
	Life insurance trust	Not applicable	No	No		Only on interest	On excess of cash over premium

[1] In some states, death benefits are not exempt from state inheritance tax.

[2] Loans are not taxed if seven-pay test is met.

other than the insured, a partner of the insured, a partnership in which the insured is a partner, a corporation in which the insured is a shareholder or officer, or a Qualified Domestic Relations Order (QDRO). If this *transfer for value* occurs, the amount by which the death benefit exceeds the tax basis of the policy is recognized as taxable income.

Distribution during Life

Policy Dividends. Dividends either distributed in cash or used to purchase additional insurance or invested in the policy are considered a nontaxable return of capital until they exceed the policy owner's tax basis. Any amount received in excess of the tax basis is taxed as ordinary income.

Policy Withdrawals/Loans. Withdrawals, until the total amount withdrawn exceeds the tax basis in the policy, are generally not taxable. Withdrawals in excess of tax basis are taxed as ordinary income. Policy loans are generally not taxable.

Interest on Policy Loans. Tax laws distinguish between Single Premium Insurance policies (where substantially all of the premiums are paid within four years from the purchase date) and non-Single Premium policies. In the case of the latter, the IRS does not allow any deduction for interest if the loan was taken against an increase in the policy's cash value.

In any event, in all cases the general limitations on interest deductions apply. For example, if the funds were used to purchase investment securities or a personal asset like an automobile, the interest would be treated as nondeductible personal interest.

Sale or Disposition, Surrender, Maturity. Insurance contracts are treated as non-capital assets. If a policy matures, or is surrendered, or disposed of, any cash or value received that exceeds the tax basis in the contract must be reported as ordinary income.

Exchange. Generally, no gain or loss is recognized in an exchange of policies if (1) it is a like-kind exchange (e.g., one life insurance contract exchanged for another); (2) the insured and owner remain the same; and (3) no cash, or debt reduction, is received as part of the transaction. In situations where cash is received, or a debt reduction is granted, the amount by which the total cash received exceeds the tax basis is recognized as taxable gain. After the exchange, the basis of the new policy becomes the basis in the old policy, adjusted for the cash receipt and debt reduction.

MECs. Until the mid-1980s, insurance companies were promoting life insurance policies like Single Premium life on the basis of the benefits of cash accumulation, loan provisions, and investment choices, rather than on traditional death benefits. As stated earlier, in order to discourage the purchase of life insurance as a tax-sheltered investment, legislation was enacted in 1988 that created a new class of life insurance contract, called *Modified Endowment Contracts* (MECs).

MECs do retain some of the attractive tax benefits available to all life insurance products. For example, both the accumulation of cash value and the benefits payable at death are exempt from federal income taxes. Policy withdrawals and loans, however, are treated as taxable distributions if they represent taxable earnings accumulated in the policy. The balance of the distribution is considered a tax-free return of the owner's investment in the policy.

LIFE INSURANCE AND ESTATE TAXES

If the deceased had no ownership in the policy, and the insurance proceeds are not received by the estate, then (with one exception) for estate tax purposes the insurance proceeds are not included in the gross estate of the deceased. However, if within three years of the decedent's death the insurance policy was gifted or transferred to a different entity like a trust, then the proceeds are included in the gross estate of the decedent. It is important to note that, because life insurance is a contract, death benefits completely bypass the probate process, as long as the beneficiary is a person or a trust. This subject will be discussed in detail in Chapter 8.

SWITCHING OF POLICIES

A well-planned life insurance program requires much thought before the policy is put into effect. Insurance policies should therefore be treated as long-term purchases and held on a permanent basis. While this statement is generally true, there are circumstances which might call for switching of policies.

The most compelling reason for the reexamination of an existing policy is the steady decline in the cost of life insurance. As compared to 1958, today the new mortality table reflects an average of a 15 percent drop in the number of deaths per 1,000 people. As a consequence, the premium rates have dropped for many types of insurance contracts. For this reason, periodically it pays to investigate the possibility of switching old policies for new ones.

The current trend of replacing whole life policies with universal life and other attractive policies is the second reason for switching life insurance policies. The old traditional whole life policies are complex, inflexible, and costly. In 1979 a Federal Trade Commission study, which was somewhat controversial, concluded that in 1977 the rates of return on these policies averaged 1.3 percent. Also, in a whole life policy the premium payments, death benefits, and the number of required payments remain fixed as long as the policy remains in force. The newer universal life policies are not only flexible with respect to both the death benefit and premium payments, but they also can generate more competitive rates of return.

Changing family conditions may be the third reason for switching policies. A policy covering a spouse's life may no longer be necessary if the children are grown. Some of the old riders which initially made sense may no longer be appropriate. Even the amount of coverage may have to be modified to suit the family's changing insurance needs.

The switching of policies may have several drawbacks as well. Most policies provide for a two-year period of contestability after which the insurer cannot refuse to pay the benefit except for the nonpayment of premium. The old policy may have superior settlement options, disability provisions, suicide provisions, and other terms which cannot be duplicated in a new policy. Also, because the new policy will be purchased at an older age and will generate new commissions or sales costs, premium payments for the new policy will most likely be higher. In addition, the old policy may still have a contingent deferred sales load associated with it which would become payable if it is switched for a new policy. Also, as already mentioned, when a whole life policy is switched into a universal life policy, investment and mortality costs are shifted from the insurer to the insured.

Finally, switching a policy might convert it into a Modified Endowment Contract (MEC). So, if the new policy is considered MEC, distributions from this policy would be treated as taxable income. Only distributions in excess of the accumulations in the policy would be treated as a nontaxable return of principal. In addition, unless a policy is directly exchanged for another policy, which is known as a 1035 exchange, if a distribution is taken prior to age 59-1/2, the IRS would impose an additional ten percent early withdrawal penalty. Consequently, extreme caution is advised before switching an existing policy because it may not be affected by the 1988 tax law creating MECs and might have other advantages just discussed.

Interestingly, initially stung by adverse publicity, several years ago the life-insurance industry started its own education campaign against policy replacements. MetLife and Prudential sent anti-churning notices to millions of policyholders, conducted internal reviews, and laid down the law to the agents. The American Society of Chartered Life Underwriters and Chartered Financial Consultants offered one of the most ambitious new tools. The Bryn Mawr (Pa.) trade group developed a six-page worksheet aimed at identifying pitfalls in replacement proposals.

With the worksheet, which is available free by calling 800-392-6900, agents begin by listing possible advantages of a new policy, such as high death benefits, lower premiums, or stronger issuer finances. A series of questions underscores some of the biggest risks of replacement. For instance, since issuers may contest claims made during the first two years of a new policy, consumers who surrender their old policies can lose the protection these policies enjoy. Also, because the growth in cash-value insurance is tax-deferred, the policyholder may owe taxes on the old policy if it is replaced. However, the worksheet covers grandfathered tax rules that apply to policies purchased in the 1970s and 1980s, and might be *long-winded and complicated* for routine use.

RATINGS OF INSURANCE COMPANIES

An Overview

Life insurance companies have always been a powerful force in our society, faithfully paying out retirement income, current income, and death benefits down through the generations. Americans have always believed that their policies were grounded in a bedrock of sound investments. That is why a few years ago the financial woes of several giant insurance companies sent shockwaves throughout the financial services industry.

Understandably, high anxiety sweeps this country in the wake of occasional runs by policyholders and state takeovers of insurance companies. The present patchwork of state regulations of the insurance industry leaves some policyholders protected and others holding the bag. The poet Edna St. Vincent Millay struck a right note for describing the status of the financial services industry. "It is not true that life is one damn thing after another," she writes, "It's one damn thing over and over."

Role of Guaranteed Funds

The insurance industry does maintain guaranteed funds, but they operate by rules far different than those applied by Federal Deposit Insurance Corporation. The key rules are as follows:

- State rules govern the insurance-finance guaranty funds. These rules vary considerably from one state to another. In fact, only a handful of state insurance funds cover guaranteed-insurance contracts, or GICs.
- In order for an insured to collect, the insurance company must be in liquidation. For instance, at one point policyholders were not authorized to collect from Mutual Benefit because it was in default but not in liquidation.
- In general, an insured is protected for only up to $100,000 in annuities and insurance cash values, $300,000 in death benefits, and $300,000 for all claims combined per company.

Rating Agencies

Amid all the worry and confusion surrounding the insurance industry, policyholders actually can safeguard their assets by relying on the opinions of the following rating agencies: A.M. BEST, Standard & Poor's, Duff & Phelps, and Moody's Investor Services.

A.M. BEST Company. In existence for the longest time, BEST rates 1,379 (out of 2,300) insurance companies on a scale ranging from A++ down to E. In addition, BEST has ten *ratings not assigned classifications*, which means that these insurance companies do not meet BEST's minimum size or the minimum financial requirements. For more information one can contact A.M. BEST Company, Ambest Road, Oldwick, NJ 08858. Tel: (908) 439-2200.

Duff & Phelps. Reporting since 1986, Duff & Phelps has claims-paying ability ratings on about 60 companies. The ratings range from AAA down to CCC. However, the company claims that in the foreseeable future it will be rating 90 percent of the major US insurance companies.

The ratings of Duff & Phelps can be obtained via the Claims Paying Ability Rating Service, or the quarterly issues of the company's Insurance Company Claims Paying Ability Rating Guide. For more information, one can contact Duff & Phelps Credit Rating Company, 55 East Monroe Street, Chicago, IL 60603. Tel: (312) 263-2610.

Moody's Investor Services. Evaluating life insurance companies since the 1970s, Moody's currently rates 72 companies. Ratings range from Aaa down to C. The company refers to these ratings as *financial strength ratings*.

Moody's offers a variety of publications, including an Insurance Credit Report Service. Further information can be obtained from Moody's Investor Services, 99 Church Street, New York, NY 10007. Their phone number is (212) 553-0300.

Standard & Poor's Corporation. S&P has been providing ratings for financial strengths and credit quality for more than 50 years. The firm currently rates 480 companies with rating from AAA down to C. In April 1992, S&P introduced *Qualified Solvency Ratings* which are based on the statistics obtained from the National Association of Insurance Commissioners (NAIC). Any company without a claims-paying ability rating from S&P is given one of the three qualifying solvency ratings: BBBq -- above average; BBq -- average; and Bq -- below average.

S&P offers several publications, including S&P's Insurance Book, Select Reports, and S&P's Insurer Rating List. For more information, one can contact Standard & Poor's Insurance Ratings, 25 Broadway, New York, NY 10004. Tel: (212) 208-1524.

Weiss. The latest entry with the insurer rating field is Weiss Ratings, Inc. While its rating system is comparable to others, it does not yet have the prestige or popularity enjoyed by other rating companies.

Every quarter Weiss evaluates the financial strength of more than 15,000 life insurance and other institutions and rates them from A+ to E and U (unrated).

Ratings by A.M. BEST, Duff & Phelps, Moody's, Standard & Poor and Weiss are provided in Table 4-5.

A.M. Best	Duff & Phelps	Moody's	Standard & Poor's@	Weiss
A++ Superior	AAA Highest	Aaa Exceptional	AAA, AAAq Superior	A+ Excellent
A+ Superior	AA+ Very high	Aa1 Excellent	AA+ Excellent	A Excellent
A Excellent	AA Very high	Aa2 Excellent	AA, Aaq Excellent	A- Excellent
A- Excellent	AA- Very high	Aa3 Excellent	AA- Excellent	B+ Good
B++ Very good	A+ High	A1 Good	A+ Good	B Good
B+ Very good	A High	A2 Good	A, Aq Good	B- Good
B Adequate	A- High	A3 Good	A- Good	C+ Fair
B- Adequate	BBB+ Adequate	Baa1 Adequate	BBB+ Adequate	C Fair
C++ Fair	BBB Adequate	Baa2 Adequate	BBB, BBBq Adequate	C- Fair
C+ Fair	BBB- Adequate	Baa3 Adequate	BBB- Adequate	D+ Weak
C Marginal	BB+ Uncertain	Ba1 Questionable	BB+ May be adequate	D Weak
C- Marginal	BB Uncertain	Ba2 Questionable	BB, BBq May be adequate	D- Weak
D Very vulnerable	BB- Uncertain	Ba3 Questionable	BB- May be adequate	E+ Very weak
E State supervision	B+ Risk	B1 Poor	B+ Vulnerable	E Very weak
	B Risk	B2 Poor	B, Bq Vulnerable	E- Very weak
	B- Risk	B3 Poor	B- Vulnerable	F Failed
	CCC Substantial risk	Caa Very poor	CCC, CCCq Extremely vulnerable	U Unrated
		Ca Extremely poor	R Regulatory action	
		C Lowest		

@ Standard and Poor publishes two ratings. The first indicated above is the *claims-paying ability rating*, which is computed at the insurer's request and is based on public and nonpublic data provided by the insurer. The second is a quantitative rating (indicated by a q in the rating), which is composed solely from public data.

SECTION II
LIFE INSURANCE PLANNING

DETERMINATION OF LIFE INSURANCE NEEDS

Traditionally, many rules have been devised to determine the true insurance needs of a family. Families often receive simple advice on how to allocate their insurance nest-egg dollars. For example, one insurance counselor suggests spending each year a sum equal to six percent of a breadwinner's gross income, plus one percent for each dependent—a total of $900 a year for a sales clerk who earns $10,000 a year and has a spouse and two children. Another counselor argues the rule of thumb for coverage is four to six times annual income. A third counselor maintains that the breadwinner should have three or four times the annual income in insurance, while a fourth asserts that five percent of one's take-home pay should go for life insurance premiums. But such guidelines are at best of limited value because individual needs vary considerably between families. Also, insurance counselors applying standard rules of thumb also disagree sharply on how much insurance should be carried by a family with certain basic responsibilities.

Before attempting to determine the life insurance needs of a family, a word of caution is in order. Practically every head of a family dreams that, in the event of a premature death, even if the surviving spouse is unwilling or unable to work, the financial lifestyle of the family would not be adversely affected. This dream can be realized only if the current flow of income to the family continues unabated. While a breadwinner may want the family to receive the same income should he or she die prematurely, it is unwise to determine the family's *life insurance needs* on this basis. A more logical objective would be to plan for providing family income (including Social Security survivorship benefits, investment income, and other income sources) in the range of, say, 60 to 75 percent of the insured's gross pay at the time of death, after taking care of final expenses, debt payments, and children's education.

At a basic level, the key objectives of buying cash value life insurance are to (1) achieve financial security for the family, and (2) receive retirement income. In order to meet these objectives, answers to the following questions should be obtained: (1) In the event of death, how much income would the remaining family need to maintain the desired standard of living? (2) How long would this income be needed? (It should at least last until the children are out of high school, and preferably until they finish college.) (3) How much Social Security income can be expected until the children are no longer covered? (4) How much income will the spouse need after the children are on their own? Answers to these questions will provide the basis for determining the life insurance needs.

There are two time tested methods available for determining how much life insurance is needed: *Human Value Approach* and *Capital Needs Analysis*. The former is based on the income potential of the client; it takes into account the maximum future earnings that would be lost if the income earner were to die today. The calculation requires estimating the present values of all the expected earnings by using an assumed discount rate and aggregating these discounted present values. However, the main problems with this approach are that it is nearly impossible to accurately estimate the future lifetime income of a breadwinner and it does not take into consideration other existing sources of income. Because of this drawback, the Capital Needs Analysis approach is generally preferred for determining the amount of life insurance that should be recommended for a family.

Capital Needs Analysis

Basic considerations. In the event of death of the breadwinner, the insurance coverage should be sufficiently large to handle the family's economic needs. Hence, the starting point in capital needs analysis is a valuation of income needs against the estimated income to be received upon the death of the breadwinner.

The typical income needs of a family and the various sources of income expected to be received by the surviving spouse are listed in Table 4-6. The excess of income needs over the expected income must be covered by income from new investments made by using the insurance proceeds received by the surviving spouse.

The lump sum required to generate a predetermined monthly income would depend upon whether the surviving spouse wishes to preserve the capital or deplete it over a predetermined period. In the former case, the monthly income generated would be far less than in the case of depleting capital where a part of the monthly income would represent a return of the principal. For instance, if a surviving wife wishing to preserve the capital invests $100,000 in a balanced fund generating nine percent, she will receive $750 a month from this investment for, say, ten years and the principal would be returned at the end of that period. If, however, $100,000 is annuitized over a ten-year period, the spouse may receive $1,270 per month but the principal would be exhausted in ten years.

In purchasing life insurance one should recognize that the financial needs of a family change over time. For instance, group health insurance may expire some time after retirement. Social Security no longer pays benefits to the surviving spouse when the youngest child reaches age 16. The surviving spouse may not be able to work while the children are at home. Also, if the spouse joins the work force on a full-time basis, the Social Security benefits may be reduced by a significant amount. In addition, during the Social Security "blackout period," Social Security benefits are eliminated. Finally, annual investment returns, adjusted for inflation, can widely

TABLE 4-6   Expense Needs Versus Sources of Income

Expense needs	*Sources of income*

A. Single-Period Needs
    i. Administrative/Final Expenses*
    ii. Estate Settlement Costs*
    iii. Debt Liquidation*
    iv. Emergency Fund*
	A. Social Security: Survivor's Income
	B. Group Life Insurance
	C. Spouse's Earnings
	D. Investment Income

B. Multiple-Period Needs
    i. Educational Cost
    ii. Surviving Spouse's Income Needs
    iii. Children's Income Needs
    iv. Retirement Needs	

* Life insurance does not necessarily need to cover these expenses. These items should be considered optional in determining the life insurance needs of a family.

fluctuate, depending upon the nature of investments and changing market conditions. The concept of varying life insurance needs to accommodate changing financial conditions of a hypothetical family is depicted in Figure 4-6. For example, the chart indicates the amount of income needed in constant dollars, the amount available from Social Security and other sources, and the amount of unfilled needs to be met by life insurance.

Capital needs analysis, which is designed to accurately calculate a family's life insurance needs, is based on the application of the present value concept presented in detail in Chapter 3. Now that we have learned about the basics of Capital Needs Analysis, it is appropriate to demonstrate its use in calculating the amount of coverage needed to fulfill the financial objectives of a family. This family consists of John, age 30, Mary, age 29, and two children, Jeff, age four, and Nancy, age two. This real world example will be presented later in the chapter after we have covered other important aspects of life insurance planning.

COST OF LIFE INSURANCE

Basic Considerations

The cost of buying life insurance can be easily obtained from various insurance companies. However, it is difficult to obtain the *real cost*—or *net cost*—of life insurance, as we shall now discover.

The net cost of carrying insurance can be significantly lowered by (1) realizing good investment returns, (2) minimizing mortality risks, and (3) maintaining low operational costs.

The cost of an insurance policy depends not only on realizing successes in the areas just identified, but also on the size of the company. Smaller companies often

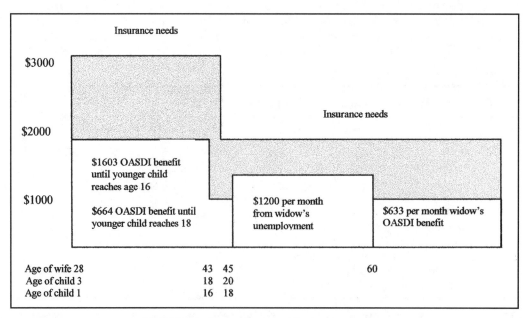

FIGURE 4-6   Determination of life insurance need

have relatively higher expenses than their more mature counterparts, due in part to the expense associated with running a small organization, management inexperience, and higher overheads. Another important expense item is the percentage of new premium dollars spent in attracting new business. Newer companies have the tendency of using a larger percentage of premium dollars for attracting new business. Finally, the death rates among a company's policyholders also affect the cost of insurance for the surviving policyholders. If mortality among the company's policyholders is excessive, the increased cost of insurance is generally met by reducing dividends on existing policies or by increasing the premium rates on future policies.

For these reasons, an uncritical comparison of premium rates per $1,000 of coverage quoted by different companies is an inefficient method of shopping for a cost-effective insurance policy. For instance, a 21-year-old male shopping for $100,000 policy coverage might be quoted the following rates:

Policy	Year	
	One	*20*
5-year Renewable Term	$ 150	$ 350
5-year Renewable and Convertible Term	235	990
Whole Life	950	950
Limited Pay Life (Paid Up at Age 65)	1,150	1,150

Obviously, these rates are not comparable, because in some cases they represent pure protection, whereas in other cases they also take cash value into account.

Essentially, four factors determine the true cost of a policy: (1) premiums, (2) dividends, (3) the cash value, and (4) the opportunity cost of investing in the policy; that is, the rate of interest the policyholder could earn by investing the funds elsewhere. The two most popular methods used for comparing costs of insurance policies are the *Net-cost Method* and the *Interest-adjusted Cost Index*.

The Net-Cost Method

The net cost, which is calculated for a given point in time (say, at the end of the tenth year) during the life of the policy is given by the following:

Net Cost = Premiums Paid – (Accrued Dividends + Cash Value)

For instance, if John Jones has been paying an annual premium of $1,000 for 10 years in a participating policy, and the accrued dividend and cash values at the end of the tenth year are $5,000 and $15,000, respectively, then the net cost of the policy is – $10,000:

$$\text{Net Cost} = \$10,000 - (\$5,000 + \$15,000)$$
$$= -\$10,000$$

A negative net cost, of course, does not imply that the company was actually paying the insured for the insurance, because the Net Cost Method ignores the time value of money. That is, it does not take into account the opportunity cost of making premium payments in excess of the amount necessary to buy pure life insurance. For this reason, the Interest-adjusted Cost Index is preferable.

Interest-Adjusted Cost Index

A more realistic method of calculating the net cost is to follow the *Interest-adjusted Cost Index method*, shown in Table 4-7. The table shows that for a person 35 years of age the true cost of buying a $1,000 participating whole life insurance

---

TABLE 4-7 Net Costs Versus Interest-Adjusted Cost Method

(A) Net Cost Method

1. Total premiums for 20 years ($240/year)	$4,800
2. Less dividends for 20 years ($75/year)	− 1,500
3. Net premiums for 20 years (1–2)	$3,300
4. Less cash value at end of 20 years (given)	− 3,600
5. Insurance cost (3–4)	−$ 300
6. Average cost per year (1/20)	−$ 15
7. Cost per year per $1,000 of insurance divided by number of thousands of face amount of policy (10 in this case)	−$ 1.50

(B) Interest-Adjusted Cost Method

1. Total premiums for 20 years, each accumulated at 4%	$7,147[1]
2. Less dividends for 20 years, each accumulated at 4%	−$2,233[2]
3. Net premiums for 20 years (1–2)	$4,914
4. Less cash value at the end of 20 years (given)	−$3,600
5. Insurance cost (3–4)	$1,314
6. Amount to which $1 deposited annually will accumulate in 20 years at 4%	$ 31[3]
7. Interest-adjusted cost per year: divide $1,314 by $31	$ 42
8. Cost per year per $1,000 (1/10): divide $42 by 10	$ 4.20[4]

Note: The illustration is based on a $10,000 policy bought at 35 years of age. The policy is assumed to have been cashed in after 20 years. Cash value at the end of 20 years equals $3,600.

(1) PMT = $240, n = 20, i = 4, fv = 7,147
(2) PMT = $75, n = 20, i = 4, fv = 2,233
(3) PMT = $1 (beginning of year, or annuity due), n = 20, i = 4, fv = 31
(4) This figure is rounded off. The exact cost is $4.24 as shown here:

Line	Amount (2 decimals)
1	$7,146.74
2	2,233.36
3	4,913.38
4	3,600.00
5	1,313.38
6	30.97
7	42.41
8	4.24

policy is $4.20 per thousand, and not – $1.50, as calculated under the Net Cost Method. While it is true that the participating policy costs are based on estimated dividends and that cash surrender values depend somewhat on the number of years a policy is kept in force, the *true* Net Cost Method can be used as an index for measuring the cost of one policy versus another policy.

Clearly, the Interest-adjusted Cost Method of calculating insurance costs is superior to the Net Cost Method. However, even this method has certain shortcomings. For one thing, the choice of a specific period for comparison, such as ten or 20 years, is arbitrary. Some companies might look better or worse when a different period is chosen. For another, this method ignores mortality rates and policy lapse rates (although these factors are taken into account in making dividend projections), factors that could be used to produce a more sophisticated index. Nevertheless, because of requirements in some states, and due to voluntary actions in others, responsible associations such as the Consumers Union consistently publish insurance costs calculated by the Interest-adjusted Cost Method so that prospective insurance buyers can compare the costs of different insurance policies.

Benchmark Method

Professor Joseph M. Belth has developed a Benchmark Method for comparing the cost of a universal life or a variable life policy against a *benchmark* which deserves special mention.[2] Under this method, the cost per $1,000 of protection each year is computed by dividing total charges under the policy by the amount of pure life insurance protection. The annual charges are determined by analyzing changes in the cash value. Since, at any point in time, the cash value of a policy is equal to the accumulated premiums plus interest less any charges, the cost of a policy can be calculated by analyzing changes in the cash value during a given year. Belth's formula for computing the cost per $1,000 of protection is given by:

$$YPT = \frac{(P + CVP)(1 + i) - (CV + D)}{(DB - CV)(0.001)}$$

YPT = Yearly price per $1,000 of protection

P = Annual premium

CVP = Cash value at the end of the preceding year

i = Assumed interest rate expressed as a decimal

CV = Cash value at the end of the year

D = Dividend for the year

DB = Death benefit at the end of the year

---

[2] Joseph M. Belth, "Universal Life and Variable Life—How to Evaluate the New Wave of Products," *Insurance Forum*, Vol. 11, No. 6, June 1984, pp. 21-24. It might be appropriate to add here that the College for Financial Planning no longer discusses this method.

For instance, assume the following information:

Annual premium = $370
Cash value at the end of previous year = $675
Cash value at the end of current policy year = $915
Annual dividend = none
Interest rate = 6 percent
Death benefit at the end of the year = $50,000

The cost of this whole life policy per $1,000 of coverage is $3.93:

$$\frac{(\$370 + \$675)\,(1 + .06) - (\$915 + 0)}{(\$50,000 - \$915)\,(.001)}$$

$$= \$3.93$$

The $3.93 cost of protection per $1,000 can now be compared with *benchmark* costs that are computed with *normal* assumptions to determine if the cost of this policy is reasonable. In general, as compared to the benchmark price:

If the policy cost is:	*Then the mortality and loading charges are:*
Same or lower	Small
Higher but less than 200 percent of the benchmark cost	Medium
Higher than 200 percent of the benchmark cost	High

LOANS FROM A LIFE INSURANCE POLICY

The cash value that grows tax-deferred inside an insurance policy acts as an attractive tax shelter. But what really makes a cash value insurance policy an attractive savings vehicle is that the accumulated cash value can be withdrawn as a loan, often at a *net borrowing cost* of around two percent. When compared to the currently prevailing rate on unsecured personal loans, or the six to seven percent on popular home equity loans, insurance policy loans appear to be very attractive. Equally important is the fact that obtaining a policy loan is easy and the loan never needs to be repaid. Of course, any unpaid loan is deducted from the face amount of the policy upon death.

Of the many advantages of an insurance policy loan just cited, the low net cost of borrowing is misleading, because the Net Cost Method ignores the opportunity cost of borrowing money. Here is a hypothetical example to illustrate the point.

A policyholder wishes to borrow $10,000 from the cash value of a variable life policy earning 11 percent. The loan interest is eight percent. However, the company will reduce the interest on the cash value from 11 percent to 5.5 percent as long as the loan remains unpaid. In this case, using a hypothetically high interest rate, the true cost of borrowing would be 13.5 percent.

Pre-loan return (1)	*Post loan return* (2)	*Loan rate* (3)	*True cost of loan* (1 – 2 + 3) (4)
11.0%	5.5%	8.0%	13.5%

There are two additional disadvantages of taking out a policy loan. First, the primary reason for buying life insurance is to receive the death benefit. A policy loan automatically reduces the death benefit by the amount of the loan, thereby partially defeating the purpose of carrying a certain amount of insurance protection. Second, policy loans taken from contracts issued after June 20, 1988 that violate the seven-pay test are taxed at the highest marginal tax bracket. Still, policy loans may be desirable in those cases where an urgent need for a loan exists and alternative sources of loan are not available.

LIFE INSURANCE SETTLEMENT OPTIONS

Basic Considerations

The main purpose of purchasing life insurance is to create an estate, preserve an estate, or transfer an estate. More specifically, life insurance can be used to provide funds for: (1) meeting the insured's death expenses; (2) paying unpaid debts; (3) paying taxes; (4) creating an emergency fund; (5) generating life income to maintain the desired lifestyle; (6) providing income for children until they are independent; and (7) financing college expenses. All of these needs are not necessarily present in every case. For instance, in one case the surviving spouse may be a career person who would not need life income from life insurance. In another case, the family may not have any children. In a third case, if grandparents take responsibility for educating their grandchildren, there might not be a need to provide for children's education.

Regardless of how many needs are present in any given situation, the manner in which the life insurance proceeds are distributed makes a difference between complete protection and partial achievement of one's stated goals. For example, if the insured has chosen a lump-sum payment option, it might impose an unreasonable burden on the beneficiary who must invest the proceeds wisely in order to obtain the desired income. In contrast, an annuity option, which locks in a fixed interest rate, may be unwise if the surviving spouse is an astute investor and can realize a significant growth by investing the lump sum in growth securities. For these reasons, every policyholder should select the settlement options most appropriate for prevailing economic conditions, desired tax benefits, and the beneficiary's investment skills. In the following pages, we will discuss the key settlement options available to life insurance policyholders.

Lump-Sum Payment: Tax-Free

Lump-sum payment is by far the most popular life insurance settlement option. A cash settlement enables the beneficiary to retire outstanding debts, pay off administrative and funeral costs, meet federal estate and state inheritance tax liabilities, and provide emergency funds. In addition, the lump sum payment provides funds for creating a diversified investment portfolio to achieve the multiple objectives of growth, current income, liquidity, and diversification. Of course, a policyholder opting for this type of settlement must make sure that the beneficiary or the associated advisor is sufficiently sophisticated to construct and manage such a challenging investment portfolio.

Fixed Annuity: Partially Taxable

For those who do not wish to put an enormous burden of investment management on their beneficiaries, the fixed annuity settlement option is desirable. This option offers three distinct choices, each of which is partially taxable.

Fixed period option. Under this option, first the period of payment is selected, and the amount of each payment is so calculated that both the principal and interest are paid up at the end of the period. This option is appropriate for providing income for raising children or buying time until the surviving spouse can join the labor force.

Fixed income option. Under this form, after selecting the installment amount, payments are made until the principal and interest are exhausted. This option is more appropriate in situations where the main objective is to provide temporary readjustment income for the surviving spouse.

Life-income option. Both options listed above suffer from a basic deficiency: The income may cease before the need for it expires. Under the life income option, the beneficiary cannot outlive the income, since the payments are made as long as the beneficiary is alive. The amount of each installment is determined by the age and sex of the beneficiary. And since the income payments continue until the death of the beneficiary, the life income option generates a lower monthly income than other types of options.

The life-income option assures that the beneficiary dependent solely upon this source would never outlive this income. This is particularly attractive in cases where the beneficiary lives an exceptionally long life. However, there are at least three problems associated with this option. (1) If the beneficiary dies at an early age, a substantial portion of the principal would be forfeited. (2) Over time, inflation would certainly erode the value of the monthly income. (3) The recipient is never permitted to invade the principal. For those who are concerned with these shortfalls, a variant known as *life-income-with-installment-certain option* is available. This option guarantees that payments will continue for *at least* a specified period (usually ten, 15, or 20 years) if the principal beneficiary dies early. Of course, the insurance company would still continue to make payments after the expiration of the minimum guaranteed period for as long as the primary (or secondary in the case of joint life) beneficiary lives. An overview of the fixed-annuity option and the variable-annuity option (discussed next) is presented in Table 4-8.

TABLE 4-8   Fixed and Variable Annuity Options

Basic considerations	Fixed annuity	Variable annuity
Investment Products	Long-term bonds, mortgages.	Stocks, bonds, mutual funds, zero coupons, money-market investments).
Flexibility of Investment	None.	Excellent. Insured directs movements of funds.
Safety of Cash Value	High.	Low to moderate.
Potential Rate of Return	Moderate.	High, over long periods.
Advantages	Guaranteed interest and principal.	Potentially high rate of return. Control of investments. Flexibility.
Disadvantages	Limited inflation hedge. Potential drop in rate of return. Earns below competitive rates of return.	No guaranteed cash value. Amount of monthly payment not guaranteed. Requires familiarity with investments. Elements of risk are always present.
Appropriate Buyer	People who (i) want to follow a conservative policy, (ii) need guaranteed monthly income, (iii) want a tax-deferred cash value fund and can tie up funds until annuitizing.	People who (i) need a monthly income, (ii) are investment-oriented, (iii) want flexibility, (iv) want a tax-deferred fund and can tie up funds until annuitizing, and (v) are well diversified in other areas (e.g. carry fixed-income-type investments).

Variable Annuity Option

One of the major limitations of the fixed annuity option is that it is, in effect, a savings account that earns a fixed interest rate for a specified period. Consequently, it does not provide a satisfactory hedge against inflation. An alternative to the fixed annuity is the variable annuity option, which provides an individual with both an accumulation option and a distribution option. In the first case the value of units increases with positive investment results, whereas in the second case the units remain fixed and the additional income is periodically distributed. Simply stated, a variable annuity is a family of mutual funds (separate accounts) within an annuity contract. Under this option, the insurance company offers an assortment of stock, bond, and money market funds and transfers investment risk to the policyholder. Values of a variable annuity contract fluctuate with the funds' performance. When annuitized, the annual payouts also vary with the portfolio's performance. For a mortality and risk fee of 0.8–1.4 percent of assets, most variable annuities provide a guaranteed death benefit (if death precedes annuitization) which would be equal to the greater of the value of the account or the initial investments, less any withdrawals. The fee also guarantees that annuity payments will not be decreased should the insurance company incur adverse mortality experience or increase in administrative costs. A summary of fixed and variable annuity options is presented in Table 4-8.

Indexed Annuity

Both fixed and variable annuities have special advantages and drawbacks, but neither provides the opportunity for market participation with *no downside risk*. However, since the marketplace demanded such a product, some years ago the insurance industry invented what is popularly known as *Indexed Annuity*.

The basic features of the Indexed Annuity (IA) are straightforward. Assume an investor purchases an IA today for $100,000 and the stock market, represented by S&P 500, goes up by two percent. On the anniversary date the policy would be credited by an amount equal to 70 percent of the two percent increase in the S&P 500 over that period (one year from the initial purchase date), subject to a maximum rate of 14 percent. Then at the beginning of year two the policy value would be increased to $101,400 ($100,000 plus 70 percent of two percent, or $1,400). However, if the S&P 500 increases by, say, 40 percent, the 14 percent cap would be imposed so the policy value would increase by $14,000 (14 percent of $100,000 dollars), and the next year's value would stand at $114,000.

The 70 percent limit and the 14 percent cap are specific to one IA policy. Companies set their own rates, caps, and method of recognizing equity growth, and add bells and whistles to their policies. But all IA policies have one thing in common: each policy offers a guaranty that the adjusted base amount would not decline, even when the market declines.

Other Options

Insurance companies offer other creative annuity options which should be explored. For instance, one company guarantees a five percent increase if you annuitize a variable annuity after ten years. Another company guarantees a fixed rate for a pre-specified period after which it is converted into a variable annuity. These examples can be easily multiplied.

Funds Left with Insurance Company

The final option for the beneficiary is to leave the funds with the insurance company at a stipulated rate of interest. The rate offered by the company may vary, depending upon prevailing market conditions; however, the *guaranteed* minimum interest rate is four percent. This option is the least attractive and is generally not preferred by most policyholders unless it is used to temporarily park the funds.

Life Insurance in Irrevocable Trust

One of the key insurance planning ideas is to create an irrevocable life insurance trust. Such a trust transfers the ownership of the insurance to the trust, and the current owner, who is generally the insured, gives up all rights to change the beneficiary and other terms of the policy. The irrevocable life insurance is designed to reduce estate taxes by removing the insurance proceeds from the owner's estate. In the case of large estates this could ultimately result in significant tax savings for the beneficiaries. Figure 4-7 demonstrates how a life insurance trust works.

While the irrevocable life insurance trust is a valuable planning tool, it does have several drawbacks. First, creating such a trust is an irreversible decision, and it

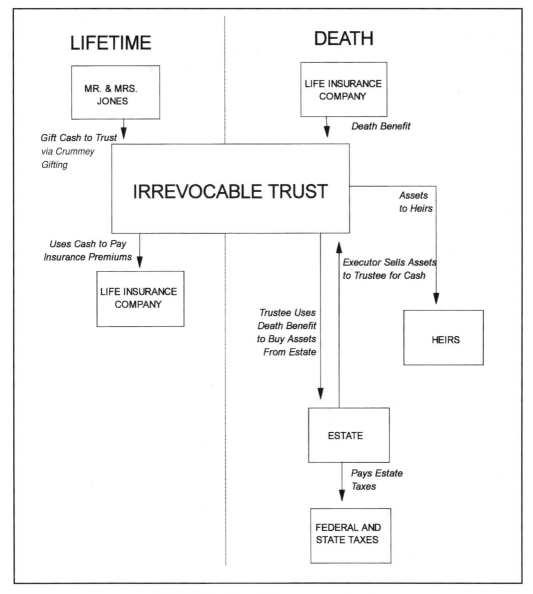

FIGURE 4-7   How a life insurance trust works

may prove to be costly if conditions subsequently change. Second, possible gift taxes might have to be paid when a policy is transferred to a trust. Third, in the event life insurance is transferred to a trust within three years of the transferor's death, the proceeds are brought back to the owner's gross estate when computing estate taxes. Fourth, if following the transfer of the policy to an irrevocable trust the previous owner is required to make a gift of more than $11,000 to help the trust make the premium payments, taxes would be imposed on gifts exceeding that amount. However, this gift can be reduced by using Split-Dollar techniques (discussed later) to avoid paying gift taxes on larger gifts. Fifth, an irrevocable trust can create a major problem if it becomes necessary to change the beneficiary or the face value. Despite these shortcomings, however, irrevocable life insurance trust remains a valuable planning tool.

ADDITIONAL LIFE INSURANCE PLANNING TECHNIQUES

Life insurance can be used in many creative ways to accomplish a variety of objectives. Since it is beyond the scope of this book to undertake an in-depth analysis of these planning techniques, only a brief discussion of some of the more important techniques is undertaken.

Buy-Sell Agreement

The death of the principal owner of a business can create serious financial problems for the business as well as the survivors of the deceased owner. Usually, the deceased's interest in the business is a dominant portion of his or her total estate. The estate tax liability can place a substantial burden on the estate, and a sale of the business to outsiders could jeopardize the interests of the surviving shareholders.

These problems can be handled with buy-sell agreements, which provide for the orderly transfer of the deceased's business interest to surviving partners, stockholders, or key employees at a fair value determined in advance. It is used for the disposition of a business interest in the event of the owner's death, disability, retirement, or upon withdrawal from the business at some point in time. Buy-sell agreements can be: (1) an agreement between the business itself and the individual owners (either a corporate stock redemption agreement or a partnership liquidation agreement), frequently called an "entity" plan; (2) an agreement between the individual owners (a cross-purchase agreement); (3) an agreement between the individual owners and keepers, family members, or outside individuals (a "third-party" business buy-out agreement); (4) a "wait and see" arrangement; or (5) a combination of the foregoing.

In the case of corporations, the most common types of buy-sell agreements are stock redemption plans, often called stock retirement plans, or shareholder cross-purchase plans. The distinguishing feature of the redemption agreement is that the corporation itself agrees to purchase or redeem the stock of the withdrawing or deceased shareholder. In this case, the corporation is the owner and the beneficiary of each policy. In a cross-purchase plan, the individuals agree between or among themselves to purchase the interest of a withdrawing or deceased shareholder. They are the owners and beneficiaries of each other's policies.

Section 419 Plan

Assume a trust company could contribute a significant amount of money just for the benefit of a few selected key people on a tax-deductible basis. Assume further that the money contributed would accumulate tax-free, would be distributed tax-free at a later date, and if any of the people died, would go to their heirs both income and estate tax free. Finally, assume that these funds and benefits would be secure from the hands of creditors. This trust is called a Section 419 Plan, or a Welfare Benefit Trust (WBT), created in 1974 by ERISA.

Section 419 Plans must meet the following conditions:

1. The eligible individuals are common law employees of the employer, and the benefits they receive under the plan are reasonable compensation for services rendered to the employer when considered with the employees' other compensation from the employer.
2. Death benefits are the only benefits provided under the Plan. They are funded with the purchase of individual whole life, term, universal or variable universal life insurance policies for insurable participants at standard life insurance premium rates published by the insurer and with annuity contracts for uninsurable participants.
3. No employer contributes more than 10 percent of the total annual contributions to the plan.
4. Employer contributions equal the premiums to be paid for its employees.
5. Gains from the sale or surrender of policies for individuals who lose their eligibility to participate in the plan belong to the Trust and are applied to cover Trust expenses.
6. No employer is directly or indirectly a beneficiary of any policy owned by the trust.

To recapitulate, to be tax deductible, a company must make contributions to a Welfare Benefit Trust known as a Multiple Employer Trust (commonly called a 419 Plan) of more than ten employers, with no one employer contributing more than ten percent to the Trust. Thus, through utilizing a properly established 419 Multiple Employer Welfare Benefit Trust, a company can make a large tax-deductible contribution primarily for the benefit of one or several individuals, with the money accumulating tax-free and the benefits distributed income and estate tax free to the named beneficiaries.

Insurance in Qualified Plans

In preparation for retirement, people invest in stocks, bonds, mutual funds, real estate, hard assets, and other products. Retirement planning also involves contributions to qualified (pension and profit sharing) plans, which accumulate on a tax-deferred basis. Life insurance plays an important role in the operation of many qualified plans.

There are four principal ways in which qualified plans can be funded with insurance: (1) individual policies; (2) group permanent insurance; (3) group annuities; and (4) deposit administration contracts. Of these, the first two are self-explanatory. The group annuity contract is a method of pension funding in which units of individual annuity contracts are accumulated each year and are fully paid for on a regular basis. In contrast, a deposit administration contract is a form of *group* annuity in which the employer makes the contribution into a deposit administration fund, which is a single fund for all employees in the group. When an employee reaches the retirement age, sufficient funds are withdrawn to provide the retiring employee with the annuity.

An essential feature of a life insurance policy in a qualified plan is that the law requires death benefits provided in these plans to be incidental. In a defined benefit plan, which prespecifies the monthly income to be received upon retirement, the incidental test is satisfied if the benefit does not exceed 100 times the expected monthly pension benefits. In a defined contribution plan, which specifies the annual contribution, the insurance premiums are limited to a certain portion of the contributions.

One of the advantages of having insurance in a pension plan is to provide a large benefit for the beneficiaries of those relatively young employees who die before their money in the qualified plan has a chance to grow. Another advantage of this strategy is to offer insurance protection for the key employees who are rated and can only obtain insurance by paying significantly higher premiums. Naturally, in this case the premium payments are treated as tax deductible contributions. However, the distributed cash value is taxable, but the difference between the face value and the cash value is treated as a tax-free distribution.

A relatively new development relates to the use of life insurance policies in Tax Sheltered Annuity (TSA) plans. Previously, employees of school districts could not be covered by life insurance coverage when they left their school system. Now, on a discriminatory basis an employer can put money into a TSA as long as no more than 25 percent of the contributions go toward paying life insurance costs. And since in a TSA life insurance can be purchased on a before-tax basis, the practice of buying insurance policies in TSAs is likely to grow over time.

Key Man Insurance

All business owners provide for adequate insurance to cover possible loss of assets, operating facilities, and profits in the event of fire, theft, or other natural disaster. Similarly, through life insurance, business owners frequently protect themselves against the loss of a partner, an executive, or other key employees. Typically, the company that owns the insurance policy is the sole beneficiary and receives the full proceeds in the event of the death of the key employee. In addition, by using cash value the company can provide a cash reserve to fund additional retirement benefits for the key employee in the event that he or she lives for a long time.

Deferred Compensation

As a way of providing a powerful incentive, sometimes corporations offer their executives what is known as deferred compensation. A deferred compensation plan is an arrangement whereby the company promises—but does not guaranty—to pay a predetermined compensation to the key employee after retirement. This helps both parties, since the corporation does not incur salary expenditures until later, and the executive does not pay taxes until the deferred compensation is actually paid out. Deferred compensation payments are tax deductible for the corporation at the time the payments are actually made.

A deferred compensation agreement is only as good as the financial arrangements that support it. An employer can promise benefits, but the ability to carry out the commitment depends on the company's solvency at the time payments become due. Another potential drawback is that deferred compensation becomes a part of the general assets of the corporation and hence can be attacked by its creditors. These problems can be solved by buying life insurance, although the creditors may still be able to get to the cash value of the insurance policy.

Insurance on the lives of the key executives who receive deferred compensation can provide a reserve fund to make payments when they are required. The company sets up the fund on the installment plan through annual deposits to the insurance company. The funds become available when the employees involved retire or die.

Split-Dollar Life Insurance

An Overview. Typically a contract between an employer and an employee, a Split-dollar life insurance is an arrangement under which the cash value, death benefit, and premiums may be split between the parties, even when the employer pays the whole premium. Under the typical arrangement, the employer pays the portion of the annual premium that equals the current year's increase in the cash surrender value of the policy; the employee pays the balance of the premium. This offers the key employees an incentive on a selective basis, and provides a means of offering stockholder employees substantial life insurance at a minimum cost.

An important feature of split-dollar insurance is that it is not a qualified employer benefit plan; consequently it can be used without concern for the anti-discrimination rules established by ERISA. Another advantage is that the employee is permitted to name the beneficiary, thereby providing insurance protection for the family. A third advantage is that an employee participating in split-dollar insurance pays only the taxes on the cost of the least expensive one-year term insurance policy using Table 2001 (now PS 58). The IRS has also ruled that the employer will receive no deduction for premiums it pays on a split-dollar insurance. When cash values are withdrawn, however, they are nontaxable.

An important amendment to the split dollar design specifies that split dollar between an employer and employee will now be taxed as a loan. If a split dollar arrangement is not taxed as a loan, then any additional benefit interest in the policy's cash surrender value transferred to the employee will be taxed as compensation. That is, "equity" in equity-split dollar is taxed when its growth exceeds the annual premium of the policy.

Benefits. Split dollar plans are often used for helping selected employees purchase inexpensive life insurance protection, or providing an additional employee fringe benefit for key employees. A split dollar plan can also provide four valuable benefits to an employer. (1) This plan can be offered to selected employees, since an employer does *not* have to offer this plan to all employees. (2) The employer's portion of the cash value of the policy can be carried as an asset on the company's books. (3) The employer can receive a complete refund of its cost in the future when the plan is terminated, although the employer does forego earning interest income on its contributions. (4) Split dollar plans are relatively easy to implement and do not have to comply with the onerous rules applicable to qualified plans.

The major benefit to the employee is that substantial amount of life insurance coverage can be acquired at a nominal cost, or at no cost. The only actual cost of insurance to the employee relates to the *value* of the life insurance coverage received. This amount may be significantly less than the actual premium (premium payment options and related income tax consequences are discussed below). Additionally, a split dollar plan can be established to provide an employee with a retirement income stream when the plan is terminated.

A split dollar plan can satisfy many needs. In an employment context, this plan is generally recommended when the employee's income tax rates are greater than the rate applicable to the employer's income.

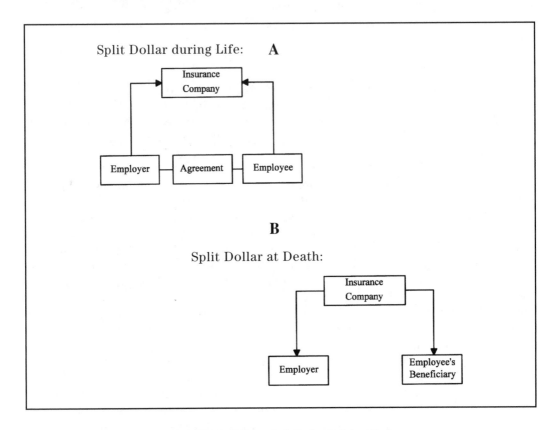

FIGURE 4-8 How to Split Dollar Policies Work

Mechanics. The basic element of a split dollar plan is a division between the employer and the employee of the benefits (death proceeds and cash value) and costs (premium payments) of a permanent life policy. Figure 4-8 illustrates a typical split dollar plan.

As noted in the figure, the employee designates who will receive the employee's share of the death benefit. Typically, the employee is entitled to the entire death benefit less the amount payable to the employer. In most cases, the business will be entitled to recover its costs, without any interest earnings, upon the death of the employee.

During the employee's life, the policy's cash value can generally be split in one of three ways:

1. Under the "original" form of split dollar plans, the employer is entitled to the entire cash value (this type of plan is rarely used today);

2. Under the "classic" split dollar plan, the employer is entitled to the greater of the total premiums paid or the cash value of the policy at any given time;

3. Under an "equity split dollar" plan, the equity is now taxed. That is, any additional beneficial interest in the policy's cash surrender value transferred to the employee is taxed as compensation.

Whether the "classic" or the "equity" approach should be used in a given situation would depend upon the analysis of prevailing economic environment, current and future needs, and desired benefits.

Ownership Methods. A split dollar plan is a legal agreement which splits the interests of a life insurance policy between the employee and the employer. A key issue relates to the actual ownership of the policy. Two common methods of implementing a split dollar plan are the *Endorsement Method* and the *Collateral Assignment Method.*

Under the Endorsement Method, the employer usually owns the policy. An endorsement is filed with the insurance company specifying the division of ownership of cash value and death proceeds between the employer and the employee. Also, the employer has control over this type of policy. Often the employer owns a life insurance policy on a key person and finds that the person's importance has changed. After the importance of the key person coverage has declined, the policy may still be valuable under a split dollar arrangement. In such a case, if an employer owns an existing policy, the endorsement method may be easier to implement than the collateral assignment method.

Under the Collateral Assignment Method, the employee, or a third party, such as a spouse or an irrevocable trust, owns the policy. The employee files a document with the insurance company called a collateral assignment and assigns a portion of the policy to the employer according to the terms of the split dollar plan. This method is easier to implement if the split dollar plan uses an existing policy owned by the employee, the spouse, or the irrevocable trust. Also, when compared to the endorsement method, the collateral assignment method may produce more favorable income tax consequences to the employee.

Conclusion. Split dollar plans offer an attractive way for employers and employees to share the costs and benefits of life insurance products. The benefits of such a plan are that it is easy to implement, provides a way for employers to offer low cost insurance for selected employees, and makes life insurance protection more affordable for the employees. It should also be mentioned that under certain conditions, split-dollar cash value increases above premium payments are now taxable. Therefore, each case should be carefully examined before making a final decision.

Insurance for the Professional

The need of life insurance coverage for professionals and small business owners is significantly different from the need for coverage for corporate employees and large business owners. The reason is that, except for the equipment and furnishings, a professional practice or a small business does not usually have much resale value. Even under the best of circumstances, the price at which the business can be sold is minuscule as compared to the income needs of the professional family.

The solution to this problem lies in the purchase of life insurance to generate a monthly income sufficient to help the family maintain the desired standard of living in the event of an untimely death of the professional. In addition, the professional person may need life insurance to guarantee a secure retirement. This is because, unlike the corporate executive, the professionals cannot depend on the corporate qualified plans and must create their own retirement funds. Consequently, professionals can supplement life insurance by other qualified (e.g., Keogh) plans to create a *balanced* retirement plan.

SECTION III
LIFE INSURANCE NEEDS: A REAL WORLD EXAMPLE

We have learned that the capital needs analysis technique can be applied to determine the life insurance needs of a family. We will now illustrate this point by using a real world example.

John Smith, 30, and Mary Smith, 29, have two children. Jeff is four and Nancy is two years old. The Smiths' family and financial data are presented in Table 4-9, while the technique for arriving at the new capital needed for John Smith is demonstrated in Table 4-10. This technique is discussed next.

> *Step 1: Final Expenses.* The final expenses are estimated to be $27,000. Since the Smiths have $2,500 in liquid assets and an additional $255 is expected to be received from Social Security, additional capital needed to meet the final expenses is $24,245 (Line A).
>
> *Step 2: Housing.* The Smiths have a $70,000 mortgage loan and they would want it to be paid off in case of John's death (Line B).

Each problem has hidden in it an opportunity so powerful that it dwarfs the problem. The greatest success stories were created by people who recognized a problem and turned into an opportunity.

Joseph Sugarman

TABLE 4-9   Family and Financial Data of John Smith

	Family data	
	John Smith	Age 30
	Mary Smith	Age 29
	Jeff Smith	Age 4
	Nancy Smith	Age 2

Financial data

Assets		Liabilities and net worth	
Cash/Liquid Assets	$ 2,500	Home Mortgage	$ 70,000
Invested Assets	0	Other Liabilities	12,000
Other Assets	20,000	Net Worth	30,500
Home	90,000		
	$112,500		$112,500
Life Insurance Coverage = $50,000			

Step 3: Education. The Smiths estimate that it would cost $32,000 to educate Jeff and Nancy. It is assumed that educational funds would earn interest at an after-tax rate of five percent and the rate of inflation would be three percent; that is, the real rate of return (actual rate minus the inflation rate) would be two percent. Finally, the Smiths decide that they would like to have $32,000 in approximately 14 years when Jeff will turn 18 and Nancy will be 16 years old (Line C).

Using a financial calculator (see Chapter 3 for details), we find that the present value of $1 growing at 2 percent per year for fourteen years is .757875. Multiplying the present value interest factor (PVIF) by $32,000, we determine that the capital required today to educate the two children is $24,252 ($32,000 x .7578754).

Step 4: Monthly Expenses for Mary Smith. If John Smith were to die today, for the next 14 years until Jeff is 18, Mary Smith will receive $1,043 per month from Social Security and $1,067 in today's dollars from her place of employment. However, the Smiths have decided that the family needs a monthly income of $2,200 to raise the two children. The resultant shortfall of $90 per month ($2,200 – $1,043 – $1,067) can be obtained by purchasing an annuity for $13,200. The calculation method is shown at the bottom of Table 4-8, Line D.

Using the same technique, we can calculate that Mary will receive a monthly income of $611 for two years after Jeff leaves home at 18 and Nancy becomes 18 by annuitizing a lump sum of $14,387. Finally, Mary will receive $483 per month for 20 years until she is 65 by annuitizing a lump sum of $95,636; similarly, she will receive $855 per month for 15 years until age 80 (life expectancy assumed by her) from a lump sum of $133,087.

Adding all the family's needs together, the total capital need of the Smith family equals $374,807. This fact is revealed in Table 4-11.

Further sophistication. In the preceding illustration we made several simplified assumptions which can be refined to calculate a more accurate capital needs

TABLE 4-10   Capital Needs Analysis of John Smith

| | | Years income needed | Amount needed | Available sources | | | Additional needed | Capital required |
Line	Income needed			Social Security	Employ-ment	Other sources		
A.	Final Expenses		$27,000*	$ 255	0	$2,500	$24,245	$ 24,245
B.	Housing		70,000*	0	0	0	70,000	70,000
C.	Education		32,000*	0	0	0	32,000	24,252
	Monthly income for Mary Smith							
D.	Until Jeff is 18	14	2,200	1,043	$1,067	0	90	13,200
E.	Nancy between 16 and 18	2	2,200	522	1,067	0	611	14,387
F.	Alone, age 45 to 65	20	1,550	0	1,067	0	483	95,636
G.	Alone, age 65 to 80	15	1,550	695	0	0	855	133,087

Assumptions:
1. Capital amounts needed for monthly expenses are assuming that the capital will be exhausted when Mary Smith is 80 years old.
2. Capital funds are assumed to earn interest at an after-tax, inflation adjusted rate of 2%.
3. Client is eligible for Social Security.
4. Client wishes to pay off the mortgage immediately.
5. Education fund available as lump sum when Jeff reaches the age of 18—that is, in 14 years.
6. Wife does not receive Social Security between ages 45 and 65 (20 years).
7. Wife's life expectancy is 80 (15 years since age 65).

Capital Required Calculations

Line A: Capital immediately required. No calculation necessary.
Line B: Capital immediately required. No calculation necessary.
Line C: FV(PVIF). PVIF (n = 14, i = 2%) is .757875 $24,252 = 32,000 (.757875)

	PMT (Begin Mode)	I(%/mo)	N	PV
Line D:	90	2/12	14 × 12	13,200
Line E:	611	2/12	2 × 12	14,387
Line F:	483	2/12	20 × 12	95,636
Line G:	855	2/12	15 × 12	133,087

Note: Figures are rounded off.
* Optional at the discretion of the surviving spouse.

analysis. Here are a few examples of assumptions which are different from those made in the previous example:

1. The Smiths do not wish to invade the principal in generating the required income.
2. Appropriate education funds become available at the beginning of age 18 for Jeff and Nancy.
3. The PVAD of monthly income is discounted by inflation-adjusted interest rate (lines E, F & G).
4. Capital funds earn interest at an after-tax rate of, say, eight percent.
5. The inflation rate is a more realistic five percent.
6. Spouse's employment income keeps pace with inflation.

TABLE 4-11

Needs		Particulars	Capital reqd.
Final Expenses		Immediate need	$ 24,245
Housing		Liquidation of mortgage	70,000
Education		Lump sum available when Jeff is 18—in 14 years	24,252
Monthly Income	#1	Monthly income until Jeff is 18	13,200
	#2	Monthly income when Nancy is between 16 and 18	14,387
	#3	Monthly income when Mary is between 45 and 65	95,636
	#4	Monthly income when Mary is between 65 to 80 **	133,087
		Total	374,807
		Less existing insurance	− 50,000
		Additional insurance need	$324,807

Note: Figures are rounded off.

** Because the starting of this income is 36 years away when Mary turns 65, it is assumed that $133,087 expected at age 65 is discounted back to the present at the after-tax, inflation-adjusted, rate of 0%. Hence the present value Today of $133,087 needed at Mary's age 65 is also $133,087. This assumption makes it a highly conservative estimate of Mary's income needs far into the future.

7. The true inflation-adjusted interest rate is 2.857 percent [(1.08/1.05 − 1) x 100], instead of two percent assumed.

We can also use the following nine step formula on the HP 12C to come out with the same result:

Step 1)   1.08
Step 2)   enter
Step 3)   1.05
Step 4)   divide
Step 5)   1
Step 6)   –
Step 7)   100
Step 8)   multiply
Step 9)   result = 2.857

If further sophistication is desired, varied assumptions can be made about different tax rates and more realistic annual rates of return, depending upon the sophistication of the surviving spouse. Fortunately, these and other assumptions can be incorporated with relative ease in the capital needs analysis by using the time value of money tool developed in Chapter 3.[1] Also, once the insurance need is determined, other techniques used in this chapter can be used to complete the life insurance planning process.

SECTION IV
MISCELLANEOUS LIFE INSURANCE ISSUES

CAPITAL MAXIMIZATION STRATEGY (CMS)

Introduction

In the wealth transfer markets, life insurance professionals encounter a number of challenges. The lack of liquid assets to meet wealth transfer costs is one limitation that with proper planning can be avoided. Large estates are generally subject to transfer and income taxes at the death of wealthy individuals. After all non-insurance estate-planning techniques have been employed, many wealthy individuals determine that life insurance can be a good way to minimize the impact of transfer taxes. However, these individuals may be reluctant to liquidate high-performing investment portfolios or business assets to purchase life insurance, creating a liquidity challenge.

The Capital Maximization Strategy Plan is designed specifically to create the necessary estate liquidity while preserving estate assets.

The Basic Framework

The CMS Plan creates an alternative method of paying life insurance premiums. Rather than using or liquidating current assets, the funds needed to pay the premiums are borrowed so the client's investment portfolio or other assets could remain intact.

Advantages of the program include:

- Reduced current net out-of-pocket cost for the needed life insurance coverage.
- Little or no impact on current investment portfolio.
- Potentially favorable gift tax consequences.

---

[1] It should be mentioned that the technique used by the College for Financial Planning in performing the Capital Needs Analysis differs slightly from the one presented here. However, it is beyond the scope of this book to compare various techniques for capital needs analysis and present pros and cons of using these techniques. But it is important to add that the technique just presented is sufficiently sophisticated to satisfy our needs.

Who Should Consider A CMS Plan?

The CMS Plan is designed for use in wealth transfer cases where the need for life insurance has been established, but the funds required to pay premium might necessitate the liquidation of estate assets. The plan requires the insured to borrow funds to pay life insurance premiums, thereby potentially reducing their net out-of-pocket expenses. Interest paid on borrowed funds is not deductible for income tax purposes.

This program is designed for persons with a minimum net worth of $5 million and with a minimum life insurance premium to be financed of $100,000. Clients must qualify both financially and medically to participate in this program.

How the Loan Works?

The lender begins a financial review of a loan application after the related life insurance application is approved for issue. Under the CMS Plan, the lender reviews the future stream of premium payments required to purchase the life insurance policy and the total loan reflected on an illustration. Each application to borrow an annual premium is treated by the lender as a separate financial transaction and requires a separate underwriting decision.

Only life insurance premiums can be borrowed. Each year the borrower is required to pay the annual interest in advance. In addition, the lender requires the life insurance policy as collateral for the loan, and may also require additional collateral. The loan can be repaid over time or can continue until death. Loan interest rates are fixed on an annual basis, but they can vary from year to year based on fluctuation in the LIBOR (London InterBank Offer Rate).

The lender may require the cash value of the life insurance policy and the death benefit as collateral for the loan. However, often the lender will require additional assets from the borrower. As an alternative, the borrower may pledge assets other than the life insurance policy's cash value as collateral for the loan. The lender makes all such collateral decisions on a case-by-case basis.

LIFE SETTLEMENT OPTIONS

In the typical life settlement, the policyholder:
- is over 65 years of age;
- has experienced an adverse change in health, but is not terminally ill;
- owns a policy with a face amount of $250,000 or more;
- no longer wants -- or can afford -- the insurance policy.

That's a pretty broad net. Indeed, a recent study found over 89 percent of universal life policies issued ultimately do not pay a death claim. Those policies are surrendered or permitted to lapse. Another study published in December 1999 found that more than 20 percent of the policies owned by seniors have life settlement values in excess of their cash surrender values.

A life settlement can be a good option for a variety of reasons. The insured may have outlived the risk insured against; the spouse has passed away; the children have completed their education; the business partnership has dissolved; or an insured, key employee, has retired after a long career.

In other cases, investment projections may have proven unduly optimistic in the current low-interest, average-market environment. So-called "vanishing" premiums have not vanished, and the financial plan built around the policy is not being met. In any such case, the owner may want out of his policy, either to move the value into another asset or to buy a more apporpriate insurance policy.

Appraisal

There is a new reality to life insurance policy ownership, and all clients age 65 or older should have their policies appraised. Obtaining a policy valuation is a straightforward process. Some basic information about the policy, a policy illustration run to maturity, along with health details similar to what would be used to place a substandard insurance case (without a medical exam), are submitted to a life settlement provider for valuation. The resulting valuation is the amount that the provider would likely pay to acquire the policy. Armed with this information, the policyholder can decide how best to use the newly discovered value.

The market value of a life insurance policy is the difference between the present value of the death benefit and the present value of the anticipated premiums. (This simplification ignores the existing cash value, and the real cost of carrying a policy is not the premiums paid but the charges assessed for insurance protection.) The amount is very sensitive to the insured's life expectancy. A shorter life expectancy means that a smaller discount will apply to the death benefit and fewer premiums will probably need to be paid. The insured's life expectancy depends on his or her age, sex, smoking status, and health history. The anticipated premiums depend on the specific provisions and cost structure of the subject policy.

Providers

Because the seller of a life insurance policy receives cash and has no ongoing financial commitment to pay premiums, it might seem that the only relevant feature of a life settlement offer is the amount. But there are other aspects that the fiduciary would want to consider while considering the sale of a policy.

There is, for one thing, the question of privacy. Sellers should make sure that only institutional funding would be used and that the life settlement provider will guarantee in writing that no ownership or identifying information about the insured would be provided to individual investors.

Security is important. The seller should make sure that the life settlement provider places the settlement funds in an escrow account to assure that they are available before the seller permits transfer of the policy. (In ascertaining that institutional funds are being used, the seller should not mistake an institutional escrow agent for an institutional source of funds.)

In this context professional liability insurance should also be considered. The seller should make sure that both the provider and broker have adequate Errors and Omissions coverage.

Taxes

The sale of a life insurance policy may be a taxable event. Tax experts disagree on the details of taxation, but there is a general consensus that if the cash surrender value of the policy exceeds the premiums paid on it, the life settlement proceeds will be taxed as follows:

- The portion exceeding the investment in the contract but not exceeding the cash surrender value, will be taxed as ordinary income.
- The portion exceeding the cash surrender value will be treated as a capital gain.

Where the cash surrender value of the policy is less than the investment in the contract, the I.R.S. may take the position that only the cash surrender value represents a tax-free return of basis, and everything else is gain on the sale of the asset. This stance is not universally accepted, so professional advice on any particular situation is in order[1].

LIVING BENEFIT PROVISION (GUARANTEED MINIMUM INCOME BENEFIT)

Variable annuities come with a host of optional features that one can select for an additional annual fee. One common and very popular type of variable annuity feature is the living benefit provision, also known as a GMIB (Guaranteed Minimum Income Benefit). The GMIB is exactly what the name implies -- a guaranteed minimum level of annuity payments by the insurance company, regardless of the performance of the annuity.

Not every insurance company offers living benefit provisions. Most insurance companies that do offer living benefit provisions allow them to be added to most, if not all, of their variable annuity products. Note that living benefit or GMIB provisions go by different names, depending on the insurance company that provides them: "GRIP," "GIA," "RIG," "MAP," and "Income Guard" are all examples of names of living benefit features given by insurance companies. They all refer to the same type of living benefit features.

Living benefit provisions are typically exercisable after the tenth year and require that the insured annuitize the entire contract. There are a multitude of payout options from which to choose, such as payments for a certain period of time (typically five to twenty years "period certain"), payments for the rest of the insured's life, the spouse's life, or any combination of the two.

The insured can even choose between a fixed payment that does not vary, or a variable payment that is based on market performance. There is at least one product that allows the insured to annuitize on a variable basis and receive market upside, while guaranteeing a minimum payment regardless of market performance. This is particularly attractive to investors interested in keeping up with inflation.

[1]Source: Alan H. Buerger. Trusts and Estates, November 2002

Managing Transfer Assets in a "B Trust"

The "B Trust" (sometimes called the "Credit Shelter Trust," "Family Trust" or "By-pass Trust") is the foundation for many well-constructed marital estate plans. Upon the death of the first spouse, the deceased spouse's estate is divided into two shares. The *Applicable Exclusion Amount* ($1,500,000 in 2005) passes to the "B Trust." The rest of the assets pass to the surviving spouse outright, or in a trust ("A Trust") that qualifies for the *Marital Deduction Amount*. The following chart illustrates the concept.

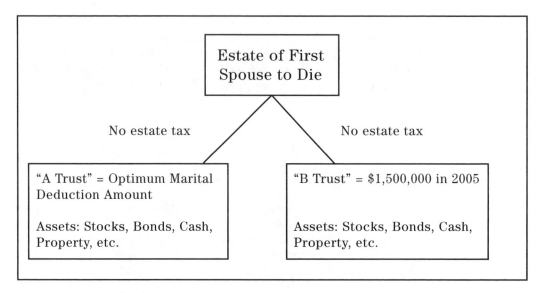

NEW ALLURE FOR DEFINED BENEFIT PLANS

Provisions of the Economic Growth and Tax Relief Reconciliation Act of 2001 let business owners and professionals make larger tax-deductible contributions to defined benefit (DB) plans.

DBs assume that the plans' assets will earn a predetermined rate and accumulate to fund pre-determined retirement income benefits of up to $160,000 annually at age 62 for participants. These plans are appropriate for entrepreneurs who are seeking to defer each year more income from taxes than they can with a defined contribution plan. For 2005, the maximum defined contribution deferral is $40,000, or for age 50 and up, $41,000.

A DB plan can be used for any type of business entity, even if there are no employees. Certain costs of new plans established by businesses with 100 or fewer employees may qualify for a tax credit during the plan's first three years, or for the first two years plus the year before the plan became effective.

The catch is that contributions to a defined-benefit plan are mandatory, although creative actuaries typically build in flexibility so that a smaller amount, or none at all, will be due in a lean year. Moreover, the plan is a promise by the business to provide a specified benefit; if the plan's assets do not earn the actuarially assumed rate of return, the employer has to make up the difference with additional contributions.

Another reason that DBs are best for businesses with a history is that over the years, the Internal Revenue Service has taken the position that these plans must be established with the intent to provide a permanent program of pension benefits. In other words, a DB requires a long-term commitment to the funding obligation. A plan can certainly be terminated after several years, and in practice, many are terminated. But it is wise to do so only for a valid business reason that was not contemplated when the plan was established.

New Split Dollar Regulations

On September 11, 2003, the IRS released the final split dollar regulations. These regulations largely follow the proposed regulations issued in July 2002 and the supplemental proposed regulations released on May 8, 2003, although there are a few differences and additions in the September 2003 release.

Effective Date. The final regulations apply to any split-dollar arrangement entered into after September 17, 2003, and to any arrangement entered into before September 18, 2003 that is materially modified after September 17, 2003. IRS Notice 2002-8 provided a valuable grandfathering provision to split-dollar arrangements terminated or converted to loan regime arrangements before January 1, 2004.

Definition of Split-Dollar Arrangement. Generally, the final regulations agreement define a split-dollar arrangement as any agreement between an owner of a life insurance contract and a non-owner, under which either party to the arrangement pays all or part of the premiums and one of the parties paying the premiums is entitled to recover (conditionally or unconditionally) all or any portion of those premiums, and such a recovery is to be made from, or is secured by, the proceeds of the life insurance. This broad definition is intended to capture most premium sharing arrangements.

The final regulations also retain the special rule definition of split-dollar arrangements that captures compensatory and shareholder arrangements not covered by the general rule. The preamble to the final regulations specifically excludes key man insurance owned by an employer where the employee has no rights in the policy.

Two Mutually Exclusive Tax Regimes. The final regulations retain the provisions of the proposed regulations that require the imposition of two mutually exclusive tax regimes with respect to split-dollar arrangements; namely, the economic benefit regime and the loan regime. As with the proposed regulations, the final regulations provide that the identity of the owner (actual or deemed) of the life insurance policy generally determines which tax regime will be used. The economic benefit regime is required in a compensatory arrangement where the employer is the owner of the policy and in a private arrangement where the donor is the owner of the policy (endorsement arrangements). The loan regime applies to situations previously known as equity collateral assignment arrangements.

Determination of the Policy Owner. The final regulations retain the provisions of the proposed regulations with respect to the definition of the owner of the policy; namely, the owner of record is presumptively the owner for tax purposes, *except* where the owner's right to the policy is limited to current life insurance protection. Where two or more owners are listed, each with all incidents of ownership of an undivided interest in the contract for tax purposes, each owner is treated as the owner. If two or more owners are listed, and each does not have all incidents of ownership of an undivided interest in the contract, then the first owner listed is recognized as the owner.

Taxation under the Economic Benefit Regime (Endorsement Split Dollar). The final regulations retain the rules of taxation under the economic benefit regime, namely, the value of the economic benefit to the non-owner, reduced by any consideration paid by the non-owner, is treated as being transferred by the owner to the non-owner. Of course, the nature of the relationship between the owner and the non-owner determines the character of the transfer. For example, if the non-owner is the employee of the owner, the transfer is treated as taxable compensation to the employee. If the non-owner is the trustee of the owner's trust, then the transfer is treated as a gift.

Calculation of Economic Benefit. The value of the economic benefit is calculated the same way as it has been since Revenue Ruling 64-328 with a minor modification. The final regulations provide that the value of the economic benefit is calculated from the death benefit on the last day of the tax year (or the policy anniversary date if the parties so elect).

Taxation of Amounts Received under the Life Insurance Contract. Any amount received under the life insurance contract (other than the amount received by reason of death) and provided, directly or indirectly, to the non-owner is treated as being paid from the insurance company to the owner and then paid by the owner to the non-owner. The final regulations apply this rule to *specified policy loans* where (1) the proceeds of the loan are distributed directly from the insurance company to the non-owner; (2) a reasonable person would not expect that the loan will be repaid by the non-owner; or (3) the non-owner's obligation to repay the loan to the owner is satisfied upon repayment by either party to the insurance company.

Likewise, the final regulations retain the rule that death benefit proceeds paid to a beneficiary are excluded from the beneficiary's gross income from income tax purposes under IRC 101(a) only to the extent that the payment is allocable to current life insurance protection provided to the non-owner under the agreement and either (i) the cost of such protection was paid by the non-owner, or (ii) the non-owner accounted for the value as an economic benefit (income to the employee, gift to the donee, etc). The character of the death benefit transferred is determined by the relationship between the owner and the non-owner.

NO – LAPSE GUARANTEED OPTION

Some insurance companies now offer a new feature on variable universal life insurance: A guaranteed death benefit, regardless of how the stock market affects the policyholder's account.

The no-lapse guarantee rider or policy option that is available for an additional premium on certain variable universal life products allows the insured to choose either a *lifetime* or a 20-year death benefit guarantee. Without such a safety net, significant stock market losses over time could cause a variable life insurance policy to lapse.

A variable life insurance with a no-lapse guarantee is attractive to those who believe in the long-term potential of equities but wish to protect themselves from the potential effects of short-term market volatility on their life insurance coverage.

The rider's *lifetime* option guarantees death benefit for as long as the insured lives or until the policy matures, whichever comes first. If an insured is 70 or younger and elects the 20-year option, the insured will receive a death benefit guarantee for the lesser of 20 years or until age 80. If the age is between 71 and 85, the insured will receive a no-lapse guarantee for the lesser of 10 years or until age 90.

At the end of the guarantee period, the insured is automatically offered a guarantee extension, provided the policy has a positive balance. The length of the extension is determined by the amount of funds available in the account.

In this chapter we have presented the structures and concepts of various types of life insurance policies and discussed key life insurance planning strategies. Issues concerning other forms of insurance will be presented in the next chapter.

If a man is called to be a streetsweeper, he should sweep streets even as Michelangelo painted, or Beethoven composed music, or Shakespeare wrote poetry. He should sweep streets so well that all the hosts of heaven and earth will pause to say, here lived a great streetsweeper who did his job well.

Martin Luther King, Jr.

CHAPTER 5

Health, Homeowner's, Automobile, and Liability Insurance: Structure, Concepts, and Planning

GENERAL PRINCIPLES

INTRODUCTION

Buying casualty and property insurance is a challenging undertaking for four main reasons. First, it takes special skills to determine the amount of insurance one really needs. Second, as mentioned in Chapter 4, since the money spent on buying insurance is usually diverted from investment, it is rarely desirable to buy as much insurance as one can afford. Third, in buying insurance, a person must not get carried away by emotion. Fourth, considerable savings in premium dollars can be achieved by shopping around and buying the least expensive yet quality insurance for the needed coverage. For these reasons, it is desirable—in fact imperative—that in buying insurance every individual apply the basic principle followed by business professionals: namely, obtain the best value for the premium dollars spent on insurance.

In this chapter, we will present the structure, concepts, and planning strategies for health, disability, long-term care, homeowner's, auto, and liability insurance. In our presentation we will emphasize that in buying property and casualty insurance people should (1) insure against *significant* risks while bearing the *small* risks themselves; (2) compare the rates before making a commitment; (3) reduce the risks through preventive measures, and (4) periodically review their coverage.

Before embarking upon a discussion of insurance against significant risks, a brief mention should be made of the principle of indemnity. In the case of property, casualty, health, disability and long-term care insurance, the insurance company merely indemnifies the insured for the actual loss and *does not* generate a profit for the insured. This principle of indemnity, however, does not apply to life insurance, since there is no way to determine the actual value of a human life.

INSURANCE AGAINST SIGNIFICANT RISKS

Insuring against small losses wastes valuable resources that can be better spent on buying protection for larger risks. Of course, only the insured can determine which losses are large, since the amount one can afford to cover depends primarily on income and the existing coverage. Therefore, the extent of health and homeowner's insurance coverage should be based upon how much risk the insured can afford to assume. Also, while casualty losses exceeding ten percent of the adjusted gross income are tax-deductible, these losses rarely exceed that limit and therefore remain nondeductible.

In buying casualty/property insurance, it is possible to reduce the cost of coverage through the manipulation of insurance deductibles. For instance, the potential premium savings from increasing deductibles on an auto policy are presented in Table 5-1. This table shows that if the deductible is reduced from $200 to $100 and if an accident occurs in, say, three years, the cost savings are a negligible $13. That is, the insured must commit an additional $87 ($447 – $360) in three years for a potential net savings of only $13. This is indeed wasteful.

The money saved by increasing the deductible can be employed in expanding the coverage on larger risks. The standard homeowner's policy includes $25,000 of personal liability insurance for accidents both at home and elsewhere. The insurance company will defend the homeowner when charged with the responsibility for the accident and will pay claims up to the $25,000 limit. The company will also pay up to $500 medical expenses per person on a no-fault basis up to a total of $25,000 on each accident. However, even if the injured person wins a $300,000 judgment against the homeowner—and that is a distinct possibility—the company would pay only $25,000 and the owner would have to pay the remaining $275,000. The payment of such a large amount could be financially disastrous. For about $10 more a year, the coverage can be increased from the standard $25,000 to $300,000 liability insurance for each accident—a very worthwhile use of premium dollars.

SHOPPING FOR INSURANCE

Casualty/property insurance should be purchased with two cardinal rules in mind. First, insurance prices vary widely, and a great deal can be saved by shopping around. Second, due diligence is required before selecting a policy, because many seemingly identical policies differ markedly on crucial points. For example, all disability policies pay an income when the insured becomes disabled, but a particular illness or injury may not qualify as a disability under every company's definition. Thus, it is imperative for the insured to select a policy which is not only cost effective but also provides *all the desired coverages.*

TABLE 5-1   Potential Savings from Raising Deductibles

	One auto accident within			
	1 year	2 years	3 years	4 years
Cost: $200 Deductible				
Total premiums paid	$120	$240	$360	$480
Deductible payment	200	200	200	200
Total cost (A)	$320	$440	$560	$680
Cost: $100 Deductible				
Total premiums paid	$149	$298	$447	$596
Deductible payment	100	100	100	100
Total cost (B)	$249	$398	$547	$696
Added cost (savings) with $200 deductible:				
Cost (A) − Cost (B)	$ 71	$ 42	$ 13	($ 16)

LOSS CONTROL THROUGH PREVENTIVE MEASURES

The premium for an insurance contract is based upon the size and number of claims resulting from accidents and other losses. Consequently, one can help reduce premium costs by reducing the hazards that cause the damage. For instance, car losses can be reduced by defensive driving and by installing in the car an anti-theft system. Similarly, home losses can be reduced by the use of fire-resistant construction materials and furnishings, and by the installation of security devices involving police, fire departments, and hospitals. Likewise, health losses can be reduced by periodic physical check-ups, dietary control, regular exercise, and taking prompt care of illnesses.

ORGANIZATION OF PERSONAL RECORDS

Record-keeping is an onerous chore which most of us would prefer to ignore. But in the areas of health and property casualty insurance it is essential to maintain up-to-date, accurate, and detailed records. This is especially important when submitting a claim, because the extent of reimbursement by the insurance company would largely depend upon the ability of the policyholder to produce documents supporting the claims.

For these reasons, every homeowner should keep an up-to-date inventory of all the personal possessions. This would involve (1) maintaining an inventory book, (2) recording the purchase price and the date of purchase of every household item of value, and (3) taking a color video or photograph of every room in the house. The insured should also maintain an accurate record of the purchase price and the cost of all improvements made to the house. It is equally advisable to keep the inventory listing in a safety deposit box or at the office.

Record-keeping is extremely important for auto insurance. This is especially true when a claim is submitted after a car is destroyed in an accident. The adjuster bases the replacement value of a car not only on its *market value* but also on the optional equipment it carried and on how well the car was maintained. Consequently, accurate service records can add significant value to the auto insurance policy.

As in the case of homeowner's and auto insurance, accurate record-keeping helps expedite a health insurance claim. This is because the reimbursement of a health-related expense is directly dependent upon the actual cost of sickness or injury covered by the policy.

SECTION I
HEALTH INSURANCE

INTRODUCTION

Even though we live in a health-conscious society, every day millions of people are afflicted with injuries and illnesses. By 2004, the annual expenses paid for health care in the U.S. were approaching $1.8 trillion, and by 2008, these expenses are expected to exceed $2.2 trillion. According to one source, government provides health care insurance to one-third of the U.S. population in the form of Medicare, Medicaid, government worker coverage, and military coverage. Private employers provide health insurance for 43 percent of Americans. Approximately seven percent buy health insurance on their own, and almost 20 percent are uninsured. Health insurance provides protection against financial losses caused by illness, injury, and disability.

The concept of health insurance was not established until the 1930s. The first health maintenance organization (HMO) and the first Blue Cross plan were both introduced in 1929. Subsequently, in 1935, with the passage of the Social Security Act, the federal government became part of the health insurance system.

Since numerous types of injuries and illnesses can affect people, health insurance has become the most complicated form of insurance. Today, health insurance policies offered to the public come in various sizes and forms. Consequently, before selecting a health insurance company, individuals should determine what type of protection will best satisfy their personal and financial needs.

NEED FOR HEALTH INSURANCE

Individuals must consider a variety of financial and economic factors before determining whether or not they need health insurance. With rare exceptions, it is essential to buy adequate health insurance coverage, because the risk of suffering severe financial losses due to health-related incidents is always present.

In purchasing health insurance, it is important to have the following types of coverages: unlimited coverage, comprehensive coverage, reasonable deductibles, and an acceptable stop-loss provision. These items will be elaborated on the following pages.

This section was critically reviewed by Rick Laidler, C.I.C., C.L.C., Owner, Community Insurance Center, Ltd., 90 S. Washington Street, P.O. Box 20, Oxford, Mich., 48371. Tel: (248) 628-2505. However, the authors are solely responsible for the contents.

TYPES OF HEALTH INSURANCE

Hospital Insurance

Hospital insurance covers the cost incurred during a hospital stay. Examples of expenses covered are room and board charges, operating room charges, nursing services, and drugs. The majority of Americans have some sort of hospital protection, although reportedly many of them have insufficient coverage.

Hospital insurance is divided into three categories: hospitalization insurance, hospital indemnity insurance, and hospital-service-incurred plans. These plans are described next.

Hospitalization insurance is sold in two forms: expense reimbursement contracts and service contracts. The former are offered by commercial insurers that pay for hospital costs when the insured is confined to a hospital. The insurance company pays a flat daily rate up to a maximum amount and the insured pays any amounts over that amount. By comparison, under the service contracts, the reimbursement amount equals total expenses of the hospital stay less any deductible and coinsurance. Expenses covered under this protection pay for per diem hospital room fees, operating room fees, and costs of medical supplies. Frequently, restrictions are placed on hospital expenses, which include a daily maximum reimbursement, an overall per stay maximum, and a maximum number of days for which expenses are to be paid.

Hospital indemnity insurance offers a specific amount of cash payment for each day of hospitalization up to a stated maximum number of days. If the stated reimbursement does not cover the daily expenses, the policyholder must make up the difference. Of course, the policyholder can keep the excess if the reverse is true. Hospital indemnity contracts often carry limited payout clauses, which can take the form of payments to cover only the costs resulting directly from an accident.

Hospital-service-incurred plans pay the hospital directly for services provided and the policyholder makes up the shortage. Except for this difference, these plans are very similar to the hospitalization insurance plans. This type of plan provides actual hospital services to the insured for a set number of days at a rate prenegotiated with the hospital. Blue Cross plans fall under this type of arrangement. In these plans, member hospitals agree to accept scheduled fees from Blue Cross in full payment for the services rendered to the patient.

While all hospital insurance policies cover the expenses associated with hospitalization, the total coverage, deductibility, or method of payment varies, depending on the types of coverage offered by various groups. For instance, Health Maintenance Organizations (HMOs) offer medical services on a prepaid basis. In contrast, Preferred Provider Organizations (PPOs) provide complete coverage if participating providers are used, and a partial coverage when nonparticipating doctors are involved. HMOs and PPOs are explained more fully in a subsequent section.

Surgical Insurance

Surgical insurance protects people from the heavy financial burden associated with surgical procedures. One form of this coverage, known as *surgical expense insurance*, sets up a maximum amount for each procedure, and reimburses patients directly (less deductibles) for up to 50 listed operations. In addition, specific methods are used for figuring out the amount of reimbursement to be paid for procedures that are not listed. Another type of surgical insurance, called the **surgical-service-incurred plan**, directly pays the operation service providers. The reimbursement amount is calculated on the basis of the fees charged by most service providers for similar services in that geographic area.

Medical Expense Insurance

Medical expense insurance pays for doctors' services, excluding surgical charges. These plans (excluding HMOs and PPOs) usually include a maximum limit, a coinsurance clause, and a deductible. In most cases, the deductible clause is written on an item basis, which means that the insured is required to pay the charges incurred during the first few office visits, the number varying with different companies. Medical expense insurance is another coverage that may be written on a service-incurred basis.

Major Medical Expense Insurance

Major medical expense insurance provides reimbursements for all-encompassing medical treatments. In general, this type of coverage is used as a supplement to hospital, surgical, and medical expense insurance and pays only the charges not covered by the other basic forms.

Major medical insurance provides for quality medical care appropriate for individual needs, diagnosed and approved by qualified physicians. In addition, many policies provide for second surgical opinions, pre-admission testing, extended hospital care, home health care, and hospice care.

Major medical expense insurance sets a high limit, such as a $1–$2 million lifetime benefit for each covered person. Certain inherent restrictions are built into this type of policy primarily as a cost control device. For instance, a deductible amount of $100 to $2,500 applies to each covered person during each calendar year. Deductibles may be waived after three deductibles have been imposed on a family during a given calendar year.

The annual reimbursement for each covered person after the deductible is generally 70 to 80 percent of the first $5,000 of all covered expenses and 100 percent thereafter. Furthermore, certain types of covered expenses may not be subject to the above deductible. The basic concept of coinsurance is demonstrated in Figure 5-1. Clearly, without the coinsurance clause, there would be little incentive for the insured to keep the expenses under control.

Incidentally, insurance companies now offer *cancer insurance,* which is a covered medical expense under the major medical coverages of most policies. This development is an industry response to heavy medical expenses that go hand in hand with the greying of America. As people live longer, the odds are that many of them will become cancer victims and will have to pay for expensive cancer treatment. Cancer insurance pays for a significant portion of these expenses.

Comprehensive Health Insurance

Although no longer popular, a comprehensive health insurance plan combines hospital insurance, surgical insurance, medical expense insurance, and major medical expense insurance into one single package. This type of insurance coverage has deductibles ranging from $100 to $200 and coinsurance requirements of around 20 percent. This feature of cost sharing helps the insurance company in providing affordable and reasonable coverage. Comprehensive health insurance plans are usually

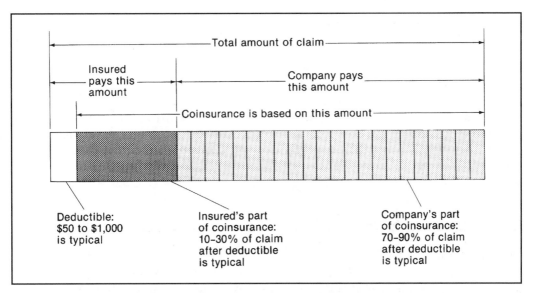

FIGURE 5-1   Summary of health insurance deductibles and coinsurance

offered on a group basis by businesses willing to offer their employees or members complete health insurance protection.

The following example articulates the cost-sharing arrangement between the insurance company and the insured. Assume the insured is offered $1,000,000 maximum coverage, $250 deductible, 80 percent insurer coinsurance, and a $5,000 stop loss limit on a $10,000 loss. In this case, the insured would be responsible for paying $1,250:

Claim	*Insurance Company Pays*	*Consumer Pays*
$ 250	- 0 -	$ 250
$ 5,000	$4,000	$1,000
$ 4,750	$4,750	- 0 -
$10,000	$8,750	$1,250

Dental Expense Insurance

Dental expense insurance makes cash payments for dental care expenses. It is similar to other health insurance policies in that it includes deductibles, coinsurance requirements, and maximum limits. In most instances, dental expense insurance, which pays for dental care, is offered by employers only on a group basis.

Eye Care Insurance

Eye care insurance provides protection from expenses connected with the purchase of prescription glasses and contact lenses. The coverage includes various eye examinations, the fitting, and the cost of lenses and frames. Eye care insurance, too, is generally offered by employers on a group basis.

Supplemental Health Insurance

Supplemental health insurance plans fill the void left by the basic insurance plans. These plans, advertised through the mail or on television, pay for surgery, hospital stay, treatment for accident, etc. regardless of the existence of other medical coverages. An example of supplemental health insurance is AFLAC, which is heavily advertised on television.

In most instances, supplemental plans are not as attractive as they first appear to be. Premiums are very high and many restrictions are imposed on the coverages they provide. Consequently, there is very little demand in the marketplace for supplemental health insurance plans.

DISABILITY INCOME INSURANCE

The Basic Need

Not all illnesses or injuries are curable or arrestable. Some may result in permanent or long-term disability. In fact, for most individuals, the chance of becoming disabled prior to retirement is greater than the chance of death. Because long-term disability can be catastrophic to the wage earner, strategies must be developed for covering the costs associated with *living death*. In fact, once disabled, the breadwinner may not be able to work again for a long time. To cope with such situations, besides medical coverage one also needs coverage for loss of income.

There is no regular medical health program that offers income during periods of loss of income. All conventional protections have limitations. Social Security has a waiting period, and only 30 percent of all disability claims filed are approved because of their restrictive definition of disability. Workers' compensation handles only work-related injuries. Company sickness or accident plans also have waiting periods. Finally, disability income riders on life insurance do not cover catastrophic illness or injury. The only safe way to be assured of adequate protection against a loss of income due to long or permanent illness is to purchase a disability income policy.

Types of Disability Insurance

There are two types of disability policies. A short-term disability policy provides for a relatively short disability benefit period, such as 13 weeks, 26 weeks, or one to two years. A long-term disability policy provides for longer disability periods, such as five years, ending at age 65, or for life. Of the two, the long term disability is the more important, but is also the one that is most often neglected.

Waiting Period

Waiting period, or elimination period, is the amount of time the insured must wait after becoming disabled before disability benefits begin. It works like a deductible in the sense that the insureds are held responsible for funding their expenses incurred during the elimination period. The following example illustrates the point:

Amount of loss	$30,000
Less: Deductible	$ 250
Expense over deductible	$29,750
Insured pays 10% of expense over deductible (up to $10,000)	$ 2,975
Insurer pays the balance	$26,775

Short-term disability insurance usually has a waiting period of zero to thirty days. Long-term disability coverage has a waiting period of one, three, or six months, but most typically three months. As a general rule, the three-month waiting period buys the best value for the premium dollars paid for that type of policy.

Definition of Disability

The definition of disability is the most important feature of a disability income policy. Most definitions of disability fall into two categories. The company will pay disability benefits only if the insured cannot perform *any job;* or the benefits will be paid if the insured is unable to perform the occupation for which he or she has been trained. The latter definition, called *own occupation*, is preferred by most consumers.

Some companies market disability policies by using a combination of both definitions. Typically, these policies provide the *own occupation* type benefits for two or three years. Any disability claims made thereafter switch to the *any job* definition.

Regardless of which definition of disability is used, it is always desirable to select the guaranteed insurability option. This option allows the insured to purchase additional amounts of disability insurance at stated intervals without the proof of insurability.

An important aspect of disability insurance relates to partial disability. Most companies pay total disability income even after the disabled person returns to work but makes less than 50 percent of normal income. If the income earned is between 50 percent and 85 percent of the previous income, however, a proportionately reduced disability income is paid by the company. Another feature of disability insurance is *residual disability* which refers to the amount of income lost by the disabled person. In this case, benefits are paid on the basis of decreased earnings.

If the policyholder pays the disability premium, it is not deductible from income tax, but the disability income is treated as a tax-free income. However, disability income is taxed as ordinary income to the disabled employee if premiums are paid by the employer.

Integration with Social Security

Some disability policies coordinate their total benefits with Social Security. Integration of a disability policy with Social Security means that the policy will pay a set benefit *minus* any payments which are received from Social Security. For instance, suppose John Kline has a disability policy which provides $3,000 in monthly benefits. John might expect to receive $4,500 per month in disability benefits if for disability his Social Security pays him $1,500 a month. This will, however, not be the case if the policy is integrated with Social Security. That is because each dollar of Social Security payments will be a direct offset to the insurer's obligation to pay. However, disability policies coordinated with Social Security could offer the best value for the money, if the insured could count on receiving Social Security benefits. Unfortunately, conditions for receiving disability payments under Social Security are so restrictive that it is advisable not to depend on these payments.

Determining the Income Need

A simplified method for determining the disability income need is presented in Table 5-2. Assume John Roe would have a monthly income of $1,300 if he becomes disabled today, whereas his monthly expenses would be $4,600. That is, he would need to have an additional monthly income of $3,300 if he were to become disabled. Since his current monthly income is $4,000, he would be able to purchase disability coverage for only $2,400. That would leave a shortfall of $900 per month in his budget, which would have to be met from other sources.

Features of a Good Policy

It is not always easy to select the best disability income policy because of the difficulties in determining how much disability income coverage is desirable, what it would cost and from whom to buy it. Before selecting this kind of insurance,

---

TABLE 5-2 Disability Insurance Need

Current Monthly Income Available

Group disability coverage	$ 500	
Individual disability coverage	$ 0	
Spouse/other family member income	$ 700	
Investment income	$ 100	
A. Total Monthly Income Available		$1,300

Monthly Expenses

Mortgage/rent	$1,750	
Insurance (life, health, home, auto, liability, etc.)	$ 635	
Car payments/other loans	$ 690	
Utilities	$ 250	
Other (education, home maintenance)	$ 475	
Savings/investments	$ 800	
B. Total Monthly Expenses		$4,600
C. Need for Additional Income Replacement due to Disability (A - B)		$3,300

Disability Coverage Available

Salaried Income	$4,000	
D. Maximum Disability Allowed: 60% ($4,000)		$2,400
Shortfall in Disability Coverage per Month (C - D)		$ 900

TABLE 5-3 Features of a Good Disability Policy

Key questions	Suggested recommendations
1. How does the policy define disability?	Select the policy that covers partial disability, not the one that specifies benefits only for total disability.
2. What job definition does the company use?	Select the company which uses the "own occupation" definition, not the "any job" definition.
3. Is the policy noncancelable and guaranteed renewable?	Choose a policy that guarantees that the policy will be renewed at the rates guaranteed in the policy up to the age specified (usually 65).
4. Does this policy cover disability resulting from both accident and illness?	Select the company that covers both forms of disability.
5. For what period of time will the policy pay?	Select the policy that covers at least through age 65.
6. How much will the policy pay?	Select the company which pays at least 60% of take-home pay at the time of accident or illness.
7. How long is the waiting period?	A three-month waiting period is preferable.
8. Does the company offer cost-of-living adjustments?	The basic benefit should rise automatically by a set percentage or in step with inflation.
9. Does the policy offer standard-of-living adjustments?	After a policy has been in force, the insured should be able to boost the monthly benefit by a certain amount at standard rates without a medical exam.

every person should at least check the vital points listed in Table 5-3 to ensure that the policy fills the gaps in the regular health insurance plan. Of these, the noncancelable and guaranteed renewable clause is one of the most important features of a disability policy.

Cost of a Disability Policy

The typical long-term disability policy provides for payment of a stated percentage of a specified monthly salary or a specified amount per month. The cost of a policy depends upon the amount of coverage, the duration of payment, and the additional riders selected. For instance, a standard *own occupation* type of disability policy for a 45-year-old male may cost $1,800 per year. This policy will (1) pay a disability income of $2,300 per month, (2) cover the insured until age 65, (3) have a five percent annual inflation adjustment factor, and (4) be noncancelable and guaranteed renewable.

Generally, disability insurance policies purchased on an individual basis are fairly expensive. By comparison, larger groups get much better terms, as revealed

TABLE 5-4   Disability Insurance for Large Groups

Number insured	Maximum benefit period		Maximum monthly benefit
	Accident	Sickness	
25–49	10 years	10 years*	$ 500
50–99	To age 65	10 years*	750
100 and over	To age 65	To age 65	1,000

* Payment stops when the insured reaches age 65.

by Table 5-4. Consequently, whenever possible, disability insurance should be purchased on a group basis.

Coordination of Benefits

Persons who are either currently employed, or have been previously employed, are entitled to a variety of health benefits. This section describes the most important features of these benefits.

Social Security Benefits. Social Security insurance includes Medicare, which provides medical insurance benefits to persons age 65 or older, or to those who are disabled for 24 months before age 65. Medicare benefits come in two major parts: Part A Hospital Insurance, and Part B Supplementary Medical Insurance. Benefits under Part A are automatic and free. Benefits under Part B are optional and must be applied for within three months before or after the 65th birthday or during the first three months of any calendar year thereafter. Most insurance companies offer packages that coordinate their benefits with Social Security benefits.

Workers' Compensation Benefits. Workers' Compensation policy covers accidental injuries and illness caused by one's employment. These programs are controlled by individual states, and funds are provided by states through employee contributions. Most states, though not all, allow full coverage of any job-related accident or illness.

DISABILITY-TO-LTC "CONVERSION" POLICIES

Some of today's individual income protection policies are designed to address a variety of incomes and life stages. They do this in a hybird design that provides income protection that can start early in the client's career, be upgraded as income rises and be converted to long-term care protection during retirement. These contracts represent a new generation of income protection insurance called "conversion" policies. These contracts evolve as people age and needs change, and they address underserved segments of the disability income market at the same time.

This conversion feature should be of particular interest to younger people who are becoming more aware of the need for LTC coverage, perhaps through witnessing parents or grandparents undergo an LTC event. They see that the need for LTC can erode life savings. As a result, they realize that, in retirement, what will matter most is preserving assets, not protecting a paycheck.

FILLING DISABILITY BENEFIT GAPS

Disability insurers usually limit benefits to 60 percent of the insured's gross income in order to give insureds a financial incentive to return to work.

Some insurers help insureds fill the gap by offering extra features that can increase insured's quality of life without putting incentive-killing cash in their bank accounts.

Some of the most common gap fillers are extra education benefits for the insured's children and benefits that keep up a claimant's retirement plan contributions.

Other companies offer dependent education benefits together with comprehensive group long-term disability insurance. Still others offer 401(k) contribution replacement benefits through annuity riders or basic policy provisions.

GROUP HEALTH INSURANCE

An Overview

Most employers offer one or more types of group health insurance plans. For an employee who is relatively young, a nonsmoker, and has no prior history of major sickness, an individual health insurance policy may be cheaper than a group policy. This is because in a group policy the risk of insuring older employees and those with a medical history is spread across the board, so the younger employees in good health have to bear the additional burden. Nevertheless, a group policy might be cheaper than an individual policy for a number of reasons. First, a company issuing a group policy significantly reduces its expenses by writing one policy covering a large number of people. Second, by spreading the risks over a large number of diverse people, it might enjoy substantial cost savings, thereby enabling it to offer cheaper rates to the group members.

Third, group coverage is usually more comprehensive. As compared to individual policies, there are fewer exclusions and limitations in group policies. Preexisting conditions, exclusions, and waiting periods are less frequent in a group policy, although there might be waiting periods for maternity coverage. Also, in group policies the insured is rarely required to take a physical or provide a detailed statement on existing physical condition. Nearly all accidents or illnesses, including heart conditions, are covered. Generally, the only eligibility requirement is that a person be an active employee when coverage begins.

Group health insurance has one major disadvantage: Leaving the place of employment automatically leads to a loss of the group coverage. However, usually the employee is able to convert the health coverage to an individual policy with the same company within 30 days, although the coverage may not be as good as the

INSIDE TOP DISABILITY POLICIES

The rates shown here for two top-quality, noncancelable policies are for a 35-year-old non-smoker, man or woman, doing professional or managerial work. There's a big difference in premiums for the basic benefit of $2,500 per month after 90 days of disability until age 65. But the policies cost about the same when the most desirable options are added.

Features	Annual Premiums	
	ABC	*XYZ*
Monthly benefits to age 65	$1,305	$1,074
Lifetime benefits	257	175
Residual benefits	0	115
"Your occupation" guaranty	61	150
$500 extra per month until Social Security disability benefits begin	100	210
Automatic cost of living increase while disabled	266	275
TOTAL PREMIUM	$1,989	$1,999

group coverage and the premium payments will most likely be higher. Generally, insurance companies point out the gaps between private and group coverage and offer recommendations most suited to the applicant's needs.

Not all group plans are alike and not all group plans are bargains. For instance, some group plans provide a major medical plan along with more basic coverage, while others do not. Also, many plans exclude maternity coverage, cover maternity costs inadequately, or provide for problem pregnancies only. Even the flat maximum payments for maternity found in group coverage sold by many commercial companies are often less than the full cost of pregnancy and childbirth. If the coverage is inadequate under a group plan, it is important to supplement that coverage to fill the gaps.

Quality is never accident; it is always the result of high intention, sincere effort, intelligent direction and skillful execution; it represents the wise choice of many alternatives.

Willa A. Foster

Important Developments

In this section we will present several new developments which have taken place in the area of group health insurance.

Cobra. Consolidated Omnibus Budget Reconciliation Act (COBRA), which was passed in 1985, made it possible for workers and their covered spouses and children to remain on a former employer's healthcare plan for a set period of time. Under this arrangement, a person pays the monthly insurance premium cost by sending funds to the former employer. The person is granted the same benefits and coverage received when employed. Generally, COBRA is available for up to 18 months. If the person is determined as disabled by Social Security, an additional 11 months of COBRA eligibility may also apply.

HIPAA. The Health Insurance Portability and Accountability Act (HIPPA), which became effective in July 1997, protects an insured person's insurability. Under this Act, if a person has been insured for the past 12 months, a new insurance company cannot refuse to cover the person and cannot impose pre-existing conditions or a waiting period before providing coverage.

Conditions are considered pre-existing only if an individual receives medical care, treatment, consultation, or prescription drugs during the six-month period immediately preceding that individual's effective date of coverage. Also, pre-existing condition waiting period cannot apply to pregnancy, newborn children, or newly adopted children. Finally, pre-existing conditions must be reduced by each month that an individual was continuously covered under creditable coverage prior to his or her date of enrollment. When individuals are no longer covered by a group plan or when they leave COBRA coverage, they are entitled to written certification of coverage by the provider.

NMHPA. The Newborns' and Mothers' Protection Act of 1996 (NMHPA) requires group health insurance plans and health insurance carriers that offer maternity benefits to allow 49-hour hospital stays after regular deliveries or 96-hour hospital stays following cesarean deliveries. The plans may not require providers to obtain pre-authorization for stays up to this amount of time. The minimum stay rules can be waived, but only by way of consultation between the provider and the mother. The rules also provide that a plan or an insurer may not offer less generous benefits for any portion of an extended hospital stay than those benefits provided during the preceding portion of the stay. Although participants remain responsible for paying deductibles, coinsurance, or other cost-sharing expenses, these expenses cannot be greater than those for any preceding portion of the hospital stay.

WHCRA. Women's Health and Cancer Rights Act of 1998 (WHCRA) applies to insured and self-insured plans and HMOs provided by private and governmental employees. For women who are eligible for mastectomy benefits under the group medical coverage and who elect breast reconstruction, the law requires that the reconstruction of the breasts and treatment for physical complications of all stages of mastectomy be covered.

SOURCES OF HEALTH INSURANCE

At a macro level, sources of health insurance can be classified into three broad categories:

Traditional or Major Medical Care. These are referred to as the *American Express* of coverage. Participants choose any doctor or hospital that accepts the card. The insurance company picks up a percentage of the costs, and the participants make up any difference in costs. This can be the most expensive plan, but it is also the most flexible.

Preferred Provider Organizations or PPOs. Participants choose any physicians from the PPO directory and they can switch to other doctors from the directory. The insured can visit any hospital involved in the plan. A standard discount on care is applied per visit. Costs can be slightly higher than an HMO.

Health Maintenance Organizations. Participants choose one primary care physician from a directory. No matter what the problem is, the insured must first see the primary care physician. Also, the participant must use referrals approved by the primary care physician. The physician is paid an annual fee per registered patient. Premiums are most economical under this type of plan, and they do not rise just because the insured gets sick or frequently uses the HMO services.

There are six types of organizations from which one may obtain health insurance. These are: Blue Cross and Blue Shield, Health Maintenance Organizations (HMOs), hybrid companies like Preferred Provider Organizations (PPOs), commercial insurance companies, Government Health Care Insurance, and self-funded employee health benefits. These sources are presented in Table 5-5.

Blue Cross and Blue Shield

Blue Cross and Blue Shield is the largest single health insurance plan existing today. In many states Blue Cross primarily offers hospitalization, whereas Blue Shield provides surgical and general medical insurance. Organized as a nonprofit corporation, Blue Cross and Blue Shield cooperates in issuing joint plans for comprehensive medical care through contracts with hospitals. These member hospitals agree to accept scheduled fees from Blue Cross as satisfactory payments for the services they render.

Health Maintenance Organizations (HMOs)

HMOs were designed to provide good quality medical care at a reasonable cost. They combine financing of health care with a delivery system to provide that care. Specifically, HMOs provide comprehensive health care in return for a prepaid prenegotiated periodic payment. In most instances, the insured individuals pay a prespecified amount per month in advance and are permitted to use the HMO for all of their medical services. In some cases, patients pay a minimal ($1–$5 per visit) fee and are also required to make small co-payments. Care is provided by a primary care physician (PCP), who is responsible for determining what care is to be provided and when the insured should be referred to specialists.

The organization of HMOs has several attractive features. Patients save time because physicians, labs, and pharmacies have been organized within a system, often under one roof. Clients choose a physician within a system, and most HMOs have evening hours with at least one doctor on 24-hour duty. The fixed-price contract overcomes the patient's reluctance to seek medical advice for minor ailments or preventive medical check-ups. HMOs also permit doctors not engaged in private

TABLE 5-5 Sources of Health Insurance*

Type	Particulars
Blue Cross/Blue Shield	Producer cooperatives that provide health care protection on a service-incurred basis. These are nonprofit organizations, providing both individual and group health coverage.
Health Maintenance Organizations (HMOs)	HMOs provide health care on a prepaid basis. A monthly fee is charged for services. There are no deductibles or coinsurance costs.
Preferred Provider Organizations (PPOs)	PPOs are a group of medical care professionals who contract with health insurance companies for providing services at a discount. Premiums are generally lower than comparable policies.
Commercial Insurance Companies	These are companies (such as Travelers and Aetna) providing health protection for half the U.S. population. They get most of their business through advertising on television and radio.
Government Health Care	This source provides health care for people at the local, state, and federal levels. Services include Social Security, disability income, Medicaid, and Medicare.

* The self-funded employee health benefit, another source of health insurance, is explained later in the chapter.

practice to spend more time with their patients because these doctors are not paid on the basis of the number of patients they treat on a daily basis.

A major disadvantage of an HMO is that, except in the case of an emergency, the insured is restricted to using doctors and hospitals associated with an HMO. In many instances, true doctor-patient relationships do not develop because the insured is not guaranteed to see the same primary care physician every time care is needed.

Preferred Provider Organizations (PPOs)

The Preferred Provider Organization (PPO) plan features a network of physicians, hospitals, and other providers of health care services who agree to provide medical care at discounted rates. In return, the employer or insurer promises to increase patient volume by encouraging insureds to seek care from the preferred provider network.

To be sure, an insured does have the complete freedom to use any provider either inside or outside the network. However, the plan encourages the use of participating providers by paying a higher level of benefits when these designated providers are used. For instance, when *non-participating* providers are used, and the basic PPO requirements are met, a calendar year deductible applies, a co-payment ratio of 20 percent is used (that is, the insured pays 20 percent of the charges), and the insured is required to obtain a pre-treatment review and certification. None of these restrictions applies when the participating provider network is used.

In the event the insured uses the participating providers in the network, the plan directly pays 100 percent of all covered charges, although the insured may be required to pay a small service fee. The PPO covers both hospitalization and outpatient care, and is reimbursed on a fee-for-service basis, so it does not have to assume any risk.

A careful blending of a PPO plan with a major medical insurance plan can provide outstanding value for the participants. In fact, many employers now provide a comprehensive health care plan using the combination just cited.

A Point-of-Service (POS) plan incorporates the features of both HMO and PPO plans. Under the PPO portion, the insured is free to choose a participating physician from among the list of network preferred providers. But under the HMO plan, the insured is required to go through a primary care physician before seeing a specialist. Under a POS plan, the penalties for using a non-network provider are greater than those imposed by a PPO plan. Consequently, cost containment is a major consideration of this type of plan.

Self-Funded Employee Health Benefits

Another important health insurance plan is known as Self-Funded Employee Health Benefits (SEHB). Traditionally, protection and cost control in health care services have meant providing conventionally insured group health care plans to employees as a part of fringe benefits. Today, under a novel alternative to group health care, the employer provides a unique plan design, claims management, and the monitoring of the utilization and provider performance.

In a partial SEHB plan, the employer assumes the degree of risk (claims) that can be anticipated. Stop loss insurance is then obtained to cover claims which exceed the actuarily predetermined level of risk. A specific stop loss provision protects the plan against an individual catastrophic claim. An aggregate stop loss provision provides coverage for claims exceeding a given amount on the entire covered group, thus limiting overall costs of claims.

In a SEHB, claim reserves are managed by the employer, which leads to greater financial control. Funds may be contributed to an employer-established account, which can be used to pay claims. Excess funds remaining in the account earn interest. In addition, cost savings are realized because (1) in most states premium tax, usually two to six percent, does not apply to self-funded claim funds, (2) the cost of self-operating the plan is generally lower, and (3) insurance carrier profits and risk charges are significantly reduced. It is little wonder that many large corporations have adopted SEHB plans.

Commercial Insurance Companies

Commercial insurance companies provide health insurance coverage for a large segment of the U.S. population. These companies, which include such household names as Travelers and Aetna, obtain most of their participants through advertisement on TV and radio. Under this arrangement, a policyholder can receive medical care from any place of his or her choice and does not have to be treated by a preassigned hospital or doctor. However, with the emergence of other types of plans, the popularity of this type of plan at best has been limited.

Government Health Care Insurance

The government health insurance plan refers to the services provided under Medicare, which is a federal health insurance program for people age 65 or older and certain disabled people. It has two parts: hospital insurance provided by Medicare, and medical insurance offered under Medicaid. In view of its importance as a provider of comprehensive medical coverage, it is appropriate to discuss Medicare in some detail.

At the heart of Medicare is the *allowable charge.* Under the program, Medicare scrutinizes each bill to determine the allowable portion of the total cost of the service. For hospital services, Medicare pays the entire bill less a deductible. For most physicians' services, it pays 80 percent of an allowable charge, while the beneficiaries pay the remaining 20 percent and any excess of each bill plus any physician's fee. The 20 percent of the allowable charge to be paid by the beneficiaries is called *coinsurance.* Beneficiaries must also pay deductibles, which are subtracted from the allowable charge before Medicare determines its 80 percent payment.

The particular deductibles, coinsurance, and excess charges depend on the type of service covered under Medicare. Part A covers care in hospitals as an inpatient, skilled nursing facilities, hospice care, and some home health care. Part B covers doctors' services, outpatient hospital care, and some services not covered by Part A.

Types of coverages under Medicare, and the gaps in these coverages, are summarized in Table 5-6. As a general rule, medical hospital insurance pays for five kinds of care: (1) Inpatient hospital care; (2) medically necessary inpatient care in a skilled nursing facility after a hospital stay; (3) private duty nursing care; and (4) hospice (doctor and medical services) care and 5) blood after patient pays for 1st three pints. Medicare covers all necessary hospitalization, except deductibles. It also covers up to 100 days (except deductible) in a skilled nursing facility and 100 percent of approved medical services. In addition, it covers (not shown in Table 5-6) 80% of doctor bills after a $100 deductible and for prescriptions it pays 75% of up to $1,500 after a $250 deductible. It is important to note that Medicare does not cover the biggest catastrophic cost of all—long-term nursing home care which averages about $57,000 a year. Nor does it cover the following: (1) private-duty nursing; (2) skilled nursing care beyond 100 days; (3) treatment outside the U.S.; (4) most dental work; (5) most immunizations; (6) cosmetic surgery except after an accident; (7) routine foot care; (8) eye and hearing exams; and (9) prescription glasses and hearing aids.

Medicare's hospital benefits (Part A) are financed solely out of Social Security payroll taxes. The Medicare portion of Social Security taxes flows into a separate trust fund which is used to pay the hospital costs. Medicare's medical benefits (Part B) are financed from general tax revenues and by the beneficiaries themselves. Part B coverage is optional. Those who wish to buy this coverage pay a monthly premium of $66.60 (2004), which is scheduled to rise every year.

Gaps in Medicare

Medicare does not cover all medical costs. The significant gaps in Medicare's coverage include the items discussed next.

Part A: Hospital services. During the first 60 days in the hospital, a patient must pay a $876 deductible. For a hospital stay of 61 to 90 days, the patient pays a daily coinsurance charge of $219. If the patient uses his or her 60 "reserve days" (91st to 150th day), the daily coinsurance charge jumps to $438. For stays beyond 150 days in the hospital, the patient pays for all costs. The 60 reserve days are a once-in-a-lifetime item; when they are used up, the patient pays all costs of any subsequent stays beyond 90 days.

Part A hospital coverage is based on a *benefit period*. This period begins on the first day the patient receives inpatient services in a hospital and ends once the patient has been out of the hospital or skilled nursing facility for 60 days in a row. Thus, a person could have more than one benefit period during the year, and pay more than one deductible or series of coinsurance payments in one year. The exception is the once-in-a-lifetime 60 reserve days.

TABLE 5-6   Medicare—and the Gaps

Service	Medicare pays	You owe
Hospital insurance	Everything except deductible	$876 deductible for days 1-60 $219/day for days 61-90 $438/day for days 91-150 All cost beyond 150 days
Skilled nursing facility care	Post-hospital care in skilled nursing facility	$0 for days 1-20 $109.50 for days 21-100 100% of all costs thereafter
Home health care	Full cost of medically necessary home health visits by a Medicare approved home health agency	Nothing
Custodial nursing care	Nothing	All costs
Hospice care	Covers all costs for individuals with a life expectancy of six months or less. Benefits are provided for up to two 90-day periods, plus an unlimited number of 60 day periods	Copayment of $5 for outpatient prescription drugs and 5% of Medicare-approved amount for inpatient respite care
Blood deductible	All but first three pints under Part A; 80% of approved amount after $100 deductible under Part B	Under Part A; first three pints (unless replaced); under Part B: approved amount (after $100 deductible)
Medical services	80% of approved charges after $100 deductible including doctor services, inpatient & outpatient medical and surgical services and supplies, physical & speech therapy, diagnostic tests durable medical equipment and other services	20% of approved charges, plus $100 deductible

Note: Each individual has a once-in-a-lifetime reserve for 60 days for inpatient hospital care. The insured is responsible for the first $35 a day. The insurer pays all costs over and above that amount.

2004 MEDICARE PART A

Part A is Hospital Insurance and covers costs associated with confinement in a hospital or skilled nursing facility.

When you are hospitalized for:	*Medicare pays*	*You owe*
1-60 days	Most confinement costs *after* the required Medicare Deductible.	$876 deductible
61-90 days	All eligible expenses, *after* the patient pays a per-day copayment.	$219 a day copayment as much as: $6,570
91-150 days	All eligible expenses, *after* patient pays a per-day copayment. (These are Lifetime Reserve Days which may never be used again.)	$438 a day copayment as much as: $26,280
151 days or more	Nothing	You pay all costs
Skilled Nursing Confinement: When you are hospitalized for at least 3 days and enter a Medicare approved skilled nursing facility within 30 days after hospital discharge and are receiving skilled nursing care.	All eligible expenses for the first 20 days; then all eligible expenses for days 21-100, *after* patient pays a per-day copayment.	After 20 days $109.50 a day copayment as much as: $8,760

2004 MEDICARE PART B

Part B is Medical Insurance and covers physician services, outpatient care, tests and supplies.

On expenses incurred for:	Medicare pays	You owe $100 annual deductible plus
Medical Expenses Physician's services, inpatient, outpatient medical/surgical services, physical/speech therapy, diagnostic tests	80% of approved amount after $100 deductible/year Reduced to 50% for most outpatient mental health services	20% of approved amount and limited charges above approved amount
Clinical Laboratory Services Blood tests, urinalysis and more	Generally 100% of approved amount	Nothing for services
Home Health Care Part-time or intermittent skilled care, home health aide services, durable medical supplies and other services	100% of approved amount; 80% of approved amount for durable medical euipment	Nothing for services; 20% of approved amount for durable medical equipment
Outpatient Hospital Treatment Services for the diagnosis or treatment of an illness or injury	Medicare payment to hospital based on hospital costs	20% of billed amount
Blood	After first 3 pints of blood, 80% of approved amount	First 3 pints plus 20% of approved amount for additional pints

On all Medicare-covered expenses, a doctor or other health care provider may decline Medicare "assignment." This means the patient will be required to pay the entire charge at the time of service.

Source: All about Medicare, P.O. Box 14367, Cincinatti, Ohio 45250-0367.

Part A: Skilled nursing facility services. Under Part A's Skilled Nursing Facility Services coverage, Medicare pays for the first 20 days of skilled nursing-home care. For days 21 to 100, the patient pays $109.50 a day, and beyond 100 days, the patient pays all costs. As with Part A hospital coverage, skilled nursing facility services are based on a benefit period.

For Medicare to pay for nursing home care, the following strict requirements must be met: the stay must be in a facility approved by Medicare, the patient's doctor must indicate that skilled care is needed on a daily basis, the patient must have been in a hospital for three days prior to the nursing home stay, not counting the day of discharge, and the patient must have been admitted to the facility within 30 days after the discharge from the hospital for the same condition for which the patient was hospitalized.

Part B: Medical services. For Part B services, the patient pays a $100 annual deductible, 20 percent coinsurance on approved charges, 100 percent of nonapproved charges, and 100 percent of costs of prescription drugs and biologicals (vaccines) that can be self- administered (with a few exceptions).

One potentially costly area can be doctor's charges not approved by Medicare. Many physicians accept Medicare assignment; that is, they agree to accept the approved fee determined by Medicare. But many nonparticipating physicians do not accept the *assignment*, and the patient must pay the excess charges. However, there are limits on the fees charged by nonparticipating physicians. The general limit is 115 percent of the assignment rate, although this can still be a significant out-of-pocket expense for many people. A person would be well-advised to use a doctor who accepts Medicare assignment.

RECENT IMPROVEMENTS IN MEDICARE

In 2003 President Bush Signs the Medicare Prescription Drug, Improvement, and Modernization Act of 2003, accomplishing four important goals for our health care system.

The following are excerpts from comments made by President Bush:

1. Prescription drug benefits under Medicare.

    Drug coverage under Medicare will allow seniors to replace more expensive surgeries and hospitalizations with less expensive prescription medicine. Even more important, drug coverage under Medicare will save our seniors from a lot of worry. Some older Americans spend much of their Social Security checks just on their medications. Some cut down on the dosage to make a bottle of pills last longer. Elderly Americans should not have to live with those kinds of fears and hard choices. This new law will ease the burden on seniors and give them the extra help they need.
2. More health care choices so older Americans can find the health coverage that best meets their needs.

    Every senior needs to know: If you don't want to change your current coverage, you don't have to change. You're the one in charge. If you want to keep your Medicare the way it is, along with the new prescription benefit, that is your right. If you want to improve benefits – maybe dental coverage, or eyeglass coverage, or managed care plans that reduce out-of-pocket costs — you'll be free to make those choices as well. And when seniors have the ability to make choices, health care plans within Medicare will have to compete for their business by offering higher quality service. For the seniors of America, more choices and more control will mean better health care.

3. More efficient Medicare, by providing screenings that will enable doctors and patients to diagnose and treat health problems early.

For years, our seniors have been denied Medicare coverage ... for a basic physical exam. Beginning in 2005, all newly-enrolled Medicare beneficiaries will be covered for a complete physical. The Medicare system will now help seniors and their doctors diagnose health problems early, so they can treat them early and our seniors can have a better quality of life. For example, starting in 2004, everyone on Medicare will be covered for blood tests that can diagnose heart diseases. Those at high risk for diabetes will be covered for blood sugar screening tests. Modern health care is not complete without prevention — so we are expanding preventative services under Medicare.

4. Opportunity to pay for out-of-pocket health care expenses through new Health Savings Accounts.

Our laws encourage people to plan for retirement and save for education. Now the law will make it easier for Americans to save for their future health care as well. A Health Savings Account is a good deal, and all Americans should consider it. Every year, the money not spent would stay in the account and gain interest tax-free, just like an IRA. And people will have an incentive to live more healthy lifestyles because they want to see their Health Savings Account grow.

MEDICARE ACT CREATES HEALTH SAVINGS ACCOUNTS

President George W. Bush signed the highly-debated Medicare Prescription Drug, Improvement, and Modernization Act of 2003 (Medicare Act). Overshadowed by the changes to Medicare is the fact that the Medicare Act also provides for new Health Savings Accounts (HSAs) for virtually anyone with a *high deductible* health insurance plan. The new HSAs are very similar to the Archer Medical Savings Accounts (Archer MSAs); but they come without the latter's restrictions or limits on participation. HSAs may be funded by tax-deductible contributions from either employees or employers, including by cafeteria plans. Distributions from HSAs to reimburse participants for medical care expenses are tax-free. Undistributed balances may be carried forward from year to year.

The Medicare Act creates a new Section 223 of the Internal Revenue Code providing for HSAs. Under Section 223, any *eligible individual* with a *high deductible health plan* can contribute to an HSA. A high deductible health plan is one with a deductible of not less than $1,000 for individual coverage or $2,000 for family coverage. This plan cannot require total annual out-of-pocket expenses, including the deductible, of over $5,000 for individual coverage or $10,000 for family coverage.

With a high deductible health plan in place, an eligible individual can contribute and deduct from income the amount of his or her deductible to an HSA, not exceeding $2,250 for individual coverage or $4,500 for family coverage. The deduction limitation actually applies on a monthly basis, so an individual with a high deductible health plan for less than an entire calendar year may only deduct 1/12th of the above amounts for each month of coverage. An individual who turns 55 before the end of the calendar year may also deduct an additional contribution of $500 for 2004. The maximum additional contribution increases by $100 every year until it reaches $1,000 in 2009.

Distributions from an HSA are excluded from income to the extent that they are for *qualified medical expenses*, as defined in IRC Section 213(d). The reference to IRC Section 213(d) implies the same broader definition of qualified medical expenses that the IRS recently approved for Health flexible spending accounts, including the cost of over-the-counter drugs. With certain exceptions, qualified medical expenses do not include payments for health insurance coverage, so the HSA could not be used to pay the premium for the high deductible health plan. The exceptions apply to the payment of premiums for the following coverages:

- COBRA continuation coverage

- a qualified long-term care insurance contract

- any health plan maintained while the individual is receiving unemployment compensation

- for those eligible for Medicare, any health plan other than a Medicare supplemental policy.

As mentioned, HSAs permit contributions by eligible individuals, their employers, or both, including contributions made through pre-tax salary reductions under cafeteria plans. The Medicare Act amends Section 125 of the Internal Revenue Code to add HSAs as a qualified benefit under cafeteria plans. Interestingly, this amendment permits long-term care insurance premiums to be paid through an HAS funded through a cafeteria plan, even though long-term care insurance is expressly excluded as a qualified benefit under Section 125.

HSAs under new Section 223 are very similar to the existing Archer MSAs plans under Section 220, but the former are not limited to self-employed individuals or small employers. Because Archer MSAs and HSAs serve the same function, allowable contributions to HSAs are reduced by any contributions to an Archer MSA in the same year. An existing Archer MSA balance can also be rolled over to an HAS.[1]

---

[1] *This article was produced by John H. Fenton.*

MEDICARE PRESCRIPTION DRUG IMPROVEMENT & MODERNIZATION ACT OF 2003

(H.R. 1 CONFERENCE REPORT) ACHP SUMMARY

Prescription Drug Benefit. Beginning in 2006, beneficiaries may voluntarily enroll in a prescription drug plan (PDP) as a supplement to traditional fee-for-service (FSS) Medicare that offers the following prescription drug benefit (with special subsidies for low-income beneficiaries): a $250 deductible; 75 percent coverage up to $2,250 of drug costs; and 95 percent (catastrophic) coverage exceeding $5,100 of drug costs. Private health plans must offer at least one health plan in a service area that provides the prescription drug benefit. Retiree health plans that provide a prescription drug benefit will receive a 28 percent subsidy on drug costs between $250 and $5,000, excludable from taxation. Prior to 2006, beneficiaries may purchase a Medicare-endorsed drug discount card.

Institute of Medicine Study on Performance Measures. Eighteen months after enactment, the Institute of Medicine must report to Congress on a study, done in consultation with the Medicare Payment Advisory Commission (MedPAC), of performance measures used in the public and private sectors and policy options in Medicare that would align payment with performance.

AHRQ Study on Clinical Effectiveness and Health Outcomes. In 2004, $50 million was appropriated to the Agency for Healthcare Research and Quality (AHRQ) for conducting research to address the scientific evidence and information needs of the Medicare, Medicaid, and State Children Health Insurance Programs. The research will relate to the outcomes, comparative clinical effectiveness, and appropriateness of health care services, including prescription drugs. It will also relate to strategies for improving the ways in which health care services are organized, managed, and delivered.

Quality Improvement. Effective Jan. 1, 2006, all private health plans must have a chronic care improvement program as part of an ongoing quality improvement program. Private health plans must adhere to current quality reporting requirements, with new regional PPOs requirements not exceeding current reporting requirements for local PPOs. Private accrediting organizations may continue to use health plans in compliance with certain Medicare regulations, including quality improvement.

Medicare Cost Contracts. Health plans reimbursed on the basis of reasonable cost may continue to serve Medicare beneficiaries indefinitely, but after 2008 they will be permitted to operate only in areas that are not served by two local health plans or two regional health plans.

Medicare Advantage Plans. In 2004, Medicare+Choice payment rates will include a fourth option of 100 percent of FFS county rates, including costs for those beneficiaries who received care in military facilities, and thereafter updated by the growth rate in FFS Medicare. Beginning in 2006, new regional PPOs may serve beneficiaries within certain geographic regions established after a market study.

In 2006 and 2007, no new local PPOs may be established. In 2006, payment rates will be adjusted for demographic factors and health status (full risk-adjustment).

Starting in 2006, private health plans will be paid according to how their bid compared to a benchmark. Plans that bid below the benchmark will be paid their bids, plus 75 percent of the difference, which must be returned to beneficiaries as additional benefits or reduced premiums. Plans that bid above the benchmark will be paid the benchmark, and the beneficiary will pay the difference as a premium. For local plans, the benchmark will be the highest of the four payment rates. For regional PPOs, the benchmark will blend the weighted average of local plan benchmarks and the weighted average of plan bids, each adjusted to reflect market share.

Medicare Supplement Policies

Through the Omnibus Budget Reconciliation Act of 1990 (OBRA '90), Congress ordered the National Association of Insurance Commissioners (NAIC) to standardize Medigap policies to make it easier for consumers to select a policy. In July 1991, the NAIC came out with the "Medicare Supplement Insurance Minimum Standards Model Act" and the "Model Regulations to Implement the NAIC Medicare Supplement Insurance Minimum Standards Model Act." The purpose of these regulations was to provide "for the reasonable standardization of terms and benefits of Medicare supplement policies."

Medicare Supplement policies are specifically designed to fill the gap in expenses not covered under Medicare Parts A and B. Because of abuses related to sales practices and policy benefits, the NAIC created a model (which many states adopted) to establish uniform provisions consisting of basic *care* benefits of optional benefit packages that could be added to the core benefits. States that do not adhere to the NAIC model must follow federal standards created as part of OBRA.

There are several types of medigap policies that can be sold. All insurance companies must offer the same benefits in all the plans. However, the insured needs to shop around, because premiums may vary from one policy to another.

Plan A, which offers the most basic core benefits, must include the following five coverages:

1. Reimbursement for insured's share of hospital charges (coinsurance) under Medicare Part A for days 61–90+ the lifetime 60-day reserve.
2. Coverage for all charges for additional days in a hospital, up to 365 days.
3. Reimbursement for the first three pints of blood for hospital insurance.
4. Reimbursement for the first three pints of blood for medical insurance.
5. Reimbursement for 20 percent coinsurance charge the insured required to pay under Part B.

Details of medical supplement policies are presented in Table 5-7.

Long-Term Health Care

An Overview. As the U.S. population ages, many of us potentially face another major expense in addition to the escalating cost of medical care: Long-term custodial and nursing home care for ourselves, our spouses, and elderly members of our family. Even more important, today long-term care refers to not only skilled nursing care, but also rehabilitative services, adult day care, home care, and housing options such as assisted living.

The projections for the growing needs for long-term care (LTC) are indeed sobering: (1) As many as half of all Americans now in their fifties will need such care during their lifetime. (2) By 2030, when the baby boomers reach 65, long-term care costs could potentially wreck the financial lives of some 77 million members of this group. (3) The U.S. Bureau of the Census estimates that by 2060, as many as 24 million people will need long-term care services. These statistics should be supplemented by the following grim facts: Approximately 11 percent of people between the ages of 65 and 74 and still living at home have some sort of long-term care need; this rises to 22 percent for those between the ages of 75 to 84, and to 49 percent for community-based residents age 85 and older. It is easy to see why LTC coverage should be treated as an integral part of overall planning, especially because LTC is an insurable, high-probability and potentially high-cost risk.

Cost of Care. LTC comes with a big price tag. Projections estimate that spending for long-term care in the U.S. will reach $207 billion in 2020 and $346 billion in 2040. Costs paid directly by individuals for nursing-home care are estimated to reach $158 billion by 2030. According to the U.S. Bureau of the Census, the average cost of a year in a nursing home is $57,000—an amount that could double or triple by the time many baby boomers reach age 65, while the median amount of assets earmarked for retirement by baby boomers is $30,000. The average male can expect to spend almost $57,000 on long-term care, while the average female should expect a LTC bill of almost $125,000.

TABLE 5-7 Medicare Supplement Policies

Benefits Included	Plan
Core benefits	yes
Skilled nursing facility coinsurance (days 21-100)	yes
Part A deductible	optional (additional premium required)
Part B deductible	optional (additional premium required)
Part B excess charges	optional (additional premium required)
Foreign travel emergency	optional (additional premium required)
At-home recovery	40 visits in addition to Medicare
Prescription drugs (within dollar limit)	yes
Preventive medical care	no

The spirit, the will to win, and the will to excel are the things that endure. These qualities are so much more important than the events that occur.

Vince Lombardi

MEDICARE AT 65 — COVERAGE

- Part A: Hospital Insurance
  - Inpatient Care
  - Followup home care
  - No monthly premium
  - 1997 deductible: $760 per stay
- Part B: Medical Insurance
  - Physician's and outpatient services
  - 1997 monthly premium: $43.80
  - 1997 annual deductible: $100 per person, then Medicare pays 80% of allowable

"MEDIGAPS"

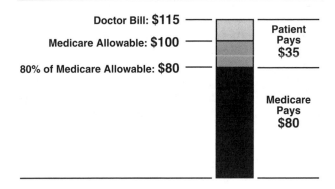

Doctor Bill: **$115**

Medicare Allowable: **$100**

80% of Medicare Allowable: **$80**

Patient Pays $35

Medicare Pays $80

FILLING THE MEDIGAP

- Self-pay
- Suplemental insurance
- Managed Care
  (HMO or equivalent)
- LTC Insurance
  (Long Term Care)
- Medicaid or QMB coverage
  (for low-income)

Who Should Buy LTC? Medicare provides for up to 100 days of care each calendar year in Medicare-certified skilled nursing facilities, and only if admission follows a hospital stay. However, severe restrictions are imposed on the Medicare recipients. For one thing, in order to qualify, people must spend down most of their assets. For another, Medicare pays the full cost only for the first 20 days, after which the individual and Medicare share coverage for up to 100 days. Supplemental Medicap plans, which can be purchased from private insurers, pay a portion of the medical expenses not covered by Medicare. However, a basic Medigap policy excludes long-term custodial and nursing home care.

For these reasons, the United Seniors Health Council, a non-profit group, recommends that people buying LTC insurance meet a minimum threshold: at least $75,000 in assets in addition to a home, plus a yearly income of $25,000 for singles and $35,000 for couples. The reason is that if a person cannot afford the premium with ease, then because of financial pressures, eventually the LTC policy would be dropped.

The Timing Issue. In the case of a LTC policy, sooner the better advice does not always apply. In fact, most professionals advise buying such a policy around age 60. This is because at earlier ages (say, age 40) it is difficult to forecast how much coverage a person would need and what the facilities would be. Likewise, waiting for too long (say, age beyond 65) could become very expensive.

Size of Coverage. Because LTC policies are so complicated, it is important to consult with either a financial planner or an insurance agent specializing in LTC policies. However, some professionals use a standard approach to estimating the amount of LTC needed to protect an individual or a couple. For instance, by one estimate, a person would spend $486,000 in a LTC facility, if the following assumptions are made: current monthly cost of care: $4,500; inflation factor: three percent; typical length of care: three years.

Private Long-Term Care Coverage

Because of the long-term care coverage limitations presented above, it is desirable for individuals to purchase private long-term care coverage for themselves, their spouses, and their parents. A long- term care insurance policy should be reviewed in light of the features discussed below.

Guaranteed Renewability. The policy should be guaranteed renewable for life. Except for nonpayment of premiums, this feature prevents the insurer from canceling the policy.

Deductible Period. The deductible or elimination period provides that a specified length of time must lapse before the insurer begins to make payments. This period varies from 21 to 365 days, depending on the policy. Generally, a 90-day waiting period offers the best value for the premium dollars paid.

Custodial Care Coverage. The policy should provide coverage not only for skilled and intermediate care but also for custodial care which does not require the engagement of licensed medical professionals.

Home Care. Long-term care in the individual's home, instead of in a residential or nursing facility, can be an attractive provision. Most policies offer this coverage only as a rider for an extra charge, or as a percentage of the normal coverage.

Pre-hospitalization. Some policies pay benefits only if the individual has been in a hospital before receiving long- term care. However, since many individuals do not go to long-term care facilities directly from the hospital, this requirement can result in a denial of benefits at a crucial time. Therefore, a good policy should not require the insured to be hospitalized before entering a nursing home care.

Alzheimer's Coverage. A good policy provides long-term care coverage for the Alzheimer's disease. This disease is generally described in policy language as *organically based mental conditions*. If such language is not specifically included in the policy, probably Alzheimer's coverage is not provided.

Inflation Protection. This feature provides for the anticipated rise in the cost of long-term care. However, a rider to offset inflationary increases can cause the premium to increase by as much as one-third. Still, a compound inflation, rather than a simple inflation, protection is recommended.

Other policy features may include:

- Clauses limiting coverage based on pre-existing conditions or medical history
- Waiver of premiums in the event of disability
- Premiums that remain level for life
- A maximum benefit period for one stay of at least four years
- A daily nursing home benefit of about $125
- A grace period, giving the policyholder some protection against overlooking payment of a premium.

In passing, it should be mentioned that today it is possible to buy only home health care, assisted living, or nursing home care, or a combination of all of them.

THE IDEAL HEALTH INSURANCE COMPANY

There is no magic formula by which one can identify the best and the least expensive health insurance company. Often big, financially strong, companies offer attractive premiums, good policies, and excellent service. But some of the small companies also meet these same criteria, so it is not possible to select a good company merely on the basis of size.

In selecting an insurance company it is best to avoid those companies that have a poor financial record and have a history of fighting their customers' claims. Also, one should not buy insurance from a company that would not be able to withstand higher than expected losses or would consistently generate lower than anticipated investment income. So one should select a company that is financially strong, offers liberal benefits, and charges reasonable premiums. Also, it should be fair, efficient, and courteous in handling its claims.

An indication of the financial strength of insurance companies is the rating they receive in *Best's Insurance Report*, the leading authority on the subject. A high rating from *Best's* may mean that the company is less likely to become bankrupt. One should try to avoid companies that do not receive either the *most substantial* (A+) or the *very substantial* (A) rating from *Best's*. These ratings are available in most public libraries.

To conclude, in making the final selection of a health insurance company, it is desirable to obtain an affirmative answer to each of the following questions:

1. Is the company's loss ratio high? The loss ratio is the percentage of premiums that a company pays back in benefits to its policyholders. A loss ratio of over 50 percent is desirable.
2. Does the company receive one of the two highest ratings for financial stability from *Best's Insurance Report?*
3. Does the company offer efficient, fair, and courteous claim service?
4. Is the company prevented from canceling a policy?
5. Does the company have a policy of not raising premiums based on claims?

THE IDEAL HEALTH INSURANCE PLAN

The ritual of picking an *ideal* health insurance plan is challenging for a number of reasons. First, the employer may offer several plans like HMO, PPO, Blue Cross, or some variant of these plans. Second, each plan has some advantages and drawbacks, and it is difficult to sort them out before making a rational decision. Third, if a family member suffers from a chronic illness, it might be necessary to select the plan that is best suited to handle that illness. The following section presents a five-step process which might be followed for selecting the best plan, notwithstanding the various problems cited above.

Step 1. Select the appropriate plan. The first order of business is to select from the employer's list the type of plan that suits the family. These plans include major medical care, preferred provider organizations (PPOs), health maintenance organizations (HMOs), Blue Cross and Blue Shield, or any other plan offered by the employer. On the basis of the earlier discussion of each plan, it should be possible to identify the type of plan preferred by the family.

Step 2. Analyze the coverage. The coverage offered by the plan should be checked against the medical needs of the family to ensure that the coverage required by the family is being offered by the plan. In this context, each plan's annual and lifetime caps should be carefully checked. Also, restrictive caps on mental-health care should be noted. Other restrictions, such as limits on outpatient visits for the year, should also be examined.

Step 3. Examine the costs. Total costs vary—sometimes considerably—between different types of plans. These costs include not only the premium costs but also additional costs which are passed on to the participants by the employers by means of co-pay, deductibles, drug coverage, and other expenses. It is best to choose a plan which is reasonably priced but also offers the services most desired.

Step 4. Check quality of plans. The National Committee for Quality Assurance, a nonprofit agency, issues report cards on insurers based on access to care, quality of service, preventive programs and so on. The quality of a plan can be checked by logging on to www.ncqa.org.

Step 5. Convenience factor. Finally, it is important to check the location and easy accessibility of the medical facility which the family members would be required to visit to get the medical care. In addition, if the HMO or the PPO requires the use of a specific hospital, then the quality and location of that hospital should also be checked.

To recapitulate, a time-tested approach is to select a good health insurance company which has been stable in the health care market for a long time. Once such a company is selected, the limitations and exclusions in its policy should be carefully analyzed vis-a-vis the cost of buying the policy. If the company also passes the five selected criteria just presented, it would be a prime candidate for ultimate selection.

A PLANNING STRATEGY

Self-Analysis

For financial planning purposes, the best strategy is to make sure that the family has adequate coverage for medical and hospital expenses, for loss of income caused by disability, and for long-term care. Even more important, young families should buy adequate medical and disability coverage even if it means a sacrifice of the life insurance coverage. This is because to a young family, a long-term disability is likely to be more devastating than death. A convenient worksheet is provided in Table 5-8 which can be used to determine if individual levels of coverage match the desired levels of coverage.

SECTION II
THE HOMEOWNER'S POLICY

INTRODUCTION

A homeowner or renter is exposed to many types of risk. Damages may occur to the property and its structures due to fire or storm. Losses may be generated by injuries suffered on or off the premises. Personal property may also be lost because of theft or fire.

The main elements of a homeowner's policy are coverage: (1) on the house, (2) for personal property, (3) against the homeowner's liability, and (4) for medical payments for bodily injury or property damage caused to other people or property. The standard homeowner's (HO) policy is a *package deal* containing all four types of coverage. The standard renter's or condominium policy offers only the last two types of coverage. The first two elements are covered under Section I of the HO

This section, and the one that follows, were critically reviewed by Sam Palise, State Farm Insurance Company. However, the authors are fully responsible for the contents.

TABLE 5-8 Health Insurance Worksheet

	Current coverage	*Desirable coverage*
Hospital Expense:		
Amount per day	————	100% of semi-private room
Maximum number of days	————	365 days; thereafter 80%
Additional expenses	————	Reasonable
Diagnostic X-ray and lab work	————	
Deductible	————	
Surgical Expense		
Highest surgical fee	————	100%
Regular Medical		
Dollars per day	————	100%
Number of days	————	30 days
Major Medical Coverage		
Major medical (deductible)	————	$300 per illness
Maximum	————	$1 million lifetime per family
Coinsurance Percentage	————	80% up to breakpoint, after which insurer pays 100%
Disability Income Benefit:		
Short-term disability	————	60% of earned income
Long-term disability	————	60% of earned income
Disability Benefit Period:		
Short-term disability	————	1 year
Long-term disability	————	Until age 65
Waiting Period		
Short-term disability	————	7 days, unless company provides sick pay for a week
Long-term disability	————	90 days
Disability Policy Definition	————	Own occ.
Key features		
Non-cancellable	————	(Yes/No)
Guaranteed renewable	————	(Yes/No)

policy, while Section II of the policy covers the remaining elements. The coverage under Section II is identical under all forms, whereas forms differ under Section I. A health insurance worksheet is presented in Table 5-8.

THE POLICY FORMS

As revealed by Table 5-9, the package policy, known as the homeowner's policy, comes in two forms: broad and special. The *broad* form is the least expensive. It covers the homeowner against personal liability and damage or loss due to the most common risks. This form includes the perils from its predecessor dwelling policy of fire and lightning, plus risks covered by the acronym WHARVES (windstorm, hail, aircraft, riot or civil commotion, vehicles, explosion and smoke, which were originally part of a policy known as the *basic* policy). In addition, it includes falling objects, weight of ice, snow or sleet, accidental discharge or overflow of water and steam, air conditioning systems and appliances, damage from artificially generated electricity and volcanic eruption. The *special* form, which can be expensive, includes all perils except those that are specifically excluded, such as damage due to earthquake or flood.

TABLE 5-9   Forms of Homeowner's Policies

	Broad Form	Special Form
COVERAGE FOR:		
Dwelling	Yes	Yes
Replacement cost of dwelling	Yes	Yes
Related private structures	Yes*	Yes*
Personal property on premises	Yes	Yes
Personal property away from premises	Yes	Yes
Improvements made by tenant	Yes	Yes
Lawns, plants, shrubs, trees	Yes–limited perils	Yes–limited perils
Rental value	Yes–either rental value or additional living expense*	Yes–either rental value or additional living expense*
Additional living expense	Yes–either rental value or additional living expense*	Yes–either rental value or additional living expense*
Contents removed to new principal residence	30 days coverage at both locations	30 days coverage at both locations
Jewelry and furs	Yes	Yes
PERILS COVERED:		
Fire and lightning	Yes	Yes
Windstorm	Yes	Yes
Outside antenna windstorm damage	Only by endorsement	Only by endorsement
Hail	Yes	Yes
Riot and civil commotion	Yes	Yes
Explosion other than steam boiler	Yes	Yes
Explosion of steam boiler	Yes	Yes

TABLE 5-9   *(continued)*

	Broad Form	Special Form
Bursting of steam or hot water appliances and heating systems	Yes	Yes
Smoke—sudden and accidental damage:		
From industrial operations	No	Contents only
From fireplaces	No	Yes
From heating or cooking unit	Yes	Yes
Aircraft	Yes	Yes
Sonic boom	Yes	Yes
Vehicle damage by other than occupant of property to:		
Building	Yes	Yes
Personal property	Yes	Yes
Fences	Yes	Yes
Driveways	Yes	Yes
Walks	Yes	Yes
Lawns	Yes	Yes
Trees, shrubs, and plants	Yes	Yes
Vehicle damage to house or garage by dwelling occupant	Yes	Yes
Vandalism and malicious mischief	Yes	Yes
Water:		
Surface water or flood	No	No
Backing up of sewers or drains	No	No
Leakage from plumbing or heating systems	Yes	Yes
Rain through doors, windows, bad roof	No	Yes—building only
Freezing of plumbing, heating systems	Yes	Yes

TABLE 5-9   *(continued)*

	Broad Form	*Special Form*
Falling objects (from outside)	Yes	Yes
Weight of ice, snow, sleet	Yes	Yes
Collapse of building	Yes	Yes
Landslide	No	No
Earthquake	No, except by endorsement	No, except by endorsement
Residence glass breakage	Yes	Yes
Sudden and accidental damage from artificially generated electrical current	Yes	Yes
Burglary damage	Yes	Yes–including theft of part of completed and occupied structure
Unspecified perils	No	Yes ("all risk" coverage)

* This is an additional amount of insurance.
** Extended Coverage perils and Vandalism and Malicious Mischief are optional under DP-1.
Source: Compiled from homeowner's policies of various insurance companies.

There are five types of homeowner's policies: HO-2, the broad form; HO-3, the special form; HO-4, the contents broad form; HO-6, coverage for condominium owners; and HO-8, for older homes. HO-2, HO-3, and HO-8 are for people who own their homes; HO-4 is for people renting homes or apartments; and HO-6 is for condominium owners. The salient features of several of these forms are presented in Table 5-10.

The key elements of the five different types of policies just mentioned are as follows. In most forms of homeowner's policies the insured is entitled to compensation for a loss caused by a specifically named peril. HO-3 provides all-risk coverage for the dwelling but not the contents or personal property. However, if one desires to purchase an *all-risk* policy covering all losses except those that are specifically excluded, then the HO-5 policy should be purchased.

In order to get full coverage, the insured cannot buy less than the amounts of minimally specified insurance. If the coverage for a particular category of claims is calculated as a percentage of the insurance on the house, usually that coverage can be increased for an additional premium without raising the amount for the house. In the event the home is damaged by fire or other disaster and the owner has to rent living quarters while it is being repaired, the company covers the living expenses.

TABLE 5-10   Homeowner Coverages

Coverage	HO-2 (broad form)	HO-3 (special form)	HO-4 (contents broad form)	HO-6 (unit owner's form)	HO-8 (modified coverage form)
	Section I Coverages			*Section I Coverages*	
A. Dwelling	$15,000 minimum	$20,000 minimum	Not applicable	Not applicable	Same as HO-1 except losses are paid based on the amount required to repair or replace the property using common construction materials and methods
B. Other structures	10% of A	10% of A	Not applicable	Not applicable	
C. Personal property	50% of A	50% of A	$6,000 min.	$6,000 min.	
D. Loss of use	20% of A	20% of A	20% of C	40% of C	
Covered perils	Fire or lightning	Dwelling and other structures covered against risks of direct physical loss to property except losses specifically excluded	Same perils as HO-2 for personal property	Same perils as HO-2 for personal property	Same perils as HO-1 except theft coverage applies only to losses on the residence premises up to a maximum of $1,000; certain other coverage restrictions also apply
	Windstorm or hail				
	Explosion				
	Riot or civil commotion				
	Aircraft				
	Vehicles				
	Smoke	Personal property covered by same perils as HO-2 plus damage by glass or safety glazing material, which is part of a building, storm door, or storm window			
	Vandalism or malicious mischief				
	Theft				
	Breakage of glass or safety glazing material				
	Falling objects				
	Weight of ice, snow, or sleet				
	Accidental discharge or overflow of water or steam				
	Sudden and accidental tearing, cracking, burning, or bulging of a steam, hot water, air conditioning, or automatic fire protective sprinkler system, or appliance for heating water				
	Freezing				
	Sudden and accidental damage from artificially generated electrical current				
	Volcanic eruption				
	Section II Coverages			*Section II Coverages*	
E. Personal liability	$100,000	$100,000	$100,000	$100,000	$100,000
F. Medical payments to others	$1,000 per person	$1,000 per person	$1,000 per person	$1,000 per person	$1,000 per person

Here are some of the additional features of various types of policies. HO-2, HO-3, and HO-8 may be written only for the owner-occupant of a dwelling used exclusively as a private residence. Special exceptions for persons doing business in the home can be added through endorsements. The dwelling may not contain two families. HO-4 may be written for a tenant residing in a rented dwelling or an apartment. HO-6 is only for condominium unit owners and members of cooperating housing units. HO-8 is offered for older homes or lower-valued dwellings. Incidentally, HO-5 is designed to provide replacement cost on contents coverage. This form (HO-5) can also supplement an HO-3 policy to provide complete replacement cost on both the dwellings and the contents.

Returning to the central theme, the two sections of the homeowner's policy (see Table 5-10) contain six different coverages (A-F). Coverage A includes both the dwelling (including one under construction) and the structures attached to the dwelling as well as materials and supplies located on or adjacent to the premises, such as those used in construction, alteration and repair of the dwelling.

Coverage B relates to structures completely separated from the building by a clear space. Examples include a detached garage and a detached fence. However, detached garages rented to other persons for a fee are excluded from coverage.

Coverage C insures a scheduled amount on personal property—both owned and non-owned—anywhere in the world, except for personal property located at a secondary residence. The coverage may vary depending on the type of property, and is limited to ten percent of the amount of personal property, subject to a $1,000 minimum. However, the coverage may be increased through the purchase of endorsements.

Certain types of property are excluded from coverage under homeowner's insurance, and special limits of liability exist on other types of property. Excluded property includes motorized vehicles, sound equipment in an automobile, and property rented to others. In addition, the following dollar limits of coverage generally apply: $100 on money, bank notes, and coins; $1,000 on securities; $500 on watercraft; $2,500 (varies by states) on theft of jewelry and furs (aggregate); $2,500 on theft of silverware and goldware; $2,000 on firearms; $10,000 on oriental rugs (aggregate); and $3,000 on home computers and equipment. A standard homeowner's policy covers personal property away from home up to ten percent of the amount specified in the policy or $1,000, whichever is greater. However, if the property is stolen from a car, one must show proof of forced entry into the car, unless the person has the extended theft endorsement.

Coverage D insures the loss of use and provides protection against losses involving both the premises occupied by the insured and those rented to others. If the premises are occupied by the insured, the company pays for the additional living expenses incurred by the family to maintain its normal standard of living. However, if the property is rented to others, coverage is limited to the fair rental value of the property.

Coverage E makes all payments, up to the limit of liability, that become the insured's legal obligation because of bodily injury or property damage falling within the scope of the coverage. The normal limit of $100,000 applies to this coverage. Personal liability protection means that if someone outside of the family is injured in an accident on the property, or in an accident (but not an auto accident) off the premises that is caused by a member of the family, the homeowner's policy covers the insured against a lawsuit.

Coverage F relates to medical payments to anyone (other than the insured's family) who are injured while on the premises with the permission of the insured, or who are injured away from the premises if the injury results from an activity of the insured's family. An amount of $1,000 is the basic limit of this coverage.

The insurance company covers medical expenses of people hurt by a member of the owner's family, or the pets, on or away from the home, even when they are not legally responsible for the injury. It also pays for damage to the property of others, even if the owner is not legally at fault. However, the insured does not personally receive any money from policy sections covering personal liability and damage to property of others and medical payments. The compensation is for injury to people other than family members living with the homeowner, and the money is paid directly to the injured person.

MAJOR PROVISIONS

The Home

The coinsurance clause. The *Rule of 80* specifies that, in order to receive full payment for any partial damage to the house, the house must be insured for at least 80 percent of its full replacement value, not including the cost of the lot. For instance, if the $150,000 home is insured for at least $120,000 and fire destroys the recreation room, causing $20,000 in damage, the entire $20,000 less the deductible would be covered. However, if the home was insured for, say, $100,000, then only a percentage of the $20,000 would be covered.

If separate building structures exist on the residential property, such as a detached garage, then annexed private structures coverage should be purchased, assuming that the value exceeds the coverage specified in the policy. Such a coverage would provide insurance in the amount equal to ten percent of the dwelling amount on separate building structures. Of course, this percentage can be increased to a higher amount by paying an additional premium.

Inflation guard policies. In view of the ever-increasing cost of replacing a home, it is advisable to purchase coverage for the actual replacement value of the house (excluding the lot). This is accomplished by keeping the insurance updated through an inflation-guard endorsement, so at all times the home will remain adequately insured. This provision increases the amount of the coverage by eight to ten percent every year. The cost of the endorsement will vary, depending on the type of coverage and variations in the cost-of-living index.

Unscheduled Personal Property

Market value. This coverage refers to those personal household contents that are not specifically listed by name and value in the policy. The homeowner's policy provides insurance on these items equal to 50 percent of the amount of insurance on the house. However, when a property is destroyed, the company asks for some type of proof of ownership and an estimate of the depreciated value of such property. For this reason, a complete video, or an updated itemized inventory of personal property, should always be maintained.

Replacement cost. A policy covering the actual cash value, that is, the replacement cost less depreciation, of a property leaves a great deal to be desired. For one thing, such a method requires the owner to maintain detailed records of the date of purchase, purchase price, estimated percentage depreciation on the date of loss, and other related bookkeeping records. For another, the reimbursement amount is likely to cover only a fraction of the replacement cost of the article. For these reasons, several years ago insurance companies started to offer replacement cost coverage. For instance, for an additional premium representing five to 15 percent of the policy's total premium, the homeowner could receive the actual replacement cost of a destroyed or stolen item. However, even those homeowners who purchased a replacement cost policy were well advised to maintain a detailed inventory of personal effects and video tape all the contents (both front and back) located inside the house.

Unfortunately, today insurance companies are covering themselves first and shifting more of the final burden to homeowners. Many insurers are phasing out *guaranteed replacement* policies that had firms paying whatever it took to restore structures to their original condition. Some also are changing dollar-based deductibles to percent deductibles, which typically require consumers to pay more money out-of-pocket when catastrophes strike.

Instead of guaranteed replacement, firms such as Travelers, All State, State Farm and Farmers are offering *extended replacement*, where they limit the buffer to 20 or 25 percent above the rebuilding cost to account for potential price-gouging in a disaster.

There are special discounts available for new or updated utilities. Also, a special coverage pays for damage by water backing up from sewers and drains. And building ordinance and law coverages protect homeowners against code changes.

As a result of these changes in home replacement cost policies, homeowners need to reexamine their coverage and consider insuring their homes closer to their full value.

Floater policies. In situations where personal properties are valued in excess of the coverage or limitations offered by a typical homeowner's policy, two types of floater policies are available. The *personal articles floater* provides all-risk protection for each article specified on the face of the policy. In contrast, *personal property floater* offers protection on *all* articles on a worldwide basis. Because these policies can be expensive, it is best to cover only those articles that warrant special coverage, such as original paintings, authentic artifacts, jewelry, furs, and boats. However, an insurance company may require the homeowner to have these items appraised before insuring them.

In the average homeowner's policy the minimum personal liability coverage is $25,000. This amount should be increased to at least $1 million, especially since the cost of raising it to that level is relatively modest.

The Cost Issue

Of all the proven strategies for reducing the cost of a homeowner's policy, selecting the most economical policy from a group of alternative quotations for identical coverage tops the list. Another strategy for cost reduction is to increase the deductible from $250 to, say, $500 which can significantly cut annual premiums. In general, because small losses significantly increase administrative costs, thereby jeopardizing the renewal of a policy, wherever possible, a $500 or a $1,000 deductible policy should be considered.

Special Insurance

Replacement cost. The contents of a home are generally insured for 50 percent of the dwelling's coverage, although the coverage can be raised to 70 percent. Consequently, if the home is insured for $100,000, without additional coverage the most one could collect on the contents would be $50,000. But that is only one type of limitation of a homeowner's policy. In most states there is a $2,500 limit on furs and jewelry lost in a single theft. Also, for certain losses the company pays only a fixed sum: $100 for coins and money, $500 for stamps, $2,000 for firearms, $2,500 for jewelry and furs, and $1,000 for manuscripts. Other limits are also imposed on this type of coverage. Collectible coins are grouped with regular money, bullion, and bank notes. Stamps are classified with securities, evidence of debts, deeds, and tickets. Other valuables and collectors' items, such as fine art, antiques, cameras, and musical instruments, can be claimed up to their insured cash value, provided a sales receipt can be produced.

After taking an inventory of the valuables, a homeowner may feel the need for additional coverage; in that case, there are two viable alternatives. The basic homeowner's coverage may be raised, which would automatically raise the unscheduled personal property protection. Additionally, the owner may have valuables—furs, jewelry, fine art, silverware, cameras, stamps, coins, and sports and hobby gear—listed individually in special endorsements or *floaters*. When buying floaters it is advisable to get the inflation-guard endorsement, assuming rising replacement values. Although it may vary from one company to another, for five percent of the regular premium, the amount of coverage can be adjusted upward on a regular basis.

Crime insurance. Burglary and robbery insurance for up to $10,000 is available to homeowners and tenants in certain states such as Florida and New York.

Flood and earthquake insurance. In 1969 the federal government and the private insurance industry introduced a joint program to make flood insurance available at rates subsidized by the government, since it was not available through homeowner's policies. To qualify, the property must be located in a community that has declared its intentions to carry out land-use control measures to reduce future flooding.

In contrast to the way flood insurance is written, earthquake insurance is usually written as an addition to a fire or homeowner's policy, with minimum payments of as low as $.03 per $100 for dwellings. That is, the coverage for a $100,000 dwelling would cost $300.

Miscellaneous Considerations

Private mortgage insurance. Home buyers who make a down payment of less than 20 percent of the purchase price are required to buy a private mortgage insurance (PMI). At a cost of $50 to $100 for every $100,000 borrowed, this insurance protects the lender against the potential default on the mortgage. The cost of this insurance may appear to be insignificant if compared with the monthly mortgage for an expensive home. But PMI adds up, simply because it can take years to reach that magic 20 percent equity threshold where it is not longer required. In fact, HomeGain, a real estate Web site, estimated (2001) that 2.7 million homeowners were paying PMI needlessly. Indeed, 58 of the 61 cities HomeGain examined registered increases in median sales prices from 1997 to 2000 sufficient to give many payers 20 percent or more equity ratios.

Fortunately, there is an effective way of getting out of this obligation, thanks to the recent appreciation in home values. According to the National Association of Realtors, the median sales price for a home rose five percent, from 1999 to 2000, and as high as 27.5 percent in some parts of the country. As a result, the equity in an average home has gone up sufficiently to exceed that 20 percent of the home's value. Therefore, by spending a mere $100 to $300 for a new appraisal, and petitioning the lender for a waiver, a homeowner should be able to cancel the PMI for good.

High valued dwelling. A house is likely to be the single biggest investment most of us make. The general rule of thumb with homeowner's insurance is not to skimp on the adequate coverage of the home. This rule is even more important for high-valued dwelling.

Most large insurance companies use some form of an estimator for determining the estimated replacement cost of homes of higher quality than those considered by the replacement cost calculator. While homes such as these may have some unique or unusual features, more of them will also have multiple levels, ornate staircases, top quality windows and doors, and many other features which are extra in homes of less value. Most of the typical additional features like air conditioning, intercom, porches and similar items are included in the base cost for each of these classes of high valued dwellings. Only a few extra features are listed for such features as garages, fireplaces, and so on.

Replacement cost of a high-valued dwelling is defined as the amount that would actually be expended to repair or replace a damaged or destroyed building in new condition with materials of the same size, kind, and quality as those that have been destroyed. The special model called by such names as the Estimator and Expensive Home Valuer is used to help the homeowners estimate the value of their expensive home. The results of this valuation method, generally used for homes valued from $500,000 to $1 million or more, are not construed as a substitute for a detailed appraisal or a quality survey where more details and specifics are necessary to complete the appraisal. For homes exceeding $1 million, it is needed to use some other means, such as an appraisal, contractor's costs and so on to determine a reasonable estimate of the replacement cost.

Policy Details. Our homes are safe havens, and it requires special policy considerations to adequately protect them. Here are several items a homeowner should look for in selecting a policy. (1) Most insurers cap coverage at 120 percent of the value of the house. It is important to purchase extra coverage if the appraisal is low, or if the home has handcrafted cabinetry or other expensive features. (2) It can take months or even years to rebuild or repair a home. A loss-of-use clause covers living expenses over and above the normal costs. This insurance is usually capped at 20 percent of the home's coverage, but some insurance companies do allow homeowners to purchase more. (3) If the homeowner works from home, a home-business endorsement should be purchased to cover the business equipments and liability. (4) Homeowners policies do not cover flood, earthquake and, in most cases, sewer or storm-drain damage. Flood insurance can be purchased from the

Federal Emergency Management Agency (www.fema.gov; 800-427-4661). The policy costs an average of $372 a year. Earthquake insurance is sold by private insurers. A sewer endorsement could be purchased at a cost of five percent in additional premium. (5) There are several ways in which premium costs could be pared down. These include the following: Alarm systems can reduce costs by as much as 20 percent. Simple safety devices like smoke alarms and deadbolts can save five percent. Many insurers give 5-15 percent breaks if two or more policies are purchased from the same company. Finally, increasing the deductible from $500 to $1,000 can save up to 15 percent in premiums.

Gaps in homeowners' policies. A typical homeowner's insurance policy might not cover the following items. Hence, it is important to buy special coverages for these items. (1) Especially pricey items such as big-screen television and extra fancy stereo equipment are often excluded from policies, or at least, inadequately covered. The same goes for antiques, collectibles, expensive jewelry and furs. To protect these and other items that a policy does not cover, riders should be obtained that specifically cover these items. (2) A backed-up sewer can send waste spewing into the house. It is essential to buy sewage and drain backup coverage if the home has a finished basement that contains valuable furniture or equipment that could be destroyed. (3) Most people who live near a river or coastline know that homeowner's policies do not cover flood damage, so they buy flood insurance through the National Flood Insurance Program. Flood insurance is sold by private insurance agents at set prices, depending on the proximity to a flood zone; a homeowner could pay more than $800 a year for $100,000 coverage if the home is in a flood plane, or as little as $230 if it is in a low-risk area. For more information on this coverage, the homeowner could log on the NFIP's Web side (www.fema.gov/nfip) or call 888-225-5356. (4) Homeowner's policies typically cover only $1,000 to $2,000 for theft of jewelry, and they offer no protection in case of a mysterious disappearance such as a ring falling down the drain. Additionally, if jewelry was not stolen and there is no police report, it may not be covered. The homeowner can buy a rider to cover such losses and tie the coverage level to the jewelry's appraised value. The cost is about $15 per $1,000 of the jewelry's value. (5) Some policies are called *all risk*, which means they cover damages caused by almost any situation except those specifically excluded in the policy. But others are named perils policies, which cover only damages caused by particular situations—such as fire, theft, vandalism, a plane crashing into the house and more than a dozen other circumstances. The laundry list seems to include everything, but inevitably leaves out some scenarios. In this case, getting an all-perils rider typically adds about 20 percent to the annual premium.

Home office protection. A great deal of home office equipment, such as computers, fax machines, copy machines and the like, are generally excluded from most conventional homeowner's policies. Homeowner's and renter's policies typically cap coverage for business property at $2,500. The coverage drops even more if the homeowner removes any of the property from the house. For instance, the policy would pay only $250 if the laptop was stolen while the owner was away on a business trip. A typical policy provides no liability coverage for business-related claims, either. For instance, if a deliveryman slips on the front door while delivering a business package, the policy may not cover that liability.

In order to solve this problem, the homeowner may wish to obtain separate insurance. This additional insurance becomes particularly important if the owner sees clients in the home office. For a low-risk home business, a rider that would increase business-property and liability coverage to the same amounts as stated in the homeowner's policy, would probably cost $100 per year.

THE PLANNING STRATEGY

Self-Analysis

For financial planning purposes, the best strategy for carrying a satisfactory homeowner's policy is to make sure that the family has adequate coverage against all major risks associated with owning a home. A convenient worksheet is presented in Table 5-11 which can be used to determine if individual coverages match the desired levels of coverage.

Annual Check-up

In addition to self-analysis, it is advisable to have an annual check-up of the homeowner's policy by an insurance professional. We will briefly review here the annual check-up process for the family of John and Betty Smith. We will review

TABLE 5-11 Homeowner's/Renter's Insurance Worksheet

	Current coverage	Desirable coverage
Home Replacement Value	$_____	100% of Replacement Cost
Type of Coverage	HO-2, HO-3	HO-3
Renter's/Condo Insurance	HO-4, HO-6	HO-4, HO-6
Personal Property:	$_____	50% of face amount
Cash	$_____ Limit	Increase limits to suit personal needs
Financial Documents	$_____ Limit	Increase limits to suit personal needs
Boats	$_____ Limit	Increase limits to suit personal needs
Jewelry and Furs	$_____ Limit	Increase limits to suit personal needs
Silverware and Gold	$_____ Limit	Increase limits to suit personal needs
Musical Instruments	$_____	Increase limits to suit personal needs
Fine Art	$_____	Increase limits to suit personal needs
Other	$_____	Increase limits to suit personal needs
Liability Insurance	$_____	$300,000 plus $2 million under umbrella policy

only the homeowner's policy here. Auto and umbrella liability policies will be examined in subsequent sections.

Recently the Smiths received the following letter from John Sipe, their insurance agent.

January 2, 2004

John and Betty Smith
1234 Gross Avenue
Minneapolis, MN 55441

Dear Mr. and Mrs. Smith:

As part of my continuing service to you, I review your file from time to time. Presently you have the following policies with me:

AUTO	1993 MERCEDES, 2002 MAZDA, 2004 INFINITI
FIRE	HOMEOWNER'S (HO-5), PERSONAL LIABILITY
	UMBRELLA
LIFE	NONE
HEALTH	NONE

I feel a thorough review of all your present policies would be very beneficial at this time. We call this service the Free Family Insurance Check-up service. To set up a convenient time for us to get together, give me a call at (248) 643-1234, or stop by to set up an appointment soon.

Remember, our company offers economical protection for all your insurance needs . . . car, home, health, life, boat, and even your business. I am attaching the following for your review:

Form A: Family Insurance Check-up Check List
     B: HO Policy Status
     C: Auto Policy Status
     D: Umbrella Policy Status

Thank you for allowing me to serve you.

Sincerely,

Jim Sipe
Friendly Insurance Agent

Form A: Fire

You should consider	
Replacement cost on dwelling:	Watercraft:
Replacement cost on contents:	Oriental rugs/personal computer:
Higher liability limits:	Jewelry/furs/fine arts/silverware:
Higher deductibles:	Sports equipment/musical instruments:
Mortgage disability/life:	Tools/equipment/goods for sale:
Umbrella coverage:	Pets:
	Smoke alarms/extinguishers:
Do you have?	Dead bolts/security systems:
	Firearms:
Other buildings on premises:	Woodburning stove/kerosene heater:
Improvements since insured:	Roomers/resident employees:
Photo inventory:	A need for professional liability:
Coins/gold/silver:	Office/business:
Cameras:	Childcare in the home:
Stamp collections/collectibles:	Sewer/drain/sump pump problems:
Trailer (not boat):	Earthquake/flood:
	Other homes/rental property/farms:

The Smiths met with Jim Sipe to review their homeowner's policy covering the home located at 1234 Gross Avenue, Minneapolis (see table). After some discussion the Smiths agreed to make the following changes in their policy in order to bring the coverage to a comfortable level.

1. Personal property coverage was increased to $200,000
2. Optional coverages were increased on:
   a. Jewelry and Furs: $5,000/$10,000
   b. Silverware/Goldware: $5,000
   c. Home Computers and Equipment: $10,000
   d. Property used in business: $5,000
   e. Face value of coverage: $300,000
   f. Liability: $2 million
3. Art and other highly valued items were reviewed, and floater policies were purchased.

SECTION III
AUTOMOBILE INSURANCE POLICY

INTRODUCTION

Every year Americans set a new record for the number of automobile accidents, as well as the number of injuries and deaths they cause. In 2004 there were millions of injuries causing economic losses amounting to billions of dollars, and these losses continue their upward journey. These statistics should be kept in mind as we discuss the need for having basic automobile insurance coverage. Additional

---

Form B: Homeowner's Policy Status

Date	January 2, 2004
Address	1234 Gross Street, Minneapolis, MN
Type	40-5
Premium	$554 Deductible: $500
Renewal date	January 2, 2003
Mortgage	Interfirst, Federal Savings
Policy No.	82-ET 5000-1 Z

Description of home	1) Year built: 1990; 2) No. of stories: 2; 3) Construction: masonry; 4) Ground floor sq. ft.: 2,292; 5) No. of corners: 4
No. of families	One
Special features	1) Bedrooms adjoining a bathroom or sitting room; 2) Masonry fireplaces; 3) Brick or stone exterior walls; 4) Hardwood floor; 5) Stained/varnished woodwork
Speciality rooms	1) Den; 2) Dining room; 3) Large foyer; 4) Office; 5) Exercise room; 6) Grand room; 7) Laundry room; 8) Recreation room; 9) Library; 10) Study
Other features	1) Deck; 2) Masonry chimney; 3) Kitchen package; 4) Central air; 5) Fireplace hearth; 6) Three-car attached garage; 7) Composite shingle roof; 8) Finished basement
Policy discounts	1) Sprinkler: 10%; 2) Home alert: 10%; 3) Home-auto discount: yes
Value covered	$190,900
Special coverages	1) Building ordinance: 10%; 2) Silver/goldware: $2,500; 3) Firearms: $2,500; 4) Jewelry/furs: $2,500/$5,000; 5) Home computer: $5,000; 6) Personal property amount: $143,175; 7) Deductible: $500; 8) Liability: $500,000; 9) Medical payment: $1,000
Endorsements	1) Back-up of sewer: $10,000; 2) Jewelry/Furs: $1,000; 3) Personal injury; 4) Nurses professional liability; 5) Theft; 6) Rented Personal Property

---

Cost of Policy Coverage

	Limit	*Annual Premium*
Dwelling	$190,900	$528.00
Dwelling extension	19,090	
Personal property	143,175	
Liability	500,000	25.00
Medical payment	1,000	
Deductibles	500	
Credit: Home alert	2%	(11.00)
Home/auto		(26.00)
Homeowners 369	7%	(37.00)
Total (annual)		**$554.00**

---

coverages—such as collision, comprehensive, uninsured motorists, and medical payments—are also important. As a matter of public policy, many states encourage the purchase of automobile insurance by imposing financial responsibility laws, and a few states make the purchase of auto insurance mandatory through compulsory liability insurance laws.

Determining the *basic* coverages of an automobile insurance policy, known as Personal Auto Policy (PAP), is not easy, for there is more to choosing the right policy than meets the eye. As can be seen from Table 5-12, there are two types of damages that could result from an auto accident: (1) Property damage (including damage to the automobile); and (2) bodily injury (including death). These damages could be the result of the driver's negligence or that of *the other guy*. Accidents also happen due to circumstances beyond the control of the drivers involved. Add to these complications other factors such as: The *other guy* happens to be an uninsured motorist, or the motorist is encouraged by a lawyer to build up a claim because he or she perceives the driver to be wealthy. That gives a fairly good idea of what is involved in selecting a good automobile insurance policy.

The selection of a good auto policy can begin with the minimum coverage. Thereafter, this coverage can be expanded in various directions, subject of course to the family's budget constraints and special needs.

BASIC COVERAGES OF PERSONAL AUTO POLICY

There are six major parts to a Personal Auto Policy (PAP). These are discussed next.

Liability Coverage (Part A)

Under the PAP, the following persons are covered:

1. The named insured
2. The spouse living in the principal household
3. The relatives of the first person named in the declaration
4. Any other person who obtained the consent of the insured or the spouse
5. Any other person or organization liable for the use of such a car by one of the previously mentioned insureds

TABLE 5-12   Summary of Basic Automobile Insurance Coverages

Coverages	Principal applications	
	Policyholder	Other persons
Bodily Injury		
Bodily injury liability	No	Yes
Medical payments	Yes	Yes
Protection against uninsured motorists	Yes	Yes
	Policyholder's Automobile	Property of Others
Property Damage		
Property damage liability	No	Yes
Comprehensive physical damage	Yes	No
Collision	Yes	No

The coverage is not extended to automobiles used in any business or occupation, or to persons working in any car business.

A significant feature of PAP is the *single limit* coverage for both bodily injury and property damage. The limit of liability included in the policy is the maximum limit of liability for bodily injury and property damage resulting from any one accident. Each of the two liabilities is discussed next.

Bodily injury liability. In buying auto insurance the major concern should be to protect against others' claims arising from bodily injury or death caused by the members or employees of the family. When a policy is purchased that includes liability, the insurance company promises to honor the claims of the aggrieved party or parties up to the financial limits stipulated in the policy. These limits are often expressed as a split limit, such as 25/50, which means that the insurance company is liable for up to $25,000 for any one person injured, and up to $50,000 for all persons injured in the same accident. While most states now prescribe the minimum amount of liability insurance that residents must carry, as a bare minimum one should carry at least a 100/300 coverage, which means $100,000 coverage for one person and up to $300,000 for all persons per accident. The insurance agent should analyze the net worth and annual income of a family in order to determine the satisfactory level of liability insurance for that family.

Property damage liability. This coverage applies when a car damages the property of others. The property may be the car of the other person or it may be other properties, such as lamp posts, buildings, or telephone poles. Property damage liability coverage provides protection in the form of legal defense and indemnification through the payment of damages for which the driver is legally liable. This coverage can be purchased in amounts ranging from $10,000 to $50,000 or more. Here again, a minimum $50,000 coverage is recommended.

Medical Payments (Part B)

Unlike homeowner's insurance which provides coverage for medical payments to others, medical payments in the auto policy cover the cost of medical services for the insured, relatives, and anyone else in the insured's car. It does not apply to pedestrians or to occupants of the other vehicle. The advantage of having automobile medical payments coverage in addition to liability insurance is that the payment is prompt, since no time is wasted in determining liability.

Uninsured Motorists (Part C)

Under this coverage the insurance company protects the driver against losses inflicted by someone who has no insurance, or has insurance with a carrier that is insolvent. However, in order to collect on a claim, it is necessary to show that the other driver was at fault. This type of policy applies only to bodily injuries, and the payment for injury by the insurance company under this coverage is limited to the state's maximum liability amount. A variation of this feature protects against underinsured motorists, where the other driver is at fault and does not have sufficient insurance to cover the losses.

Coverage for Damage to Insured's Auto (Part D)

Comprehensive physical damage. Comprehensive insurance (also called *other than collision*) protects the car against theft, vandalism, falling objects, fire, lightning, and so on. However, this coverage does not apply to cars damaged in a collision with another car or object, or to cars which lose value because of normal wear and tear. The extent of the coverage is specified in the policy, and the amount of deductible varies from policy to policy. Some comprehensive fire and theft policies also reimburse the policyholder for a rental car during repair or until a new car can be purchased.

Collision/overturn. Generally speaking, if the car is damaged by a person other than the driver, it should be possible to get the car repaired or replaced at the cost of the person at fault, provided he or she has coverage. If liability insurance is nonexistent, the person may refuse to pay for the damages. It is also possible that the insurance company representing the driver at fault may delay paying for the damages, in which case the driver would have to finance the auto repair. For these reasons, and also because the driver may be responsible for damages to the car, it is desirable to purchase collision insurance, which is a pledge by the insurance company to pay for any damage to a car should it collide with another vehicle or object, regardless of who is responsible for the accident.

Collision insurance normally has a deductible amount of $100 or more. An efficient way to reduce the auto premium is to take a higher deductible, such as $250 or $500. The insured risks losing the amount of the deductible if the car is damaged, but the premium savings are substantial. Another sensible strategy is to skip the collision coverage if the car is several years old. This decision can easily be made by comparing the market value of the car with the collision premium charged.

Duties after Accident or Loss (Part E)

In case of a claim, a policyholder must:

1. Send the insurance company accident-related paperwork, duly filled out.
2. Authorize the insurance company to obtain medical and other pertinent records.
3. Submit proof of loss.
4. Cooperate with the insurance company in every way.

General Provisions (Part F)

The key provisions of a PAP are listed below:

1. The terms of a policy may be changed or waived only by an endorsement signed by the company.
2. The policyholder does not have a right of action against the company until all the terms of the policy have been met, and under the liability coverage, until the damage amount an insured is legally liable to pay has been finally determined.
3. The policyholder may cancel the policy by notifying the company in writing of the date to cancel, signing a lost policy release, or returning the policy.

Factors that Affect Premiums

The cost of auto insurance depends in part on whether the insured has a high or low probability of being involved in an accident. Factors considered by insurers when categorizing drivers and determining premiums include age, gender, and marital status. Individuals over age 25 are less likely to be involved in an accident than younger drivers. Women have fewer accidents than men, and married drivers have fewer accidents than single drivers. Insurers also consider:

Personal Driving Record—Drivers with a history of accidents and/or traffic violations (especially driving under the influence offenses) are more likely to incur losses than those with clean records. Some insurers give discounts for completing defensive driver or driver education courses.

Type of Vehicle—High-performance vehicles and sports cars are considered higher risk. Insurers may offer preferential rates for vehicles that have certain safety features (e.g., anti-lock brakes, air bags).

Cost to Repair Vehicle—Repair expenses can vary widely, even among vehicles that have comparable original purchase prices.

Vehicle Use and Location—Daily commuters in densely populated urban areas pose a higher risk than occasional drivers in rural areas.

Other Insurance Purchased—Those who purchase their homeowners and auto policies through the same company generally receive preferred rates.

Miscellaneous Considerations

Cost of auto insurance. Every state requires that drivers have some sort of automobile insurance in place. And even if they did not, it would be sheer madness to drive without some form of protection, because a single accident could bankrupt the driver.

For many the auto policy is quite expensive. The biggest bite of auto insurance comes from liability protection, which is effectively divided into bodily injury protection and property protection. This is one element of auto insurance no driver can afford to shortchange.

However, to reduce the cost, one should consider raising the deductibles, which is the portion of the expense the driver has to pay before coverage kicks in. Pushing up deductibles to $500 or even higher can significantly cut the premiums. Another way to reduce the premium is to eliminate collision coverage if the car is a few years old.

Other ways of cutting cost include: (1) Good safety record, because drivers with good records get better rates. (2) Insuring every car with the same company, since multi-car packages often mean lesser premiums. (3) Avoiding smoking, because smokers reportedly have more accidents than non-smokers. (4) College study, because if the driver were in college and getting good grades, the insurance company would most likely reduce the premiums.

Loopholes in auto insurance. Generally, when someone drives a person's car with owner's permission, the insurance company covers the driver. However, if the driver lives in the same house and is not listed on the policy, then the general rule may not apply. Therefore, it is important to get this matter resolved by the insurance company. Experts recommend that the children should be included in the policy of the owner even if they are away to school. Also the insurance company should be informed if a nanny or a housekeeper will be using the car regularly.

One area of contention is when the car is used in business driving. The company might not cover the car for accidents that occur during business use. Another area of concern is when a traveler rejects insurance coverage by a car rental company on the assumption that his own policy will cover it. In many cases that is a wise decision, but not always. Typically, American auto insurance policies cover damages only in the U.S. and Canada and not in other countries. Even in the U.S., drivers should consider those options if they have an old car and have dropped collision and comprehensive coverage on the policy.

NO-FAULT INSURANCE

In those states that do not have no-fault insurance, an insurance company must reimburse the policyholder for damages only if the insured is at fault. However, determination of fault is not always easy. It may require legal negotiations, and could possibly lead to costly lawsuits. Furthermore, the problem becomes more complicated if neither motorist is at fault, or when both parties are at fault. For this reason, and also to reduce the number of cases which overburden our court system, many states have adopted no-fault insurance laws.

There are four essential elements in the basic no-fault plan: (1) An accident victim's losses should be paid for by his or her insurance company; this makes court action unnecessary to determine liability. (2) The right to sue for additional compensation is significantly limited. (3) No-fault insurance is mandatory, thus insuring payment to all accident victims without recourse to courts. (4) Insurance companies must provide safeguards against cancellation or nonrenewal so that all drivers can possess the required insurance.

The original idea of pure no-fault insurance was to eliminate lawsuits and have victims reimbursed by their own insurance companies for their medical expenses, without any reimbursement for *pain and suffering*. This eliminated the *fault* concept and allowed immediate reimbursement for bodily injuries. However, no state has adopted this version of no-fault. Every state allows lawsuits if there are severe injuries, prolonged disability, or large expenses accumulated for a given accident. States that have adopted such no-fault laws include Colorado, Connecticut, Florida, Georgia, Hawaii, Kansas, Kentucky, Massachusetts, Michigan, Minnesota, New Jersey, New York, North Dakota, Pennsylvania, Puerto Rico, and Utah. In these states, no-fault insurance is compulsory and has proved to be an effective way to compensate auto accident victims.

Coverage limits and deductibles, which range from $50 to $2,000, vary from state to state. This represents the amount the injured person must pay before making a no-fault claim. Coverage for personal injuries may range from $10,000 to $25,000 for an individual, and from $20,000 to $50,000 for injuries to two or more persons.

Some states have adopted a more liberal no-fault insurance known as *add-on no-fault*. This type of no-fault insurance gives the injured party the right to sue the party at fault. These states, together with the states already mentioned, account for over half of the states having some form of no-fault insurance.

A Summary

The most common form of property insurance purchased by Americans is a personal automobile policy. Certain basic coverage is mandatory in most states, but insurance companies offer options to extend protection beyond the legal minimum levels.

Insurers offer the following types of auto insurance:

Types of Insurance	Items/Events Covered
Liability	Injuries to others and damage to their property
Medical payments	Medical and/or funeral expenses incurred because of an auto accident, regardless of who is at fault
Uninsured and underinsured motorist	Expenses (liability and/or physical damage) incurred when the insured is the victim of an accident involving an uninsured vehicle, or a vehicle that has insufficient coverage
Physical damage	Damage to the insured vehicle from an accident (collision) or causes such as theft, fire, or vandalism (comprehensive)

Other options are available as endorsements or "add-ons," such as coverage for glass breakage, temporary replacement vehicles, and towing expenses.

Before purchasing or renewing an automobile policy, the following items should be reviewed:

- Available coverages (for gaps in current coverage)
- Current coverages (for excess or overlapping coverage)
- Maximum limits on current coverages (for appropriateness)
- Drivers covered under the policy (for additions or deletions)
- Vehicles covered under the policy (for additions or deletions)
- Need for collision and/or comprehensive coverage
- Appropriateness of increasing deductibles for physical damage coverage
- Factors that affect premiums

THE PLANNING STRATEGY

Self-Analysis

Planning for adequate auto insurance coverage involves making sure that the existing coverages compare favorably with the desired limits. A convenient worksheet is presented in Table 5-13 for completing the task.

Annual Check-up

It is necessary to have the auto policy revised annually by an insurance professional. We refer to John Sipe's letter to the Smiths presented earlier to which he attached the Family Insurance Check-Up list (Form A) and the Automobile Policy Status (Form C).

TABLE 5-13　Automobile insurance Worksheet

	Current Coverage	Desirable Coverage
Liability Insurance:		
Bodily injury	————	100/300
Property damage	————	$100,000
Umbrella policy*	————	$1 million
Collision	————	$500 deductible
Comprehensive	————	$100 deductible
Uninsured Motorists' Coverage	————	Same as liability coverage limits
Underinsured Motorists' Coverage	————	Same as liability coverage limits
Medical Payment Coverage	————	N/A
No-Fault Insurance:		
Medical expense	————	Coordinated
Other coverage	————	Full

* Insurance companies generally require higher limits (e.g., 250/500) in order to provide an umbrella policy.

The Smith family met with Jim Sipe to discuss their auto policy. Following the meeting, a number of changes were made, as listed next:

1. The bodily injury liability and the property damage liability on the 1991 Mercedes were increased from 100/300/50 to 100/300/100 to make them consistent with the coverage on the other cars.
2. Limited property damage coverage (Y) was increased for the Mercedes which had a lower coverage.
3. Comprehensive coverage on the 2004 Infiniti car was increased because it was a "fancy" car.

Form A: Auto

How many cars are in the household:	Uninsured 100/300
Are cars driven to work/used for business: One car	Death, dismemberment, loss of sight: None
Which children drive/which cars:	Loss of earnings: Full coverage to state maximum
Other regular drivers: H/W	Other coverages:
Annual mileage: Under 7,500 each	Nonowned auto coverage:

You should consider	*Do you have?*
High liability limits:	Motorcycle/scooters:
Higher medical/no-fault coverage:	Trucks/RVs/motorhomes/campers:
Higher deductibles comp./collision:	Other vehicles/trailers:
Emergency road service:	Cellular phone/CB/cassette radios:
Rental/travel expense coverage:	Plans to purchase new car:

Form C: Auto Policy Status, January 1, 2002

	Infiniti I30 *Car, 2004*	*Mercedes Benz* *Car, 1993*	*Mazda* *Car, 2004*
Policy Number	0139849	0298379	0391365
Class	6A	6C	6B
Vehicle Description	Infiniti, G20 4D SED	Mer. Benz 350 SD	Mazda 626 "LX" 4D SED
Total Premium	584.08	522.88	719.86
Covered Date	8-1-02	8-1-02	8-1-02
Birthdate	2-14-35	5-13-30	5-13-30
Bodily Injury Liability (A)	100/300/100	100/300/50	100/300/100
Limited Property Damage (B)	500 limit	100 limit	500 limit
Comprehensive Deductible	100	100	100
Collision Regular Deductible	500	500	500
Uninsured Motorist	100/300	100/300	100/300
Personal Injury Protection	Active	Active	Active
Property Protection	Active	Active	Active
Catastrophic Claim	Active	Active	Active

Applicable Discounts: 1) Multi-car discount; 2) Multiple line discount; 3) Accident-free discount; 4) Vehicle safety; 5) Anti-theft; 6) Safety belt discount

The Smiths also discussed the advisability of purchasing a 2001 Mercedes 380 SE. However, when they discovered that it would cost $2,400 a year to insure this car, the idea was quickly dropped.

SECTION IV
MISCELLANEOUS INSURANCE COVERAGE

UMBRELLA LIABILITY INSURANCE

Under the property-casualty insurance policies, there are recommended liability and property damage coverage limits to provide adequate protection for claims made against a policyholder resulting from loss of property or personal injury. However, coverages provided by these policies may still be insufficient for reimbursing the aggrieved parties. An umbrella policy supplements, but does not replace, an insured's homeowner's, auto, boat, aircraft, and other nonbusiness policies.

Typically, umbrella coverage limits are $1 million to $5 million, and this policy is relatively inexpensive. The amount of coverage desired under this policy depends on the insured's risk exposure. Basic coverage under an umbrella policy extends to bodily injury, mental anguish, shock, sickness, disease, disability, false arrest, false imprisonment, wrongful eviction, detention, libel, defamation of character, and invasion of privacy. A typical umbrella policy excludes the insured's obligation for worker's compensation and disability benefits, damage to property of the insured, and product failure.

The umbrella policy fits over a homeowner's policy (with a minimum of $100,000 personal liability coverage) like an umbrella of added coverage, and is activated when the coverage under the homeowner's policy has been exhausted. Assume an insured is sued for $1 million and is carrying both a $100,000 personal liability coverage under the homeowner's policy and a $1 million umbrella policy. The insurance company will pay $100,000 under the homeowner's policy and $900,000 under the umbrella policy.

As in the case of the homeowner's policy, an umbrella policy supplements the coverage provided by an auto policy. If an insured person carrying a 100/300 auto policy and a $1 million umbrella policy is sued for $750,000 in an auto accident, the insurance company will cover $100,000 per person under the auto policy and $650,000 under the umbrella policy. Without this umbrella coverage, the driver would have to pay that amount out of personal funds, and hence could become financially crippled.

It is imperative that liability limits under the homeowner's and automobile policies be coordinated with the underlying deductible of the umbrella policy. Assume an insured has a $100,000 limit under both the homeowner's and automobile policies and a $300,000 underlying deductible under the umbrella policy. If this insured files a claim, the first $100,000 is covered under either the homeowner's or the automobile coverage, and amounts over $300,000 are covered under the umbrella policy, thereby leaving a significant gap of $200,000 between the policies. As a result, it is recommended that all property and casualty insurance, such as, homeowner's, automobile, and umbrella policies, be purchased through one insurance company in order to minimize the possibility of any gaps in coverage.

DIRECTOR'S LIABILITY INSURANCE

This type of insurance is used to protect officers and directors of business entities from claims of wrongful acts such as error, neglect, or omission while performing their duties. In today's litigative society, this insurance coverage is almost routinely provided for the directors by corporations, banks, and other institutions. Board members of Condo Associations, Subdivision Associations, and Charitable Organizations should also be covered by this type of insurance. A large deductible for the director's liability policy is the only way to keep the premium at an affordable level.

PROFESSIONAL LIABILITY INSURANCE

Today, many professionals, like doctors, lawyers, and financial planners, are exposed to malpractice suits and other associated risks, and they need protection against these risks. Incorporating a professional business does not provide the necessary protection because the corporate status does not shelter the corporate officer from malpractice suits. Most professional liability policies are written on a claims-made basis, which means that the insurance company is only responsible for claims made during the policy period. Costs of professional liability insurance policies are fairly high. Consequently, professionals shopping around for these policies should thoroughly investigate various options, including those offered by their respective professional associations, before selecting the right policy.

THE PLANNING STRATEGY

Self-Analysis
The adequacy of the personal liability umbrella coverage should be checked at the time of the annual review of homeowner's and auto policy. A $1 million policy is an absolute minimum; however, depending on circumstances, the possibility of increasing the coverage should also be explored. Individuals should also make sure that they carry Worker's Compensation for household help, outdoor help, and babysitters.

Annual Check-up
John and Betty Smith received the accompanying personal liability umbrella policy details (Form D) from Jim Sipe, their insurance agent. After a brief discussion, John Smith decided to increase the policy coverage to $1.5 million, since this amount of insurance could be purchased at an additional cost of only $26 per year.

Form D: Personal Liability Umbrella

Term:	Continuous		
Renewal date:	2-26-04	Date paid:	7-20-04
Premium:	$196	Amount paid:	$196
Bill to:	Insured		
Present liability:	$2,000,000		
Self-insurance:	$500		
Rate class:	II		
CL:	Y		

In this chapter the planning issues relating to health, homeowner's, automobile, and liability insurance were discussed. However, because of space limitations, not *all* issues relating to these types of insurance were fully covered. For those wishing to obtain additional information, advice, and translation of fine prints, the sources listed in the Appendix might be useful.

In the next chapter issues relating to educational planning will be undertaken.

There are four steps to accomplishment: Plan Purposefully. Prepare Prayerfully. Proceed Positively. Pursue Persistently.

Unknown

APPENDIX TO CHAPTER 5:
ADDITIONAL SOURCES OF INSURANCE INFORMATION

National Insurance Consumer Helpline
110 William Street
New York, NY 10038
800/942-4242
Guidance in homeowner, auto, property, life and health insurance.
Helpline: 8 a.m. to 8 p.m. EST, M-F

Insurance Information Institute
1101 17th Street NW, Suite 408
Washington, DC 20036
202/833-1580
Property casualty policies (auto, home, business).

Health Insurance Association of America
1025 Connecticut Avenue NW, Suite 1200
Washington, DC 20036
202/233-7780
Health coverage, individual or group.

American Council of Life Insurance
1001 Pennsylvania Avenue NW
Washington, DC 20004-2599
202/624-2000
All types of life insurance.

Federal Emergency Management Agency (FEMA)
500 C Street SW
Washington, DC 20472
202/646-4600
Agency that handles emergency insurance from hurricanes to floods.

Federal Insurance Administration, part of FEMA
800/638-6620
Runs the National Flood Insurance Program.

National Insurance Consumer Organization
121 N. Payne Street
Alexandria, VA 22314
703/549-8050
Life policies analyzed for $35.

National Association of Life Underwriters (NALU) and
  Association of Health Insurance Agents (AHIA)
1922 F Street NW
Washington, DC 20006
202/331-2162
Information on life and health insurance products and agents.

Standard & Poor's
25 Broadway
New York, NY 10004
212/208-1527
Free ratings of insurers. Reports also available in libraries.

CHAPTER 6

Educational Planning

INTRODUCTION

Most Americans consider a college education extremely important—and understandably so. It broadens a person's perspective of the world, widens his or her appreciation of all that it offers, and enhances self-esteem. Besides, according to National Commission on Responsibilities for Financing Post-Secondary Education, college graduates on average earn more than twice the amount earned by high school graduates.

Unfortunately, financing a college education defies the law of physics. When it comes to college costs, what goes up just keeps going up. If they continue to climb at the five percent annual average rate of the past 15 years, by 2014 parents will have to spend more than $151,000 just to put today's newborn through the typical public university. And if the baby is destined for an ivy-clad campus like Harvard, the parents could be looking at a four-year bill close to $360,000. This expense, of course, is just for one child. That college cost, multiplied by the number of children a family has, is sufficiently scary to make most parents throw up their hands in despair.

Fortunately, the bleak picture painted above need not lead one to desperation and inaction. It is of course true that for many American families a college education is the second largest expense they will undertake, next to the purchase of their home. And given the astounding cost involved, funding the four years of college for a child frequently represents a formidable financial goal. With careful planning, however, it can be prevented from becoming an overwhelming financial burden.

So, the message about education funding is simply this: Whether a family will need to meet college costs in the next decade or within a few short years, the best way to pursue this goal is to start the planning process *today*. The reason is that the sooner the planning process begins, the closer the family will move towards the goal of having the money for college. And this is a goal worth pursuing, because a college education is one of the greatest gifts a child will ever receive.

COLLEGE COSTS

As mentioned, putting a child through college is one of the biggest costs most families will ever face. Expenses at public colleges have nearly tripled over the last fifteen years, according to the U.S. Department of Education, and are up even more at private colleges.

Estimates of how much four years of college will cost are available from various public and private sources. For instance, Figure 6-1 indicates that, according to the College Costs and Financial Aid Handbook, 2004, by the year 2024, the four-year cost in private colleges would amount to $316,515, whereas the comparable cost at public institutions would be $146,850. By contrast, in 2004, these costs amounted to, respectively, $110,708 and $51,364. No matter what estimate is used, every parent should make a concerted effort to ensure that funds are available for financing the institution of choice when the child is ready to enter college.

It should now be clear that in the future college costs will rise, and parents will continue to be shocked by the price tags attached to educating their children. Consequently, a financial planner would be wise not to start a discussion on educational planning by showing parents what it is going to cost them and how difficult it would be for them to reach their educational goals. Instead, it is recommended that financial planners adopt an alternative approach. First, they should emphasize that parents who have time on their side should capitalize on the magic of compounding. Second, planners should explain to parents that they do not have to *save it all*. In fact, saving is only one of five ways to pay for college. The others are: pay as you go, or funding college out of earned income; financial aid; borrowing; and letting someone like grandparents pay the bills. In the next section, the power of compounding in educational planning will be discussed. Other ways of paying for college will be discussed later in the chapter.

THE MAGIC OF COMPOUNDING

In educational planning, as in every other segment of financial planning, it is *time in*, and not *timing*, that makes all the difference. The following illustration demonstrates this concept.

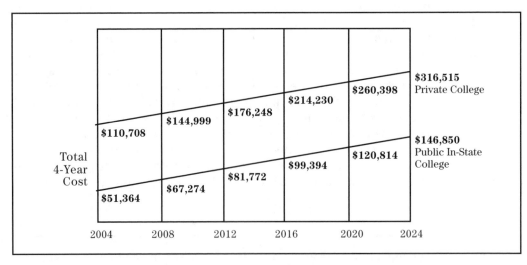

FIGURE 6-1   The cost of a future education

Consider the case (Figure 6-2) where investor Sylvia just gave birth to a son. She starts saving for his college education by investing $100 a month in a mutual fund. If she continues to set aside the same amount every month for 18 years, she will have invested a total of $21,600 ($100 x 12 x 18). Assuming an after-tax annual rate of six percent, the total value of the portfolio at her son's college age would be $38,929.

Now consider the case of John who just became a proud father of a cute girl. John wants to save for her college, but because of other commitments, he plans to start investing ten years from now. Fortunately, John is able to invest $225 per month (instead of Sylvia's $100 per month) for the next eight years, or a total investment of $21,600, the same amount Sylvia invests in her mutual fund. However, to John's great surprise, even though his investment also generated an after-tax annual rate of six percent, when his daughter is ready to go to college, the total value of his investment amounts to only $27,775—almost 36 percent less than Sylvia's investment.

This illustration clearly demonstrates that because Sylvia started early, time was on her side, and she was able to capitalize on the magic of compounding. What this implies is that Sylvia reinvests the earnings in her account along with her original principal, so the investment gains build up over time not only on the money she originally invested, but also on the gains she made in previous years.

The power of compounding over time can be demonstrated both in terms of the number of years of investing *and* the amount of periodic investment. Table 6-1 reveals that an individual would have $38,929 if a monthly investment of $100 were made for 18 years and an after-tax six percent annual return were realized. If that

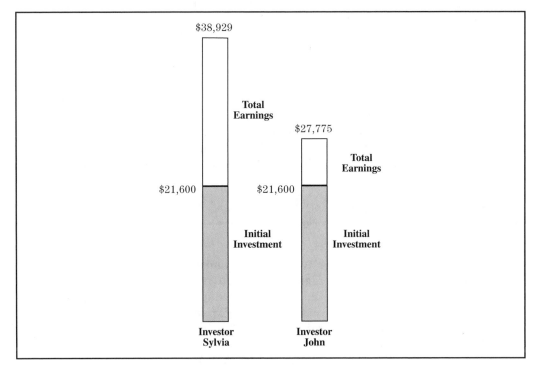

FIGURE 6-2 Investing for a college education

TABLE 6-1 Growth of Investments Over Time

Monthly Investment	Number of Years Investing					
	3	6	9	12	15	18
$100	$3,953	$8,684	$14,345	$21,120	$29,227	$38,929
$200	$7,907	$17,386	$28,691	$42,240	$58,455	$77,858
$300	$11,860	$26,052	$43,036	$63,360	$87,682	$116,787
$400	$15,813	$34,736	$57,381	$84,480	$116,909	$155,716
$500	$19,776	$43,420	$71,727	$105,600	$146,136	$194,645

Note: Annual after-tax return is eight percent

individual would like to have a slightly higher amount ($43,036) in nine years, then the amount of monthly investment would have to be increased to $300, or three times the monthly investment in the previous case.

SAVING FOR COLLEGE COST

Let us establish a framework for determining the amount of savings required to pay for the full projected costs of college education. For this analysis, it is necessary to determine the four-year public or private education costs, which will be assumed to increase at five percent per year. Also, because of the availability of Section 529 plans, which allow a tax-free accumulation of educational funds, a before-tax rate of return of eight percent will be assumed.

Table 6-2 presents the framework for determining for the Wood family how much monthly savings are necessary to meet the shortfall in their child's educational funding cost. Their son, John, is expected to be a public school in-state resident in nine years. The Woods have already saved up $25,000 for John's college and expect this fund to earn a before-tax annual return of eight percent. Based on these assumptions, an educational funding calculation (Table 6-2) shows that every month the Woods would have to invest $171 to reach their educational funding goal.

COLLEGE SAVINGS PLANS

UGMA and UTMA

The Uniform Gifts to Minors Act (UGMA) and Uniform Transfers to Minors Act (UTMA) are two vehicles designed to set up custodial accounts in a child's name for the benefit of the child. Both provide a simple and inexpensive method of making a gift or bequest to a minor without the expense of a trust.

For investments held in a child's name, the first $750 (2005) in earnings in these plans is free of federal income tax, and the second $750 is taxed at the child's rate, presumably ten percent. Earnings above that are taxed at the parents' rate until the child reaches age 14. At that point, all investment income after the first

TABLE 6-2 Education Funding Cost Calculation

I.	Cost of Education in Nine Years	
	1. Current Cost in Public Institution	$50,000
	2. Number of Years Until College	9
	3. College Inflation Rate	5 percent
	4. College Cost in Nine Years	$77,566
II.	Value of Savings in Nine Years	
	5. Current Value of Savings	$25,000
	6. Before-tax Rate of Return	8 percent
	7. Number of Years Until College	9 years
	8. Future Value of Savings	$49,975
III.	Additional Savings Required	
	9. College Cost in Nine Years (Line 4)	$77,566
	10. Value of Savings in Nine Years (Line 8)	$49,975
	11. Savings Shortfall (Line 9 minus 10)	$27,591
	12. Annual Savings Required (assume i = 8%, n = 9)	$ 2,046
	13. Monthly Savings Required (Line 12/12)	$ 171

$750 is taxed at the child's rate. Thus, a child earning $1,200 would pay just $45 in federal income tax [ten percent of (1,200-750)], compared with the tax bill for $348 for a parent in the 29 percent bracket who earned the same amount.

There are also compelling arguments against investing in a child's name. Money transferred to a child's custodial account is considered an irrevocable gift. Once the children reach the age stipulated by law—it is usually 18 or 21—the money is theirs to do with as they please. When a parent puts money into a custodial account, there is no guarantee the child will use that money for college.

Not only can parents provide no guarantee on how today's baby will turn out in 18 years, they also cannot foresee future events that could upset even the best-laid savings plan. Assume that a parent saves in the name of his four children. If three of his four children decide against going to college or get funding from a variety of sources, the parent will not be able to spend the savings for any other purpose because all the educational funds were saved in the children's names.

Ownership of assets also has implications for college financial aid. In calculating *estimated family contributions* toward college costs, the standard federal aid formula requires children to pay 35 percent of savings held in their name. Parents, on the other hand, contribute only 5.6 percent of their assets, after various allowances. The values of certain assets, such as tax-deferred retirement plans, annuities, cash-value life insurance and home and farm equity, are excluded from the formula before calculating the parents' required contribution.

Education IRAs

The Taxpayer Relief Act of 1997 (TRA '97) created a tax-favored education individual retirement account (Ed-IRA) designed to help taxpayers save for children's education. Money contributed to an Ed-IRA is nondeductible from taxes but earnings accumulate tax-deferred.

Contributions to an Ed-IRA are treated as nontaxable gifts to the beneficiary and, when distributed, may be received by the beneficiary free of federal income tax. In general, if earnings are distributed to pay qualified post-secondary educational expenses, they are excluded from the beneficiary's income, and are received free of federal income tax. It should be noted that the contributor must be related to the beneficiary, and that there is no limit on the number of individual beneficiaries for whom one contributor may set up Coverdell Ed Savings Account.

For 2005, the law limits contributions to a Coverdell Ed Savings Account to $2,000 per beneficiary per year. The contributions must be in cash, and may be made up to April 15 of the year following the year for which the contribution is made. Other restrictions include the following: (1) Multiple Ed-IRAs may not be used to exceed the $2,000 limit for any one beneficiary. (2) The $2,000 per year limitation is phased out for taxpayers with an adjusted gross income above certain levels. For joint filers, the contribution is phased out when AGI is between $190,000 and $220,000. (3) No contribution to an Ed-IRA for a beneficiary is permitted in any year in which a contribution is made for the same beneficiary to a qualified state tuition program, such as the 529 plans. (4) Ed-IRA coordinates with HOPE and Lifetime Learning Credits for education expenses with the exclusion for Ed-IRA distributions, so no tax benefits could be derived for the same expenses.

Distributions from an Ed-IRA are considered to be a combination of the original contributions and earnings. If for a given year the qualified education expenses exceed the total amount distributed from the Ed-IRA, then all of the distributed earnings are excluded from the beneficiary's income. However, if the qualified education expenses are less than the amount distributed, then a portion of the distributed earnings is included in the beneficiary's taxable income for the year. An additional ten percent tax is added to the portion included in the taxable income.

Ed-IRA funds cover qualified educational expenses. These include books, tuition, equipment, computer hardware and software, and supplies. Room and board may also qualify, if certain requirements are met. The program qualifies elementary and secondary schools and institutions that award bachelor's degrees, graduate-level education, or professional degrees. Certain vocational institutions also qualify.

Any earnings distributions included in a beneficiary's income because they are not used for qualified educational expenses are subject to an additional ten percent tax. Certain exceptions apply, including death or disability of the beneficiary.

Another aspect of Ed-IRA is that if a beneficiary does not use the funds held for him or her in an Ed-IRA, the money may be rolled over into a new Ed-IRA for a different beneficiary. If the rollover occurs within 60 days of the distribution, and if the new beneficiary is a member of the original beneficiary's family and has not yet attained age 30, the distribution is not taxable to the original beneficiary. The same objective may be reached by simply changing the beneficiary of an Ed-IRA. As long as the new beneficiary is a member of the original beneficiary's family, the change is not treated as a taxable distribution.

The exclusion from income for distributed earnings from an Ed-IRA is available for any tax year in which a taxpayer claims either the HOPE credit or the lifetime educational credit for a particular beneficiary, as long as it is not claimed for the same expense. If a beneficiary reaches the age of 30 and there are still funds remaining in the Ed-IRA, the law assumes that the funds remaining in the Ed-IRA have been distributed, and thus become subject to tax for that year. The ten percent additional tax also applies to amounts so distributed, assuming that the beneficiary had reached the age of 30. If a beneficiary dies before age 30, within 30 days any remaining Ed-IRA balances must be distributed to the beneficiary's estate and taxed.

Section 529 Plans

At last count, almost all states (48) had either adopted a college tuition plan or had enacted legislation authorizing the implementation of such a program. Although there are differences in these college education programs, they all have one thing in common: Every state's program must meet the regulations of Section 529 of the Internal Revenue Code defining a *qualified state tuition program*, or QSTP. These regulations are extremely important because they describe the rules that the state programs and individual taxpayers must follow in order to be in compliance with Section 529.

The benefits. Section 529 offers significant benefits to qualified state tuition programs and to the participants. The key tax benefits are summarized next.

1. Every QSTP is provided a tax-exempt status by the IRS. In 1994, the IRS had argued *(Michigan vs. United States)* that the Michigan Education Trust was not a state instrumentality. The government could have challenged other state programs as well. However, that issue is no longer relevant, because Section 529 protects all state programs created for funding college educational programs.
2. All earnings of the QSTP are tax deferred.
3. Distributions or education benefits received from state-sponsored qualified tuition programs are excludable from gross income.
4. Section 529 plans extend tax-exempt status to qualified tuition programs funded by private institutions. Distributions from these programs sponsored by private institutions would be excluded from gross income, starting in 2004.
5. Contributions to a Section 529 plan are considered a completed gift for estate and gift tax purposes. This rule applies despite the fact that the owner retains ownership rights which would normally be treated as part of his or her estate. In addition, the funding of the account is treated as the gift of a present interest qualifying for the annual $11,000/$22,000 tax exclusion.
6. Section 529 provides that the contributor may elect to treat the gift as occurring ratably over a five-year period, so that the $11,000/$22,000 exclusion can be leveraged to as much as $55,000/$110,000 in one year.
7. The contributor of a 529 plan is allowed to replace the current designated beneficiary with a new beneficiary who is a member of the family. A member of the family is broadly defined as someone who is a son or a daughter, a brother or sister, the father or mother, a niece or nephew, an aunt or uncle, or a son- or daughter-in-law. In addition, the Tax Act of 2001 expanded the definition by including first cousins of the original beneficiary as a member of the family. An account owner may also "rollover" the funds from one state's program to another state's program within 60 days with a new qualified beneficiary.
8. The Tax Act of 2001 allowed tuition credits or other amounts to be transferred tax free from one qualified tuition program to another qualified program for the same beneficiary.
9. The use of 529 plans does not affect the ability of the beneficiary to claim the Hope Scholarship credit or the Lifetime Learning credit. Education expenses qualifying for credit can be paid for with 529 plan withdrawals.

Tuition vs. savings plan. Section 529 plans come in two forms. A *prepaid tuition plan* guarantees that the money saved today will match the growth in tuition inflation at state-run colleges. Currently (2003 - 2004 academic year) that translates into an average 14.1 percent return. In most cases the participants can also use the money for out of state institutions. Prepaid plans appeal especially to people with modest incomes who are aiming for a state college or university.

In contrast, a *college savings plan* allows a person to contribute to a pool of money that is managed by the state treasurer or an outside investment advisor. A typical savings plan invests in stocks when the child is young, then progressively moves toward bonds and cash, as the child gets older. But some plans do let the contributor choose all stock or bond accounts. The funds in a plan can be used at any accredited school for tuition, room, board, books and supplies.

One of the factors that distinguishes the two plans is the way colleges treat them for awarding college aid. In the case of a prepaid plan, every dollar used for tuition takes a dollar away from the student's eligibility for aid. That could mean smaller work or study grants, smaller subsidized student loans and lower probability of obtaining funds from the college.

By contrast, in the case of a college savings plan, only a portion is counted toward the student's eligibility for aid. If the plan is in a parent's name, the college will count no more than 5.6 percent of the money each year. If, on the other hand, the plan is in the child's name, each year the school might want 25 or 30 percent of the money, and some schools may want much less than that. Therefore, as a general rule, as compared to a prepaid tuition plan, a student qualifies for more aid in a college savings plan.

Section 529 vs. UGMA/UTMA. Section 529 plans are so tax efficient that they could literally buy a student an extra year of college. Assume a parent invests in a 529 plan $60,000 for his son and the portfolio doubles in value ($60,000 gain) by the time he goes to college. If it had been invested in an UGMA account, the gain would have been taxed at his son's marginal tax rate of 15 percent, reducing the account by around $9,000. However, under 529, because the earnings grow tax-deferred, taxes would have been avoided altogether.

A study conducted in 2001 by T. Rowe Price contrasted the advantage of investing in 529 over investments in UGMA/UTMA and a taxable account. This study assumed 28 percent federal and five percent state taxes with no state tax on 529 withdrawals, which were made in equal amount over four years. An amount of $5,000 was invested in three different accounts (Section 529, UGMA, and a taxable account) on an annual basis. Annual returns were ten percent with distributions based on average growth fund. The study revealed that if college savings were started when the child was born, then after 18 years the 529 plan would have $287,000. This amount would be $37,500 and $63,200 higher, respectively, than investments in UGMA and taxable accounts. Table 6-3 contrasts 529 plans with the traditional education IRAs and UGMA plans.

Major drawbacks. The 529 plans have several drawbacks which should be explicitly recognized. (1) It is a long-term plan, and in order to derive significant benefits, the plan should be started when the child is ten years old or younger. (2) While withdrawals from 529 are tax-free, they are still treated as income to the child, and hence could hurt in figuring financial aid. (3) Section 529 plans typically

TABLE 6-3 Best Place to Invest College Funds

	529 Plans	UGMA/UTMA	EDUCATIONAL IRAs
NATURE OF PLAN	A 401(K) - type savings plan sponsored by most states that offers a limited choice of investments.	A custodial account that lets you invest on behalf of a child.	Like other IRAs, this is a tax-deferred plan to set up thru a financial service firm.
MAXIMUM CONTRIBUTION PER ACCOUNT	Varies by state-generally ranges from $100,000 - $250,000	Unlimited, subject to Annual Maximum Contribution Per Donor (see below).	$500 per year, contributions must stop when child turns 18. Starting with 2002, it increased to $2,000/yr.
LIMITATIONS ON INCOME	None	None	Adjusted gross income limits apply.
AGE LIMITATIONS	Varies by plan.	None	No contributions after age 18. All distributions must be made by age 30.
ANNUAL MAXIMUM CONTRIBUTION PER DONOR	$50,000 per beneficiary in the first year of a five-year period to avoid federal gift tax consequences ($100,000 per married couple).	$11,000 per beneficiary ($22,000 per married couple) to avoid federal gift tax consequences.	$500. Increased to $2,000 in year 2002.
TAXES	Investments are tax-deferred. Earnings withdrawals will be free of federal income taxes.	Investments are taxable, but are assessed at the child's rate after age 14.	Investments are tax-deferred, and withdrawals are tax-free for qualified educational expenses.
INVESTMENTS	Many state plans offer only 3 or 4 investment options, and once money is invested, it's difficult to move.	You decide where to establish the account, and which stocks, bonds, or mutual funds to invest in.	You decide where to establish the account, and which stocks, bonds, or mutual funds to invest in.
QUALIFIED USE OF PROCEEDS	Any accredited post-secondary program in the U.S., and some overseas programs.	Limited to expenses for child only. Cannot be used for parent's expenses.	Any accredited post-secondary program in U.S., and some overseas programs.
PARENTAL CONTROL	Person funding the account controls it.	Child takes control of assets at the age of consent (18 or 21).	Person making the contribution controls it.
FINANCIAL AID	Assests belong to parents, which helps with financial aid qualification. But the income is considered child's which hurts those seeking aid.	Assets belong to child, which is bad for getting financial aid.	The asset and income belong to the child, which adversely affects financial aid application.
FUNDS REMOVED FROM DONOR'S ESTATE	Yes	Generally no, if the donor dies while acting as custodian.	Yes
DONOR MAY CHANGE BENEFICIARY AT ANY TIME	Yes	No	No
BOTTOM LINE	On average, the best of all available choices. But due diligence is strongly advised.	Appropriate for parents who are starting saving late, not counting on financial aid, and want maximum flexibility.	Because of its $2,000 limitation, it may not provide sufficient income to pay for college.

provide very few investment choices and little flexibility in creating special portfo-lios favored by the participants. (4) Once a participant joins a program, it becomes very difficult to transfer it to another program. (5) Currently, there is a ten percent penalty on Section 529 program distributions included in income. (6) The 2001 tax law *sunsets* on January 1, 2011, which means that on that day Congress could make withdrawals from these accounts taxable.

TAX RELIEF RECONCILIATION ACT OF 2001

The Tax Act made major changes in tax laws affecting educational funding. Several of these changes have already been introduced in previous discussions. Three ad-ditional changes are discussed next.

Employer-Provided Educational Assistance

Employer-paid educational expenses are generally deductible by the employer and are excludable from the employee's income, up to $5,250 annually, if certain requirements are met. The exclusion did not apply to graduate courses and was scheduled to expire with respect to undergraduate courses that start after Decem-ber 31, 2001. The Tax Act extended the exclusion to graduate courses and made the exclusion for undergraduate and graduate courses permanent, effective for courses starting in 2002.

Student Loan Interest Deduction

Within limits, interest paid on qualified education loans is tax deductible. The deduction, which may be claimed whether the taxpayer itemizes or not, is allowed for up to $2,500 of interest paid each year during the first 60 months in which inter-est payments are required. Voluntary payments of interest do not qualify. Eligibil-ity for the deduction is phased out for taxpayers with AGI of $40,000 to $55,000 for unmarried taxpayers and $60,000 to $75,000 for joint filers (adjusted for inflation.)

The new law repealed the 60-month limit, as well as the restriction that volun-tary interest payments are not deductible. The income phaseout ranges were in-creased to $50,000 to $65,000 for unmarried taxpayers and to $100,000 to $130,000 for married couples filing jointly.

Deduction for Higher Education Expenses

In general, education expenses are not tax deductible. (Certain exceptions exist—for example, if the education qualifies as an employee business expense). While the HOPE and Lifetime Learning Credits are available for qualifying expenses, in some cases a deduction for the expenses would provide a greater tax benefit.

Recognizing this, Congress included in the Tax Act a new deduction for quali-fied higher education expenses (defined in the same manner as for the HOPE Credit) that are paid during the year. The deduction may be claimed whether or not the taxpayer itemizes deductions. However, no education expense deduction may be claimed in a year in which a HOPE or Lifetime Learning Credit has been claimed for the same student. The maximum amount of the deduction—and the maximum income a taxpayer may have and still claim the deduction—are as follows:

Year	*Maximum Deduction*	*Income Limit (AGI)*
2004-2005	$4,000	Not exceeding $65,000 ($130,000 for joint filers)
	$2,000	Over $65,000 ($130,000 for joint filers) but not exceeding $80,000 ($160,000 for joint filers)

Those with AGI exceeding the maximums (and married-separate filers) may not claim any deduction. The deduction expires for tax years beginning after 2005.

INSTRUMENTS OF EDUCATIONAL INVESTMENT ALTERNATIVES

There are many financial products available to the family seeking to save for future college costs. In addition to UTMA/UGMA, Section 529 plans and educational IRAs already discussed, a number of other investment choices are available for financing education. The key investment alternatives available to a family for this purpose are discussed next.

The Zero Coupon Option

An option with an iron-clad guarantee is to invest in a zero-coupon Treasury bond, with maturity dates corresponding to the child's years of college. Assume a father who prefers safe investment buys four Treasury zeros for his new-born daughter. These bonds will deliver to the daughter approximately $45,000 a year during her four years in college. It is, of course, true that, like all bonds prices, during the intervening years prices of these Treasury zeros will rise and fall with fluctuations in interest rates. However, these fluctuations can be ignored, because their maturity prices will not be affected by fluctuations in interest rates.

Savings Bonds for Education

In 1990, the Treasury department announced the *Education Bond Program*. This program allows interest to be completely or partially excluded from federal income tax when the bond owner pays qualified higher education expenses at an eligible institution or a state tuition plan in the same calendar year the bonds are redeemed.

Series EE bonds issued since January 1990 and all Series I Bonds are eligible for this program. Bondholders do not have to indicate that they intend to use the bonds for educational purposes when they buy them. But they should comply with all the requirements for the program when they buy the bonds.

In order to qualify, a person has to be at least 24 years old. If the bonds are intended for a child's education, they must be registered in the name of either the purchaser or the spouse. If the bond is to be used for the education of the purchaser, then it must be registered in his or her name.

Post-secondary institutions, including colleges, universities, and vocational schools that meet the standards for federal assistance qualify for the program. Qualified educational expenses include tuition and fees. The expenses may be for the benefit of the bondholder, the spouse, or a dependent. The costs of books and room and board are not qualified expenses. These expenses are reduced by the amount of any scholarships, fellowships, employer-provided educational assistance, and other forms of tuition reduction.

The full interest exclusion is only available to married coupes filing joint returns with a modified adjusted gross income of less than $119,750 (2005). The tax exclusion will be phased out for incomes between $89,750 and $119,750. For single filers, the modified adjusted gross income should be between $59,850 and $74,850. Both the principal and interest from the bonds must be used to pay qualified expenses in order to exclude the interest from gross income.

Treasury Inflation Indexed Securities

In January 1997 the U.S. Treasury introduced a new type of security known as Treasury inflation-indexed securities (TIPS). For the first time these securities were designed to help protect investors against the inflation risk of owning bonds, and these are particularly suited for saving for college. TIPS pay a fixed rate of interest on a principal amount that is continuously adjusted for inflation. The Treasury expects the securities to help investors diversify fixed income portfolios and reduce the Treasury's own borrowing costs.

Inflation-indexed securities are issued with maturities ranging from two to 30 years. As with most conventional Treasury notes and bonds, these securities are sold in minimum denominations and multiples of $1,000, and the timely payment of interest and principal is guaranteed by the full faith and credit of the United States. However, unlike traditional Treasury securities, the inflation-indexed securities are structured to help interest and principal payments keep pace with inflation.

Interest on inflation-indexed securities, like the interest on all U.S. Treasury securities, is exempt from state and local income taxes. For federal income tax purposes, semiannual interest payments are taxable in the year they are received. However, the greatest drawback of TIPS is that the inflation adjustments to principal are taxed like interest in the year in which the adjustments occur, even though these principal adjustments will not be paid until maturity. Because of this adverse tax treatment, TIPS are more appropriate for tax-deferred accounts.

Low-load Insurance

Another choice available, especially to older parents who also need insurance, is the low-load universal life policy. While there are drawbacks to investing educational funds in cash value policies, the following illustration demonstrates how it might work in cetain cases.

Assume John Jones is a healthy forty-year old man and he needs a $500,000 life insurance policy. John buys a low-load universal life policy with $500,000 in death benefits. Next, he puts as much cash into the policy as the federal law allows to prevent it from becoming a Modified Endowment Contract (MEC). That means that John would have to follow a complicated payment schedule: $19,277 per year for the first four years; $3,275 the fifth year; nothing for six years; $1,921 the twelfth year; then $6,859 for the remaining eight years. At the end of ten years, the cash value should approximate $130,000; after 20 years, it should be $310,000. John can pay the college costs by borrowing against, or withdrawing tax-free, the policy's cash value. A *buy term and invest the difference* strategy would provide John with the same amount if he earned an after-tax annual return of 4.7 percent for 20 years. However, in that case, at age 60 his term insurance would start costing him $4,550 a year, and at age 65 it would become prohibitively expensive. So, in John's case, a low-load insurance policy would be preferable, because it would provide him the desired protection and also the vehicle for funding college costs.

CollegeSure CD

Another novel idea relates to the purchase of CollegeSure CD, marketed by College Savings bank. CollegeSure CDs are sold in whole *units* and *fractional units*. One unit pays for one year of tuition, room, board, and fees at an average private college; 0.40 units pays approximately one year at an average in-state public college; and 1.42 units pays approximately one year at an Ivy League school. The cost of a unit or a fractional unit is based on when the parents want the CD to mature. Parents can buy CollegeSure CDs (available in maturities of one to 25 years) that will mature at the time the youngster enters college. This product can be purchased from College Savings Bank, 5 Vaughn Drive, Princeton, New Jersey, 08540. Telephone number: 1-800-342-6670, or www.collegesavings.com.

Parents do not have to buy CollegeSure CDs in one lump sum. They can invest as little as they wish, and when they wish. Once the transaction is completed, they get a confirmation informing them what fraction of the unit they own, and how much it will provide upon maturity. The minimum for opening an account is $500, but that is waived if the parent signs up for an automatic deposit program.

College Savings Bank calculates the annual interest rate on a CD on the basis of the Independent College 500 Index. The Index measures the average total cost and the annual rate of change for tuition, fees, room and board paid by full-time freshman students at 500 widely attended private colleges in the U.S.

The most attractive feature of CollegeSure CDs is that there is no limit on how much a CD can earn. Even if college costs hit double-digit increases, the CD is guaranteed to keep up. And if costs do not increase in any given year, the CD is still guaranteed to earn a minimum of four percent.

CollegeSure CDs are insured by the FDIC for up to $100,000 and, like bank CDs and EE bonds, investors pay no fees or commissions. Also, if the child earns a scholarship to go to college, the parents get back *all* the money they have invested plus the accumulated interest.

Section 2503 (c) Minor's Trust

A Section 2503 (c) minor's trust is a gift tax tool that enables a grantor to make a gift to a minor in trust and still obtain the annual gift tax exclusion. This trust is used when a person wishes to make a gift to a minor children and when the grantor's income tax bracket is high and the recipient's tax bracket is low. It is also used when the grantor owns an asset which is likely to appreciate substantially over a period of time but does not want the appreciation included in the gross estate.

The tax implications of the minor's trust are enormous. If the income of the trust is distributed each year, it is taxable to the recipient who by definition is in a relatively low tax bracket. If the income is accumulated, it is taxed to the trust. Gifts to the trust constitute a present interest. Therefore the annual gift tax exclusion of $11,000 applies as long as the conditions are met. Finally, appreciation on property from the date it is placed in trust is removed from the grantor's estate.

ASSET ALLOCATION STRATEGY

Saving for college is not an end in itself. These savings must be properly invested so the after-tax return assumed in required savings calculations could be realized. There is, of course, no magic formula for investing college funds. But there is the eternal truth: Higher returns are generally associated with higher risks. And because college costs must be paid when they are due, caution should be exercised in assuming above average risks when investing college funds. In this section, a brief review of several investment options will be undertaken.

Numerous studies have demonstrated that, in the long run, stocks handsomely beat all other forms of investment. But these studies also reveal that stocks are far more volatile than bonds and money-market securities.

One of the keys to sound investing for college funding is to have an intelligent investment strategy, which aims at maximizing returns for the level of risk acceptable to the family. Generally, this involves diversifying across three different asset classes—stocks, bonds, and money market securities. This point requires elaboration.

As mentioned, history has shown that while the highest growth potential is in stocks, they are also the riskiest of the three asset classes. In contrast, money market securities carry no risk, but they also generate lowest return. Consequently, a rational strategy would be to invest almost exclusively in stocks when the child is relatively young. As the child grows older, however, the proportion of stocks should gradually drop, while the share of bonds and money market securities should gradually increase. An example of this strategy being applied to a child at various ages is presented in Figure 6-3.

Incidentally, people saving for college generally prefer mutual funds over individual stocks and bonds. This is because mutual funds offer diversity, permit investment of relatively small amounts at desired intervals, and if invested in a family of funds, provide an easy way to rebalance the portfolio over time. Also, as a child gets closer to college, with relative ease the parent can shift from a growth mutual fund to an income mutual fund.

FINANCIAL ASSISTANCE

It is by far the best policy to plan for financing educational costs. However, sometimes the families who do plan, and certainly those who fail to plan, find it necessary to look for alternative sources of funding education costs. Fortunately, there are several options, such as grants and scholarships, loans, and work-study programs that can be explored. Figure 6-4 presents a pictorial view of the major sources of student aid.

Grants and Scholarships

Pell Grants are federal monies usually awarded to students of low income families and are currently given in amounts of up to $3,750 per year. Colleges award and administer Supplemental Education Opportunity Grants provided by the Federal government. Students receiving Pell Grants get priority, and the awards range from $100 to $4,000 per year.

It is important to scrutinize state scholarship programs, college grants and, of course, private grants. Some of these grants may be based not on financial needs but on merits, such as the National Merit Scholarship Award which is determined by the student's academic performance.

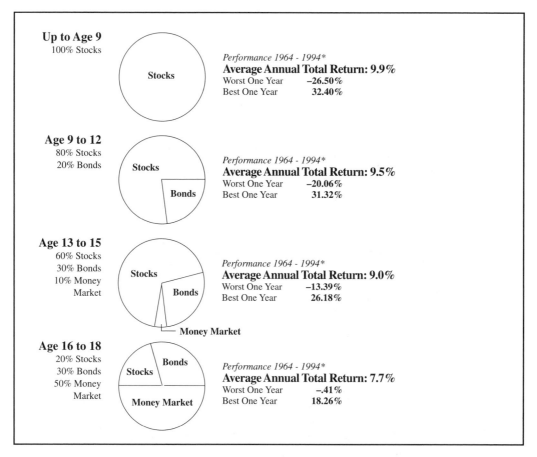

Up to Age 9
100% Stocks

Performance 1964 - 1994*
Average Annual Total Return: 9.9%
Worst One Year   −26.50%
Best One Year   32.40%

Age 9 to 12
80% Stocks
20% Bonds

Performance 1964 - 1994*
Average Annual Total Return: 9.5%
Worst One Year   −20.06%
Best One Year   31.32%

Age 13 to 15
60% Stocks
30% Bonds
10% Money
Market

Performance 1964 - 1994*
Average Annual Total Return: 9.0%
Worst One Year   −13.39%
Best One Year   26.18%

Age 16 to 18
20% Stocks
30% Bonds
50% Money
Market

Performance 1964 - 1994*
Average Annual Total Return: 7.7%
Worst One Year   −.41%
Best One Year   18.26%

FIGURE 6-3   Investment strategies for educational funding.

Student Loans

Student loans constitute a substantial source of college funding. Perkins loans are granted and administered by colleges or universities, while the funds are provided by the Federal government. These loans depend on a student's financial need. An undergraduate may borrow up to $4,000 a year for each year of undergraduate study up to a maximum total of $20,000 after two years of undergraduate work, or $6,000 before that time period. Perkins loans only charge a five percent annual interest—much lower than other loans—and allow a grace period of nine months after graduation before loan payments are due.

Federal Stafford Loans, formerly known as Guaranteed Student Loans, are low interest loans available through the *subsidized* Stafford Federal Loan Program, with the government paying the interest while the student is in school. The *unsubsidized* Stafford Federal Loan Program is intended for students who do not qualify for the subsidized loan or need additional funds. The student can apply for this type of loan through a bank, savings and loan institution, or a credit union.

Students who need more than $23,000 may want to explore the Federal Parent Loans to Undergraduate Students (PLUS) loan program. These ten-year loans, which are also offered through some employers, allow parents to borrow 100 percent of the cost of the college less the amount the student has received from Stafford and Perkins

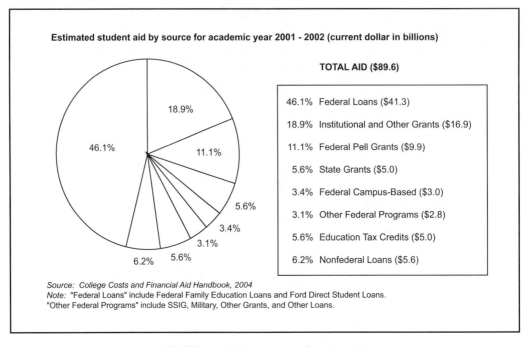

Estimated student aid by source for academic year 2001 - 2002 (current dollar in billions)

TOTAL AID ($89.6)

46.1% Federal Loans ($41.3)

18.9% Institutional and Other Grants ($16.9)

11.1% Federal Pell Grants ($9.9)

5.6% State Grants ($5.0)

3.4% Federal Campus-Based ($3.0)

3.1% Other Federal Programs ($2.8)

5.6% Education Tax Credits ($5.0)

6.2% Nonfederal Loans ($5.6)

Source: College Costs and Financial Aid Handbook, 2004
Note: "Federal Loans" include Federal Family Education Loans and Ford Direct Student Loans.
"Other Federal Programs" include SSIG, Military, Other Grants, and Other Loans.

FIGURE 6-4   Major sources of student aid

loans and other aid sources. The interest is variable, but it is guaranteed not to exceed nine percent. The time to pay off the debt depends on the amount borrowed: twelve years for a $7,500 loan, and thirty years for loans of $60,000 or more.

The financial aid officers at the college can identify private scholarships and grants. Also, the parent may wish to consider a home equity loan, because interest payments on these loans are tax deductible. Finally, funds can be borrowed from the 401(k) retirement fund, but this option should be exercised only as a last resort.

Work Study Programs

Work Study programs, also known as cooperative education programs, are available at many colleges. Students can earn money to finance their education by working part-time or alternating semesters of work (related to college studies) with regular semesters of classroom study. Finally, while acceptance is very difficult, if a student attends a U.S. military academy such as Annapolis, West Point, or the Air Force Academy, tuition is free and the student receives a monthly allowance for living expenses. Of course, as part of the commitment, a certain number of years of military service must be performed after graduation. If the child decides to attend a public or private college, he or she can enroll in the Reserve Officers Training Corps (ROTC) and receive scholarships in return for military service.

Further information on the various sources of financial aid available today can be obtained from the Federal Student Aid Information Center at 1-800-433-3243 which publishes a Student Guide or at their website, www.ed.gov/prog-info/sfa/studentguide.com. In addition, the local library or high school guidance counselor's office should carry information on private and public scholarships.

FAMILY'S EXPECTED CONTRIBUTION

Families that adequately save have no difficulty financing their children's education. Not everyone is that disciplined, however. In many instances, families with other, more pressing, commitments are unable to save the necessary funds and hence must fall back on other means of support for financing their children's education. If these families wish to receive financial aid, then they should be aware that the current Federal Direct Student Loan Program has cut in half the fees on all subsidized Stafford Student Loans. However, the law also states that in analyzing a family's student loan application, the processing firm will use the federal methodology formula known as the *expected family contribution*, which is assumed to be the amount the family can afford to pay toward the child's educational bills.

Convenient worksheets are available which can be used to estimate a family's expected contribution. The amount of total contribution expected from a family can be reduced by taking the following steps: (1) The government's aid formula assumes that, to meet college bills, parents can tap as much as 47 percent of after-tax income, but no more than 5.6 percent of assets. Since the formula treats capital gains as income, it is wise to cash in investments for college bills as early as possible so these gains would not be included in the income figure. (2) If a family expects to be eligible for aid, then it is prudent not to save money in the child's name. The formula calls on students to contribute 35 percent of their assets to college—over six times the amount expected of parents. (3) Families should invest as much as possible in a 401(k) or other tax-sheltered retirement plans because the federal formula exempts them in calculating the total value of assets owned by the parents. Details of family's expected contribution can be obtained from www.collegeboard.org.

REPAYMENT OF STUDENT LOANS

Obtaining a student loan is no easy task. But the repayment of the student loan can be even more challenging, since the amount could run as much as $100,000 for those graduating from law or business school, and $200,000 or more for those graduating from medical school.

Student loans are, of course, granted on the assumption that every recepient will make a good faith effort to repay the loan in a timely fashion. However, in today's uncertain economic environment, many graduates find that either they do not have a job or are not earning enough to make systematic loan payments. For them, certain other options are available, which are discussed next.

Deferment

Unlike mortgages, which never have cancellation or deferment options, student loans do accommodate special financial needs of people. If the graduate does not have a job, he or she may be eligible for a deferment. That means that the graduate does not have to pay immediately, and in some cases the interest meter may be turned off for a while. The government grants deferments on its loans for about a dozen reasons, including returning to school, being pregnant if recently out of school, being temporarily disabled, or serving in the military.

Forbearance

People who cannot make ends meet, but do not qualify for a deferment, may be able to get the forbearance. That suspends principal and interest payments, although interest continues to accrue. Some borrowers actually get loans forgiven if they meet certain specific conditions, such as teaching in a particular area or going into the military.

Graduated Payment

Lenders also offer the option of graduated payments, featuring low monthly payments that gradually increase. For instance, a $5,000 loan at eight percent would normally carry a monthly payment of $60.67. In contrast, a new graduate opting for a graduated repayment would pay only $35.50 a month at first and end up with a final payment of $101.92 after ten years.

Consolidation

One of the major problems of managing student loans is that most students put together a portfolio of loans, and end up writing several checks each month in order to satisfy a variety of terms and conditions. That is one reason why some graduates choose to consolidate their student loans. Under this federal program available through lenders, school loans totalling $7,500 or more can be combined so the borrower would be required to write only one monthly check. However, the normal ten-year repayment period could then be extended to 20 or even 30 years.

Consolidation offers a good compromise for people who cannot cover their current monthly payments. However, consolidation does have a cost. The Loan Counseling Task Force provides the following information: A person with $23,000 in school loans from three different programs pays $84.42 less a month by consolidating and extending payments for 20 years. But over the life of the loan, that person also pays $14,336 in additional interest charges.

REDUCTION OF COLLEGE DEBTS

It has been observed that no matter how much a family has been able to accumulate, they may still find it necessary to borrow to pay for college expenses. While there may be no alternative to incurring a college debt, as described below, there are several debt-cutting tools available to families.

Financial Aid

The first strategy is to obtain the least expensive form of financial aid. It is generally a mistake to assume that, unless someone has a direct influence of the financial aid officer, the application would automatically be rejected. Even families with high income sometimes qualify for low-cost loans and grants. After a student is accepted at a college, a financial aid officer sends an aid package describing school grants, loans, and campus work-study programs. Families can negotiate with the aid officer to substitute grants and work-study programs for loans.

Tuition at Freshman Rate

With tuition costs escalating at five percent per year, a tuition freeze could save a family thousands of dollars. Guaranteed tuition plans come in two forms. At some schools, the freshman rate can be fixed through senior year for a fee, but tuition is still paid annually. Other schools allow payment for four years up-front, but the student locks in the freshman rate.

Lower Tuition Rate

Many schools offer tuition discounts of one form or another. The most common variety is available to students over age 25. Sometimes a student can save after crossing state lines. Specifically, a network of 56 institutions in Colorado, Nevada, Wyoming, and seven other Western states increased tuition for out-of-state students far less than are charged by non-participating colleges.

Teaching Position

California, Florida, New York, and more than 30 other states sponsor loan-forgiveness programs for future teachers, especially of science, math, and foreign languages. For instance, in Florida, juniors and seniors can borrow $4,000 a year if they attend Florida schools that the state approves, and after graduation they do not have to repay the loan if they teach in the state public schools for four years.

EDUCATIONAL PLANNING: A REAL WORLD EXAMPLE

In this section we will present an educational funding plan for the Bloom family. Jack and Beth Bloom have two children, John, age two, and Katie, age one. Recently the Blooms had a discussion with their financial planner, Tim Miffin, regarding the steps they should take now to plan for their children's education. Results of this discussion, and the plan that followed, are presented below.[1]

The process started with the Blooms filling out a Confidential Education Funding Worksheet (Table 6-4). On the basis of this data Tim developed an education funding plan which is presented in Table 6-5. This plan indicates that since the Blooms have already saved $5,000 for his education, John's four-year education would be adequately financed if starting this year the Blooms invested $2,916 per year in an investment earning an after-tax annual return of 6.5 percent. He also pointed out (not shown in the table) that the Blooms could achieve their goal by making a one-time deposit today of $31,721, or making monthly contributions of $243 until John graduated from college. For Katie, since the money already on deposit is $2,000, her education funding would require an annual investment of $2,797, or a one-time investment of $33,740. A summary of this analysis is presented in Table 6-6.[2]

In conclusion, it should be pointed out that the education funding plan presented above is only the beginning. Decisions must still be made regarding the selection of investment products, management of educational portfolios, and adjustment of planning parameters as conditions change. Regardless of which method is used, however, there is no substitute for a careful analysis, and starting the funding process when the children are relatively young.

In this chapter we have discussed the key issues relating to educational planning. In the next chapter, cash management, savings, credit, and debt planning issues will be discussed.

---

[1] The analytical framework was supplied by Raymond James Financial Services.
[2] See Table 6-6.

TABLE 6-4 Confidential Education Funding Worksheet

NAME: Jack & Beth Bloom   **Date: Jan - 2005**

This projection will find the amount of contribution that should be made at the beginning of each year to fund future education expenses. Education assets and annual deposits will compound at the annual growth rate indicated. Total future costs will be computed based on today's annual cost and estimated college cost inflation rate.

	John	Katie
Child's Name	John	Katie
Child's Birthdate	7/19/1999	3/21/2004
Child starts school at what age?	18	18
Number of years in college	4	4
Annual college cost today	$11,916	$11,916
Current value of education fund (if any)*	$5,000	$2,000
Annual after-tax return on investments	6.5%	6.5%
Annual college cost inflation rate**	4.6%	4.6%
Continue funding through college years?	(Yes)/ No	(Yes)/ No
Increase deposits by what annual rate?	0%	0%

  * Enter the total amount of assets you have set aside and earmarked for child's education.

  ** The College Board's 2003-2004 figures show that college costs increased at a rate of 5.35% from 1958 to 2004, college costs increased on average at 6.86%.

COMMENTS:

_____

_____

_____

TABLE 6-5   Education Funding Plan

Jack & Beth Bloom Annual Education Fund Schedule- January 2005							
John				Katie			
Age	Annual Deposit	$11,916 Tuition at 4.6%	Year End Balance at 6.5%	Age	Annual Deposit	$11,916 Tuition at 4.6%	Year End Balance at 6.5%
5	2,916		8,241	1	2,797		4,927
6	2,916		11,693	2	2,797		8,044
7	2,916		15,369	3	2,797		11,364
8	2,916		19,284	4	2,797		14,900
9	2,916		23,453	5	2,797		18,665
10	2,916		27,894	6	2,797		22,676
11	2,916		32,623	7	2,797		26,946
12	2,916		37,659	8	2,797		31,495
13	2,916		43,023	9	2,797		36,339
14	2,916		48,735	10	2,797		41,498
15	2,916		54,819	11	2,797		46,993
16	2,916		61,298	12	2,797		52,844
17	2,916		68,199	13	2,797		59,076
18	2,916	(21,382)	54,166	14	2,797		65,713
19	2,916	(22,365)	38,238	15	2,797		72,781
20	2,916	(23,394)	20,245	16	2,797		80,309
21	2,916	(24,470)	7	17	2,797		88,326
22		(91,611)		18	2,797	(26,773)	70,091
				19	2,797	(28,005)	49,439
				20	2,797	(29,293)	26,157
				21	2,797	(30,614)	13
						(114,712)	

TABLE 6-6   Education Funding Summary

Jack & Beth Bloom
Education Funding Summary - January 2005

	John	Katie
Current Age	5	<1
Start school at age	18	18
Number of years in school	4	4
Annual college costs* today	$11,916	$11,916
Value of education fund	$5,000	$2,000
Current after-tax return	6.50%	6.50%
Assumed college cost inflation rate	4.6%	4.6%
Make deposits through college years	Yes	Yes
Annual % increase in deposits	Level	Level
Your child will enter College in	13 Years	18 Years
Future first year cost	$21,382	$26,773
Future total cost of College	$91,611	$114,712
To reach your future education fund objectives, you must		
Make an additional **one-time deposit** today of **OR** begin making **annual** contributions of	$31,721 $2,916	$33,740 $2,797

* 2004 College Board Annual Survey of Colleges estimates annual college costs (ie, tuition, fees and on-campus room and board) to be $29,791 for private schools and $11,916.

CHAPTER 7

Cash Management, Savings, Credit, and Debt Planning

INTRODUCTION

In the last thirty years or so, financial planning has come of age. And yet, the majority of us have only a vague idea of how we stack up financially. The reason is not hard to find. Given the constant barrage of bad financial news in the media, most Americans worry about inflation, rising health care costs, exploding college tuition, investment risks, threat of a recession, and the complexities of ever-changing tax laws. A national survey conducted by the International Association for Financial Planning discovered that, by two to one, consumers say their net worth is not what they would like it to be. The uncertain economy and the desire to maintain a progressively higher standard of living make it hard for them to save. And two out of five people fear, above all else, that they would outlive the funds earmarked for retirement. To put it bluntly, most people are making more money than ever before but claim that they are not getting ahead.

This pervasive sense of financial uneasiness explains why the average person takes a haphazard approach to money management. Some find even filing income tax returns overwhelming, let alone constructing net worth statements to determine their financial progress. Others confuse documentation of every expense item with budget planning. Clearly, the problem is that most people do not handle their personal affairs as a business and hence do not enjoy the benefits that come from analyzing an annual income statement and a balance sheet.

This chapter was critically reviewed by Charles G. Dharte, Jr., retired Chairman of the Board and CEO of Huntington Bank of Michigan. However, the authors are solely responsibile for the contents.

In this chapter we will discuss issues relating to cash management, savings, credit, and debt planning. In the first part we will analyze the techniques of net worth and cash management planning. Systematic savings planning techniques will be presented in the next part. Finally, in the last part, we will discuss the issues relating to credit and debt planning.

NET WORTH AND CASH MANAGEMENT PLANNING

Effective cash management has two primary objectives: (1) Maintain a cash reserve sufficient to meet emergency needs, such as illness, injury or death, or as a cushion for possible loss of employment. (2) Create and maintain a systematic surplus of cash directed toward capital investment. The three primary components of cash management are: budgeting, cash flow analysis, and planning. These components are a prerequisite to the development of a comprehensive personal financial plan.

NET WORTH PLANNING

The Basic Concept
Net worth planning involves calculating current net worth, setting a realistic net worth goal for the following year, and developing specific strategies for meeting that goal. The main reasons for undertaking net worth planning are to: (1) establish a financial discipline; (2) organize a financial life around a future target; (3) measure financial progress on a regular basis; and (4) feel financially secure about the future. Clearly, the starting point of net worth planning is the calculation of net worth.

Calculation of Net Worth
Net worth is the total fair market value of all assets owned, such as a home, stocks, bonds, and real estate investments, minus all outstanding liabilities, such as mortgage and revolving-credit loans. That is, net worth is the amount by which assets exceed liabilities at a specific point in time.

The process of calculating net worth begins with pulling together the relevant financial records. These include the latest tax records, bank statements, canceled checks, credit card information, other itemized living expenses, brokerage accounts and mutual fund records, mortgage payments, real estate closing records, insurance policies, pension account records, and loan repayment schedules. Gathering all this information may seem daunting, but it is an integral part of net worth planning. Also, these records not only help us calculate net worth but also provide valuable data needed to analyze other planning areas.

The statement of net worth, presented in Table 7-1, has several important features: (1) Assets are categorized as liquid, investment, or personal assets. (2) Investment assets are further classified as short-term and long-term. (3) Long-term assets are termed equity, debt, or miscellaneous assets. (4) Liabilities are categorized as either short-term or long-term. Subtracting total liabilities from total assets provides the value of net worth for the family as of a given date.

The Planning Strategy

The net worth figure just derived provides the basis for developing an appropriate planning strategy. If net worth is negative, which is a distinct possibility, it need not necessarily imply that the family is on the verge of declaring bankruptcy. It does mean, however, that attention should be paid to developing more aggressive strategies that would lead to debt reduction, higher investment return, and revised goal setting.

Just as a negative net worth does not signal an impending disaster, simply having a positive net worth does not mean an end to the financial planning process. In fact, a positive net worth figure for a given year should be compared with that of the previous year. If the annual rate of growth in net worth meets the prespecified target, consideration should be given either to maintain the existing rate of growth or devise improved strategies for accelerating the rate of growth. If, however, the current rate of growth in net worth falls short of the target set by the family, a conscious effort should be made either to develop new strategies for correcting the situation or set a more realistic net worth goal.

There is little benefit to calculating net worth unless it is done at least on an annual basis. For only then can one determine if the savings, credit, investment, and other related programs measure up to the short- and long-term financial objectives set by the family.

CASH MANAGEMENT PLANNING

The Basic Concept

The net worth statement determines the value of assets and liabilities at a given point in time, whereas a cash flow statement paints a picture of the cash flow over a period of time. The only way the net worth can grow is when the annual cash inflow exceeds the annual cash outflow. And that is precisely the basis for using cash management planning as a dynamic financial planning tool.

If during the year total savings fall short of the amount necessary to achieve the targeted growth in net worth, then corrective actions must be taken to rectify the situation. Such actions can take the form of reduction of expenses, increase in income, or a combination of both. If, however, these strategies fail to generate additional savings necessary to meet the goal, then the family may have to reevaluate its net worth goal. And, even in those cases where adequate savings are being generated, cash management planning can help a family reach a higher level of net worth by generating larger savings.

The premise of financial planning is built on cash flow management. It is through the generation of surplus funds that clients can accomplish specific financial goals. This will ensure that the client has enough cash and other liquid assets to: (1) conduct ongoing family operations; (2) have an adequate emergency fund to meet unforeseen contingencies; (3) acquire productive assets; (4) prevent illiquidity from becoming a problem; and (5) set aside adequate funds for children's education, retirement and other long-term goals.

Cash flow management also helps clients achieve financial independence by converting positive cash flows into productive investments. If, however, the net cash flow is negative, then the net worth would fail to grow, thereby making it impossible for clients to achieve their financial independence goal.

TABLE 7-1 Statement of Net Worth

Assets			Liabilities		
Items	Current value	%	Items	Current value	%
I. LIQUID ASSETS			**I. SHORT-TERM**		
1. Cash and Checking Accounts	___		1. Current Bills	___	
2. Savings Accounts	___		2. Credit Cards	___	
3. Credit Union	___		3. Installment Loans	___	
4. Money Market Funds			4. Other	___	
5. TOTAL (1-4)	___		5. TOTAL (1-4)	___	
II. INVESTMENT ASSETS			**II. LONG-TERM**		
A. SHORT-TERM			1. Mortgage	___	
1. CDs	___		2. Life Insurance Loans	___	
2. Treasury Bills	___		3. Borrowing from Qualified Plans	___	
3. Cash Value-Life Insurance			4. Loans to Purchase Investment	___	
4. Other			5. Other	___	
5. TOTAL (A1-4)	___		6. TOTAL (1-5)	___	
B. LONG-TERM			**III. NET WORTH** (Total Assets minus Total Liabilities)	___	
(i) *Equity*					
1. Common/Preferred Stock	___				
2. Mutual Funds—Stock	___				
3. IRA-Stock	___				
4. Pension/Profit Sharing- Stock					
5. Other					
6. TOTAL (B-i-1-5)	___				

(ii) *Debt*

1. CDs-Long-Term _____
2. Corporate/Government/
   Muni. Bonds _____
3. IRA-Bonds _____
4. Pension/Profit Sharing-
   Bonds _____
5. Other _____
6. TOTAL (B-ii-1-5) _____

(iii) *Miscellaneous*

1. Limited Partnerships _____
2. Tangible Assets _____
3. Business Ownership _____
4. Real Estate (ex. Residence) _____
5. Other _____
6. TOTAL (B-iii-1-5) _____

III. PERSONAL ASSETS

1. Residence/Vacation Home _____
2. Automobiles _____
3. Personal Property _____
4. Other _____
5. TOTAL (1-4) _____

Total Assets _____ 100

Total Liabilities & Net Worth _____ 100

Planners can take several steps to assist their clients reposition their cash flow so that their financial planning goals can be achieved with greater efficiency. First, the planner can underscore the importance of exercising greater control over cash management, because serious financial problems result from a lack of control over cash disbursements. In fact, inadequate income, unwise investments, and catastrophic changes in circumstances are not the real causes of most financial disasters. Instead, as mentioned, it is the lack of control over cash flows that creates most financial problems.

Second, the planner should explain to the client the probability of achieving various goals based on the available financial resources. The planner should also assist the client in setting up a cash flow strategy that would help generate the desired level of savings. If, however, the revised cash flow budget proves to be inadequate, the planner should help revise the clients' objectives to make the savings and financial goals mutually consistent.

The process of cash management consists of budgeting, cash flow analysis, and cash flow management. Each of these areas is discussed next.

Budgeting

The budgeting process involves projecting cash flows, documenting actual receipts and disbursements, and monitoring expenditures and savings. Additionally, by comparing the actual expenditures with the corresponding budgeted items, this process identifies any discrepancies between them. Clearly, this task can be accomplished only if the client maintains both accurate and detailed accounts of income and expenditure. However, a collection of these data may not be as difficult as is generally perceived by clients. This is because budget-related data can be easily retrieved from income tax returns, home improvement records, financial statements, insurance policies, retirement and Social Security information, pension benefits, credit card records, investment data, and check book records. In the final analysis, an examination of the comprehensive budget provides the client with a unique perspective for constructing future budgets.

Successful budgeting involves controlling expenditures to enable clients to live within their budget. However, in order to achieve this objective, the expenditure estimates must be realistic. If these estimates reveal that expenditures will most likely exceed income, the planner should help the client identify those expenditures that can be reduced or eliminated. Also, since budgeting is a dynamic process, the planner should periodically review the budget and, when warranted, recommend its reorganization.

In passing, it should be mentioned that if a client is burdened with excessive debt, has marginal success in controlling budget expenditures, or presents a complicated situation that is beyond the capacity of the planner to handle, then the case should be referred to a counseling service for proper guidance and assistance.

Cash Flow Analysis

Once the planner has developed a functional budget in collaboration with the client, a cash flow analysis can be performed. This involves: (1) gathering from the client information on cash inflow and outflow; (2) development of a cash flow statement; and (3) calculation of the net cash flow. And since most clients are oblivious to their net cash flow position, this exercise can constitute a valuable learning experience for them.

The planner should be mindful of the fact that net cash flow can always turn out to be negative. If that happens, the planner should develop a more realistic estimate of the expected income or expenses. However, even after that exercise, if it appears that the available discretionary income is less than the amount required to meet the budgetary expenses, then the planner would have to develop a more stringent strategy for helping the client achieve a positive cash flow position.

Steps in Cash Flow Analysis

There are three key steps to cash flow analysis: (1) Gather current cash flow data. (2) Estimate future income and expenses. (3) Create a comprehensive cash flow statement. Each step is discussed next.

Step 1. The first step involves gathering from the client data relating to current cash inflows and outflows. In the process of providing the necessary data, the client is likely to develop an understanding of various sources of cash flows. This, in turn, should help the client make decisions regarding short-term spending priorities and learn how they lead to the development of long-term strategies.

When gathering income data, the planner should take into account all possible income sources, verify each of them from past income tax returns, and include this information in a cash flow statement. Also, in collecting data relating to expenditures, the check book, charge cards, and petty cash statements should be examined to establish the basic spending pattern. Finally, tax-deductible expenditures should be differentiated from non-tax-deductible expenditures, so the information could also be used for tax planning.

Step 2. The second step involves estimating future income and expenses, which could pose a special problem. Therefore, to keep the task simple, initially a distinction should be made between fixed and variable expenditures. The former are defined as those necessities over which the client has little control. Examples of these expenses include rent, mortgage, food, clothing, auto payments, insurance, utilities, taxes, loans, and charge accounts. By contrast, variable expenditures are items over which the client has at least some degree of control. If needed, these expenses could be modified, or even indefinitely postponed.

The collection of fixed and variable expense data should be used as the basis for making three-to-five-year expense projections. In making these projections, expected future changes in inflation rates, tax rates, salary income, and other possible areas should be taken into account. Also, changes in living expenses may include possible care for aging parents, future college expenses, additions to the family, purchase of a new car or a home, and other related changes which would increase living expenses. These projections should then be analyzed against the client's preestablished long-term goals.

When projecting future expenditures, the client should take into account contingency plans, which refer to the need for having in place an emergency fund and adequate insurance coverage. The emergency fund is intended to meet those expenses that are not included in the family budget, such as unexpected repairs, maintenance, or loss of employment. This fund should equal at least six months of expenses and should be placed in money market securities.

TABLE 7-2 Statement of Cash Flow

Inflow		Outflow	
	Amount		*Amount*
I. SOURCES, BEFORE TAX		I. FIXED EXPENSES	
1. Salary-Husband	_____	A. FAMILY NEEDS	
2. Salary-Wife	_____	1. Food	_____
3. Self Employment	_____	2. Clothing	_____
4. Divided/Interest	_____	3. Auto	_____
5. Capital Gains/	_____	4. Other	_____
Losses		5. TOTAL (1-4)	_____
6. Rents/Annuities/	_____	B. HOME	
Pension		1. Mortgage	_____
7. Bonus/Gift/Misc.	_____	2. Insurance	_____
Income		3. Utilities	_____
8. Alimony/Child	_____	4. Tax	_____
Support		5. TOTAL (1-4)	_____
9. TOTAL (1-8)	_____	C. INSURANCE PREMIUMS	
II. TAXES		1. Life	_____
1. Federal	_____	2. Disability	_____
2. State	_____	3. Health	_____
3. Local	_____	4. Auto	_____
4. Social Sec./	_____	5. Liability	_____
Disability		6. TOTAL (1-5)	_____
5. TOTAL (1-4)	_____	D. OTHER DEBTS	
III. INFLOW, AFTER		1. Installment	_____
TAX (I minus II)	_____	Loans	
		2. Charge	_____
		Accounts	
		3. Other	_____
		4. TOTAL (1-3)	_____
		II. FLEXIBLE EXPENSES	
		A. FAMILY NEEDS	
		1. Vacation	_____
		2. Entertainment	_____
		3. Gifts	_____
		4. Other	_____
		5. TOTAL (1-4)	_____
		B. EDUCATION	
		1. Tuition	_____
		2. Other Expenses	_____
		3. TOTAL (1-2)	_____

TABLE 7-2   *(continued)*

Inflow		Outflow	
	Amount		*Amount*
		C. MAJOR APPLIANCES & EXPENDITURES	
		1. Appliances _____	
		2. Other _____	
		3. TOTAL (1-2)	_____
		D. MISCELLANEOUS	
		1. Charity _____	
		2. Other _____	
		3. TOTAL (1-2)	_____
		III. TOTAL SAVINGS (Total Inflow minus Total Outflow)	_____
TOTAL INFLOW	_____	TOTAL OUTFLOW & SAVINGS	_____

Step 3. The last step in analyzing cash flow involves the construction of a cash flow statement, which is presented in Table 7-2. It shows the net change in inflows and outflows over time as determined by the client's receipts and disbursements. For comparison purposes, expenditures and income data should be condensed into general categories. Examples of inflows on the cash flow statement include salary or self employment income, interest, dividends, net rental income, and income tax refunds. Outflows include housing, food, clothing, transportation, insurance, taxes, savings and investments. Analyzing a cash flow statement helps clients better understand their spending habits over time. The cash flow statement records changes over time whereas a balance sheet presents a snapshot or a picture at a given point in time.

Cash Flow Planning

Once the client's current cash flow information has been analyzed and a cash flow statement prepared, the planner can start the cash flow planning process. This involves using specific strategies to maximize the client's discretionary income, and comprises the following three steps: (1)Implementation of strategies to maximize the discretionary income and minimize the expenditures; (2) revision of client's goals, assuming that Step 1 fails to achieve the desired goals; and (3) monitoring the cash flow plan periodically to ensure that the client is staying on track for accomplishing the established goals.

Step 1. Various strategies can be employed to maximize the discretionary income or minimize the expenditures. For instance, if the available discretionary income is less than the amount required to meet the client's financial goals, the following alternative strategies might be considered: (1) Debt restructuring. (2) Asset reallocation. (3) Qualified plan options. (4) Employee benefit plans. (5) Incorporating children's assets. (6) Income tax planning. (7) Expenditure control. Each alternative is discussed next.

Debt Restructuring. This technique involves paying off all outstanding credit card balances by consolidating debt into one low personal line of credit by refinancing the personal residence, discontinuing the use of credit cards, and deferring major purchases on credit as long as practical.

Asset Reallocation. This strategy includes repositioning of assets for improving cash flow. This is accomplished by switching the underperforming assets into more productive investment assets, thereby improving the investment return. In addition, growth and taxable investments might be substituted for, respectively, income producing and tax-exempt investments to achieve a similar objective.

Qualified Plan Options. Here the objective is to utilize qualified plans to a greater degree. For instance, if the client is not contributing the maximum allowable amount into a 401(k) qualified plan, then he or she should be encouraged to do so. Also, qualified plans need not consist only of 401(k) plans. Self-employed clients can also invest in a Keogh or a simplified employer-sponsored plan. Finally, IRAs, deferred compensation plans, and non-qualified savings plans might be available to both employed and self-employed clients.

Employee Benefit Plans. In this case, the client's benefit plans are used to pay for expenses with before-tax (as opposed to after-tax) dollars. Examples include using 401(k), 403(b), or SEP, or Flexible Spending Account through an employer, for paying allowable child care or medical expenses.

Incorporating Children's Assets. This technique involves saving for a child in a custodial account or a trust. The reason is that, for a child over age 14, and for children under 14 (up to the allowable amount), the marginal tax bracket applicable to the taxable investment earnings is likely to be lower.

Income Tax Planning. In this case, the objective is paying for expenses on a pretax basis (such as permitted by Section 125 or a cafeteria plan) or bunching of certain expenses in alternate years to take advantage of the so-called income tax effects.

Expenditure Control. This idea focuses on making a good faith effort to reduce consumption expenditure. This can be accomplished by emphasizing upon the client the important role a higher level of savings can play in building wealth.

Step 2. The second step constitutes helping the client revise or re-prioritize the stated goals. Here the objective is to ensure that the client is able to achieve all of the important goals. Examples of goal revisions include: eliminating negative cash flows, reducing income taxes, obtaining comprehensive insurance coverage, repositioning investment portfolio, and accumulating funds for a major purchase or target—be it a child's education, an early retirement, or a significant wealth transfer upon death.

Step 3. The final step is to monitor the plan. Monitoring should be done on an ongoing basis, because only through this process can one determine if the cash flow plan is functioning properly. Variances from the original targets should be investigated, and if appropriate, corrected. The results of the plan should be measured against the client's objectives to ensure that the client is satisfied with the way the plan is operating.

The primary motivation for undertaking cash management planning is to determine the adequacy of savings to meet the desired growth of net worth. The net worth growth target can be further refined by setting up more focused investment, educational, and retirement goals. An integral part of achieving these financial goals is to have adequate funds available, and cash management planning can help provide the necessary funds in a systematic and efficient manner.

Cash management planning can also be used as an important diagnostic tool. For instance, if negative savings are currently being generated, a close scrutiny of fixed and variable expenses can determine how the current situation can be reversed. The cash flow diagnostic tool can also be used to identify areas of excess spending so the spending patterns can be restructured to reduce the cash outflow to a more desirable level.

To recapitulate, cash flow management is crucial for the long-term success of a comprehensive financial plan. Laying a solid foundation for cash flow planning can go a long way toward accomplishing the client's financial short- and long-term objectives.

SYSTEMATIC SAVINGS PLANNING

INTRODUCTION

As a general rule, the majority of people who maintain a monthly budget consider savings to be their primary target. We have clearly demonstrated that preparing a monthly budget is only a means toward achieving a much broader, and a far more valuable, objective. The key to long-range financial success is the development of a systematic savings planning strategy. This strategy refers to the creation of specific plans to: (1) generate the required savings; and (2) systematically direct these savings toward the targeted areas so the specific financial goals can be achieved.

THE STARTING POINT

Systematic savings planning begins with net worth planning, because the desired annual rate of growth of net worth determines the rate at which savings should be generated. This point requires elaboration.

Let us assume John Client has a net worth of $750,000 and he wishes it to grow annually by a predetermined rate. John can achieve his objective only if savings increase at an accelerated pace. This fact is clearly revealed by Table 7-3. For instance, starting with a base of $750,000, if John wants his net worth to grow by ten percent a year, he would have to generate a positive savings of $75,000 during the first year—a formidable target indeed. Even more serious is the fact that during the fifth year savings must equal $109,000 if the ten percent growth rate in net worth is to continue. By comparison, a base of $400,000 would require additional savings of $40,000 during the first year and larger amounts in subsequent years if the net worth is expected to grow by ten percent, still a big challenge for most people. It is therefore important to set a realistic target for the growth of the net worth, so the family does not despair and give up savings planning altogether.

GOAL SETTING

Setting the overall savings target begins the systematic savings planning process at the macro level. However, it is the micro-level goals which are challenging and difficult to achieve.

TABLE 7-3 John Client: Net Worth Planning

Target: Annual Growth: 5%

		('000) Projected				
	Current	Year 1	Year 2	Year 3	Year 4	Year 5
Net Worth	$750	$787.5	$826.9	$868.2	$911.6	$957.2
Additional Savings Required	—	+37.5	+39.4	+41.3	+43.4	+45.6

Target: Annual Growth: 10%

	Current	Year 1	Year 2	Year 3	Year 4	Year 5
Net Worth	$750	$825	$907	$998	$1,098	$1,207
Additional Savings Required	—	+75	+82	+91	+100	+109

Positive savings increase the level of net worth in one of three ways: an increase in assets, a decrease in liabilities, or a combination of both. Therefore a family should give due consideration to setting appropriate goals in the first two areas. A goal-setting worksheet, presented in Table 7-4, not only specifies the amount of savings needed to finance each of the stated objectives, but also commits future savings to these objectives.

TABLE 7-4 Goal-Setting Worksheet

Goal	Amount needed $	Savings period: months	Expected after-tax return %	Monthly savings required $
I. Home				
II. Appliance				
III. Major Purchases				
1.				
2.				
3.				
4.				
IV. Vacation				
V. Education				
1.				
2.				
3.				
VI. Retirement				
VII. Charity				
VIII. Other _____				
Other _____				
Other _____				
TOTAL:	$ _____			$ _____

The next step in the goal-setting process is to calculate the amount of savings required to achieve each of the specific goals and record them in the last column. This can be accomplished by using the future value annuity factor (FVAF) concept developed in Chapter 3. Assume that the objective is to save $50,000 by the end of ten years to finance a child's education. If three percent compound interest can be earned on monthly educational savings net of inflation and taxes, and if money is saved at the end of every month, then by using HP-12C calculator we can determine that the monthly savings required to achieve this objective are $357.80, as shown in Table 7-5. The same technique can be used to determine the savings required for meeting other financial goals listed in Table 7-4.

The total *annual* savings required to meet all the stated objectives (Total Monthly Savings Required x 12 in Table 7-4) can now be compared with the total annual savings available (Item III of Outflow column in Table 7-2). If the available savings are greater than, or equal to, the savings required, consideration might be given to further improvement of the savings situation. If total available savings fall short of savings needed, however, specific steps must be taken to correct the problem.

Adequate Savings Scenario

Even when current savings are sufficient for meeting both short- and long-term financial goals and net worth growth targets, refinements in savings plans can still be made to further improve the situation. The reason for this is that we have never been taught to treat *savings as a fixed expense.* We seldom recognize the idea that we must *pay ourselves first* in the form of savings in order to ensure our own financial security. The result is that normally we live up to our means and go into debt whenever we need replacement of big ticket items or have to meet a major financial crisis. Since this is not a desirable long-term approach, a better strategy is to treat savings as a fixed expense and not as a residual amount after all other needs have been met. This strategy can help generate additional savings which, if properly channeled, could accelerate the rate of growth of net worth.

Inadequate Savings Scenario

If savings are inadequate to meet the stated goals, drastic steps need to be taken to bring savings up to the desired level. For convenience, these steps are divided into several broad categories.

TABLE 7-5

Step 1: Identify known variables
Future value: $50,000
Interest rate: 3%/12 months
Number of periods: 10 years × 12 months

Step 2: Clear calculator [f] [CLX]

Step 3: Enter data
Press
[5] [0] [0] [0] [0] [FV]
[3] [g] [i]
[1] [0] [g] [n]
[PMT]
Answer: $357.80

Expense reduction. The first order of business is to carefully analyze current expenses. The main emphasis should be placed on those flexible expenses that can be reduced without seriously affecting the desired lifestyle. These generally include personal expenses like clothing, personal care and entertainment, but they may also include the purchase of big ticket items, home remodeling, and expensive vacations. It also pays to improve the savings picture by cutting down some of the fixed expenses, although such an action may require moving to a smaller home or giving up some of life's amenities which we take for granted.

A practical expense reduction strategy is to make a monthly estimate for each major expense category and then compare the estimate with the actual expense in each category. If the *actual* expense for a given category consistently exceeds the *estimated* expense, then a conscious effort should be made to either reduce the actual expense or, if justifiable, increase the level of estimated expense. A convenient worksheet is presented in Table 7-6 which can be used to develop a meaningful expense reduction strategy.

Increase in income. Families generally assume that the income flow will remain relatively stable, especially if the breadwinners earn salaried income. This is not always a valid assumption. In the following section we will discuss how income can be augmented even for salaried employees.

An effective way in which returns on investments can be improved is by selecting investments that offer higher interest rates but have an acceptable risk level. The income situation can also be improved by reducing the checking account balance to the minimum and shifting the rest of the liquid funds into higher-yielding money market funds and short-term Treasury bills.

The level of income can also be raised by reorganizing the investment portfolio, a detailed discussion of which will be undertaken in Chapter 14. At this time it would suffice to identify some of the strategies for accelerating the growth of investible funds or increasing the cash flow generated by these funds.

In the investment world risk and reward are positively related. This means that an investor can obtain higher returns by moving the funds from low-risk to higher-risk investments. The success of this strategy, of course, depends on an accurate determination of the investor's risk tolerance level. A sensible strategy is to move the funds into those investments that are in the highest risk categories acceptable to the investor.

The second strategy is to become yield conscious. For instance, the annual return on a five-year, five percent, certificate of deposit with quarterly compounding is 5.094 percent, but the same CD with daily compounding could yield 5.126 percent. Similarly, yields on brokered CDs could be much higher than those offered by local banks.

The third strategy is to concentrate on tax savings. Assume that an AAA-rated, ten-year corporate bond is currently (2004) yielding 4.5 percent. Switching the money to a municipal bond of similar quality and maturity and yielding 3.5 percent would increase the yield from five percent to 5.33 percent, assuming a 25 percent tax bracket. Tax savings can also be realized by investing part of the money into limited partnerships which generate tax-sheltered cash flow, although the attendant risks of these investments should never be overlooked.

The fourth strategy is to convert a growth-oriented stock portfolio into an income-oriented stock portfolio or a bond portfolio. Typically, growth-oriented stock

TABLE 7-6 Expense Reduction Worksheet

Expenses	Jan.		Feb.		Mar.		Apr.		May		June		July		Aug.		Sept.		Oct.		Nov.		Dec.		ANNUAL		
	B	A	B	A	B	A	B	A	B	A	B	A	B	A	B	A	B	A	B	A	B	A	B	A	B	A	S/D
I. FIXED EXPENSES																											
A. FAMILY NEEDS																											
1. Food																											
2. Clothing																											
3. Auto																											
4. Other																											
5. TOTAL (1-4)																											
B. HOME																											
1. Mortgage																											
2. Insurance																											
3. Utilities																											
4. Tax																											
5. TOTAL (1-4)																											
C. INSURANCE PREMIUMS																											
1. Life																											
2. Disability																											
3. Health																											
4. Auto																											
5. Liability																											
6. TOTAL (1-5)																											
D. OTHER DEBTS																											
1. Installment Loans																											
2. Charge Accounts																											
3. Other																											
4. TOTAL (1-3)																											
II. FLEXIBLE EXPENSES																											
A. FAMILY NEEDS																											
1. Vacation																											
2. Entertainment																											
3. Gifts																											
4. Other																											
5. TOTAL (1-4)																											
B. EDUCATION																											
1. Tuition																											
2. Other Expenses																											
3. TOTAL (1-2)																											
C. MAJOR APPLIANCES & EXP																											
1. Appliances																											
2. Other																											
3. TOTAL (1-2)																											
D. MISCELLANEOUS																											
1. Charity																											
2. Other																											
3. TOTAL (1-2)																											

B: Budget   A: Annual   S/D: Surplus or Deficit

portfolios have low dividend yields. By converting such a portfolio into an income-oriented portfolio the investor can increase current cash flow.

The final strategy relates to the switching of non-income-producing investments, such as gold, coins, and antiques, into income-producing assets. These non-income-producing investments may be inappropriate for persons with cash flow problems, and substitution of income-producing assets like bonds and utility stocks can generate much-needed additional income.

EFFECTIVE SAVINGS STRATEGIES

Several *common sense* strategies can help increase personal savings. These strategies are outlined next.

Goal Setting

Unrealistic goal setting is perhaps the most important reason for the failure of savings strategies. The planner should assist the client in setting realistic savings goals. For example, setting a 20 percent annual savings goal for a family that is experiencing difficulty in making both ends meet is bound to fail. The best rule is to set a savings goal which is achievable with a concerted effort by the family.

Self-Rewarding Plan

Saving for college education, retirement, or vacation, or for purchasing a big ticket item always constitutes a difficult undertaking. Consequently, if a family exceeds the targeted savings goal, it should reward itself by spending the extra savings. This practice provides an added incentive for the family to meet the savings goal.

Savings-First Approach

We live in a consumption-oriented society in which it is relatively easy to buy goods on credit. But few of us realize that our savings would dramatically increase if we make cash purchases. The reason is simple: By saving first and paying cash, we would not only avoid paying high interest charges on loans but would also earn interest by investing the savings.

Automatic Savings Plans

A relatively painless way of saving is to have the money deducted directly from the paycheck and invest it in an appropriate vehicle. Money saved this way has a tendency to grow steadily, in the end surprising everyone.

Several vehicles are available for implementing automatic savings plans. One of these is the Series EE savings bonds. If these bonds are held for five years or longer, the return is based on the average yield of five-year Treasury notes. The yield cannot dip below a minimum rate specified by the government. Also, the interest is exempt from state and local taxes. Contribution to company qualified plans is the second method of instituting an automatic savings plan. A qualified plan can take the form of a pension, profit sharing, thrift, or 401(k) plan. Many plans allow participants to choose among various investments, including stocks, bonds, and mutual funds, company shares, and guaranteed investment contracts. Earnings in qualified investments grow tax-deferred, and coupled with the power of compounding, can make a significant difference in the way savings would grow over time.

A third technique for instituting an automatic savings plan is to instruct the bank to automatically switch each month a predetermined amount into designated mutual funds and enjoy the benefits of dollar cost averaging. This will not only help the net worth grow faster, but will also assist the saver in achieving with greater ease the long-term financial goals like educational funding and retirement.

EMERGENCY FUNDING STRATEGIES

Occasionally, even the best structured budgetary plans face temporary difficulties due to circumstances beyond ones control. In these situations it might be necessary to tap the liquid funds that were saved for a *rainy day*. If these funds are exhausted, then it would become necessary to raise additional funds. For this reason, it pays to become familiar with some of the better known sources of emergency funds that are easily available.

One such source is a home equity line of credit. Once the loan is approved, the homeowner can borrow up to 70 or 80 percent of the home's market value. A home equity loan is always considerably cheaper than a personal loan. Besides, interest is fully tax-deductible on equity loans of up to $100,000.

Another major source of emergency fund is the accumulated cash value in a life insurance policy. Loans from insurance policies issued prior to June 20, 1988 are completely tax-free, and most insurance companies charge low interest rates on these loans. Loans against cash values in policies issued after that date are still cheaper than personal or credit card loans, although some policies may not enjoy the tax-exempt status of the pre-June 1988 policies.

A third source of funds is company savings plans. Many companies allow their employees to borrow against their vested profit sharing, 401(k) or company stock plan assets up to $50,000.

A fourth source of emergency funds is the money earmarked as IRA investment. No loan interest needs to be paid on this money. And as long as the funds are returned within 60 days, there would be no tax liability triggered by this withdrawal.

CRITERIA FOR SAVINGS MEDIA SELECTION

The primary reasons for saving are to: (1) accumulate funds for meeting emergencies; (2) have funds available for purchasing consumer items; and (3) increase net worth, which is often referred to as capital formation. Savings strategies designed to achieve the first two objectives are significantly different from those associated with capital formation. This is because the major emphasis for saving for the first two reasons is on popular liquid assets, whereas the main criterion for capital formation savings is long-term growth, for which the more traditional long-term investment vehicles are used.

There are six major criteria for determining where money should be saved: safety, liquidity, return on savings, simplicity and minimum balance requirements, special service features, and tax considerations. These criteria are discussed next.

Safety

At the present time, all national banks and many state banks are members of the Federal Deposit Insurance Corporation (FDIC). This means that the checking, savings, and certificate of deposit accounts maintained at these banks are insured against bank failure for up to $100,000 on each account. Similarly, savings and loan associations are insured for the same amount by the Federal Savings and Loan Insurance Corporation (FSLIC). By using various combinations of accounts (individual, joint, trust, revocable, and so on) in banks and savings and loan associations, a typical family of four can insure up to $1.4 million of personal savings. In addition to the deposits insured by various government agencies, savings put into various types of government bonds are completely safe. However, money market accounts at various brokerage firms and other financial institutions are neither insured nor completely safe.

Safety concerns were foremost on the minds of the American public when in 1988 widespread savings and loans association and bank failures were reported by the media. The Bush Administration quickly moved to institute a plan to bail out the failing institutions to ensure that no one lost their savings. However, this incident, labeled the "Savings and Loan Mess," created deep concerns among the public; fortunately, confidence in savings institutions have now been fully restored.

Liquidity

If one desires to convert savings into cash quickly without losing the principal, checking and savings accounts in banks and credit unions as well as money market accounts provide a high degree of liquidity. In contrast, certificates of deposit provide higher interest rates but restrict withdrawal privileges. Similarly, various types of U.S. government bonds lack complete liquidity in that an early conversion may result in a partial loss of return.

Return on Savings

An important criterion in selecting a savings institution is the return it offers. Actually, the true return on savings depends not only upon the advertised rate, but also upon other considerations, including the type of account used for accumulating savings. This point requires elaboration.

Bank savings accounts. The most traditional of all bank savings accounts, which were previously called passbook accounts, form the backbone of bank savings. Until the interest rate ceiling was removed in April 1986, the maximum legally allowable rate on regular savings in federally insured institutions was 5.5 percent. However, even with the legal ceiling removed, most banks now pay 2 percent or less on savings accounts.

Bank checking accounts. Contrary to commonly held belief, interest can be earned on checking accounts, but only if certain stated criteria are met. Generally, a *regular checking* account pays no interest and usually costs about $5.00 per month. This cost is generally waived by the bank if a minimum balance of $400 to $500 is maintained. In contrast, *NOW* (Negotiated Order of Withdrawal) accounts pay interest and also allow check withdrawals. Often they waive maintenance fees if a minimum balance of $1,000 is maintained. Another variety, popularly known as *MMDAs* (money market deposit accounts) are not full-fledged checking accounts because they limit the depositors not only to three checks and three preauthorized transfers per month, but also require a minimum balance of $300 to $500. However, these accounts pay the highest rates of any bank account on which checks can be written.

For those with $5,000 to $20,000 in cash and securities, *AIOAs* (All-In-One Accounts) provide the best alternative. These accounts consist of a package of automated cash management, preferential personal treatment, and certain investment services provided by the bank or an outside firm that offers such services for the bank. On the cash management side, the bank covers the check written by the depositor by transferring exactly the right amount from the money market balance to the checking account. On the investment side, the depositor can use the bank facilities not only for trading securities but also for financial planning, managing real estate investments, and trust and estate planning. Even more important, dividends, interest, and proceeds from the sale of securities are deposited directly into the interest-bearing money market account.

The real yield. One of the most difficult tasks savers face is to figure out the real yield on their savings. The reason is not hard to find. Fierce competition for available savings often prompts financial institutions to make exaggerated claims which must be decoded to identify the real yields.

Simple versus compound interest. A common practice among financial institutions is to advertise a high interest rate on multi-year accounts; but it is only simple interest, and not compound interest. This practice can be utterly misleading to the neophyte and the unsuspecting saver. For instance, if ABC bank pays 5-3/4 percent simple interest on its five-year CD, and XYZ bank pays only five percent interest on its CD compounded annually over the same period, to the uninitiated the former bank looks more attractive. But based on what we learned in Chapter 3, in reality it is the XYZ bank which offers a better deal.

Delayed deposit credit. The real yield on a deposit also depends upon the number of days the money is allowed to earn interest. Some banks wait several days before crediting the account with the new deposit. This practice could significantly cut the yield on the deposit.

Minimum monthly balance requirement. Basically, there are six methods for paying interest: (1) low quarterly balance, (2) low monthly balance, (3) pro rata balance—FIFO, (4) pro rata balance—LIFO, (5) day-of-deposit to day-of-withdrawal balance, and (6) average daily balance. For instance, assume a $10,000 deposit is made on January 1 at 5-1/4 percent, and no additional deposits or withdrawals are made for a year. If interest is compounded and paid quarterly, under each of the preceding six methods the annual interest would be $535.42. Differences among these methods result from deposits or withdrawals of funds during the interest period and their effect on the final amount of interest paid, depending on which method of calculation is used.

The best savings method for depositors is the average daily balance method, in which the bank calculates the ending balance for each day, and then computes the average balance for the period to get the amount for which it is paying interest. The worst of course is the low balance method, in which the bank pays interest based on the lowest daily balance on deposit each day.

Grace period allowance. Grace days are also important in determining how much interest an account will earn. A grace period for deposits allows savings institutions to pay the interest from the first calendar day of the month and also on deposits withdrawn during the month's last three business days (called dead days). When a bank allows a grace period, it automatically boosts the real yield.

Other factors. Other factors that affect real yield include charges for excess withdrawals, penalties for premature closing of accounts, and other assorted charges. The impact of these charges and penalties on the real yield can vary greatly depending upon individual policies adopted by various financial institutions.

Money market mutual funds. A money market fund is a mutual fund that invests only in short-term money market instruments. Investors purchase and redeem these shares without paying a sales charge. Minimum initial investments for most funds vary from $500 to $5,000. Generally, these funds have a check writing option that enables individuals to write checks of $300 or more. Shares can also be redeemed from most money market funds by telephone or wire request, in which case the fund either mails the payment to the investor or remits it by wire to the investor's bank account.

Money market fund rates are generally higher than those offered by banks on their savings accounts. However, unlike bank accounts, money market accounts are not insured by the Federal Deposit Insurance Corporation (FDIC).

Certificates of deposit. Certificates of deposit (CDs) significantly differ from savings accounts in one respect: They must remain on deposit for a specified period of time. Consequently, investors earn a higher return on CDs than on savings. The difference in the rates depends on a CD's amount and the length of maturity. However, a substantial interest penalty is imposed on a CD's early withdrawal, and in certain instances early withdrawal may even result in partial loss of the principal.

In this connection, mention may be made of brokered CDs which have gained considerable popularity in recent years. Brokered CDs are simply CDs issued by a bank or a savings and loan association through a middleman—a broker—who gets paid a commission by the issuing institution. As long as the issuing bank is covered by the FDIC, brokered CDs are also fully insured by the FDIC up to the usual $100,000 limit.

The incentive for investing in a brokered CD does not come from a superior return, for generally the returns on these CDs are not appreciably higher than those on ordinary CDs. Their main attraction is that investors can liquidate them at any time without incurring the usual early withdrawal penalty associated with ordinary CDs.

Treasury bills. U.S. Treasury bills are the shortest-term marketable U.S. obligations offered and, by law, cannot exceed one year to maturity. The most frequent and most popular Treasury bill issues are three-month and six-month maturities which are offered on a weekly basis. Bids (tenders) for both issues are usually invited approximately one week prior to the auction. At that time, the amount offered and the terms of the offering are announced, with the terms for the two issues being similar. Treasury bills are sold on a discount basis. This means that investors pay a discount price for a bill but receive the face value upon maturity. The difference between the discount and maturity prices, or the additional cash received, as a ratio of that investment is the return on the Treasury bill. Incidentally, the minimum denomination of a Treasury bill is $10,000, followed by increments of

$5,000. It should also be noted that although Treasury bills are perfectly liquid and absolutely safe, an investor compelled to sell them before maturity could incur a loss.

Simplicity and Minimum Balance Requirements

It is simple to deal with all of the various institutions under consideration. In most instances, in order to transact business with them, the depositor need only present the passbook, have the account number put on a withdrawal/ deposit slip, call the broker to deal in U.S. Treasury bills, or fill out a simple application to open a money market account with check writing privileges.

Regarding minimum-balance requirements, banks and credit unions require a small minimum balance to open an account and a reasonable balance to maintain it. Savings bonds and U.S. bonds can be purchased for amounts ranging from a low of $25 (Series EE bonds) to $10,000 for Treasury bills. Finally, money market accounts generally require a minimum balance of $500, although the minimum may be as high as $5,000 with some funds.

Special Service Features

For providing special services, no other institution can match those offered by commercial banks, or what are frequently called full-service banks.

In addition to the traditional banking services, most banks offer special services that add to their quality. These include twenty-four-hour banking through automatic teller machines (ATMs), good deals on loans, travellers checks, income tax preparation services, investment management services, and even travel advice and airline tickets. Of course, many non-bank institutions provide similar types of services as well.

Tax Considerations

Of all the savings alternatives just discussed, only interest income received on a *tax-exempt* money market fund is exempt from federal income taxes. The simplest way to decide the relative attractiveness of a tax-exempt money market fund is to convert it into a fully taxable equivalent. This can be easily done by using the following equation:

$$\text{Equivalent Fully Taxable Yield} = \frac{\text{Tax Exempt Yield}}{1 - \text{Marginal Federal Tax Rate}}$$

Thus, if the yield on a tax-exempt money market fund is 4.5 percent and the investor is in the 25 percent tax bracket, the equivalent fully taxable yield is 6 percent: [4.5%/(1–.25)].

It is equally simple to calculate the after-tax equivalent yield from a fully taxable investment. For instance, suppose the taxable yield on a money market fund is six percent. For an investor in the 25 percent tax bracket, the after tax yield is 4.5 percent: [6(1–.25)].

Summing Up

Deregulation of financial institutions has brought about widespread changes in the financial services industry. Today's financial institutions provide a wide variety of choices and their services are superior to what they were even a few years ago. An overview of the popular liquid assets available today is presented in Table 7-7.

TABLE 7-7   Selection of Savings Media

	Safety	Liquidity	Simplicity	Special Services	Rate of Return	Minimum Required	Federal Tax Advantage
Commercial Bank	A	A	A	A	C	A	C
Mutual Savings Bank	A	A	A	B	A	A	C
Savings and Loan Association	A	A	A	B	A	A	C
Credit Union	A	A	A	B	A	A	C
Series EE Bonds	A	C	B	C	C	B	B
Series HH Bonds*	A	C	B	C	C	C	C
Treasury Bonds*	A	C	C	C	C	C	C
Municipal Bonds*	A	C	C	C	C	C	A

Differences have been ranked on an A, B, or C scale, with A denoting the highest and C the lowest degree of characteristic.

* These investments are not discussed in the text, and are included here merely for comparison.

Record Keeping

Accurate record-keeping assists the client in achieving long-term goals and objectives. The planner should provide guidance and checklists to assist the client in establishing an effective record-keeping system. Good record-keeping can help the planner recognize the hidden problems, retrieve important information, and assist the client in tax preparation.

Record-keeping, which can be linked to budgeting, should be done on a monthly basis. Use of computer programs, such as Quicken, can help the client analyze all existing information and determine what percentages of funds are spent on various expenses.

CREDIT AND DEBT PLANNING

INTRODUCTION

Shakespeare's Polonius was adamant on the subject of credit. "Neither a borrower nor a lender be," he cautioned his son. And many parents today believe that is still good advice for their children.

Unfortunately, such advice on credit is no longer sound. In our society, credit provides a valuable financial planning tool that should be used judiciously to maximize our welfare. The history of credit in the U.S. is presented in Table 7-8.

TABLE 7-8　History of Credit in the U.S.

1780:	George Washington's campaign is financed with a loan arranged by Robert Morris.
1800:	The first bankruptcy law is adopted.
1812:	The first installment furniture sales goes into effect in New York.
1831:	The first building and loan association is formed, offering mortgages with fixed monthly payments.
1856:	I.M. Singer & Company launches an installment selling campaign, allowing suitable buyers to take home a sewing machine for $5 down and monthly payments for the balance plus interest.
1857:	Remedial loan societies are created to grant credit to small borrowers.
1911:	Sears starts installment selling.
1914:	Western Union issues the nation's first charge cards.
1919:	General Motors launches the GM Acceptance Corporation to help buyers finance car purchases.
1950:	The Diners' Club introduces its travel and entertainment card.
1958:	American Express introduces its charge card. Bank of America mails the first 60,000 "Bank Americards" to Fresno, California residents.
1970:	President Nixon bans mass mailings of unsolicited credit cards, requiring banks to ask customers if they actually want a card before sending one.

Credit, whether it is buying now and paying later or borrowing money to pay for it, allows us to have *what* we want and *when* we want it. Our primary objective, then, should be to weigh the cost of borrowing money against the benefit to be derived from it, and obtain credit when the benefits exceed the cost of borrowing money. We should also protect our credit rating so we would maintain the highest level of creditworthiness at all times.

A DEBT OR A CREDIT?

A convenient way of stretching income is to borrow—commonly known as consumer credit or debt. Since there exists a great deal of confusion about the real distinction between debt and credit, we shall begin by defining both terms.

Formerly, debt was taboo, and no one liked to be in debt. Today, old attitudes have changed. Most people now believe that debt allows families to raise their living standards and increase their productive capacities. In fact, debt has become such an integral part of our lives that it is not even considered cynical to ask: Remember when people worried about how much it took to buy something instead of how long?

While debt has generally contributed to growth and prosperity, it has also created financial difficulties. Everyone at some time has seen the disastrous consequences of excessive debt accumulation by a person or business. Most families filing for bankruptcy are generally overextended. Their debts accumulate to the point where they cannot pay them back without resorting to the court system. Thus, debt appears to be both good and bad—a paradox that must be resolved before debt can be used as a financial planning tool.

In our society, people who borrow are often looked upon as lacking thrift and a sense of responsibility, while those who are creditworthy are viewed with respect. Yet such perceptions are really two sides of the same coin: to incur credit is to incur debt. It is now easy to see why debt is inherently neither good nor bad. What is important is the relationship between debt and one's ability to adequately service it and ultimately liquidate it with assets.

Of all the different types of debts that exist today, consumer debt or *consumer credit* is of special interest, because it refers to the use of credit by individuals for personal needs, in contrast to credit used by business or government. We will now undertake a discussion of consumer credit.

SOURCES OF CONSUMER CREDIT

Commercial Banks

The term *bank* refers to commercial banks and mutual savings banks. These are full service institutions offering a variety of loans—secured, unsecured, installment, and non-installment—to consumers and businesses. Many banks allow their depositors to use passbook savings accounts as collateral for loans, and consequently charge a lower interest rate. Most banks also make automatic overdraft loans, which permit depositors to write checks in amounts larger than the funds in their accounts. Typically, banks tend to make loans to their own customers, although loans are also made to others who are good financial risks.

Consumer Finance Companies

These are lending institutions specializing in small loans, and they make secured and unsecured loans on an installment basis. There are limits on the maximum amount that can be loaned ($2,000 to $5,000) and on the maximum interest that can be charged (48 percent on loans of less than $500).

Credit Unions

Another important source of credit is credit unions, which are cooperative thrift and loan associations limiting their loans to their own members. The annual percentage rate charged by these unions is six to 12 percent, although federal credit unions are legally permitted to charge up to 21 percent. In general, charges by credit unions are lower than those charged by commercial banks and finance companies.

Savings and Loan Associations

Savings and loan associations make mortgage loans, although they are also permitted to make other types of loans. These institutions also make certain types of home improvement and mobile home loans, as well as some personal and education loans using passbook savings as collateral. Typically, savings and loans charge seven to 12 percent on consumer loans, depending upon the borrower's creditworthiness and the terms of repayment.

Life Insurance Companies

Whole life insurance policies can serve as excellent collateral for inexpensive loans. Most insurance companies let their policyholders borrow most or all of the accumulated cash value at five or six percent. These loans are easy to obtain, and technically they do not even have to be repaid. However, financial protection is reduced by the loan amount, and that reduces the attractiveness of loans against insurance policies.

Auto Dealers

Loans from auto dealers are easily obtainable for financing automobiles. The formalities for obtaining these loans are kept at a bare minimum. However, auto loans are frequently expensive, and they may run as much as two percentage points above a typical bank installment loan used to finance new cars. It should be mentioned here that frequently new car dealerships advertise low financing rates (2.9 to 4.9 percent) for certain dealer-selected models, and these loans can be attractive.

Summing Up

On the basis of a discussion of the major sources of consumer credit just presented, it is possible to argue that no one source of credit is best for every occasion. Individual family situations vary considerably, and each of the sources listed previously satisfies a specific family situation. For instance, credit unions lend to their members only, while banks grant loans only to those who qualify. Persons with poor credit ratings and a desperate need for money are left with little choice but to borrow from pawnbrokers or loan sharks, and families with limited payment capacity in need of small loans often find it more convenient to borrow from small loan companies.

CREDIT HISTORY

Its Importance

Sooner or later everyone uses credit to acquire both consumer goods and capital assets. Even the few consumers who usually pay cash eventually wind up making installment purchases. If these credit-conscious consumers have not already established a credit rating, it may be difficult for them to borrow money.

Opening that first charge account, or getting that first charge card, is not always simple. Factors such as age, income, address, and employment stability, are important to credit managers. Traditionally, there have been noticeable biases against young, single or married adults of either sex, against divorced women, against ADC (aid to dependent children) mothers, and against persons with legal problems, although existing laws relating to credit prohibit these biases. However, some of these biases still prevail, and in our credit-oriented society, in spite of these difficulties, establishing a good credit rating is a must for everyone.

Factors Influencing Credit History

Consumer credit is based on faith in the consumer's good intentions to repay. In this sense, each prospective debtor is judged in terms of "the four Cs of credit." These are:

Character as judged by honesty, reliability, responsibility, and record of financial responsibility.

Capacity as measured by the financial ability to meet obligations; that is, it is based on the present and future earning power.

Capital as judged by the financial resources that can serve as collateral or security for the loan.

Credit rating as judged by the overall capacity to repay the loans.

The credit rating standards (recommended for the use of bankers) constructed from various banking and credit union publications are presented in Table 7-9.

Protection of Credit History

Denial of credit by a finance company may hurt a consumer badly, especially if it is based upon an incorrect credit report. The Federal Fair Credit Reporting Act of 1971 directs any credit company denying a loan to inform the consumer that the loan application was rejected on the basis of information contained in a credit report. The applicant is then free to contact the local credit bureau for further details. The bureau, in turn, must disclose all the information (excluding medical) in the file. If the file contains incorrect or incomplete information, the applicant has the right to ask the bureau to check the facts and, if warranted, make suitable adjustments in the record. If the bureau's information cannot be verified, these items must be dropped.

TYPES OF CREDIT

The Basic Issue

In our credit-oriented society, frequently we find it desirable or necessary to borrow; hence it is important to understand the nature of credit and learn the art of using it judiciously. This involves an appreciation of the *true* cost of credit and the knack of discovering the source of credit that is not only the cheapest but also right for the type of credit being sought.

There is no such thing as the *single cost of credit*. Costs vary according to a host of factors, such as types and sources of credit, the prevailing prime interest rate, duration of loans, credit rating of the borrower, and even the value and type of collateral offered. In fact, sometimes credit may even be costless. We will now discuss various categories of credit available, and the principal ways in which credit costs are calculated and expressed.

Categories of Credit

All consumer credit transactions fall into two broad categories: *sales credit* and *cash credit*. Sales credit is granted by department stores, automobile dealerships, repair shops, and other types of businesses in connection with the purchase of goods or services. In contrast, cash credit is extended to individuals by lending agencies in the form of cash.

Cross-dimensionally, sales and cash credits could be classified as *non-installment credit* and *installment credit*. The former is single-payment credit and is used for charge accounts, utility bills, bills for professional services, and single-payment cash loans. On the other hand, installment credit is used for paying off loans over time, granted for the purchase of durable goods, and for paying off major expenditures. A variant of installment credit is the *check credit plan*, under which the credit user

TABLE 7-9　Credit Rating Standards

	Favorable	*Unfavorable*
Employment	With good firm two years or more. Job involves skill, education.	Shifts jobs frequently. Employed in seasonal industry such as construction work. Unskilled labor.
Income	Steady; meets all normal needs.	Earnings fluctuate, depend on commissions, tips, one-shot deals. Amount barely covers requirements.
Residence	Owns own home or rents for long periods in good neighborhoods.	Lives in furnished rooms in poor neighborhoods. Changes address frequently.
Financial structure	Has savings account and checking account that requires minimum balance. Owns property, investments, life insurance.	No bank accounts. Few, if any, assets.
Debt record	Pays bills promptly. Usually makes large down payment. Borrows infrequently and for constructive purposes.	Slow payer. Tries to put as much on credit as possible. Frequent loans for increasing amounts.
Litigation	No suits by creditors.	Record of suits and other legal action for nonpayment. Bankruptcy.
Personal characteristics	Family man. Not many dependents relative to income. Mature.	Large number of dependents. Marital difficulties. Young, impulsive.
Application behavior	Seeks loan from bank with which he regularly deals. Answers all questions fully and truthfully.	Applies for loan at banking office far removed from his residence or place of business. Makes misstatements on application. In great hurry to obtain cash.

Source: Constructed from various banking and credit union publications.

is authorized to write checks against the credit limit as long as the amount for which checks are written does not exceed the approved limit.

Within these major categories, depending upon borrowers' preferences, credit-granting institutions offer one of three types of sales credit.

Thirty-day or regular charge accounts. Most Americans use credit generously as a convenience, especially when they are not charged for the use of such credit. A universal built-in feature of all regular charge accounts is that the seller of goods or services promises to deliver these products on credit without charge, provided their customers pay for them within a stated grace period. This arrangement obviates the need for carrying cash and also helps consumers consolidate their payments at regular intervals. This credit for convenience is an excellent idea, although one must never lose sight of the fact that the credit user will be charged a very high rate of interest (18 percent or more) on the unpaid balance of the loan if payments are not made by the due date.

Revolving and optional charge accounts. Revolving accounts revolutionized our major stores. They not only boosted sales but also changed the budget styles of consumers. Under this arrangement, businesses allow their customers to make repeated purchases as long as the total does not exceed the limit established when the account was opened. Furthermore, there is no finance charge if the payment is made within a stated grace period. But if a customer chooses not to pay for the purchases either partly or in full within the grace period, then a finance charge is imposed on the unpaid balance. Charges computed at 1, 1-1/2, or 2 percent monthly are equivalent to annual rates of 12, 18, or 24 percent, respectively.

Installment purchases or time-payment plans. The most popular demand for credit, of course, stems from the use of installment credit for buying durable goods. A sharp rise in personal expectations and demands for durable consumer goods, coupled with the inability of most buyers to pay cash for them, has been instrumental in the phenomenal growth of installment credit. In all cases installment credit or buying on time—as it is popularly called—is payable in several predetermined installments, hopefully, but not necessarily, spread out over the useful life of the durable goods being financed.

As mentioned, there are two methods of financing installment credit: buying on time directly from the seller, and borrowing money from a credit institution. In either case there is a cost involved in incurring a debt. This cost, which has several names—simple interest, add-on interest, interest discounted, monthly interest, finance charges, and points—is not a uniform charge.

Regardless of which payment method is selected, the consumer will probably have to go through sales finance agencies to make the specific choice. A large number of retailers and other businesses find it uneconomical to extend their customers credit by tying down their working capital, and hence they transfer their loan business to sales finance agencies. If an account is transferred to a finance company, the consumer will become responsible to that company for the repayment of the loan.

An important alternative to paying directly to sales finance companies is the credit card, the issuer of which honors the customer's creditworthiness. There are several advantages to using credit cards, chief among them being convenience, creation of instant credit, flexibility, ease of payment, and emergency use. Not all credit cards are cost-free, however. Travel and entertainment cards charge an annual fee—usually $15 to $75—but no interest on the loan. There is also a fee for cards issued by banks; in addition, there is an interest charge if payment is not made within a specified time. Typically, this ranges from one to 1-1/2 percent per month—a 12 to 18 percent annual rate. The same is true of most retail store cards.

The planner can assist the client in credit management techniques. This would include ensuring that credit is used properly, reviewing the current debt structure, establishing banking relationships, projecting borrowing needs, advising on borrowing sources, and helping with financial emergencies.

EFFECTIVE INTEREST RATE

John and Janet Client recently shopped around for a quality stereo system The information they gathered about the cost of credit is summarized in Table 7-10. If they took out a two-year simple interest loan from a credit union at a 12 percent interest rate, the $1,000 stereo would cost them $1,125. The same stereo would cost them $1,131.15 at an interest rate of 12.59 percent, $1,190.63 at 18.3 percent, and $1,256.25 at 24.6 percent. The Clients also discovered that the longer the repayment period, the higher the cost. The finance charge on a 12 percent $1,000 loan for one year was $65; if the time period was extended to three years, the finance charges almost tripled. Understandably, the Clients were confused by all of these numbers and had difficulty in deciding which method of financing the stereo was best for them.

Like the Clients, millions of American consumers when confronted with such decisions are unable to cope. However, for an intelligent buying decision there is no substitute for recognizing *effective* or *real* rates of interest under various types of loan provisions.

Interest represents the price borrowers pay to lenders for credit over specified periods of time. The amount of interest paid depends on a number of factors: the dollar amount lent or borrowed, the length of time involved in the transaction, the stated or nominal annual rate of interest, the repayment schedule, and the method used to calculate interest.

THE BURDEN OF DEBT

An Overview

We have learned that consumer credit is a powerful financial planning tool. However, used unwisely, it can create a nightmare for the family. Therefore, every family should limit their debt to the level they can conveniently handle. Unfortunately, no simple formula or all-purpose table is available that can neatly determine how much debt is safe for a family. Given the psychological make-up, financial resources, values, goals, and willingness to accept discipline, each person must establish his or her credit capacity.

Guidance from the Business World

One way to determine how much debt one can afford is to borrow from the business model. A business reaches its debt limit when its debt reaches its level of

TABLE 7-10   Cost of Borrowing $1,000

I: High interest rates raise total cost of credit

Total amount borrowed	$1,000	$1,000	$1,000	$1,000	$1,000
Interest rate (annual)	12%	12.59%	18.3%	24.6%	40%
Finance charge	$ 125.00	$ 131.15	$ 190.63	$ 256.25	$ 416.67
Total payment (principal and interest)	$1,125.00	$1,131.15	$1,190.63	$1,256.25	$1,416.67

Note: A two-year simple interest loan is used in this illustration.

II: Longer time payments raise total cost of credit

Total amount borrowed		$1,000	$1,000	$1,000
Interest rate (annual)		12%	12%	12%
Financed over		1 year	2 years	3 years
Finance charges		$ 65.00	$ 125.00	$ 185.00
Total payment (principal and interest)		$1,065.00	$1,125.00	$1,185.00

Note: Finance charges are calculated by using a complex system consisting of: (1) declining balance method; (2) a point system; and (3) a varied loan payment method.

equity. In other words, financial lenders consider businesses with a debt/equity ratio equal to or greater than one to be non-creditworthy and do not grant them additional loans. Consumers may regard their personal debt/equity ratio, calculated from their net worth statement, as a yardstick for determining their credit capacity. Note, however, that in calculating the debt/equity ratio the value of the home (an asset) and its mortgage (a liability) should be excluded, since financing a home falls into a category separate from borrowing for acquiring other assets.

The Rule of Thumb Approach

Another approach, based upon personal experiences of financial planners, involves setting the consumer installment debt limit as a fixed percentage of monthly income. Experts say the debt payment should be no more than ten to 15 percent of net monthly income. These payments should include all items purchased on credit except home mortgages. Net monthly income can be calculated by subtracting all taxes, Social Security taxes, IRA contributions, and contributions to pension and profit sharing plans. A debt limit calculation worksheet is presented in Table 7-11 which can be used to determine the maximum debt limit permissible for a given family. If debt to equity ratio exceeds 44 percent, then immediate action should be taken to correct the situation and seek the assistance of a professional.

BANKRUPTCY

The Modern Interpretation

Formerly, a debt was supposed to be honored by all means, and bankruptcy was taboo. Thus it seemed to Mark Twain, who, to his disbelief, was forced into bankruptcy in 1894. His creditors were happy to come to a compromise with him,

TABLE 7-11   Debt Limit Calculation Worksheet

1.	Monthly mortgage/rent	$ _____	Debt to income ratio
2.	Monthly credit card payments (average)	$ _____	Line 5/Line 12: _____
3.	Monthly auto lease or loan payments	$ _____	
4.	Monthly "other" obligations	$ _____	Less than 35%: Excellent
5.	Monthly debt payments (Lines 1+2+3+4)	$ _____	35% - 44%: Okay
			45% - 49%: Poor. Take
6.	Annual gross salary	$ _____	immediate action
7.	Bonus	$ _____	Over 50%: Danger zone.
8.	Overtime	$ _____	Seek professional help.
9.	"Other" income	$ _____	
10.	Alimony received	$ _____	
11.	Total income (Lines 6+7+8+9+10)	$ _____	
12.	Monthly income (Line 11/12)	$ _____	

but he promised to return *100 cents on the dollar*, and at the age of 59, despite uncertain health, he embarked on a 13-month foreign lecture tour to earn the necessary money. He did not return to the United States until after he had fulfilled his vow to return "100 cents on the dollar," not even when he learned of the illness and subsequent death of his beloved daughter.

Today, the honorable man who wrote *Huckleberry Finn* would probably be regarded as a nut. The stigma once attached to taking a financial bath no longer seems to be an important consideration for many modern-day debtors. Bankruptcy courts are filled with petitions from real estate agents, contractors, schoolteachers, journalists, stockbrokers, architects, engineers, and financial planners. In fact, even wealthy movie stars, professional athletes, and prominent business people have declared—and others like them continue to declare—bankruptcy.

While bankruptcy is no longer taboo, it still should be avoided. In the following section we will address this issue.

Avoiding Bankruptcy

Road to Recovery. There is an old cliche in the financial world which states that people cannot correct dangerous behavior unless they recognize that it is harmful. One simple way to find out if a person has a debt problem is to determine if there is enough money to pay off all the monthly expenses plus the minimum credit card and other debt obligations.

Obviously, not all financial difficulties result in bankruptcies. Financial problems may arise when expenses and obligations consistently exceed income, and the ability to make payments becomes a major issue. Such a situation may be created by either a mismanagement of finances or a set of circumstances totally beyond one's control. Whatever the reason, an individual can avoid a lot of grief by knowing some basic facts about the alternatives available to a person with serious financial difficulties.

Repayment Account. If money can be saved from cutting back on unnecessary expenditures, then automatic monthly deposits can be made into a separate bank account. Instead of using this money to pay monthly bills, it should be used to pay more than the minimum required on credit cards and increase the emergency fund.

Be a banker. Many 401(k)s allow participants to borrow against them. They will be repaying the loan with after-tax dollars. However, these retirement funds typically charge loan rates of eight or nine percent, much less than credit cards. And the borrowers would be paying themselves, rather than a bank.

Adopt creative measures. One way to reduce the burden of heavy debt is to switch to a less expensive house or a modest car and use the funds to reduce debt. Another idea is to prioritize debts and start paying off the bad debts which charge exorbitant rates of interest (such as credit card debt). A third debt reduction idea is to freeze the credit cards so they could not be used on an impulse.

The objective approach. It is impossible to solve a financial crisis by juggling books or by making random payments to only some of the creditors. These creditors are professional people who can easily outwit debtors when it comes to confronting such delinquent payers with legal claims. The best thing is to make a statement showing the money that can be spared for loan payments and the total monthly payments that must be made. This statement will clearly reveal where the consumer stands with respect to outstanding debts.

Informal arrangements with creditors. When financial difficulties are experienced that can no longer be handled by the consumer, an informal arrangement should be made with the creditors that can be settled out of court. If the necessary goodwill is shown by working with creditors rather than avoiding them, they may be willing to defer payments or refinance the debt to reduce the size of monthly payments. To reduce the debt, these creditors may also permit the return of some of the merchandise bought on credit.

If the informal arrangements fail to resolve the overextended debt problem, it may be possible to find a lending agency that could arrange for lower monthly payments extended over a longer period of time.

Credit counseling. If the first two steps fail, the next recourse should be to seek the help of a community credit counseling service, which provides expert, confidential guidance for little or no charge. It can be located through a banker or a lawyer, or the National Foundation for Consumer Credit—8701 Georgia Avenue, Suite 507, Silver Spring, MD 20910—and it can be contacted for obtaining a copy of their clinic directory.

Credit counseling services operate at two levels. First, through recasting the budget at a more modest level, the service may be able to help one keep the spending plan at a realistic level, thereby enhancing one's ability to meet financial obligations. Second, if expenses far exceed income and there is no way to bring the two together, the counseling service will try to arrange new repayment schedules with the creditors. If this is possible, the debtor may be asked to give the service a predetermined amount every month. According to an established plan acceptable to the creditors, the service will then distribute the amount to creditors.

Wage-earner plan. The last step before filing for bankruptcy is the wage-earner plan, a form of debt consolidation allowed under Chapter XIII of the Federal

Bankruptcy Act. Under this plan, under the guidance and protection of the Bankruptcy Court, and with the assistance of an attorney, the debtor draws up a budget for paying all the debts, along with meeting the normal living expenses for a period of three years. If this plan meets with the approval of the court and the creditors, interest and late charges on the debts are suspended, and each month the debtor turns over to a court trustee the predetermined installment payments for distribution to the creditors. The important feature of this plan is that the consumer does not give up any assets and a bankruptcy is not declared.

In this chapter we have presented issues relating to budgeting, credit management and debt planning. The topic of estate planning will be undertaken in the next chapter.

I don't know what your destiny will be, but one thing I know; the only ones among you who will be really happy are those who will have sought and found how to serve.

Albert Schweitzer

APPENDIX TO CHAPTER 7:
ROAD TO A SECURE FINANCIAL FUTURE

There is no doubt that the United States of America is the most economically advanced nation in the world. It is also evident that currently we enjoy the highest standard of living, and this trend towards prosperity will certainly continue in the 21st century.

It is therefore somewhat disconcerting to read the following story which recently appeared in a leading newspaper. Steve Yam has lots of debt. The 30-year old real estate broker, whose annual income is approximately $40,000, owes a total of $45,000 on eight credit cards. He owes another $6,000 on a debt-consolidation loan he took out years ago. But that does not stop him from accumulating more debt by using credit cards to pay for gas, entertainment, large purchases and vacations.

But wait! Steve cannot be totally blamed for this fiscal indiscipline. None of his money worries and irresponsible spending habits have kept him from getting new solicitations in the mail each week from banks and other financial institutions eager to give him yet another pre-approved credit card. And that is not all. A local store is willing to sell him new furniture with no down payment until 2006, and the loan would be advanced at zero percent interest.

It is practices like these that have allowed Americans to continue borrowing to pay for homes, cars and other big-ticket items, bolstering the weakened economy. But the resulting growth in consumer credit—to a record $2.039 trillion (excluding loans to secure real estate) at the end of 2001—also has exposed a potential new economic fault line.

Unfortunately, people do not fully realize the dangers of the credit that is available to them. Many consumers know that they are acting irrationally but they do not have any qualms about going deeper into debt. But these debts take a heavy toll on the family budget. American households spend nearly 14 percent of their disposable income servicing debt. From the president of the U.S. to the bankers and businessmen—all these people are telling us to spend, spend and spend, and we are listening to them. It is little wonder that for many consumers this irrational exuberance directly leads to the bankruptcy courts.

But it should not have to be this way, especially since we are an enlightened, affluent nation. The chapter on cash management, savings, and debt planning provides us with a solid platform on which to build our short- and long-term financial objectives framework.

There is no question that the discipline of creating monthly and annual budgets and living within our means is extremely important. However, including in one's expenses a line item for savings is, in my opinion, critical to accumulating cash reserves which are vital for achieving personal financial goals.

Mr. Charles G. Dharte, Jr. retired as Chairman of the Board and CEO of Huntington Bank of Michigan. Because of his lifelong devotion to establish fiscal discipline in personal financial planning, he was invited to write this section. We are certain that the reader will greatly benefit from his observations.

To be sure, individuals who desire to develop a sound wealth creation strategy must reconcile their differences between current *needs* and current *wants*. In a society promoting products and services that are quite appealing, and with the easy availability of credit, consumers must make informed choices that would lead to personal success in wealth creation. The harmonious use of cash management, savings, and credit can provide a concise snapshot of the family's financial position. In such a framework, when a spending or borrowing decision is made, the financial risk that is assumed in the process becomes quantifiable.

Consider, for instance, the problem of choosing between a new car and a two-year old car in a mint condition which still has its warranty in place. While the pleasure of driving a brand new car cannot be totally denied, the premium that must be paid to experience that pleasure should never be overlooked. In fact, making such a financial choice represents a lifestyle decision, and only an in-depth financial plan can provide the framework for making such a decision in a rational manner. Regardless of what the decision is ultimately made, the individual with a comprehensive budget plan would make the choice knowing full well that a sizeable premium must be paid if a used car is rejected in favor of a new automobile.

This, then, is the backdrop against which responsible financial decisions should be made. And it is the discipline of the informed choice prior to making the premium payment that leads to sound decision-making and ultimately to wealth creation.

The discussion on credit undertaken in the chapter makes a powerful point. The primary purpose of using credit should be to achieve one's personal financial goals and not merely to enhance the currently prevailing lifestyle. The selection of the most appropriate credit option (such as credit card, debit card, line of credit, home equity loan, mortgage loan, and so on) should be made with great care. This is because, for best results, the right credit option should be ready for use on a when-needed basis, so consumers would not be compelled to assume excessive credit risk in an emergency and ruin their credit rating in the process.

In conclusion, it can be said without equivocation that we live in a great nation that gives us the freedom to make our own choices. I sincerely hope that we will always have the courage to be honest with ourselves insofar as our needs and wants are concerned. I further hope that we will have the good judgment to implement some of the recommendations contained in this chapter. In the final analysis, if we develop the fiscal discipline by implementing a functional budget, using credit wisely, and making rational final choices, then we will succeed in creating wealth and establishing a long and secure future.

CHAPTER 8

Basic Structure of Estate Planning

INTRODUCTION

As a general rule, the estate of a person consists of personal assets, real property, joint interests, qualified retirement plans, life insurance owned by the individual, life insurance policies gifted within three years of death, and any business interests. Upon death, the estate will pass by different means to other family members, friends, and designated entities. This estate can be likened to a funnel shown in Figure 8-1, through which all of the assets will pass. What emerges at the bottom of the funnel is the amount of the estate remaining to be distributed. The amount of property actually distributed can be significantly affected by the form of ownership and the means chosen by the decedent to effectuate the transfer.

The strategies developed for establishing various forms of ownership and legal titles are commonly referred to as *estate planning*. The objectives of estate planning include: (1) protecting the family; (2) providing for an efficient utilization of assets during lifetime; (3) ensuring that the estate property is adequate for family needs; (4) arranging for an orderly distribution of assets to the beneficiaries; and (5) taking steps to ensure that, upon death, the surviving family members would be able to obtain proper guidance and advice from trusted professionals.

UNAUTHORIZED PRACTICE OF LAW

The financial planners must avoid performing services for their clients that constitute an unauthorized practice of law. It is clear that the drafting of documents by

This chapter, and the one that follows, were critically reviewed for technical accuracy and enhancement by Salvatore J. LaMendola, Esqr., J.D., C.P.A., Attorney at Law, Cox, Hodgman & Giarmarco, Tenth Floor, Columbia Center 101 West Big Beaver Road, Troy, Mich. 48084-4160. Tel: (248) 457-7000. Also, the authors greatly benefited from the thoughtful criticisms of Julius H. Giarmarco, Esqr., J.D., LL.M. The review was completed in 2001. However, the authors are solely responsible for the contents.

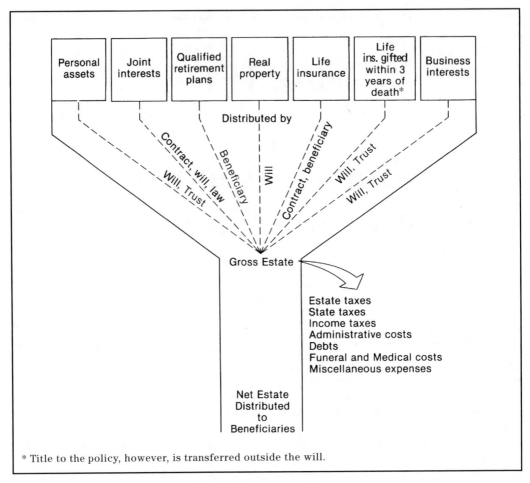

FIGURE 8-1 Estate distribution

someone other than an attorney is the unauthorized practice of law. The task for the planner, however, normally relates to the review of a will or a trust instrument and the advice rendered relative to the desirability of specific clauses. Generally, when a statute or legal interpretation applies to the specific situation, the planner should always take a conservative approach by consulting an attorney.

HISTORY OF ESTATE TAXES

Taxation of property transfers at death can be traced back to 700 B.C. in ancient Egypt. The following are the major developments which took place in the U.S. since 1797.

1797. First estate tax in the U.S. was a stamp tax, requiring use of federal stamps on wills and other documents related to inheritances. It was created to finance a defense against France. This tax was repealed in 1802.

1862. With expenses from the Civil War mounting, a new tax on intergenerational transfers of wealth was imposed. It was expanded in 1864. The tax was repealed in 1870.

1898. Another estate tax was enacted during the Spanish-American War. Estates under $10,000 were excluded, as were bequests to a surviving spouse. This tax was repealed in 1902.

1916. The beginning of modern estate and gift taxes, legislation established rules for valuing an estate, created exemptions and deductions and imposed progressive rates ranging from one percent to ten percent. Estates up to $50,000 were exempt from taxation. By the following year rates ranged as high as 25 percent on estates over $10 million.

1924. Top rate was raised to 40 percent on estates of more than $10 million. Gift tax was added, repealed in 1926 and was reintroduced in 1932.

1934. Rate on estates over $10 million was raised to 60 percent, and to 70 percent on estates over $50 million a year later.

Early 1940's. The top rate was raised to 77 percent on large estates.

1948. Marital deduction was added, permitting as much as one-half the value of an estate to pass to a surviving spouse free of taxation.

1976. Estate and gift taxes were combined under a single rate schedule, with the top rate set at 70 percent on amounts greater than $5 million. The amount exempt from taxation was raised from $60,000, increasing gradually, to about $175,000 in 1981.

1981. The unified tax credit was increased, effectively raising the amount exempt from taxation gradually to $600,000 in 1987. Limits on transfers to a surviving spouse were eliminated. Reduction of the top rate to 55 percent for the largest estates was phased in over three years.

1997. Exemption amount was raised to $625,000 beginning in 1998, with increases in several steps to reach $1 million in 2006.

2001. Exemption amount for 2002 was raised to $1 million.

2002. Exemption amount for 2003 is $1 million.

2003. Exemption amount for 2004 was raised to $1 million.

2004. Exemption amount for 2005 was raised to $1 million.

DEALING WITH DEATH: PSYCHOLOGICAL IMPLICATIONS

The estate planning process can help the client come to terms with the financial problems created by death. In many respects, the client must accept the fact that death is inevitable, and the estate planning process should begin *now*. The planner's role is to raise the issues associated with death and dying to help the client come to personal realizations and conclusions. Reducing fear and anxiety about death can help the client fully enjoy the pleasures of life. A plan that structures the future and provides support for the survivors upon death can be psychologically satisfying to the client.

AN OVERVIEW OF ESTATE PLANNING

ESTATE PLANNING: OBJECTIVES AND TOOLS

The Common Misconceptions

A popular myth that is widely prevalent is that estate planning makes sense only for wealthy people. That is simply not the case. In fact, even those people at lower financial levels need to plan for their estates. Besides, not every estate is as small as it might appear, since appreciated values of solely-owned homes, stocks and bonds, life insurance proceeds, and the prorated portion of jointly held properties are included in every estate.

Those who believe that estate planning can be dispensed with if husband and wife own everything jointly are also mistaken. In fact, when property is held by non-spouses as joint tenants with rights of survivorship, upon the death of the first joint tenant the entire value of the joint property is included in the decedent's gross estate, unless the surviving joint tenant can prove that he or she contributed to the joint property. Property jointly owned by spouses is subject to federal estate tax at the surviving spouse's death.

Some people believe that purchasing life insurance constitutes a complete estate plan. They are grossly mistaken. True, insurance proceeds paid to a named beneficiary do not have to pass through probate, since a life insurance policy is a contract. But it is still subject to federal estate taxes if the deceased had incidents of ownership at the time of death. Choosing the right options on a policy is also part of estate planning. Should it be paid to the beneficiary in full or in installments? Should the beneficiary be solely responsible for managing the money, or should a trustee be given that task? These and other related questions are answered as part of estate planning.

Finally, a myth that never dies is that making a will completes the estate planning process. A will does not govern the distribution of all assets. Retirement and profit sharing benefits or assets transferred to a living trust, for example, are not subject to the manner of distribution provided for in the will. The fact is that a will documents an individual's wishes relating to certain assets, but by itself it is not an estate plan. The will does not cover all the aspects of estate planning, since some of the assets may pass outside the will or may not be coordinated with the transfer of other assets to the beneficiaries.

Objectives of Estate Planning

The primary objective of a comprehensive estate plan is to make sure that the maximum value reaches the intended beneficiaries in a manner directed by the deceased. In order to accomplish this goal, it is necessary to carefully consider the impact of federal estate and state transfer taxes so as to legally minimize the impact of current estate tax laws. The planning process can be both cumbersome and technical. It is therefore advisable to seek the help of a practicing estate planning attorney or a financial planner specializing in estate planning.

Tools of Estate Planning

The word *estate* refers to everything solely or jointly owned by a living person. An effective estate plan lays the foundation for an orderly transfer of an estate upon death in accordance with the wishes of the deceased.

A person's estate comprises two types of property: one type passes through probate (probate estate), and the other type passes outside the probate estate. The former type consists of assets owned outright by a person. These assets can be disposed of by the person as desired. The latter type of assets includes, but is not limited to, life insurance policies, jointly owned property, retirement benefits payable to designated beneficiaries, and assets transferred to an inter vivos trust, commonly called a *living trust*, which designates how the property is to be treated upon death. Incidentally, those properties that pass outside probate could still be subject to federal estate tax.

The following are four basic tools of estate planning:

The Will
Joint Ownership
Trusts
Lifetime Gifts

In addition, when creating an estate plan, a skillful estate lawyer can create other documents designed to save thousands of tax dollars and make the estate plan more efficient. For instance, there are a number of ways to transfer assets from one spouse to the other which will qualify for the unlimited marital deduction. Assets which pass in this manner will avoid the payment of federal estate taxes at the time of the transfer.

At this point it is useful to make a distinction between assets which go through probate and those that completely bypass it. Both types of assets are included in the gross estate of the decedent as can be seen from Figure 8-2.

We will now turn to a discussion of the structure of each of the four basic tools of estate planning just listed. Use of these tools for developing effective estate planning strategies will be discussed in the next chapter.

THE WILL

Importance of a Will

Every person, single or married, old or young, healthy or sick, needs a will, which is a legal document that disposes of an individual's property activated upon death. This document can be used to designate: (1) to whom the property should go; (2) when it should go; (3) in what amount it should go; (4) how it should be safeguarded; (5) by whom it should be handled; and (6) who should be the guardian of minor children. By creating a valid will, a person exercises the legal right to transfer assets upon deserving or needy relatives, friends, or other beneficiaries, and designating a guardian responsible for taking care of minor children until they reach adulthood.

Absence of a Will

Even when a person does not have a valid will, some form of will is provided by the state to distribute the estate. So when a person dies without a will, state statutes known as the *laws of intestacy* determine how the estate is to be distributed. Frequently, the state's notion of how the estate should be handled, and the minor children supervised, are at odds with how the deceased would have proceeded.

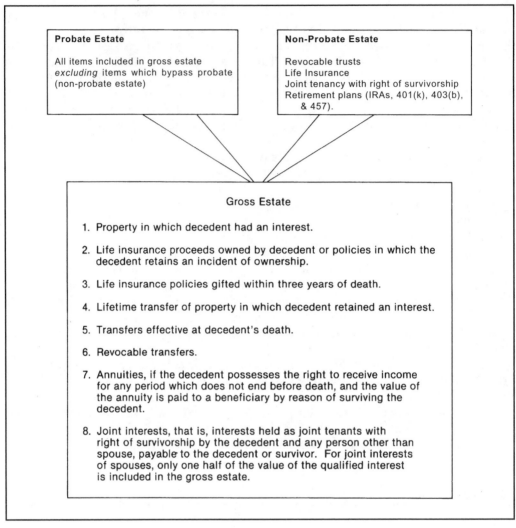

Probate Estate

All items included in gross estate
excluding items which bypass probate
(non-probate estate)

Non-Probate Estate

Revocable trusts
Life Insurance
Joint tenancy with right of survivorship
Retirement plans (IRAs, 401(k), 403(b),
   & 457).

Gross Estate

1. Property in which decedent had an interest.

2. Life insurance proceeds owned by decedent or policies in which the
   decedent retains an incident of ownership.

3. Life insurance policies gifted within three years of death.

4. Lifetime transfer of property in which decedent retained an interest.

5. Transfers effective at decedent's death.

6. Revocable transfers.

7. Annuities, if the decedent possesses the right to receive income
   for any period which does not end before death, and the value of
   the annuity is paid to a beneficiary by reason of surviving the
   decedent.

8. Joint interests, that is, interests held as joint tenants with
   right of survivorship by the decedent and any person other than
   spouse, payable to the decedent or survivor. For joint interests
   of spouses, only one half of the value of the qualified interest
   is included in the gross estate.

FIGURE 8-2   Gross estate

In particular, in the absence of a valid will, charitable organizations and individuals other than relatives receive nothing. Consequently, dying intestate can be a real tragedy.

The distribution of an estate when a person dies intestate is shown in Figure 8-3. While the laws of descent and distribution vary between states, without a will, most states make the spouse share the estate with children, siblings, or parents.

There are other disadvantages to not leaving a valid will. Upon dying intestate, the estate will be handled by a court-appointed personal representative who may not have been approved by the deceased. Another disadvantage is that legal procedures may force the personal representative to sell and distribute the estate or convert it into *legal investments* (government bonds, checking accounts, and so on) in accordance with the law. Most states limit the types of investments in which a personal representative can invest estate assets. Furthermore, the personal representative may be required to sell non-income producing assets because there is

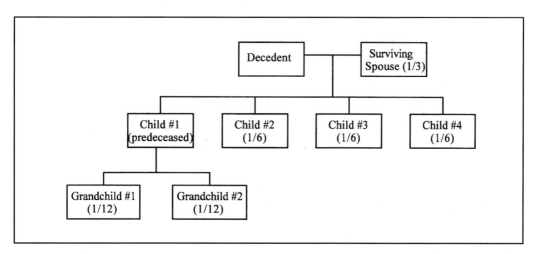

FIGURE 8-3 Typical scheme of distribution for intestate succession. Paul J. Lochray, *The Financial Planner's Guide to Estate Planning*, Prentice Hall, 1987, p. 67.

no provision in the will authorizing the representative to retain them. Thus, an investment which the decedent would have retained in the family, such as a closely-held business, might have to be sold and the proceeds invested within prescribed statutory limitations. Finally, without the protection of a will, the estate could be reduced substantially by unnecessary administrative expenses and estate taxes, thereby reducing the value of the net estate.

Drafting a Will

To draft a valid will, one must have the *testamentary capacity*. That is, it must be demonstrated that at the time the will was drawn the individual recognized the natural objects of his or her bounty, was knowledgeable about the assets comprising the estate, and was certain of how the assets were to be distributed. Although there exists a wide variety of wills, they can be classified into four categories, as described next.

Simple will. A simple will is signed by the maker or testator before the required witnesses, usually two in most states. This will specifies the disposition and the distribution of the estate involved. This is usually the shortest and easiest will to execute and is appropriate for small estates.

Reciprocal will. When two persons—most often husband and wife—simultaneously execute their own wills, frequently they leave their respective and totally distinct estates to each other. A reciprocal will can be drawn up as a unified document, although the most common practice is to draft two separate wills. This type of will is valid even when the estates of the two parties are not commonly owned. For instance, there could be separate property such as inheritances from previous wills, an estate that is not related to the present marriage, or any other related holdings.

Mutual will. A mutual will is a single instrument created by two parties to dispose of their respective properties. Mutual wills, or joint wills, are neither the simplest nor the most efficient form of will to draft, and if possible, they should be avoided.

Holographic will. This type of will is written entirely by hand by the individual, known as the testator or testatrix. Various states have differing opinions on their acceptability, and many legal battles have evolved over their validity. It is advisable to avoid making this type of will.

Basic Structure of a Will

A will can be a long, complicated document, or it can consist of a single phrase, "I leave all my personal property and belongings to my spouse." Regardless of its degree of complexity, the basic structure of a will should contain the following common clauses.

Exordium Clause. This clause identifies the name, address, and domicile of the testator. It also invalidates all prior wills and declares the current will as the testator's will.

Payment of Debt and Taxes Clause. This clause directs the payment of debt and taxes.

Disposition of Personal and Real Property Clause. This clause provides for the disposition of personal property, such as furniture, jewelry, automobiles, and clothing. It also directs the disposition of real estate property.

Trust Clause. This clause sets out the terms of any trusts created by the will.

Appointment of Fiduciary Clause. This clause designates the person or the fiduciary who will serve as the personal representative.

Powers Clause. This clause details the powers to be exercised by the personal representative. These include managing and selling property, handling the investable funds, and borrowing and lending of funds.

Appointment of Guardian Clause. This clause designates who will serve as guardian of minor children, if any.

Common Disaster Clause. This clause specifies which spouse would be presumed to have survived the other in the event of simultaneous death.

Testimonium and Attestation Clause. This clause establishes that the testator recognized the will and provides for compliance with other requirements, such as signatures of witnesses.

Codicil

Occasionally, even the best-drawn wills run into unexpected problems. Marriage or divorce might render a will obsolete. Other changes in the family, financial or business situation, or tax law changes might require revision of the existing will. An instrument, known as codicil, can be used to make these alterations in the existing will, thereby avoiding the problem of creating a new will. The codicil should be drawn up by a lawyer, properly witnessed, and attached to the will. Of course, there are certain situations in which it is more appropriate to draw up a new will rather than to alter the will by means of a codicil. The planner should be aware that the law of each state governs the validity of will provisions.

Letter of Last Instructions (Memorandum)

Settling an estate is no easy chore, and it can become complex and time consuming. Since a person's interests are best served when family members promptly receive what is due them without losing an excessive amount in taxes and court costs, the beneficiaries should assist the personal representative in every possible way. A person may also wish to assist in carrying out the surviving spouse's responsibilities specified in the will. The creator of the will can achieve these objectives by writing a letter of last instructions. Although not legally binding, this letter is usually addressed to a surviving spouse, and a copy is provided to the personal representative.

Ideally, a letter of last instructions should be both informative and directive. It should guide the surviving spouse in locating the will and other important papers (such as birth certificate, Social Security card, marriage certificate, naturalization papers), finding the safety deposit box, arranging for organ donations, and making the funeral and burial arrangements. This letter should also contain details of at least the following documents: life insurance, bank accounts, savings and loan association accounts, securities, savings bonds, real estate, Social Security, homeowners' insurance policy, health and auto insurance, and financial obligations.

MAKING A WILL: SOME POINTERS

Estate planning attorneys recommend that the following points be kept in mind when making a will.

1. The individual should work closely with the family, as the will is written by a professional. That way, family objectives can be met regardless of who dies first.

2. A beneficiary should not be chosen as a witness. If called upon to validate, the person may not be able to collect the inheritance.

3. The maker would be well advised to use in the will both percentages and absolute amounts rather than simply dollar amounts. For instance, if $25,000 is left to a charity and the remainder to the spouse, nothing would be left for the spouse if the estate shrinks to that level. Of course, these percentages and dollar amounts should be periodically reviewed to avoid such problems as the possibility of making a charitable contribution of a larger dollar amount than anticipated if the estate value rises in the future, or the shrinkage of the estate below a given level.

4. The will should be as flexible as possible. For instance, the heirs may suffer if the will insists on their holding certain stocks for the long term.

5. The will should be altered by a codicil and not by writing on the document itself.

6. The will should be kept up-to-date. Also, it should be reviewed whenever there are significant changes in the family and in the tax laws.

7. All will-related affairs should be kept in order. This includes making an inventory of all assets and purchasing additional life insurance to provide liquidity to compensate for an estate consisting largely of illiquid assets.

8. The will should dispose of property in accordance with the maker's wishes.

9. The will should dispose of the maker's property in a way that would avoid conflicts among the maker's family and friends.

10. If consistent with the objectives of the maker, the will should minimize or avoid altogether estate taxes.

Upon death, this information will be of great value and assistance to both the family members and to the personal representative.

The Personal Representative

An important aspect of setting up a will is the appointment of a personal representative. The personal representative can either be one or more individuals, or it can be a corporate fiduciary such as a trust company. Designating a personal representative, of course, is not a precondition for setting up a will, and a will would be valid even if the appointment of a personal representative is omitted. However, in that case the court would appoint a personal representative to administer the will.

The main responsibilities of a personal representative are as follows: (1) Probate, or prove, the will's validity in probate court. (2) Assemble all property belonging to the estate, including life insurance benefits, household effects, securities, mortgages, real estate interests, and cash. (3) Collect money owed the estate. (4) Appraise, manage, and protect business interests. (5) Liquidate or invest funds in accordance with the will. (6) Pay all debts, federal, state, and local taxes, and all death-related expenses. (7) Defend against claims when necessary. (8) Distribute the remaining properties and close the estate.

Because the personal representative plays such an important role in overseeing the orderly distribution of an estate, this person can certainly benefit from having access to an up-to-date data sheet. A condensed and simplified version of such a sheet entitled Estate Planning Data Requirements, is presented in Table 8-1.

Power of Attorney

People often worry about the onset of a physical or mental disability as they advance in age. In particular, they fear that the management of their assets and decisions about their financial well-being may be taken out of their hands without regard to their personal preferences. For these people drawing up a power of attorney document may provide an ideal solution.

A power of attorney is a written agreement that allows a trusted individual (the attorney-in-fact) to act on behalf of the principal (the person who created the power of attorney). This agreement may be either special, applying to only certain situations, or general, giving the attorney-in-fact virtually limitless control over the principal's financial affairs. It may also be either indefinite or for a specified length of time. The power of attorney is used in those situations in which the principal is incapable of carrying out his or her own financial, legal, or other responsibilities. Examples of incapacity are heart attack, an extended vacation, or unexpected detention in a foreign country.

Durable Power of Attorney

A durable power of attorney (DPOA) is used to select someone to make financial decisions for the principal in case of incapacity. A DPOA can be drafted to become effective immediately or only upon incapacity of the principal.

A DPOA must generally be in writing. It is also recommended that it be dated, signed by the principal, and acknowledged before a notary public.

A durable power of attorney for healthcare (DPAHC) is used to nominate someone to make healthcare decisions for the principal. The DPAHC can give a person the authority to determine what medical treatment to consider should the principal become incapacitated.

TABLE 8-1   Estate Planning Data Requirements

Personal data:
Names, addresses, phone numbers, family consultants
Family birthdates, occupations, health problems, support needs
Citizenship, marital status, marital agreements, wills, trusts, custodianships, trust beneficiary, gifts or inheritances, Social Security numbers, education, and military service.

Property (except life insurance or business):
Classification, title, indebtedness, basis, date and manner of acquisition, value of marketable securities, and location

Life insurance

Health insurance:
Disability income
Medical expense insurance

Business interest:
Name, address, ownership
Valuation factors; desired survivorship control; name, address, and phone number of business attorney and accountant

Employee census data

Employee benefits

Family income:
Income of client, spouse, dependent children, income tax information

Family finances:
Budget information, investment preferences
Ranking of economic objectives, capital needs, other objectives

Income and capital needs:
Retirement: Age, required amount, potential sources
Disability: Required amount, sources
Death: Expected sources of income

Liabilities:
Classification of liabilities, creditors, amounts, whether insured or secured

Factors affecting plan:
Gift propensity, charitable inclinations, emotional maturity of children, basic desires for estate distribution

Authorization for information:
Life insurance

Receipt for documents:
Personal and business

Source: Copyright © 1988 by The American College. Reprinted with permission. The Financial and Estate Planning Fact Finder is part of the Advanced Estate Planning course.

Guardian for Minor Children

It is customary to assume that a parent is the best person to act as guardian for his or her minor children. While this is generally true, under certain circumstances it might be advisable to appoint someone other than the parent to perform this task. For instance, both husband and wife might die simultaneously, in which case the court might appoint a guardian not acceptable to either of them. Naming an alternative person directs the court to consider appointing an acceptable person as a guardian. In a different situation involving divorce, for some time the surviving parent may not have been involved with the care and rearing of the children of a previous marriage. In such a case, or in the case where the surviving parent is ill-prepared to deal with both the children and the property, an individual has the opportunity to designate separate persons as guardians of the children and the conservators of the *property*. These individuals will be entitled to be compensated for their services. Separating the responsibility of managing the money from managing the children provides an added degree of protection for the family. Clearly, the well-being of the children and the children's property are of great importance, and it is imperative that careful consideration be given to the selection of a guardian who will efficiently perform both tasks. A will establishes the guardianship of minor children, subject to court approval.

Probate

An estate plan deals with two kinds of property—probate and nonprobate assets. The personal representative disposes of the probate assets in accordance with the instructions contained in the will. Nonprobate assets bypass probate, and contractual arrangements by the testator, such as, beneficiary designations for insurance, frequently control their transfer to specific individuals.

The literal meaning of probate is *to prove*. Probate occurs under the supervision of a local court known as probate, surrogate, or orphan's court. It is a procedure established by law for the orderly distribution of estates. The probate process is designed to assure that all of the deceased's properties are collected and protected; that all debts and taxes are paid; and that the beneficiaries promptly receive the designated assets.

Upon death of an individual, the personal representative submits the will to the court and asks that it be probated. Before the court can probate a person's estate, however, it must be satisfied that the will submitted by the executor is indeed the final will. Therefore, the court makes sure that the will is valid, avoids all restricted actions, and recognizes the limitations on the types of property (Social Security, qualified plan benefits, and so on) that may pass through the will. The court also provides the opportunity to all interested parties to contest the will. If all goes well, the will is probated and the personal representative is granted *Letters Testamentary*—the legal authority to act on behalf of the deceased.

In addition to approving the will, the probate court rules on the legitimacy of creditors' claims and oversees the activities of the personal representative until the estate is distributed. If minor children are involved, the court also supervises the guardian until the property is finally distributed to the children after they reach their age of property distribution specified in the will.

The probate process is usually long, complicated, and costly. Consequently, in most instances, it makes sense to take the necessary steps to avoid delay in the probate process. These steps include assigning broad powers to the personal representative to settle disputes, keeping the will up-to-date, maintaining a complete inventory of all assets, and purchasing life insurance to provide additional liquidity for the estate. In addition, people can include in their will directives to adopt a streamlined independent probate process.

The technique of bypassing probate as an estate planning tool will be discussed in the next chapter.

JOINT OWNERSHIP

Introduction

The gross estate consists of those assets to which a person has title or legal rights of ownership. These rights depend not only on the method by which the property was acquired but also on state statutes governing marital property. Some states consider marital property to be community property while others do not. Because the form of ownership is crucial to how property will pass at death, planners should have a basic understanding of the forms and kinds of property ownership, both from a practical and a tax viewpoint.

Community Property States

In the nine community property states (Arizona, California, Idaho, Louisiana, Nevada, New Mexico, Texas, Washington, and Wisconsin), both spouses own a separate, undivided, *equal* interest in the property. Generally speaking, property acquired during marriage is treated as community property and is equally owned by both spouses. Property acquired by either spouse as a gift or inheritance retains its status as separate property. The basic principle of community property is that each spouse owns an undivided one-half interest in the property.

At the death of one spouse, the surviving spouse owns half of all community property outright, and the other half is included in the decedent's estate. Therefore, the decedent's one-half interest is subject to testamentary disposition. Thus, each spouse controls the one-half interest owned; it does not pass by operation of law to the surviving spouse.

The most important implication of community property is that it receives a complete step-up in basis for both halves of the community property upon the death of the first spouse. This is in contrast to jointly held property, in which only half of the property receives a step-up in basis. Furthermore, even if only one of the spouses initially acquires property or earns income, community property states emphasize that it is the efforts of both spouses that lead to the acquisition of property. Also, not only do both spouses have equal rights of ownership in the community property and the earnings, but they also share equal ownership rights in the income derived from salaries, wages, or other compensation for services.

Common Law States

In the common law states, the nature of distribution of assets held jointly depends on the form of joint ownership. Of the three types of joint ownership permitted in these states, one is designed specifically to process all assets through probate, whereas the other two completely bypass probate. Each of the three types of joint ownership has its own distinct characteristics.

Joint tenancy with rights of survivorship. This type of ownership can be set up by any two or more persons. Each owner is known as a joint tenant and owns an equal share of the property. Co-owners who are not married may sell or give away their interests with the other co-owner's permission. When death occurs, the share of the deceased owner automatically passes to the surviving joint owner. It is possible to have more than two joint owners. Upon the death of a joint owner the existing owners continue to own the property as joint co-owners. This type of ownership completely bypasses the probate process, but (as between non-spouses) the property is included in the gross estate of the deceased for estate tax purposes at either the proven portion of ownership, or at 100 percent of the market value if it is not possible to prove the percentage of ownership. Thus, a joint tenant's interest in the property does not pass by will or intestacy, but by operation of law. Generally, it is not a recommended form of ownership except under certain circumstances.

Tenancy by the entirety. This form of joint tenancy differs from the former type in two respects. First, in those states that permit it, tenancy by the entirety can be established only by married couples. Second, neither spouse can sell or give away any property without the consent of the other. When death occurs, the deceased's share passes to the survivor. This form, too, completely bypasses probate.

Tenancy in common. This type of ownership directs all property not to the co-owners but rather to the heirs named in the will or to the heirs at law if the person died intestate. Each tenant in common owns an undivided interest in the property. Consequently, its major objective is to insure that all assets pass through probate court. Hence, tenancy in common is not designed either to save on probate costs or to avoid delays by bypassing probate.

A comparison of the advantages and disadvantages of sole ownership, joint tenancy, and tenancy in common is presented in Table 8-2. This table suggest that several factors should be considered before selecting for the client the most appropriate form of property ownership.

Community Property and the Transitory Couple

If a couple acquires property in a community-property state and subsequently relocates to a common-law property state, the classification of property becomes somewhat difficult. Generally, the character of the asset acquired as community property does not change because the couple relocates to a common-law state. Also, property acquired in a common-law state retains its character if the couple moves to a community-property state. The major exception is the introduction of quasi-community-property which applies only in Arizona (upon divorce), and California and Idaho (upon divorce or death). In these states, property acquired during marriage in a common-law state is treated as community property.

TRUSTS

An Overview

An important cornerstone of estate planning, trusts are used when there is a desire or legal need to split the beneficial interest from the management of the property. A trust is a legal entity created to hold, manage, and eventually (upon death) distribute assets to the beneficiaries in accordance with the wishes of the grantor who sets up the trust. Assets included in the trust—stocks, bonds, real estate, life insurance, business interests, artwork, and so on—are called trust property, principal, or corpus. The basic elements of a trust are presented in Figure 8-4.

Trust property is managed by a trustee, who must carry out the grantor's instructions contained in the trust. These include the management of trust property and its distribution to the beneficiaries, who benefit from the distribution of trust property. The law does not place any restrictions on who, or how many people, might benefit from a trust. Thus, beneficiaries of a trust might be the spouse, children, brothers and sisters, other relatives, charitable and educational institutions, or business associates. Finally, the trustee controls and manages the trust in accordance with the conditions specified in the trust document.

There are two principal forms of trust: *inter vivos* or living trust and *testamentary trust*. The former comes into effect immediately upon its creation, whereas the latter is written into the will and comes into existence upon death.

The living trust has two advantages. First, property held in a living trust avoids probate. This means that property can be distributed to the beneficiaries without approval from the probate court. Because the trustee can make decisions without court approval, there are no court costs or executor fees with a living trust.

Second, a living trust protects the privacy concerns of the decedent. A living trust is a private document. No one has the right to see the trust document except the trustee and beneficiaries. A will, on the other hand, is public record and can be

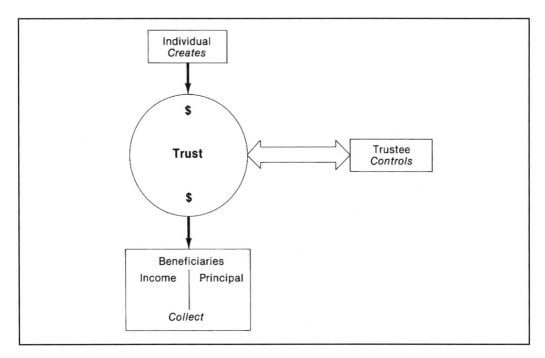

FIGURE 8-4 Diagram of a trust. Paul J. Lochray, *The Financial Planner's Guide to Estate Planning*, Revised Edition; © 1989, p. 68. Reprinted by permission of Prentice Hall, Inc., Englewood Cliffs, New Jersey.

TABLE 8-2 A Comparison of the Advantages and Disadvantages of Sole Ownership, Joint Tenancy, and Tenancy in Common Property

	Sole ownership	Joint tenancy WROS	Tenancy in common
Avoids probate?	No	Yes	No
Can be disposed of by will?	Yes	No	Yes
Does decedent have postmortem control?	Yes	No	Yes
Receive a partial step-up in basis at decedent's death?	Receives step up in basis on entire amount when it passes to beneficiary or heir	Yes	Same as sole ownership on the tenant's proportional interest
Consent of others needed prior to conveyance?	No	Yes—if there is a spousal joint tenant	No
Amount included in gross estate of decedent?	All	One-half if spouses; otherwise, the portion or percentage which is proved as actual contribution; if survivor cannot prove contribution, then all	Tenant's undivided fractional interest
Survivorship rights upon death of decedent owner?	No	Yes	No

If gifted, subject to payment of gift tax?	Yes	No—if gifted to spouse; otherwise, yes	Yes
Effective means of splitting income?	No	Yes	Yes
Reduced administrative expenses and costs?	No	Yes	No
Difficult to dispose of or convey?	Generally, no	Generally, no	Can be a problem if tenants in common cannot agree to buy or sell their interest to others—can result in a co-ownership discount
Can interest qualify for marital deduction?	Only if bequeathed to spouse in decedent's will or if transferred to spouse pursuant to intestacy statute	Yes—if surviving joint tenant is spouse	Yes—if tenant in common bequeaths it to spouse in will or if transferred to spouse pursuant to intestacy statute
Subject to creditors' claims?	Yes	No—possibly free in some states, but state law must be checked	Yes
Lifetime control?	Yes—total	Yes—partial	Yes—partial

Source: Paul J. Lochray, *The Financial Planner's Guide to Estate Planning*, Revised Edition, © 1989, pp. 121–22. Reprinted by permission of Prentice Hall, Inc., Englewood Cliffs, New Jersey.

read by anyone. This distinction may be extremely important to wealthy individuals and people who have public recognition.

The living trust, which begins to operate during the owner's lifetime, can be either revocable or irrevocable. The owner or grantor, who creates the trust, frequently acts as his or her own trustee. The owner can also name another trustee to manage the assets in the event of disability or incompetence. Assets are held in the trust during the owner's lifetime and, upon death, the trust estate avoids probate, but the assets are included in the deceased's gross estate. In contrast, an irrevocable living trust can be created to pass assets free of federal estate taxes to the beneficiaries. In creating this trust, in most—though not all—instances, a person gives up any right to trust income and principal as well as the right to change the beneficiary or other terms of the trust agreement. For example, in one case, the settlor retains the right to trust income despite the fact that the trust is irrevocable.

Purpose of a Trust

It is not necessary for everyone to create a trust for an orderly transfer of an estate to the beneficiaries. However, most people have specific objectives which are difficult—in fact, nearly impossible—to carry out without a trust. For instance, with the help of a trust, a person can provide a life income for the spouse and children. Subsequently, the assets could pass to the grandchildren. In another instance, if the spouse is inexperienced or incapable of managing investments, a trust can safeguard investable funds by letting a trustee manage them while providing adequate income for the spouse and children. A trust might also become necessary where a person has remarried. In this case, a trust can provide life income to the second spouse and upon the death of this spouse distribute the assets to the children of the first marriage. Another situation in which a trust can be extremely useful relates to the care and support for a physically or mentally incapacitated person. Finally, a trust becomes an essential document where there is a possibility of a simultaneous death of both spouses. It is therefore safe to conclude that most people need some type of trust as an integral part of their estate plan.

Selection of a Trustee

The decision to create a trust—be it inter vivos or testamentary—carries with it the task of selecting a trustee. The duties and responsibilities of a trustee may vary, depending upon the size and complexity of the trust. However, it is highly desirable that the trustee be sensitive to the needs of the beneficiaries and possess financial savvy. A trustee can also become an all important person if the grantor of the trust is suddenly incapacitated and is unable to manage the trust properly.

As a general rule, it is always desirable to engage as a trustee a fiduciary company with perpetual life or a professional financial advisory firm. Such a trustee can not only manage a trust professionally but can also provide continuity, which is always desirable. However, annual fees for professional trustees can range from about one percent to four percent of a trust's assets. Consequently, people with relatively small trusts may wish to sacrifice the use of a professional trustee and select a friend or a relative for little or no compensation. Of course, a professional financial advisor can act as a trustee provided there is no conflict of interest present in that relationship. Regardless of how a trustee is selected, wherever feasible, it is prudent to leave the original trust agreement with the trustee, keep the first copy of the trust with the attorney, the second copy with the grantor, and the third copy in a safety deposit vault.

The use of a trust as a tool of estate planning is discussed more fully in the next chapter.

LIFETIME GIFTS

Another effective tool for reducing the size of the estate is gift giving. During one's lifetime, gifts can be given in a variety of ways to individuals and institutions. However, there are pitfalls in giving gifts, and these must be carefully considered when designing a program of lifetime giving.

The law allows (2005) every person to gift each year up to $11,000, gift tax-free to any person, or $22,000 for a gift split between husband and wife. The law does not limit the number of people to whom gifts can be made during a given year. However, gifts exceeding $11,000 for a single person, or $22,000 for a married couple, are considered taxable gifts.

When a gift exceeding $11,000 ($22,000 per couple per year) is made during lifetime, a gift tax becomes payable. However, instead of actually paying the gift tax to the IRS, the donor can have the unified credit amount reduced by the gift tax due. For instance, let us assume that John made a gift to his son, which generated a gift tax liability of $20,000. Instead of sending to the IRS a check for that amount, John can deduct $20,000 from his unified credit. In this case, John would not pay any gift tax, but the unified credit available to him during that year would be reduced by the gift for tax amount.

The IRS makes an important distinction between gifts made within three years and after three years of death. All gifts which use the unified credit are included back into the estate tax computation. However, in those cases where death occurs after three years of making the gift, the donor is not penalized for making the gift, and the gift taxes paid are *excluded* from estate tax calculation. In sharp contrast, gift taxes paid by the decedent within three years of death are *included* in the decedent's gross estate. The effect of this is to make gifts made within three years of death tax-inclusive rather than tax-exclusive. This rule eliminates one of the key benefits of making lifetime gifts. It should be mentioned, however, that the appreciation on the property after the gift escapes taxation.

COMPUTATION OF ESTATE TAX

FEDERAL ESTATE TAXES

An Overview

The estate built during one's lifetime may not entirely be passed on to the beneficiaries. The federal government and at least one state government have the right to claim their shares before the estate can be distributed.

The federal estate tax is a tax on the right to transfer property at death, and not on the right of the beneficiary to receive the property. The federal estate tax must be paid by the estate. In addition, an estate is also subject to a state inheritance tax, which will be discussed in a subsequent section.

For purposes of calculating federal estate taxes, an estate includes not only real estate, bank deposits, personal property, and other obvious types of assets, but also insurance proceeds, interests in trusts, and jointly held property. In addition, certain interests a deceased may have in other estates are also included in the estate.

The 1976 Tax Act created a *unified* federal estate tax rate schedule applicable to both lifetime gifts and transfers at death. This provision was adopted to discourage the transfer of assets *in contemplation of death.* The tax on gifts is imposed on the right to transfer property and is measured by the value of the property transferred. The donor is primarily liable for the tax. A graduated table of rates is used for calculating both gift and estate taxes and is known as the unified rate schedule.

Economic Growth and Tax Relief Reconciliation Act of 2001

The Economic Growth and Tax Relief Reconciliation Act of 2001 (the "Act") was signed into law by President Bush on June 7, 2001. Beginning in 2002, the new Act increased the estate tax applicable exclusion amount and reduced the top estate tax rate by eliminating the five percent surcharge for estates above $10 million. Table 8-3 illustrates the applicable estate tax and generation skipping tax (GST) *deathtime* rates.

The federal estate tax and generation-skipping transfer tax will be repealed effective January 1, 2010. Following that repeal, the present law providing for a stepped-up basis for property acquired from a descendent will also be repealed. This point requires elaboration.

Currently, for federal income tax purposes, when an heir receives an asset from an estate, the basis of the asset (e.g., stocks) is not computed on the decedent's date of purchase. Instead, the basis is assumed to be the fair market value of the asset on the decedent's date of death or on the alternative valuation date six months later. For example, if in the past the decedent purchased stock valued at $100,000 and the stock's value on the date of death, or alternate valuation date, is $200,000, the heir's basis for future gains or losses is $200,000. If the heir sells the stock for, say, $250,000, capital gain taxes will be levied only on the $50,000 profit.

TABLE 8-3   Applicable Exclusion Amounts and Highest Estate and Gift-Tax Rates

	Esate Tax		Gift Tax	
Calendar Year	Applicable Exclusion Amount	Highest Esate Tax Rate	Applicable Exclusion Amount	Highest Gift Tax Rate
2002	$1 million	50%	$1 million	50%
2003	$1 million	49%	$1 million	49%
2004	$1.5 million	48%	$1 million	48%
2005	$1.5 million	47%	$1 million	47%
2006	$2 million	46%	$1 million	46%
2007	$2 million	45%	$1 million	45%
2008	$2 million	45%	$1 million	45%
2009	$3.5 million	45%	$1 million	45%
2010	- 0 -	- 0 -	$1 million	35%
2011	$1 million	55%	$1 million	55%

Starting in 2010, under the Act, this so-called *stepped-up* basis tax break will be modified to allow for a total of $1.3 million in basis step-up on aggregate transfers to any beneficiaries, and an additional $3 million of basis step-up on transfers to a surviving spouse, for a total of $4.3 million of basis *step-up*. These amounts will be adjusted for inflation after December 31, 2010. For all other assets transferred at death, the value of an heir's basis in a decedent's assets will be the *lesser* of the decedent's basis in the property or the fair market value of the property on the date of the decedent's death.

Under the Act, the gift tax will *not* be repealed. Moreover, the applicable exclusion amount for gifts is *not* the same as that for estate taxes. The gift tax exclusion of $1 million will remain at that level. The highest gift tax rates match the highest estate tax rates (see Table 8-3) until January 1, 2010, when the gift tax rate will equal the highest individual *income* tax rate. Essentially, after January 1, 2010, this will operate as a flat 35 percent gift tax on all gifts above the applicable lifetime exclusion amount of 1$ million. Finally, since January 2002, the exclusion amount and the highest rate for estate and gift taxes have become identical.

Another provision of the Act deals with family-owned business. Under the Taxpayer Relief Act of 1997, family-owned businesses got an immediate break. Effective January 1, 1998, the law added $600,000 credit plus an additional $700,000, or a total of 1.3 million estate tax exemption for small businesses and family farms. The family-owned business estate tax deduction was repealed on January 1, 2004.

Clearly, the Act fails to provide certainty. This lack of certainty derives from the *sunset* provisions of the new Act which was necessary to comply with the Congressional Budget Act of 1974. The estate tax repeal, effective 2010, and the new carry-over basis system which takes effect on January 1, 2010, will *expire* on December 31, 2010, unless these are re-enacted by a future Congress. Therefore, the integrity of estate tax repeal is dependent upon both the political landscape and the economic strength of the nation nearly a decade from the initial passage of the Act.

Estate Tax Calculation

The federal estate tax is calculated by: (1) adjusting the value of the gross estate in order to determine the tentative tax base; (2) calculating the tentative tax; and (3) arriving at the net tax liability by subtracting the gross tax paid during lifetime as well as the applicable tax credits. The format for calculating the federal estate tax is presented in Table 8-4. We will now discuss the key items associated with the calculation of federal estate tax.

TABLE 8-4   Computation of Federal Estate Tax

Gross estate
   Less deductions
Equals taxable estate
   Plus adjusted taxable gifts
Equals tentative tax base
   Times rate of tax
Equals tentative tax
   Less gift tax paid after 1976
Equals gross tax
   Less credits
Equals net tax liability

Gross Estate

Includible items. The key items to be included in the gross estate are listed in Table 8-5. While most of the items are self-explanatory, it may nevertheless be of some interest to make a few basic comments about them.

As a general rule, items included in a gross estate are cash, real estate, securities, rights in property, collectibles, life insurance payable to anyone if the deceased owned the policy, and gifts of life insurance made within three years of death. Assets which are gifted away but in which the deceased retained some control are also included in the gross estate. The value of an annuity payable to any beneficiary upon death is included in the gross estate if during life the deceased had the right to receive income from the annuity. However, only the share of the annuity that was purchased by the individual is taxable. In the case of jointly owned property, one-half of the value of the property is included in the gross estate if the parties are a married couple. If the joint tenants are not a married couple, the entire property is included in the gross estate of the deceased unless the survivor can claim to have paid for the property. Finally, if the deceased died owning an interest in a trust that allowed the deceased to specify the future recepient of the interest, then the assets over which the deceased had the power to specify would be included in the deceased's estate.

Valuing the estate. The process of calculating estate taxes begins with determining includibility. Once it is determined which assets are to be included, the values of the items comprising the gross estate can be calculated. In most instances, such as in the case of bank deposits, investments, pension, profit sharing, Keogh, 401(k) plans, and life insurance proceeds, determining the market value poses no problem. In the case of certain other assets, however, determination of fair market value at the time of death, or an alternative date six months after death, may be more difficult. Examples of these assets include family businesses, farm land, and stocks in closely held corporations.

TABLE 8-5   Includable Items in Gross Estate

  I. Property in which decedent had an interest
   a. Personal assets
   b. Real property
   c. Intangible property
   d. Retirement assets
   e. Closely-held business
   f. Equity investments
   g. Hard assets
  II. Gifts of life insurance made within three years of death
  III. Incomplete lifetime transfers
  IV. Annuities payable to beneficiary
  V. Half of joint property (married couple)
  VI. Power of appointment (general) trust
  VII. Proceeds of life insurance owned by deceased

The method of determining a couple's gross estate is presented in Table 8-6. Naturally, the method would be a lot more involved in the case of a more complicated estate. However, the *process* would be very similar to the one presented here.

Deductions

The IRS allows certain expenses and liabilities to be deductible from the gross estate. The key deductions are listed in Table 8-7. Most of the items listed in this table are self-explanatory. A few, however, require a brief explanation.

Claims against the estate. Claims against the estate are limited to a legitimate contractual obligation for which there was full consideration in money.

Charitable deductions. The estate is allowed to take an unlimited deduction for property donated to a *qualified* charity. However, unlike the income tax charitable deduction, no percentage limitations are placed on the estate tax deduction for charitable gifts.

Marital deduction. The estate may deduct *all* property bequeathed to a surviving spouse. This is known as the unlimited marital deduction.

Power of appointment trust. The unlimited marital deduction will be available for a Power of Appointment Trust if: (1) the surviving spouse is entitled to all of the income from the trust; (2) the spouse actually receives the income at least annually; and (3) the surviving spouse's Power of Appointment is unconditional.

Qualified terminable interest property (QTIP) trust. Property included in this trust will qualify for the estate tax marital deduction. This is because the entire interest and the property—both income and remainder—is treated as passing to the spouse.

Estate Tax Calculation

A single rate schedule is applied to a decedent's estate and all the post-1976 lifetime gifts over the annual gift tax exclusion. Under the current gift and estate tax system, the overall tax on the taxable estate is calculated whether or not a lifetime gift is made. Of course, lifetime gifts that reduce the taxable estate may reduce the estate tax.

For those estates where lifetime taxable gifts (that is, gifts in excess of $22,000 per year for married couples) are nonexistent, the estate tax equals the gross estate less the allowable deductions. The applicable credit amount is subtracted from the tax calculated on the taxable estate. Other credits, including the state death tax credit, further reduce the estate tax.

The estate tax is cumulative for those estates that have taxable lifetime gifts. In these cases, the applicable tax rate is applied to the sum of the taxable estate at death and taxable lifetime gifts made after 1976. Of course, gifts that are already included in the gross estate are excluded from this calculation. Also, gifts made within three years of death are added back into the estate for estate tax purposes. The tax calculated on the combined estate is reduced by gift taxes payable on gifts made after 1976. The applicable credit amount and other credits are then subtracted from the tentative federal estate tax in order to arrive at the final federal estate tax liability.

TABLE 8-6 Property Ownership and Gross Estate

Property		Ownership			
				Property	
	Est. Current Value	Community	Joint	Husband's	Spouse's
1. Net worth					
a. Liquid assets other than cash value of life insurance	$30,000		$30,000		
b. Investment assets, other than retirement funds	$230,000	$230,000	$50,000		$30,000
c. Personal assets	$500,000	$500,000			
d. Total assets	$760,000	$650,000	$80,000		
e. Liabilities	($100,000)	($100,000)			
f. Total	$660,000	$550,000	$80,000		$30,000
2. Insurance owned					
a. On husband's life	$500,000			$50,000	
b. On spouse's life	$300,000				$300,000
c. Total	$800,000				$300,000
3. Other estate assets					
a. Retirement plans	$290,000			$290,000	
b. Other					
c. Total	$290,000			$290,000	
4. Total gross estate	$1,309,000		$80,000	$790,000	$330,000
5. Total gross estate for husband and spouse					
a. Husband's gross estate	$1,105,000	$275,000	$40,000	$790,000	
b. Spouse's gross estate	$645,000	$275,000	$40,000		
c. Total	$1,750,000	$550,000	$80,000	$790,000	$330,000

TABLE 8-7 Allowable Deductions from Gross Estate

1. Funeral expenses
2. Expenses of last illness
3. Casualty losses
4. Administration expenses
5. Claims against the estate
6. Mortgage and other indebtedness
7. Charitable deductions
8. Marital deduction
9. Power of appointment (general) trust
10. Qualified terminable interest property (QTIP) trust
11. Sale of employer's stock to ESOPs (50 percent)

TABLE 8-8 Estimated Federal Estate Tax: Husband's Estate

1. Gross estate		$1,105,000
2. Deductions		
a. Funeral expenses	$5,000	
b. Administrative expenses	$15,000	
c. Total expenses	$20,000	
3. Martial deduction for property passing to spouse:		
a. Jointly held property	$40,000	
b. Transferred by contract (and life insurance)	$790,000	
c. Community property	$255,000	
d. Total martial deductions	$1,085,000	
4. Charitable deductions	0	
5. Total deductions		$1,105,000
6. Tentative taxable estate		0
7. Post-1976 taxable gifts other than gifts includible in gross estate		0
8. Total taxable estate		0
9. Tentative federal estate tax		0
10. Less:		
a. Gift taxes paid on post-1976 gifts	0	
b. Unified credit	$555,800	
c. Total		$555,800
11. Federal estate tax*		0

* This illustration assumes death in 2004.

Federal estate taxes. The process of calculating the federal estate tax on the estate of the husband, presumed to die first, and on the estate of his spouse upon her death, is presented in Tables 8-8 and 8-9. The estate tax is calculated by using the unified gift and estate tax rates presented in Table 8-10. Because of the existence of a comprehensive estate plan, there was no federal estate tax due on the $1,105,000 estate upon the first death. And, even though the surviving spouse's gross estate was $1,730,000, the federal tax was only $90,000.

State inheritance taxes. In the U.S., most states impose an inheritance tax, often based upon federal estate tax liability, which is payable by the recipient of the inheritance. The size of the state tax is determined by the amount the heir inherits and the heir's relationship to the deceased. State inheritance taxes are deductible in determining federal estate taxes.

TABLE 8-9   Estimated Federal Estate Tax: Wife's Estate

1. Gross estate		$1,730,000
2. Deductions		
a. Funeral expenses	$5,000	
b. Administrative expenses	$25,000	
c. Total expenses	$30,000	
3. Martial deduction for property passing to spouse:		
a. Jointly held property	0	
b. Transferred by contract (and life insurance)	0	
c. Community property	0	
d. Total martial deductions	0	
4. Charitable deductions	0	
5. Total deductions		($30,000)
6. Tentative taxable estate		$1,700,000
7. Post-1976 taxable gifts other than gifts includible in gross estate		0
8. Total taxable estate		$1,700,000
9. Tentative federal estate tax		$645,800
10. Less:		
a. Gift taxes paid on post-1976 gifts	0	
b. Unified credit	$555,800	
c. Total		$555,800
11. Federal estate tax*		$90,000

     * It is assumed that death takes place in 2004.

STATE INHERITANCE TAX

Each year nearly 400,000 retirees move to those states where both the weather and the economic climate are better. And because retirees carry their pocketbooks and brokerage accounts, their former home states lose income taxes, sales taxes and driver's license fees. In order to keep retirees from taking away their valuable resources, many states have reduced or eliminated their inheritance taxes, and many more are in the process of eliminating it.

In this chapter we have presented the basic structure of federal estate taxes. The next chapter will be devoted to a detailed discussion of estate planning techniques.

TABLE 8-10   Estate and Gift Tax Rates

1993 and thereafter

If the amount is: Over	But not over	Tax	Plus % on excess over
0	$ 10,000	0	18
$ 10,000	20,000	$ 1,800	20
20,000	40,000	3,800	22
40,000	60,000	8,200	24
60,000	80,000	13,000	26
80,000	100,000	18,200	28
100,000	150,000	23,800	30
150,000	250,000	38,800	32
250,000	500,000	70,800	34
500,000	750,000	155,800	37
750,000	1,000,000	248,300	39
1,000,000	1,250,000	345,800	41
1,250,000	1,500,000	448,300	43
1,500,000	2,000,000	555,800	45
2,000,000	2,500,000	780,800	49
2,500,000	* * * * *	1,025,800	50

The only good luck many great men ever had was being born with the ability and determination to overcome bad luck.

Channing Pollock

CHAPTER 9

Estate Planning: Concepts and Strategies

INTRODUCTION

The major objectives of estate planning are to preserve the assets accumulated during a person's lifetime and to develop strategies for passing them on to the intended beneficiaries. Minimizing estate taxes is also an important estate planning goal, although it should not take precedence over other personal and financial goals. Upon death, a will becomes the primary document for passing the estate to the beneficiaries, but it is an integral part of, and not a substitute for, estate planning.

A basic estate plan includes four documents: a will, a living trust, a financial power of attorney, and a health care power of attorney. A comprehensive estate plan can involve a number of complex documents. Consequently, drafting an estate plan requires the working knowledge of several fields, including finance, law, economics, accounting, insurance, and taxes. In addition, depending upon individual circumstances, the estate plan may contain provisions for such esoteric topics as generation skipping tax, qualified terminable interest property trusts, and buy-sell or business continuation agreements. It is therefore highly desirable, if not mandatory, for an individual to seek the help of a competent estate planning attorney, a financial planner, or an accountant for developing an effective estate plan. In fact, complex estate planning is frequently a team effort, and an individual may need the help of all three professionals working together to design a sophisticated estate plan.

This chapter is divided into three parts. First, we will present estate tax reduction strategies. Next, we will analyze estate preservation and distribution rules. Finally, we will present miscellaneous estate planning techniques.

ESTATE TAX REDUCTION STRATEGIES

INTRODUCTION

One of the major objectives of estate planning is to eliminate, or significantly reduce, potential estate tax. Direct lifetime gifts can be made to remove from an individual's estate future appreciation on property. Ownership of life insurance can be changed to avoid paying estate tax on life insurance proceeds. The will may provide for bequests that will qualify for the marital and charitable deductions.

To be sure, maximum reduction of the estate tax upon the first death is not always the most preferred strategy. In some instances it might be desirable to pay the estate tax upon the first death if that would help minimize the total estate taxes payable upon both deaths. At other times, paying estate taxes may well be the appropriate strategy for achieving other objectives. Nevertheless, it is appropriate to discuss here the key estate tax elimination and reduction strategies, because for most people that constitutes one of the primary objectives of estate planning.

MARITAL DEDUCTION

The 1981 Economic Recovery Tax Act (ERTA) made it possible to totally eliminate estate taxes upon the death of the first spouse. Property passing to a spouse is generally free from federal estate or gift taxes because of an unlimited marital deduction. To qualify for the marital deduction, the property must be given to the spouse outright or by other legal arrangements that are equivalent to ownership in law. There is an exception in the case of income interests in Charitable Remainder Annuity or Unitrusts and in Qualified Terminable Interest Property (QTIP), for which the executor makes an election. If the spouse is made the unconditional beneficiary of life insurance proceeds with unrestricted control over any unpaid proceeds, then life insurance proceeds will also qualify as marital deduction property.

We have already learned that transfers between spouses are exempt from both federal estate and gift taxes. The unlimited marital deduction opens up exciting ways for large estates to save on taxes—especially when the deduction is combined with the unified credit. However, despite the availability of the unlimited marital deduction and the applicable exclusion amount, for most families estate planning is still essential. The reason is that, while there is no estate tax when the property passes to the surviving spouse, significant estate taxes might become due when the property is transferred to the beneficiaries upon the death of the second spouse. We will illustrate this point by using three examples.

Example I. Mr. John Becker's entire estate worth $2,000,000 is left outright to his wife, Betty Becker. Betty's will provides for everything to be left to the children. In this case, upon John's death, because of the unlimited marital deduction, the entire estate of $2,000,000 passes to Betty free of estate taxes. However, upon Betty's death, only $1.5 million (2004) will pass estate tax-free to the children. The balance of $500,000 will be subject to estate taxes. Note that if John had used both a will and a trust, and the trust sheltered his $1.5 million exemption, upon his death that amount would have been transferred to a bypass trust (discussed later) for Betty, and only $500,000 would have been used for the marital deduction. In that case, upon Betty's death, the $500,000 amount would pass estate tax-free to the children (because of her $1.5 million unified credit). In addition, the balance of $1.5 million in the bypass trust would also pass to the children estate tax-free, since this amount was not a part of Betty's estate. Clearly, by not using the bypass trust strategy, John Becker wasted his own $1,500,000 exemption.

Example II. In this example, John Becker leaves $1.5 million to his wife and the balance of $500,000 to his children. In this case, no estate taxes would be payable upon either death. However, since $500,000 is left to John's children, Betty receives no economic benefit from this money. A better strategy would be to put $500,000 in trust for the children (explained more fully in the Trust section), with Betty Becker receiving income from the trust during her lifetime. Such an arrangement would give Betty the right to the income from the trust, an option to receive five percent of the principal every year, and the right to receive principal for her health, education, support, and maintenance. Under such an arrangement, $1.5 million would pass tax-free from John to Betty because of the unlimited marital deduction, and subsequently to the children under Betty's estate tax credit umbrella. And so does the $500,000 in John's estate. The reason is that John's $1.5 million applicable exclusion amount shelters the $500,000 he has transferred in trust to his children, and it bypasses Betty's estate. However, the trustees of the trust have the limited right to invade the principal of the trust for Betty's benefit.

Example III. The third example refers to a large estate of $2.5 million. The estate is almost entirely owned by John Becker whereas Betty Becker has a negligible estate. If John leaves his entire estate to Betty, upon John's death his estate would pay no tax. But Betty's estate would pay tax on the full $2.5 million less her $1.5 million exemption. However, if John were to leave $1.25 million to Betty and the rest to his children, and then she leaves her $1.25 million to her children, the Beckers would succeed in sheltering $1,250,000 in each estate, thereby avoiding the estate taxes.

To recapitulate, when using the marital deduction, the consequences of leaving a large estate to a surviving spouse should be carefully weighed. This is especially true when the spouse does not have the skills or the interest for managing a large estate. In that situation, upon the death of the first spouse it might be better to leave the assets in a trust that is equivalent to total ownership, and thereby completely avoid paying estate taxes.

JOINT OWNERSHIP

In Chapter 8 we learned that upon death the nature of distribution of assets held jointly depends on the form of joint ownership. We will now discuss some of the advantages and disadvantages of joint ownership.

Key Advantages

There are several advantages to joint ownership of property. First, if property is held in joint tenancy with right of survivorship, which is often the case between family members, upon death the surviving joint owner automatically owns all the jointly owned property without the necessity of probate. The reason is that, under the law, there is a presumption that the decedent intended the property to automatically pass to the surviving joint owner. Second, property held jointly by married couples cannot be taken away in settlement of a debt. For example, if a person owes a certain amount of money to a loan company and becomes delinquent on loan payments, the company cannot seize the car, or some other property to cover the loan if the person jointly owns these properties with the spouse. However, jointly held property can be subject to a debt claim where the debt is incurred jointly by the same parties. This would be the case where the lender has both spouses sign the note. Third, if a person is the sole owner of a vacation home located out of state, the will must be probated in two states. Joint ownership would eliminate this requirement. Fourth, joint ownership can be used to shift income to a family member in a lower tax bracket. For instance, a father and his son age 15 holding stock jointly would each be taxed on only half the dividends, frequently resulting in significant income tax savings. Finally, joint property can be used to achieve special objectives. If a mother wants to gift $11,000 to her daughter, but still wants to be able to use the money for her own benefit, she can place the money in a joint bank account in both names. The mother can then draw money from this account, or if she wants to minimize her access to that money, she can have it set up so that both the mother's and the daughter's signatures are required for withdrawal.

Key Disadvantages

There are also disadvantages to joint ownership of property. Since jointly owned assets automatically pass to the surviving joint tenant, the survivor could end up with an estate exceeding $1.5 million (2004) if the couple had all of their assets in joint tenancy. This may result in higher estate taxes upon the death of the surviving spouse. Another disadvantage of joint ownership is that people often tend to use this as a substitute for a valid will. In situations where all properties are jointly owned and there is no will, if both spouses die in an accident the entire property would be distributed according to rigid, unalterable rules commonly known as the laws of intestate succession, also known as the laws of intestacy.

An important problem associated with joint ownership of highly appreciated assets involves both federal income and federal estate taxes. Assume John and Betty Jones bought a house for $30,000 in 1966 and held it jointly until John died in January 2004, when the house was worth $200,000. Half of the house's value ($100,000) was included in John's gross estate, leaving Betty with his $100,000 interest plus her own $100,000 interest in the house. The IRS assumes that Betty bought her interest with $15,000 (one-half of $30,000) in 1966. If in 2004 she sells the house for $200,000, she incurs $85,000 ($100,000 – $15,000) in capital gains which will be taxed at the 20 percent capital gains tax rate. This tax liability could have been avoided had John owned the house alone and bequeathed it to Betty via a will. In that case Betty's cost basis for the house—known as the step-up basis—would have been $200,000 and the sale would not generate any taxable profit. Of course, Betty could also avoid paying taxes on this amount if under the Taxpayer Relief Act of 1997 she used her $250,000 exclusion pertaining to the capital gains realized from the sale of her principal residence.

It is apropos to add here a little unknown rule. If a couple transfers property out of a joint name into the name of one of the spouses, and that spouse dies within a year of the transfer, there is no step-up in basis with respect to the spouse receiving back her or his interest. For instance, John and Betty own a joint property and the property is transferred to John. If John died more than one year after the transfer, then Betty would receive the step-up in basis. But if John died less than a year after the transfer, then Betty would not receive a full step-up in basis; instead, she would receive a step-up only with respect to John's share.

Another disadvantage of joint tenancy is underscored by the following example. Suppose the mother, father, son and daughter all own an asset as joint tenants. It is the parent's intention that the asset passes equally to son and daughter upon their death. In this case, if the son predeceases all three, and the parents die in a common accident, the daughter would receive the entire asset and the son's family would be unintentionally disinherited. This example clearly demonstrates that joint tenancy does not provide complete control over the asset because the order of deaths can significantly change the outcome.

Finally, unmarried joint tenants can increase estate tax liability for their heirs by owning property jointly. The face value of a jointly owned property is included in the estate of the decedent, except where it can be demonstrated that the surviving joint owner contributed to the purchase of the property.[1]

Having completed a review of the key advantages and disadvantages of joint ownership, we now turn to a discussion of the major estate planning strategies involving joint ownership with right of survivorship.

Planning Strategies

We have learned that only one half of the value of the property held in joint tenancy by husband and wife is included in the gross estate of the first spouse to die. Generally, the decedent's surviving spouse has an income tax basis that consists of two elements: (1) One-half of the original cost of property (that is, the surviving spouse's half); plus (2) one-half of the fair market value of the property at the time of death (that is, the half that is included in the estate). An example should make this clear.

Assume several years ago John and Betty Roe bought some property as joint tenants. The cost of the property was $10,000 and at John's death the fair market value of that property is $100,000. One-half, or $50,000, of the value of this property is included in John's estate, but this amount will pass to Betty free of federal estate tax because of the unlimited marital deduction. Betty's income tax basis for the entire property is $55,000—$5,000 representing half of the original cost plus $50,000 representing one-half of the value of the property at John's death. If Betty sells the property for $100,000, she would have a taxable long-term capital gain of $45,000 ($100,000 minus $55,000).

The tax situation just described could be dramatically improved if John holds the property only in his name. In that case, upon his death the property valued at $100,000 would be included in his gross estate. However, it will still be sheltered by the unlimited marital deduction. In addition, for income tax purposes Betty's step-up cost basis on this property will be $100,000. So, if she sells it for $100,000, she will not realize any capital gains and no income tax will be due on the sale of this property.

---

[1] This section assumes that everyone is a married and family joint tenant. Therefore, the major disadvantages of joint tenancy are not discussed here.

Another strategy concerning joint ownership involves splitting the property down the middle during the individuals' lifetimes. Each spouse then leaves his or her estate in trust to the children with an income interest to the other spouse. The result is a total avoidance of estate taxes upon both deaths. Here is an illustration to demonstrate this point.

Let us assume Sam and Sue Becker are both 55 years old. Sam owns property worth $1.5 million and Sue owns none. Instead of owning this property jointly, Sam makes a gift of one-half ($750,000) of his assets to his wife. His will provides that his $750,000 in assets goes to his children in trust. Sue has the right to the trust income, and the right to receive a limited amount of principal. Upon Sue's death, the $750,000 in trust goes to the children. Sue's will reads exactly the same way. If she dies first, her $750,000 in assets goes to the children in trust with Sam's right to trust income during his lifetime.

There is no estate tax involved in this case, no matter which spouse dies first. This strategy also assures the surviving spouse the full use of the estate for life. If Sue dies first, her $750,000 goes directly to the trust for the children. This amount is sheltered by the applicable exclusion amount and passes automatically to the children when Sam dies. Thus, Sam owns $750,000 outright and is entitled to life income from the $750,000 Sue left in the trust. When Sam dies, the $750,000 left in trust bypasses his estate and goes directly to the children. The remaining $750,000 goes directly to the children under the terms of his will, since it is fully sheltered from estate taxes by the unified credit. The situation is reversed if Sam dies first, but the end result is the same. The children ultimately receive everything, and the estate completely escapes federal estate taxes.

LIFETIME GIFTS

An Overview

The tool of the lifetime gift, initially discussed in Chapter 8, is extremely valuable for reducing the overall estate taxes. Here is a summary of the rules governing lifetime gifts.

1. Annual gifts of $11,000 per donee—or $22,000 per married couple for split gifts—are exempt from gift taxes. Thus, an individual can give away multiples of $11,000 (or $22,000 for married couples) annually to an unlimited number of people and pay no gift taxes. However, in order to qualify for an annual exclusion, the gift must provide the recipient with a present interest, such as outright interests or current income interests in a trust. No taxes are due on transfers until the aggregate transfers by the donor have exceeded $1.5 million (2005).

2. In addition to the annual gifts of up to $11,000, ($22,000 for married couple), an individual can also make lifetime gifts, although these gifts are added back to a decedent's estate for estate tax purposes.

3. If death occurs within three years of a lifetime gift of a life insurance policy, the insurance proceeds are added back in the estate of the donor-insured.

4. For taxable gifts, the date-of-gift value of the property, and not the date-of-death value, is added back to a decedent's estate for purposes of calculating estate taxes.

Gift Tax Calculation

The gift tax applies to all gifts of property which exceed the $11,000 annual exclusion and the allowed deductions. The value of the gifted asset or property is its fair market value on the date the gift is made. However, the basis of the gift is the donor's cost, unless the gift tax is paid by the donee. The gift tax is assessed on the basis of the gift tax rate schedule and is reduced by the allowable credits. As already mentioned, gifts made within three years of death are added back to the estate for calculating estate taxes.

Gifts of tuition to educational institutions or money paid to hospitals for healthcare do not count as gifts for annual exclusion purposes. Also, variable exclusion gifts can be used to fund Section 529 Education Savings Accounts or Education Savings Plans. It is important to note that an individual is entitled to making an unlimited amount of transfers to educational institutions or hospitals for the benefit of someone else with no gift tax consequences if the gift is made directly to these institutions.

The federal gift tax is computed by using the following steps:

Step 1. Determine the amount of taxable gifts for a given period. Taxable gifts refer to the gross amount of the gift made less the allowable deductions and exclusions.

Step 2. Determine the sum of the taxable gifts for each of the preceding calendar years.

Step 3. Add the amounts determined under Steps 1 and 2.

Step 4. Compute the tax on the Step 3 amount using the gift tax rate schedule.

Step 5. Compute the tax on the Step 2 amount using the gift tax rate schedule.

Step 6. Subtract the Step 5 tax amount from the Step 4 tax amount. The difference, less any available applicable credit amount, is the gift tax for the period for which the return is being prepared.

Incidentally, if the gift tax is paid, the recepient is entitled to add that tax (with some limitations) to the basis of the property received.

Planning Ideas Involving Gifts

The twin goals of estate planning are to provide for the passage of assets in accordance with the estate owner's wishes and to minimize the tax liability. Strategies that an estate owner can use to dispose of the assets are: (1) Lifetime gifts, in which the donee becomes the absolute owner of the property given during the lifetime of the donor, and (2) Testamentary gifts, which involve the disposition of an estate owner's property at death through the provisions of the will.

Giving property away during one's lifetime can have substantially different tax consequences from the disposition of the same property at death. In many situations, significant tax savings can be achieved by means of lifetime gifts which are not available if disposition is deferred until death. In addition, there might be non-tax reasons for making lifetime gifts, such as to provide support for parents or to assist children with special needs.

Annual exclusion. The annual exclusion of a $11,000 gift per person provides an excellent planning opportunity. Assume George and Betty have two children and an estate of $2.0 million. They make gifts of $22,000 to each child for eight years, or a total of $352,000, thereby reducing the estate to $1.648 million. George leaves $1.5 million directly to his wife and the balance of $148,000 in a credit shelter trust. The $1.648 million ($1.5 million + $148,000) goes to the children at the deaths of the parents. The result is that the entire $2.0 million ($1.648 million plus total gift of $352,000) is transferred to the children, and no gift or estate tax is paid either when the lifetime gifts are made or when the $1.648 million passes to the children.

Other advantages of making lifetime gifts include the following: (1) Probate and administrative costs on transferred property are eliminated. (2) Frequently, state death taxes are reduced. (3) If the property generates tax preference income and creates an alternative minimum tax liability, the transfer may relieve the donor of such liability.

Special property. Another strategy relates to the gift of property with a potential for significant appreciation. Assume Lisa Brown owns an undeveloped real estate property which she hopes will significantly appreciate in value. The current value of the property is $300,000 and she gifts it to her daughter. Two years later when Lisa dies, the fair market value of the property is estimated at $1 million. However, the gift is added back to Lisa's estate at the original value of $300,000 and not at the fair market value of $1 million estimated at the time of her death.

Gifting via a trust. Gifting to minors via trusts constitutes the third gift planning strategy. Trusts permit the grantor to postpone the donee's receipt of the trust property until a prespecified age is attained. Under the terms of a trust, a trustee can be given broad investment powers, and through the use of a trust the donor can designate the distributions of trust property to the minors at the ages considered most desirable by the donor.

Gifts to charity. Gifts to qualified charities offer the fourth important estate planning strategy. As a general rule, gifts to qualified charities are deducted from the gross estate before estate taxes are calculated. These gifts can be made either outright or through the use of a trust. Depending upon the type of charitable trust selected by the donor, the trust property can assure an income stream to the donor, the surviving spouse, or other beneficiaries. For instance, an *inter vivos* or living charitable remainder trust (explained later in the chapter) provides a current income tax deduction equal to the present value of the remainder interest gifted to the charity. In this case the donor's estate is reduced by the value of the property transferred, and future income from the asset is taxed to the income beneficiary rather than to the donor.

Disadvantages of Gifts

While gift giving has great potential for reducing the donor's income tax and future estate taxes, it does have several drawbacks: (1) Without proper consideration for future needs, a person may gift away too much property during earning years and, as a result, experience financial strains later in life. (2) If a husband decides to give substantial gifts to his wife under the assumption that both will continue to live together, but later on is divorced, then he will have given the gift to someone who no longer shares his life. (3) If a taxable gift or bequest is given to grandchildren, a generation skipping tax may be imposed on the gift. The tax is imposed at a flat rate of 50 percent, but there is a $1.1 million exemption to be allocated amongst all of the grandchildren. It is therefore safe to conclude that lifetime gifts should not be allowed to compromise the tradeoffs among various objectives established for maximizing the financial welfare of all the concerned parties.

Other disadvantages of giving gifts include the following: (1) A lifetime gift could ultimately lead to a higher overall transfer tax liability. This may occur if the value of the transferred property is lower on the date of the donor's death than it was on the date of the gift. (2) The loss of the stepped-up income tax basis to the decedent's heirs. Property acquired by gift carries over the donor's basis for purposes of determining gain, while property acquired upon death gets a stepped-up basis. (3) The loss of control of the property, without a corresponding tax advantage. This can occur if, at death, the decedent's gross estate is not sufficiently large to be subject to estate tax. It can also occur if under the unlimited marital deduction provision, the gifted property could have been passed on to the surviving spouse without generating an estate tax liability.

Estate with and without Lifetime Gifts

The following illustration underscores the differences in gifting during lifetime and after death.

John, age 70 and a widower with three children, has a potential taxable estate of $2,000,000. If he dies in 2002 without having made lifetime gifts, the estate would be subject to a federal estate tax of $225,000:

Taxable estate	$2,000,000	
Estate tax on $2,000,000	$780,800	
(marginal bracket: 45%)		
Less: unified credit	(555,800)	
Net estate tax		**$225,000**

Now assume that John decides to give each of his three children an annual gift of $11,000, which is covered by the annual gift tax exclusion. Through this means John gifts away $528,000 of his estate by the time he dies 16 years later, which coincides with his life expectancy. Upon his death, assuming that neither his estate nor the gifted amount appreciated in value, the estate tax was calculated to be zero:

Taxable estate ($1,500,000 - $528,000)	$1,472,000	
Estate tax (marginal bracket: 43%)	$543,760	
Less: unified credit	(555,800)	
Net estate tax		**None**

Thus, by making judicious use of the $11,000 annual gift exclusion, John was able to save $225,000 in estate taxes. But if other factors were taken into account, even this impressive tax saving amount would pale by comparison. For instance, assuming a six percent after-tax return on the gifted amounts, upon John's death the value of the gifts would have been $847,193. At John's marginal tax bracket of 43 percent, the potential estate tax would be $364,293. Another drawback of John's not gifting during lifetime would be that, upon death, his estate would be much higher, thereby putting him potentially on the 49 percent marginal estate tax bracket.

In conclusion, gifting during lifetime, when sheltered by annual gift tax exclusions or by the applicable exclusion amount, enjoys significant tax advantages and should be given serious consideration. Of course, the advantages of gifting should be balanced against the drawback that, once the process is completed, the gifted property is permanently removed from the estate of the owner.

Conclusion

As part of an overall estate plan, lifetime and testamentary gifts should be made on a selective and coordinated basis with careful regard to the tax and personal considerations of both the donor and the donee. Federal and state gift, estate, generation-skipping, and income, tax—all play a part in the timing and amount of gifts and in the selection of the property to be given away.

TRUSTS

The use of the right type of trust is one of the most valuable estate planning tools. This section will discuss in detail how different types of trusts can be used to reduce or eliminate federal estate taxes.

Estate Taxes and Trusts

The law provides a variety of trust-related tools that can be used to minimize federal estate taxes. These tools, presented in Table 9-1, are discussed in detail in the following pages.

The key issues. The avoidance of the federal estate tax frequently involves two key features: the gift/estate tax applicable exclusion amounts of $1,000,000 and/$1,500,000 (2005), respectively and the unlimited marital deduction. The law offers a credit that allows every person to give away during his or her lifetime, or after death, up to $1,000,000 to beneficiaries free of federal gift taxes, or $1,500,000 at death free of federal estate taxes. The second feature is even more generous. It states that a person can leave an unlimited amount of assets to the surviving spouse free of federal estate taxes. These two provisions of the law allow married couples to pass to the non-spousal beneficiaries an estate up to $3 million without federal estate taxes. Frequently a trust commonly known as a *bypass or family* trust is used to accomplish this objective.

Bypass trust. A bypass or family trust is created as a testamentary trust which comes into existence upon death. Following death, the decedent's assets are reallocated in such a way that no estate taxes would be due upon the first death, and estate taxes would be either eliminated or minimized upon the second death. An illustration should make this clear.

Suppose John Jones owns $3 million, and Betty Jones does not own any assets. If John's assets are transferred to Betty upon John's death, no estate taxes would be due because of the unlimited marital deduction. However, upon Betty's death, only $1.5 million (2005) would pass estate tax-free, thereby subjecting the balance to estate taxes.

TABLE 9-1 Trusts and Taxes

Type of trust	Nature of trust	Advantages	Disadvantages	Included in gross estate	Qualifies for marital deduction	Recipient of income	Recipient of assets
Bypass (family) trust	Property allocated to this trust so as to not overqualify for marital deduction.	Bypasses the survivor's taxable estate.	Surviving spouse does not have ownership of trust property.	Yes, subject to $600,000 exclusion.	No	Personal choice[+]	Personal choice[+]
Marital trust	Surviving spouse receives all income and the right to designate the beneficiary.	All income goes to spouse. Also, this trust, plus the pour-over trust,* can eliminate estate tax.	Spouse does not receive property outright.	No	Yes	Surviving spouse	Surviving spouse's choice
QTIP trust	This trust controls the distribution of property upon death of second spouse. Surviving spouse receives all income.	Property owner can direct distribution of property after death of surviving spouse.	Surviving spouse has no control over property.	No	Yes	Spouse	Personal choice[+]
Estate trust	This trust terminates on the death of the surviving spouse at which time assets and accumulated income are paid to the probate estate.	Appropriate where current income is not desired. Trust is not required to distribute income.	Tax rates are steeper.	No	Yes	Spouse	Surviving spouse's choice
Life insurance trust	Irrevocable inter vivos trust funded by life insurance policy.	Proceeds bypass estates of both spouses, if trust is irrevocable.	Loss of control over policy.	No (except when death occurs in 3 years).	No	Personal choice[+]	Personal choice[+]

* Proceeds from other trusts (e.g., life insurance trust) can pour over into this trust upon the occurrence of certain events such as death.
[+] Choice of the person who creates the trust.

The Joneses can adopt an alternative strategy to minimize estate taxes. John modifies his estate plan to create a bypass trust. Upon John's death, $1.5 million worth of assets will be transferred into the bypass trust, while the remaining $1.5 million would be directly received by Betty. The situation would now be as follows. Assets received directly by Betty would qualify for the marital deduction and would escape estate taxes upon John's death. Although assets transferred into the bypass trust would not qualify for the marital deduction, these assets would also escape estate taxes because John is entitled to the $1.5 million applicable exclusion amount. That is, upon John's death, the entire $3 million would be available for Betty's benefit free of federal estate taxes.

The story would be repeated upon Betty's death. If she does not remarry, Betty would not have a marital deduction but would be entitled to the $1.5 million estate tax exclusion. Assuming that Betty's estate was not more than that amount, the entire estate would pass to her beneficiaries estate tax-free. The tax code excludes the assets in the bypass trust from Betty's estate because she does not have control of the property in that trust. In addition, the bypass trust would remain free of federal estate taxes no matter how large the assets grow, as long as the initial size of the trust was limited to $1.5 million. These facts are clearly illustrated in Table 9-2.

Power of appointment trust. The marital deduction is allowed for a transfer to a power of appointment trust. This trust is a type of marital trust in which the surviving spouse is entitled to income for life, payable at least annually, and in which the surviving spouse has a general power of appointment over the entire interest. A power of appointment trust allows the surviving spouse to give trust property to any person at will. Also, the holder can exercise this power in favor of himself or herself, the estate, the creditors, or the creditors of the estate.

Marital trust. In the previous illustration, Betty received $1.5 million from John's estate with complete control over this estate. If for medical or psychological reasons John did not want Betty to have unlimited powers over these assets, he

TABLE 9-2   Use of Bypass Trust

	Property willed to Betty Jones		Use of bypass trust	
	John Jones	Betty Jones	John Jones	Betty Jones
Estate value	$2,000,000	$2,000,000	$2,000,000[1]	$1,000,000[1]
Marital deduction	$2,000,000	0	$1,000,000	0
Taxable estate	0	$2,000,000	$1,000,000[2]	$1,000,000
Tax, before credits	0	$780,800	$345,800	$345,800
Unified credit	0	$345,800[3]	$345,800[3]	$345,800[3]
Estate tax	0	$434,200	0	0

[1] Property passing directly to Betty.

[2] Property in a bypass trust.

[3] The $555,800 unified credit refers to the estate tax on a $1.5 million estate (2005). This is another way of stating that up to $1.5 million of an estate passes federal estate tax-free.

could have transferred these assets into a *marital trust*, also known as *power of appointment* trust. Under the marital trust provisions, Betty would have the right to designate by will who would receive the assets of the marital trust (hence the name "power of appointment" trust) and such appointment may be made to anyone she chooses. Betty would receive all of the income from the marital trust and may also be given the right to withdraw any part of the trust's assets during her lifetime. The concept of marital trust is presented in Figure 9-1.

The marital, or power of appointment, trust is an extremely valuable estate planning tool. However, the law specifies that in order for the marital trust to qualify, the following strict conditions must be fully met:

1. The surviving spouse must be entitled to all of the income produced by the assets and it must be distributed at least once every year.
2. The surviving spouse must be given a general power to appoint the property to: (1) herself or himself; (2) the estate; (3) the creditors; or (4) the creditors of his or her estate.
3. No one else can appoint any part of the trust assets to anyone except the surviving spouse.

Tax considerations of a marital trust are indeed significant. Initially, assets transferred to a marital trust qualify for the marital deduction, even though the surviving spouse does not directly control the assets. This is because, in the eyes of the law, the spouse receives sufficient benefits from this trust to warrant such a classification. Upon the death of the surviving spouse, however, the assets of the marital trust would be added to his or her estate. Naturally, the entire estate would pass to the beneficiaries tax-free if the total value of the marital trust added to the value of other assets does not exceed $1.5 million (2005).

QTIP trust. A marital trust gives the surviving spouse unlimited power to dispose of the assets in any manner he or she chooses, including to a new partner after remarriage. For instance, if John creates a marital trust, he will have no guarantee that after his death the assets will ever reach his children. To allay that fear, John can create a *qualified terminable interest property* trust, or QTIP trust, also known as the current interest trust. The QTIP trust agreement, and not the surviving spouse, controls the distribution of the assets upon the death of the QTIP trust creator.

Assets transferred into a QTIP trust qualify for the unlimited marital deduction, provided all of the income of the trust is paid, at least annually, to the surviving spouse. Also, no provision for invasion of the trust assets can be made for anyone other than the surviving spouse. Finally, if the assets of a QTIP trust qualify for the marital deduction, then these assets must be included in the estate of the surviving spouse. The concept of QTIP trust is presented in Figure 9-2.

A QTIP trust is generally used as an estate planning tool for one or both of the following reasons:

1. The trust allows the marital deduction to apply to the value of QTIP trust property, even though the client making the will controls who will be the trust's ultimate beneficiary.
2. The trust allows the personal representative of the estate to decide if the property would be included in the estate of the decedent or in the estate of the surviving spouse.

The Marital - Family type of Trust is designed to make certain that the $1,500,000 exemption (2004) of each spouse is used, while allowing the surviving spouse to have use of all of the deceased spouse's assets during the remainder of his or her lifetime. The Family Trust (Trust B) is generally not taxed at either death. The Marital Trust (Trust A) is generally taxed at the surviving spouse's death.

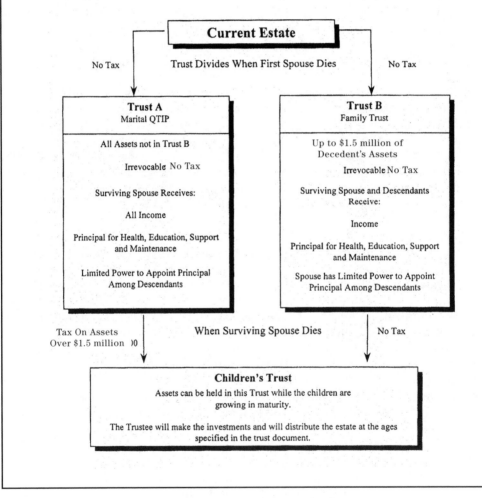

FIGURE 9-1 Marital/Family Living Trust

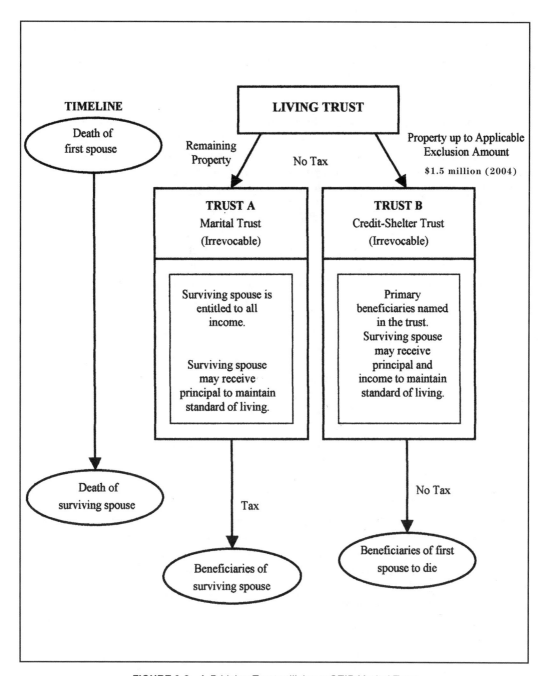

FIGURE 9-2 A-B Living Trust utilizing a QTIP Marital Trust

Here is an example to illustrate the use of a QTIP trust. Assume John and Mary Dow have two children, Jeffrey and Lisa. Also, from previous marriages, John has a daughter, Cindy, and Mary has a son, Robert. John is afraid that, upon his death, Mary will favor her son Robert in her will. John can allay his fears by providing in his will that certain property can go into a QTIP trust. This trust will pay Mary income for life, with the remainder of the trust going to Cindy, or if John prefers, to Cindy, Jeffrey, and Lisa, upon Mary's death. If the trust satisfies all the legal conditions, the value of the property going into the QTIP trust will qualify for the marital deduction.

Estate trust. An estate trust terminates upon the death of the surviving spouse at which time assets are transferred to the spouse's estate. The estate trust is particularly suitable in situations where there is a desire to invest in non-income producing property and the surviving spouse does not need the income from the trust. An added advantage is that since the trust is not required to distribute income, the trust can be created as a separate taxpaying entity.

A significant disadvantage of the estate trust is that the trust assets must be paid to the surviving spouse's probate estate. This can delay the distributions to the beneficiaries, increase the costs to the estate, and defeat one of the primary reasons for setting up a living trust in the first place (that is, to avoid probate).

A comparison of the salient features of the four types of trust just discussed is presented in Table 9-3. In each case it is assumed that the surviving spouse is the income beneficiary of the trust. This table reveals that no one trust is superior to the others, since individual circumstances dictate the selection of the best trust.

Life insurance trust. The trusts described thus far are primarily designed to shelter up to $3 million (2005) from federal estate taxes. One asset, which can easily push the estate beyond that limit, is a sizable life insurance policy. The trust designed to solve that problem is known as *life insurance trust.*

TABLE 9-3 Comparative Features of Key Trusts

Particulars	*Bypass trust*	*Marital trust*	*QTIP trust*	*Estate trust*
Value of trust property subject to marital deduction?	No	Yes	Yes	Yes
Value of trust property included in decedent's taxable estate?	Yes	No	No	No
Trust income must be distributed annually?	No	Yes	Yes	No
Remainder of trust distributed to persons named by decedent?	Yes	No	Yes	No
Remainder of trust distributed to persons named by surviving spouse?	No	Yes	No	Yes
Value of trust property included in surviving spouse's estate?	No	Yes	Yes	Yes

To shelter life insurance proceeds from estate taxes, one must sacrifice ownership rights, such as the right to change beneficiaries, the right to surrender or cancel the policy, the right to assign it, and the right to borrow against it. This may be accomplished by irrevocably transferring the ownership of a policy to a life insurance trust. If the insured's death occurs more than three years from the time of the transfer, the life insurance proceeds are included in the trust, completely bypassing the estate of the deceased. The surviving spouse may continue to receive income from this trust for life, and the trustees may be given the discretion to invade the principal in accordance with the trust's provisions. After the surviving spouse dies, the assets are distributed to the named beneficiaries.

An important limitation imposed by law on life insurance trusts relates to the timing of the assignment of the policy. The law states that the assignment must occur more than three years prior to the death of the insured in order to exclude the proceeds from the estate of the deceased. Consequently, it may be wise to arrange the plan in a way that would automatically transfer the life insurance proceeds into a marital trust should death occur within three years of the trust's creation. If the plan is arranged in this manner, even when death occurs within three years of transfer of a life insurance policy, the estate of the deceased would escape the estate tax via the marital deduction route. The concept of life insurance trust is presented in Figure 9-3.

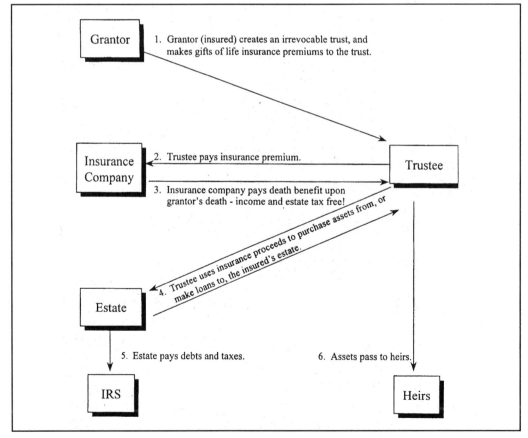

FIGURE 9-3 The Irrevocable Life Insurance Trust

Charitable trust. The life insurance trust is but one way to reduce the estate tax burden on sizable estates. An estate can also be reduced by outright gifts to individuals and charities as well as by creating charitable trusts. Gifting to charities as an estate planning tool was discussed in a previous section. Charitable trusts are discussed in this section.

Charitable trusts involve an *income interest* and a *remainder interest*. The former is the right to receive the earned income, while the latter refers to a claim on the property that remains after the income interest is satisfied. Through the use of a charitable trust, a person can currently receive an income tax benefit for contributing a remainder interest or income interest to charity while retaining the other interest for personal use.

There are four types of charitable trusts which can be used to qualify for the unlimited estate tax charitable deduction. These are described next.

Charitable remainder annuity trust. This trust permits the annual payments of a fixed income to one or more beneficiaries during their lifetime or for a term no greater than 20 years. The trust assets cannot be invaded, nor can the trust be amended or revoked. Upon the termination of the trust the assets are transferred to the designated charity. In this type of trust the donor retains a life income interest in the contributed property. Consequently, the entire value of the assets is included in the person's gross estate. However, for federal income tax purposes, the donor receives a charitable deduction for the present value of the property passing to the charity as a remainder interest in the year of the transfer to the trust. It should be added here that the donor cannot make additional contributions in an annuity trust.

In order for a charitable remainder annuity trust to qualify as an estate deduction it must meet the following tests:

1. A fixed amount or fixed percentage of the beginning value of the trust must be paid to the non-charitable beneficiary.
2. The annuity must be no less than five percent of the initial fair market value of the property transferred to the trust.
3. There is a maximum payment of 50 percent.
4. The percentage now has to result in a present value of the remainder interest equal to at least ten percent of the additional contribution value.
5. The specified amount must be paid at least annually.
6. The trust must be irrevocable.
7. The trust must be for the benefit of one or more individuals named in the trust.

At this point, it is important to make a distinction between charitable remainder trusts that are established by spouses and trusts that are established by a parent or child. When the former trusts are established, there are no gift or rebate tax implications, and they are included in the estate upon the death of the surviving spouse.

Charitable remainder unitrust. In this trust, the individual or other designated beneficiaries receive variable—rather than fixed—annuity income. The variable amount is determined by taking a specified (not less than five) percentage of the fair market value of the trust's assets. Thus, a unitrust must revalue its assets annually to determine its income payout amount. Other than these provisions, a unitrust is similar to the charitable remainder annuity trust. Incidentally, a donor can make future contributions in addition to the initial contribution in this trust. The concept of charitable remainder trust is presented in Figure 9-4.

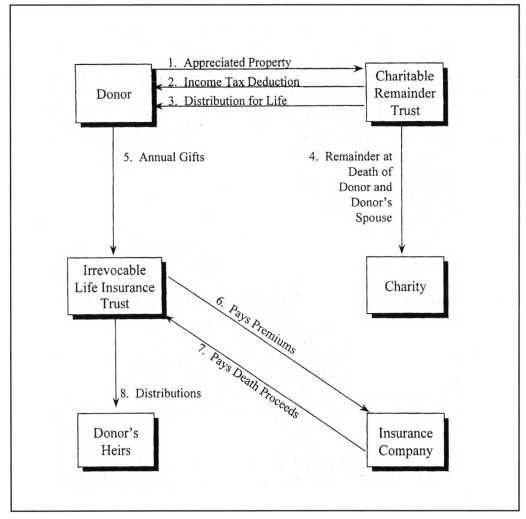

FIGURE 9-4 Charitable Remainder Trust

Charitable lead trust. A charitable lead trust is different from a charitable remainder trust. Instead of transferring the remainder interest to charity, the lead trust distributes an income interest to charity while the remainder interest is retained by the donor or the beneficiaries. Since the charitable income interest must be in the form of an annuity or unitrust interest, there is the possibility that very little trust income will be distributed to the donor or other beneficiaries.

Pooled income fund. A pooled income fund is a remainder trust created and maintained by a public charity. These investment funds consist of funds pooled together from the contributions of many individuals. Since a donor's retained life estate is based upon the trust's income, a pooled income fund is of particular benefit to an individual with limited assets. The deduction of property transferred to a pooled income fund is equal to the difference between the fair market value of the property contributed and the present value of the retained income interest. The gift and estate tax consequences are the same as for transfers to a charitable remainder trust.

The donor to a pooled income fund is entitled to an income and gift tax deduction if the following requirements are met:

1. The donor must contribute an irrevocable remainder interest to the charitable organization.
2. The property transferred by the donor must be commingled with the property transferred by other donors.
3. The fund cannot invest in tax-exempt securities.
4. No donor or income beneficiary can be a trustee.
5. The donor must retain for himself or herself, or other named beneficiaries, a life income interest.
6. Each income beneficiary must be entitled to receive a pro rata share of the annual income based upon the rate of return earned by the fund.

Irrevocable Gift Trust

An irrevocable gift trust can be created for passing significant amount of assets free of federal estate taxes to the beneficiaries. In creating this trust, a person gives up any right to trust income and principal as well as the right to change the beneficiaries or other terms of the trust agreement. Clearly, upon the transferor's death, gift-tax paid on the assets transferred into the trust for longer than three years is not included in his or her estate.

Basically, to keep the property out of the estate, the grantor cannot: (1) retain a reversionary interest in the assets; (2) retain the power to amend, revoke, or change the trust; (3) maintain a right to the income or enjoyment of the property; (4) retain the power to control the disposition of the property; and (5) maintain any incidents of ownership in insurance included in the trust.

There are two major advantages to creating an irrevocable gift trust over outright gifts. First, the individual can have the income distributed from the trust to one or more beneficiaries. Second, the person can specify who would inherit the principal upon death. The law does not require the ultimate beneficiaries to be the same persons as those who receive the income from the trust.

SOPHISTICATED ESTATE TAX REDUCTION STRATEGIES

FAMILY LIMITED PARTNERSHIPS

While not a new concept, recently *family limited partnerships* (FLPs) have become an important tax-planning tool where transfer of property to junior generations at a substantially reduced transfer tax cost is a major consideration. Among the reasons for this popularity is the clarification by the IRS (Revenue Ruling 93-12) of its position on whether minority discounts applied to transfers to family members, and the further compression under the *Omnibus Budget Reconciliation Act of 1993* (OBRA '93) of income tax rates applicable to trusts. The basic structure of an FLP is presented in Figure 9-5.

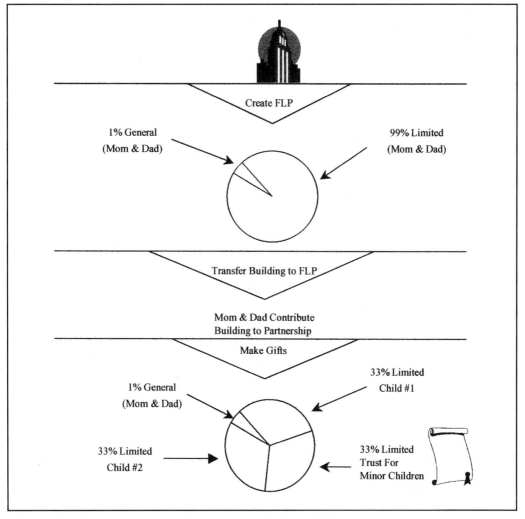

FIGURE 9-5 The Family Limited Partnership

Advantages. The key advantages of using FLP as an estate planning tool are presented below.

1. An individual can discount gifts of limited partnership interests and thus transfer property to the intended beneficiaries at a significantly reduced transfer tax cost. The following illustration underscores this benefit.

   Assume Bob and Jane, both 45 years old, own a real estate business with a fair market value of $2 million. Their CPA has advised them that upon their death in, say, 25 to 30 years, the property could create an estate tax liability in excess of $4 million. The couple wishes to reduce their estate tax liability, without giving up the management control over their business.

   In 1998, Bob and Jane transfer the business to an FLP in exchange for general partnership and limited partnership interests. As general partners, parents retain management control over the business, and they gift limited partnership interests to their children to reduce their gross estate. After formation of the FLP, the couple uses their unified credits to gift limited partnership interests worth $1.25 million, the maximum amount they can transfer in 1998 using their respective unified credit without paying any gift tax. If a qualified appraiser determines that the gift of the limited partnership interests is entitled to a discount for lack of marketability and lack of control, the couple would be entitled to use the discounted value for determining the gift tax value. If a 33 percent discount is assumed, the initial gift, shielded from gift tax by their unified credits, is leveraged. Although the couple transfer limited partnership interests to their children valued at $1.25 million, the transferred limited partnership units represent approximately $1.9 million of pro rata value in the real estate business. Parents can additionally leverage their annual exclusion gifts of $10,000 per parent, per beneficiary, and effectively transfer about $59,000 of value in real estate business to their son and daughter each year without paying gift tax. If each parent continues to make annual exclusion gifts to son and daughter until his or her death, they both can transfer to the children their entire interest in the business without paying any gift or estate tax. This strategy saves the family in excess of $4 million in taxes, assuming that the real estate business is the sole asset of the parents, the value of the business appreciates at 5 percent per year, and the husband and the wife die in 2023 and 2028, respectively.

2. An individual can freeze the value of property by passing future appreciation to the intended beneficiaries. Historically, this has been achieved by recapitalizing the business, which gives the business owner preferred stock, while the other family members receive common stock, which will appreciate as a result of the future growth of the company. Once the process of stock distribution is completed, the business owner receives dividends on the preferred stock holdings and pays tax at both corporate and individual levels. Using an FLP, the business owner can effectively create the equivalent of cumulative preferred stock by retaining a GP interest, thereby avoiding the problem of double taxation altogether. It is

vital, however, that the limited partner family members be treated as true partners, and that gifts of limited partnership interests be complete and unrestricted.

3. An individual can reduce his or her gross estate without giving up control of the underlying property held by the FLP. If a donor retains control over gifted assets, upon death the fair market value of these assets would be included in the donor's estate. However, the situation is different in the case of an FLP. In this case, although a general partner retains effective control of property gifted to the limited partners, the limited partnership interests gifted during life are not included in the gross estate of the donor. This is because the actions of the general partner represent the fiduciary duties of the partners. Consequently, the value of the limited partnership interests that the general partner transfers during his or her lifetime is not included in the donor's gross estate upon death.

4. An individual can reduce the gross estate while protecting the underlying property from creditors and non-family ownership. An FLP can provide some degree of creditor protection, because usually a creditor's only remedy against a limited partnership interest is a court order requiring that all distributions from the partnership to the debtor-partner be made to the creditor until the debt is discharged. However, in this case, the creditor will not receive any cash or property if the FLP does not make any distributions to the partners.

5. An FLP can result in substantial savings in taxes. As a flow-through entity, all FLP income is taxed directly to the individual partners. Unless they are in the highest tax bracket, because of the flow-through provision, as compared to a trust, an FLP may produce significantly higher income tax savings. This advantage has become even more pronounced under OBRA '93, which effectively subjected all taxable income of trusts (over an exemption limit of $8,650) to the top tax bracket.

Disadvantages. An FLP is not for everyone, however. Experienced legal and tax counsel are required to ensure that the FLP is recognized for both state law and tax purposes. For example, counsel must ensure that the FLP has a legitimate business purpose, conducts business in a formal and businesslike manner by holding periodic meetings, and annual partnership tax returns are prepared and filed in a timely fashion.

WEALTH REPLACEMENT TRUST

A wealth replacement trust (WRT), also known as asset replacement trust, is an irrevocable life insurance trust, which is put into place in conjunction with a charitable remainder trust (CRT), to replace the assets the heirs of the donor of a CRT would be losing by the assets passing to the charity after the noncharitable income beneficiaries' death.

For example, assume George, who is in a 55 percent federal estate tax bracket, transfers $1 million worth of appreciated stock to a charitable remainder annuity trust, retaining a 6 percent annuity trust for himself. After his death, assets pass to a charity of his choice. Had he not created the trust, his heirs would have inherited $450,000 ($550,000 would have been paid as federal estate tax). Therefore, to replace the amount by which his heirs would have been disinherited, he created an irrevocable life insurance trust, which can purchase a sizeable insurance policy on his life.

Incidentally, since George receives immediate tax benefits upon establishing a charitable remainder trust through an income tax distribution, and since he would have an increased cash flow with the trust because the trust paid no income tax on the sale of the assets, which could be reinvested at a potentially higher yield, the funding for the life insurance premium could be achieved by using the tax savings and the increased cash flow, without any additional outlays by the client.

Replacing Gifted Assets

In order to establish a WRT, an individual sets up an irrevocable trust, naming the heirs as beneficiaries. A life insurance policy is purchased within the trust with a face value equal to the value of the securities in the CRT. This insurance policy can be funded by the investment income of the CRT. A true WRT would replace the wealth net of estate taxes that would have been received by the children or family members. That is, assuming the highest estate tax bracket of 48 percent (2004), the WRT would have to replace only 48 percent of the assets transferred to the CRT.

Since the insurance policy is placed inside an irrevocable trust, upon death it is not included in the estate of the insured. The insured's heirs receive the death benefit from the life insurance policy without having to go through probate, thereby effectively replacing the charitable gift.

Covering Estate Taxes

An estate with potential estate tax problems can be served by using a similar approach. First, in order to significantly reduce estate taxes, a living trust is established with a provision (called A-B provision) to transfer $1 million to a by-pass trust. This enables the trust's owner to take advantage of the $1.5 million (2005) exemption equivalent twice and eliminate the tax liability for $3.00 million of the estate. Next, using a portion of the income from the initial trust, an Irrevocable Life Insurance Trust is established, naming the intended heirs as beneficiaries. The trust can be funded with a life insurance policy—popularly known as survivorship policy, or second-to-die policy—that pays upon the death of the second spouse.

Upon the death of the second spouse, the assets of both spouses' trusts will pass to the heirs without going through probate. At the same time, the death benefit from the insurance policy in the WRT can be used to pay estate taxes on those estates that exceed $3.00 million.

SPRINKLING TRUSTS

A sprinkling trust is not a trust by itself; rather it is a provision that may or may not be contained within a trust. However, by using this type of provision the trust maker grants discretionary powers to the trustee concerning the disbursement of trust funds. These powers can then be used to achieve both tax and non-tax objectives. Because trustees may use their own judgment when distributing funds among the beneficiaries, the trust's resources can better serve those with greater financial and material needs. In addition, if trust income is dispensed in amounts inversely related to each beneficiary's tax bracket, it could result in valuable income tax savings. Finally, the trustees are empowered to retain income in the trust for future disposal. Deferring payments can also result in tax deferral, and ultimately in tax savings.

The tax consequences of the sprinkling trust, however, could also turn out to be detrimental. If trustees can be proved to be related or subordinate to the grantor, the power vested in them to sprinkle the trust's income and principal could conceivably make the trust taxable to the grantor. On the other hand, if the trustees are sufficiently independent of the grantor, then they may be too far removed from the beneficiaries to adequately judge their needs. For that reason, many grantors are reluctant to give to a bank or a trust company the power to sprinkle income among their heirs or beneficiaries.

THE CRUMMEY TRUST

The Crummey Trust is a popular device used in making certain types of gifts that qualify for the $11,000 annual exclusion from gift tax. Significant tax benefits could be derived if these annual gifts could be used for making life insurance premium payments. The Crummey Trust takes its name from a court case upholding this type of trust and supporting its tax benefits.

An irrevocable life insurance trust is a vehicle for holding life insurance policies. The primary goal of such a trust is to shift the ownership of the policies from the insured's generation to a lower generation in order to remove the policy proceeds from taxation at the death of the insured and the spouse. This result can be achieved by gifting policies to the children.

Where a life insurance policy continues to require payment of premiums after the gift, the plan would call for the insured to make annual gifts to the trust to cover the premium payments. In order to make those gifts qualify as a present interest gift, the trust will have a "Crummey" withdrawal power in the beneficiaries (usually the children).

With a Crummey withdrawal power, each time a contribution is made to the trust the beneficiary has a temporary right to demand withdrawal from the trust. If the demand right is not exercised, the annual transfer for that year remains in the trust for management by the trustee. Once the withdrawal right lapses, the trustee is then free to use the funds which were contributed to pay the premiums on the life insurance policies.

The beneficiaries generally recognize that the withdrawal of funds would jeopardize the viability of the life insurance policy which was taken out specifically to benefit them; for that reason, usually they let the withdrawal right lapse. Because the right of withdrawal is usually not exercised, the trustee of a Crummey Trust generally uses the funds for the purpose desired by both the trust grantor and the beneficiaries. When the grantor-insured dies, the insurance proceeds are used to provide benefits to the surviving spouse, children, and grandchildren. If the life insurance is on the life of the surviving spouse or on the joint lives of both parents, upon the death of the surviving spouse the insurance proceeds are used to pay the federal estate taxes due.

A reduction of the grantor's estate tax liability is the main reason for setting up an irrevocable trust. As long as the grantor establishes such a trust and retains no incidence of ownership over the property and no powers over the funds in the trust that could be construed as ownership, the assets placed in the trust are not included in the gross estate of the grantor.

In funding a Crummey trust, the vehicle of choice is invariably permanent life insurance for the following reasons: (1) It increases substantially in size upon death. (2) It can be funded with installments qualifying for the $11,000/$22,000 annual exclusion per beneficiary. (3) The cash or side fund permits funds flexibility. (4) The insurance proceeds, which represent discounted dollars, can eventually be used to pay estate taxes.

GENERATION SKIPPING TRANSFER TAX

A generation skipping transfer (GST) is any transfer of property by gift or at death, to any person who, under federal tax law, is assigned to a generation that is two or more generations below that of the transferor. There are three levels where GST techniques are useful. First, where a person stands to inherit a substantial estate from a parent but already has a substantial estate, a GST would be set up for the parent's property for the benefit of the person. Second, a GST may be used where parents wish to minimize transfer taxes in a child's estate but still give the child the use and benefit of the property, or where the parents wish to protect the property from a spendthrift child. Third, a person may wish to make direct transfers to a grandchild or another person two or more generations below for the beneficiary's education, support or enjoyment, or in order to avoid tax in the estate of the intervening generation.

The generation skipping transfer tax (GSTT), enacted in 1976, is designed to prevent the transfer of wealth without tax to successive generations. Following is a summary of the GSTT rules:

1. Under the current law every individual is entitled to make cumulative transfers (by lifetime gifts or death time bequests) of up to $1,100,000 without paying GSTT.
2. The rate of tax on generation skipping transfers is now equal to the maximum gift and estate tax rate applicable at the time of transfer. It is a flat tax of 55 percent. GSTT is in addition to any other tax that may be due on the transfer.

Here is an example of how GST works. An inter vivos trust is usually used to establish the method of trust distribution during life as well as to avoid probate of trust assets at death. In many cases, the trust is created as a receptacle for lifetime gifts and to receive assets at the death of the donors. The trust instrument would provide for the creation of two separate trusts. An amount equal to the child's share of the donor's GSTT exemption ($1,000,000 in 2005) would be allocated to one trust (the exempt trust). The other trust would be the non-exempt trust for GST purposes. For optimal results, it is best to fund the exempt trust with assets with the greatest growth potential. This concept allows the maximum amount of assets to pass to the future generations without transfer tax, because once the exemption is allocated to the trust, the growth is also exempt.

The exempt and non-exempt trusts are established so that they have GSTT inclusion ratios of zero and one respectively. When the exempt trust is established with an inclusion ratio of zero, that trust maintains its total immunity from GSTT as long as there are no later additions of non-exempt property.

The concept of generation skipping trust, also called the Dynasty Trust, is presented in Figure 9-6.

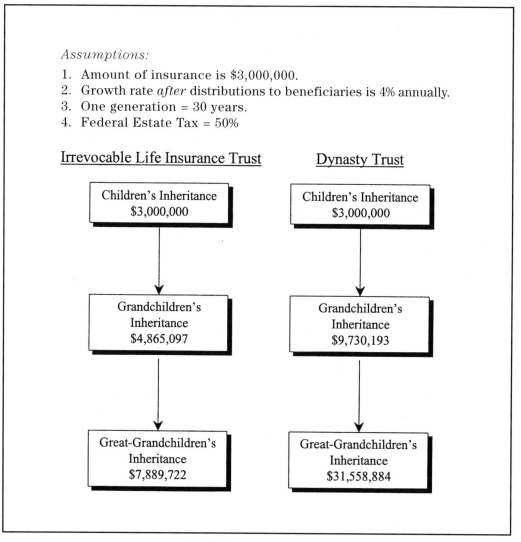

FIGURE 9-6 Dynasty Trust

DYNASTY TRUST LEVERAGING THE GSTT EXEMPTION

A Crummey Trust funded with life insurance can leverage a grantor's GSTT exemption. For example, a married couple could give up to $3,000,000 (2004) to a Crummey Trust. The trustee could in turn use that amount to purchase, say, a $15 million joint and survivor life insurance policy on the grantors' lives. Upon death of the surviving spouse, the following benefits would ensue:

1. The face value of $15 million received by the Crummey Trust would be income tax free under Section 101(a) of the Internal Revenue Code.
2. The entire proceeds would be estate tax free because the grantors did not own the policy.
3. There would be no GSTT because the grantor's GSTT was used to make gifts to the trust.
4. The children and grandchildren would receive the income from the trust and any principal needed to maintain their standard of living.
5. Upon the death of the children, the property (including any appreciation) would pass *estate tax free* to the grandchildren, and perhaps even to the great-grandchildren.

Incidentally, if a Dynasty Trust is formed in a jurisdiction that has no rule against perpetuities, such as the situation in Wisconsin, South Dakota, Delaware, Illinois, Idaho, and Alaska, then this type of trust does not have to terminate with a distribution to the grandchildren or great grandchildren.

SPLIT DOLLAR ARRANGEMENT

Split dollar life insurance is an arrangement, typically between an employer and an employee, under which cash values, death benefits, and premium costs may be split between the parties. Typically, the employer pays that part of the annual premium which equals the current year's increase in the cash surrender value of the policy. The employee pays the balance, if any, of the premium.

Essentially, the premiums on the life insurance policy are treated as interest-free loans to the owner of the policy (that is, the insured's Crummey Trust). The trust gives the corporation a security interest (called collateral assignment) in the policy so that at the insured's death, the Crummey Trust repays the corporation its loans. It should be added here that the IRS is beginning to question the tax-free treatment of split dollar, and care should be taken in using this strategy. The tax consequences of a split dollar arrangement are as follows:

1. The premiums advanced by the corporation are non-deductible. Thus, in a Subchapter S corporation, the premiums paid by the corporation would be taxable to the shareholders on a pro-rata basis (as would be corporate earnings).
2. The insured must report as income the lower of the so-called PS 58 cost of the policy or the insurance company's cost of carrying a one-year term policy. This is the equivalent of the term insurance rate for the face amount of the policy. In a joint and survivor policy, this rate will be a very small fraction of the actual premium.

3. The value of the gift by the insured to the Crummey Trust is the same as the PS 58 cost each year.

4. Clearly, more insurance can be purchased within the Crummey Trust because the $11,000/$22,000 annual exclusion per beneficiary is measured by the lower PS 58 cost (as compared to the actual premium). This is known as trust packing.

DISCLAIMER

A disclaimer is a beneficiary's unqualified refusal to accept an inter vivos or testamentary transfer of property. A beneficiary making a qualified disclaimer is treated as if the disclaimed interest in property had never been received. The property then passes as though the disclaimant predeceased the decedent. A disclaimer would be used on one of the following situations: (1) The entire estate was left to the surviving spouse. (2) A marital deduction was claimed for the entire amount and the unified credit was not used. (3) The estate was left to the decedent's children, and because they have sufficient assets on their own, they chose not to use the decedent's GSTT exemption. A disclaimer must be irrevocable, in writing, and made no later than nine months after the date on which the transfer was made (corresponding to the filing of an estate tax return).

GRANTOR RETAINED ANNUITY TRUST (GRAT) AND GRANTOR RETAINED UNITRUST (GRUT)

An Overview

A grantor retained annuity trust (GRAT) is an irrevocable trust to which an individual transfers property but retains a fixed annuity interest for a specified term not to exceed life expectancy, with the remainder interest passing to specific beneficiaries. While there is an initial gift tax imposed when the property is transferred to the GRAT, ownership of the transferred property passes to the grantor's beneficiaries without the imposition of additional gift tax if the grantor survives the selected term. If, however, the grantor fails to survive the selected term, the value of the transferred property is included in the grantor's gross estate. A GRAT is a useful tool because it allows a grantor to transfer property and all the property's appreciation to the beneficiaries at a reduced transfer tax cost.

Here is an example to illustrate the tax benefits of a GRAT. Assume a 65-year old father, Sam, has a sizeable estate, which includes a tool and dye shop valued at $500,000. His son Mike operates the tool and dye shop. Sam would like Mike to own the shop, but he would have to pay a gift tax if he made an outright gift of the shop to Mike since Sam has exhausted his unified credit.

Instead of making an outright gift, Sam transfers the shop to the GRAT, retaining a ten percent annuity interest ($50,000 per year) for ten years, and naming Mike as remainder beneficiary. Sam's gift to the GRAT is substantially less than the fair market value of the tool and dye shop because his retained annuity interest reduces the value of the gift by 65 percent. If Sam survives the ten-year term, ownership of the shop will pass to Mike without the imposition of any additional gift tax. If the value of the shop appreciates at the rate of five percent per year to approximately

$800,000, and Sam passes away immediately after the ten-year term, under certain assumptions the potential transfer tax savings would be 43 percent of the appreciated value.

If Sam passes away during the term so that the value of the tool and dye shop is brought back into his estate, his estate would receive a credit for any previously used unified credit. Therefore, from a transfer tax perspective, the GRAT strategy creates a win-win situation. If Sam survives he clearly wins, and if he does not, the transfer tax on his interest in the shop does not increase. Figure 9-7 presents an overview of the GRAT strategy.

A grantor retained unitrust (GRUT) works very much like a GRAT. The basic difference is that a GRUT provides the grantor with a fixed percentage of the value of the trust on an annual basis for a set period of time.

Key Advantages
The key advantages of GRAT are presented below.

1. The grantor can pass property to the intended beneficiaries at a reduced transfer tax cost. As observed, the taxable gift the grantor makes of the

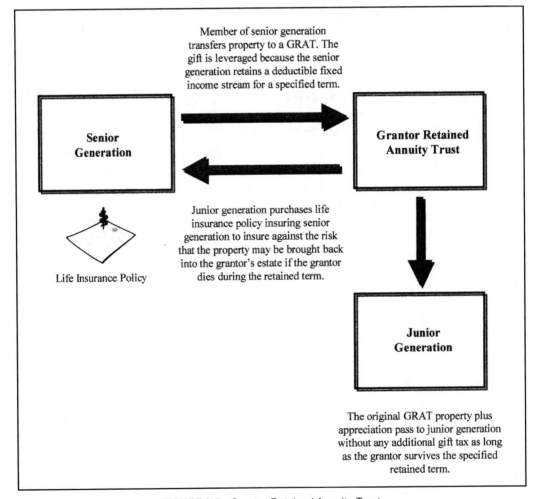

FIGURE 9-7   Grantor Retained Annuity Trust

remainder interest in the GRAT is significantly less than the fair market value of the transferred property, since the grantor retains the right to a fixed annuity for a specified number of years.

2. The grantor can freeze the value of the gifted property and pass all future appreciation to his intended beneficiaries. The size of the gift of the remainder is based upon the fair market value of the transferred property at the time the grantor transfers the property to the GRAT. Regardless of the amount by which the transferred property appreciates over the term of the GRAT, if the grantor survives the selected term, there will be no additional gift tax imposed when ownership of the GRAT property is transferred to the grantor's beneficiaries.

3. The grantor can retain an income stream from transferred property for a specified period but exclude the transferred property from the gross estate. A wealthy person may wish to reduce the estate by transferring certain property to the beneficiaries, but may be reluctant to make a current gift of the property. A GRAT provides the person with the opportunity to make a leveraged gift of property currently, yet retain the right to an income stream for a specified time period.

INSTALLMENT SALES AND SCINS

An Overview

The installment sale is a device for spreading out taxable gain, thereby postponing the income tax on gain from the sale of property. The key ingredient in an installment sale is that the seller must receive at least one payment after the taxable year in which the sale occurs. The self-cancelling installment note (SCIN) is a variation of the installment sale. When it is used, the note contains a provision under which the balance of any payments due at the date of death is automatically cancelled. Typically, under the SCIN strategy, the individual sells a valuable asset to a youngster for installment payments with the provision that the installment obligation will cease in the event of the owner's death. This results in a tax-free transfer of the value of the property above the installments already received.

Here is an example to illustrate the use of installment sales strategy. Assume Judy Brown wants to sell a piece of property for $100,000, which has a cost basis of $50,000. In this case she would have to report a taxable gain of $50,000. However, since she is tax conscious, Judy sells the property for $100,000 and simultaneously agrees to accept $10,000 a year for ten years plus appropriate interest on the unpaid balance. In this case, since her ratio of gross profit ($50,000) to contract price ($100,000) is 50 percent, she will report $5,000, or 50 percent, of each $10,000 payment she receives as capital gains (interest is ignored for simplicity).

Advantages

There are several advantages to using an installment sales strategy. Some of these advantages are presented below.

1. An installment sale strategy is used when a taxpayer wants to sell property

to another individual who may not have sufficient capital to purchase the property outright. For instance, the installment sale provides a way for employees with minimal capital to buy out a business owner who, in return for allowing a long-term payout, may receive a higher price for the business. This device is often used to create a market for a business where none exists at the time this strategy is put in place.

2. In another situation, an installment sale is used where an individual in a high income tax bracket holds substantially appreciated real estate or securities, other than marketable securities. In such a case, a portion of the tax on a sale of such property can be spread over the period of installments.

3. An installment sale can be an effective estate freezing device where the sale is between family members and involves rapidly appreciating closely held stock, real estate, or other assets. The value of the property transferred in an installment sale is established at the time of the sale. The installment payments are not adjusted to reflect changes in the value of the transferred property. Thus, any appreciation on the transferred property is excluded from the transferor's gross estate, even if the transferor dies before full repayment of the balance due on the note.

4. If an installment sale is properly structured, an individual can transfer property to the intended beneficiaries without paying gift tax or using the unified credit. A transfer of property in this transaction will not be a gift if the transferor receives full and adequate consideration in exchange for the transferred property.

5. A SCIN is appropriate in instances where the seller desires to retain a payment stream, which will not continue beyond his or her death and may end at an earlier date. Unlike a private annuity, the SCIN allows the buyer to depreciate assets based on the purchase price paid and to deduct the portion of payments attributable to interest expense. The SCIN is most appropriate when the seller is not expected to outlive the term of the transaction.

POWER OF APPOINTMENT

A power of appointment is a right given in a will or a trust by one person (the donor) to another person (the donee) allowing the donee to name the recipient (appointee) of the donor's property at some future date. Thus, it is the right to dispose of someone else's property and is, therefore, a way to give someone other than the grantor a right to complete the provisions of the will or trust. This authority over the disposition of property can provide substantial flexibility in an estate plan and serve as an important tax-saving tool.

There are many special situations where the power of appointment strategy can be used with great results. For instance, this strategy makes sense when an estate owner would like someone other than himself or herself to make decisions concerning the property. Also, when the estate owner is not clear what the future needs of the intended beneficiaries would be, a power of appointment can be used to handle that uncertain situation. Finally, a power of appointment might be used when the estate owner desires to qualify assets for the marital deduction but would like to provide both asset management through a trust and have the right to designate who will receive the property if the spouse does not exercise the power.

A possessor of a power of appointment has differing amounts of flexibility, depending on whether the power is general or limited. The holder of a general power of appointment can exercise the power in favor of any person desired, including the holder of the power. Only general powers of appointment are significant for transfer tax purposes, because these possessors are authorized to appoint the property to themselves, their estates, their creditors, or the creditors of their estates. Possession of a general power of appointment leads to the inclusion of the property in the gross estate of the power holder.

The holder of a limited power of appointment can only exercise the power in favor of the persons or classes of persons the transferor specified in the instrument creating the power. Limited powers are usually restricted to children and/or descendants. A limited power of appointment does not lead to the inclusion of the property in the gross estate of the holder. Clearly, for a limited power of appointment to be effective, it must forbid the powerholder to appoint property to himself, his estate, his creditors, and his estate's creditors.

QUALIFIED PERSONAL RESIDENCE TRUST (QPRT)

A qualified personal residence trust (QPRT) is an irrevocable trust to which an individual transfers his or her residence, reserving the right to live in the residence rent-free for a term of years, the remainder interest passing to specified beneficiaries. While there is an initial gift tax imposed upon the transfer of the remainder interest in the QPRT, ownership of the residence eventually passes to the grantor's beneficiaries without the imposition of additional gift tax if the grantor survives the selected term. If the grantor dies before the term expires, the value of the residence is included in the grantor's gross estate. Figure 9-8 presents the QPRT strategy.

The following example illustrates the potential tax benefits of this type of trust, with a term of ten years or the death of the grantor, should it occur earlier:

Value of residence	$500,000
Age of grantor at beginning of trust	55
Term of the trust	10 Years[1]
Gov't. rate for valuing remainder interest	4.2%[2]
Value of Retained Interest	$206,115
Value of Remainder Interest (Gift)	$293,885

Potential Estate Tax Savings = $223,119[3]

[1] If death occurs before ten years, residence reverts to grantor's estate.
[2] This rate generally changes monthly.
[3] 40% x [$740,122 Profected Future Value (4% ROR) - 293,885]

Assuming the grantor lives beyond the ten-year period, he or she will have removed from the taxable estate a $500,000 asset plus its growth potential for ten years.

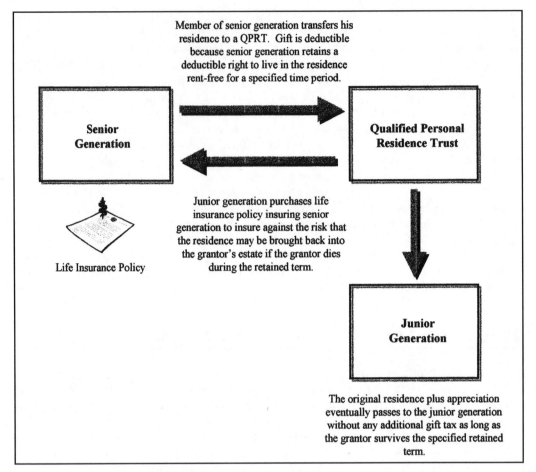

FIGURE 9-8   Qualified Personal Residence Trust

The QPRT must prohibit the holding of any property other than personal residence, and it must contain the following provisions: (1) No distributions to other persons are permitted. (2) Cash can be held for the initial purchase of the residence within three months, or purchase of a replacement residence within three months of the date the cash is added to the trust. (3) If the property is sold or insurance proceeds are received, a two-year replacement period is permitted. Excess cash must be distributed at least quarterly or at the termination of the trust to the term holder. (4) If the property is no longer used as a personal residence, the trust must terminate and its assets be distributed to the term holder, unless converted into a qualified annuity trust.

The QPRT instrument should be drafted so as to make it a grantor trust. This makes the trust income taxable to the grantor but also allows the person to deduct mortgage interest and property tax payments made by the trustee. The grantor will also qualify for the benefits associated with IRC Section 1034 if the property is sold and another one is purchased for equal or greater value.

RECAPITALIZATION

An estate freeze is any planning device that lets the owner of property freeze the present value of the estate and shift the future growth to successors, generally the next generation. It may also involve the retention of some form of income stream or cash flow from the property.

Recapitalization involves a gift or sale of a business interest. Such a sale has the effect of freezing the value of a transferor's estate by removing some of the income and appreciation from the maker's estate. Recapitalization is designed to minimize taxes when control of an asset is passed on from one generation to the next. It is normally used when a future generation is expected to continue the family business. The older generation recapitalizes the business with preferred and common stock or partnership interests (this will not work for an S corporation because of the two classes of stock prohibition), retains the preferred interest, and sells or transfers the common interests to the younger generation. The preferred stock value is frozen for valuation purposes because the appreciation element is transferred to the common stock. The post transfer income and appreciation of the business is not included in the estate of the transferor. Since the rules require that actual payments be made to the newly created preferred interest holders, a steady cash flow from the recapitalized entity is essential and a high appreciation potential of the organization is preferable.

SALE/GIFT LEASEBACK

A sale-gift leaseback is a sequence of transactions beginning with the transfer of an asset through a formal sale or gift and the subsequent leasing back of the same property to the seller/donor. It is used to provide current liquidity, minimize income taxes by shifting income to a lower tax bracket, or remove from the seller's estate future appreciation of the property. It is also used to generate current cash flow through a sale and still retain the use of the asset. An equally attractive opportunity for using this tool is created when a purchaser does not wish to record in the balance sheet an asset and a corresponding liability.

Incidentally, the sale/leaseback is similar to passing property at death, because in such a transaction the purchaser receives a step-up basis (not available in the case of a gift). This type of transaction frequently occurs between related parties and should be completed in two separate transactions with legitimate business purposes.

There are specific requirements associated with this technique. The transaction must have validity to avoid litigation and conflict with the IRS. There must be a completed and irrevocable sale and a legally enforceable lease agreement. In the case of a sale, the transaction must represent a necessary business operation and not one designed solely to shift income tax liability. Finally, the terms of the transaction, and especially the amount of the lease payment, must be arrived at in an arm's length, bona fide manner.

Another form of recapitalization involves splitting voting common stocks into voting shares and non-voting shares. This is a popular technique among S Corporations that do not permit the existence of two classes (common and preferred) of stock. It does not create a second class of stock and is also a useful technique for retaining controls in the hands of the older generation while passing the majority of the stock to the younger generation through gifting techniques.

SECTION 303 STOCK REDEMPTION

Section 303 stock redemption can provide cash and other property from the corporation without resulting in dividend treatment, so the executor will have liquid funds to pay estate taxes and other expenses. It is used when there is a desire to keep control over a family corporation after death. It can also be appropriate when the corporation's stock is a major estate asset, and a forced sale or liquidation of the business to pay the estate taxes could create a serious problem. Finally, this technique could be used when a tax-favored withdrawal of funds from the corporation upon death of the shareholder would be desirable.

The requirements of Section 303 stock redemption are stringent. The redeemed stock must be included in the decedent's gross estate for calculating estate taxes. The value of all stock of the corporation included in the gross estate must be more than 35 percent of the excess of the value of the gross estate over the sum allowable as a deduction. For instance, assume the gross estate is $2 million, the administrative and funeral costs are $150,000, and there are no other deductible expenses. To qualify for Section 303 redemption, the value of the stock must exceed $550,000 (that is, it must be more than 35 percent of $2 million less $150,000). Finally, redemption under Section 303 will qualify for favorable tax treatment only to the extent that the interest of a shareholder whose stock is redeemed is reduced either directly or indirectly through a binding obligation to contribute toward the payment of the decedent's administration expenses and estate taxes.

Under Section 303 stock redemption, the amount paid to the estate is not treated as a dividend, but rather as an exchange price for the stock. However, since the value of the stock receives a step-up in basis upon death by reason of being included in the shareholder's estate, no capital gains are generated when the stocks are redeemed. This is the basis for the effectiveness of this technique as a valuable estate tax reduction tool.

SPECIAL USE VALUATION

Special use valuation allows an executor to value qualified real property based on the use for which it qualifies, rather than its highest and best use value. The maximum reduction in value provided by the special use valuation provision is $750,000. This proves to be beneficial because property normally included in a decedent's gross estate is valued at fair market value. It is normally used to value real property used in a farm or other trade or business when the value of the property based on its current use is less than its value determined under any alternative valuation method.

PRIVATE ANNUITY

Private annuity refers to a situation where an individual transfers property to another individual or entity in exchange for an unsecured promise to a stream of income for the transferor's lifetime. If the obligor is concerned that the transferor may outlive his life expectancy, the arrangement can be structured as a private annuity for a stated term that is at least equal to the transferor's life expectancy.

Private annuities are most commonly used by a senior generation family member with a shorter than average life expectancy to transfer appreciated property to the junior generation.

Private annuity arrangement is used to achieve at least four major objectives. First, the transferor can remove property from the estate without incurring gift, estate or GST tax liability. This is because the property is transferred in exchange for the private annuity, the present value of which equals the fair market value of the property. Second, the transferor can freeze the value of the transferred property and pass all the future appreciation to the intended beneficiary. Third, the transferor can retain an interest similar to a life estate without causing the property to be included in the gross estate. Fourth, the junior generation may possess the requisite maturity to manage the property but lack the financial means to purchase the property outright. The private annuity arrangement allows the obligor to purchase the property over the transferor's lifetime.

ESTATE PRESERVATION AND DISTRIBUTION STRATEGIES

In the previous section we discussed various strategies for reducing federal estate taxes. In this section we will analyze strategies for preservation and effective distribution of an estate.

THE WILL

Regardless of the size of an estate and the kind of property included in it, the best way to protect a family's interest is for each spouse to have a will. A valid will is the basis for answering four critical estate-related questions: (1) Who will get the property? (2) Who will raise the children? (3) Who will administer the estate? (4) How much estate tax will be paid? Clearly, the importance of a valid will cannot be overemphasized. The topic of wills was presented in Chapter 8 in detail. We will now discuss the use of the will in the development of estate planning strategies.

There is no simple way to summarize the salient features of a will that is appropriate for the estate planning needs of all families. Single persons and young couples may get by with a fairly simple will. The estates of a couple can escape estate taxation as long as a person's bequest does not raise the surviving spouse's estate beyond the $1.5 million exclusion (2005).

The importance of making a more comprehensive will increases as soon as children enter into the picture. The family then has to make several difficult decisions: (1) Who will raise the children should both parents die? (2) Where do the children best fit in? (3) How do the parents like the job the candidates are doing raising their own children? Additionally, at this time a revocable trust should be drawn up that takes effect if both parents die, to support the children until they are mature.

As the estate approaches the $1.5 million (2005) level, the will can be supplemented by a bypass trust. If the bypass trust is set up before death, upon the death of the first spouse up to $1.5 million (2005) can be transferred into this trust, which escapes estate taxes because it falls within the limits of the estate tax exclusion. The property in the bypass trust will support the surviving spouse, upon whose death the money will pass to the beneficiaries.

Finally, for estates over $3 million, the will can be supplemented by other, more sophisticated, instruments like a marital deduction trust, QTIP trust, and life insurance trust. These trusts, like others just described, are part of a valid estate plan designed to preserve and distribute the estate in an orderly fashion.

PROBATE

In Chapter 8 we learned that an estate plan deals with two kinds of property: probate and non-probate assets. The former are those assets that pass to the personal representative, who helps them pass through the probate court and then disposes them in accordance with the instructions contained in the will. Non-probate assets are those that bypass probate, either by operation of law, such as joint tenancy, or by contract, such as life insurance beneficiary designations.

Advantages of Bypassing Probate

There are several important reasons as to why people may wish to bypass probate. (1) The probate process is both slow and expensive. It involves attorney's fees and court costs. There are still more costs involved if the court finds it necessary to appoint a personal representative for the estate or a guardian for the children. (2) Some of the heirs may not have access to their full inheritances until the long and arduous probate process is completed. (3) If the property is owned in more than one state, the heirs have to contend with two or more probate procedures. (4) Probate court records are fully open to everyone, from curious neighbors to newspaper reporters and business competitors.

Disadvantages of Bypassing Probate

While there are many reasons for bypassing probate, for the following reasons it may not always constitute the best strategy. (1) Where substantial assets are involved, it may be better to go through probate and not leave everything to the spouse. (2) There may be large estate tax savings in more efficiently arranging the disposition of some of the assets. (3) In the case of a common disaster where both spouses die simultaneously, a joint ownership without a will instituted to bypass probate may spell disaster, because it may increase the estate tax liability upon the death of the last person.

Incidentally, some of the disadvantages of bypassing probate can be minimized by administering the system known as *independent probate*. This system allows for privacy and expeditiousness, with minimal court intervention. It is advisable to scrutinize every situation carefully before deciding whether or not bypassing the probate strategy constitutes the best strategy.

REVOCABLE LIVING TRUST

Perhaps the most effective method for estate preservation and distribution is the creation of a revocable living trust. Two trusts which fall in this category are presented in Table 9-4.

TABLE 9-4 Trusts and Estate Preservation

Type of trust	Nature of trust	Advantages	Disadvantages	Included in gross estate	Gift taxation	Income taxation	Estate taxation
Revocable Inter Vivos	May be revoked by grantor.	Avoids probate. Permits flexibility.	No tax benefits.	Yes	None	Grantor pays taxes.	Grantor
Minor's Trust 2503(c)	Income or principal may be paid out or accumulated before minor attains age 21; any property left is payable to minor.	Protects children's inheritances. Qualifies for annual exclusion.	If minor dies, property may pass to parents.	Yes*	Value of principal taxable; annual exclusion available.	Beneficiary if distributed; trust if undistributed.	If minor dies property may be included in parent's estate.

* Since the trust qualifies for the annual gift tax exclusion, it would not be excluded in the gross estate of the parent. However, if the beneficiary dies, it would be included in the gross estate of the beneficiary.

As a general rule, a revocable living trust is created to inform the trustee: (1) to whom the income and principal are to be distributed; (2) when the distributions are to be made; (3) how the property held in trust should be managed; and (4) how long the trust should be continued. A revocable living trust provides no federal tax advantages to the creator of the trust, since the creator has the power to revoke the trust at any time. Since the creator is in control and owns all of the trust property, trust income is taxable to the creator no matter who receives the income. Also, upon death, for federal estate tax purposes, the trust assets are included in the creator's gross estate.

There are additional advantages to creating a revocable trust. First, property placed in a revocable trust bypasses probate. This can avoid delays and probate costs. Second, a revocable trust can be used as a depository of a variety of cash assets. Third, a person can act as trustee when in good health, but a successor trustee can take over the management functions of the revocable trust if the owner becomes incapacitated.

Even though a revocable trust is designed to act as a substitute for a will, the creator of the trust still needs a will, since an individual may neglect to put all of the present and future possessions in the trust. The will should include a *pour-over* provision that will sweep any remaining property into the trust at the owner's death. The will can also be used to distribute personal belongings, name guardians for children, and provide for a personal representative to take care of any unfinished business.

Setting up a revocable trust requires a great deal of effort. The lawyer must draft a trust document that names the owner, the trustee, and others as co-trustees. The document must include instructions on how to manage the property if the owner becomes disabled, and also after the owner's death. The owner also has to change bank accounts, brokerage accounts, and retitle other assets to the name of the trust. So long as the owner of the trust retains the power to alter, amend, revoke, or terminate the trust, the owner (and not the trust) is required to file an annual tax return. Every time a new account is opened or a property is purchased, it must be purchased in the name of the trust.

STANDBY OR CONVERTIBLE TRUST

A major drawback of a revocable trust is the hassle of transferring all assets into such a trust at a time when a person is healthy and feels no compulsion to do so. This problem can be obviated by the use of a standby or convertible trust. Simply stated, an attorney simultaneously creates two documents: a standby trust and a durable power of attorney. The former stands unfunded, whereas the latter gives a designated person the power of attorney over the property. No further action is necessary at this time. If the grantor of the revocable trust becomes incapacitated, the designated person transfers the assets into the standby trust. The outcome is the same as though all the assets had been systematically transferred to the revocable trust in the first place.

MINOR'S TRUST (POWER IN TRUST)

Sometimes a parent may be fearful that a court-appointed guardian, or one appointed by the parent, may misuse the assets left for the benefit of minor children. These fears can be allayed by the establishment of a minor's testamentary trust. As the name implies, this trust is activated upon the person's death. The trustee is required to follow to the letter all the instructions contained in the trust agreement. This insures that the assets are managed and ultimately distributed according to the wishes of the deceased. Note, however, that since the trust assets are controlled by the owner, upon death they are included in the estate of the deceased and, consequently, this trust does not avoid estate taxes.

MISCELLANEOUS ESTATE PLANNING ISSUES

In this concluding section we will discuss several important issues which must be taken into consideration when developing a comprehensive estate plan. While some of these issues have been mentioned in previous discussions, they will now be brought into sharper focus to wrap up our discussion on estate planning.

ESTATE LIQUIDITY

At death, there will be an immediate need for ready cash to pay off the expenses before the estate can be distributed to the beneficiaries. Typically, these expenses include funeral costs, administrative expenses, liquidation of debts and liabilities, and cash bequests to heirs. In addition, ready cash must also be available to pay for personal income, state inheritance, and federal estate taxes.

Several major sources are available to meet the liquidity needs of an estate. These include: (1) Ready cash, such as bank accounts, money market accounts, and certificates of deposit. (2) A broad range of assets that can be turned into cash quickly without sacrificing value. (3) Life insurance proceeds which provide instant liquidity upon death. (4) Proceeds of buy-sell agreements which generate ready cash. (5) Other convertible assets. In most instances, the first four sources listed here should provide sufficient liquidity to meet the estate liquidity needs. However, if insurance is heavily relied upon to provide liquidity, the amount of life insurance carried should be reviewed on a periodic basis and adjusted upward when necessary.

FEDERAL INCOME TAX CONSIDERATIONS

After death of a person, one of the most important decisions to be made by a personal representative relates to the filing of a single or joint federal income tax return. Since the surviving spouse's taxable income does not end upon death of an individual, it is possible to minimize the federal income tax liability by manipulating income and deductions in order to utilize the joint tax rates.

In filing an income tax return, it is desirable to take full advantage of all the allowable deductions. For instance, medical expenses paid within one year of death are deductible. So are the bad debts or investments that have become worthless in the year of death as well as all the administrative expenses relating to the settlement of the estate.

Acceleration or postponement of income is another strategy relating to the reduction of the federal income tax liability. The law states that any income *constructively* received prior to death must be treated as income, even if such income is actually received *after* death. Consequently, if reduction of income is desired, and if it can be demonstrated that some of the incomes were not constructively received by the decedent, then these can be excluded from the final tax return. In addition, if the decedent was receiving an annuity, but had not received all of the investment, the unrecovered portion of the annuity can be deducted on the decedent's final return.

STEPPED-UP BASIS RULES

For income tax purposes, the basis—or cost—of property acquired from a decedent is the fair market value of the property as of the date of the decedent's death or, if elected by the personal representative, the alternative valuation date. This rule, known as the *stepped-up basis rule* (not available for gifting), offers an extremely valuable estate planning tool. Here is a simplified example to illustrate this point.

Several months ago Steve Stahl purchased 1,000 shares of a NASDAQ stock for $10 a share which has now appreciated to $110 a share. Assuming his marginal income tax bracket to be 28 percent, if Steve were to sell the stock now for $110 a share, after paying a 28 percent tax on the profit ($28,000) he would realize $82,000 ($72,000 profit plus the $10 of cost recovery). Assuming an estate tax rate of 50 percent, upon death Steve's heirs will receive only $41,000 (50 percent of $82,000). If, however, Steve keeps the stock until death, the stepped-up basis for that stock will be $110 per share. Estate taxes of 50 percent will consume half of the total value of $110, so the beneficiaries will receive a net amount of $55,000. Hence, the net savings on this transaction will be $14,000 ($55,000 minus $41,000).

SURVIVORSHIP LIFE INSURANCE

A popular concept in estate planning, called *survivorship* or *second-to-die* insurance, is a form of whole life insurance policy that pays off only after the death of both spouses. The premium, cash values, and dividends are based on the *joint equal age concept*. That is, the insurance company has to set aside reserves for only one death benefit payment, rather than two separate ones payable under traditional life insurance policies covering two lives. Consequently, the premium cost is only 50 or 60 percent of what two people would pay to purchase the same amount of individual whole life coverage.

Survivorship insurance can be used effectively in estate planning. For instance, if a couple buys a survivorship policy with the children or an irrevocable life insurance trust as the owner, the proceeds are exempt from both estate and income taxes of the parents. So, a policy geared to the estimated size of the estate taxes can provide the heirs with liquid cash to cover the estate taxes after both deaths.

ESTATE PLANNING FOR BUSINESS OWNERS

Finally, estate planning strategies used for business owners might be discussed. Clearly, these are sophisticated strategies and their implementation requires both technical knowledge and a high level of competence. Our objective is to present here only a highly simplified—and therefore somewhat distorted—view of several key strategies.

Installment Sale

A common estate planning problem is the distribution of a closely held business to family members when only some of them are directly involved in running the business. The technique used in such a case is known as the installment sale.

As mentioned, the installment sale is a device whereby the purchase price is paid by the buyer in a series of installment payments over a period of several years. Typically, this device is used to spread out the taxable gain and thereby defer the income tax on the sale of property. But it can also be used to sell the closely held business to those family members who are involved with the business and invest the money for the benefit of *all* the children, including those who are not associated with the business. Another attractive feature of this strategy is that it removes the future appreciation of the business from the seller's estate without triggering a gift tax. The installment sale is subject to specific IRS rules.

Private Annuity

We have learned that private annuity is an arrangement between two parties, neither of whom is an insurance company. The transferor or annuitant transfers complete ownership of a property to a transferee who, in turn, promises to make periodic payments to the transferor for a period of time. Usually, this period is the transferor's lifetime or the lifetime of both spouses.

A private annuity is an excellent estate planning tool for removing a sizable asset from the estate of a wealthy individual. For instance, assume John Kerr is the sole shareholder of the closely held business called Real Estate Corporation. He has two sons presently working in the business. He could sell his company to his sons in return for their agreement to pay him an annuity for life. This will result in a reduction in John's estate because the value of the business will be removed from his estate for federal estate tax purposes. At John's death, annuity payments will cease and neither the closely held corporate stock nor the promised payments will be included in his estate.

Business Purchase Agreement

A business purchase agreement, commonly known as a stock purchase or a buy-sell agreement, is an arrangement for the disposition of a business interest in the event of an owner's death, retirement, or upon withdrawal from the business. Such an arrangement is frequently structured in one of the two following forms:

1. *Stock Redemption Agreement.* This agreement is reached between the company and the individual owners.
2. *Cross-Purchase Agreement.* This arrangement is made between individual owners.

A business purchase agreement is used when it is desirable to *peg* the value of the business for federal estate and state inheritance tax purposes. It is also used to create a market for the sale of a business interest in the event of death or retirement.

A simple example will illustrate the use of a business purchase agreement in estate planning. John and Bob are equal stockholders in a business valued at $500,000. The business purchases $250,000 of life insurance and a policy providing $2,850 a month of disability insurance on both men. At John's death, his stock passes to his estate. The proceeds of life insurance on John's life are paid to the business. Then the business pays the cash proceeds to John's estate according to the agreement. In return for the cash, John's personal representative transfers the stock to the business. Consequently, Bob ends up with ownership of all of the outstanding voting stock.

Under the buy-sell agreement, should John become totally disabled prior to retirement, he would receive his full salary for one year. At the end of the year of total disability, John's interest would be sold to the business. The business would pay at least $25,000 (ten percent of $250,000) as a down payment to John. The business would also issue John a ten-year note for the remaining value of the stock, $225,000. The business would pay nine percent interest on the note. Thus, John would receive approximately $2,850 a month for ten years. In order to help pay off the note, the business would receive $2,850 a month of disability income insurance proceeds from a policy owned by, and made payable to, the business.

PREPARING THE FAMILY

The Basic Needs

Some people have the short-sighted attitude that what they earn they should enjoy by spending it now. Many, however, know that such a pleasure is really enjoyed at their own or another's expense. But not everyone knows how to strike a balance between immediate enjoyment and the future comfort of their dependents after they are gone.

A husband, for example, owes his wife more than an insurance policy. He should present her the opportunity for full financial security. He should share with her the full range of information involved in financially managing a family. Consequently, for the husband much more is expected than simply preparing a will or designating her as the beneficiary of his insurance policy.

Young families stand to lose more than the retired couples when the breadwinner dies. As is often the case, a young widow finds that she must shoulder full family responsibilities. Younger children require more care. Fewer years have passed for building an estate and accumulating resources. In fact, young families tend to be chronically in debt. And a young widow faces many more years of struggling alone with young children than does a widow in the middle or later years. Furthermore, should a young widow with children remarry, the new family may have additional members, making its future even more precarious. What is essential at such a time is an effective estate plan. An example of the key elements of an estate plan designed to help a family is presented in the accompanying boxed insert.

Preparing the Wife

A typical husband is about four or five years older than his wife. It is thus likely that a wife will be a widow for a decade or so (five years plus the difference in spouse's ages). For a husband, then, an essential aspect of estate planning is to prepare his wife to be a widow so that she may be *financially* prepared when his death occurs.

At a time of deep shock a widow must perform three major tasks: pay the

---

PREPARING THE FAMILY
FOR BREADWINNER'S DEATH

Name	Purpose or relationship	Method of assistance	Timing of assistance	Payment	Type of property
Betty	Wife	Provide lifetime income.	During Betty's lifetime, starting with John's death.	Income from bypass trust.	Mutual funds, bonds, income producing real estate.
Robert	Son	Gift.	Upon death.	Transfer of property.	Car (collector's item), china, furniture.
Susan	Daughter	Increase her income.	Upon death.	Transfer of assets to trust with provisions to make annual distribution of income.	Bonds, income producing real estate.
Bhutto	Adopted son	Help his parents raise the boy.	Upon death.	Transfer life insurance proceeds in a trust.	Life insurance.
MMC School	Charity	Assistance to needy students.	Upon death.	Trust setting up a scholarship fund.	Life insurance.

bills, distribute the assets according to her husband's wishes, and maintain continuity in the lives of survivors. These are onerous tasks under the best of circumstances, and the widow deserves all the help she can get from her husband.

Paying the Bills

Upon the husband's death, the wife must pay funeral expenses, probate costs, and estate taxes. These costs can easily run into thousands of dollars, not to mention the delays in meeting the family's normal expenses. To defray these expenses, as well as to meet other contingency expenditures, there should be some money in a checking or savings account, or some other liquid form, that is in the spouse's name only. That is because, for administrative reasons, at least half of any joint account with the deceased's name on it as well as any account in his name alone could be frozen for some time.

Locating Important Papers

Taken by itself, a widow's task of clearing her husband's estate through the probate court, paying all the legal taxes, and distributing the remaining assets according to her husband's wishes is a formidable one. If she does not have a personal financial planner who maintains up-to-date records, or if she cannot locate all the important papers and quickly gather all the relevant information, this job can turn into a nightmare. The two most important papers that a widow must be able to locate quickly are the will and the letter of last instruction. In addition, a widow must have: (1) details of the life insurance policies in existence; (2) names and account numbers of bank accounts; (3) accounts with savings and loan associations and credit unions; (4) the name of her husband's stockbroker; (5) a list of stocks and bonds and investments in mutual funds; (6) Social Security information; (7) the number of his safety deposit box; (8) information on investments in real estate property; (9) bills owed; and (10) other miscellaneous information such as the names of the professional advisors and various obligations to others.

The Survivors

After the estate plan has been executed and the initial expenditures have been paid, the lives of the survivors must go on. The widow can bear this burden more gracefully if she had previously discussed with her husband how she might meet both the financial and emotional challenges of maintaining the family during widowhood. There are various ways in which these responsibilities can be met. For instance, a trust can be set up to handle the family finances. A guardian can be appointed to oversee the welfare of the minor children. Perhaps a combination of these, as well as access to good advice from close family friends, would be ideal.

Preparing the family to face the death of the breadwinner or a life partner is both important and essential. Consequently, a detailed discussion of this topic is presented in Chapter 20 entitled, "Planning for Widows."

ADVANCED STRATEGIES

John Kirk explained that there are a number of sophisticated strategies which should be used to accomplish all the objectives established by the Johnsons. These include family limited partnership (FLP), grantor retained annuity trust (GRAT), qualified personal residence trust (QPRT), private foundation, charitable lead annuity trust (CLAT), and irrevocable life insurance trust (ILIT). While each of these provisions has been included in the estate plan, because of space constraints, only three strategies will be discussed here.

Grantor Retained Annuity Trust (GRAT). This trust pays the grantor a fixed annuity for a specified number of years, after which the remaining trust property passes to the grantor's descendants free of additional gift tax. This could result in substantial savings, as explained next.

Assume Betty transfers personal investments worth $1 million to a GRAT. She will receive an annuity of $125,000 for ten years, with the remaining assets payable to a grant trust she established for the children. After ten years, a portion of Betty's applicable exclusion will shelter the taxable gift, so no gift taxes will be due.

There is, however, an important drawback to GRAT which should be addressed. If the grantor does not survive the trust term, all of the trust assets are included back in his or her taxable estate. In order to eliminate this risk, John suggested that a *guaranteed* GRAT should be established which would completely eliminate the mortality risk.

Irrevocable Life Insurance Trust. John explained that, notwithstanding all the sophisticated strategies that the Johnsons intend to put in place at this time, there is a distinct possibility that estate taxes would be due upon both deaths. An extremely efficient means of accumulating funds for paying the estate taxes is via an irrevocable life insurance trust (ILIT).

In an ILIT, first, a life insurance trust would be set up. Next, a survivorship life insurance policy, also known as a second-to-die policy, would be purchased on the lives of George and Betty Johnson and placed in the insurance trust. It is recommended that a $1 million policy be purchased with an annual premium of $12,000. In order to avoid any incidence of ownership, the trust would be set up as an irrevocable life insurance trust, with children as the owner of the trust.

Each year, the Johnsons will gift $11,000 to the children-owners, which would qualify for the annual gift tax exclusion (2004). After waiting for a reasonable period, the children would withdraw the gifted money from the trust and pay the insurance premium to keep the policy in force. Finally, after the death of both spouses, tax-free life insurance proceeds worth $1 million would be paid to the children-owners of the policy. This money could be used to pay the estate taxes, if due, or for any other purposes the children see fit. This is a fine example of paying estate taxes with *leveraged dollars*. The reason is that all taxes (both income and estate) are eliminated on the life insurance proceeds and, depending upon when the deaths occur, the insurance proceeds could represent a multiple of the insurance premiums paid during the time the policy was in force.

Private Foundation. Since the Johnsons are charitable-minded, this strategy takes on a special meaning for them. A private foundation is a tax-exempt entity established to receive charitable contributions, which can be used to finance charitable causes. The funds contributed to the private foundation can be left in the foundation for future use. However, the law requires that each year at least five percent of the funds be distributed as grants to the preferred charities.

The private foundation can be titled as George and Betty Johnson Family Foundation to perpetuate the family name so the family would be recognized and appreciated for its generosity. Furthermore, the legitimacy associated with private foundations results in an access to information that is not as readily available to individuals. This enables the foundation to learn more about substantive areas of interest and provides a means to direct the foundation's contributions. Finally, a private foundation can be used as a means to develop and reinforce family unity through regular meetings, informal discussions and decision-making process.

A REAL WORLD ESTATE PLAN

In this chapter a number of advanced estate planning strategies have been presented. In this section some of these strategies will be used to develop a real world estate plan.

AN OVERVIEW

George and Betty Johnson have requested their estate planner John Kirk to develop a comprehensive estate plan that upon their death would efficiently transfer their assets to their loved ones and minimize the estate taxes. George and Betty, both U.S. citizens, are, respectively, 62 and 60. George is an executive with GM, earning an annual salary of $500,000, and he plans to retire at 65. Betty actively raises funds in the community foundation and the couple donates to the foundation an impressive sum of $40,000 per year.

George and Betty have three married children and four grandchildren. The Johnsons are an affluent couple. Their combined estate, valued at $5 million, consists of personal residence valued at $750,000 and personal investments of $4.25 million, and they equally own these assets. In addition, George owns a $2 million term life insurance of which Betty is the primary beneficiary. For this policy George pays an annual premium of $5,000.

The Johnsons are anxious to transfer significant amount of assets out of their estate without affecting their life style. Their objective is to disinherit the IRS to the extent allowed by law. They fully understand that changes in a number of estate tax law provisions are in the air and that their estate plan expected to be completed in September, 2004 will not reflect these changes.

The estate plan developed by the estate planner can be conveniently grouped into three sections. In the first section, the traditional estate planning strategies will be covered. In the second section, we will present the sophisticated strategies. Finally, in section three, strategies for formalizing their philanthropic bent will be discussed.

TRADITIONAL ESTATE PLANNING STRATEGIES

After carefully reviewing the financial data provided by the Johnsons, estate planner John Kirk recommended that the following steps be taken to complete the traditional, or basic, elements of the estate plan.

Wills and Revocable Trusts. John recommended that a marital trust be established for Betty that would qualify for marital deduction. In addition, a bypass trust should be set up in order to utilize the remaining applicable credit of $1,500,000. Without the bypass trust, the credit of the first spouse to die would be wasted. Any property passing to the surviving spouse above and beyond the amount passing to the bypass trust will be transferred to the marital trust and qualify for the estate tax marital deduction.

Gifts of Assets to Grantor Trust. John explained that the current law (2004) allows each spouse to gift up to $1,500,000 free of gift tax. This amount is scheduled to increase to $2 million by 2006-2008, and $3 million in 2009, and an unlimited amount by 2010. In addition, George and Betty have an exemption that allows each to transfer $1,500,000 of property (2004) to grandchildren free of generation skipping tax (GST), or to allocate the exemption to property transferred in trust and thereby shelter the trust property from all future transfer taxes.

John suggested that a grantor trust be established to maximize estate tax benefits. When a grantor trust is set up, the grantor pays income taxes due on the assets held by the trust so the trust assets could grow tax free. Once a grantor trust is set up, the Johnsons should transfer $1,500,000 worth of private investments to the grantor trust. George would be allowed to pay income tax due on the trust investments so they would grow tax-free. In addition, George could allocate a portion of his GST exemption to the trust. The trust assets would not be subject to GST and would grow tax-free. This strategy would result in substantial savings in both income taxes and estate taxes.

Annual Gift Exclusions. Since the Johnsons are interested in transferring substantial amounts of assets to their children and grandchildren as soon as possible, they should gift up to $11,000 per year (2004) free of gift taxes, known as gift tax annual exclusion, to each of their children and grandchildren.

In this chapter we have presented basic and advanced estate planning strategies. Basic structure of retirement income will be presented in the next chapter.

There's no thrill in easy sailing when the skies are clear and blue; there's no joy in merely doing things which anyone can do. But there is some satisfaction that is mighty sweet to take, when you reach a destination that you thought you'd never make.

Spierlla

CHAPTER 10

Basic Structure of Retirement Income

INTRODUCTION

Of all the many strategies which might be developed to meet different financial objectives, none are more difficult than those relating to financial independence and retirement planning. This is because, for most people, financial independence or retirement seems far away, and in these uncertain times planning for the distant future is virtually impossible. However, no matter how far away retirement age seems at the moment, we should prepare for the day *now*. There is nothing worse than discovering on the 65th birthday that, given the existing financial position, it is impossible to maintain a desired standard of living.

The argument for planning early for retirement is indeed compelling. In 2001, a report prepared by AARP (American Association for Retired Persons) found that Americans older than 50 are better off today than 20 years ago but many are ill-prepared for old age, with only a third having private pensions and Social Security amounting to more than half of their retirement income after 65. There are growing inequalities between the rich and the poor in old age, with many low-income people relying solely on Social Security benefits from the government.

The biggest single area of concern was among the lowest 25 percent of wage earners in the 50-61 age range who had poor wages, no pension coverage, and no health insurance, and were less likely to own homes. According to this report, income grew 17 percent from 1980 to 2000 among people 50 and older, but it grew substantially faster in the top income group with a 28 percent rise versus the lower income group at 11 to 20 percent.

This chapter, and the one that follows, benefited from a significant contribution by Mr. David C. Fillo, QPA, QKA, CEBS, CLU, ChFC, Vice President, Great Lakes Pension Administrators, Inc., 37935 W. Twelve Mile Road, Farmington Hills, Mich. 48331-3033. Tel: (248) 553-8070. However, the authors are solely responsible for the material presented here.

Another report pointed out that in 2002 about 76 million Americans, or 28 percent, were older than 50, and by 2020 there will be 40 million more in that group, amounting to 36 percent of the population. Many Americans will remain low-income people, with no home ownership, no health insurance, and very little income outside of Social Security income and other government-sponsored programs.

A third report published in 2000, called Retirement Confidence Survey, made the following disturbing observation: The amounts that workers have accumulated for retirement are generally low, and many people appear to be falsely confident about their retirement security. Workers may also find that their retirement planning has been inadequate because they hold false expectations about the age at which they will be eligible for full Social Security retirement benefits, the age they will retire, the length of their retirement, and the sources of their retirement income.

While it may be difficult for a 30 or 40-year-old to visualize life after 25 or 30 years, it is imperative that planning for the future is started without delay. This is because financing the lifestyle a person hopes to lead will have a dramatic impact on the rate of accumulation of savings needed for retirement. For instance, if a 30-year-old (in 2005) earning $40,000 a year hopes to retire at age 65 with an annual income of $50,000 in today's dollars, assuming a four percent inflation-adjusted interest rate and a life expectancy of 85, at age 65 (year 2040) this youngster would need to amass savings of $2.68 million as shown next:

Step 1

$$PV = \$50,000$$
$$n = 35$$
$$i = 4$$
$$FV = \$197,304$$

Step 2

$$PMT = \$197,304$$
$$n = 20$$
$$i = 4$$
$$PV = \$2,681,425$$
$$\text{or } \$2.68 \text{ million}$$

This gloomy picture dims even further when we add to this scenario the fact that pensions and Social Security might not provide enough of a cushion for retirement. On the expenses side, a key concern is the health care cost during retirement which has been increasing above the rate of inflation. Today, Medicare pays only part of the retiree's medical bills (see Chapter 5). Many of the costs of long-term care, such as that required for Alzheimer's disease and for nursing care, are not covered at all. When we put it altogether, we begin to realize how important it is to develop and implement an effective retirement plan at the earliest possible opportunity.

Planning for retirement involves taking four major steps: (1) The preretirement expenses should be estimated. (2) On the basis of Step 1 monthly or annual retirement expenses needed to maintain the desired standard of living should be determined. (3) The total expected income from all sources, including government-sponsored plans (such as Social Security), corporate retirement plans, personal retirement plans (such as IRAs and Keoghs), personal savings, and employment during retirement should be estimated. (4) If the expected income falls short of the expected expenditure needs, appropriate steps should be taken *now* to alleviate the anticipated retirement income deficit problem. This concept of planning for retirement is presented in Figure 10-1.

This chapter will be devoted to a discussion of the major sources of retirement income. The techniques of estimating capital needs during retirement, taxation of a distribution from qualified plans, and the key retirement planning techniques will be discussed in the next chapter.

The key sources of income available upon retirement can be conveniently classified into the following categories: (1) government sponsored plans; (2) corporate retirement plans; (3) personal retirement plans; (4) personal investment; and (5) employment during retirement. These sources are listed in Figure 10-2. Of these, personal investment strategies will be fully discussed in Chapters 12, 13, and 14, while employment during retirement needs no further consideration. Consequently, in the first, second, and third parts of this chapter we will analyze the first three sources of income just listed.

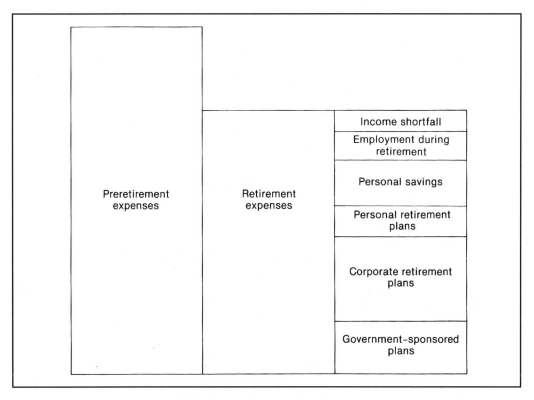

FIGURE 10-1 Planning for retirement

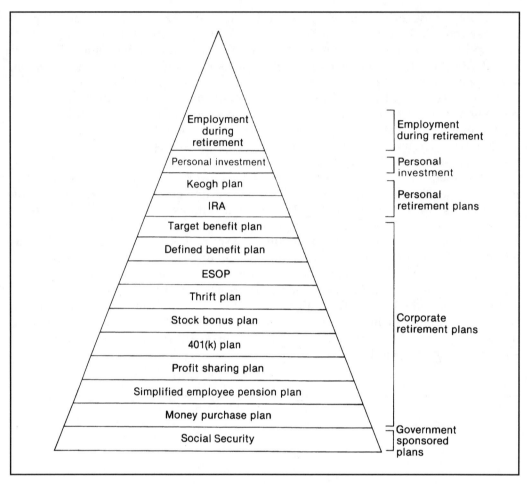

FIGURE 10-2 Retirement earnings tree

GOVERNMENT SPONSORED PLANS

SOCIAL SECURITY

General Remarks

President Franklin Roosevelt's Social Security Act of 1935 was a historic land-mark with a modest beginning. In 1940, the first year of the benefits, barely one person in six hundred received assistance, compared with one in less than three in 2001. The maximum monthly Social Security payment in 1940 was $41. In 2005, it was $1,784.

"The essence of Social Security insurance" said Winston Churchill, "is bring-ing the magic of averages to the rescue of millions." This statement brings to mind the long soup lines in which old people were forced to stand for hours to receive their handouts. Actually, Social Security is anything but a scheme to rescue millions of impoverished people. It includes old age retirement, survivors' benefits, disability insurance, and Medicare—all of which are administered by the Federal Government. In addition, Social Security includes state and local government administered programs, such as unemployment insurance and public welfare.

Even a casual review would show that the growth of Social Security over half a century has been phenomenal. However, such an overview conceals a basic fact. Data show that through 1949, no worker paid into the System more than $30 a year. The maximum Social Security tax in 2004 was $6,724 (wages over $87,900 pay and additional 1.45 percent for the Medicare tax)—over 224 times the original tax. Furthermore, in 2004, a couple could get the maximum monthly benefit of only $3,569, not an attractive return on the thousands of dollars contributed over the working life of an average couple.

An overview of Social Security is presented in Table 10-1. We will now present the key features of Social Security plans.

The Eligibility Issue

Commonly called OASDHI (Old Age, Survivors', Disability, and Health Insurance), the Social Security program is financed by payroll taxes. Social Security taxes are paid by both the employer and the employee in equal amounts. In 2004 the tax rate including Medicare was 7.65 percent each for the employer and the employee and the maximum wage base on which the tax was imposed was $87,900. The Medicare portion of the Social Security tax is 1.45 percent for all wages above the $87,900 wage base.

Before a person or family becomes eligible to receive monthly cash benefits under Social Security, a minimum amount of work credit must be earned. Social Security credit is measured in "quarters of coverage." In 2004, employees and self-employed persons received one quarter of coverage for each $900 of annual earnings subject to Social Security taxes. The amount of earnings needed to receive a quarter of coverage will increase automatically in the future in order to keep pace with average wages.

TABLE 10-1 Retirement Plans: Social Security

Title	Major responsibility for funding rests on	General characteristics	Where appropriate	Vesting rules
Social Security	Federal Government	Starting at the earliest age of 62, upon application, payments begin. Monthly income is based on several factors. No age restrictions apply for payments due to disability or death.	Every working person is entitled to Social Security benefits.	$8\frac{1}{4}$ to 10 years of work.

No more than four quarters of coverage can be credited for one year. In 2004, 40 quarters of work credit were necessary to become eligible for Social Security. For instance, if a person becomes disabled before age 24, only 1-1/2 years of work out of the three-year period ending when the disability begins are required for receiving disability benefits. Persons meeting the minimum work credit requirements are called *fully insured*, while those meeting the disability requirements are called *currently insured*. These work credit requirements and other related data are presented in Table 10-2.

Types of Benefits

Basically there are three types of benefits offered by Social Security: (1) The Old Age and Survivors Insurance Trust Fund provides monthly checks to retirees, their families, and to families of deceased workers. (2) The Disability Insurance Trust Fund pays benefits to disabled workers and their families. (3) The Hospital Insurance Trust Fund pays Medicare claims.

Retirement benefits. Social Security offers pension benefits to workers who are fully or currently insured. If born prior to 1939, an insured worker can retire any time on or after the 65th birthday with full benefits. The maximum monthly Social Security benefits in 2004 were $1,784 for an insured worker retiring at age 65. The normal retirement age is gradually being raised to 67 (persons born beginning January 1, 1960 or later).

The minimum—or early—retirement age is 62, regardless of the normal retirement age. The monthly benefits for an early retiree are anywhere between 70 to 80 percent of the maximum benefits. For instance, if the normal retirement age is 66, the worker will receive 75 percent of the full benefits if an early retirement is taken at age 62.

The law does not make it mandatory for anyone to retire at age 65. If a person continues to work past the normal retirement age, the Social Security Administration would raise the monthly benefits. The increase is six percent a year for each month of working past the normal retirement age. The increase is not available past age 70. The present six percent per year increment for each additional year of work past the normal retirement age will be increased to eight percent for those born in 1943 or later.

An increase in the monthly benefits for persons working beyond the normal age constitutes only one side of the story. On the other side, the law taxes the earned incomes retirees receive to supplement their benefits. This topic will be discussed in a subsequent section.

Benefits for spouse and children. Social Security benefits of a fully insured retiree are extended to spouse and children as well. If the insured worker applies for Social Security at age 65, the spouse receives 50 percent of the retiree's primary insurance amount (PIA). The PIA is reduced by 25/36th of one percent for each month before age 65, or if a spouse applies for Social Security benefits before age 65. In addition, a child under age 18 (or under 19 if in high school), or a child of any age if disabled mentally or physically before age 22, is entitled to 50 percent of the insured's PIA.

In the case of death or divorce, a widow, widower, or surviving divorced spouse will receive 100 percent of PIA of the deceased or divorced spouse, if the benefits

TABLE 10-2 Length of Work Requirements for Social Security Benefits

Type of benefits	*Payable to*	*Minimum years of work under Social Security*
Retirement	You, your spouse, unmarried children, under age 18, or 18 if in high school, or who are disabled before age 22, dependent spouse 62 or over, or of any age if caring for a child who is under age 16 or who is disabled before age 22, or unmarried divorsed spouse, at least age 62, if married for at least 10 years.	10 years (fully insured status)
Survivors[a] Full	Widow(er) 60 or over Widow(er) if caring for child 16 years or younger Unmarried children under 18, or disabled before 22, or 18 if in high school Dependent widow(er) 62 or over Disabled spouse at age 50 Dependent parent(s) at 62 or older	10 years (fully insured status)
Current	Widow(er) caring for child 18 years or younger Dependent children	1-1/2 years of last 3 years before death (currently insured status)
Disability	You and your dependents	If under age 24, you need 1-1/2 years of work in the 3 years prior to disablement. If between ages 24 and 31, you need to work half the time between when you turned 21 and your date of disablement. If age 31 or older, you must have 5 years of credit during the 10 years prior to disablement.
Medicare Hospitalization (Part A: automatic benefits)	Anyone 65 or over (whether) working or retired) plus some others, such as the disabled.	Anyone qualified for the Social Security retirement program is qualified for Medicare Part A at age 65. Others may qualify by paying a monthly premium for Part A.
Medical expense (Part B: voluntary benefits)	Anyone eligible for Part A and anyone else 65 or over. (Payment of monthly premiums required.)	No prior work under Social Security is required.

[a] A lump-sum death benefit no greater than $255 is also granted to dependents of those either fully or currently insured.

began at age 65. If the distribution of the benefits begins before age 65, a different formula is applied by Social Security Administration to determine the benefit amount.

Disability benefits. A *covered* individual who suffers from long-term disability can collect for life disability benefits of 100 percent of the PIA, regardless of age. An individual qualifies for disability benefits in any month if the individual: (1) would have been fully insured had he or she attained age 62 and filed an application for retirement benefits on the first day of the month; (2) has at least 20 quarters of coverage in the 40-quarter period ending with the quarter in which disability began (less stringent requirements if disability occurs between ages 24 and 31); (3) has a medically determinable physical or mental impairment that is expected to result in death or last for at least 12 months; and (4) has been disabled for at least six months.

Disability benefits offered by private insurance companies were discussed in Chapter 5 in detail. Disability benefits under Social Security are similar to private disability policies in some respects but are different in other respects. For instance, under Social Security rules, after becoming eligible for disability benefits, an individual or family can receive benefits for the duration of the disability, even if it lasts for life. In contrast, a private insurance policy issued to age 65 would automatically lapse upon the insured's attaining that age. Also, under Social Security the amount of the monthly family benefit paid on behalf of the disabled worker, say, under age 35, would range between 40 and 80 percent of the pre-disability monthly earnings. The private disability policy would pay only the monthly amount specified in the contract. Finally, all disability payments under Social Security are automatically adjusted periodically to reflect increases in the cost of living. In contrast, only those privately insured policies which have a COLA (cost of living adjustment) feature will make a predetermined inflation adjustment in disability payments.

Medicare

Medicare is a two-part, government sponsored, health insurance program for persons over age 65 and certain disabled persons. The basic plan provides automatic coverage of hospital and nursing care expenses when a person becomes eligible. The other part of the program, the supplementary plan, is voluntary and covers only those individuals who make the required premium payments. The Medicare service is handled by the Health Care Financing Administration, and not by the Social Security Administration.

The hospital insurance part of Medicare pays for the cost of inpatient hospital care and certain kinds of follow-up care. The medical insurance part of Medicare helps pay the costs of physicians' services, outpatient hospital services, and for certain other medical items and services not covered by hospital insurance. Premiums are paid by eligible individuals for appropriate coverage, whether or not they are currently receiving Social Security benefits.

Taxation of Social Security Benefits

Social Security benefits consisting of retirement, disability, and survivor payments are currently subject to federal taxes if the annual income from other sources exceeds $32,000 for married taxpayers filing jointly or $25,000 for a single taxpayer (zero for married taxpayers filing separately). For the purposes of Social Security taxes, the annual income comprises adjusted gross income, all municipal bond and other nontaxable interest income, and up to 85 percent of the Social Security benefits received in excess of the income limits.

Wage earners under age 65 lose $1 in Social Security benefits for every $2 in earnings above the annual limit ($11,640 in 2004). Also, a modified test is applied for the year an individual reaches age 65. One dollar in benefits is lost for every $3 in earnings above the limit ($31,080 in 2004). This reduction only applies for the months prior to attaining age 65. However, there are no earnings limits for retirees age 65 and over.

The boxed insert presents a convenient worksheet for calculating the tax on Social Security benefits.

Social Security Income Estimate

The success of retirement planning depends partly upon an accurate estimate of Social Security income to be received upon retirement. In addition, knowing where one stands with Social Security is essential for analyzing life insurance and disability insurance coverage.

Fortunately, the Social Security Administration promptly mails a personalized accounting of Social Security payments and expected income. All the person has to do is mail a completed Form SSA 7004 entitled, *Request for Earnings and Benefit Estimate Statement*. This form can be obtained by calling 1-800-772-1213. If the Administration has made an error in correctly recording past payments, this error should be promptly rectified to avoid future problems.

CORPORATE RETIREMENT PLANS

GENERAL DISCUSSION

Corporate retirement plans, commonly known as qualified plans, provide an excellent means of accumulating wealth on a tax-deferred basis. Furthermore, the distribution of this wealth can be timed so the owner receives during retirement the maximum after-tax income. Finally, distributions under the plan may be accorded favorable tax treatment.

Corporate retirement plans offer tax advantages both to the employer and the employee. The company gets a current tax deduction for amounts contributed to the plan, while the employees are not taxed on their contributions to the plan at the time the contributions are made. Also, the plan is not taxed on its earnings, so there is a tax-deferred buildup of retirement benefits. At the time of distribution of retirement benefits, depending on the method of distribution, lump sum distribution rules or annuity rules apply, unless the benefits are rolled over into an IRA or another qualified plan. In Chapter 11 these tax distribution rules will be discussed in detail.

Taxation Of Social Security Benefits

A portion of Social Security benefits may be subject to income taxation. The following worksheet will assist in determining that tax.

1. Social Security benefits for the year $ _____
2. 50% of line 1   _____
3. Modified adjusted gross income:
    a. AGI less net Social Security benefits received   _____
    b. Tax exempt interest and dividends received or accrued   _____
    c. Line 3a plus line 3b   _____
4. Provisional income (line 2 plus line 3c)   _____
5. Applicable "first-tier" threshold[1]   _____
6. Line 4 less line 5 (not less than zero)   _____
7. 50% of line 6   _____
8. Amount of benefits subject to tax (smaller of line 2 or line 7)   _____

If the "provisional income" (line 4, above) does not exceed the corresponding "first-tier threshold" (line 5, above), no amount is taxable. However, if provisional income exceeds the corresponding threshold, continue with the worksheet below.

9. Applicable second-tier threshold[1] $ _____
10. Line 4 minus line 9 (if less than zero then enter zero)   _____
11. 85% of line 10   _____
12. Amount taxable under first-tier (from line 8, above)   _____
13. Applicable dollar amount[1]   _____
14. Smaller of line 12 or line 13   _____
15. Line 11 plus line 14   _____
16. 85% of line 1   _____
17. Amount of benefits subject to tax (smaller of line 15 or line 16)   _____

Filing Status	First Tier Threshold (for line 5)	Second Tier Threshold (for line 9)	Applicable Dollar Amount (for line 13)
Married filing jointly	$32,000	$44,000	$6,000
Married filing separately (but lived together part of the year)	$0	$0	$0
All others	$25,000	$34,000	$4,500

Note: This is not an official IRS worksheet.

Caution: Any increase in income, such as from the sale of stock or a retirement plan distribution, may subject one to an unexpected tax on the Social Security benefits.

[1] See boxed information.

Source: Kettley Publishing Co., 2001 - Back Room Technician. Reproduced with permission.

SPECIFIC REQUIREMENTS

All retirement plans must comply with minimum participation standards set out in Employee Retirement Income Security Act (ERISA) and the Tax Reform Act (TRA) of 1986. To be sure, the law does not require a company to provide retirement benefits, and in fact certain provisions appear to discourage retirement plans. However, if an employer elects to provide retirement benefits, the minimum requirements set by ERISA or TRA must be met if the plan is to be considered qualified.

The basic requirements under ERISA, which have been significantly changed by subsequent tax laws, are presented in Table 10-3. The table reveals that many of the requirements are both stringent and complicated. Clearly, ERISA sets rigid standards of fiduciary responsibility, imposes restrictions on certain types of investments, prohibits discrimination against non-highly paid employees, and penalizes especially prohibited transactions.

PARTICIPATION REQUIREMENTS

All qualified plans must cover employees who have reached the age of 21 and have one year of service. However, the law allows one exception to this general rule. If a plan provides for immediate vesting, two years of service may be required for coverage. That is, if eligibility requires two years of service, the participant becomes 100 percent vested after two years.

COVERAGE REQUIREMENTS

A plan must satisfy one or more of the following tests in order for it to be considered qualified.

Ratio Percentage Test

The plan must cover a percentage of non-highly compensated employees that is at least 70 percent of the percentage of highly compensated employees covered. Employees who do not meet the plan's minimum age or service requirements are not counted. Union members do not count if retirement benefits have been the subject of good faith bargaining between the company and the union.

The Average Benefits Test

The plan must benefit a non-discriminatory classification of employees. In addition, the average benefit, as a percentage of compensation, for all non-highly compensated employees of the employer must be at least 70 percent of that for highly compensated employees.

Minimum Participation Test

Currently, this test is only applicable to Defined Benefit Plans. A plan meets the test if it does not discriminate in favor of highly compensated employees. For plans that began in 1989 or after, the following requirement has been added as a qualification. The plan must benefit the lesser of: (1) 50 employees of the employer; or (2) 40 percent or more of all employees of the employer. This percentage may not be satisfied by aggregating comparable plans.

TABLE 10-3   Basic Requirements Under ERISA and Internal Revenue Code

Category	*Key factors*	*Special rules*
Participation Requirements	1. Employees 21 or older and with one year's service must be covered. 2. A plan providing for immediate vesting may require two years of service for coverage.	
Coverage Requirements	1. *Percentate Test.* Either (1) 70% or more of all employees participate; or (2) the percentage of non-highly compensated employees who benefit under the plan must equal at least 70% of the highly compensated employees who benefit under the plan.	1. Special definition for highly compensated employees.
	2. *Ratio and Average Benefits Test.* A plan meets the test if (1) the plan does not discriminate in favor of highly compensated employees; and (2) the average benefit percentage of non-highly compensated employees is at least 70% of the average benefit percentage for highly compensated employees.	2. Special rule for SEP
	3. *Minimum Participation Requirement.* The 1997 law drops the minimum participation rule for defined contribution plans and modifies the rule for defined benefit plans. A defined benefit plan will satisfy the minimum participation requirement if it benefits the lesser of: (1) 50 employees, or (2) the greater of (a) 40 percent of all employees of the employer or (b) two employees (one employee if there's only one employee).	
Vesting Requirements	1. *Five-year vesting.* An employee must be fully vested after five years of covered service. 2. *Graded vesting.* Employees are vested depending on their years of service. Graded vesting begins after three years of service, while full vesting begins after five years.	Special values apply to certain types of plans.

TABLE 10-3   (continued)

Category	Key factors	Special rules
Funding	1. *The minimum funding requirement* is the sum of normal costs of plan, experienced gains and losses and amounts necessary to amortize past service costs. 2. Not every retirement benefit is subject to minimum funding standards. Plans exempt from this requirement include profit sharing plans, government plans, unfunded plans, and IRA plans.	
Maximum Contributions and Benefits	1. Defined Contribution Plans: the lesser of $41,000 (2004) or 100% of compensation. 2. Defined Benefit Plans: the lesser of $90,000 (adjusted for inflation [$165,000 in 2004]) or 100% of average compensation for highest three consecutive years of service (taking into account only the first $200,000 [2004] of compensation), actuarially reduced for retirement before age 62.	A combined limit is applied where an employee participates in both types of plans. For employees of less than ten years of work the limit is proportionately reduced.
Nondiscriminating Rules for 401(k)	The plan must meet *one* of the two criteria to be nondiscriminatory: 1. The contribution percentage for highly compensated employees is no greater than 125% of the contribution percentage for all other eligible employees. 2. The contribution percentage for highly compensated employees is no greater than the lesser of 200% of the contribution percentage for all other eligible employees (or this percentage plus 2%).	Different rules apply to simple and save harbor 401(k) plans.

VESTING REQUIREMENTS

For plan years that began in 1989 or after, currently there are two permissible minimum vesting schedules: (1) Full vesting upon the completion of five years of service; or (2) graded vesting beginning at 20 percent per year after three years of service and increasing by 20 percent for each subsequent year of service until full vesting is attained after seven years of service.

Incidentally, a few types of plans provide for immediate 100 percent vesting. These are plans requiring two years of service before participation, plans maintained by certain educational organizations, simplified employee pension plans, simple plans, and some employee stock ownership plans. Other plans, called top heavy plans, must provide either for 100 percent vesting after three years of service or for 20 percent vesting after two years of service and 20 percent additional vesting each year. This is known as the six-year vesting rule. Current rules provide that 401(k) matching contributions must vest at least as rapidly as the top heavy vesting requirements.

FUNDING REQUIREMENTS

There are several plans which are not subject to minimum funding requirements. These include profit sharing plans, government plans, unfunded plans, and IRA plans. The minimum amount that an employer is required to contribute annually to a plan subject to a minimum funding requirement is the sum of two elements: (1) Normal costs of the plan which consist of current contributions; and (2) amounts necessary to amortize past service costs representing payments for costs of the employees' services prior to the adoption of the pension plan.

In general, all plans are concerned with the general funding rules. Additionally, employers have to fund their defined benefit, money purchase, and target benefit plans by contributing annually an amount at least sufficient to fund the normal costs of the plan.

The IRS charges employers with interest for underfunding their plans. Conversely, an employer who has funded more than the maximum permitted contribution is charged a ten percent excise tax for overfunding. These penalties will be discussed more fully in a subsequent section.

PLAN INVESTMENT RULES

In developing plan investment strategies, federal regulations require that the plan trustee exercise care, skill, prudence, and diligence. In addition, federal guidelines indicate that investments should be: (1) sufficiently liquid to allow for timely distribution of benefits; (2) sufficiently diversified to minimize risk potential; and (3) sufficiently conservative to provide dependable growth without undue risk. Within these guidelines, plan contributions can be invested in a bank account, stocks, bonds, mutual funds, government securities, life insurance, money market funds, and fixed and variable annuities.

TYPES OF PLANS

There are two major categories of qualified plans: defined contribution plans and defined benefit plans. A third category, target benefit plans, is a hybrid of a money purchase (a form of defined contribution) and defined benefit plans. These categories are presented in Figure 10-3. A defined contribution plan provides an individual account for each participant and for benefits based solely upon the amount contributed to the participant's account, plus any income, expenses, gains and losses, and forfeitures which may be allocated to the account. In contrast, defined benefit plans specify the benefits to be paid to plan participants at retirement. These plans pay the plan participants the specific benefit which is promised, or defined, in the plan document.

Defined Contribution Plans

The annual contribution to a defined contribution plan is usually a percentage of the compensation of plan participants. For a money purchase plan, the legal document establishing the plan describes the percentage of compensation which the employer (business) is required to contribute. Allocations to all other plans are determined by a formula. The mechanism for determining the plan contribution by the employer is presented next, assuming a ten percent contribution for participants earning $125,000:

Percentage specified in plan document	x	Compensation of plan participants	=	Annual contribution to plan
10 %	x	$125,000	=	$12,500

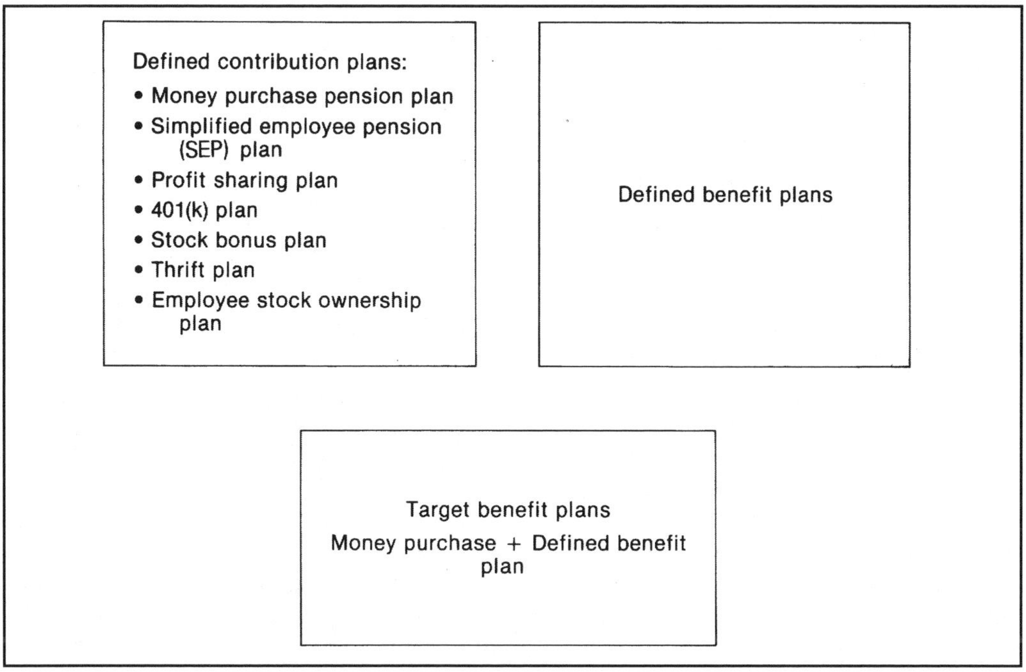

Defined contribution plans:
- Money purchase pension plan
- Simplified employee pension (SEP) plan
- Profit sharing plan
- 401(k) plan
- Stock bonus plan
- Thrift plan
- Employee stock ownership plan

Defined benefit plans

Target benefit plans
Money purchase + Defined benefit plan

FIGURE 10-3   Major categories of corporate retirement plans

Federal regulations limit the maximum tax-deductible contribution which a business can make to a defined contribution plan. As mentioned, the annual addition to each participant's account is comprised of the employer's contribution, any employee contribution, and any forfeiture allocation. The maximum limits under different types of plans (except SEP plans) are as follows:

Type of plan	*Maximum annual addition*
Money Purchase	Lesser of 100% of compensation, or $41,000 as indexed (2004)
Profit Sharing	same
Target Benefit	same
Money Purchase and Profit Sharing	same

During any given year the maximum annual addition for certain employees in a profit sharing plan could be as much as 100 percent of their compensation or $42,000 (2005), whichever is less. However, the overall annual deduction is limited to 25 percent (2005) of the total compensation of all eligible employees of the corporation. In the case of a SEP plan the maximum allowable contribution is the lesser of (1) $42,000 (2005), (2) 13.04 percent of the owner's net profits, or (3) 25 percent of an employee's taxable wages.

Except for a profit sharing plan, the plan document defines the amount of the employer's contribution to be allocated to each participant's account. It is defined as a percentage of compensation, as shown here:

$$\text{John's compensation} \times 10\% = \text{John's allocation}$$

The employer's contribution may also be defined as a proportional amount of the contribution:

$$\frac{\text{John's compensation}}{\text{Total compensation}} \times \frac{\text{Total plan}}{\text{contribution}} = \text{John's allocation}$$

Similarly, amounts forfeited by terminating participants who are not yet eligible for full benefits under the plan may also be allocated proportionately to each participant based on compensation:

$$\frac{\text{John's compensation}}{\substack{\text{Total compensation} \\ \text{of all participants}}} \times \substack{\text{Forfeitures} \\ \text{to be} \\ \text{reallocated}} = \substack{\text{John's share of} \\ \text{forfeitures}}$$

Incidentally, forfeitures may also be used to reduce the employer's required contribution.

Each participant in a defined contribution plan is considered to have an individual account. Every year all the investment data for the plan for the 12-month period is reviewed. The gain or loss of the plan's assets is calculated and allocated among the individual participant accounts. The allocation is determined by using the following formula:

$$\frac{\text{Individual participant}}{\text{account value}} \quad x \quad \frac{\text{Investment}}{\text{gain/loss}} = \frac{\text{Participant's}}{\text{gain/loss}}$$

For instance, suppose the following information is provided:

Account value of Employee #1 = $10,000

Account value of Employee #2 = 8,000

Account value of Employee #3 = 2,000

Total assets of the plan = $20,000

Investment gain for the year = $2,200

Based on the preceding data the following allocations are made:

$$\text{Employee \#1:} \frac{\$10,000}{\$20,000} \text{ x } 2,200 = \$1,100$$

$$\text{Employee \#2:} \frac{\$8,000}{\$20,000} \text{ x } 2,200 = \$880$$

$$\text{Employee \#3:} \frac{\$2,000}{\$20,000} \text{ x } 2,200 = \$220$$

The benefit which a participant receives at retirement or termination is the current value of the account in which the participant has a vested interest. The value of the account is the sum of the annual contributions made to the account, its share of the forfeitures, and its share of the investment return of the plan assets. The calculation is done in two steps:

Step 1

$$\frac{\text{Sum of}}{\text{contributions}} + \text{Forfeitures} + \frac{\text{Investment}}{\text{gains/losses}} = \frac{\text{Participant's}}{\text{account balance}}$$

Step 2

$$\frac{\text{Participant's}}{\text{account}} \quad x \quad \frac{\text{Vested}}{\text{percentage}} = \frac{\text{Participant's}}{\text{benefit}}$$

To conclude, defined contribution plans have certain basic characteristics which are common to all plans included in this category. For instance, the contribution to be made, as defined in the plan document, is usually defined or allocated as a percentage of compensation. In addition, the value of a participant's individual account is the benefit to be paid out at the time of retirement or termination of employment. However, each type of defined contribution plan has its own unique characteristics, as is revealed in Table 10-4. We will now undertake a detailed discussion of each type of defined contribution plan.

TABLE 10-4   Defined Contribution Plans

Title	Major responsibility for funding rests on	Types of investment permitted	General characteristics	Where appropriate	Vesting rules
Money Purchase Pension Plan	Employer.	Determined by trustees.	This plan fixes the employer's contribution by a predetermined (flat amount or flat earnings) formula. The benefit depends upon the length of service, annual contributions of each employee, and corporate earnings.	All employees can benefit from it.	Minimum vesting rules apply.
Simplified Employee Pension Plan (SEP)	Employer.	Only highly risky investments are not permitted.	A SEP is an IRA funded by employer. An IRA account is set up by an employee. Then employer makes an annual contribution of 25% of salary or $40,000 (2004), whichever is less.	All employers unable or unwilling to pay lawyer's fees and annual administrative fee can set up SEPs.	Immediate.
Profit Sharing Plan	Employer.	Determined by trustees.	Through this plan, employers allow their employees to participate in the profits. Employer contributions to the plan are allocated among the employees under a defined formula. The benefit is equal to the value of contributions, plus earnings, that have accumulated in each account. The company must make recurring and substantial contributions to keep the plan in force.	This plan is appropriate where employers want their employees to share in the success of the company. A company need not have made a profit to take advantage of making a deductible contribution.	Minimum vesting rules apply.
401(K) Plan	Employee.* Employer may match a portion of employee's contribution.	Employee's choice of stock or bond mutual funds, fixed income account, or company stock.	401(K) plan may be a part of a profit sharing or a stock bonus plan. Majority of contributions come from employees, so the employer's cost is low. This plan allows employees to defer taxation on part of their compensation, while still providing access to the money for certain emergencies.	Employees in need of sheltering part of their taxable income while retaining the right to borrow from the plan for specified reasons may select this plan.	Immediate. Minimum vesting rules apply to the employer contributions.

Plan	Contributor	Investment	Description	Appropriateness	Vesting
Stock Bonus Plan	Employer.	Corporation's stock or cash.	Stock bonus plan provides benefits similar to a profit sharing plan, except that employer's contributions are not necessarily dependent upon profits and benefits are distributable in company stocks.	This plan is appropriate where employers want their employees to share in the success of the company but wish to retain cash in the company.	Minimum vesting rules apply.
Thrift Plan	Employer. Employees may make contributions with after-tax dollars.	Determined by trustees.	This plan is hybrid of pension, profit sharing, and stock bonus plans.	This plan is appropriate where the important features of several types of plans are described.	Minimum vesting rules apply. Immediate vesting for employee contributions.
Employee Stock Ownership Plan (ESOP)	Employer.	Company stock.	Employer contributions of company stock are discretionary and don't have to be made from profits. Starting at age 55, employees must be given a choice of investments other than company stock for a portion of their account balance.	Employers interested in retaining employees on a long-term basis may opt for this plan.	Immediate. Minimum vesting rules apply.
Savings Incentive Match Plan for Employees (Simple Retirement Plan)	Employer.	Only highly risky investments are not permitted.	This plan can either be set up as an IRA for each employee or as part of a 401(k) plan to which employees may make pretax contributions of up to $10,000 (2005), per year. These plans have easy discrimination rules and no heavy reporting requirements.	All employees can benefit from it	Immediate.

* Employee contributions are tax-deductible

15 KEY QUESTIONS

How much do you know about your own pension plan or that of a prospective employer? Here's what to ask your plan's administrator:

1. What type (or types) of plan do I have? (Remember, if it's a defined benefit plan, benefits are guaranteed and insured by the government.)
2. When will I become eligible?
3. When will I be vested?
4. What happens if my employment is interrupted?

Source: Changing Times, January 1988, p. 82. Reprinted with permission.

5. What provisions are there for early retirement?
6. How much would I receive if I decided to retire early?
7. Can I receive benefits if I keep working after age 65?
8. Is there any inflation protection?
9. Are disability benefits provided?
10. What about death benefits?
11. How is the plan funded?
12. How fast are benefits accrued?
13. What is the current financial condition of the plan?
14. Do you anticipate any difficulty in paying benefits?
15. Do I have any say in how my share of the money is invested?

Money purchase pension plan. The money purchase pension plan permits the employer to make a tax-deductible contribution according to a predetermined formula. An employee's benefit depends upon: (1) the length of time the employee worked while covered under the plan; (2) the amount of money contributed each year by the employer; (3) forfeitures; (4) contributions; and (5) investment results.

The contribution formula can take one of two forms. Under the *flat amount formula*, a set amount of money is contributed to the plan each year on behalf of each participating employee. This formula does not recognize either the length of service or the income of an employee and is therefore considered not as attractive as the *flat percentage of earnings* formula form. The latter type fixes the percentage of income contributed annually to the plan by the employer on behalf of the employee. Maximum contribution under either formula is the lesser of 100 percent of the participant's compensation or $41,000 (2004) per year.

The four major characteristics of money purchase pension plans are summarized below:

1. They may permit a contribution formula of up to 100 percent of compensation, or $41,000 (2004), whichever is less.
2. They require a *fixed* annual contribution commitment by the employer, regardless of the performance of the business.
3. The plans' investment gains or losses are proportionately allocated among the participants.
4. Forfeitures may either be reallocated to the accounts of the remaining participants or used to reduce the employers' required contribution.

Simple Retirement Plan. Currently, a Savings Incentive Match Plan for Employees (SIMPLE) can be adapted by employers who had 100 or fewer employees earning at least $5,000 of compensation) during the preceding year. Employers who no longer qualify have a two-year grace period to continue to maintain the plan.

A SIMPLE plan can be set up either as an IRA for each employee or as part of a 401(k) plan to which employees may make pretax contributions of up to $9,000 (2004) per year. In either case, the employer will not be subject to complex nondiscrimination testing as long as: (1) the employer matches employee contributions up to three percent of the employee's contributions, or (2) the employer makes non-matching contributions equal to two percent of the employee's compensation.

Simplified Employee Pension Plan. A simplified employee pension (SEP) plan combines the simplicity of an IRA with the generous contribution limits of a formal pension plan. Essentially, SEPs allow employers to use IRAs to build tax-sheltered retirement funds for themselves and their employees with minimal paperwork and cost. A SEP plan is adopted by the employer with each eligible employee establishing an IRA to receive his or her share of the employer's contribution. Having individual IRAs as the funding vehicle obviously minimizes the record-keeping function, as the employee's *account balance* at any time is the value of the IRA at that time. No earnings allocation is required to be made by the company. The level of effort involved in the implementation and administration of SEP plans directly depends on whether the employer uses as the plan document either the IRS model SEP Form 5305-SEP or the presumably simpler SEP prototype.

The law requires that SEP plans cover all employees at least 21 years old who have worked for three of the past five years.

Employer contributions to the SEP must be made according to a written allocation formula. The maximum allowable contribution is the lesser of $41,000 (2004), 13.04 percent of the owner's net profits, or 15 percent of an employee's taxable wages.

Distributions from a SEP plan are covered by the same rules as those governing IRAs. Each SEP participant has the right to extend payments over the beneficiary's life.

Profit sharing plan. A major type of defined contribution plan is a profit sharing plan. In this type of plan, each year the employer is permitted to make contributions to the retirement plan trust whether or not the company realizes a profit for that year. Employees are not taxed on employer's contributions, and the contributions grow tax-deferred until they are distributed.

The company has a choice of selecting a definite contribution formula. For example, a profit sharing plan may provide for a flat percentage of pre- or post-tax profits to be contributed to the plan. Alternatively, it may have a sliding scale formula which increases as profits rise, or it may provide that profits are to be shared only if they exceed a predetermined level. Generally, the employer's overall annual contribution to a profit sharing plan is limited to 25 percent of the total compensation of all *eligible* employees of the corporation.

Under the profit sharing plan rules, a company is not required, but may choose, to make contributions whether or not the company makes any profit. However, the law does state that the continuation of such a plan is contingent upon the company's making recurring and substantial contributions, and many employers make a contribution even when the associated companies had an operating loss.

In the case of five-year vesting in a non-top heavy plan, the vesting rules covering a profit sharing plan require a complete vesting of each year's contributions to an employee's account by the end of the fifth plan year of service. The plan may also choose a seven-year graded vesting, in which case seven-year vesting rules will apply. If an employee leaves the firm before his or her contributions are fully vested, the funds are "forfeited"; these funds are typically used to increase other participants' accounts.

It is interesting to note that three other plans—401(k), stock bonus, and employee stock ownership plans—operate as profit sharing plans, but each has its own unique characteristics, as we shall now observe.

401(k) plan. A 401(k) plan may be part of a profit sharing or a stock bonus plan. Under this arrangement, the tax law allows the employee to contribute up to $13,000 (2004), which is annually adjusted for inflation. The employee agrees to take a salary reduction equal to the contribution and is not taxed on the contribution except for F.I.C.A. (Social Security) taxes. In addition, the company may match part of the employee's contribution. However, the sum of the employee's contribution plus the company's contribution is limited to the maximum of 100 percent (2005) of the eligible compensation. The law also allows a plan to accept after-tax employee contributions, on a nondiscriminatory basis, which grow tax-deferred.

Income earned on the 401(k) plan accumulates tax-deferred until it is withdrawn. Funds may be withdrawn after an employee reaches the age of 59-1/2, is separated from service, becomes disabled, or demonstrates financial hardship. Withdrawals are also allowed if the plan is terminated.

The Tax Act of 2001 provides for higher contributions to 401(k) plans, as presented below. As can be seen from this table, the contribution limits gradually rise until 2006. The Act also adds a catch up feature for workers age 50 and older, which is even more generous than the one for IRAs:

New Contribution Limit	Beginning	Savers Age 50+ can add
$11,000	2002	$1,000
$12,000	2003	$2,000
$13,000	2004	$3,000
$14,000	2005	$4,000
$15,000	2006*	$5,000

Contribution limits adjusted annually for inflation in $500 increments in subsequent years.

Stock bonus plan. A stock bonus plan is similar to a profit sharing plan except that the employer's contribution may be made in either stock or cash. A "cashless" contribution in the form of stock keeps needed cash in the company, but still provides the company with the same tax deduction. The amount of the employer's contribution is the fair market value of the stock.

An interesting feature of the stock bonus plan is that the contribution is generally fully invested in the employer's stock. This is in contrast to a profit sharing plan which cannot invest more than ten percent in employer stock. Another feature of this plan is that if a distribution is made in a lump sum, the appreciation realized while the stock was held in the trust is usually not taxed until the stock is sold.

Thrift plan. A thrift plan is a hybrid of pension, profit sharing, and stock bonus plans. It may resemble a profit sharing plan by making employer contributions contingent on current profits or accumulated earnings. It resembles a stock bonus plan by allowing employer securities as an investment. Finally, it resembles a pension plan by making employer contributions mandatory.

In thrift plans, which are also called savings plans, contributions by employees must be made with after-tax dollars, although these contributions grow on a tax-deferred basis. Also, employees may withdraw their own contributions at will, although they may forfeit employer contributions by doing so.

Employee stock ownership plan. An employee stock ownership plan (ESOP) is an employee benefit plan designed to invest primarily in the common stock of the corporation sponsoring the plan. An ESOP must meet all the IRS rules requiring non-discrimination, vesting, and participation, as well as other rules applicable to ESOPs.

Generally, the basic element of an ESOP is a stock bonus plan. It may also be a combination of a stock bonus plan and a money purchase pension plan. As mentioned, a stock bonus plan is established and maintained to provide benefits similar to those of a profit sharing plan. The exception is that employer contributions are not necessarily dependent on profits, and benefits can be distributed in the form of employer stock.

Essentially, an ESOP is a defined contribution plan. The maximum contribution allocated to one person is the lower of $41,000 (2004) or 100 percent of the compensation. The maximum contribution the employer can make to the plan and receive a deduction is 25 percent of the total eligible compensation.

Defined Benefit Plans

A defined benefit plan is a qualified employee pension plan that guarantees a specified benefit level at retirement. For an older, highly compensated employee, this type of plan will allow the maximum amount of tax-deferred retirement saving. However, if an employee changes jobs every five years—as is the case with average Americans—then such a plan would penalize the employee because it would result in a lower pension benefit. This is because defined benefit plans reward long-term employees with larger retirement benefits.

Defined benefit plans differ significantly from defined contribution plans. For example, the benefit an employer wishes an employee to receive upon retirement is first established, and then the contributions are set at the level necessary to achieve the targeted benefits. The benefit formula consists of either a flat dollar amount or a flat percentage of earnings. The maximum annual deductible contribution for retirement at age 65 (provided the person was born prior to 1939) is limited to the amount it takes to generate the lesser of: (1) an annual income of $165,000 (2004) adjusted for inflation; and (2) 100 percent of the average employee's compensation for the three highest consecutive years.

In a defined benefit plan, the value of accrued benefits is determined by one of three rates of accrual tests: the 3 percent method, the 133-1/3 percent rule, or the fractional rule.

Defined benefit plans include: (1) fixed benefit plans in which all employees receive the same benefits; (2) flat benefit plans in which the benefit is a percentage of salary; and (3) unit benefit plans in which the benefit depends on the income (optional) *and* time of service.

The basis of the contributions made by the employer to a defined benefit plan is the total amount of benefits which must be paid to all participants when they retire. The employer must contribute the amount necessary to fulfill the benefit promises specified by the plan. The amount of the employer contribution is determined annually by an actuary. Salient features of a defined benefit plan are presented in Table 10-5.

Since the funding method of a defined benefit plan is so different from that of a defined contribution plan, it is appropriate to briefly comment on the actuarial method of calculating a plan contribution. Every year an actuary reviews the plan to calculate the portion of the ultimate assets needed by the plan which should be contributed in a specific year. The actuary bases the amount of the plan contribution on several factors which include: (1) the benefits promised by the plan; (2) the ages, sex, salaries, and retirement ages of the participants; and (3) the assumptions, or mathematical projections, of the interest to be earned by the plan's assets, future salary increases of the participants, and the projected mortality of the plan's participants. This calculation method is summarized below:

Benefit formula provisions	+	Characteristics of plan participants	+	Assumptions of future plan performance	=	Contribution required to fund future benefits

In a defined benefit plan, the participant receives the promised income upon retirement. However, if the service is terminated prior to the anticipated retirement, the participant receives only the present value of the vested *accrued benefits*. The value of accrued benefits is determined by a mathematical formula utilizing one of the three accrual methods mentioned above.

At this point, it is apropos to comment on a provision in the tax law which concerns defined benefit plans. The tax law could spark a comeback for the old-style pension plan. That, at least, is the view of some benefits consultants and actuaries who point to a tax incentive for employers offering traditional *defined-benefit plans*, the kind that pay retirees a fixed monthly amount, based on salary and years of service.

The incentive is a little-noticed technical provision that gradually lifts the cap on employer pension-fund contributions from 150 percent to 170 percent of the plan's current liabilities. After 2003, this full funding limit was repealed. Amounts beyond the caps are subject to stiff penalties. This seemingly small change could enable some companies to better fund their plans, thereby receiving a bigger tax break for those contributions. It can be reasonably expected that the increase would most likely prompt more small companies to adopt new plans, because the funding limitation is one of the biggest problems that is associated with a defined-benefit pension plan.

In recent years, most employers creating retirement plans for workers have avoided old-fashioned defined-benefit pensions in favor of simpler 401(k) retirement-savings plans. However, under the current law, not only does a higher limit make it more likely that small and midsize companies will adopt new pension plans, but it also helps ensure that large companies with pension plans will keep them.

TABLE 10-5 Defined Benefit Plans, TBP, and TSA

Title	Major responsibility for funding rests on	Types of investments permitted	General characteristics	Where appropriate	Vesting rules
Defined Benefit Plan	Employer.	Determined by trustees.	This plan defines the benefit to be received at retirement. Then the actuary determines what contributions must be made each year to meet the benefit target.	This plan is especially beneficial for highly paid employees who are 50 and over. They can shelter a significant portion of their taxable earnings by participating in this type of plan.	Minimum vesting rules apply.
Target Benefit Plan (TBP)	Employer.	Determined by trustees.	This plan is a hybrid of defined benefit and money purchase plan. Benefits targets are established and contributions are set at levels necessary to meet the target. However, the benefits actually paid are not necessarily equal to the target chosen but depend on the account upon distribution.	This plan is best for older clients with a budget. Target plans are also suitable where maintenance of individual participants' accounts is desired.	Minimum vesting rules apply.
Tax-Sheltered Annuity (TSA or 403(b) Plan)	Employee. Employer may elect to contribute as well.	Employees's choice of almost any type of investment	Employees of Section 501(c)(3) organizations and public school teachers can buy special, nonforfeitable, tax-deferred annuities or face amount certificates of mutual funds to provide funds for their retirement.	All eligible employees may take advantage of TSA to plan for retirement.	Immediate.

The so-called full-funding limits are troublesome for many employers because they are based on a plan's *current* liabilities, which refers to the amount a plan would owe this year if its entire work force retired all at once. A plan's current liabilities can vary significantly from year to year, depending on the demographics of a company's work force. For example, a company with a large number of young workers may not be able to contribute much money, if any, to a pension today because its work force has not accrued big pension benefits. But as those employees age, and as the company hires older workers, other federal pension rules, such as the so-called minimum-contribution requirements, could suddenly force it to put in large sums into a plan to make up for lower contributions during earlier years.

An attractive feature of all plans is the loan provision. An employee may be permitted to borrow from the plan up to a maximum amount. The loan amount is limited to the lesser of: (1) $50,000, reduced by the employee's highest loan balance during the past 12 months; or (2) 50 percent of the present value of the employee's vested interest in the plan, or $10,000, whichever is greater. Interest, which is usually charged at a rate slightly higher than the prime rate, is not deductible. With the exception of money borrowed to purchase a home, the loan must be repaid within five years, and the interest and principal must be amortized at least on a quarterly basis.

Age-Weighted Profit Sharing Plans

Age-Weighted Profit Sharing Plans offer some of the best features of profit sharing and defined benefits plans. IRC Section 401(a)(4) allows employers to utilize the flexible contribution aspect of a profit sharing plan and the *age-based* funding methods of a defined benefit plan. This is particularly attractive to owners of businesses since they allow for contributions not only based on compensation, but also on the participant's age at entering the plan. Thus, employers can contribute larger amounts for valued older employees, including themselves. In addition, they can control the contributions to the qualified plans from year to year. For instance, if the business is profitable during a given year, maximum allowable contribution to a qualified plan could be made for that year. However, no contribution need be made during the year in which the business is not profitable. Another important feature of these plans is that the owner can reward older valued employees without *over compensating* the younger employees.

Age-Weighted Profit Sharing Plans are cheaper than the traditional defined benefit plans. The employer can save on PBGC premiums and administrative fees. In addition, the IRS regulatory requirements normally associated with Age Weighted Plans are less rigorous than those associated with defined benefit plans.

The Age-Weighted Profit Sharing Plan must meet all the requirements applicable to a regular profit sharing plan. These are listed below:

1. The maximum annual deduction is 25 percent (2004) of covered payroll.
2. Each year the employer maintains discretion over making contributions to the plan.
3. The maximum individual allocation for any one participant is $41,000 (2004) or 100 percent of salary, whichever is less.

4. Top heavy plans must satisfy the three percent top-heavy minimum requirement for all non-key employees.
5. Forfeitures from non-vested accounts are allowed to be reallocated, or they may be used to reduce future contributions.
6. Investment earnings are allocated to participant accounts.

An Illustration

The following illustration demonstrates the benefits of a Age-Weighted Profit Sharing Plan. Assume John Jones, Inc. has the following employee compensation scheme:

	Age	Compensation	Traditional Contribution
Owner	55	$150,000	$15,000
Employee 1	45	45,000	4,500
Employee 2	40	40,000	4,000
Employee 3	35	35,000	3,500
Employee 4	30	30,000	3,000
Employee 5	25	25,000	2,500
Employee 6	20	25,000	2,500
Totals		**$350,000**	**$35,000**

Currently, John Jones has a traditional profit sharing plan. Under this plan, a contribution of $35,000 would provide each employee with exactly ten percent of pay. However, if this plan is replaced by an Age-Weighted Profit Sharing Plan, the total contribution of $35,000 would be redistributed in favor of the owner. This fact is demonstrated in the following table:

	Age	Compensation	Traditional Plan Cont.	Age-Based Cont.
Owner	55	$150,000	$15,000	$25,939
Employee 1	45	45,000	4,500	3,442
Employee 2	40	40,000	4,000	2,035
Employee 3	35	35,000	3,500	1,184
Employee 4	30	30,000	3,000	900
Employee 5	25	25,000	2,500	750
Employee 6	20	25,000	2,500	750
Totals		**$350,000**	**$35,000**	**$35,000**

The Distribution Rules

The Unemployment Compensation Amendments Act of 1992 mandated new rules regarding the taxation of distributions from qualified plans. The rules were designed to increase revenues to pay for the extended unemployment benefits. The Act did not increase the amount of taxes on distributions; it merely accelerated tax collection.

Prior to the enactment of these rules, an employee could receive a lump sum distribution from a qualified plan and then rollover the proceeds to a new qualified plan within 60 days without triggering tax consequences. The current rules have made this method of transfer very expensive, as will shortly become clear.

The law has affected several key areas of distribution, which are discussed below.

Direct Rollovers

The current law requires every qualified plan to provide each participant the option of transferring funds *directly* to another qualified plan, or to an IRA. This is commonly known as a *trustee-to-trustee* transfer. This rule primarily affects defined contribution plans, since these plans are most frequently eligible for rollover. In contrast, in defined benefit plans, employers must offer the direct rollover option if the proceeds are less than $5,000 or a lump sum option is available. Since an IRA is not sponsored by an employer, the direct rollover option does not apply to distributions from IRA plans.

Mandatory Withholding Rules

If a participant does not elect to transfer funds directly to another trustee, the law mandates that 20 percent of the taxable amount be withheld from every eligible distribution. Consequently, the law essentially makes the traditional *rollover* of qualified plans somewhat obsolete.

To carry this discussion one step further, under the law an employee has three options available to rollover funds from a qualified plan into another qualified plan, or IRA. These options are discussed next by using the following case.

John Client, age 50, has accumulated $100,000 in his retirement plan over a 20-year period. In 2004, John decided to move to a more promising job and transfer his old qualified plan into a qualified plan offered by the new employer. Prior to joining the new firm, John requested the trustee of the old plan to rollover the proceeds using the traditional rollover method. He received a check from the employer and deposited the check into his new plan within 60 days. Since he did not request a direct trustee-to-trustee rollover, under the new law, the plan trustee was required to withhold 20 percent ($20,000) of the proceeds so he was able to mail a check to John for only $80,000 ($100,000 – $20,000).

Upon receipt of the check John had two options to choose from, as discussed below.

Create a Taxable Event. John could simply rollover $80,000 into the new qualified plan. He could do so by depositing the check into the new plan. This option is not particularly attractive because the IRS assumes that the employee took an early distribution of $20,000 that was withheld by the old trustee. Consequently, for the 2004 tax year, John would be required pay ordinary income taxes on $20,000.

Worse still, since John had not attained age 59-1/2, the ten percent early withdraw penalty would also apply.

The story of qualified plan distribution in the manner just described unfolds in the following manner. During 2005, when John files his 2004 tax return, he will get a refund of $20,000 that was withheld by the old plan trustee minus the applicable taxes. After taxes, this refund would only amount to "$11,800," as stated below:

Amount of tax withheld by trustee	$20,000
less early withdraw penalty (10% x $20,000)	– 2,000
less income tax at 31% (31% x $20,000)	– 6,200
Net cash due	$11,800

Make Up The Difference. As an alternative to creating a taxable event, under the rules John could continue to shelter from taxes the entire amount of $100,000. If he chose this method, in rolling over his old qualified plan funds he would add $20,000 of his own money to the $80,000 being released by the trustee, thereby starting his new qualified plan at the $100,000 level. Under this scenario, when John files his tax return in 2005, he will receive a tax refund of $20,000 that was withheld by the old trustee. It is important to note, however, that while no taxes will be due on the $20,000 originally withheld by the trustee, John would nevertheless lose the use of his $20,000 from the day it was paid to the new fund until the refund check was received from the IRS.

Direct Transfer. If John elected to have a *direct* trustee-to-trustee transfer (as opposed to the traditional rollover described above), the total balance of $100,000 would be transferred from the old qualified plan to the trustee of the new qualified plan. Even more important, this method would trigger no tax liability or early withdrawal penalties, and there would be no need for the old trustee to withhold any taxes. That is why this is considered to be the most efficient and cost effective method of transferring funds from one qualified plan to another fund, or to an IRA.

The current distribution rules, and their associated tax consequences, are summarized in the following table.

Target Benefit Plans

Target benefit plans are a combination of defined benefit and money purchase plans. In this type of plan, the benefit is established and then contributions are set at the level necessary to achieve the targeted benefit. But the benefit actually paid out is not necessarily the selected benefit. The amount finally distributed depends on the amount that has accumulated in the account.

In a target benefit plan, the contribution is fixed and not related to the plan's actual investment return. It must be made each year regardless of the business situation. Target Benefit plans permit a maximum contribution up to the lesser of 100 percent (2004) of compensation or $41,000 for each participant. However, the deduction remains at 25 percent of total participation compensation.

An important feature of target plans is that individual account balances are kept for all participants. The contribution is allocated into separate accounts for

Choice for Handling a Lump- Sum Distribution	
Options	Consequences
Leave money in former employer's plan	Money continues to grow tax deferred; can later be moved to new employer's plan or to an IRA.
Take the cash	Payout cut by 20% because of new income tax withholding requirement; entire withheld amount subject to income taxes in year received; plus 10% penalty if recipient is under the age 59 1/2.
Begin periodic withdrawals	Pay tax on distribution, but no 10% penalty (distributions must continue until age 59 1/2, or for five years, whichever is later).
Take the cash and put it into an IRA or another qualified plan	Payout cut by 20% withholding, but money can be refunded after tax return for the year is filed if amount equal to entire distribution was put into IRA or new plan within 60 days; money continues to grow tax deferred.
Transfer directly into IRA or another qualified plan	Money continues to grow tax deferred.

each participant. All accounts share in the investment gains, losses, expenses of the plan assets, and forfeitures if they are reallocated. The benefit provided to the participant is the balance in the account at retirement which, as mentioned, could be different from the targeted amount.

Tax-Sheltered Annuity

A tax-sheltered annuity (TSA) represents a special retirement plan open only to the employees of certain nonprofit, religious, charitable, and educational institutions specified in Section 501(c)(3) of the IRS code as well as teachers of public school systems.

An employee may contribute the lesser of up to $11,000 or 25 percent of annual compensation to a TSA under a salary reduction agreement. For 2004, the contribution is limited to $13,000 or 100 percent of pay. Participation by the employer may be in the form of additional, matching, or total contributions. Premiums paid by employers to buy TSAs are excluded from the employee's gross income up to the employee's *exclusion allowance* for that year. The exclusion allowance equals

20 percent of the employee's annual compensation times the years of service, less the amount contributed by the employer and excluded from income by the employee in earlier years. The total contributions by the employer are determined by a sophisticated formula. It is important to note that for TSA plans, beginning in 2002, the exclusion allowance has been repealed.

The laws governing distribution from TSAs are similar to those relating to withdrawals from an IRA. For instance, in both cases early withdrawals prior to age 59-1/2 are subject to a ten percent penalty, and minimum compulsory distributions must begin at age 70-1/2.

A TSA account can be rolled over into another TSA account or into an IRA. A TSA can also be rolled over into another pension or profit sharing plan. A rollover from a TSA account must be completed within 60 days of receipt of the funds from that account.

TSA funds can be invested in life insurance annuity contracts or in mutual funds. Other forms of basic investments, such as investments in stocks, bonds, GNMAs, and real estate investment trusts, are also approved for this plan.

Table 10-6 presents a summary of various qualified plans and their key features. Also, Table 10-7 presents the phase-in of retirement savings provisions which became law after the passage of the Economic Growth and Tax Relief Act of 2001.

PERSONAL RETIREMENT PLANS

INDIVIDUAL RETIREMENT ACCOUNT (IRA)

An Overview

Anyone who has earned income is eligible to open an individual retirement account (IRA), whether self-employed or an employee, full-time or part-time. The key restriction on an IRA is that a tax-deductible IRA contribution cannot be made in any year in which the person is eligible to participate in a tax-qualified plan and earns more than a specified amount, as described next.

The provisions regarding the deductibility of an IRA are summarized in Table 10-8. The following facts are revealed by the table. First, if neither spouse is covered by a qualified plan, the law allows a taxable income deduction of $3,000 per worker or $6,000 for married couples, regardless of income. Second, married couples covered by a corporate plan, and having an adjusted gross income in 2004 of less than $65,000 ($33,000 on a single return), keep the full deduction. The caps climb gradually to $80,000 ($50,000 for singles) over the next eight to ten years.

As mentioned, the IRA contribution limit of $3,000 (2004) rises to $4,000 in 2005 and $5,000 in 2008. Thereafter, contribution limits will continue to rise in line with inflation. In addition, workers age 50 and older can add an extra $500 to their IRAs for the 2005 tax year and an additional $1,000 beginning in 2006.

Finally, joint filers who make less than $50,000 ($25,000 for single filers) will receive an additional incentive to contribute to an IRA or an employer-sponsored retirement savings plan. Depending on the income a wage earner may be able to get a non-refundable tax credit of up to $1,000 a year. The tax credit is available even if the contribution is tax deductible. The new tax credit is designed to make it easier

TABLE 10-6 Qualified Plans and Key Features

Plan	IRA	SEP	SAR-SEP	403(b)
2002 Plan Contribution Limits	$3,000 or 100% of compensation, whichever is less	15% or $30,000 (indexed), whichever is less (based on the first $200,000 of compensation)	15% or $11,000 whichever is less	100% or $11,000 whichever is less
Contribution Deadline	Tax filing deadline, no extensions	Tax filing deadline, plus extensions	Salary Deferrals may only be made on a calendar year basis	Salary Deferrals may only be made on a calendar year basis
Deadline to Set Up Account	Tax filing deadline, no extensions	Tax filing deadline, plus extensions	No new SAR-SEP plans may be established after December 31, 1996.	There is no deadline to establish. Salary deferral contributions are always current year.
Maximum Eligibility	*must be under 70 1/2 to contribute *must have earned compensation during the year	Employers must include all employees who: *Are over 21 *Have performed service in 3 of the past 5 years *Have total compensation during the year exceeding $400(indexed) *May exclude union employees *May exclude nonresident aliens	Employers must include all employees who: *Are over 21 *Have performed service in 3 of the past 5 years *Have total compensation during the year exceeding $400(indexed) *May exclude union employees *May exclude nonresident aliens	Only employees of public schools or tax-exempt organizations (under IRC 501 (C)(3) may participate
Required Reporting	*contributions and rollovers reported on form 5498 *distributions reported on form 1099-R	*Rollover contributions reported on form 5498 *Distributions reported on form 1099-R	*Rollover contributions reported on form 5498 *Distributions reported on form 1099-R	*Distributions reported on form 1099-R *5500 reporting required if employer is making non-elective contributions.
Distribution Events	*Normal-attainment of age 59 1/2 *Premature-prior to age 59 1/2 , may be subject to 10% penalty *Death *Permanent Disability	*Normal-attainment of age 59 1/2 *Premature-prior to age 59 1/2 , may be subject to 10% penalty *Death *Permanent Disability	*Normal-attainment of age 59 1/2 *Premature-prior to age 59 1/2 , may be subject to 10% penalty *Death *Permanent Disability	*Attainment of 59 1/2 *Financial Hardship *Permanent Disability *Death *Separation from service

TABLE 10-6   *(continued)*

Profit Sharing	Money Purchase	401(k)	SIMPLE IRA	SIMPLE 401(K)
25% or $40,000 (indexed), whichever is less (based on the first $200,000 of compensation)	25% or $40,000 whichever is less (based on the first $200,000 of compensation)	*$11,000 deferral limit *100% or $40,000 per individual limit (including employee deferrals, employer contributions and forfeitures) *The maximum employer contribution is 25% of total eligible payroll	*$ 7,000 deferral limit *Employer must match deferrals up to 3% of compensation (can be lowered to 1% in 2 out of 5 years OR employer can make a contribution for each eligible employee of 2% of compensation	*Lesser of $7,000 100% deferral limit *Employer must match deferrals up to 3% of compensation (match must be 100% vested) OR the employer can make a cont. for each eligible employee of 2% of compensation
Tax filing deadline, plus extensions	Tax filing deadline, plus extensions	Tax filing deadline for employer contributions	Tax filing deadline for employer contributions	Tax filing deadline (incl. extensions) for employer contributions
Plan must be adopted by year end	Plan must be adopted by year end	Plan must be adopted by year end	SIMPLE plans must be established 60 days before the start of a particular calendar year	SIMPLE plans must be established 60 days before the start of a particular calendar year
Employers must include all employees who: *Are over 21 *Have completed 1 year of service (must have worked at least 1000 hours each year) *May exclude union employees *May exclude nonresident aliens	Employers must include all employees who: *Are over 21 *Have completed 1 year of service (must have worked at least 1000 hours each year) *May exclude union employees *May exclude nonresident aliens	Employers must include all employees who: *Are over 21 *Have completed 1 year of service (must have worked at least 1000 hours each year) *May exclude union employees *May exclude non-resident aliens	Employers must include all employees who: *Earn at least $5,000 during two preceding years and can reasonably expect to earn at least $5,000 in current year. *May exclude union employees *May exclude non-resident aliens (no age requirement)	Employers must include all employees who: *Are over 21 *Same as regular 401(k) plan. *May exclude union employees *May exclude non-resident aliens
*5500 reporting required unless exception applies *Distributions reported on form 1099-R	*5500 reporting required unless exception applies *Distributions reported on form 1099-R	*5500 reporting required. *Distributions reported on form 1099-R	*5500 reporting NOT required. *Distributions reported on form 1099-R	*5500 reporting required. *Distributions reported on form 1099-R
*Separation from service or Attainment of plan's normal retirement age *Permanent Disability *Death *Plan Termination *Financial Hardship	*Separation from service or Attainment of plan's normal retirement age *Permanent Disability *Death *Plan Termination	*Separation from service or Attainment of plan's normal retirement age *Permanent Disability *Death *Plan Termination *Financial Hardship	*Normal-attainment of age 59 1/2 *Premature-prior to age 59 1/2, May be subject to 10% penalty OR 25% penalty if distribution is taken prior to 2 years of participation. *Death *Plan Termination *Permanent Disability	*Normal-attainment of plan's normal retirement age *Permanent Disability *Death *Plan Termination *Financial Hardship *Separation from service

TABLE 10-7   Phase-in of Retirement Savings Provisions

Type of Account	New Contribution Limits	Beginning	Savers Age 50+ Can Add	Beginning
IRAs	$3,000	2002	$500	2002
	$4,000	2005	$1,000	2006
	$5,000	2008[1]		
401(k), 403(b), 457	$11,000	2002	$1,000	2002
	$12,000	2003	$2,000	2003
	$13,000	2004	$3,000	2004
	$14,000	2005	$4,000	2005
	$15,000	2006[1]	$5,000	2006
Simple IRA	$7,000	2002	$500	2002
	$8,000	2003	$1,000	2003
	$9,000	2004	$1,500	2004
	$10,000	2005[1]	$2,000	2005
Profit-sharing and Money Purchase Pension	$40,000 or 100% of compensation, whichever is less	2002	$2,500	2006[1]

[1] Contribution limits adjusted annually for inflation in $500 increments in subsequent years.

for younger workers to save for retirement as well as for families in lower income brackets.

The Act also treats more fairly those couples where both spouses work but only one has a retirement plan. The spouse without a plan will not be penalized by restrictions on IRA eligibility. However, to take advantage of this change, the couple's joint income must be below $150,000.

In addition to the regular IRAs, the current law permits contributions to the Roth IRA, which is designed to help a large group of eligible taxpayers who currently do not qualify for tax-deductible contributions to traditional IRAs. These taxpayers can put $3,000 (for 2004) a year into a Roth IRA on a non-deductible basis and avoid federal taxes altogether upon distribution on the earnings as long as the money is used for retirement or other qualifying purposes.

In 2001, participants in corporate retirement plans could make a fully deductible IRA contribution only if their income was below $53,000 ($33,000 for singles). In contrast, the full $3,000 (for 2004) non-deductible contribution to a Roth IRA can be made by taxpayers with AGI of as much as $150,000 on joint returns and $95,000 on individual returns. It should be noted here that higher earners who are not covered by a company plan are permitted to make deductible IRA contributions regardless of the size of their income.

The Roth IRA earnings grow tax-free, if the money remains in the account for at least five years, and is then withdrawn: (1) after retirement, (2) past age 59-1/2 for educational expenses, or (3) for the purchase of a first home. The Roth IRA's

TABLE 10-8 Deductibility of IRA

		Participating in pension plan?	
	Adjusted gross income	*Yes*	*No*
Joint	$50,000 or less (Indexed)	$3,000	$3,000
	Above $50,000	Varies	$3,000
Single	$30,000 or less (Indexed)	$3,000	$3,000
	Above $30,000	Varies	$3,000

tax benefits remain intact in later years even if the holder's income soars above the contribution limits.

For individuals who can choose between a deductible IRA and a Roth IRA, it appears that, as a general rule, tax-free growth in the future can be more valuable than getting a tax deduction during the year the contribution is made and pulling money out later at ordinary income tax rates. However, persons expecting to pay taxes at a significantly lower rate in retirement might be better off taking the deduction at the present time.

There are two additional advantages to the Roth IRAs. First, investors can pull out an amount up to their original contribution at any time without triggering a tax consequence. Second, there is no requirement, as there is with a deductible IRA, for distributions to begin at age 70-1/2.

Deduction limits for an active participant in a qualified plan who is married and files separately are not as straightforward as those for the categories just discussed. In general, for such a person no deduction is allowed if the AGI is over $10,000. If the AGI is less than $10,000, a partial deduction is allowed, and the amount of the deduction is calculated by using a special formula. For instance, suppose John Johnson is married, files a separate return, and is an active participant in an employer plan. John's AGI is $7,500. The maximum deductible IRA contribution is $500:

Step 1: $7,500 ($7,500 – $0)
Step 2: $2,500 ($10,000 – $7,500)
Step 3: $500 ($2,500 x .20)

Long-Term Accumulation

The magic of compounding and the concept of the time value of money are demonstrated nowhere more clearly than in the long-term accumulation in an IRA account. For instance, Table 10-9 reveals that $2,000 invested at the beginning of every year at ten percent for 30 years would total $361,887. If the investment earns a 12 percent return, in 30 years the IRA fund would grow to approximately half a million dollars.

Deductible versus Nondeductible Contributions

As mentioned, qualified plan participants whose AGI exceeds designated amounts can no longer make tax-deductible contributions into an IRA. However,

TABLE 10-9 Long-Term Accumulation of IRA Contribution

Investment return	Years					
	5	10	15	20	25	30
7%	$12,307	$29,567	$53,776	$ 87,730	$135,353	$202,146
8	12,672	31,291	58,649	98,846	157,909	244,692
9	13,047	33,121	64,007	111,529	184,648	297,150
10	13,431	35,062	69,899	126,005	216,364	361,887
11	13,826	37,123	76,380	142,530	253,998	441,826
12	14,230	39,309	83,507	161,397	298,668	540,585

Note: Annual contribution of $2,000 is made at the beginning of each year.

their contributions are still allowed to grow tax-deferred until distribution. For these people, to contribute to an IRA or not becomes the key question.

The difference between the tax-deferred and taxable IRA contributions is presented in Table 10-10. In this illustration it is assumed that the investor is in the 27.5 percent tax bracket and the investment grows at ten percent. According to this table, in ten years the excess of savings will be $14,464; in 30 years these savings will amount to $149,278. Of course, taxes on before-tax IRA contributions would have to be deducted before the amounts in Column 2 can be compared with those in Column 1 in order to arrive at more accurate excess savings figures. Also, on the negative side, the investor will be required to keep very detailed records: income tax forms and a copy of Form 8606 for any year with a nondeductible contribution; Forms 1099-R and W2P, showing distributions from the IRA, and Form 5498, showing the value of the IRA at the end of each year. On balance, nondeductible IRA contributions do offer economic benefits, but the burden may prove to be onerous. Incidentally, a tax-deferred annuity may be a better alternative than a nondeductible IRA, since unrestricted amounts may be invested in an annuity which grows tax-deferred.

Types of IRAs

IRA assets must be invested in one of two plans: an individual retirement account that has a bank or other qualified organization as trustee or custodian; or an individual retirement annuity.

Individual retirement plan. An IRA account must be a trust or custodial account, although it may be in a self-directed IRA. The individual's interest in the account must be non- forfeitable. Unless the contributor becomes disabled or dies, the account must be held exclusively for the purpose of providing retirement benefits. The IRA benefits can be distributed starting with the earliest of 59-1/2 years or time of death or disability. In addition, the distribution must begin by no later than age 70-1/2.

An IRA trust may accept only cash contributions. The IRA funds may be invested in savings accounts, stocks, bonds, mutual funds, real estate, limited partnerships, approved government coins, gold, and endowments. However, the rules

TABLE 10-10 IRA: Before versus After-Tax Contribution

Years (1)	IRA: Before-tax (2)	IRA: After-tax (3)	Difference (4)
10	$ 52,594	$ 38,130	$ 14,464
20	189,008	137,031	51,997
30	542,830	393,552	149,278

Note: 1. Investor's marginal tax bracket remains constant at 27.5 percent.
2. Annual contribution of $3,000 before-tax, or $2,175 after-tax, is made at the beginning of each year.
3. IRA funds grow at a constant return of ten percent.
4. This illustration does not take Roth IRA into account.

prohibit the investment of IRA funds in highly speculative products including collectibles, art, and gems.

Individual retirement annuity plan. This is an annuity issued by an insurance company. It may be either an individual annuity contract or a joint and survivor annuity for the benefit of the annuitant and spouse. The investment must be nontransferable and its distribution must begin when the annuitant is no older than 70-1/2.

Rollover versus Transfer

The terms *rollover* and *transfer* are applied to any movement of funds from a qualified plan or an IRA to another IRA investment. There are, however, important distinctions between a rollover and a transfer.

An investor rolls over an IRA when a plan is liquidated and a check or wire transfer is sent by the trustee to the IRA investor. This would be the case when a lump sum distribution is received from a qualified plan or the money is withdrawn from an IRA investment. In this case, from the time the money is received, the investor has 60 days to reinvest in another IRA account without paying current taxes on the rollover amount. Only one rollover is allowed per year per IRA account. Thus, if a person has five separate accounts, the person could roll over each account once a year. Incidentally, taxable IRAs can also be rolled over into a qualified plan.

In contrast, an IRA is *transferred* when the money is sent directly by one trustee to another trustee, completely bypassing the investor. There are no legal restrictions on the number of times a transfer can take place in a year. However, some custodians impose restrictions on how many transfers will be permitted during any given year and may also impose fees on such transfers. It is therefore advisable to investigate these restrictions and costs before transferring IRA funds.

An important caveat should be added here. An employee receiving a lump sum distribution from a qualified plan can roll over part or all of the distribution into an IRA, thereby deferring taxation on the amount rolled over into an IRA. Any amount not rolled over is currently taxed as ordinary income. However, by rolling over the lump sum distribution into an IRA, the employee forfeits the right to subject this amount to a favorable tax treatment known as ten-year forward averaging, which is explained in the next chapter.

TABLE 10-11 Keogh Plan: An Overview

Type	Who is interested?	Its nature	Maximum annual contributions	Maximum Vesting	Legal reporting
Keogh: Money Purchase	Persons who can commit to a fixed annual obligation.	Contributions are a fixed percentage of compensation and must be made annually.	Lesser of $40,000 or 20% of net profit for owner and 25% of total taxable wages for employees.	Full vesting after three years, or six-year graded vesting. Part-time and seasonal employees may be excluded.	Form 5500 must be filed annually.
Keogh: Profit Sharing	Persons who wish to tie contributions to profits or are unable to commit to a fixed obligation.	Discretionary contributions are based on profits. No contributions during a given year are permitted.	Lesser of $40,000 20% of net profit for owner and 25% of total taxable wages for employees.	Same as above.	Same as above. If both money purchase and profit sharing plans are adopted and the accounts are at different institutions.
Keogh: Defined Benefit	Persons 50 and over who are anxious and able to make the highest contributions possible.	Contributions must be made annually to fund a predetermined retirement benefit.	Amount necessary to fund a maximum benefit of $165,000 (2004), (indexed for inflation), per year at retirement, up to 100% of income.	Same as above.	Form 5500. Also, annual review by an actuary to determine annual contributions.

KEOGH PLAN

Introduction

If IRAs are the best tax shelter for employees, Keogh or H.R. 10 plans are the best plan for the self-employed. A Keogh plan, or more accurately, the qualified plan of an unincorporated entity, is simply a retirement plan for self-employed business people or professionals. The self-employed person gets a deduction for the contributions and the earnings in the fund accumulate on a tax-deferred basis.

The ceilings on Keogh contributions have been made competitive with those of tax-protected corporate pension plans. This means that a self-employed person can make an annual contribution of up to the lesser of $40,000 or 25 percent.

Types of Keogh Plans

An overview of Keogh plans is presented in Table 10-11. The simplest Keogh plan is a *defined contribution* plan. There are three kinds of defined contribution plans: money purchase, profit sharing, and target benefit. In a money purchase or target benefit plan, the participant must contribute the same minimum percentage each year, or risk a fine, equal to ten percent of the amount of any under-funding.

The maximum deductible contributions of defined contribution Keogh plans are as follows: (1) For profit sharing plans, 25 percent (after contribution) of net self-employment income up to $205,000 (2004) or $40,000, whichever, is less. (2) For other defined contribution plans, 25 percent (after contribution) of net self-employment income up to $200,000 (2002) or $40,000, whichever is less. However, in practical terms, the dollar limit on contributions to profit sharing plans is $40,000 (20 percent of $200,000 [2002]).

For the defined benefit Keogh, the maximum allowable contribution limit is actuarially determined.

Those who wish to avoid the risk of a penalty, or who like to tie their contributions to the profitability of their enterprise, prefer the profit sharing Keogh. In this plan the limits are the lower of $41,000 or 20 percent of the owner's net profits (or 15 percent of total employees' taxable wages).

Frequently, employees of corporations who are also self-employed business persons wish to shelter most or all of their self-employed earnings. This is especially true for older self-employed persons who also have secured positions with corporations. For them, the *defined benefit* Keogh provides a rare opportunity. With this type, the individual decides not how much to put in the plan each year, but how much the plan should pay out on maturity—up to the maximum allowable benefit limit of $165,000 a year (2004), adjusted for inflation. Annual contributions to this plan will vary according to the age of the participant and other factors, such as the return on the plan investment. For this reason, defined benefit Keoghs require detailed actuarial computations every year in order to determine how much contribution would be legally allowed for that year.

In this chapter we have analyzed in detail the basic structure of retirement income. In the next chapter we will undertake a detailed review of the key concepts and strategies relating to retirement planning.

When nothing seems to help, I go and look at a stonecutter hammering away at his rock perhaps a hundred times without as much as a crack showing in it. Yet at the hundred and first blow it will split in two, and I know it was not that blow that did it—but all that had gone before.

Jacob Riis

CHAPTER 11

Retirement Planning: Concepts and Strategies

INTRODUCTION

For the past couple of generations, Americans have relied on the venerable three-legged stool to provide for their retirement: Social Security benefits, private pensions, and personal savings. Many factors currently threaten the stability of this stool. For instance, retirees of the 21st century will grow far older. When Social Security was enacted in 1935 and retirement was set at 65, the average male that age could expect to live an additional 12 years. In 2004, he could live for 18 more years, and by 2025, that period could be extended to 20 more years. At the same time, the age at which full Social Security benefits can be collected is rising to 67, and the portion of benefits individuals sacrifice when they retire will be greater.

Longer lives will require more financial support. Yet the ability of Social Security to provide this expanded support appears questionable. Three people now work and pay Social Security taxes for each retiree collecting; by 2030, that ratio will drop to 1. In addition, the viability of many corporate plans is in doubt.

Clearly, anyone with a sizable retirement plan and/or IRA benefits should begin planning early in order to maximize the value of those benefits, by avoiding penalty taxes and taking advantage of beneficial tax treatments. In some cases, payment of taxes on appreciation in employer stock may be appropriate. However, most individuals would achieve greater value by a tax-free rollover to another qualified plan or IRA, which would further defer taxation on the amounts rolled over, thereby permitting additional tax deferred earnings.

The distribution of rollover IRA account balances can be planned to maximize the total value received by the individual, the individual's spouse, and their beneficiaries. In general, this planning entails delaying the start of distributions and stretching them out as long as possible under the IRS Code's minimum distribution rules.

Deferral of income taxes on retirement contributions and the accumulated earnings is the major benefit of qualified retirement plans and Individual Retirement Accounts (IRAs). Accordingly, if the money is not needed for living or other expenses, receipt of retirement benefits should be deferred as long as possible. Because retirement distribution rules are complex, however, professional assistance may be necessary to achieve the best results.

The *Internal Revenue Code* limits deferrals by requiring that minimum distributions be made by April 1 following the calendar year in which the client attains the age of 70-1/2, or if later, the year the participant terminates employment. In addition, minimum distributions for subsequent calendar years must be made *no later than the last day of each calendar year*. Usually, one should plan to avoid *doubling up* of the first-year and second-year payments in the same calendar year. These requirements are enforced with severe penalty—a 50 percent excise tax on minimum amounts not distributed on time.

Retirement planning, or planning for financial independence, is one of the key areas of personal financial planning. We work all our lives, expecting to earn the privilege of maintaining a desired lifestyle upon retirement. It is conceivable, however, that without proper planning, this retirement dream could turn into a nightmare. For instance, without proper planning and systematic directive actions, a retiree might not have an adequate income upon retirement. An accumulated capital fund might not last as long as both spouses live. Retirees might not make the right decisions with regard to: (1) tax-wise distribution of retirement funds; (2) picking the right retirement age; and (3) selecting the appropriate strategies for investing retirement funds.

In retirement planning, individuals first define their goals for quality of life after retirement. Next, they measure their ability to meet their goals and develop strategies for improving their performance. In the final analysis, success in retirement planning is assured if the individual is able to retire at the desired retirement age with the expected level of income.

This chapter is divided into four parts. First, an in-depth analysis of retirement income needs is undertaken. Then, distribution requirements and tax implications of retirement fund distribution are explored. Next, several methods of receiving retirement income are presented. Finally, several retirement planning strategies are discussed.

At this point it is necessary to make an important assumption. Any sophisticated discussion on retirement planning should take into consideration the differences in individuals planning for retirement, such as: (1) the financially sophisticated person; (2) the dual-career couple; (3) the highly compensated executive; (4) the owner of a professional practice; (5) the owner of a closely held business; and (6) the salaried employee. However, since such sophistication is beyond the scope of this book, in our discussions on retirement planning *we will treat all individuals as part of a homogeneous group*. While that will inevitably create distortions, by so doing we will be able to focus our attention on the major issues relating to retirement planning.

RETIREMENT INCOME NEEDS ANALYSIS

RETIREMENT BUDGET

The retirement income needs analysis begins with the construction of a realistic retirement budget, which involves the estimation of income and expenses during retirement years. We will now turn to the construction of such a retirement budget for a hypothetical family. John and Betty Jones are an average couple. John is a corporate employee and Betty is a dental hygienist. Both participate in corporate retirement plans. John is 40 and wishes to retire in 20 years. Betty is 30 but intends to retire with John.

Retirement Expenditure Analysis

We will begin with the Jones's current expenditures, which are presented in Table 11-1. These expenditures are strictly for the Jones family and do not necessarily represent either a national average or an ideal expenditure pattern. In fact, in analyzing retirement budgets it may be counterproductive for financial planners to make value judgments about their clients' expenditure patterns.

Once the current expenditures are recorded, our next task is to estimate the expenditures expected during retirement. There are, of course, no hard and fast rules for estimating these expenses. The accepted rule of thumb is that a retiree is likely to spend 60 or 70 percent of the preretirement expenditure level. This rule, however, appears too rigid and often misleading, because it does not specifically recognize the differences between (1) various categories of expenditures, and (2) people who aspire to maintain different—and richer—lifestyles after retirement.

A better approach to estimating expenditures during retirement is to divide fixed and flexible expenditures into several key categories and encourage the client to estimate the retirement expenditure in each category. This approach provides individuals with an opportunity to fine tune their retirement income estimates. For instance, Table 11-1 reveals that the Joneses plan to keep on making mortgage payments after retirement; consequently, after retirement their housing expenditures will remain virtually unchanged. For another family expecting to own a home free and clear before retirement, these expenses would be drastically reduced after retirement. Another area of interest is entertainment expenditure. Some families may wish to drastically reduce their entertainment expenses after retirement, while others may plan to spend a great deal more by undertaking world travels or developing other expensive hobbies like golf or scuba diving.

Returning to the Jones family, we find that after retirement the Joneses expect to spend $73,804 per year, which is 46.3 percent of their current expenditure.

Retirement Income

We now turn to an estimate of the retirement income for the Joneses. The family expects to receive an annual income of $55,800 from corporate and noncorporate qualified plans as well as from Social Security, as shown next:

Social Security	$10,200
Pension/Profit Sharing Plans	32,400
401(k) Plan	9,000
IRA Plan	4,200
	$55,800

The Social Security benefits can be calculated with the help of a Social Security pamphlet called *Estimating Your Social Security Retirement Check*. The company's benefits department can estimate the income from pension, profit sharing, and 401(k) plans. Annual income from IRA and Keogh plans can be calculated by estimating the value of each plan upon retirement and acquiring from a life insurance company the lifetime annuity value for the accumulated amount.

To sum up, at retirement, the Joneses expect to have annual expenses of $73,804, whereas their incomes from corporate and noncorporate qualified plans and Social Security are expected to be $55,800. The balance of $18,004 must come from personal investment to enable the family to meet its retirement goals.

The Potential Shortfall

Now that we have learned that the Joneses must receive $18,004 every year from personal investments in order to meet their retirement goal, we can determine if they can reasonably expect to meet this goal.

The analytical framework for calculating the savings required for retirement is presented in Table 11-2. In constructing this table we have made the following assumptions: (1) The Joneses' current personal, nonqualified savings amount to $85,954; (2) number of years to retirement is 20; and (3) both qualified and personal savings will grow at an inflation-adjusted real rate of three percent. As we can see, in this table line 3 confirms that after retirement the Joneses must receive an annual income of $18,004 from nonqualified investment sources.

We recall that John Jones is 40 and wishes to retire in 20 years. Assuming his life expectancy to be 80, the first step is to determine how much savings is required at the beginning of year 21 to generate $18,004 a year at the end of each year for 20 years. We calculate that amount to be $267,854:

$$PMT = 18,004$$
$$i = 3$$
$$n = 20$$
$$PV = 267,854$$

Next, we estimate the value of personal savings on the day of retirement. Currently, personal savings of the Joneses are $85,954 (line 5). If these savings grow at an after-tax, inflation-adjusted rate of return of three percent, the value of the savings in 20 years will be $155,242:

$$PV = 85,954$$
$$i = 3$$
$$n = 20$$
$$FV = 155,242$$

TABLE 11-1 Retirement Budget Estimate

Income/expenditures	Current year	At retirement
Current Income	$196,396	$55,800*
Expenditures		
Housing		
Rent, mortgage, property taxes, utilities (gas, oil, electricity and water), telephone, home furnishings, household services, maintenance, improvements	39,012	36,904
Clothing		
Purchases and cleaning	1,846	1,100
Food	7,800	8,000
Transportation		
Car repair and maintenance, installment payments, gas, commuting costs, etc.	3,854	1,200
Gifts	2,700	1,500
Contributions	4,188	1,500
Education, books, subscriptions	6,456	1,500
Insurance		
Life, medical, auto, property, liability	4,236	950
Medical and dental care		
Premiums, deductible and out-of-pocket costs	132	350
Loan-repayment costs	2,880	0
Personal care		
Grooming, health club, other	0	0
Entertainment		
Vacations, dining out, movies, plays, concerts, sports events, cable TV, videocassettes, entertaining, sports, hobbies, other	11,244	10,000
Domestic help	0	200
Savings and Retirement		
Contribution to company plans IRAs, Keoghs, SEPs, other savings	17,000	0
Taxes		
Federal, FICA, state, local	53,500	8,600
Miscellaneous	4,500	2,000
Total expenditure	159,348	73,804
Surplus(+)/deficit(−)	+ 37,048	− 18,004

* Expected income from corporate and noncorporate qualified plans, and Social Security and IRA plans.

TABLE 11-2 Determination of Savings Required for Retirement

Line 1	Annual budget after retirement		$ 73,804
Line 2	Annual distribution from:		
	a. Social Security	$10,200	
	b. Pension/profit sharing plans	32,400	
	c. 401(k) plan	9,000	
	d. Keogh plan		
	e. IRA plan	4,200	
	f. Total:		55,800
Line 3	Annual income needed from nonqualified Investments (#1 minus #2f)		18,004
Line 4	Savings required by retirement date, in current dollars PMT = 18,004, i = 3, n = 20, PV = 267,854		267,854
Line 5	Current personal savings		85,954
Line 6	Value of personal savings at retirement PV = 85,954, i = 3, n = 20, FV = 155,242		155,242
Line 7	Amount of savings required to cover the deficit (#4 minus #6)		112,612
Line 8	Savings required each year FV = 112,612, i = 3, n = 20, PMT = 4,191		4,191

Assumptions: 1. Current personal savings = $85,954
2. Years to retirement = 20
3. Inflation-adjusted real rate of return = 3%

We have determined that, at retirement, the Joneses need a total personal savings of $267,854 (line 4), whereas their expected savings would be only $155,242 (line 6). That is, the expected shortfall of savings is $112,612 (line 7). This shortfall can be met if each year the Joneses save an additional amount of $4,191 for 20 years and realize an after-tax, inflation-adjusted rate of return of three percent:

$$FV = 112,612$$
$$i = 3$$
$$n = 20$$
$$PMT = 4,191$$

An oversimplified framework for the retirement income shortfall is presented in Figure 11-1. This figure reveals that without additional savings the Joneses would experience an annual shortfall of $7,569 when they retire in 20 years. While the Joneses realize that the additional annual savings of $4,191 required to meet their retirement goal can quickly change with a change in the key variables (e.g., inflation rate or family situation), this analysis does provide them with a basis for effective retirement planning.

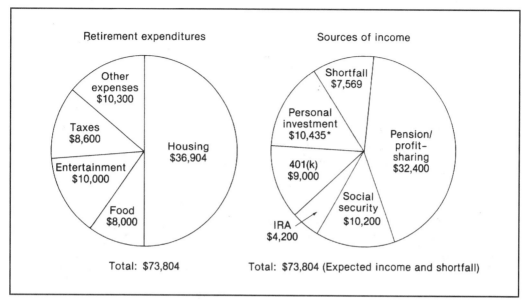

FIGURE 11-1   Retirement income needs analysis

Given the basic assumptions made in this example, the Joneses have four distinct options:

Option 1: They can retire on time if they manage to save an additional $4,191 per year and make it grow at a three percent after-tax real rate of return.

Option 2: Even if the Joneses cannot save additional funds, they still can conceivably meet their retirement goal if they succeed in having their savings grow at a rate faster than the three percent after-tax real rate assumed in the previous discussion.

Option 3: The Joneses can lower their retirement income goal.

Option 4: John Jones can extend his desired retirement age beyond age 60.

To recap, a potential shortfall in the retirement budget requires the development of specific strategies to solve the problem. These strategies can be conveniently divided into the following categories.

1. *Tax-Advantaged Investment Planning.* This strategy requires that the family consider the possibility of making the maximum contribution to their qualified plans and IRAs, if that is not currently being done.

2. *Savings Planning.* Increasing the amount of annual savings may entail a thorough examination, and eventual reduction, of current monthly expenses. A more austere budget may force the family to choose between nonessential current expenditures and a better standard of living at retirement.

3. *Asset Repositioning Planning.* A review of the existing investments may induce the family to shift the current portfolio into more aggressive investments if there are strong feelings about the desired level of

retirement income. Of course, if these planning strategies do not produce the desired results, the family would be forced to lower the desired retirement income or advance the retirement age, neither of which might offer an attractive alternative.

The Potential Surplus

Not every retirement plan has a potential shortfall. For instance, assume the Joneses wish to have annual retirement expenses of $73,804 (Table 11-2), but at retirement expect to receive an income of $75,800 instead of $55,800. In that case they will have a potential surplus in their retirement budget, and no further action will be necessary on their part.

DISTRIBUTION FROM QUALIFIED PLANS

INTRODUCTION

Qualified plans are subject to strict rules about when and how they can make distributions to participants. As a general rule, some deferral is required before employees can receive distributions. Also, employee contributions are generally subject to fewer restrictions than employer contributions. In addition to these general rules, however, there are specific rules which apply to different types of qualified plans. A description of various types of plans and the key distribution rules governing them is presented next.

PENSION PLANS

Pension plans are subjected to the most stringent distribution rules. Furthermore, within the pension plans, rules applying to defined benefit plans are stricter than those applicable to the defined contribution plans. As a general rule, the law allows distribution from a pension plan: (1) at retirement; (2) upon the attainment of normal retirement age; (3) upon the separation of service; (4) upon death; (5) in the event of permanent disability; or (6) upon the plan's termination.

PROFIT SHARING PLANS

The rules governing profit sharing plans are less restrictive than those governing pension plans. In general, distribution from a profit sharing plan is allowed: (1) upon the attainment of age 59-1/2; (2) when certain specified events like layoff, illness, disability, or termination of employment occur; or (3) after the passage of a prespecified time period.

OTHER QUALIFIED PLANS

Other types of qualified plans are subject to varying distribution rules. For instance, 401(k) plans cannot make the distributions because of the passage of time, but these plans can make distributions at retirement, death, disability, separation from service, or attainment of age 59-1/2. Also, because of hardship, these plans are allowed to distribute elective contributions, but not earnings on them. Obviously, these rules apply only to 401(k) plans. Other plans, such as thrift plans, ESOPs, SEPs, and so on are governed by a slightly different set of rules.

Employee contributions to various types of plans are not subject to the same restrictions as those imposed on employer contributions. However, a waiting period is generally imposed before employee contributions can be distributed.

REQUIRED DISTRIBUTIONS

All qualified plans are required to make compulsory distributions to the participating employees when certain conditions are met. Chief among these conditions is the participants' attaining age 70-1/2.

Minimum Distribution Rules

An overview. On January 11, 2001, the IRS released new regulations which significantly altered the method of calculating required minimum distributions (RMDs) for IRAs and other tax-favored retirement plans. Under the new regulation, most account holders will be able to take smaller distributions allowing for greater tax deferred growth, while the beneficiaries have been given greater flexibility in deferring distributions after an account holder's death.

To calculate RMDs under the current regulations, an account holder multiplies the fair market value (FMV) of the account as of the prior year-end by a factor obtained from the Uniform Life Expectancy Table (formerly known as the "MDIB table"). The calculation is made each year to determine a new RMD. The only time the Uniform Table is not used is when the account holder names a spouse as beneficiary and the spouse is more than ten years younger than the account holder. In this situation, the account holder is entitled to use a Joint Life Expectancy Table which would produce even lower RMDs.

The current regulations also provide benefits to non-spousal beneficiaries who inherit retirement plan benefits. IRAs can be split into separate IRAs following the account holder's death in order for multiple beneficiaries to use their own separate life expectancies for determining required distributions. If the division does not occur by the end of the year following the year of the account holder's death, or if a qualified trust is named as beneficiary, plan benefits will be paid over the oldest beneficiary's life expectancy. IRA beneficiaries are no longer forced to take lump sum distributions out of an IRA at an account holder's death simply because of the RMD options selected upon the account holder's required beginning date. The current regulations also allow for greater use of disclaimers to facilitate tax planning strategies.

In situations where a non-qualified trust, a charity, or an estate is named as beneficiary and an account holder dies before attaining age 70-1/2, plan benefits must be distributed in accordance with the old five-year rule. For account holders that die after age 70-1/2, benefits must be paid to the non-qualified trust, charity, or estate over the remaining term certain period of the account holder.

Defined benefit plans. Different rules apply for calculating required distributions from defined contribution plans, such as profit sharing and 401(k) plans, than for defined benefit plans. These rules generally anticipate that minimum distributions from defined contribution plans will be in the form of installment payments and that minimum distributions from defined benefit plans will be in the form of annuity payments. Previous rules governing annuity distributions from defined benefit plans are not substantially changed by the new regulations.

Defined contribution plans. The new method of calculating required distributions is similar to the old method—the payment amount is still calculated by dividing the participant's account balance at the end of the preceding calendar year by a life expectancy factor. What is different is the use of a single table of life expectancy factors based solely on the participant's current age. The required minimum distribution is the amount the participant must withdraw each year after reaching the required beginning date. The participant can always withdraw more than the required minimum.

Distributions to beneficiaries. Under the current regulations, different death benefit payment rules apply, depending on whether the participant dies before or after the required beginning date. Regardless of whether the employee's death occurs before or after the required beginning date, the beneficiary may receive the payments over the beneficiary's life expectancy, based on a single life expectancy table provided by the IRS.

The current rules permit the beneficiary (for life expectancy purposes) to be determined as late as the end of the calendar year following the year of the employee's death. This delay facilitates administration of situations where one or more beneficiaries cash out benefits or give up rights to the benefit in favor of another beneficiary by making a disclaimer before December 31 of the calendar year following the year of the participant's death.

Assume the participant designates his spouse as beneficiary and their children as contingent beneficiaries. After the participant's death, the spouse disclaims the benefit. The eldest child's life expectancy is used to calculate the required distributions to the children. Since the child has a longer life expectancy, the required distributions will be much lower.

In the event of death on or after the required beginning date, distributions must begin by the end of the calendar year following the calendar year of the participant's death and distributed over the oldest designated beneficiary's life expectancy determined as follows:

- *Nonspouse beneficiary:* based on the beneficiary's life expectancy using the age on his or her birthday in the calendar year following the calendar year in which the participant died, reduced by one year for each later year.

- *Spouse beneficiary:* If the spouse is the sole beneficiary, based on the spouse's life expectancy using the age of his or her birthday in the calendar year following the calendar year in which the participant died, redetermined each year based on the spouse's age falling in that year.

In the event of death before the required beginning date, since the participant dies before reaching the required beginning date, life expectancy payments for nonspouse and spouse beneficiaries as described above may be elected. The beneficiary may instead elect a five-year cash out under which the beneficiary must be paid the entire balance by December 31 of the year containing the fifth anniversary of the participant's death.

If the spouse is the sole beneficiary, distributions may also be postponed to December 31 of the year in which the participant would have reached age 70-1/2.

Failure to make distributions. If required distributions are not timely made, the participant must pay a 50 percent excise tax on the amount of the required distribution not made. Although the IRS does not always assess these severe penalties, plan administrators should take steps to ensure that required distributions are properly made.

TAXATION OF PLAN BENEFITS

The tax consequence of a distribution from a pension plan depends upon the mix of before-tax and after-tax dollars used to make the contributions. If the employer uses before-tax dollars to fund the entire cost of the retirement plan, upon distribution, qualified plan benefits to the recipients become fully taxable. However, if the employee made contributions to the plan with after-tax dollars, or was previously taxed on benefits, such as life insurance premiums, and the benefits represent both types of contributions, only that part of each distribution representing the employer's contribution becomes taxable. Of course, all earnings accumulated in a qualified plan on a tax-deferred basis are fully taxable as ordinary income.

Once the amount of distribution subject to taxation has been identified, the tax treatment of this amount would depend upon whether the distribution is taxed under the lump sum distribution rules or the annuity rules. The tax treatment under each method is discussed below.

Lump Sum Distribution

Although the law does not require them to do so, as an alternative to the annuity option, many qualified plans offer persons who have been participants for at least five tax years—the minimum required for lump sum distribution—a choice of receiving the money in the form of a lump sum distribution. Under IRS rules, employees favoring this option may choose between two methods of computing the tax: as part capital gain, or as all ordinary income subject to the ten-year forward averaging rule.

Capital gains treatment. The portion of a lump sum distribution attributable to employer contributions for service before 1974 is eligible for capital gains treatment. This treatment was phased out over a six-year period which began in 1987. But employees who attained age 50 before January 1, 1986, can choose to remain eligible for capital gains treatment.

Participants who choose the capital gains tax option are permitted to use 20 percent as the favorable tax rate to compute the tax separately on accumulations eligible for capital gains in their plan accounts.

Forward averaging. Participants of qualified plans can choose the alternative method of taxation known as forward averaging. For distributions after 1986, employees who attained age 50 before January 1, 1986 can elect to use the ten-year averaging method. However, in that case, they must use the tax rates in effect on December 31, 1986.

Annuity Distribution

The second option available to plan participants is to receive the distribution as an annuity. Distributions received as an annuity, less the return of the participant's cost basis, are taxed as ordinary income. This cost basis represents the contributions made by the employees with after-tax dollars and the previously taxed employer's contributions. Income tax consequences for annuities are discussed in a subsequent section.

Rollovers

It is possible to postpone the taxation of qualified plan benefits at the time of lump sum distribution. This is accomplished by rolling over within 60 days the total distribution into an IRA or into another qualified pension or profit sharing plan. The earnings will then continue to accumulate tax-deferred until withdrawals are made.

It is not necessary for a plan participant to roll over the entire retirement fund. However, partial distributions have several restrictions associated with them:

1. They can be rolled over only into an IRA *or* into another qualified plan.
2. The partial rollover is allowed only if the distribution is due to the participant's death, disability, separation from service, or the distribution is after a fixed number of years.
3. After a partial rollover, no part is eligible for ten-year averaging or capital gains treatment.

TAXATION OF IRAs

Earnings in the IRA accounts are tax-deferred until withdrawn; upon distribution, all earnings are taxed as ordinary income.

The rules governing the taxability of IRA contributions are a little more involved. If contributions were made with tax-deductible dollars, upon distribution these are fully taxed. Distributions attributable to nondeductible contributions are treated as a return of capital basis and are not taxable. Finally, if nondeductible and deductible contributions are made by the same individual, all distributions are apportioned between them.

TAXATION OF KEOGH PLANS

Since Keogh plans are for the self-employed, for such a plan there is no lump sum distribution after retirement. Consequently, the treatment is limited to distributions by reason of death, attaining age 59-1/2, or disability.

Keogh plan withdrawals must begin by April 1 of the year after a person reaches 70-1/2. If the participant is married, a minimum withdrawal is based upon the life expectancy of the individual and the spouse. According to the new rules mentioned earlier, all deductible Keogh contributions and earnings are taxed as ordinary income. However, nondeductible contributions are distributed tax-free.

As in the case with corporate plans, the ten-year forward averaging rule also applies to Keogh plans. However, a person can take advantage of a special tax break only once, whether it applies to a lump sum distribution from a Keogh plan or a corporate plan. Because of this limitation, depending on individual circumstances, it may be advisable to roll over the corporate lump sum payment into a Keogh plan if one is available. That way the ten-year forward averaging rule can be applied to the lump sum distributions from *both* plans.

OTHER TAX CONSIDERATIONS

Premature Distributions

If an individual makes a withdrawal from an IRA account prior to reaching age 59-1/2, an additional early withdrawal penalty of ten percent is imposed on the taxable portion of the withdrawal. Of course, this penalty is waived if the distribution is: (1) triggered by either death or disability; (2) used to purchase a single or joint lifetime annuity; (3) rolled over within 60 days into another IRA; (4) due to hardship; or (5) made to someone besides the participant under a qualified domestic relations order.

The ten percent penalty tax on early distribution is also imposed on qualified defined benefit and defined contributions plans, tax-sheltered annuities, SEPs, and custodial accounts. However, the exceptions to this additional tax are: (1) death; (2) disability; (3) single or joint lifetime annuity distributions; (4) distributions to employees who have attained age 55, separated from service, and who received the distributions as part of an early retirement arrangement; (5) distributions made to pay deductible medical expenses; (6) distributions of dividends from profit sharing or stock bonus plans; (7) distributions from ESOPs (employee stock option plans) that have been invested in employer securities for five years; and (8) made to a former spouse, child or other dependent of the participant under a qualified domestic relations order.

Excess Contributions

If contributions made to a qualified plan exceed the maximum allowed by law, the excess contribution is subject to a ten percent excise tax. In the case of an IRA, an individual can avoid paying this tax by withdrawing the excess from the IRA account before the deadline for the IRA contributions, which is April 15 of the year following the year for which the contribution is made.

The IRS provides a formula which can be used to determine how the *earnings* relating to the excess contributions to qualified plans must be withdrawn. Also, if the client is under 59-1/2 years of age, then the withdrawal of earnings is treated as a premature distribution and a ten percent penalty tax is imposed on them. Form 5329 is required to be filed distinguishing between the: (1) IRA earnings; (2) IRA distribution; and (3) the penalty tax. These steps are necessary to cover timely removal of the excess contributions.

Insufficient Distributions

When an individual reaches age 70-1/2, the law requires that compulsory minimum distributions from qualified plans, tax-deferred annuity plans, IRAs, SEPs, and governmental deferred compensation plans begin in one of the following forms: (1) full distribution; (2) minimum distribution; or (3) individual or joint and survivor annuity. If the actual distribution falls short of the minimum required distribution, there is a penalty tax of 50 percent on the shortfall. This shortfall represents the difference between the amount that has been calculated as the minimum distribution and the amount actually distributed from the plan.

RETIREMENT INCOME: THE ULTIMATE DECISION

INTRODUCTION

As retirement age draws near, every individual is faced with the dilemma: How can one make a rational decision on the most efficient means of distribution of qualified money? As revealed by Figure 11-2, the major sources of retirement income consist of income from personal investment, corporate sponsored qualified plans, Keogh plans for self-employed income earners, IRAs, and Social Security. Of these, personal investment income will be discussed in detail in Chapters 12, 13 and 14 and need not be repeated here. The rest of the choices will be discussed in this section. Also, since there is little difference between corporate sponsored qualified plans and Keogh plans insofar as distribution of retirement income is concerned, no distinction will be made between them.

Company Sponsored Qualified Plan and Keogh Plan

There are three principal ways in which an individual can withdraw retirement money: an annuity, lump sum distribution, or IRA rollover. At stake is the bulk of the retirement wealth. Furthermore, since the choices open to the retiree are almost always irrevocable, and the outcomes of the distribution decisions are vastly different, great care should be exercised in making this important decision. We will now discuss in detail each of the three key distribution choices available to a retiree.

Annuity

The annuity principle. Life insurance enables an individual to purchase a contract providing a definite sum of money at the time of death. Such contracts are possible because the mortality of a large group of individuals can be predicted with reasonable accuracy.

A different problem, however, faces the individual who has accumulated a sum of money and wants to determine how much can be safely spent each year during lifetime so he or she will not run out of money. If the money is spent too rapidly, some day the funds will be exhausted—possibly with several years of life remaining. In contrast, if the funds are disbursed too slowly, at the time of death a portion of the funds will be left, money that could have been used to maintain a higher standard of living.

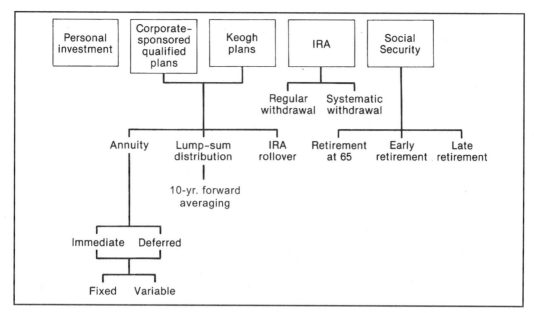

FIGURE 11-2 Major sources of retirement income

Confronted with this problem, no one person can be certain as to what sum can be *safely* spent each month. However, this uncertainty does not apply to a large group. Through the use of mortality tables, in return for the payment of a lump sum or a series of payments, insurance companies can make *guaranteed life-income payments* to various individuals, because the mortality rates of each group can be predicted with reasonable accuracy. Put differently, the greater total sums paid to those who live to unusually advanced ages can be balanced by the smaller payments made to those who die relatively early. Such payments are called annuities.

The word *annuity* implies payments made by an insurance company at fixed intervals, such as monthly, quarterly, or yearly. When a life insurance policy is purchased, payments are made to the insurance company during the policyholder's lifetime, and the company pays a stipulated amount when the policyholder dies. With an annuity, an individual pays a given sum to the insurance company, and in return receives an income according to various options (discussed below). An annuity contract, therefore, is essentially the reverse of a life insurance policy, although it is *not* an insurance policy.

Under the classic, or original, type of annuity, the income ceases with the death of the annuitant, and the insurance company is under no further obligation. Fortunately, however, many important variations of the original type are available in the marketplace today, as revealed in Figure 11-3. This figure reveals that annuity contracts vary according to how the payment for the annuity is made, how the proceeds are distributed, how earnings accrue, and when the benefits are received by the annuitant or beneficiary. Of these features, disposition of proceeds is of special interest for the individual planning to retire.

It might be interesting to think of an annuity as a *liquidating* retirement payment plan, illustrated in Figure 11-4. Assume Betty Jones retires at age 65 with an after-tax lump sum distribution of $100,000. She purchases an annuity

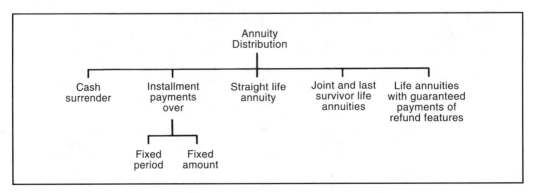

FIGURE 11-3 Forms of Annuities

which guarantees an income for 20 years. During this 20-year period, in addition to receiving her principal of $100,000, Betty will receive an additional $10,185 representing the return on the principal in the form of dividends and interest. Put differently, the monthly income received by Betty will consist of interest, dividends, and a portion of the original investment. Consequently, at the end of the 20-year period, the entire investment will have been liquidated and the company will owe nothing to Betty Jones.

Disposition of proceeds. Various options available under an annuity plan, which were briefly discussed in Chapter 4, are presented in Figure 11-5. The figure reveals that the annuity can be either *fixed* or *variable*. The former refers to an annuity contract which promises a fixed return during the life of the contract and is therefore not dependent upon the results of the vehicle in which the money is invested. However, typically the return is fixed on an annual basis (with a minimum guaranty of four percent) so the fixed return can—and often does—vary from year to year. In contrast, a variable annuity is a form of contract that is invested in one or several mutual fund portfolios. In this case, payments can vary in size, depending upon the rate of return on the portfolios selected. In both cases, the options available to the annuitant are identical, although generally the amount of the annuity payments will vary—sometimes greatly—between the two methods of payment. We will now discuss the key choices available to an annuitant.

- *Life only* pays for the annuitant's lifetime and pays nothing to the surviving spouse or other heirs.
- *Joint and survivor* pays a reduced amount to the annuitant during his or her lifetime and then continues 100 percent, 66-2/3 percent, or 50 percent of the original sum over the remaining lifetime of the surviving joint annuitant. Payments stop after the death of the annuitant *and* the joint annuitant, and the company owes nothing to the beneficiaries.
- *Joint and survivor period certain* promises that payments will continue for at least the minimum (for instance, ten, 15, or 20 years) guaranteed period even if the annuitant (or both annuitants) dies during this period. If the annuitant survives longer than the specified period, the annuity continues to pay the same amount until death. Joint plus survivor period certain is a variant of life period certain in that payments are made at least for a specified period or until the death of both parties.

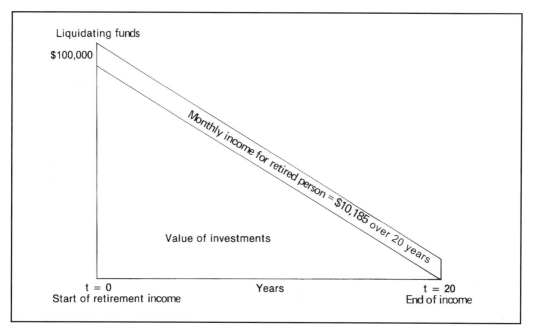

Liquidating funds

$100,000

Monthly income for retired person = $10,185 over 20 years

Value of investments

t = 0
Start of retirement income

Years

t = 20
End of income

FIGURE 11-4 Liquidating retirement payout plan

- *Life period certain* pays the annuitant for as long as the annuitant lives, or a minimum number of payments, whichever is longer.

Tax Treatment of Annuity Payments

Each annuity payment represents a combination of the return of principal and interest on the principal. If the principal has already been taxed, it is not taxed again when the payment is received. The following table illustrates how the payments are spread out over the life of the annuity.

Age on Annuity Starting Date	Number of Anticipated Payments
Not more than 55	360
More than 55 but not more than 60	310
More than 60 but not more than 65	260
More than 65 but not more than 70	210
More than 70	160

Variable Annuity. Under the variable form of annuity payments, the monthly payments are made from a variable account which fluctuates on the basis of investment results. As such, the expected return cannot be accurately determined in advance. Therefore, Treasury regulations make the assumption that the expected return is equal to the investment in the contract. The excludable portion of each payment is calculated by dividing the investment in the contract by the anticipated number of months times the monthly payout. Assume the monthly payout of a five-year variable annuity is $990.02 and the initial lump sum payment is $50,000. In this case the $50,000 investment would be divided by the five years of payout [$50,000/($990.02 x 12 x 5) = 84.17%] and 84.2 percent of each monthly

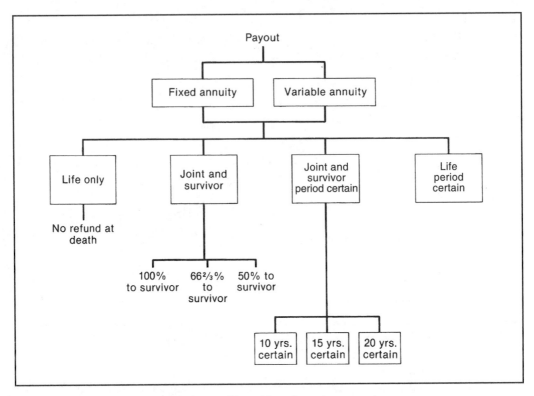

FIGURE 11-5   Disposition of annuity proceeds

payment of $990.02, or $833.30, would be excluded from gross income. Essentially, the tax treatment is the same for both fixed and variable annuities.

The best choice. Clearly, the best choice of an annuity option depends upon the objective of the annuitant and the total amount of retirement income expected to be received from other sources. Individuals who wish to receive a guaranteed income for life to supplement Social Security and other investment income should choose either the life only or joint and survivor option, possibly with a minimum period of guaranty of ten or 15 years. However, those who have other sources of income and wish to use up the lump sum in a relatively short period of time may choose a guaranteed income for, say, five or ten years.

Finally, if the retiree can assume the market risk, a variable annuity should be considered, because there is a potential for growth in this type of annuity.

Lump Sum Distribution

An overview. One of the valuable options available to most retirees is to receive the nest egg in one lump sum instead of as an annuity. If a decision is made to receive the lump sum, then the retiree comes to the second crossroad: whether to pay the tax on the lump sum right away or to postpone the tax by rolling over the money into an IRA. If the latter decision is made, the money must be directly transferred or rolled over into an IRA within 60 days. If the first choice is preferred, however, the employee must resort to a rather sophisticated tax planning strategy, as described next.

Forward averaging option. With the exception of IRAs, SEPs, and 403(b) plans, distributions from qualified funds receive a special tax treatment provided they meet certain eligibility requirements. For a plan to be eligible, a distribution must be of the *entire* account balance, made within one taxable year, on account of retirement, or upon death or disability. In addition, to be eligible, the participant is required to be in the plan for at least five years. Finally, the participant must be 59-1/2 or older; otherwise a ten percent penalty could be imposed on the distribution.

Effective January 1, 2000, the law has disallowed five-year averaging for lump sum distributions from qualified plans. But the crackdown does not affect plan members who reached age 50 before 1986. Ten-year averaging will continue to be available as under prior law.

People who participated in their employer's pension plan before 1974 have yet another option. They can elect to have the portion of the sum attributable to the pre-1974 contributions taxed as capital gains at the top 1986 rate of 20 percent. Taxpayers in this category can then use ten-year forward averaging for the remainder of their payout.

The ten-year forward averaging method requires taking the following steps:

Step 1: Divide total distribution by 10.

Step 2: Add $2,480 to this amount.

Step 3: Compute tax on this total by using 1986 (not current) single taxpayer rates (even if the retiree files joint returns).

Step 4: Multiply the tax calculated in Step 3 by 10.

IRA Rollover

The third distribution option is to directly transfer or roll over the funds into an IRA within 60 days of receiving the lump sum distribution. With a rollover IRA the retiree avoids paying current taxes on the distribution. Instead, taxes are paid when money is withdrawn. The advantage in choosing this option is that no penalties are imposed for the rollover and the individual can choose how the money is invested through a self-directed IRA account. Most important, the entire distribution continues to grow tax-deferred over the life of the IRA. A disadvantage of this option is that all IRA conditions are imposed on such rollovers.

LUMP SUM VERSUS IRA: A TAXING DECISION

The discussion undertaken in the previous section underscored an important point: To choose between a lump sum distribution and an IRA transfer or rollover is a taxing decision. There is no clear choice and the best alternative depends on a host of tax-related factors, as revealed in the following discussion.

Let us examine the case of John and Betty Jones, both of whom were 65 and were set to retire on December 30, 2000. John's employer offered to make a monthly payment of $2,000 to him for life or pay him a $250,000 lump sum. These choices with related data are presented in Table 11-3. Receiving the annuity would shrink the annual income of $24,000 ($17,280 after taxes, assuming a 28 percent tax bracket) to $10,608 in 2000 dollars by the time John reaches 75 if inflation were to run at a 5 percent a year annual rate ($FV = \$17,280$, $i = 5$, $n = 10$, $PV = 10,608$).

If John Jones chose to receive the lump sum, he would have many investment options open to him for the retirement fund. Let us examine the two choices presented in Table 11-3.

The first choice relates to the payment of federal income tax by using the preferential treatment under the ten-year forward averaging rule. John's CPA has determined that the tax (2000) on the $250,000 lump sum distribution would be $50,770, so the *net* amount of distribution would be $199,230 ($250,000 – $50,770).

Next, John contacts his financial planner and asks him to recommend a municipal bond fund which would permit him to withdraw tax-free $17,280 per year—the same income he would receive under the lifetime annuity plan. John further specifies that his annual withdrawals should increase by five percent, so his income would keep up with the expected annual inflation rate of five percent. That is, during the tenth year, at age 75, John would receive $28,147, which would have the purchasing power of $17,280 in today's dollars. Finally, John asks his financial planner to ascertain how much money would be left in the fund if he were to die at, say, age 75, assuming the mutual fund maintains its historical track record. The information supplied by the financial planner is summarized in Table 11-3.

A comparison of the results achieved by selecting the annuity option and the lump sum with ten-year forward averaging reveals the following interesting facts: (1) The income under the lump sum choice keeps up with inflation, whereas the annuity income is not protected against inflation. (2) If death occurs at age 75, John's heirs will receive a significant amount of money under the second choice ($87,552), whereas they would receive nothing if the annuity choice was selected. (3) Although not shown in the table, it is conceivable that at some point (say, around age 80) the money under the second choice would run out, whereas under lifetime annuity John could never outlive his annuity income.

Table 11-3 reveals that John could also transfer or roll over the total lump sum amount of $250,000 into an IRA, and immediately start withdrawing the desired after-tax annual income of $17,280. In this case John would not have to pay tax upon distribution. But if the money is invested in a fully taxable corporate bond fund, John would have to withdraw every year $24,000 to net an after-tax income of $17,280 ($24,000 – 28% x $24,000), assuming John continues to be in the 28 percent marginal federal income tax bracket. When compared with the first two choices, this last option offers the best alternative.

TABLE 11-3   Retirement Distribution Choices

Option	Initial tax	Net sum invested	at age 65*	at age 75*	at age 75**
Pension (Annuity)	$0	$0	$17,280	$10,608	$0
Lump sum with 10-year averaging	50,770	199,230	17,280	17,280	87,552
IRA rollover with immediate withdrawals	0	250,000	17,280	17,280	148,759

  * In after-tax 2000 dollars, assuming inflation of 5% a year.
 ** Assuming the mutual fund performance matches its historical record.

Before leaving this topic, an important caveat should be added. Besides the three choices presented here, John and Betty have other important choices which should be explored before making the final decision. More important, even the best choice under one set of circumstances could turn out to be the worst under a different set of circumstances. For instance, if John lives to age 100, the lifetime annuity, which appears to be the worst choice, would turn out to be his best option. Consequently, care should be exercised in making sure that the client clearly understands all the underlying assumptions before making the final decision.

To recap, the decision to annuitize, take a lump sum distribution and invest, or transfer or roll over into an IRA, must be made on an individual basis. In addition to examining the numbers, in those cases where the retirees cannot be expected to manage their own funds and need the assurance of an uninterrupted flow of current income until death, the annuity route may provide the best alternative. However, people who can afford to have their investment managed by a professional should either take a lump sum distribution or roll it over into an IRA, depending upon their current and future tax situation.

IRA DISTRIBUTION

The distribution rules from IRA funds are straightforward. At the lower end, except in the case of death or disability, any distribution prior to age 59-1/2 is subject to a ten percent early withdrawal penalty. At the upper end, the individual's funds in the account must be distributed starting no later than age 70-1/2. If not paid in a lump sum, the payments must be distributed over a period that does not exceed the life expectancy of the individual or of the individual and the spouse, if the individual is married. If the individual, or the individual and the spouse, die before receiving the entire amount, unless the five-year method is especially elected, the current rules allow ongoing required minimum distributions to be based on the life expectancy of the designated beneficiary with the shortest life expectancy.

It should now be obvious that, subject to the restrictions just specified, an individual is free to choose any suitable distribution method for the IRA funds. However, purely for illustrative purposes, we will present here only two methods which are frequently used by IRA fund owners.

Systematic Withdrawal: Personal Investment

Let us take the case of John Klein. At age 45 he started investing $2,000 at the beginning of every year into an IRA investment which grew at an annual rate of ten percent. Now, 20 years later, the IRA investment has grown to $126,005 ($PMT = 2,000$, $i = 10$, $n = 20$). Now that John is retired he decides to start receiving, say, $500 per month from his IRA investment. Also, since the long-term inflation rate is expected to be around six percent, John wants his initial monthly income of $500 to increase by six percent every year so he could maintain the purchasing power of the monthly income at the current level. After some investigation John has identified the ABC stock mutual fund which has consistently generated a long-term annual return of ten percent. Satisfied with this record, John invests $126,005 into ABC stock mutual fund and simultaneously sets up a systematic withdrawal plan. Through this plan John will achieve his retirement objective of receiving an inflation-adjusted monthly income of $500 (that is, income increasing at six percent every year), and his IRA funds will hopefully last beyond John's 90th birthday.

Systematic Withdrawal: Insurance Plan

In the second illustration, we assume that John Klein, age 65, has decided to withdraw $126,005 from an IRA fund and invest it in a systematic withdrawal plan with ABC Insurance Company. In this case, the ABC Company guarantees that John will initially receive $524.99 per month, or $6,299.89 during the first year. However, the annual income John receives will increase every year to a peak of $18,732.42 at age 85. Furthermore, even though John is receiving annual payments, the funds in the annuity will continue to exceed $126,005 through age 84.

To sum up, the systematic withdrawal plan selected by an IRA investor can be tailor-made to suit the family's needs. A wide variety of options is currently available, and possibly with external assistance, a withdrawal plan can be selected to achieve the family's stated objectives.

SOCIAL SECURITY BENEFITS

For purposes of receiving Social Security benefits, the current normal retirement age is 65. However, retirement age will increase in steps for workers born in 1938 and later years. For workers who reach 62 in year 2022, that is, those born in 1960 or later, the retirement age is 67. Social Security benefits expected to be received at the normal retirement age were discussed in detail in Chapter 10 and need not be repeated here.

In order to derive the maximum retirement benefit, the decision to start Social Security benefits at retirement, at age 62, or after the normal retirement age, should be coordinated with distribution from qualified plans and IRAs. Also, the taxability of Social Security benefits should be taken into account in making this decision.

RETIREMENT PLANNING STRATEGIES

In this concluding section we will analyze several basic strategies which can be used to accomplish a variety of retirement planning objectives.

LOANS FROM QUALIFIED PLANS

Loans within limits are permitted by qualified plans to all employees. According to the current rules, an owner-employee of five percent shareholder may qualify for a "prohibited transaction" exemption relating to loans from plan participants if the Department of Labor approves a special exemption.

As a general rule, loans must be repaid within five years in equal payments at least quarterly over the term of the loan, except for loans used to acquire a principal residence of the participant. Also, the $50,000 maximum loan limit on exempt loans must be reduced by the highest outstanding loan balance during the immediately preceding 12 months.

Following the passage of TRA of 1986, the rules for taking out loans from qualified plans significantly changed. Today, the advisability of borrowing from a plan depends on the individual's tax bracket, the time of contribution to the plan, and the type of the company savings plan from which the individual intends to borrow the money.

The pros and cons of withdrawals and loans from the three most popular types of retirement plans are presented in Table 11-4. In general, withdrawing money from a company plan makes sense only if it is an after-tax account and the employee is taking out money contributed before 1987. The reason is that money invested after 1986 in an after-tax plan must include a prorated portion of the employee's account's earnings, and, if the money was matched, employer contributions. For instance, assume an employee withdraws $1,000 from an after-tax plan in which he or she has a $10,000 balance: $7,000 from the employee's own post-1986 contributions, and $3,000 from earnings and the employer's contributions. Of the money the employee takes out, $700 would be considered a non-taxable withdrawal of after-tax contributions and $300 will be taxed at the employee's bracket. In addition, if the employee is under age 59-1/2, a ten percent penalty on $300 would be imposed on the withdrawal.

Withdrawing from a 401(k) plan may be a viable alternative, but the employee must prove that financial hardship is the basis for the withdrawal. Still, all withdrawals are taxable and a ten percent penalty is imposed if the person is under age 59-1/2 except when the money is used to pay for unreimbursed medical expenses exceeding 7.5 percent of the person's AGI.

Taking out a loan from a qualified plan may be a better alternative than withdrawal, since no tax or penalty is imposed on a loan. As Table 11-4 indicates, the maximum amount that can be borrowed at any time is the lesser of: (1) $50,000 minus the highest outstanding loan balance over the previous 12 months; or (2) half of the invested plan balance or $10,000, whichever is greater.

In deciding whether to borrow from a qualified plan an employee must take both loan costs and deductibility of interest into account. In general, most plan loans charge an interest rate equal to one or two percentage points higher than the prevailing prime rate. Incidentally, consumer interest paid on a loan from a qualified plan is not deductible from individual federal taxes.

PENSION ENHANCEMENT STRATEGY

We have learned that one of the distribution options of a retiree is to choose the joint and survivor annuity. This option continues to pay the spouse a stated percentage of the original monthly benefit (including 100 percent) after the death of the annuitant. However, this option generates a lower monthly payment than the life only option. An interesting alternative is to choose the life only option, and purchase an appropriate amount of cash value insurance policy with the higher monthly payout to duplicate the benefits of the joint and survival option.

An example should make this clear. Let us suppose John Quinn, age 55, intends to retire at age 62. His wife, Jane, is age 50. If upon John's retirement they select a joint and survival payout option that pays Jane 75 percent of their initial benefit at John's death, their annual retirement income while both are alive will be $26,671. If they select a life only option their annual income will be $31,452—an increase of $4,781 per year.

TABLE 11-4   Withdrawals and Loans From Qualified Plans

Type of plan	*Withdrawals*		*Loans*	
	Restrictions	*Taxes*	*Maximum amount permissible*	*Deductibility of interest*
After-tax savings	A company may limit the number of withdrawals or prohibit an employee from making future contributions for a certain period of time.	Withdrawals of an employee's contributions are tax-free. Earnings and company contributions are taxable and have a 10% penalty if the employee is under 59-1/2. Withdrawals of contributions made after 1986 are partly subject to tax and a 10% penalty for those 59-1/2 or younger.	Companies that permit loans allow the employee to borrow the lesser of (1) $50,000 minus highest outstanding loan balance over the past 12 months, or (2) half of the vested balance over $10,000, whichever is greater.	None
401(k)	If under age 59-1/2, withdrawals are permitted for financial hardship and like profit sharing plans, funds can be withdrawn in the event of (1) termination of employment, (2) death or disability, or (3) attainment of age 59-1/2.	In addition to regular taxes, the employee must pay the 10% penalty on the amount withdrawn if under age 59-1/2.	Most companies impose the same limits as the ones on loans from after-tax plans.	None
Employee stock ownership	Few companies permit withdrawals. There is no assurance as to the frequency and amount of employee contributions, and the employer may not be financially able to repurchase the stock, even though required to do so.	Regular taxes are due upon liquidation.	Loans are seldom permitted.	None

First, we calculate the benefit of this strategy by multiplying the increase in pension income by John's life expectancy in retirement. We then estimate that $200,000 will replace Jane's survival pension benefit. This figure is arrived at taking 75 percent of the initial payout of $26,671, or $20,003, and capitalizing it at ten percent. The benefits can range from $30,000 to $89,000 over the life of the plan.

The pension enhancement plan presents an interesting retirement strategy. However, it does not provide a panacea for all annuity problems, since the outcome can change dramatically in other family situations.

SOCIAL SECURITY TAXES

For single individuals with annual incomes of less than $25,000 and married couples filing a joint return with annual incomes of less than $32,000, Social Security payments are not taxable. For incomes higher than these amounts, as much as 85 percent of Social Security income could become taxable. A base amount of zero is used for a married person filing separately if the taxpayer lived with his or her spouse at any time during the year.

Let us recall that any income over $32,000 triggers a Social Security tax for a married couple filing a joint return. For instance, suppose Bob and Jane Smith earned $40,000 from various sources. Since this income is above the $32,000 threshold, $8,000 of the Social Security income will be included with taxable income. However, if the Smiths shift their municipal bond investment into a tax-deferred investment, like a single premium deferred annuity, then the interest income from this annuity would not be included in the calculation, with the result that their taxable income might drop to below $44,000, in which case the Social Security income would completely escape taxation.

EARLY RETIREMENT

Preparing for early retirement takes extensive time and planning. Not everyone, however, has such luxury. If an employer makes an early retirement offer, the employee may only have a few weeks to make the decision to accept or reject it. This is not as farfetched as it may seem. Many companies have in recent years made such offers to their employees.

The early retirement question has two distinct dimensions: psychological and financial. Before accepting such an offer, or voluntarily deciding to retire early, one should frankly ask the following question: Am I ready to retire? If the answer is negative, or if there are lingering doubts, then the idea of early retirement should be abandoned.

Assuming that the psychological issue has been satisfactorily resolved, the financial dimension should be handled by undertaking a preliminary review of the following three key areas.

Pensions

The terms of pension payments should be explored. As a general rule, an early retirement offer should pay a pension equal to, or greater than, the amount one would receive under normal retirement. In some cases, employers calculate the benefit by adding on three to five years to the employee's age or tenure. Both types of offers can increase the pension by as much as 30 percent over the expected normal pension income.

Health Insurance

The COBRA law, passed in 1986, requires employers with more than 20 employees to continue group health insurance coverage (excluding dental insurance) at the employee's expense for up to 18 months after retirement or up to 36 months for employees who are divorced or whose retirement plans have been terminated. It is important to determine the cost and availability (regarding preexisting conditions or current health conditions) of buying individual health insurance after group coverage runs out.

Life Insurance

An early retirement may require switching from the company's group life policy to an individual policy. The cost of such a policy may run around $400 a year per $10,000 of coverage. The employer may also offer a decreasing term policy; the benefit would shrink each year and virtually disappear at age 70.

SPECIAL SPOUSAL BENEFIT

A special retirement planning strategy can be used to help a small business owner who has no other employees. This strategy involves an increase in the maximum allowable contribution to a defined benefit plan when the client's spouse is unemployed and has never participated in a defined contribution plan of the employer. In such a situation it is possible to pay the spouse a minimum salary and fund the plan to provide a $10,000-a-year retirement benefit. In order to make it a viable strategy, the business owner must provide justification that the spouse is active in the business.

NONQUALIFIED DEFERRED COMPENSATION PLAN

Certain individuals can draw on payments from a nonqualified deferred compensation plan as an additional source of retirement income. This type of arrangement is nonqualified because the company chooses to benefit a selected group of employees without regard to the anti-discrimination rules of qualified plans. A deferred compensation plan is documented by an agreement between the company and the selected employee. The essence of the agreement is that the company promises to pay the employee for currently performed services at some future date. This type of arrangement is attractive to highly compensated employees because considerable income tax savings could be realized by deferring the receipt of income to retirement years, when it might be taxed at lower rates.

Incidentally, deferred compensation can be tied to an insurance policy. If the employee dies before retirement, proceeds from the policy would be used to pay the death benefit. If the employee reaches retirement age, the company may wish to keep the policy in effect and make payments to the employee out of the accumulated cash value.

Another strategy relates to Rabbi trusts which are irrevocable trusts used to fund nonqualified deferred compensation plans. If properly structured, these trusts may provide a measure of security for the assets in executive deferred compensation plans because the employer does not have access to the assets. However, because the trust's assets are subject to claims of the employer's creditors, the funding of the trust does not constitute a taxable event for the employee.

PLANNING FOR RETIREMENT: ADDITIONAL CONSIDERATIONS

Deferral of income taxes on retirement contributions and the earnings thereon is the major advantage of qualified retirement plans and IRAs. Accordingly, if the money is not needed for living or other expenses, receipt of retirement benefits should be deferred as long as possible. Also, because retirement distribution rules are complex, professional assistance may be necessary to achieve the best results.

The *Internal Revenue Code* limits deferrals by requiring that minimum distributions must begin for the calendar year in which age 70-1/2 is attained and be paid *no later than April 1 of the following year*, and by prescribing how to calculate those minimum amounts. In addition, minimum distributions for subsequent calendar years must be made *no later than the last day of each calendar year*. Usually, one should plan to avoid *doubling up* of the first-year and second-year payments in the same calendar year.

Minimum distribution requirements are enforced with severe penalty—a 50 percent excise tax is imposed on minimum amounts not distributed on time.

Early Planning Needed

Anyone with a sizable retirement plan and/or IRA benefits should begin planning early in order to maximize the value of those benefits. The early planning strategy should strive to avoid penalty taxes and take advantage of beneficial tax treatments. In some cases, payment of current taxes using ten-year averaging or deferral of taxes on appreciation in employer stock may be appropriate. However, most individuals would achieve greater value by a tax-free rollover to another qualified plan or IRA, which would further defer taxation on the amounts rolled over and permit additional tax deferred earnings.

The distribution of rollover IRA account balances can be planned to maximize the total value received by the individual, the individual's spouse, and their beneficiary. In general, this planning entails delaying the start of distributions and stretching them out as long as possible under the minimum distribution rules.

Minimum Distribution Rules

One of the biggest outcomes of the Tax Reconciliation Act of 2001 is that no irrevocable elections take place at age 70-1/2 anymore. The required beginning date (RBD) is still April 1 of the year following the year in which age 70-1/2 is attained; however, nothing is locked at that point.

Only one method for calculating RMDs exists, with one exception. Everyone's RMD is calculated based upon the Minimum Distribution Incidental Benefit (MDIB) life expectancy factor table. Each year, the minimum distribution amount is recalculated on the basis of a new factor based on the IRA owner's age even if the IRA owner has no beneficiary. The only exception to this method occurs when a spouse is more than ten years younger than the IRA owner *and* is the sole beneficiary. In this situation, the joint life expectancy of the IRA owner and spouse may be used. With the uniform payout schedule, the existence of a designated beneficiary no longer plays a role in the calculation of lifetime RMDs.

Determination of the designated beneficiary for post-death RMDs is made on December 31 of the year following the year of the account holder's death. Beneficiaries that disclaim their interest, or take a distribution of their entire interest prior to that date, are not considered when determining the designated beneficiary whose life expectancy will be used for RMD calculations.

Unless otherwise elected, the default payout method in instances where the account owner dies before the RBD is now the life expectancy method. This means that annual distributions must be made based on the life expectancy of the designated beneficiary unless the five-year method is specifically elected. These distributions must begin by December 31 of the year following the year of the account holder's death.

Spouses who do not elect to treat the deceased owner's account as their own may take distributions based upon their recalculated life expectancy. In such an instance, if the spouse dies, distributions may continue over any remaining life expectancy, as determined according to the nonrecalculation method, starting with the recalculated life expectancy of the spouse in the year of death.

A nonspouse beneficiary may take distributions based upon his or her nonrecalculated single life expectancy as determined in the year following the year of death. If the account holder dies after his or her RBD, but does not have a designated beneficiary with a life expectancy within a year after the year of death, then distributions may be calculated based upon the single life expectancy of the account holder as determined in the year of death and reduced by one (nonrecalculated method) in each subsequent year.

COMBO STRATEGY

Basic Structure

A creative strategy, called the Combo Strategy, exists in the area of retirement planning. The traditional strategy involving annuities provides a guaranteed income for life, but it suffers from three major drawbacks. First, the annuity is a fixed monthly payment, so inflation erodes its purchasing power over time. Second, if death comes early, annuitants do not get their money's worth because annuity payments stop upon death. Third, annuities are designed to completely exhaust the capital at the completion of the annuity period, or in the case of a life time annuity, upon the death of the annuitant. Therefore, a better alternative is to use a Combo Strategy that uniquely combines the strengths of annuities and growth investments. The Combo Strategy involves a six-step process, as discussed next.

Step 1. Begin with an estimate of the client's monthly budget. The budget should include not only the client's fixed and flexible expenses but also an amount for emergencies and an allowance for "play money." Let us assume that the client's estimated monthly budget is $5,000.

Step 2. Call the Social Security Administration to obtain the client's monthly Social Security income. It will vary from one family to another, depending upon the starting age, single or joint income, and so on. Assume the client's monthly Social Security income will be $1,400.

Step 3. Instruct the client's employer to transfer the lump sum directly from the pension plan to an IRA with a money-market mutual fund that can serve as a temporary shelter for the money until it is decided as to how to invest the funds.

Requesting that the employer transfer the funds directly to a mutual fund trustee avoids the need to have 20 percent of the distribution amount withheld for taxes. Assume the lump sum due to the client is $1 million

Step 4. Calculate the shortfall in budget by subtracting from the client's estimated budget expenses, Social Security income and any other guaranteed income (such as railroad or military pensions) the client might have. Assuming no additional income, in this case the deficit is $3,600 ($5,000 – $1,400).

Next, shop around for the highest monthly annuity income the client can purchase from an insurance company that is rated at least A by two rating agencies. If shopping is done carefully, it might be possible to purchase a monthly annuity of $3,600 for, say, $600,000. That would leave the balance of $400,000 ($1 million – $600,000) for growth investment.

Step 5. At this point the assistance of an investment manager should be sought in setting up an investment portfolio that would be growth-oriented and would carry the degree of risk acceptable to the client. This portfolio should coordinate the balance of the lump sum distribution with other qualified money [IRA, 401(k), 403(k)] and personal investment. If the portfolio is diversified by investing in national and international stocks, Treasury and corporate bonds, and liquid investments, and it is managed by a professional manager for a reasonable fee, over a five-to-fifteen year period the client might reasonably expect to earn an average annual return of 10-12 percent.

Step 6. The client should plan on withdrawing from this portfolio if and when funds are needed to keep up with inflation. In addition, the client should not lose sight of the fact that at age 70-1/2 the retiree must begin minimum compulsory distribution from the portion of investment that represents IRA or other qualified funds.

Concluding Remarks

The Combo Strategy just described is merely one of many options available to a client. For instance, if the client does not need to receive a guaranteed monthly annuity income in order to be able to sleep well at night, the annuity route could be skipped altogether, and a financial counselor could start managing the investment portfolio so the client could live off the income generated by that portfolio. That way the client can not only enjoy the desired standard of living but also can set the stage for a healthy growth of the estate that will eventually be passed on to the beneficiaries. It should be remembered, however, that the more the client is concerned about outliving the assets, the more he or she should lean toward purchasing a joint life annuity. Also, since the tax implications of annuity or lump sum distribution can be complex, it is always desirable to consult a tax attorney. In the final analysis, the retirement years cannot be enjoyable unless they are also free of financial worries.

In this chapter we discussed retirement planning concepts and strategies. A discussion of investment products and financial markets will be undertaken in the next chapter.

APPENDIX TO CHAPTER 11:
CURRENT RULE REGARDING NOTICE OF
BLACKOUT PERIODS

On January 23, 2003 the Department of Labor's Pension and Welfare Benefits Administration released its final rule requiring advance written notice of blackout periods. The rule became effective on January 26. A failure to honor the new requirements can result in penalties of up to $100 per day for each affected participant or beneficiary.

1. Responsibility for Giving Notice. An administrator of an individual account plan [e.g., 401(k) plan] must provide written notice to participants and beneficiaries whose rights will be temporarily suspended or limited by a blackout period. Notice also must be given to issuers of employer securities subject to the blackout period. A "blackout period" generally includes any period during which the ability of the affected parties to direct or diversify assets credited to their accounts, obtain loans from the plan, or obtain distributions from the plan, will be restricted for more than three business days.

The final rule contains certain exclusions from the definition of "blackout period." These represent any suspension, limitation, or restriction that:

(a) occurs by reason of the application of the security laws (as defined under the Securities Exchange Act of 1934);

(b) is a regularly scheduled suspension, limitation, or restriction that has been disclosed to affected parties through the summary plan description.

(c) occurs by reason of an act, or a failure to act, on the part of any individual participant or by reason of a third party's action or claim involving the account of an individual participant.

2. Contents of the Notice. The notice to affected parties must be written in a simple language and should contain a set of important information.

3. Timing of the Notice. The notice to both affected parties and issuers of employer securities must be furnished at least 30, but not more than 60, calendar days in advance of the last date on which affected parties could exercise the rights in question.

4. Manner of Distribution. The written notice may be furnished in any manner permitted for similar types of notices, including through electronic media.

The difference between a successful person and others is not a lack of strength, nor a lack of knowledge, but rather in a lack of will.
                                                                Vincent Lombardi

CHAPTER 12

Investment Products and Markets: An Introduction

INTRODUCTION

This chapter is devoted to a broad review of the basic investment products, the security markets, and the key market indices. A detailed discussion of investment theories and concepts will be undertaken in the next chapter.

FIXED-INCOME INVESTMENTS, PREFERRED STOCKS, AND COMMON STOCK INVESTMENTS

FIXED-INCOME INVESTMENTS

Fixed-income investments have a fixed payment schedule. Although the legal strength of the promise may vary, bond investors are promised specific payments at predetermined times. The salient features of the key forms of fixed income investments are presented below.

Savings Accounts

Passbook savings accounts are the most obvious example of fixed-income investments. NOW, or SUPER NOW, accounts *(Negotiable Order of Withdrawal)* are

This chapter, and the two that follows, were critically reviewed by Dr. Joseph E. Champagne, Ph.D. Dr. Champagne serves as Chairman of the Board of Ross Controls, and also serves on the Board of Directors of the Munder Funds, a multi-billion-dollar mutual group fund. However, the authors are solely responsible for the contents.

interest-paying checking accounts that restrict the number of permitted checks, similar to conventional savings accounts, and are insured by the FDIC up to $100,000.

Certificates of Deposit

Certificates of Deposit (CDs), available from banks and savings and loans, involve minimum amounts (usually $500, or $100,000 for jumbo CDs) and specified time periods (typically six-month increments from six months to five years). The promised rate of interest on a CD is higher than for passbook savings, and the rate increases with the length of deposit of the CD.

Incidentally, savers can buy these *brokered* CDs from brokerage firms. These CDs are insured by banks or savings and loan associations and sold through a middleman—a broker—who gets paid a commission by the issuing institution. As long as the issuing bank has federal deposit insurance, brokered CDs are insured, up to the usual $100,000 limit.

Marketable Government Issues

Marketable issues, which make up about three-quarters of the federal debt, can be purchased through a dealer, a broker, or a Federal Reserve Bank without bidding for interest rates. Marketable government securities differ mainly in the length of time to maturity.

Treasury bills. Treasury bills are short-term securities which mature in 13, 26, or 52 weeks from the date of issue. Bills are sold on a discount basis; the investor pays a price lower than the face value and, upon maturity, receives the face value. T-bills are sold in a minimum increment of $10,000, with multiples of $5,000 available above the minimum, and are auctioned to the highest bidder. Consequently, the T-bill interest rates vary, depending on the amount of bid received for each issue. In both initial offerings and in secondary market trading, Treasury bills yields are quoted on a true annualized yield basis.

Certificates of indebtedness. Certificates of indebtedness with a term of one year are issued at par value and pay fixed interest, or coupon rates, which are printed on the bond and never change. The investor collects this interest by cashing in coupons at a bank, post office, or another federal office.

Treasury notes and bonds. Treasury notes and bonds are sold at par as long-term investments. Both notes and bonds may be purchased through commercial banks, brokerage firms, or Federal Reserve Banks. Bills, notes and bonds are liquid investments. Notes are U.S. government coupon obligations with an original maturity of one to ten years; they carry fixed interest rates and are payable semiannually. Bonds are long-term issues with an original maturity of more than ten years, but no longer than 30 years. Treasury bonds are used to finance the federal debt. Treasury note and bond prices are quoted in percentages of $1,000 par value, and fluctuations in their prices are expressed in 1/32s of a point.

Agency issues. Agency issues represent bonds issued by *federal agencies* and *government-guaranteed agencies*. The former include, among others, the Export-Import Bank, the Federal Housing Administration (FHA), and the Government National Mortgage Association (GNMA). Federal agencies cover a wide spectrum of activities, ranging from financing agricultural industry to providing the funds necessary to satisfy America's need for homes. Debt securities issued by the latter agencies, which include Banks for Cooperatives and Federal Home Loan Banks, are not guaranteed by the U.S. government, although they raise money under the Treasury's supervision. Most of the activities of these agencies are concentrated in the area of farm credit and housing.

Non-marketable Government Issues

Series EE bonds. EE bonds are non-negotiable zero coupon bonds with the maturity of 11 years sold at discounts from their face values of $50 up to $1,000. Currently, depending upon when it was purchased, each bond guarantees a minimum yield if held to maturity, no matter how other market interest rates may fall, but yields may rise to market rates above the stated minimum yield. The rate of EE bonds equals 85 percent of the average rate on five-year Treasury securities and is adjusted every six months. EE bonds are not subject to state income taxes, and federal income taxes on the earned interest can be postponed until maturity.

Series HH bonds. Series HH bonds pay the same interest rates as Series EE bonds. However, their term-to-maturity is ten years, and they pay semiannual coupons which are taxable. The smallest denomination Series HH bond is $500, but that bond can be purchased only in conjunction with Series EE bonds.

Series I Bonds. I Bonds are designed for investors seeking to protect the purchasing power of their investment and earn a guaranteed real rate of return. These bonds are an accrual type of security, which means that interest is added to the bond monthly and paid when the bond is cashed. An investor pays $50 for a $50 bond and it grows with inflation-indexed earnings for up to 30 years. The Treasury offers these bonds to encourage more Americans to save for the future.

The earnings rate of an I Bond is a combination of two separate rates: a fixed rate of return and a variable semiannual inflation rate. The fixed rate remains fixed for the life of the bond, while the semiannual inflation rate can vary every six months. I Bonds increase in value each month, and interest is compounded semiannually.

Earnings on I Bonds are exempt from state and local income taxes. Federal income taxes can be deferred for up to thirty years, or until they are redeemed.

Treasury Inflation-Protection Securities

All bond investors face the risk of inflation. Long-term bond investors in particular can lose a substantial portion of the purchasing power of their invested funds due to a gradual increase in prices. Treasury Inflation-Protection Securities (TIPS) are one answer to the inflation risk problem.

TIPS are marketable, book-entry debt securities, issued by the U.S. Treasury, are sold by the government at a quarterly auction, in minimum amounts of $1,000. They carry a fixed annual interest rate, and pay interest twice a year. The inflation protection is provided by adjusting the principal amount of the security according to changes in the inflation rate. The semiannual interest payment is then calculated based on the adjusted principal amount. The inflation-adjusted principal amount is paid at maturity.

Interest income from TIPS is treated in the same manner as interest income from other direct obligations of the federal government. The interest is taxable by the federal government, but is generally exempt from state and local taxes.

A unique characteristic of TIPS is that any adjustment of the principal amount is considered to be currently taxable "interest" income. For instance, if the bond-holder has $30 of taxable interest income from the bond for the first year and receives $20 of interest in cash, then the difference of $10 is treated as inflation adjustment to the principal amount.

Municipal Bonds

Municipal bonds are issued by state or political subdivisions, such as counties, airports, school districts, cities, towns, and villages, and also by state agencies and authorities. In general, interest paid on municipal bonds is exempt from both federal and local income taxes within the state of issue. Municipal bonds can be grouped into two broad categories: *general obligation* and *revenue bonds*.

General obligation bonds. General obligation bonds are backed by the full faith, credit, and taxing power of the issuing government unit. An investor can buy state issues backed by the state government, school bonds backed by the school district, city bonds backed by the municipality, or various other bonds, generally backed by the county government.

Revenue bonds. Revenue bonds are strictly dependent on the income from the issuing governmental unit or project to meet the interest and principal payments. These include both sewer and revenue bonds, as well as bonds used to finance bridges, tunnels, toll roads, airports, and hospitals.

Investors can also invest in other types of revenue bonds. For instance, *special tax bonds* are payable from the proceeds of a special tax, such as tax on gasoline, liquor, or tobacco. Local school bonds are another good example. When these issues are backed by full faith, credit, and taxing power of the issuing authority, they become general obligation bonds.

Corporate Bonds

Owners of corporate bonds expect to receive no more than repayment of the bond principal and interest from the issuing firm, because they are creditors rather than owners of the company. However, bondholders must be paid interest on their principal before dividends can be paid to the stockholders. Also, in the case of business failure or liquidation, bondholders must be repaid before the equity holders can receive any payment.

Types of corporate bonds. Some corporate bonds carry special features and privileges, while others are distinguishable by the type of security pledged against bond repayment. Bonds can be *secured* or *unsecured*. With a secured bond, the issuer reinforces its promise to pay the interest and principal by pledging specific property to the bondholders as collateral. In the case of an unsecured bond, the issuer merely promises to pay the stated interest and principal.

There are several types of secured and unsecured bonds.

Debentures. A debenture is unsecured and is backed only by the faith and general credit of the issuing company. Subordinated or junior debentures are the same as regular debentures, except that in case of liquidation their owners are paid after payments to the regular debenture holders.

Guaranteed Bonds. A guaranteed bond has interest or principal—or both—guaranteed by a company other than the issuer. The railroad industry uses this kind of bond when larger railroads, leasing sections of track owned by small railroads, guarantee the bonds of the smaller railroads.

Mortgage Bonds. A mortgage bond is a debt obligation secured by a mortgage on property. The value of the property may or may not equal the value of the mortgage bond issued against it. Because these securities are usually issued by giant utility companies, they make up a major segment of the corporate bond market.

Convertible Bonds. These debt instruments may be exchanged by the owner for common stock or another security—usually of the same company—in accordance with the terms and exchange ratios for the issue identified in the original issue. Any of the previously listed types of bonds may be convertible, although most convertible bonds are debentures or subordinated debentures.

Callable Bonds. A callable bond has a set maturity date, but it can be redeemed after sufficient notice to the bondholders by the issuer at specified periods. The call feature is stated in the original offering prospectus. The callability feature of this type of bond is likely to be exercised if current market rates are less than the coupon rate.

Junk bonds. Corporate bonds rated below Baa by Moody's or below BBB by S&Ps are characterized as *junk bonds*, whereas bonds with higher ratings are identified as investment quality bonds. The connotation *junk* comes from the investment community's belief that, under unfavorable economic conditions, market prices of such bonds will significantly drop, producing at least a paper loss.

Junk bonds should not be confused with deep discount bonds. The latter sell at discount prices because they carry a low coupon rate. By contrast, junk bonds sell well below par because they carry substantial default risk. Clearly junk bonds offer a higher yield, reflecting the substantial default risk they carry.

Zero coupon bonds. These bonds offer no periodic interest payments, are sold at a discount from their face value, and gradually increase in value representing interest income as they approach maturity. Yield to maturity is based solely on the difference between the initial investment and the amount received upon sale or maturity. These bonds do not pay interest on a semi-annual basis. However, the bondholder is required to pay taxes on the imputed annual interest payments.

Bond ratings

The two key bond rating agencies are Moody's Investor Service and Standard & Poor's (S&P). The highest quality bonds are rated AAA, while the lowest grade bonds have the rating of C (for Moody's) and D (for Standard & Poor's). The higher the rating of a bond is, the lower its default risk, and the lower the default risk premium associated with it.

As a general rule, in rating bonds, the agencies take into consideration five major factors: (1) the level and trend of fixed charge coverage; (2) the company's long-term debt-to-equity ratio; (3) the company's liquidity position; (4) the significance of the company in the industry; and (5) the nature (secured versus unsecured, and so on) of the specific debt issue.

Warrants and Rights

Warrants and rights are related to both stocks and bonds. They do not represent ownership in the issuing company, and are not a form of debt. They only represent the privilege of purchasing a specified corporate security at a particular price within a specified limit of time. Ownership of these instruments, however, is of temporary, rather than of continuous, interest.

Warrants. *Warrants* allow the holder to purchase a corporate security—usually common stock—at a given price within a specific period of time. This time period may be finite or indefinite. A company may issue warrants to shareholders or creditors when a new stock or bond issue is released as an inducement to purchase these securities. Warrants are generally traded on stock exchanges after the security has been issued.

Rights. Unlike warrants, rights have short expiration dates, generally extending between two to ten weeks. Rights to purchase a common stock are often given to shareholders when additional stock is issued. Shareholders are then entitled to purchase more stock in proportion to their current holdings in order to maintain their existing percentage equity in the firm.

PREFERRED STOCK

Preferred stock may be considered a fixed income security because the yearly payment is stipulated either as a coupon (e.g., five percent of the face value) or as a stated dollar amount. However, preferred stock is junior, or subordinate, to all bonds issued by the company. Preferred stockholders do not generally participate in company management, and they have no voting rights such as the common stockholders possess.

There are different types of preferred stock available in the market. If the stock is *cumulative*, the claim to dividends may be carried over from one year to the next; if the company falls behind in dividend payments, it must make up the entire amount before paying dividends to the common stockholders. Another variety, called *convertible preferred stock*, carries a contractual clause entitling the holder to exchange it for shares of common stock of the same company within a specified period. A third type of preferred stock is called *participating preferred stock*. Unlike typical preferred stockholders, a participating preferred stockholder not only receives dividends, but shares additional earnings with the common stockholders. Also, many preferred stocks are *callable*, and may be redeemed by the issuing company at a given "call price" within a specific number of years after issuance.

COMMON STOCK

Key Features

Common stockholders have equity in the corporation, and they are usually the only group who can participate in the increased earnings via an increase in the stock value. They are not personally liable for debts incurred by the corporation, but in the event of business failure or liquidation, common stockholders are the last to be paid. They do, however, retain residual rights to any assets that may remain after all the creditors have been paid. Owners of common stock are entitled to participate in the management of the enterprise to the extent of voting to elect directors and approving specified changes in the company's charter.

Types of Stock

Investors generally group stocks according to some of the traditional classifications used on Wall Street—for example, blue chips, growth and value stocks, income stocks, and so on. The following section briefly describes the various types of stock.

Blue chips. Blue chip stocks are high-grade investment quality stocks issued by major companies which have long unbroken record of earnings and dividend payments. Usually, these companies hold important, if not leading, positions in their industries, and can weather economic downturns and post strong earnings gains during upturns, because they have the resources to capitalize on a recovery.

Non-blue chip. These stocks include all stocks which are not classified as blue chips. In some cases, stocks may be issued by established companies with impressive earnings records and excellent future prospects. However, the company may lack the size, corporate resources, or industry position that many consider necessary to qualify the stock as a blue chip.

Under these broad general headings that divide thousands of stocks, equities can be further categorized according to other important investment features. None of these categories are mutually exclusive; it is possible for some stocks to fall under one or more of the following types.

Growth company stocks. Growth company stocks are shares in companies that exhibit above- average and accelerated growth of earnings. These companies typically pay only a small portion of earning in dividends, because they can maintain or accelerate their growth by reinvesting earnings in the business.

Cyclical company stocks. Cyclical company stocks are stocks of companies whose earnings fluctuate with the business cycle and are accentuated by it. When patterns in the economy are favorable to their industry, the earnings of cyclical companies peak. When the course of the economy changes direction, they suffer earnings setbacks and adversities.

Defensive stocks. Stocks of cyclical companies can be contrasted with recession-resistant stocks, commonly known as defensive stocks. These companies sell products and services which enjoy a demand that does not greatly fluctuate with the business cycle. Familiar examples of recession-resistant industries are those involved with health care, food, utilities and cosmetics.

Income stocks. Income stocks are characteristic of those firms that pay a high dividend relative to their stock prices. The dividend yields on these securities are above average for stocks and frequently are competitive with the returns on debt instruments. Income stocks, such as utility stocks, are purchased by the investors mainly for their current yield, rather than for their potential price appreciation.

Speculative stocks. These stocks are traded for short-term profit, and represent entities for which the purchaser is assuming an unusually large amount of risk, hoping to earn a very large return. The purchase of any stock can entail speculation; someone could buy the shares of the highest grade blue chip with the intention of selling the shares the next day for a short-term profit. However, speculative stocks generally refer to electronics, biotech, and other types of technological stocks that can widely fluctuate on a short-term basis.

MUTUAL FUNDS

INTRODUCTION

Mutual funds are companies through which investors pool their assets. A fund sells its own shares to the public and invests the proceeds. It is a fast, easy way for investors to set up comprehensive portfolios.

A mutual fund is a company that manages its shareholders' investments toward a stated objective. The aim is usually specific: to invest in stocks for capital appreciation, in bonds for regular income, or in a mixture of stocks and bonds for both growth and income. In sharp contrast to individual money management firms, the universe of mutual funds is open to anyone with money to invest. Typically, the price of admission is no more than $1,000.

CLOSED-END VERSUS OPEN-END FUNDS

Most mutual funds are called open-end, because they create more shares when investors want them. Each afternoon, these funds add up the value of their investments, divide this total by the current number of fund shares, and determine the price of a share. Investors can buy shares from the fund or sell them back for this price, which is called the net asset value, or NAV. In sharp contrast, a closed-end fund issues a set number of shares, and investors then trade those shares on a stock exchange through a broker, just as they would an individual stock. Consequently, share prices might be higher or lower than the fund's NAV, depending upon the relative demand and supply situation for that fund. A closed-end fund purchased for less than its NAV is said to be selling at "a discount;" if a higher price is paid, then it is selling at "a premium." Closed-end funds do not have to give investors their money back as open-end funds must do, so they can more easily pursue long-term investment strategies.

ADVANTAGES OF FUND INVESTMENT

Regardless its objective, every mutual fund offers investors at least three advantages, as discussed next.

Diversification

Each dollar invested buys an interest in the fund's entire portfolio. That portfolio usually contains the stocks or bonds of many dozens of companies.

Professional Portfolio Management

The fund's manager, often supported by a staff of investment analysts, decides which securities to buy and sell, and when to buy and sell them, in keeping with the fund's objective and the markets' behavior.

Liquidity

The great majority of mutual funds issue new shares and redeem existing shares on demand. The share price equals the current market value of the fund's investments divided by the number of shares outstanding (called NAV), plus any sales charges. Funds with no sales or redemption charges are called *no-load* funds.

TYPES OF FUNDS

Funds of all shapes and colors abound, but the main categories are equity funds, fixed-income funds, balanced funds, and money market funds. Most equity funds lean toward one of two basic styles of investing: value funds like to buy stocks that have dropped to bargain prices, then wait for prices to rise to their intrinsic value. Growth funds do not focus so much on price. They like companies whose earnings are growing quickly, and often buy stocks that have already risen in value.

Fixed income funds are just what their name implies. They buy interest-paying bonds issued by companies and governments. Balanced funds invest in a combination of both stocks and bonds. Finally, money market funds are essentially parking places for cash, almost like savings accounts.

Within these broad categories, there are various types of funds which can be differentiated with respect to their investment objectives and potential for volatility. These are described next.

Aggressive Growth Funds

These funds attempt to maximize the growth of investment with little emphasis on generating income. Therefore, they invest in those common stocks that have a high potential for rapid growth and capital appreciation.

Aggressive growth funds provide a relatively low stability of principal because they invest in stocks that experience wide swings. These funds often invest in small company stocks that provide low current income because they reinvest their profits in their businesses. Aggressive growth funds generally carry high risks because they make a concerted effort to secure more pronounced growth of the principal. Hence, these funds are not suitable for risk averse investors who must conserve their principal or need current income.

Growth Funds

Assumed to be more conservative than aggressive growth funds, these funds invest in more matured, established companies to achieve long-term growth. Also, they do not invest in less stable, smaller companies, which provide substantial gains over the short term but also carry with them the risk of significant declines. Growth funds are not suitable for investors who are unable to assume market risks or are dependent on investment income.

International/Global Funds

International funds seek growth through investments in companies outside the U.S. By contrast, global funds invest in securities around the world, including the U.S. Both types provide investors with an opportunity to further diversify their mutual fund portfolio, especially since foreign markets do not always move in tandem with the U.S. market.

International and global funds offer opportunities for growth and diversification. However, they also carry currency and other related risks, and are therefore not suitable for risk averse investors.

Growth and Income Funds

These funds seek long-term growth of capital as well as current income. Some funds invest in a combination of growth stocks, stocks paying high dividends, preferred stocks, corporate bonds and money market instruments. Others invest in growth stocks and generate current income by selling options. These funds are suitable for investors who can assume some risk but also want a moderate level of current income.

Fixed Income Funds

The goal of fixed income, or bond, funds is to provide high current income while aiming at the preservation of capital. Fixed income funds invest primarily in government and corporate bonds and preferred stocks. However, since bond prices fluctuate with changing interest rates, fixed income funds do carry interest rate risk.

Compared with money market funds, fixed income funds offer a higher level of current income but a lower stability of principal. Within the fixed income category, funds vary greatly both in terms of their stability of principal and in their ability to generate current income. High yield funds, which seek to maximize income by investing in lower-rated, or junk, bonds of longer maturities, entail less stability of principal than those fixed-income funds that invest in higher-grade bonds and offer lower coupon rates.

Balanced/Equity Income Funds

The main objective of these funds is to generate current income by investing primarily in those stocks that pay large dividends. Since stocks are generally more volatile than bonds, these funds are less stable than fixed income funds. Balanced and equity income funds are suitable for conservative investors who want current income with limited growth of principal.

Specialty/Sector Funds

These funds invest in securities of a specific industry or sector like health care, high technology, leisure, utilities, and precious metals. Because each specialty fund invests primarily in one sector, these funds do not protect investors from risk the way regular mutual funds do. However, sector funds do make it possible for investors to diversify among many companies within an industry, such as the computer industry or the service industry.

Asset Allocation Funds

Investors who want a fund that does it all select asset allocation funds. These funds allocate their money between stocks, bonds and cash in predetermined proportions. Often included in this category are the new life-cycle funds, which do a much better job of providing one-stop shopping than traditional balanced funds.

It is apropos to add here one word of caution. A number of asset allocation funds are either market timers or market timers in drag, and are unsuitable for serious long-term investors. However, the legitimate asset allocation funds tend to move funds between stock, bond and money market instruments in response to the fund managers' view of the relative market prospect. Hence, they may be suitable for investors who can tolerate some risk, are seeking capital appreciation, and do not need high levels of income.

Money Market Funds

For the cautious investor, these funds provide a very high stability of principal while seeking a moderate to high current income. They invest in highly liquid virtually risk-free, short-term debt securities of agencies of the U.S. government, banks and corporations, and Treasury bills. These funds have no potential for capital appreciation.

Index Funds

Long ignored or disparaged, index funds are the investment community's ugly ducklings. These funds buy and hold groups of stocks that mimic the performance of some market yardstick like the S&P 500-stock index. Clearly, that is not a prescription for excitement. But index funds tend to hold their course regardless of the currents that send high-flying funds soaring or diving. Also, advantages can include low costs and lower year-to-year taxes because holdings are not sold very often.

MUTUAL FUND FEES AND EXPENSES

Understanding mutual fund fees and their impact on investment is the key to successful investing. By learning about the types of fees associated with mutual funds, one can make the right investment choices. However, it should be remembered that, besides fees, other factors affecting a fund's long-term track record include the fund's long-term performance, its investment style, the strength of the management team, and its risk volatility profiles. Also, it is desirable to learn about additional features and services that the fund may offer, such as round-the-clock assistance, automatic dividend reinvestment, and no-fee exchanges and redemptions. Key mutual fund charges are presented in the boxed insert.

Load or Sales Charges

Mutual funds sold through brokers charging a sales commission are known as load funds. By contrast, directly marketed mutual funds are sold without a broker

---

MUTUAL FUND CHARGES

Front-end load. An initial sales expense (three percent to 8.5 percent) that is charged before the shares are purchased. Some of this money goes to managing the fund but most of it goes to paying sales commissions.

Back-end load. A deduction taken from the proceeds of the sale of shares. The percentage charged usually decreases as the length of time over which shares are held increases.

Re-load. A charge to reinvest the gain and/or cash dividends.

Exit fee. A charge to cash in any shares of the fund. It's usually a flat rate or one to two percent of the proceeds.

Managing fee. Used to cover costs like salaries, expenses, and so on.

12b-1 fee. Fee used to cover advertising, commissions, and other costs.

Transfer fee. A charge to switch from one fund in the company to another. It is usually .5 to one percent.

---

or a salesperson, and as a result, typically no sales loads or fees are deducted from the purchase. These funds are known as no-load funds.

Management Fees and Operating Expenses

All mutual funds—both load and no load—charge management fees and operating expenses. These expenses represent the amounts paid to portfolio managers for managing their portfolios, and to others for providing administrative services, such as maintaining shareholder records and furnishing shareholder statements and reports. These fees are reflected in fund's share prices and are not charged directly to shareholders. The management and operating fees usually range between 0.15 percent and two percent of a fund's total asset value.

12b-1 Fee

The SEC created this fee to help mutual funds recover the costs of promoting and selling fund shares. Most load funds, and some no-load funds, routinely charge a 12b-1 fee of up to 0.75 percent a year. Mutual funds can also tack on an additional 0.25 percent for shareholder assistance and account maintenance. When the 12b-1 fees were introduced, it was expected that as funds grew, in part through successful marketing, the portion of expenses borne by each shareholder would diminish. Unfortunately, that has not been the case. Most load funds families have merely added the 12b-1 fees to their charges, although a few have reduced or eliminated front-end loads in exchange for collecting the 12b-1 fees.

Redemption Fees

Some funds charge a fee even when shares of one fund are exchanged for shares of another fund from the same company. Other funds may charge a fee only when fund shares are liquidated and the proceeds are mailed to the investor. That is, at redemption, the investor may be charged a redemption or exchange fee, or the investor may have to pay a back-end sales charge known as contingent deferred sales charge (CDSC). The difference between the two is important.

A redemption or exchange fee is often returned to the fund itself, rather than to the management company. This arrangement benefits long-term investors in the fund because they are not paying the transaction costs attributable to investors who are getting in and out of the fund on a trading basis. By contrast, a CDSC goes to the management company to pay sales commission. The fee is imposed on shares redeemed within a specific period following their purchase and is usually assessed on a sliding scale beginning at four to five percent of the fund value in the first year, decreasing to zero over the following five or six years.

Trustee Fees

An independent board governs every mutual fund. A somewhat biased study tracking the 82 largest fund families found a correlation between the level of trustee compensation and fund expenses. In order to find out how advisors are compensated, one should consult the prospectus supplement—the Statement of Additional Information—which breaks down the costs that make up the *other* expenses.

Supermarket Charges

One-stop fund shopping allows investors to buy from various fund families and have the investments consolidated in a single monthly statement. For a fund to participate in such a supermarket, it must pay the sponsor an annual fee of 0.25 to 0.35 percent for every dollar invested. Unfortunately, investors have to pay this fee even if they bypass the supermarket and invest directly with the fund company.

EXPENSE RATIO

Mutual funds express their fees in the form of expense ratios. In order to calculate the expense ratio, a mutual fund divides its total operating expenses (salaries, research expenses, telecommunications, shareholder statements, check processing, tax reporting, and other costs of keeping the fund running) by total dollars under management. Thus, a fund with $10 million in assets and $120,000 in operating expenses will have a 1.2 percent expense ratio ($120,000/10,000,000). A fund publishes its net return in the financial press after netting out these expenses. If the fund's expense ratio is 1.2 percent, then it would have to earn 11.2 percent (ten percent + 1.2 percent) in order to deliver a ten percent net return. By contrast, a fund with expenses of 0.5 percent would have to earn only 10.5 percent to generate the same ten percent net return. This means that the higher the ratio, the better the fund manager has to perform to generate a stated return.

FEE REDUCTION STRATEGIES

There are systematic ways of reducing mutual fund fees and expenses. These are discussed next.

Select the Right Asset Class

An investor should select the share class that charges the lowest fees for the expected holding period. For example, if Class B shares of ABC Mutual Fund has a back load of six percent, which disappears after five years, and the plan is to hold this mutual fund at least for five years, the back load can be avoided altogether by investing in B shares.

Take Advantage of the Fund Break

Load mutual funds generally offer break points to investors who make large purchases of shares. For instance, a typical load mutual fund may offer the following breaks:

Investment	*Load*
Less than $50,000	5.5%
Between $50,000 and less than $100,000	5.0%
Between $100,000 and less than $250,000	3.5%
Between $250,000 and less than $500,000	2.5%
Between $500,000 and less than $1,000,000	2.0%
Over $1,000,000	None

So, it is always a good idea to pool the available resources in an attempt to reach the appropriate break point to lower the load.

Sign a Letter of Intent

If the plan is to invest $100,000 over time but there is only $60,000 to invest, one can sign a *Letter of Intent* to come up with the additional cash over the next 12 months. Then the fund will allow the investment of both the initial $60,000 and the additional $40,000 at the lower load of 3.5 percent. Later, if the investor fails to come up with $40,000 during the next 12 months, the mutual fund will merely charge a load of five percent on the initial $60,000 investment.

Carefully Time the Liquidation

If the investor originally purchased a fund that had a back load, it may pay to hold that fund until the back load disappears, or is drastically reduced. Of course, the risk of holding the fund too long should be weighed against the advantage of reducing or eliminating the back-end load altogether.

Invest Fund Distributions

Most mutual funds permit reinvestment of dividend and capital gain distributions without changing a load or investment fees. This reinvestment of distributions can significantly add to the portfolio.

Consolidate Investments

Sometimes mutual funds offer break points based upon *all the purchases* of funds in the family. If a person wishes to invest $1 million inheritance among four of American Fund's load funds, then a load of three percent per fund would have to be paid. However, if the fund accepts it as a single $1 million investment, this investment would qualify for a no-load status, saving a huge sum of money.

Utilize Group Discounts

Participants in a corporate 401(k) plan can sometimes apply the company discount to their own IRA account or taxable account. A fund may also allow a discount if the person belongs to a company retirement plan, church or an investment club. Finally, where *flesh and blood* discounts are permitted, the fund may add up investments of all the family members in order to give everyone the break-point advantage.

Find a Seller

If an investor can find a seller of a load fund, then the shares could be directly purchased without paying the normal load. The San Diego discount-broker Jack White & Company maintains a flat-fee based secondary fund trading market called Connect that crosses trades.

MUTUAL FUND ALPHABET

A-class shares have a front-end sales fee, while B-class shares sell at net asset value but with a higher 12b-1 fee and a deferred back-end charge that phases out after five years or so. Generally, the longer an investor expects to stay with a fund, the more reason there is to buy the A-class shares of that fund.

In addition to A and B shares, investors can also buy C and D shares. C shares have no front or back-end load, but a *level* load—as high as one percent of the account per year. D shares are a little like A and B shares, with higher expense deductions in the first year and a smaller back-end charge. Finally, Y shares are available to institutional investors.

READING A MUTUAL FUND PROSPECTUS

Before making an investment decision, every investor should examine the fund's goals and objectives and the ability of its management to carry them out. Additionally, one must evaluate the services provided by the fund and the costs of such services.

A wealth of information is contained in the fund's prospectus which, by law, must be furnished to all potential investors before a purchase application can be accepted by the fund. In the following paragraphs, we will discuss statements of investment objectives and policies, risk factors, investment restrictions, costs and fees, and other miscellaneous information contained in a mutual fund prospectus.

Investment Objectives and Policies

Mutual funds can be classified into various categories according to their objectives.

Capital gains or growth funds cater to the needs of those investors who prefer future long-term capital gains over immediate dividend income. Their investments are largely made in established companies that have demonstrated the ability to expand faster than the nation's economy as a whole.

Income funds basically favor securities with above-average, current income potential, although growth possibilities are not ruled out. Because their objective is to select stocks with high and stable dividend payments, income funds offer greater price stability than capital gains and growth funds.

Growth and income funds invest for a combination of capital gains and current income. Of course, some funds seek income as the primary objective and growth as a secondary aim; still others seek an even balance between the two. Funds seeking both growth and income generally invest in a more broadly diversified group of securities than funds whose principal objective is current income.

Index funds are designed to match the performance of the selected stock market index. These funds operate under the notion that matching the market averages will produce better long-term performance than the efforts of money managers who try to beat the market. An example of an index fund relates to the situation where the portfolio manager attempts to match the S&P 500 index.

Balanced funds hold bonds and preferred stocks in addition to common stocks in order to minimize market risk.

The important characteristics of objectives for various types of mutual funds are presented in the accompanying boxed insert.

Risk Factors

An important section contained in every prospectus deals with the risks fund managers are likely to assume. For instance, the fund may state that in seeking capital appreciation it will purchase stocks of small companies which may trade on the OTC market and may have a history of price volatility greater than the stocks of more mature companies. Another prospectus may assert, "We expect to be fully invested in stocks under most market conditions." Also the fund's prospectus may specify if the fund deals in call and put options. These statements should be taken into account in determining the riskiness of the fund.

Investment Restrictions

It is desirable to study the investment restrictions as well. Every prospectus contains the usual investment restrictions imposed by the Investment Company Act of 1940. In addition, it may also impose other restrictions on the portfolio managers. A list of typical restrictions is presented here:

1. The fund will not indulge in short selling.
2. The fund will not purchase securities on margin.
3. The fund's assets will be diversified so no more than 7.5 percent of the total is invested in a single industry group.
4. The fund will not borrow more than three percent of the total assets for meeting emergencies.

Naturally, these investment restrictions should be carefully studied before investing in a fund. In passing, it should also be mentioned that many funds have left these restrictions wide open.

Past Performance

Mutual funds generally present a five-year track record and compare their record with that of the Standard & Poor's 500 Index or the Dow Jones Industrial Average. In addition, the prospectus reveals such important data as the ratio of expenses to average net assets and the portfolio turnover rate. While past performance does not guarantee future success, a good track record is certainly an

CHARACTERISTICS OF SELECTED MUTUAL FUNDS		
Type		*Characteristics*
Aggressive Growth	Key Strength:	Growth potential in rising markets
	Main Weakness:	High vulnerability to slumps
	Investor Profile:	Risk takers who won't need cash for at least three years
Growth	Key Strength:	Long-term growth
	Main Weakness:	Scant protection from market drops
	Investor Profile:	Long-term investors who want capital growth with roughly market level risk
Value	Key Strength:	Buy out-of-favor stocks not widely followed or recommended by analysts
	Main Weakness:	Upturns in performance may not occur and may take considerable time for the market to recognize value, because they may be temporarily out-of-favor with investors
	Investor Profile:	Contrarians, investors who desire low P/E ratios, low price-to-book value
Total Return	Key Strength:	Comparatively steady gains in variety of market conditions
	Main Weakness:	Tepid results in high times
	Investor Profile:	Risk averse investors looking for capital growth and moderate income
International	Key Strength:	Can outpace U.S. stocks
	Main Weakness:	Vulnerable to currency fluctuations
	Investor Profile:	Growth investors who want diversity
Gold	Key Strength:	Gains not dependent on U.S. stock market
	Main Weakness:	More ups and downs
	Investor profile:	Investors who want to hedge against inflation
Bond Fixed Income	Key Strength:	Dependable monthly income
	Main Weakness:	Rising interest rates can zap principal
	Investor Profile:	Income seekers and equity investors looking to diversity

attractive feature of any fund. Also, a low ratio of expenses to average net assets of up to one percent and a moderate portfolio turnover rate (say, 30 to 40 percent) might demonstrate that the fund is being efficiently run.

Fund Information

There are several financial information services that help investors track fund information concerning fund performance characteristics and portfolio investment. These include Lipper Analytical Services, Morningstar Mutual Funds, and Value Line Mutual Fund Survey. Information contained in these publications allow investors to identify particular funds that meet their own objectives and make better informed decisions. It should be pointed out, however, that overuse of rankings and ratings generated by these fund information services can lead to poor decisions. The reason is that, as a general rule, past performance is an unreliable predictor of future performance. In addition, during short reporting periods winners tend to be highly volatile funds which often do not repeat their success. Finally, over the long run, different types of funds tend to enter into the winner's circle.

Costs and Fees

The SEC requires every fund to include a table of all fees near the front of the prospectus, followed by a hypothetical total of all fees over several years. A pure no-load fund usually indicates this fact on the cover. Front-load, low-load, and back-load funds disclose their costs inside the prospectus. The investor may also have to be creative in interpreting additional costs. For instance, instead of saying that all dividends are subject to the usual full front-end load, one prospectus puts it this way: "Dividends will be reinvested in additional full and fractional shares at the public offering price (net asset value plus a sales charge)."

Miscellaneous Information

The back pages of the prospectus contain valuable information on additional services available through the fund. These include, among other items, share purchase, sale and exchange privileges, transfer between funds within the family, participation in a systematic withdrawal plan, dividend distribution, reinvestment, and automatic deposit and withdrawal plans. Information is also provided on telephone switch, check writing privileges, and other related services provided by the fund.

MUTUAL FUND RATING SERVICES

Mutual fund ratings or other evaluations of fund performance can provide an important way for investors to compare their fund's past performance with other funds. We will now present the best known rating services that are available in the marketplace.

Morningstar

This is the industry's best print resource for comprehensive, unbiased, and accurate mutual fund information. Morningstar publishes several important reports, including Morningstar Mutual Funds, Morningstar Principia Pro for Mutual Funds, Morningstar Principia Pro for Stocks, and Morningstar Principia Pro for Variable Annuities/Life.

As an example, the Pro for Mutual Funds Report tracks 13,000 mutual funds. It provides complete securities holdings for each fund, and identifies all funds that hold a particular security. The Multi-Asset Portfolio Developer lets the user construct and analyze real-world portfolios containing mutual funds. Most important of all, the Report publishes style boxes, risk-adjusted star ratings, and category ratings to various mutual funds so their relative performance could be determined with confidence.

Lipper

Lipper is a leading global mutual fund information company analyzing fund companies and financial intermediaries. The firm tracks 47,000 funds worldwide with assets in excess of $10 trillion.

The analysis of Lipper is unmatched for its quality, reliability and level of precision. It integrates comprehensive fund research, fund performance, asset growth, portfolio composition, and expense information. It also uses customized approach which allows the user to measure and compare performance with other peer groups.

Standard & Poor's

Standard & Poor's Fund Services sets the standard as a leading global provider for mutual fund information and analysis. Through their extensive research facilities, they give investors and intermediaries the insights they need to make more informed investment decisions.

Standard & Poor's is one of the most widely accepted financial rating organizations around the globe, setting the standard in the financial markets. This gives them the ability to provide fund sponsors, intermediaries and money managers the information they need to stay ahead of the competition, and to provide investors the information they need to make more informed decisions.

S&P conducts institutional quality research and analysis on over 1,500 funds, covered by their 400 professionals in 13 countries. In addition, they provide the industry's most comprehensive database of funds with nearly 60,000 institutional, pension, insurance, and mutual funds worldwide.

Thomson Financial

Thomson Financial is a global provider of data, analysis, and information tools. It offers the most comprehensive range of indispensable, market-leading services and customizable solutions to help investors make better decisions, be more productive, and achieve superior financial results. One of the Washington, DC area's leading companies, Thomson Financial employs more than 500 people, 200 of whom are technical staff.

TRADITIONAL INDEX FUNDS

AN OVERVIEW

Traditionally, investors chose their own stocks, and held them for long periods of time. Then came the mutual fund boom, and investors began to ask mutual fund managers to do the picking for them. And, as the longest bull market in history continued through 1999 without a substantial decline, many investors decided that they no longer needed astute mutual fund managers to find the best investments. Instead, many started investing in mutual funds whose sole purpose was to mimic the performance of the stock market.

Known as index funds, these funds simply hold shares in all the companies that make up, for instance, the S&P 500 index, Wilshire 500, Russell 2000, or Morgan Stanley Capital International Europe, Australia and the Far East (EAFE) Index. In essence, these funds run on auto-pilot, giving up the chance to do any better than the market average but also promising that, except for the cost of running a fund, they will do no worse.

The popularity of index funds has come as many Americans, exuberant over the winning performance of the stock market, have become convinced that to make money in the stock market all that they have to do is be in the market—period.

It is true that index funds operate in a routine fashion. That is their beauty. They will not let investors beat the stock market by a dazzling 14 percent, as Fidelity's Magellan fund did in 1993. But neither will they let them lag the S&P 500 by ten percent, as Magellan did in 1996.

Index funds owe a great deal of their recent success to their investment style, and to the rapid rise of the stock market in the 1990's. The major advantages of investing in index funds are discussed next.

FEWER CAPITAL GAINS

Unlike other stock funds, whose managers are constantly buying and selling securities in an effort to maximize returns or minimize losses, index funds are managed very conservatively. Managers buy and hold stocks longer, selling or buying only those securities which drop out, or added to, the index.

A related advantage of index funds is that both index funds and actively managed funds lose money when the market is down. But on April 16 mostly the people who own actively managed funds wonder how they could simultaneously lose a great deal of money and still generate massive tax bills via capital gains distributions. Index fund shareholders rarely experience that problem.

Keeping Pace with S&P

Most stock mutual funds reportedly underperform the S&P 500, partly because they have to sell stocks to cover net withdrawals. For instance, the majority of stock funds failed to beat the S&P 500 from 1975 to 2004.

An S&P fund virtually guarantees that the investor will do as well as the index. The risk, of course, is that the fund will do poorly when the S&P 500 underperforms, such as in a bear market. But over time, the index fund will likely approximate the long-term market average.

Painless Strategy

The index fund investors do not have either the time or the ability to ferret out the few exceptional fund managers who regularly beat the market averages. It also makes sense to choose the largest indices, since they include companies that are followed by Wall Street and the financial press. For that reason it is best to buy an index fund that invests in large, well-known, and well-researched companies, such as those that make up the S&P 500 group.

LOWER COST

The index-fund investor's costs may be as low as 0.18 percent a year, as compared to the internal costs of 0.75-1.25 percent or more for managed funds. This implies that investors of actively managed funds rack up huge investment costs as they try to find the best investment managers.

The advantage of investing in index funds is best summarized by Loren Schweitzberg, an assistant professor of computer engineering at Wayne State University (quoted by Edward Wyatt , the New York Times): "I am 32. I think it would be hard to find an actively managed fund that does better than the index for the next 35 years—or even 25 or 20. In that sense, indexing is a more conservative option."

Names of the popular index funds can be obtained from any brokerage firm.

PITFALLS OF INDEX FUNDS

Downside Risk

Statistics show that the majority of the index fund investments have been generated since 1990. During most of the period covering 1991-2001, the major stock market indices have never fallen more than ten percent. When the overall stock market significantly declines, an index fund will decline as much as the market. This is because, unlike a general stock fund, an index fund cannot hold cash or bonds which often cushion a market fall.

The impact of a significant fall in any fund, including the index fund, is more severe than is usually recognized. For instance, if a fund were to fall 50 percent, then it would take a 100 percent increase in its value just to break even.

Skewed Weighting Systems

As in the case with the S&P index, the index funds are weighted by a company's market value. Therefore, movement in the prices of the biggest stocks, like General Electric, Coca-Cola, and Exxon, have a magnifying effect on the performance of the index. In recent times it is those big stocks that have contributed to the largest advances in the S&P index.

Divergence Between Index Funds

Contrary to commonly held belief, index funds do not always mirror the market index. In fact, over time, because of redemptions and other administrative factors, some index funds fail to keep up with the index they are supposed to match. When that happens, many planners come up with *new versions* of indexing that inject more human judgment into the formulas. This human analysis and personal analytical opinion contradict the broad assumption which is the cornerstone of managing index funds.

Tax Ramifications

One reason index funds can operate with such low costs is that they almost never sell their stocks—so investors almost never have to pay taxes on stock gains. But when nervous investors—even those who profess to be in the market for the long haul—begin redeeming their shares at the first sign of the faltering of the market, index funds are compelled to sell their shares. Then taxable index funds investors are required to pay taxes, which hurt their after-tax returns.

A Narrow Focus

Historically small-cap stocks have handsomely beaten large-caps. Also, numerous studies have demonstrated that international stocks and bonds can increase the return and lower the risk of individual portfolios. Unfortunately, these choices, as well as the choice of holding cash, are out of bounds for index funds.

Value Added by Money Managers

Selected actively managed mutual funds do beat the market on a consistent basis, even allowing for the fact that in the past ten years the broad market has outperformed its very long-term average of around 11 percent. In addition, few neophyte investors recall a period like the five years that ended in 1982, when more than 80 percent of actively managed portfolios beat the S&P 500. On this basis, a strong case can be made for active management by those money managers who have established long-term venerable track records.

Increased Volatility

S&P 500 index funds, which approximate 50 in number, are more volatile than the majority of actively managed stock funds, most of which hold around five to ten percent cash all the time. Index funds are fully invested, with very close to 100 percent of their assets invested in stocks. Managed funds also cut volatility by owning foreign stocks and a variety of fixed income securities, which index funds cannot do.

So, the question, "Are index funds right for investors?" can only be answered after taking into account all of the advantages and pitfalls of investing in these funds, and the special needs and limitations surrounding the investor.

NEW HORIZON IN INDEX FUNDS

Several years ago index funds became popular because many research studies showed that, after costs, the majority of money managers did not beat the markets in which they operated. Today, however, there is more than one way of indexing. Investors can buy classic *index funds*, or they can buy index stocks that trade on a stock exchange. Salient features of a variety of index stocks are presented next.

iSHARES

iShares are over 50 different index funds that trade like stocks. Each share represents a portfolio of stocks designed to closely track one specific stock index. iShares are like stocks in that investors can buy and sell them the same way they can buy and sell stocks of an individual company. iShares consist of stocks that represent the underlying index tracked by the fund. These Shares may use futures to simulate full investment in the respective underlying index, to facilitate trading, or to reduce transaction costs.

iShares offer two distinct advantages for investors concerned with reducing taxes. First, they are engineered to minimize portfolio turnover, which can reduce capital gains distributions. Second, investors in these iShares, like those in common stocks, pay taxes primarily on the investment's appreciation at the time of sale.

In dealing with iShares, investors can make adjustments at any time without short-term restrictions or redemption fees. Of course, a brokerage commission is charged on the sale. Also, investors can margin these iShares, in which case standard margin rules apply.

Redemption of iShares is handled differently from redemption of mutual fund shares. iShares funds are engineered to minimize portfolio turnover and potential capital gains tax consequences by restricting the creation and redemption of these iShares to large transactions carried out by institutional investors designated as "Authorized Participants." Individual investors seeking to liquidate iShares positions simply place orders through their brokerage accounts for execution on the exchange.

STANDARD & POOR'S DEPOSITARY RECEIPTS

Standard & Poor's Depositary Receipts (SPDRs), or Spiders, were created in January 1993. Each unit tracks the performance of a particular market index. The original SPDR follows the S&P index of 500 leading stocks, and investors buy them all in a single share.

SPDRs are bought through brokerage firms. A round lot may cost about $15,000 in today's prices. No-load mutual funds, on the other hand, are bought directly from the fund itself. Prices of SPDRs fluctuate daily, just like any other stock. Likewise, like a stock, investors can sell SPDRs short, write options against them, and place limit orders.

The cost of a SPDR that tracks S&P 500 is 0.12 percent a year (2004), plus brokerage commission and the "spread," which is the difference between buying price and selling price. By comparison, investors pay 0.35 percent for the Schwab 500 with no spreads or commissions.

INTERNATIONAL INDEX INVESTING WITH iSHARES MSCI FUNDS

iShares MSCI Index Funds move the concept of index investing to the international level. Each share of this fund is designed to expose investors to specific international equity markets when they purchase a diversified portfolio of stocks within that country. The MSCI indices are universally recognized benchmarks against which international money managers are measured. There are currently (2004) 23 iShares MSCI funds in existence.

EXCHANGE-TRADED INDEX FUNDS

Exchange-traded index funds (ETFs) are hybrid securities that combine the advantages of the traditional index mutual funds with many of the features of listed equity products. ETFs are baskets of stocks that allow an investor to buy or sell a portfolio of securities through a single share. However, unlike mutual funds, ETFs can be bought and sold at intra-day prices, on typically the American Stock Exchange. Some ETFs seek to track a broad market index like the S&P 500 Index or the Nasdaq 100 Index, while others target a specific sector like biotechnology or energy.

ETFs are comparable to index funds, but they do have several special advantages. First, an investor can buy a single share of an ETF for as low as $5, whereas most mutual funds require a minimum purchase of $1,000. Second, index funds may be famous for their low expenses, but ETFs beat even these funds, with an average annual expense ratio of just 0.34 percent, as compared to the average stock index fund expense ratio of 0.50 percent. Third, ETFs are highly tax-efficient. Traditional index funds are relatively tax efficient, since the fund managers do not make many trades. But if the market dives and a lot of shareholders want to redeem their shares, the manager might have no choice but to sell stocks and pass taxable capital gains along to shareholders. ETFs also refrain from trading, but redemption is not an option for ETF investors. If an ETF shareholders want to cash out, they would have to sell their shares on the open market.

Fourth, unlike mutual funds, which place limits on the frequency and size of trades, an investor can trade ETFs as often as desired. Active traders might move in and out of an ETF several times in a single day—just as they do with individual stocks. But unlike mutual funds, an investor can place an order to buy or sell an ETF at a special price.

Finally, the most important tax efficiency of ETF comes from what is known as *redemption in kind*. It is commonplace that traditional mutual funds trade at net asset value, or NAV. Occasionally, a gap opens up between the NAV and the price at which ETF is traded, and that creates a unique opportunity for investors.

Assume that such a gap has opened, and Nova Tech is trading at a slight discount—maybe one cent per Nova—to NAV. An institutional investor will jump on that opportunity, buying up 25,000 shares of Nova at the discounted price, and handing them over to the ETF company. In exchange, instead of cash, the ETF company will give the investor a basket of stocks, the same stocks that make up the EFT's index. The investor will immediately sell these stocks on the market, benefiting from the discrepancy between the price he paid for the Nova shares and the slightly higher price for which he can sell the stocks he got in exchange.

The benefits derived from this transaction should be clear. Although the institutional investor effectively redeemed his shares, the fund manager did not have to sell any stocks in order to cash him out. And because he simply traded the stocks, the transaction did not generate any capital gains on which shareholders would owe taxes. Even more important, the manager can pick the shares he handed over to the institutional investor, giving him the shares of Xerox, for instance, for which he paid the least. Over time, this can significantly lower the EFT's capital gains exposure.

VARIABLE ANNUITY AND LIFE INVESTMENT PRODUCTS

Variable annuities have become a juggernaut in the financial services industry. In 2004, variable annuity assets under management approached a record $960 billion.

Buoyed by the spectacular growth, life insurance companies have introduced several variants of the traditional contract. Since these products directly compete for the dollars earmarked for stocks, bonds and mutual funds, in this section a brief description of each of the variable annuity products will be presented.

DEFERRED VARIABLE ANNUITY

An annuity is a contract between an investor and an insurance company. A deferred annuity allows investment of money in one lump sum—a single-premium annuity— or in increments over a number of years.

There are two types of deferred annuities: fixed and variable. The former guarantees a fixed dollar amount when the fixed term expires. Variable Annuities (VAs), however, allow an investor to choose from a variety of investment opportunities, such a stocks, bonds, and managed accounts, and they offer a broad spectrum of options, including global investments and capital preservation accounts. In essence, a VA is a mutual fund wrapped inside an insurance contract that allows the earnings to compound on a tax-deferred basis.

Benefits of a VA Investment

The key advantages of VAs are presented below.

First, VAs offer many of the same benefits that mutual funds do, including access to a diversified investment portfolio run by professional money managers at an affordable cost. A VA lets an investor pick and choose any combination of varied investments. It also permits the investor to follow some type of an asset allocation strategy, thereby reducing the overall risk of the portfolio. Also, none of these reallocation movements have tax consequences, because in a VA the investment grows tax-deferred.

Second, unlike an IRA, 401(k), or other qualified contributions, there is no annual limit on how much money can be invested in a VA, or how often switches can be made between subaccounts. Even more important, unlike qualified investments, VAs are not subject to required minimum distributions at age 701/2.

Third, upon death of a VA investor, the beneficiaries are guaranteed the full amount of the original investment or the current value of the annuity, whichever is greater.

Fourth, a VA company permits the withdrawal of up to seven percent of the distribution as payout while the rest of the money, or any portion thereof, can remain invested in growth funds. This arrangement allows an investor to achieve attractive returns from equity investments while enjoying current monthly income.

Fifth, the greatest benefit derived from a VA is the appreciated income stream it generates if the funds are allowed to grow tax-deferred over some length of time. For instance, it can be demonstrated that, after a period of time, an investor could use the VA funds to generate significantly higher monthly income than would be possible if the funds were originally invested in a taxable mutual fund which generated comparable returns.

Drawbacks of VAs

There are several drawbacks to VAs as well. The key drawbacks are discussed next.

First, the main insurance cost is the mortality and expense charge (called M&E charge) which can run anywhere from 0.55 percent to 1.40 percent per year. The insurance company also levies an annual contract charge ($25 to $40 per year), and a management fee on each subaccount. All told, in a VA, investment and insurance-related expenses typically run about two percent.

Second, surrender charges, or contingent deferred sales charges (CDSC), can last anywhere from five to ten years—declining frequently by one percent per year. The average surrender charge in a VA is 5.84 percent. However, one can completely avoid these charges by withdrawing each year no more than the free withdrawal (usually ten percent) allowed until these charges disappear.

Third, if an investor is younger than 59-1/2 and withdraws an amount from VA, the IRS would impose a ten percent early withdrawal penalty on the tax-deferred interest withdrawn, except in very special cases.

Key Check Points

Investors in VAs should make sure that the insurance company is on a solid footing by checking its ratings published by A.M. Best, S&P, Moody's and Duff and Phelps. Also, the selection list should be limited to those VAs that offer at least five different subaccounts with good track records in case switching between accounts is desired at a future date. Particular attention should also be paid to the money managers and to three-, five-, and ten-year total return figures published by these managers.

Valuable information on variable annuities can be found in Morningstar Variable Annuities/Life Performance Report (1-800-876-5005) and VARDS Report (404-998-5186).

New Features

In recent years, VA companies have introduced several bells and whistles in their contracts, some of which are truly innovative. The key features are presented below.

Among the most important innovations was Hartford Life's introduction in 1997 of dollar cost averaging, which was followed by most major annuity providers. This program lets investors buy into an annuity with a lump-sum amount. The initial investment sits in a fixed-income account before it is slowly moved into equity accounts over a set period of months. Investors receive a guaranteed return over the annuity's first few months and do not have to worry about buying in at the market top.

Another feature relates to the flexibility added to the expense ratio. Annuity companies have started unbundling the insurance component of the high insurance cost, letting investors pick and choose the insurance they want and how much they want to pay. For instance, John Hancock's VA lets investors choose between a standard or an enhanced death benefit, and a nursing home waiver. As a bonus, Hancock has dropped its M&E fees to just one percent.

Finally, working with the top load and no-load fund companies, COVA Financial Services has developed a back-end computer system that is compatible with each broker-dealer client's computer system and product offering. If brokers and their customers are already working with one company for their IRA or 401(k), COVA offers to build a VA using funds of the same company.

VARIABLE IMMEDIATE ANNUITY

Variable Immediate Annuities (VIAs) are gaining increased attention in the financial planning community due to the demographics and the shifts in focus towards income. They can provide a steady stream of income and act as an ideal complement to pension and Social Security payments. This product is most appropriate for individuals who are retired or nearing retirement, and have a sum of money from which they are looking for a reliable income payout that will begin immediately.

The greatest drawback of VIAs is that buying an immediate annuity requires the adviser and client to relinquish total control of those assets—something neither is seldom willing to do. Also, these annuities do not protect annuitants from inflation and do not allow them to withdraw any portion of the principal funds even in case of an extreme emergency.

Keyport developed the Preferred Income Plan, one of the first immediate variable annuities that offer flexibility, if needed, in the income stream and future cash access. Subsequently, other companies began rolling out similar offerings, with options that allow investors partial access to their funds. For instance, some companies offer investors a guaranteed payout until they are 100, but will still let them withdraw funds in case of an emergency. There are also new products with attached death benefits attached, that assure that the beneficiaries would receive the same payments the policyholders would have received.

It is important for the holder of a VIA to establish an underlying mix of investment options providing returns that continue to keep pace with inflation. Most VIAs allow the option to create diversity in the underlying portfolio, an option that can prove to be valuable.

A prime benefit of VIAs is that the part of each income payment that represents a return of the principal is not taxable. Investors can also switch their funds from one investment option to another without having to pay taxes. For instance, if a person switches the underlying investment option from equities to fixed income, the resulting gains in equities are not taxed. The person only pays income taxes on the payouts received.

Shopping for a VIA is no simple task. Even if an investor gets monthly income quotes from a few insurers, the figures may not be comparable, because all insurers do not offer the same choice of assumed investment return. In addition, the investor needs to factor in the guarantees and flexibility that each annuity offers. More critically, everyone should weigh the initial monthly income against the annuity's total annual costs. Even if an insurer offers an attractive high first-month income, that might turn out to be a bad deal if the annuity's high costs would make it difficult to earn a decent long-term return.

EQUITY-INDEXED ANNUITY

An equity-indexed annuity (EIA) grows at the greater of an annual, guaranteed minimum rate of return, typically 3 percent, and the return from a stock market index such as the S&P 500, reduced by certain expenses and formulas. If the selected index rises sufficiently during a specific period, a greater return is credited to the contract owner's account for that period. If the stock market index registers a modest gain or declines, the value of the policy increases only by the minimum guaranteed amount. So the owner is guaranteed to receive back at least all principal plus the minimum guaranteed growth, if an EIA contract is held for a minimum period of time, known as the "penalty period."

While the concept of EIA is based on the simple notion of a limited upside and a guaranteed safety of the principal, its execution is complicated. This is because EIAs invest in a mix of zero coupon bonds and index options, and the terms, guarantees, payouts, and fees are all over the lot. That makes shopping for EIAs tricky. Fortunately, two free Web sites, www.annuityratewatch.com and www.annuityadvisoronline.com, do an excellent job of collecting data on EIA contracts and their fees and features. EIAs have fixed terms from one to ten years, and impose steep "surrender charges" for cashing out early.

Key to an EIA selection is the *participation rate*, which is the portion of the index's gain received by the annuity owner. The calculation of that percentage is also important. Some EIAs use a "point-to-point" method, which gives a flat percentage for the total return achieved by the index during the lifetime of the contract. By contrast, the "annual ratchet" method calculates the value each year. The difference between the two methods can be significant.

Let us assume that a person invested in an EIA which uses the annual ratchet method. The S&P 500 was at 1400 when the contract was issued. If on the first anniversary date the index had declined to 1100, the policy value will remain unchanged and the starting point for the second year would be 1100. The investor would benefit when the index rises above 1100. However, had the insurance company used the point-to-point method, the investor would have no gain until the index crossed 1400.

Fees and annual charges also vary—sometimes considerably—between insurance companies marketing EIAs. Some companies replace these charges with *performance caps*. For instance, the Allianz Powerhouse contract pays 125 percent of the S&P 500's average value each year but caps the gains at 15 percent.

VARIABLE LIFE INSURANCE

Variable life insurance permits the policyowner to allocate a portion of each premium payment to one or more investment options, in separate subaccounts after a deduction for expense and mortality charges.

The death benefit and cash value of a variable life policy will increase or decrease based on the performance of the investment options selected. The death benefit, however, never drops below an initial guaranteed amount, unless policy premiums are not paid, or if loans or other withdrawals are taken from the policy. The ultimate death benefit is subject to the claims paying ability of the insurer.

Because the investment options available inside a variable life policy usually involve securities, the SEC requires this type of policy to be accompanied by a prospectus. It provides detailed information on how the policy works, its risks, and all expenses or charges involved. The SEC also requires individuals selling variable life policies to be licensed to sell securities.

There are two types of variable life insurance, based on the formula used to link the amount of death benefit to the performance of the investments chosen by the policyowner. Under the *corridor percentage method*, the amount of the death benefit is periodically changed to equal a certain percentage of the cash value. Under current tax law, this percentage is 250 percent up to the insured's age 40, gradually decreasing to 100 percent, usually at age 95. By contrast, the *level additions method* uses excess investment earnings to purchase additional amounts of singe premium, paid-up insurance. In general, if investment performance is positive, the amount of the death benefit increases; if not, the death benefit amount decreases.

In passing, it should be mentioned that one big worry of consumer advocates is that many policyholders may calculate their ability to afford the premiums on variable life policies based on healthy stock market returns. If these returns do not materialize, these people might be unable to afford the insurance charges in which case the policy would lapse. Therefore, caution should be exercised in purchasing variable life insurance policies as an investment vehicle.

VARIABLE UNIVERSAL LIFE

A variable universal life insurance policy combines features of both universal life policies and variable life policies. As with a variable life policy, a variable universal contract permits a policyowner to allocate a portion of each premium payment to one or more investment options, in separate accounts, after a deduction for expense and mortality charges. An annual statement detailing the expenses, charges, and credits allows a policyowner to track performance over time.

Like universal life policies, within certain guidelines, a variable universal contract permits the owner of a policy to modify the policy's death benefit, and change the amount and timing of premium payments, to meet changing circumstances. The ultimate death benefit is subject to the claims paying ability of the insurer.

There are two primary types of variable universal life, based on the level of death benefits. Type I variable universal life, also knows as "Option A," policies pay a fixed, level death benefit, generally the face amount of the policy. Type II policy, also known as "Option B," generally pays the face amount of the policy plus the accumulated cash values. As the cash values grow, so does the potential death benefit.

SOPHISTICATED INVESTMENT PRODUCTS

REAL ESTATE INVESTMENT TRUSTS (REITs)

The passage of an Act of Congress in 1960 revived interest in the type of group real estate investments known as *Real Estate Investment Trusts*, or REITs. These institutions are exempt from taxation if they (1) have 75 percent of their assets in real estate, mortgages, cash, or government securities at the end of each quarter; (2) derive 70 percent of their gross income from real estate, and receive no more than 30 percent of their income from capital appreciation (to discourage investing in highly speculative projects); (3) distribute 95 percent of their income to shareholders (officially known as beneficiaries); and (4) have at least 100 shareholders, no five of whom can control more than half of the shares. In exempting the REITs from taxation, the lawmakers intended that these institutions be publicly held and that they be instrumental in diverting public funds primarily into the real estate industry.

There are two major types of REITs on the market: *mortgage trusts* and *equity trusts*. Mortgage trusts provide short-term financing for construction loans or for permanent mortgage loans for large projects. Equity trusts buy or build their own real estate property and hire management firms to run them.

REITs offer the investor an opportunity to invest in real estate without committing a large amount of money. Shares of REITs are generally readily marketable, especially those listed on exchanges or traded over the counter. Because a REIT is, in effect, a closed-end investment company, its price is determined on the open market. The price of REIT shares may be above or below the actual book value of the real estate holdings.

The Internal Revenue Code (IRC) contains a number of conditions which a trust must meet to qualify as a Real Estate Investment Trust, including the requirement that a REIT pay out at least 95 percent of its taxable income. If a REIT meets these conditions, the income paid to the shareholders is not taxed twice (as it would be in a regular corporation), but is taxed only once in the hands of the shareholders. That is, income from sources such as rents and mortgage interest received is only taxed to the shareholder as ordinary income. Also, capital gains from the profitable sale of real estate investments are treated as a long-term gain, regardless of the length of time an individual has owned the shares in the REIT. Of course, if a shareholder sells the shares in a REIT, the gain or loss is treated as long or short term, depending upon how long the shares were owned.

INVESTMENT DERIVATIVES

In Saul Bellow's 1956 novella, *Seize the Day*, the hero uses his last $700 to buy lard futures on the advice of a close friend. To the hero's dismay, he watches lard prices plummet, and a shocked broker closes out his account. This scenario is enough to scare a reader away from such markets for life.

But derivatives—financial instruments that, like futures, are derived from an underlying transaction of goods, currencies, stocks, bonds, or money itself—are quite popular. Originally invented for commodities providers as a hedge against price fluctuations, futures and options also gave speculators the chance to make a fortune or lose everything. Now, financial engineers are designing derivatives that ideally meet very specific investment needs.

It is difficult to summarize the arcane world of derivatives in the short space available. Consequently, as an alternative, a short description of the key derivatives is presented below.

Options. A standardized contract between a party and one of the exchanges, or a custom contract between two parties, which gives the buyer the right, but not the obligation, to exercise an option to buy or sell at a present price on a specified date. A *call option* gives the holder the right to *buy* the underlying asset by a certain date at a certain price. A *put option* gives the holder the right to *sell* the underlying asset by a certain date at a certain price. Mutual funds buy calls to take advantage of possible price increases in an underlying asset without risking more than the premium paid for the option. Puts are used to protect against price declines. Losses are limited to the premium the fund manager pays for the option, while the profits are potentially unlimited. Seller's profits are limited to the premiums they receive, but they have unlimited loss potential if a buyer chooses to exercise an option. Standardized options are widely traded on exchanges, but there is also a universe of customized option contracts traded over the counter.

Option Spreads. An infinite variety of option spreads exist today. These include yield curve spreads, money market spreads, spreads on LIBOR (London Interbank Offered Rate), T-bill and Eurodollar futures, and spreads on mortgage, swap, commodity, currency and hybrid equity and bond markets. For example, a fund manager who thinks the German bond market will outperform the U.S. bond market in terms of yield can buy an inter-governmental bond option spread. Managers with exposure to spreads can buy option spreads to hedge their bets.

Straddle, Strip, Strap and Strangle. These are a combination of option trading strategies which involve taking a position in both calls and puts on the same stock. Of these, straddle is the most common strategy; it involves buying equal amounts of puts and calls with the same strike price, the same underlying asset, index or currency, and the same expiration date.

Futures. Exchange-traded futures are standardized contracts between two financial institutions or a financial institution and a corporate client that obligate one party to buy and the other to sell a specific underlying asset at a specified date and price in the future. The right to offset, or cancel, an existing futures position (by acquiring an equal but opposite position, leaving participants with zero exposure), allows buyers, sellers and clearing houses to cut their losses or take profits without negotiating with counterparties.

Eurodollar Futures. Managers buy these exchange-traded contracts based on the rate of three-month Eurodollar time deposit funds as a way of pricing Eurodollar-based financial instruments like swaps and forward rate agreements.

Swaps. A plain vanilla interest-rate swap is when one party, B, agrees to pay another party, A, cash flow equal to interest at a predetermined fixed rate on a common principal amount for a number of years. At the same time, party A agrees to pay party B cash flows equal to interest at a floating rate on a common principal for the same period of time. The currencies of the two sets of cash flows are the same and the life of the swap can range from two to 15 years. There are currency, option, future, commodity and municipal swaps. By obtaining financing from one market and then swapping all or part of the cash flows into the desired currency denominations and/or rate indices, fund managers can diversify their activities in global markets, hedge their holdings, and increase their liquidity. Because they are tailored to a manager's projections, swaps can be a gamble if interest or currency rates widely fluctuate.

SHORT SELLING

Short selling is the reverse of the usual market transaction. Instead of buying a stock in the hope that it can be sold later at a higher price, a short trader *first sells stock* and later *buys it back* at what the seller hopes will be a lower price; that is, the short seller attempts to first sell high and then buy low. Short traders borrow stock to sell short from their brokers, who acquire stocks so they can lend them from the margin accounts. At a subsequent time period, the short seller purchases the stock to cover the sale. At that point, the short seller realizes either a profit or a loss, depending on the purchase and sale price of the stock. At that point, the borrowed stocks are returned to the broker.

RUNMONEY, FOLIOfn, ETC.

Traditionally, mutual funds have suffered from two major drawbacks. First, when it comes to taxes, they are managed inefficiently, since funds can generate capital gains even when they are losing money. Second, they charge an ongoing management fee. It is now easy to see why investors might be tempted to abandon the communal nature of mutual funds in favor of individually managed portfolios of stocks. However, the hitch has been that only wealthy investors with $1 million or more to invest could afford professional money managers.

All that is changed now. Investors with as little as $50,000 can now afford individually managed accounts through RunMoney, myMoneyPro.com, WrapManager, and PrivateAccounts.com (bought out by E*Trade).

At myMoneyPro.com, an investor can choose from a list of 20 top-ranking money management firms that focus on large-cap growth stocks, small-cap value, or other investment styles. Investors can also set preferences. For instance, if investors do not want to invest in stocks that support birth control, they can inform the managers when they initiate the account. Similarly, if an investor has accumulated capital gains elsewhere, she can request the manager to begin harvesting capital losses to offset those gains.

Another advantage is access to the composition of the portfolio on a daily basis. Mutual fund companies are required to provide progress reports to their shareholders only twice a year. By contrast, RunMoney clients, who have access to as many as 120 different money managers, can view their individually managed accounts on a daily basis.

There is yet another option available to the do-it-yourself investors who are interested in creating and managing their own stock portfolios. Until now, even if they used Charles Schwab which charges $14.95 a trade, building a portfolio of 35 stocks would cost $525 in commission. In addition, if the portfolio is rebalanced twice a year in response to changing market conditions, that could cost an additional $1,000 or more. Therefore, an investor would need at least $25,000 to create a diversified portfolio.

Today, FOLIOfn offers an attractive alternative. For $29.95 a month, and no minimum investment, this company allows an investor to create and manage up to three "folios" of up to 50 stocks each. It also lets the investor modify the portfolio as many times as desired for no additional charge during two set periods of time daily. Furthermore, because this company allows investors to purchase fractional shares of stock, it is possible to gain instant diversification for as little as $1,000.

Finally, investors participating in FOLIOfn can customize their portfolios. For instance, an account can be set up so that every time the investor sells a stock, the company executes the order in a way that maximizes capital losses and minimizes capital gains, or vice versa. In addition, other sites, such as MAXfunds.com, personalfund.com, and SmartLeaf, now offer Web-based advice to personal fund investors.

Nothing will ever be achieved without great men, and men are great if they are determined to be so.

Charles de Gaulle

SPDRs (SPY). The American Stock Exchange and State Street Bank created the SPDRs (Standard & Poor's Depositary Receipts) in January 1993. Structured as a unit investment trust, SPY is the most common exchange-traded index product that represents an investment in the S&P 500. It holds substantially all of the securities in the S&P 500 Index in approximately the same proportion as the underlying index, with the intent of closely tracking the price and dividend yield performance of the index. The index is market-cap weighted, measuring the performance of the large-cap sector of the U.S. equity market. The initial share price of SPDRs represents one-tenth the value of the S&P 500 Index. For example, if the S&P 500 is trading at 815, SPY will trade at about $82; where a 10-point move in the S&P will mean a one-point move in SPY. The expense ratio is just 0.12 percent. Liquidity on the SPDR is excellent, often being the most actively traded security on the AMEX. The first and largest of all ETFs, SPY has over $34 billion in assets.

Mid-Cap SPDRs (MDY). With the success of the original SPDR, the AMEX, with State Street Bank & Trust as the trustee, introduced the MidCap SPDRs in May 1995. Also structured as a unit investment trust, MDY holds substantially all the securities that comprise the S&P MidCap 400 Index, with the intent of closely tracking the price and yield performance of the index. The index is market value weighted, measuring the performance of the mid-cap sector of the U.S. market. The MidCap SPDRs are initially priced at one-fifth the value of the index. MDY remains a popular choice for investors to gain access to the mid cap sector of the U.S. market. When used in conjunction with a broad-based core holding, such as SPY, MDY can be used to overweight the mid cap sector. Expenses are slightly higher than the SPY at 0.25%.

Select Sector SPDRs. State Street Bank and Trust Company introduced the Select Sector SPDRs in December 1998. Select Sector SPDRs use each a sub-section of the S&P 500 as their underlying benchmark, allowing investors to closely track the performance of each of the industry sectors within the S&P 500. There are nine Select Sector SPDRs, with a combined investment in each sector equaling an investment in the entire S&P 500. The sectors include consumer discretionary, consumer staples, energy, financials, health care, industrials, materials, technology, and utilities. The initial price of select sector SPDRs is set at one-tenth the value of the underlying index. Select sector SPDRs allow for customized asset allocations to fit specific investment needs and goals. Investors are able to gain access to, or overweight specific industries within the S&P 500 that they feel may outperform.

DIAMONDS (DIA). In January 1998, the AMEX introduced DIAMONDS, structured as a unit investment trust containing all 30 stocks of the Dow Jones Industrial Average Index in approximately the same proportion as the underlying index. The index is price-weighted, containing blue-chip stocks considered to be leaders in their industry. DIAMONDS seek to closely track the price and yield performance of this popular index. DIAMONDS are initially valued at one-hundredth of the value of the Dow and have a competitive expense ratio of just 0.18%. With the Dow Jones Industrial Average being one of the most widely followed indexes, DIAMONDS have grown to a market capitalization of over $4 billion.

Nasdaq–100 Index Tracking Stock (QQQ). Created in March of 1999 by Nasdaq and the AMEX, QQQ is similar to SPDRs and DIAMONDS in that it is structured as a unit investment trust. Known as "Cubes," they hold a portfolio of the equity securities that comprise the Nasdaq-100 Index with the intention of providing, before expenses, investment results that closely approximate this index. The Nasdaq 100 Index is modified capitalization-weighted, and is composed of 100 of the largest and most actively traded, non-financial companies listed on the Nasdaq Stock Market. The share price of QQQ is initially set at approximately 1/40th the value of the index. Second only to SPY in market capitalization, the "Cubes" have close to $16 billion in assets and an expense ratio of 0.18 percent.

iShares. Barclays Global Fund Advisors began introducing its ETF lineup, called iShares, in mid-2000 through its subsidiary, Barclays Global Investors (BGI). BGI, re-branded its former WEBS series (World Equity Benchmark Shares), which track the Morgan Stanley Capital International (MSCI) country indexes, and released a wide variety of funds tracking many popular domestic and global indexes. These funds track 13 Dow Jones, 12 Russell, 19 S&P, 24 MSCI, six Goldman Sachs, three Lehman, a Nasdaq, and a Cohen & Steers index. Introduced in 2002, iShares now has four fixed-income ETFs following three Lehman Treasury indexes and a Goldman Sachs' corporate bond index. iShares have by far the most offerings in the ETF universe and now have accumulated approximately $30 billion in assets.

iShares MSCI Index Funds. Formerly World Equity Benchmark Shares (WEBS), these funds have been re-branded iShares and are managed by Barclays Global Fund Advisors. They are designed to track the MSCI Index for each country. The MSCI Indexes are globally recognized benchmarks against which international money managers are commonly measured. There are currently 24 iShares MSCI funds. Although most iShares MSCI funds are single-country investments, investors who like to invest regionally can purchase several iShares MSCI funds and utilize customized weightings to create an optimized international portfolio. Also, a MSCI EAFE Index (Europe, Australasia, and the Far East) and MSCI EMU (European Monetary Union) Index funds are available for those wanting a more broad-based international portfolio. Investors incur extra risks when investing in country-specific funds, such as foreign currency risk, as iShares MSCI country funds do not hedge currencies. Also, investment returns in international markets may be more volatile than that of the U.S. market and involve normal risks. SPDR has very low operating expenses, and are exposed to typical investment risks, such as market fluctuations due to changes in the economic and political developments in those countries with which they are associated.

streetTRACKS. In the latter part of 2000, State Street Global Advisors released its latest family of exchange-traded index funds called streetTRACKS. These funds are designed to track various Dow Jones, FORTUNE, Morgan Stanley, and Wilshire indexes. The Dow Jones indexes represented are the US Large Cap Growth and Value Indexes, US Small Cap Growth and Value Indexes, and the Global Titans Index, which consists of the 50 largest multi-nationals in the world. The FORTUNE Indexes represented are the FORTUNE 500 Index and the FORTUNE e-50 index. Also in the lineup are the Morgan Stanley Technology Index, the Morgan Stanley Internet Index, and the Wilshire REIT Index. Other ETFs with which State Street is involved, but that are not part of the streetTRACKS family include: SPDRs, the nine Select Sector SPDRs, and Diamonds.

Vanguard VIPER Shares. Released in May 2001, Vanguard's VIPER (Vanguard Index Participation Equity Receipts) shares are basically a separate share class of existing Vanguard index mutual funds and, as such, have identical investment objectives and strategies as the issuing fund. VIPERS are different than other ETFs in that an existing shareholder of a Vanguard index mutual fund that offers corresponding VIPER shares has the ability to convert existing open-end shares into VIPER shares of the same fund for a $50 fee. Depending on the brokerage firm, fractional shares may not be converted, so investors could incur a modest taxable gain on partial shares that are liquidated. Once converted, however, investors cannot convert their VIPER shares back into conventional shares. Also, conventional shares held in a 401(k) account cannot be converted into VIPER shares. Currently, there are two available VIPERs, the Vanguard Total Stock Market VIPER (VTI) and the Vanguard Extended Markets VIPERs.

Treasury FITRS. The latest fixed-income ETFs to be introduced, FITRS (Fixed Income Trust Reciepts) were brought to market in November 2002 by ETF Advisors, LP. These funds are designed to track the returns of U.S. Treasury securities with selected maturities of one year, two years, five years, and 10 years. The funds have at least 95 percent of the underlying assets in debt obligations of the U.S. Treasury, or other Federal agencies. The funds invest in a portfolio of four to 10 securities, designed to have an annual tracking error of the underlying index of less than 1 percent. FITRS allow investors to have exposure to Treasuries at key points on the yield curve. The funds distribute dividends monthly, mostly from Treasury interest, which is typically exempt from state and local income taxes. Low expense ratios are in line with other fixed-income ETFs, at 0.15 percent each.

BLDRS. Nasdaq Financial Products Services, Inc. and The Bank of New York (as Trustee) introduced BLDRS (Baskets of Listed Depositary Reciepts) in November 2002. The new family of ETFs are based on the Bank of New York ADR Index, a real time index tracking U.S. traded depositary receipts. These funds are designed to provide a low cost way to invest in foreign markets through depositary receipts. Currently, there are four BLDRS following the following Bank of New York ADR indexes: Emerging Markets 50, Developed Markets 100, Europe 100, and Asia 50. Expense ratios for the BLDRS are kept low at 0.30 percent. Each of the indexes uses a capitalization-weighted methodology designed for diversification.

EXCHANGE-TRADED INDEX INVESTING

Exchange-Traded Funds (ETFs) continue to gain popularity among individual and institutional investors alike, and the growing demand has produced a wide range of investment products. ETFs now cover virtually every equity asset class, while tracking the most popular and widely followed indexes. ETFs are hybrid securities that combine the advantages of the traditional open-end index mutual fund, while offering many trading features of listed equity products. The first ETF came to market in 1993 with the creation of the Standard & Poor's Depositary Receipts, or

SPDRs, by State Street Global Advisors and the AMEX. SPY remains the largest ETF and is among the most actively traded securities on the American Stock Exchange. According to Morningstar, through October 31 2000, 85 percent of actively-managed U.S. diversified equity funds trailed the S&P 500 over a trailing 10-year period. With the majority of managers underperforming the index they are paid to beat, investors are increasingly employing the strategy of approximating the returns of the market, instead of trying to pick the right managers to beat the market. The growing popularity of this investment philosophy has helped fuel the demand for ETF products worldwide. The following are some of the benefits that ETFs have in common:

- Trading flexibility, such as continuous pricing, intraday liquidity, margin purchases, stop and limit orders, and the ability to sell short–even on a downtick
- Tax efficiency
- Low operating costs
- Convenient access to targeted market sectors and countries
- Accurate tracking of underlying benchmark indexes, with dividends from stock holdings passed along to the investor
- Broad diversification within specific industries

Trading Flexibility. The trading flexibility of ETFs sets them apart from traditional open-end mutual funds. Unlike open-end mutual funds, which are bought and sold throughout the day at a price that is equal to the fund's NAV (determined at the end of the day), ETFs trade more like stocks. ETFs are continuously priced throughout the trading day and can be bought and sold by investors at intraday market prices. Investors can also place stop and limit orders to specify the prices at which they wish to trade. ETFs can be purchased on margin, and unlike stocks, they can be sold short–even on a downtick.

Tax Efficiency. ETFs are tax efficient in that they are designed to track an index, which normally results in lower portfolio turnover and taxable gains when compared to actively-managed funds. The fact that ETFs trade on an exchange also contributes to their tax efficiency. When an open-end mutual fund experiences large redemptions from investors for cash, the need to meet investor redemptions may force the fund to liquidate securities, which may create capital gains tax liabilities. This tax burden is then passed on to the investors who remain in the fund. Because ETFs trade on exchanges, investors simply sell their shares to other investors. This exchange-trading feature eliminates the need for the fund to liquidate holding for cash and possibly generate capital gains. Because ETF shares are created and redeemed as an "in kind" transaction, the creation/redemption process is also a nontaxable transaction.

Low Operating Costs. ETFs are designed to closely approximate the returns of well-known indexes and are passively managed. Passively managed funds are generally less likely to demand high management fees and ETFs are among the lowest cost products available. For example, the iShares S&P 500 Index Fund has an expense ratio of just 0.09 percent and SPY has an expense ratio of 0.12 percent. Costs are also kept down by the fact that ETF shares trade on an exchange, thus not incurring the expenses associated with buying and selling portfolio securities to meet investor purchases and redemptions. There are no minimum investment amounts (one can buy a single ETF share), loads, short-term restrictions, or redemption fees associated with ETFs. Instead, investors pay a standard brokerage commission.

Targeted Investing. These are exchange-traded funds that follow almost every widely followed index, allowing investors to easily move in and out of entire sectors of the economy with minimum trading costs. For example, investors can maintain a core holding of the U.S. market with an investment in SPDRs (SPY), while overweighting the energy sector with the Energy Select Sector SPDR if they prefer this sector. Investors are also able to tap into the international markets by using either broad-based international indexes such as the iShares EAFE Index Fund or by using one of the many country-specific funds, such as the iShares MSCI Hong Kong Index Fund. In addition, ETFs can be used to temporarily equitize cash in a portfolio, since there is no minimum holding period. By temporarily investing cash in a broad market ETF, such as the Vanguard Total Stock Index Viper, investors can remain fully invested in the market while planning their next investment move.

Accurate Index Tracking. ETFs consist of a basket of stocks in specific weights, designed to closely track the performance of a benchmark index. ETFs can either hold substantially all of the underlying securities in their appropriate weightings, or use a representative sampling technique to attempt to approximate the returns of the underlying index. ETFs structured as a unit investment trust, such as SPY, MidCap SPDRs, Nasdaq Index Tracking Stock and DIAMONDS hold dividends paid from constituent stocks in a non-interest bearing account and pass them along to the shareholders on a quarterly basis. DIAMONDS distribute dividends on a monthly basis. Reinvestment of dividends paid from stocks within the portfolio is not available for trusts with this structure. The ETFs structured as open-end funds (iShares, streetTRACKS, and Vipers) normally distribute dividends, less expenses, to the investor on a quarterly basis. These funds have the ability to reinvest dividends paid from stock holdings in the fund on a daily basis.

Diversification. Diversification is an important tool for reducing the risk of one or more underperformers having a large impact on an investor's portfolio. Using ETFs, investors can easily construct well-diversified portfolios within specific sectors of the market, with lower trading costs than building a diversified portfolio of individually selected stocks. By owning a larger basket of stocks within a specific sector investors capture the average return of the sector, instead of taking on the increased risk of overweighting a single loser in a smaller, more volatile portfolio of stocks. However, some ETFs are narrower in scope and may experience greater volatility than a broad-based ETF.

EXCHANGE-TRADED FUNDS COMPARED TO CLOSED-END FUNDS

Exchange-traded funds should not be confused with closed-end funds. ETF shares are continuously created and redeemed and a prospectus must accompany all sales. The creation/redemption process allows for arbitrage opportunities, and as a result, discounts and premiums that commonly exist with closed-end funds are typically not associated with ETFs. ETFs share a number of similar features with closed-end funds, but are distinctively different. Like closed-end funds, ETFs are listed on an exchange and have an underlying net asset value and market price. Both trade like stocks, offering continuous pricing, intraday liquidity, margin capability, and the ability to be sold short. However, closed-end fund shares are created in an initial public offering, following which the number of shares remains fixed. Investors who wish to buy shares after the IPO must do so by buying them from another investor on an exchange, at a price determined by supply and demand. Closed-end funds can issue new shares in a rights offering and redeem shares in a tender offer, but they do not do so on a continuous basis. Since closed-end fund shares are not redeemable directly through the fund company, they often trade at significant discounts or premiums to their underlying net asset value.

ETFs differ from closed-end funds in that ETF shares are continuously created and redeemed in large blocks, directly with the fund company. The creation/redemption feature of exchange-traded funds is a self-regulating mechanism that prevents meaningful discounts or premiums from persisting. The creation/redemption feature allows ETFs to grow when investor demand is high and shrink when demand wanes. Liquidity can become an issue with closed-end funds that have low trading volume, where a sizable order can considerably move the price of an illiquid fund. Liquidity is generally not an issue with ETFs because of the existence of creation/redemption mechanism.

EXCHANGE-TRADED INDEX FUNDS

Symbol	Fund Name
ADRA	BLDRS Asia 50 ADR Index Fund
ADRD	BLDRS Developed Markets 100 ADR Index Fund
ADRE	BLDRS Emerging Markets 50 ADR Index Fund
ADRU	LDRS Europe 100 ADR Index Fund
DIA	DIAMONDS
ICF	iShares Cohen & Steers Realty Majors Index Fund
IYM	iShares Dow Jones U.S. Basic Materials Sector Index Fund
IYC	iShares Dow Jones U.S. Consumer Cyclical Sector Index Fund
IYK	iShares Dow Jones U.S. Cons. Non-Cyclical Sector Index Fund
IYE	iShares Dow Jones U.S. Energy Sector Index Fund
IYF	iShares Dow Jones U.S. Financial Sector Index Fund
IYG	iShares Dow Jones U.S. Financial Services Index Fund
IYH	iShares Dow Jones U.S. Healthcare Sector Index Fund
IYJ	iShares Dow Jones U.S. Industrial Sector Index Fund
IYR	iShares Dow Jones U.S. Real Estate Index Fund
IYW	iShares Dow Jones U.S. Technology Sector Index Fund
IYZ	iShares Dow Jones U.S. Telecommunications Sector Index Fund
IYY	iShares Dow Jones U.S. Total Market Index Fund
IDU	iShares Dow Jones U.S. Utilities Sector Index Fund
IGE	iShares Goldman Sachs Natural Resources Index Fund
IGN	iShares Goldman Sachs Networking Index Fund
IGW	iShares Goldman Sachs Semiconductor Index Fund
IGV	iShares Goldman Sachs Software Index Fund
IGM	iShares Goldman Sachs Technology Index Fund
LQD	iShares GS $ InvesTop Corporate Bond Fund

Symbol   Fund Name

Symbol	Fund Name
SHY	iShares Lehman 1-3 Year Treasury Bond Fund
IEF	iShares Lehman 7-10 Year Treasury Bond Fund
TLT	iShares Lehman 20+ Year Treasury Bond Fund
EWA	iShares MSCI Australia Index Fund
EWO	iShares MSCI Austria Index Fund
EWK	iShares MSCI Belgium Index Fund
EWZ	iShares MSCI Brazil Index Fund
EWC	iShares MSCI Canada Index Fund
EFA	iShares MSCI EAFE Index Fund
EZU	iShares MSCI EMU Index Fund
EWQ	iShares MSCI France Index Fund
EWG	iShares MSCI Germany Index Fund
EWH	iShares MSCI Hong Kong Index Fund
EWI	iShares MSCI Italy Index Fund
EWJ	iShares MSCI Japan Index Fund
EWM	iShares MSCI Malaysia Index Fund 28
EWW	iShares MSCI Mexico Index Fund 28
EWN	iShares MSCI Netherlands Index Fund 29
EPP	iShares MSCI Pacific ex-Japan Index Fund 29
EWS	iShares MSCI Singapore Index Fund 30
EZA	iShares MSCI South Africa Index Fund 30
EWY	iShares MSCI South Korea Index Fund 31
EWP	iShares MSCI Spain Index Fund 31
EWD	iShares MSCI Sweden Index Fund 32
EWL	iShares MSCI Switzerland Index Fund 32
EWT	iShares MSCI Taiwan Index Fund 33
EWU	iShares MSCI United Kingdom Index Fund 33
IBB	iShares Nasdaq Biotechnology Index Fund 34
IWF	iShares Russell 1000 Growth Index Fund 34
IWB	iShares Russell 1000 Index Fund 35
IWD	iShares Russell 1000 Value Index Fund 35
IWO	iShares Russell 2000 Growth Index Fund
IWM	iShares Russell 2000 Index Fund
IWN	iShares Russell 2000 Value Index Fund
IWZ	iShares Russell 3000 Growth Index Fund
IWV	iShares Russell 3000 Index Fund
IWW	iShares Russell 3000 Value Index Fund
IWP	iShares Russell Midcap Growth Index Fund
IWR	iShares Russell Midcap Index Fund
IWS	iShares Russell Midcap Value Index Fund
OEF	iShares S&P 100 Index Fund
IVW	iShares S&P 500/BARRA Growth Index Fund
IVE	iShares S&P 500/BARRA Value Index Fund
IVV	iShares S&P 500 Index Fund
IEV	iShares S&P Europe 350 Index Fund
IOO	iShares S&P Global 100 Index Fund
IXC	iShares S&P Global Energy Sector Index Fund
IXG	iShares S&P Global Financials Sector Index Fund
IXJ	iShares S&P Global Healthcare Sector Index Fund
IXN	iShares S&P Global Technology Sector Index Fund
IXP	iShares S&P Global Telecom Sector Index Fund
ILF	iShares S&P Latin America 40 Index Fund
IJK	iShares S&P MidCap 400/BARRA Growth Index Fund
IJJ	iShares S&P MidCap 400/BARRA Value Index Fund
IJH	iShares S&P MidCap 400 Index Fund
IJT	iShares S&P SmallCap 600/BARRA Growth Index Fund
IJS	iShares S&P SmallCap 600/BARRA Value Index Fund
IJR	iShares S&P SmallCap 600 Index Fund
ITF	iShares S&P/TOPIX 150 Index Fund
MDY	MidCap SPDR

Symbol   Fund Name

Symbol	Fund Name
QQQ	Nasdaq-100 Shares
SPY	SPDR - S&P Depositary Reciept
XLY	Select Sector SPDR - Consumer Discretionary
XLP	Select Sector SPDR - Consumer Staples
XLE	Select Sector SPDR - Energy
XLF	Select Sector SPDR - Financials
XLV	Select Sector SPDR - Health Care
XLI	Select Sector SPDR - Industrials
XLB	Select Sector SPDR - Materials
XLK	Select Sector SPDR - Technology
XLU	Select Sector SPDR - Utilities
DGT	streetTRACKS DJ Global Titans Index Fund
ELG	streetTRACKS DJ US Large Cap Growth Index Fund
ELV	streetTRACKS DJ US Large Cap Value Index Fund
DSG	streetTRACKS DJ US Small Cap Growth Index Fund
DSV	streetTRACKS DJ US Small Cap Value Index Fund
FFF	streetTRACKS FORTUNE 500 Index Fund
FEF	streetTRACKS FORTUNE E50 Index Fund
MII	streetTRACKS MS Internet Index Fund
MTK	streetTRACKS MS Technology Index Fund
RWR	streetTRACKS Wilshire REIT Index Fund
TFT	Treasury 1 Year FITR ETF
TOU	Treasury 2 Year FITR ETF
TFI	Treasury 5 Year FITR ETF
TTE	Treasury 10 Year FITR ETF
VXF	Vanguard Extended Market VIPERs
VTI	Vanguard Total Stock Market VIPERs

APPENDIX TO CHAPTER 12:
MARKET BENCHMARKS

Russell 3000

The index of 3000 large US companies, ranked by market capitalization. It represents approximately 98 percent of the US equity market.

Russell 1000

The 1000 largest companies in the Russell 3000 index. This index is highly correlated with the S&P 500 Index.

Russell 1000 Growth

Represents a segment of the Russell 1000 Index with a greater-than-average growth orientation. Companies in this index have higher price-to-book and price-earnings ratios, lower dividend yields, and higher forecasted growth value.

Russell 1000 Value

Represents a segment of the Russell 1000 Index with a less-than-average growth orientation. Companies in this index have low price-to-book and price-earnings ratios, higher dividend yields, and lower forecasted growth values.

Russell 2000

The 2000 smallest companies in the Russell 3000 Index, representing approximately ten percent of the Russell 3000 total market capitalization.

Russell 2000 Value

Represents a segment of the Russell 2000 Index with a less-than-average growth orientation. Whereas the Russell 1000 style indices (growth and value) are categorized as being either entirely value or growth, the Russell 2000 style indices use a probability methodology that places many securities in both styles. As a result, a company's available market capitalization can be split between value and growth in proportion to its respective probabilities. With this methodology, the combined market capitalization of the Russell 2000 Growth and Value indices will add up to the total market cap of the Russell 2000.

Russell 2000 Growth

Represents a segment of the Russell 2000 Index with a greater-than-average growth orientation. Whereas the Russell 1000 style indices (growth and value) are categorized as being either entirely value or growth, the Russell 2000 style indices use a probability methodology that places many securities in both styles. As a result, a company's available market capitalization can be split between value and growth in proportion to its respective probabilities. With this methodology, the combined market capitalization of the Russell 2000 Growth and Value indices will add up to the total market cap of the Russell 2000.

Russell Mid-Cap

Index consists of the bottom 8000 securities in the Russell 1000 index as ranked by total market capitalization, and it represents over 30 percent of the Russell 1000 total market cap.

Russell Mid-Cap Growth

Represents a segment of the Russell 2000 Index with a greater-than-average growth orientation. Companies in this index have higher price-to-book and price-earnings ratios, lower dividend yields, and higher forecasted growth value.

Russell Mid-Cap Value

Represents a segment of the Russell 1000 Index with a less-than-average growth orientation. Companies in this index have low price-to-book and price-earnings ratios, higher dividend yields, and lower forecasted growth values.

Wilshire 5000

Measures the performance of all U.S. common equity securities, and so serves as an index of all stock trades in the United States. The returns for the index are total returns, which include reinvestment of dividends.

Standard & Poor 500 (S&P 500)

A broad-based measurement of changes in stock market conditions based on the average performance of 500 widely held common stocks. It consists of 400 industrial, 40 utility, 20 transportation, and 40 financial companies listed on US market exchanges (mostly NYSE issues). It is a capitalization-weighted index calculated on a total return basis with dividend reinvested. The S&P 500 represents about 75 percent of the NYSE market capitalization.

S&P 500 Growth/BARRA

The S&P 500 Growth/BARRA and the S&P 500 Value/BARRA split the S&P 500 into two mutually exclusive groups in such a way that each encompasses half of the S&P 500 total market capitalization. The S&P Growth/BARRA tracks the performance of those stocks in the S&P 500 with higher price-to-book ratios. A cap-weighted index, it is rebalanced semi-annually on January 1 and July 1, based on its price-to-book ratios and market capitalization at the close of trading one month prior. The index is adjusted each month to reflect changes in the S&P 500. Turnover has averaged about 20 percent per year (on a cap-weighted basis). This index tends to be heavily weighted in the Consumer Staple sector, which includes Food Retailing, Drugs and Health Care, Tobacco and Liquor. Inception: *January 1975.*

S&P 500 Value/BARRA

The S&P 500 Growth/BARRA and the S&P 500 Value/BARRA split the S&P 500 into two mutually exclusive groups in such a way that each encompasses half of the S&P 500 total market capitalization. The S&P Value/BARRA tracks the performance of those stocks in the S&P 500 with lower price-to-book ratios. A cap-weighted index, it is rebalanced semi-annually on January 1 and July 1, based on its price-to-book ratios and market capitalization at the close of trading one month prior. The index is adjusted each month to reflect changes in the S&P 500. Turnover has averaged about 20 percent per year (on a cap-weighted basis). This index tends to be heavily concentrated in the Energy, Utility, and Financial sectors. Inception: *January 1975*.

Standard & Poor's Midcap 400 (S&P 400)

A measurement in changes in 400 domestic stocks chosen by capitalization, liquidity, and industry group representation. It is a capitalization-weighted index, with each stock's weight proportional to its market value. The index represents approximately ten percent of the aggregate market value of US companies. Combined, the S&P Midcap 400 and the S&P 500 indices represent 78 percent of US domestic public companies.

Lehman Brothers Government/Corporate (LBGC)

A measurement of the movement of approximately 4,200 corporate, publicly traded, fixed-rate, nonconvertible, domestic debt securities, as well as the domestic debt securities issued by the US government or its agencies. Bonds included must be investment grade (Baa or higher), with amounts outstanding in excess of $1 million and at least one year to maturity. The index is rebalanced monthly by market capitalization.

Lehman Brothers Government/Corporate Intermediate

A measurement of the movement of approximately 2,800 bonds from the Lehman Brothers Government/Corporate Index with maturities between 1 and 9.99 years. The index is rebalanced monthly by market capitalization.

EAFE

A measurement of the performance of approximately 1,000 securities listed on the stock exchanges of Europe, Australia, and the Far East. It is an arithmetic average weighted by market value, and it is calculated on a total return basis, which includes reinvestment of gross dividends before deduction of withholding taxes.

MSCI World

A measurement of the performance of securities listed on the stock exchanges of Europe, Canada, Mexico, Australia, and the Far East. It is an arithmetic average weighted by market capitalization, and it is calculated on a total return basis, which includes reinvestment of gross dividends before deduction of withholding taxes. Index created by Morgan Stanley.

MSCI World ex-US

A measurement of the performance of approximately 1370 securities listed on the stock exchanges of Europe, Canada, Mexico, Australia, and the Far East. It is an arithmetic average weighted by market capitalization, and it is calculated on a total return basis, which includes reinvestment of gross dividends before deduction of withholding taxes. Index created by Morgan Stanley.

Lehman Brothers Municipal Bond

A measurement of the movement of approximately 1,100 municipal bonds with maturities between two and 30 years. It is computed from prices on these bonds supplied by Kenny Information Systems, Inc. The index is composed of approximately 50 percent revenue bonds and 50 percent state G.O.'s.

Lehman Brothers Intermediate Treasury

All bonds covered by the Lehman Brothers Government Bond Index with maturities between one and ten years. The total return calculated for the index consists of price appreciation/depreciation and income as a percentage of the original investment. It is rebalanced monthly by market capitalization.

Salomon Brothers 2 Year Treasury

Officially known as the Salomon Brothers US Treasury benchmark on the run index. It measures the total return for the current two year on the run treasury that have been in existence (have settled and formally issued for the entire month).

91 Day Treasury

Representing the monthly return equivalents of yield averages which are not marked to market, this index is an average of the last three three-month Treasury bill issues.

60% S&P 500/40% Lehman Brothers Government/Corporate

A blended index with 60 percent of the S&P 500 Index return and 40 percent of the Lehman Brothers Government/Corporate Index return.

50% S&P 500/50% Lehman Brothers Government/Corporate

A blended index with 50 percent of the S&P 500 Index return and 50 percent of the Lehman Brothers Government/Corporate Index return.

70% S&P 500/30% Lehman Brothers Government/Corporate

A blended index with 70 percent of the S&P 500 Index return and 30 percent of the Lehman Brothers Government/Corporate Index return.

60% MSCI/40% Lehman Brothers Government/Corporate

A blended index with 60 percent of the MSCI Index return and 40 percent of the Lehman Brothers Government/Corporate Index return.

30% EAFE/20% S&P 500/50% Lehman Brothers Government/Corporate

A blended index with 30 percent of the EAFE Index return, 20 percent of the S&P 500 Index return, and 50 percent of the Lehman Brothers Government/Corporate Index return.

60% S&P 500/40% Lehman Brothers Municipal Bond

A blended index with 60 percent of the S&P 500 Index return and 40 percent of the Lehman Brothers Municipal Bond Index return.

Wilshire Real Estate Index

A measurement of equity REITs and real Estate Operating Companies. No special-purpose or health care REITs are included. It is a market-cap weighted index fro which returns are calculated monthly using buy and hold methodology; it is rebalanced monthly.

In this chapter we have presented various investment products available in the marketplace. In the next chapter investment theories and concepts will be presented.

The worse you feel, usually because the news is bad, the safer the market is. The better you feel, usually because the news is good, the closer you are to a top.

John Train

Cyclical Nature of Index Performance

	S&P 500	Russell 1000 Growth	Russell 1000 Value	S&P Midcap 400	Russell Midcap	Russell 2000	Russell 2000 Growth	Russell 2000 Value	EAFE	Lehman Inter. G/C Bond	91 Day Treasury
Annual Returns											
1980	32.50	39.57	24.41	N/A	32.50	38.58	52.26	25.39	24.43	6.42	11.88
1981	-4.92	-11.31	1.26	12.46	2.40	2.03	-9.24	14.85	-1.03	10.50	15.04
1982	21.55	20.46	20.04	22.67	23.26	24.95	20.98	28.52	-0.86	26.10	11.33
1983	22.56	15.98	28.28	26.11	23.82	29.13	20.13	38.64	24.61	8.59	8.95
1984	6.27	-0.95	10.10	1.18	1.43	-7.31	-15.83	2.27	7.86	14.36	10.00
1985	31.73	32.85	31.51	35.59	32.01	31.04	30.97	31.01	56.73	18.10	7.84
1986	18.67	15.36	19.98	16.21	18.20	5.69	3.58	7.41	69.94	13.13	6.23
1987	5.25	5.31	0.50	-2.04	0.23	-8.76	-10.48	-7.11	24.93	3.66	5.90
1988	16.57	11.27	23.16	20.89	19.80	24.89	20.37	29.47	28.60	6.67	6.76
1989	31.67	35.92	25.19	35.52	26.27	16.25	20.17	12.43	10.80	12.77	8.65
1990	-3.11	-0.26	-8.08	-5.13	-11.50	-19.50	-17.41	-21.77	-23.20	9.16	7.77
1991	30.47	41.16	24.61	50.10	41.51	46.05	51.19	41.70	12.49	14.61	5.61
1992	7.61	5.00	13.81	11.92	16.34	18.42	7.77	29.14	-11.84	7.17	3.56
1993	10.06	2.90	18.12	13.95	14.30	18.89	13.36	23.84	32.95	8.79	2.94
1994	1.33	2.66	-1.99	-3.58	-2.09	-1.81	-2.43	-1.55	8.06	-1.97	4.17
1995	37.58	37.19	38.35	30.95	34.45	28.44	31.04	25.75	11.55	15.31	5.84
1996	22.97	23.12	21.64	19.20	19.00	16.53	11.26	21.37	6.36	4.06	5.26
1997	33.36	30.50	35.18	32.25	29.00	22.36	12.94	31.78	2.04	7.87	5.26
1998	28.58	38.71	15.64	19.11	10.11	-2.55	1.23	-6.46	20.34	8.41	5.06
1999	21.04	33.16	7.35	14.73	18.23	21.26	43.09	-1.49	27.29	0.38	4.73
2000	-9.09	-22.43	7.01	17.51	8.24	-3.01	-22.43	22.83	-13.96	10.10	5.94
2001	-12.36	-20.84	-6.25	7.16	-5.62	1.82	-10.08	13.62	-22.66	8.96	4.43
2002	-22.37	-27.73	-15.22	-10.46	-10.46	-20.87	-30.54	-11.92	-14.79	9.84	1.80
2003	27.74	29.19	29.55	40.05	38.62	45.39	49.29	45.96	39.29	4.31	1.11
2004	10.9	6.16	16.12	17.94	22.98	10.65	13.86	22.11	20.72	3.04	1.24

Past performance does not guarantee future results. Small Cap investing may result in greater volatility and is not suitable for every investor. Foreign investing, even in ADRs, involves additional risks including foreign money fluctuations, different accounting standards by country and possible political and economic instability.

* S&P Midcap 400 incepted February, 1981.

CHAPTER 13

Investment Management: Concepts and Strategies

INTRODUCTION

In this chapter we will present the key elements of investment concepts applicable to individual securities and efficient portfolios constructed primarily with mutual funds. We will also discuss time tested strategies that have been developed to manage these investments to maximize return for a given level of risk.

We will begin this chapter with a discussion of the concepts and strategies associated with individual securities. However, the majority of the chapter will be devoted to the theory of portfolio construction and the time-tested strategies of managing investment portfolios consisting solely of mutual funds.

Investment can be simply defined as the commitment of a given sum of money at the present time with the expectation of receiving a larger sum in the future. This definition underscores two important points. First, the process of investment involves the trade-off of *present* income for *future* income. Second, the objective of the investment is to receive a *future* flow of funds larger than that originally involved. In this context, it is important to differentiate between investment and speculation. Essentially, speculators concentrate on returns expected to be received over relatively short periods of time; in contrast, an investor's objective is to derive benefits form investment over a long horizon. Furthermore, speculators act quickly on the available information which has not yet been analyzed or acted upon by the general public, whereas investors generally base their judgment on investment analysis.

FIXED-INCOME SECURITIES

FIXED-INCOME SECURITY RETURN

It is a well-established fact that risk and return are positively related. That is, the higher the risk of a fixed income security, the higher the return demanded by bond-holders to invest in that security. The return on a bond consists of a combination of the coupon payments and the profit or loss realized if the bond is sold before maturity or if the issue defaults on the payment of interest or the principal. For instance, if an investor purchases a 30-year bond with a coupon of eight percent and holds it until maturity, then the annual return on that bond, which is known as yield to maturity, is eight percent. If, however, the issuer defaults on the coupon payments or the principal, then the annual return would be less than 8 percent, depending upon the nature and the timing of default.

FIXED-INCOME SECURITY RISK

The concept of fixed-income security risk is much more complex than the subject of bond return. Chapter 12 was devoted in part to the description of various types of fixed-income securities. But bonds are more than mere legal documents. They are analyzed in terms of risk and rates of return, or, more appropriately, income and capital appreciation, which an investor can expect to attain from them. It is of course true that many investors do not like to take risks. It is also true that virtually no investment is completely free from risk. Consequently, every serious investor must learn how to deal with fixed-income securities risk.

Even bonds with identical maturities and yield-to-maturity can significantly differ from one another because of the varying degrees of risk associated with them. Several types of risk have telling effects on bond prices, as discussed below.

Key Fixed-Income Risks

Interest rate risk. The interest rate risk refers to the possibility of variations in bond prices as a result of fluctuations in market interest rates. When market interest rates rise, bond prices decline, and the opposite is true when market

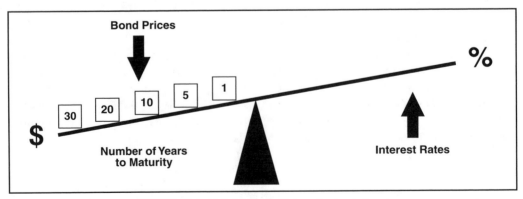

FIGURE 13-1 Relationship of interest rates to bond

rates drop. The reason is that when the interest rate rises, bonds with lower coupon rates fall out of favor, and their prices decline. Figure 13-1 demonstrates this relationship. It also shows that the longer the maturity of a bond, the higher the impact of a change in interest rates on bond prices.

The interest rate-bond price relationship conceals an important fact. Even in the case of a perfectly safe, non-callable Treasury bond, the impact of the rise in interest rates can be devastating. For instance, Figure 13-2 reveals that a mere two percent increase in the interest rate would slash the price of a 30-year, 7.5 percent Treasury bond by 18 percent. Of course, the reverse is also true. In 1991, for instance, because of steadily declining interest rates, long-term Treasury bonds racked up total returns of 19.3 percent—a stunning performance not likely to be repeated any time in the near future.

Inflation risk. The inflation risk is the impact of inflation on the coupon payments and the return of the principal. If an investor holding a ten percent bond receives an interest payment of $100 at the end of one year, and during the year the price level rises by, say, six percent, then the real interest (adjusted for inflation) would be only 9.4 percent. So, assuming that the principal is received after one year, the buying power of $1,000 would drop to $943.40 in real dollars, a loss of 5.66 percent.

Maturity risk. Because the future is assumed uncertain, investing in a bond with a longer maturity always involves a higher risk than the risk associated with a shorter-maturity bond. Because bond holders generally prefer shorter-term investments to minimize risk, they require a higher premium for investing in long-term securities. Borrowers are willing to pay the premium because they want to be compensated for the impact of future increases in interest rates.

Default risk. Yields reflect a borrower's credit quality. Lower quality, or non-investment grade bonds—those rated BB or below—generally offer higher yields than better quality issues, but they have more potential for price volatility. The higher yield compensates the investor for lending money to a company that is considered more likely to default in terms of interest and principal payments. Thus, a rising yield (or falling price) on a bond may reflect a company's deteriorating

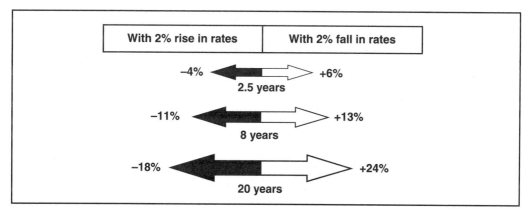

FIGURE 13-2   Bond price volatility (based on 7.5% coupon)

financial situation rather than any overall rise in market interest rates. Similarly, when a company's financial situation improves, generally the yields on its obligations decline.

Callability risk. Callability risk refers to the possibility of a bond being called before maturity due to falling interest rates, in which case the bondholder would be compelled to invest the proceeds at a lower interest rate. Typically, if a bond is called, a premium over the maturity price is paid by the issuer to the bondholder; this premium often varies directly with the remaining years to maturity. A common premium for a corporate bond called at the end of the call protection period would be one year's interest.

Liquidity risk. A bond may also be subject to liquidity risk. This risk refers to the price concession one must grant in order to quickly convert the bond into cash and receive the amount approximately put into it. In general, the less liquid a security, the higher its liquidity risk.

Table 13-1 presents a list of categories used by Moody's and S&P to rate corporate bonds. Typically, bonds carry these six types of risk which can be broadly measured in terms of the risk premiums associated with each type of risk.

Risk Reduction Strategies

Several risk reduction strategies applicable to bonds are available that have worked well over time. These are discussed below.

Laddering bond investments. Laddering bond investments—whether an investor holds individual bonds or shares in funds—is a commonly recommended strategy that may be suitable for bond investors. Laddering means buying bond investments that mature at different times. As a rule, investors adopting this strategy should buy bonds with maturities within a ten-year time horizon. That way, every other year or so, as bonds representing 20 percent of their portfolio comes due, new bonds are purchased at the prevailing rates. With this approach, investors can systematically purchase bonds at prevailing market rates, which over time can help smooth out the overall volatility of their bond portfolio.

TABLE 13-1   Investors' Services Rating Classification

Moody's	General description	Standard & Poor's
Aaa	Highest Quality	AAA
Aa	High Quality	AA
A	Upper Medium Grade	A
Baa	Medium Grade	BBB
Ba	Lower Medium Grade	BB
B	Speculative	B
Caa	Poor Standing (Perhaps in Default)	CCC-CC
Ca	(Generally) in Default	C for Income Bonds
C	Lowest Grade (in Default)	DDD-D

Diversifying with international bonds. When foreign countries are still in a recession, or are beginning to recover, higher interest rates are offered by international bonds. However, investors going overseas for bonds should not let the relatively high returns tempt them into committing too much of the bond portfolio in these potentially volatile markets. As a general rule, ten to 15 percent of the total funds invested in fixed-income securities should be sufficient to increase the foreign exposure measurably and get the diversification needed to help mitigate price and interest rate risks on the domestic holdings. Of course, in investing in international bonds, currency risk should always be taken into account.

Investing in tax-exempt bonds. Yields on tax-exempt bonds could be attractive in comparison with taxable bond yields, especially for investors who pay top tax rates. And in a high tax environment, increased demand for tax-exempt funds can help provide some support for municipal bond prices.

Adopting dollar cost averaging strategy. A simple method that can help obtain good values in the bond market is dollar-cost averaging—regularly investing a fixed amount in bonds that match investor's needs. This strategy can be particularly effective when reinvesting bonds that have come due, or shifting investments to reflect changing goals and needs. With dollar-cost averaging, investors buy more bonds or shares when prices are down, and fewer when they go up. Of course, dollar-cost averaging does not protect against a loss in declining markets or ensure a profit in rising markets, and investors may have a gain or loss when they sell their bonds.

Buying a Bond

As a general rule (with the exception of government bonds which are always presumed to be appropriately priced) it is advisable to purchase an undervalued bond. However, since bonds are long-term obligations to pay a fixed number of dollars at maturity, several special factors should be taken into account when purchasing a bond.

Bond yield. The critical variable in bond investment is its yield: Given a fixed coupon rate, the lower the price of a bond, the higher its yield. Although there are many exceptions, when the stock market is up, at least in theory, the bond market weakens and vice versa. Consequently, the stock market bears careful watching when selecting a bond.

Two important caveats of bond yields deserve special mention. First, during periods of restrictive monetary policy, interest rates generally rise, thereby depressing bond prices and pushing up bond yields. Second, when short-term interest rates decline, investors start investing in long-term securities, which ultimately leads to a decline in the long-term rates as well. These factors should help a financial planner determine the appropriate time for investing in bonds.

Bond ratings. Bond ratings regularly published by Standard & Poor's and Moody's facilitate the task of selecting attractive bonds. The ratings range from AAA for the safest bonds to D for highly speculative bonds which may even be in default. The ratings of A or better are given to investment grade bonds, while speculative bonds are rated lower than BB.

Current yield and yield to maturity. The current yield on a bond is the ratio of the current coupon payments to the current market price of that bond. For instance, if a $1,000 bond with a 20-year maturity and a coupon of eight percent is currently selling for $950, the current yield is 8.42 percent [($80/$950)x100)]. However, if the same bond is held until maturity, a different measure, known as *yield to maturity* (YTM) must be calculated. The YTM takes into account the capital gain or loss the investor would realize by holding the bond until maturity when the issuer returns to the bondholder the face value (and not the current price) of the bond. Naturally, if the maturity price of the bond exceeds the current market price, the YTM will exceed the current yield; the reverse will be true if the current price exceeds the maturity price. For instance, in the case of the preceding bond currently selling for $950, if held until maturity, the bondholder will receive the maturity price of $1,000, and the YTM will equal 8.53 percent.

Selling a Bond

Selling a bond is a complex process which requires a different discipline than that required for buying a bond. Since this is a challenging task, it is best to check the following points before making the final decision.

Underperformance. This is the most challenging task an investor faces. First of all, what period of time should be selected for checking the performance: six months, five years, or something in between? While there are no set rules to follow, some guidelines could still be provided. The shortest period is 12 months and the longest period should be no more than three years.

Change in company position. If the financial condition of the bond issuer significantly changes, resulting in the downgrading of the bond's rating, then serious consideration should be given to liquidating the holding.

Extent of loss. It is important to calculate the extent of the loss. Despite the gloom and doom publicized by the media, the *real loss* in the bond holding might be less than what appears on the surface.

The tax consequences. Whether the sale of the bond would result in a gain or a loss, it is best to assess the situation so the gain or the loss could be fully utilized by the bondholder to minimize the overall tax burden.

EQUITY SECURITIES

EQUITY RETURN

As explained in Chapter 12, equities are very different from fixed-income securities. In these securities, there are no promised coupon payments and return of principal upon maturity. Instead, the return from a stock is based primarily upon the increase over time in the sale price of the security, although dividend payments (not promised) should also be taken into account in calculating the annual return.

Calculation of a common stock return can be explained with a series of practical examples. Assume an investor paid $60 a share for ABC mutual fund and sold it for $72 a share. The percentage gain is 20 percent:

$$\text{(Gain/Original Price) x 100}$$
$$\text{or (12/60) x 100} = 20\%$$

Next, let us assume that three years ago an investor bought a stock for $5,000 and in subsequent years reinvested all dividends and capital gains. The stock is worth $7,604 today. As demonstrated below, the compounded annual rate of return is 15 percent.

Line	Items	Stock Return
1.	Original Investment	$5,000
2.	Current Market Value (including reinvested cash flow (dividends plus capital gains)	$7,604
3.	Number of years held	3 years
4.	Total Reutrn:	
	(a) Subtrace Line l from Line 2	
	(b) Divide (a) by Line 1	
	Add 1 to (b)	1.5208%
5.	Compound Annual Return:	
	Pick from compound value table (see Chapter 3, p. 3-4)	
	return associated with 1.521 (or 1.5209)	15%

Now that the technique of calculating the basic stock return has been demonstrated, a more involved case can be presented. Suppose an investor had an investment worth $10,000 at the beginning of the quarter and added a net $1,500 during the quarter. At the end of the quarter the value of the investment was $12,000. Capital gains and dividends were reinvested. As demonstrated below, the annual rate of return was 19.7 percent.

I.   Rate of Return During the Quarter

Line	Items	Stock Return
1.	Value of investment at the beginning of quarter	$10,000
2.	Value of investment at the end of quarter	$12,000
3.	Net addition or withdrawal during the quarter (withdrawal will be a negative number)	$ 1,500
4.	Multiply Line 3 by 0.5	$ 750
5.	Subtract Line 4 from Line 2	$11,250
6.	Add Line 4 to Line 1	$10,750
7.	Divide Line 5 by Line 6	1.046
8.	Subtract 1 from Line 7	.046
9.	Return during the quarter: Multiply Line 8 by 100	4.6%

II.   Return for the Whole Year

Line	Items	Stock Return
10.	Multiply Line 7 by itself three times (e.g. in sample case, it is 1.046 x 1.046 x 1.046)	1.197
11.	Subtact 1 from Line 10	.197
12.	Annual Return: Multiply Line 11 by 100	19.7%

In the previous illustration it was assumed that the quarterly returns remained unchanged. If they were different, the annual return would be calculated in the manner presented below.

III.   Compound Annual Rate of Return

Line	Items	Stock Return
13.	Return during the first quarter	4.6%
14.	Return during the second quarter	-2.5%
15.	Return during the third quarter	3.5%
16.	Return during the fourth quarter	4.0%
17.	Divide Line 13 by 100. Add 1 to the amount.	1.046
18.	Divide Line 14 by 100. Add l to the amount	.975
19.	Divide Line 15 by 100. Add 1 to the amount	1.035
20.	Divide Line 16 by 100. Add 1 to the amount	1.040
21.	Multiply Line 17 by Lines 18, 19 and 20	1.097
22.	Subtract 1 from Line 21	.097
23.	Compound Annual Return: Multiply Line 22 by 100	9.7%

The final illustration presents a *simplified* method of calculating a portfolio return during the preceding year, because this return calculation is something in which most investors are interested. However, for a more accurate return calculation , it is best to use *Quicken Deluxe* or the portfolio tracker available free on MONEY's Website (www.money.com).

To start the calculation process, all that is needed is the value of investments at the beginning and the end of 2004 and the total amount of money added or withdrawn during the year. All purchases are treated as additions. Withdrawals include proceeds from sales but not dividends, interest or capital gains distributions. If those were distributed in cash, they should be added to the year-end total. If they were reinvested, then they should not be counted separately because they will be reflected in the year-end balance. As demonstrated by the following illustration, the total return for the year 2004 was 17.78 percent.

Steps	Stock Return
1. Enter the value of portfolio at the start of 2004.	$50,000
2. Enter the value of portfolio at the end of 2004.	$62,000
3. Add to line 2 any dividends, interest or capital gains distributions that was taken in cash. The total is the ending balance.	$62,000 + 500 = $62,500
4. Enter the net total of any additions or withdrawals made during the year.	$2,500
5. Subtract Line 1 from Line 3. Divide the result in half and then add that figure to Line 1. The result is the average monthly balance.	$62,500 - $50,000 = $12,500 $12,500 / 2 = $6,250 $50,000 + $6,250 = $56,250
6. Add Line 1 to Line 4. Subtract that Total from Line 3. The result is the Total gain for 2004.	$50,000 + $2,500 = $52,000 $62,500 - $52,500 = $10,000
7. Divide Line 6 by Line 5. Multiply by 100. This is the 2004 total return percentage, before taxes.	$10,000 / $56,250 = 0.1777 0.1777 x 100 = 17.78%
Total Return for the Year	17.78%

EQUITY RISK

When investing in a stock, an investor assumes the risk of realizing less than the expected return. Closer scrutiny reveals that this risk has two important components: (1) The risk that the variability in return would be caused by factors that affect the prices of all stocks or undiversifiable risk. (2) Factors that are unique to a firm or industry, known as non-market or diversifiable risk.

Market or undiversifiable risk refers to both the economic and the market risk. The former refers to the risk that slower economic growth will cause investments in stock to decline. Recessions can adversely affect shares of growth companies, cyclical companies, and other types of companies. In addition, market risk refers to risks associated with political developments, tax law changes, investor psychology, foreign domination of the U.S. investment market, leveraged buy-outs, and insider trading fiascos. In contrast to the undiversifiable risk, the diversifiable risk refers to that portion of the variability of a stock's return which is the result of unexpected events or developments within the company or the related industry.

Interestingly, different strategies should be formulated in order to deal with the two types of risk just discussed. Investors deal with undiversifiable risks by requiring higher rates of return from investments with higher risks. The strategy, commonly known as the risk-return trade-off, refers to the higher returns demanded by investors to make it worthwhile to assume higher levels of risk. In contrast, investors attempt to reduce or eliminate diversifiable risks by constructing efficiently diversified portfolios. A risk-return pyramid, which demonstrates the risk-return trade-off between various types of investments, is presented in Figure 13-3.

Risk is the most important word in the lexicon of every serious investor. And yet, because it dampens the enthusiasm of even the most up-beat investor, few investors discuss it—and rarely with clarity of understanding.

Here is a typical scenario. Without exception, before buying a major fund most serious investors examine the fund's 1-, 3-, 5-, and (if available) 10-year returns. All financial magazines (MONEY magazine, Business Week, Kiplinger's magazine, Forbes, Fortune, and Morningstar) diligently publish these returns on a regular basis. And yet, few investors pay attention to the sections that identify risks associated with these returns. Unfortunately, looking at returns without adjusting for risk is fraught with danger and can spell disaster.

Risk is a far more complicated concept than return, simply because the former does not lend itself to an easily understandable measure. However, every serious investor must objectively deal with risk. The following are three measures of risk with which every investor should become familiar.

Key Measures

Beta. We begin with a simple equation for a straight line: $Y = a + bX$, where X and Y can be any two variables [Figure 13-4(A)]. Here the "a" represents the value of Y when X is zero, while "b" measures how fast Y changes in response to a given change in X. Now let's turn to Figure 13-4(B), where Y and X have been replaced by, respectively, XYZ stock and S&P 500, which represents the market. Fluctuations in the stock's return vis-à-vis S&P 500 return have been plotted for 5-years (not shown) and the AB line (a least squares line) has been drawn that is closest to the stock's returns during the period. In this chart, the value of beta [b in Figure 13-4(A)] represents the average percentage change in XYZ stock's return in response to a

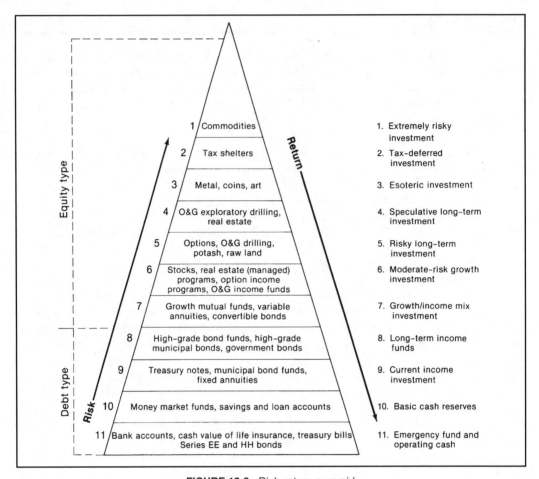

FIGURE 13-3 Risk-return pyramid

percentage change in S&P 500 return. That is, beta measures the riskiness of XYZ stock relative to the volatility, or risk, associated with S&P 500. Beta of one implies that the stock is as volatile as the market, whereas a Beta of higher or lower than one implies that the stock is, respectively, more or less volatile than the market.[1]

---

[1] For the pros, the formula for beta is as follows:

$$\beta = \frac{\sum\limits_{i=1}^{n}\left(x_i - \overline{X}\right)\left(y_i - \overline{Y}\right)}{\sum\limits_{i=1}^{n}\left(x_i - \overline{X}\right)^2}$$

where:

$\sum$ = the mean of the sum of the subsequent equation, from month 1 through month n

n = the number of months

x_i = each x observation (the excess monthly return of the benchmark index over the 90-day T-bill)

$\overline{X}$ = the average of all x observations

y_i = each y observation (the excess monthly return of the fund over the 90-day T-bill)

$\overline{Y}$ = the average of all y observations

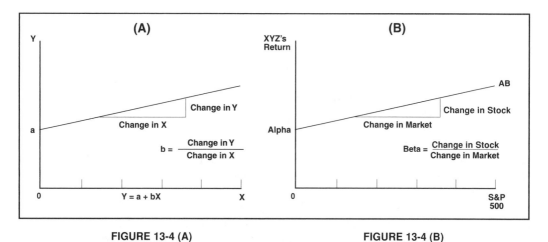

FIGURE 13-4 (A)   FIGURE 13-4 (B)

In this context, beta indicates how much the stock will rise or fall in relation to changes in the market index. Implicitly, the market has a beta of one because the market index chosen is the measure of the market's movement. In Figure 13-4(A) the stock has a beta of 0.6. This means that on average the stock moves up or down by a factor of 0.6 in the market index. Consequently, a beta of less than one results in lower *highs and lows* than the market. The opposite is true for a stock which has a beta of greater than one.

But that is not a guarantee, only a tendency. In fact, stocks seldom perform precisely according to their beta. One of the risks of high-beta investing is that stocks do not always produce as high returns as their betas suggest they would. That is, beta defines an *inexact relationship* with the market that works more on the law of averages than the law of physics.

Alpha. Alpha is a measure of the value added by the manager's luck or skill.[2] In the Figure 13-4(B), alpha [a in Figure 13-4(A)] is, say, four percent. Here alpha indicates the expected return of the stock when the market provides a zero percent return. In a different case, the alpha might be a negative number in which case it would indicate that the manager has a negative impact upon the performance of the stock.

The following equation using alpha and beta provides for estimating a stock's return:

Stock return = Risk free return + alpha + beta (Market's expected return - Risk-free return)

where Risk-free rate: 5%; alpha: 0.04; beta: 0.6; Market's return: 14%

Under these assumptions, the stock's expected return would be:

$$14.4\% = 5\% + 4\% + 0.6 \ (14\% - 5\%)$$

---

[2] In technical lingo, alpha is a measure of the difference between a fund's actual returns and its expected performance. A positive alpha figure indicates the fund has performed better than expected. In contrast, a negative alpha indicates the fund's underperformance, given the expectations. All MPT statistics (alpha, beta, and R-squared) are based on a least-squared regression of the fund's return over Treasury bills (called excess return) and the excess returns of the fund's benchmark index.

R-squared. R-square estimates the quality of the alpha and the beta by correlating the relationship of a stock's performance to the market or to another relevant benchmark. Referring back to Figure 13-4(B), if the data points fell exactly on the line, we could say that the graph shows a high correlation in the relationship of the fund to the market. But, if the data points were widely distributed about the line, we would not have the same correlation to support the relationship between the stock and the market. R-squared value ranges from zero percent to 100 percent. A high concentration of the data points about the line gives a R-squared value close to 100 percent and strengthens confidence in the relationship of a stock to the market. Conversely, the lack of concentration of data points close to the line yields a R-squared value close to zero percent and, therefore, reduces confidence in the relationship of the stock to the market.

In conclusion it should be stated that often alpha, beta and R-squared are used improperly with the result that they give out misleading signals. The most common error is comparing a stock to an index that has no relevance to it. For example, it is of little use to compare a portfolio of small-cap and international stocks and corporate bonds to S&P 500 index because the R-squared value would be close to zero. Also, alpha does not give insight as to whether the value added was due to the skill of the manager or luck. When used with care, however, these measurements can assist planners in making better investment choices for their clients.

Standard deviation. Risk, or variability, of the stock's or mutual fund's return is measured by standard deviation.[3] Figure 13-5 presents the prices of ABC and XYZ stock over a five-year period. When line A (called least squares line) is drawn that minimizes the total vertical distance between individual points that make up the curve and the line, and the exercise is repeated to complete line B, two important facts emerge: (1) The slopes (or elevation) of both lines are identical. (2) ABC stock has fluctuated much more than XYZ stock; therefore, the standard deviation (roughly, a kind of average distance between the line and individual points)

---

[3] For the pros, two equations make up the current standard deviation calculation. The first part calculates the fund's monthly standard deviation. The second part annualizes the monthly number to put it in a one-year context. The formula for monthly standard deviation is as follows:

Monthly Standard Deviation (σ) = $\sqrt{\dfrac{(x_1 - \bar{x})^2 + (x_2 - \bar{x})^2 + ... + (x_n - \bar{x})^2}{n}}$

Where:

X_1 = return for first month
X_I = return for the ith month (each month between the first and last month)
X_n = return for the last month
n = The total number of returns being used, in this case 36.

$\bar{X}$ = The average monthly total return during the 36-month period, also called the arithmetic mean. This number is arrived at by adding together all 36 monthly returns for the fund and dividing by 36. The formula for calculating $\bar{X}$ is as follows:

$\bar{X} = \dfrac{X_1 + X_2 + ... + X_n}{n}$

In the second equation, we annualize the monthly standard deviation to put the number in more useful one-year terms. The equation is as follows:

Annualized Standard Deviation = $\sqrt{[\sigma^2 + (1 + \bar{x})^2]^{12} - (1 + \bar{x})^{2^{12}}}$

Where:

σ = monthly standard deviation, from the first part of the calculation.

$\bar{X}$ = the average monthly total return, or arithmetic mean, from above.

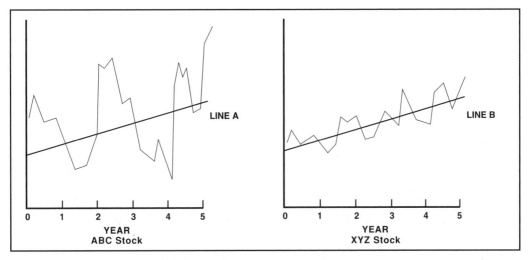

FIGURE 13-5 Stock prices over a 5-year period

of ABC is much higher than that of XYZ. This implies that ABC investors have taken a bumpier ride than their XYZ counterparts to get to the same place. So, since the slopes of lines A and B are identical, which implies that both stocks generated the same average return, it can be concluded that ABC investors were not rewarded for assuming higher risks. Put differently, risk can be thought of as the price one pays for stock performance. The more of it is assumed, the higher is the return expected in the long run.

Incidentally, standard deviation has another interpretive quality: assuming a normal distribution, 95 percent of the stock's return is expected to fall between the average return plus-and-minus two standard deviations (Figure 13-6). So, if the stock's average return is 12 percent and its standard deviation is two percent, then over time the stock is likely to return 12 percent plus or minus two standard deviations (that is, between eight and 16 percent). This information can come in handy in making investment decisions. It should be recognized, however, that the past history may not be repeated in the future.

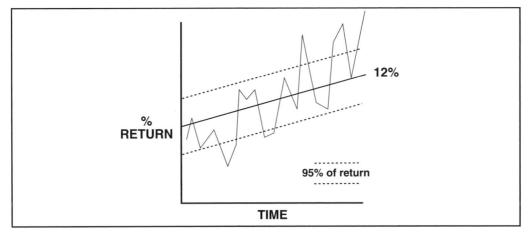

FIGURE 13-6 Standard deviation of stocks

Figure 13-7 demonstrates how standard deviation can be used as a decision-making tool in the real world.

Sharpe Ratio. Standard deviation is not without its flaws. It can be misleading because it penalizes upward moves as much as downward moves. A stock or a fund whose performance is consistently mediocre can score higher than one with a lot of upside volatility. Similarly, downside risk also can make a mediocre stock look better than one that had a few big disappointments but still soared over time.

A measure called the Sharpe ratio, named after Nobel Laureate William Sharpe, attempts to address this problem by adding performance data to the formula. This ratio is calculated by recording the difference over time between a stock's investment return and the yield on short-term Treasury bills. The average of these measures is then divided by their standard deviation. Another way of explaining this ratio is to say that it is calculated by using standard deviation and excess return to determine reward per unit of risk. The higher the Sharpe Ratio, the better the stock's historical risk-adjusted performance.

The original Sharpe Ratio has some of the same drawbacks as standard deviation, because standard deviation is part of the equation. To remedy that problem, Sharpe developed what he calls the *selection ratio* to measure risk-adjusted returns relative to a benchmark or index. This more recent version of the Sharpe ratio effectively puts all funds or stocks on an even playing field, assuming that benchmarks are correct.

Morningstar Risk-Adjusted Rating

Popularly known as Star Rating, the Risk-Adjusted Rating brings performance (returns) and risk together in one evaluation. In order to determine a fund's star rating for a given time period (three, five, or ten years), the fund's Morningstar Risk Score is subtracted from its Morningstar Return Score. The result is plotted on a bell curve to determine the fund's rating for each time period: If the fund scores in the top ten percent of its broad asset class (domestic stock, international stock, taxable bond, or municipal bond), it receives five stars (Highest); if it falls in the next 22.5 percent it receives four stars (Above Average); a place in the middle, 35 percent, earns 3 stars (Neutral); those lower still, in the next 22.5 percent, receive two stars (below Average); and the bottom ten percent get only one star (Lowest).

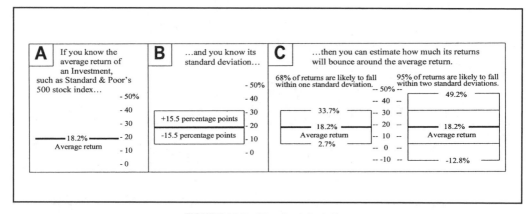

FIGURE 13-7 Standard deviation

Morningstar recognizes that no rating system can take into account all factors that one must consider before deciding to invest in a mutual fund. The Morningstar Risk-Adjusted Rating is intended as a way of identifying funds that have produced the highest level of returns relative to the risks they have taken. Investors should keep in mind that while it serves as an initial screen, the rating is only the first step toward a more comprehensive evaluation.

The following example demonstrates the use of Star rating as a planning tool. The Global Total Return A fund has a current rating of 3 stars. This is based on its three-year (three stars), five-year (four stars), and ten-year (two stars) weighted average. A fund's overall return and risk profiles stem from a weighted average of these three time periods. The ten-year statistics account for 50 percent of the overall score, the five-year figures for 30 percent, and the three-year numbers for 20 percent. If only five years of history are available, the five-year period is weighted 60 percent and the three-year period 40 percent. If only three years of data are available, the three-year figures alone are used.

The Morningstar Return figure puts a fund's returns in the context of a risk-free rate. The Morningstar Return figures also reflect the effect of loads. Listed for three, five, and ten years, Morningstar risk statistics evaluate the fund's downside volatility relative to that of others in its broad asset class. In order to calculate the Morningstar Risk score, fund's monthly returns are plotted in relation to the T-Bill returns. The amounts by which the fund fell short of the Treasury bill's return are added, and the result is divided by the total number of months in the rating period. This number is then compared with those of other funds in the same broad asset class. The risk score expresses how risky the fund is, relative to the average fund in its asset class. The average risk score for the fund's asset class is set equal to 1.00; thus a Risk Score of 1.35 for a taxable-bond fund reveals that the fund has been 35 percent riskier than the average taxable-bond fund for the period considered.

To conclude, Morningstar works on the assumption that the investors are reluctant to assume added risks unless they are compensated for such ventures. Low risk and high returns are rewarded equally. Accordingly, Morningstar's system favors all-weather funds, which tend to perform consistently over time.

TRADING IN EQUITIES

Buying a Stock

The key to successful stock market investment is the ability to size up a stock in order to determine whether or not it should be purchased. The time-tested strategy is to invest in an undervalued stock because, over time, the market price of a stock tends to gravitate toward its present value. That is, an investor should invest in a stock which is fundamentally strong and offers good value, but is currently selling below its present or intrinsic value.

It may be of some value to present here the techniques of fundamental analysis. The single most important variable in fundamental analysis is the projection of future earnings. With that in mind, the first order of business is to construct a comprehensive company profile. This profile would provide the basis for the analysis of the price/earnings ratio, the dividend yield, the growth of future earnings, and, finally, the analysis of the expected price appreciation. The company's position in the industry, the prevailing economic conditions, and the investor's risk tolerance level would help the investor calculate the discount rate with which the future earnings should be discounted to determine the present value of the stock. The final step in this analytical process is to select the stock whose present value *exceeds* its current market price.

While the identification of a fundamentally strong stock is the basis for stock market investment, the timing issue is equally important. The market does not always spot an attractive stock and frequently undervalued stocks perform poorly in a given market. Investing in such a stock at that time might mean a longer than anticipated holding period and even a temporary loss in the market value of the holding. Consequently, an attempt should be made to invest in only those stocks which are not only undervalued but also exhibit technical strength. These securities are commonly referred to as stocks which are both *fundamentally* and *technically* strong.

Selling a Stock

The first law of successful stock investing is: Buy a stock which is both fundamentally and technically strong. The buying part may be relatively easy. Without a strict investment discipline, however, determining the right time to sell a stock might be extremely difficult. For one thing, when prices fall, it appears reasonable to postpone selling in hopes of a recovery. And when prices rise, greed can get in the way of taking profits. Notwithstanding the difficulties associated with the sale of a security, for good investment results, the task must be successfully performed. The reason is that, in the final analysis, in investing the potential gain is of little value unless it is actually realized. There are several key selling strategies which provide a financial planner with broad guidelines for selling a stock.

Theory of undervalued security. A good test of the attractiveness of a security at a given time is whether or not it is still an undervalued security. That is, if a stock which was undervalued when it was first selected is still undervalued, then it makes sense to hold it until it becomes appropriately valued. If not, then it is a prime candidate for sale, regardless of how well it is performing at this time. This rule keeps emotions of greed out of the decision process.

Realization of goals. After a stock has met the investor's goals, unless there are overriding considerations, it should be sold. For instance, suppose an investor purchases a stock at $25 because its book value is $40 and it generally sells at 85 percent of its book value. There is no law that says stocks have to sell at book value. But if the company is fundamentally sound, there is good reason to believe the stock will return to near its historic price/book value ratio of 85 percent. So, if the price approaches $34 (85 percent of the book value of $40), one should seriously consider selling the stock.

Change of conditions. It is also appropriate to sell a stock if the reason for which the stock was purchased is no longer valid. Suppose an investor purchases the stock of a drug company which introduced a miracle drug on the market. If the product fizzles, it is best to face the new facts and sell the stock.

Speculator success syndrome. Quite often a spectacular price increase signals trouble for a stock. In 1985, Alfin quadrupled in a few months when a skin-care product was promoted as an anti-aging cream. Home Shopping Network stock experienced a similar success. Both stocks later traded at mere fractions of their all-time highs.

Myth of break even strategy. One of the myths that never seems to die is that a depressed stock should be held until the current losses are recouped. In order to appreciate the fallacy of this line of thinking, one needs to only consider the following table:

Current loss	*% Gain required to recoup the loss*
10%	11%
15	18
20	25
30	43
40	67
50	100
75	300

Note that if a stock loses 75 percent of its value, which was the case in 2001-02 for many stocks, then the stock must appreciate 300 percent merely to recoup the past losses. A more sensible and practical strategy would be to determine the present value of a security at a give moment and sell it when the price exceeds the present value.

In this context, a mention should be made of the use of *stop loss orders* which are designed to minimize an investor's exposure to loss. When a stock is purchased, or at any time thereafter, the investor can instruct the broker to sell the stock if the price falls to a certain level, such as five or ten percent below the purchase price. This would generally protect the investor against an extended drop, although the broker cannot guarantee a sale at the specified price. In the event of panic selling, such as that which occurred on the infamous Black Monday in 1987, there might not be any buyers. To avoid such a contingency, the investor could also place a *stop limit order*, authorizing the broker to sell at a specified price. Of course, such an order does not unconditionally guarantee that the order would be filled.

Tax considerations. While as a general rule tax considerations should not be allowed to influence a decision to sell a stock, sometimes it is desirable to resort to tax selling at an opportune time. Basically, selling at a gain or a loss is a taxable event. Consequently, if a decision has been made to sell a security on fundamental grounds, selling it at a given time (for instance, before year-end) could produce favorable tax outcomes.

LIMITING THE RISK

Weathering the market's ups and downs is a key concern for most investors, regardless of their risk tolerance level, age, tax bracket, or net worth. While the risk associated with stocks, bonds, and other investment vehicles cannot be completely eliminated, there are ways in which investors can reduce risk to manageable levels. Some of the better known techniques of weathering the market's fluctuations are discussed next.

Dollar Cost Averaging

Dollar Cost Averaging (DCA) is a systematic program of investing equal sums of money at regular intervals, regardless of the price of shares. Clearly, DCA cannot guarantee a profit or prevent a loss. However, it does reduce the effects of market fluctuations over the long term. The reason is that instead of timing the market, the individual invests the same amount of money whether the share price is high, low, or in between. Hence, the investor buys more shares when the price is low and fewer when it is high, thereby avoiding the common mistake of buying high and selling low.

The key advantage of DCA is that, in the long run, it has the effect of making the average share cost less than the average share price. Two illustrations, covering a weak market and a strong market, demonstrate this strategy. In each illustration, it is assumed that the investor has decided to invest $100 each month.

A DCA program during a period of declining market is presented in Table 13-2. After four months and a total investment of $400, the average price of this investment is $7.00 while the average cost is $6.23. This situation is the result of purchasing progressively larger number of shares for $100 as the market price consistently declines, assuming that the stock continues to be undervalued and fundamentally strong. In the second illustration presented in Table 13-3, the average cost of the investment is $12.61, but the average price is slightly higher ($13.00) than the average cost. This is the result of an appreciation in the stock price in a rising market.

A word of caution should be added here. While both illustrations demonstrate its power as an investment tool, DCA is not appropriate for short-term investments and, as mentioned, cannot guarantee a profit or prevent a loss. However, this technique does provide investors with the benefit of a disciplined investment program that eliminates the need for market timing and helps alleviate the effects of a

TABLE 13-2   Dollar Cost Averaging in a Declining Market

Investment	Total invested	Market price	Shares bought	Total shares	Average price/ share	Average cost/ share
$100	$100	$10	10.0	10.0	$10.00	$10.00
100	200	8	12.5	22.5	9.00	8.89
100	300	6	16.7	39.2	8.00	7.65
100	400	4	25.0	64.2	7.00	6.23

TABLE 13-3   Dollar Cost Averaging in an Advancing Market

Investment	Total invested	Market price	Shares bought	Total shares	Average price/ share	Average cost/ share
$100	$100	$10	10.0	10.0	$10.00	$10.00
100	200	12	8.33	18.33	11.00	10.91
100	300	14	7.14	25.47	12.00	11.78
100	400	16	6.25	31.72	13.00	12.61

fluctuating market.

Incidentally, investors who use the dollar cost averaging strategy may find that market volatility can be useful. The proof is in Table 13-4. In this table, the low-volatility case, presented on the left side, is contrasted with the high-volatility case, presented on the right side. Clearly, if the prices swing widely, by investing $12,000 over a twelve month period the investor is able to acquire 1,587 shares at an average cost of 7.56 share. When the market swings are tempered, however, the same $12,000 buys only 1,484 shares at an average cost of $8.09 per share.

Constant Ratio Plan

The *constant ratio plan* (CRP) is a variation of DCA in which the monthly contribution is equally divided between a stock fund and a money market fund. Subsequently, if an increase in the share price makes the equity portion worth considerably more than the value of the money fund, then part of the equity fund would be liquidated and the proceeds transferred into the money fund. The reverse action would be taken if equity prices drop, thereby making the money fund worth more than the equity fund.

A 55/45 ratio limit is generally applied to the CRP, although other ratios would work equally well. This means that whenever the value of either fund exceeds 55 percent of the total value of the portfolio, an automatic readjustment plan is put into motion to make the ratio equal (50 percent). For instance, if the value of the stock fund rises to 55 percent, the investor shifts cash from the partially liquidated equity fund into the money fund to make them of equal value. Likewise, if the equity fund drops to 45 percent of the portfolio, the investor quickly shifts funds from the money fund into the equity fund to make them of equal value. So, the advantage

TABLE 13-4   Market Volatility and DCA

MARKET VOLATILITY AND DCA
(Examples: $1,000 Systematic Investment Per Period)

Low- Volatility Case		High- Volatility Case	
Price	Number of Shares	Price	Number of Shares
$10	100	$10	100
8	125	7	143
6	167	5	200
8	125	9	111
10	100	11	91
12	83	13	77
10	100	9	111
8	125	7	143
6	167	5	200
6	167	5	200
8	125	9	111
10	100	10	100
Total Shares Purchased	**1,484**		**1,587**
Average Cost Per Share	**$8.09**		**$7.56**

of this strategy is that the investor automatically buys low and sells high.

Variable Installment Plan

A refined approach to investing in stocks is known as *variable installment plan* (VIP), which begins with an equal investment in both stock and money funds, but shifts the emphasis on stock investment when the fund's share price declines. A simple rule is for the investor to direct the entire monthly contribution to the stock fund whenever its share price falls by a predetermined (for example, ten percent) percentage. Similarly, the investor would skip the monthly stock fund investment if its share price rises by ten percent and invest the entire monthly contribution into the money fund.

A more sophisticated VIP strategy requires the investor to keep track of the average cost of the stock fund shares, including those purchased with reinvestment dividend and capital gains distributions. When the fund's current share price is higher than the average cost, the investor invests less in the stock fund. Conversely, when the share price is lower, more is invested in the stock fund.

A simple rule, which can be devised to determine how much of a contribution should be made to the stock fund, is described here:

$$\text{Amount of Contribution} = \frac{\text{Average Cost of Shares}}{\text{Current Price}} \times \begin{array}{l}\text{Original}\\\text{Contribution}\end{array}$$

For example, suppose an investor started investing $1,000 a month in a stock fund when the share price was $10.00. If, after a month, the price jumps to $12.00, the contribution for the second month would be $833.00 [($10/$12) x $1,000]. The difference ($167) would be invested in the money market fund.

In passing, it should be mentioned that investors can use other, more sophisticated, variations of the VIP just described. One such variation is known as the *leveraged variable investment plan* (LVIP), which requires the calculation of a leverage factor to minimize the average cost of a stock fund. In fact, an imaginative and sophisticated investor can design a variety of complex plans to suit his or her investment objectives.

Strategy of Covered Calls

The market risk can also be reduced by the sale of covered call options. A call option gives the buyer the right to purchase a stock at the *strike* or set price within the call option period. The option is covered by the stock the investor owns at the time of the option sale. A covered call option reduces the investor's risk exposure, although it simultaneously reduces the potential for profit. An illustration should make this strategy clear.

Let us assume Susan Bohn owns 100 shares of Marvin stock, trading at $30 a share. Susan sells a contract giving the buyer the option to buy these shares for $30 within the next six months; in return she receives a premium of $3 per share, or a total of $300. If Marvin's price drops to, say, $28 a share in the next six months and the option is not exercised, Susan's investment drops to $2,800 (100 shares x $28). However, the loss is more than compensated by the $300 option price, so she ends up with a profit. It should be added here that a stockholder can continue to write options to generate additional investment income. This strategy works best in a stable market.

But what if the stock price rises to $35 and the option is exercised? In that case, Susan must surrender the stock at $30 a share. The result will be that she will end up with $3,300 ($3,000 from the stock sale plus $300 option price) instead of $3,500 which she would have received from the sale of the stock had she not sold the option. It is now easy to see why a covered call option reduces the risk exposure but also simultaneously reduces the potential for profit.

Call Option with Stock Sale

A reverse strategy is to lock in profits by selling an appreciated stock and simultaneously buying call options on the same stock. As mentioned, a call option gives the buyer the right to buy 100 shares of the stock at a certain price for a fixed time period.

This strategy works in the following manner. Suppose Bob Kirk owns 100 shares of Tiger in which currently he has a $1,200 profit. Bob thinks the stock is overpriced and will eventually plunge. However, he notices that Tiger is hot and thinks it might still make one or two upward moves before taking a nose dive. Consequently, Bob sells Tiger at $40 thereby locking in the $1,200 profit and buys a six-month call option on the stock for $300. If the stock does rise, Bob will exercise the option and realize additional profit. If not, all Bob would lose would be the $300 option price but he would have locked in the $1,200 capital gain on that stock.

Mutual Fund Returns

The main purpose for investing in a mutual fund, as it is for any investment, is to realize an acceptable return. It is, therefore, important to learn how to determine mutual fund returns.

A typical mutual fund statement received by John Client on December 30, 2001, is presented in Table 13-5. Based upon the data presented in this table, John Client's rate of return on his Sensible Mutual Fund investment can be determined in the manner presented in Table 13-6.

SALE OF MUTUAL FUNDS

The Basic Issue

Buying mutual fund shares completes only half the transaction. The other half consists of the decision one faces to sell it at the most appropriate time—unquestionably the toughest decision one faces as a mutual fund investor. Unfortunately, matching the present value of a fund's share to its market price is not a viable approach. The reason is that the mutual fund is a portfolio of stocks, bonds, and other related securities, and at any given moment a portfolio is likely to contain both undervalued and overvalued securities. Consequently, different strategies must be developed to decide when to sell mutual fund shares. In the following paragraphs, we will present several of these strategies.

Change of Investment Objective

Buying into a fund, of course, is just the beginning of the investment process. A change in the stock or bond market or in the investor's risk preference might necessitate switching, or liquidating, investment in mutual fund shares because of a change of the fund manager. Each fund is committed to a particular investment philosophy which dictates the type of securities it will hold. Although its managers may alter the holdings fairly frequently, they cannot completely change direction

TABLE 13-5   Sensible Mutual Fund Account

Confirmation Date: December 30, 2004

John Client
445 South Livernois
Rochester Hills, MI 48307
Account Number: 0000213944

Page 1 of 1
2003-2004 Statement

Statement Date	Transaction Date	Transaction Detail Description	Dollar Amount of Transaction	Share Price	Shares This Transaction	Total Shares Owned
		Beginning Balance	$5,000.00			164.870
1/06/03	1/06/03	Investment	5,000.00	$26.92	185.735	350.605
4/18/03	4/07/03	Income Reinv. at .250	87.65	28.50	3.075	353.680
4/18/03	4/07/03	Short-term Cap. Gain at .450	157.77*	-	-	353.680
6/02/03	6/02/03	Investment	1,000.00	30.34	32.955	386.635
7/18/03	7/05/03	Income Reinv. at .250	96.66	31.30	3.09	389.725
10/25/03	10/11/03	Income Reinv. at .250	97.43	35.80	2.72	392.445
1/04/04	1/04/04	Redemption	1,000.00	37.90	-26.39	366.055
1/27/04	1/18/04	Income Reinv. at .200	73.21	37.92	1.93	367.985
1/27/04	1/03/04	Short-term Cap. Gain at .500	183.03*	-	-	367.985
4/27/04	4/04/04	Income Reinv. at .300	110.40	38.02	2.90	370.885
7/19/04	7/05/04	Income Reinv. at .250	92.72	37.50	2.47	373.355

* These amounts were paid in cash.

to capitalize on basic changes in investment conditions. In fact, by the terms of their prospectuses, many funds are required to invest only in certain types or grades of securities. For example, an income fund may replace certain stocks with others, but even the new stocks must be income stocks. Consequently, an income fund investor who is unwilling to hold income stocks has little choice but to move the money to another type of fund with a different goal or method of operation.

Consistent Poor Performance

Mutual fund investment is for the long term, and one or two bad quarters should not be the compelling reason for liquidating the shares. However, if the fund's performance continuously ranks in the bottom fourth or fifth of funds of its type for several quarters, serious consideration should be given to liquidating the fund. Of course, in making this decision the back-end load charges, if applicable, and tax consequences must always be taken into account.

Size of the Fund

The general maxim for mutual fund investment in stocks is, *smaller is better.* The critical size for a mutual fund appears to be assets of around $1-2 billion, as portfolio managers face increasingly difficult investment choices as the assets exceed $1 billion. Clearly, investing large amounts of money makes it more difficult to accumulate meaningful positions in individual stock issues, especially if these

TABLE 13-6 Rate of Return

	A	
Line	*Transaction*	*Result*
1.	The number of months (maximum 24 months) over which the return is calculated	19
2.	Value of investment at the beginning of the period: 350.605 sh. x $26.92	$9,438
3.	Value of investment at the end of the period: 373.355 sh. x $37.50	$14,000
4.	Dividend income and capital gains distributions paid out in cash and not reinvested	$341
5.	Net redemptions or investments, excluding reinvested distributions and initial investment: $1,000 (Inv. on 6/2/96) - $1,000 (redemption)	$0
	Computation of gain or loss:	
6.	Add line 2 to half of Line 5	9,438
7.	Add Lines 3 and 4, then subtract half of the Line 5 amount	14,341
8.	Divide Line 7 by Line 6	1.519
9.	Subtract 1 from Line 8, then multiply by 100	51.9%
10.	For annualized return, divide 12 by the number on Line 1. Multiply the result by line 9	32.7%

B
Average Cost

$$\frac{\$10,000.00 + 87.65 + 96.66 + 97.43 + 73.21 + 110.40 + 92.72}{373.355}$$

$$= \frac{\$10,558.07}{373.355}$$

$$= \$28.28$$

issues are relatively small. There are exceptions, of course, as is evidenced by the extraordinary success of Fidelity Magellan and Vanguard, which manage billions of dollars worth of assets. But these exceptions are rare, and investors would be well advised to get out when their fund gets too big for their taste. However, this small size criterion does not apply to bond mutual funds, since the more bonds a fund holds, the slimmer are the chances of its being badly hurt should some of its bond issuers default.

Miscellaneous Changes

If a fund portfolio manager primarily responsible for the fund's admirable record quits the fund, and the new manager does not have a comparable track record, it would be wise to carefully watch the fund's future performance under the new manager. Investors should also be leery of spectacular performance for several consecutive months. Such performance is usually the result of the manager's taking unusually high risks with investors' money. Finally, a change in economic conditions might warrant a shift from a stock or bond fund into a money market fund.

MUTUAL FUNDS AND TAXES

At tax time, every mutual fund shareholder is faced with a dual task: reporting fund distributions (dividend income and capital gain distribution) and calculating capital gains and losses as a result of the sale (redemption) or exchange of fund shares.

Fund Distributions

At the beginning of every year, each mutual fund sends its investors Form 1099-DIV for each of the regular, nonqualified accounts. This form lists the taxable dividend and capital gains distributions that the fund declared during the previous year and paid by January 31 of the current year. All dividend and capital gains distributions listed on this form are considered taxable even if they were reinvested in the fund, unless it is a municipal bond fund in which case dividends are treated as tax-free distributions. Currently short-term capital gains are taxed at the same rate as dividend distributions.

The procedure for reporting distributions on tax returns is straightforward. First, itemized information needs to be provided on Schedule B if the total dividend and distribution income exceeds $400. This income is the sum of all dividend and capital gains distributions, plus all other dividend income received on individual stock holdings. Second, investors should submit Schedule D if other capital gains and losses have been realized. In that case, the mutual fund capital gains distributions will also be reported on Schedule D, along with other capital gain and loss transactions.

Calculating Capital Gains or Losses on Fund Sales

In order to calculate the taxable gain or loss on mutual fund shares sold, the investor has to determine the sale price and the true cost of those shares, known as the cost basis. The former is easy to determine; the latter can cause some problems. There are three basic ways to determine the cost basis which are discussed next.

Specific Identification Method. When a capital gain is reported on a mutual fund sale, the IRS allows the investor to identify the sale of those shares for which originally the highest price was paid. Obviously, this constitutes the best strategy, since that would automatically minimize the gain and the tax liability.

First-in, First-out Method. If an investor does not, or cannot, use the first approach, by default the IRS assumes that shares sold were those that were acquired first, known as the FIFO approach. This method may maximize the tax bill, since as a general rule, the shares bought first are likely to have the lowest cost.

Average Cost Method. A better alternative might be to use the average cost approach, which requires calculating the average per-share price for all the shares of the fund. This may generate a lower tax liability than with FIFO approach.

The tax consequences of using the three approaches described in Table 13-7 are interesting. In this illustration, the Specific Identification Method resulted in a short- term gain of $400, while the Average Cost Method generated a long- term gain of $858. Finally, as expected, the FIFO method resulted in a long-term gain of $1,000.

TABLE 13-7   Mutual Fund Tax Calculation

Date	Purchase/Sale	Amount
April 2000	Purchase 1,000 shares at $20	$20,000
Sept. 2000	Purchase 100 shares at $22	$2,200
Dec. 2000	Purchase 100 shares at $22	$2,200
June 2001	Purchase 100 shares at $22	$2,200
Dec. 2001	Purchase 100 shares at $24	$2,400
Dec. 2001	Sell 200 shares at $25	$5,000

Specific Identification Method

Total funds received (200 x $25 per share)		$5,000
Less highest cost shares (100 shares at $22/share purchased June 2001 and 100 shares at $24/share purchased Dec. 2001)		($4,600)
Short- term gain		**$400**

First In, First Out Method

Total funds received (200 x $25/share)		$5,000
Less cost of first 200 shares acquired (shares purchased in April 2000 at $20/share)		$4,000
Long- term gain		**$1,000**

Average Cost Approach

Total funds received (200 x $25/share)		$5,000
Less average cost of $20.71/share (Divide total purchase price of $29,000 by 1,400 shares. That equals $20.71/share		$4,142
Long- term gain		**$858**

At this point it is apropos to add an important caveat. In determining the taxability of mutual fund gain it is extremely important to properly calculate the *tax basis* of that investment. The following example clarifies the point.

Assume an investor placed $5,000 in a mutual fund ten years ago and reinvested $4,000 received as fund distributions during the next ten years. Now if the investor sells all the shares for, say, $10,000, what would be the taxable gain? If it is figured that the taxable gain is $5,000 ($10,000 – $5,000) then it would be an incorrect answer. The cost basis is $9,000 ($5,000 + $4,000 distribution), and the taxable gain is only $1,000 ($10,000 – $9,000).

THEORY OF PORTFOLIO CONSTRUCTION

INTRODUCTION

The market can be a lot like the weather: One day, conditions are hot. The next day, the cold winds start to blow. Trying to predict the direction of the market from one day to the next is even harder than predicting the weather. Steep declines or huge gains in the market in quick succession are the reason for developing a sensible investment portfolio strategy that could serve investors over the long horizon.

Experts say that, contrary to popular belief, real investment success is not due to the ability to select the best investments at the most opportune times. Instead, most effective strategies are based on diversification and asset allocation—strategically spreading the investments across broad asset classes like stocks, bonds, and cash to achieve the investment goals. In fact, a landmark study found that over 90 percent of the *variability* in total portfolio return was determined by long-term asset allocation, while less than five percent of variability in return was the result of specific investment selection. In this section, we will present the use of the concepts of diversification and asset allocation in the construction of an efficient portfolio. Also, for pedagogical reasons, we will use only mutual funds in demonstrating the technique of portfolio construction.

THEORY OF EFFICIENT PORTFOLIO

In 1952, Harry Markowitz developed a novel approach to stock investment, which virtually revolutionized the thinking of the academic community. In fact, the basic elements of modern portfolio theory are based on a series of propositions concerning rational investor behavior that were first developed by Markowitz.

The basis of Markowitz's approach was the use of fluctuations or variability of investment returns as an approximation of the risk of investment. If Stock A is expected to yield eight percent +/- two percent (that is, between six and ten percent) and Stock B is expected to yield eight percent +/- four percent (that is, between four and 12 percent), then both stocks have the expected return of 8 percent. But because Stock B's return can fluctuate more widely than A's, B is more risky and hence less desirable than A. First, Markowitz sought to formalize this concept of risk by using the statistical concept of variance. Then he developed the portfolio theory by demonstrating that once the level of risk the investor is willing to assume is established, a computerized theoretical model could be used for selecting the optimum portfolio that would maximize the rate of return.

Once the basis for measuring risk and return of a single stock was firmly established, the academic community formally addressed the risk problem that was created by putting all the eggs in the same basket. Ultimately, diversification became as hypnotic a mantra for investors as location is for real estate buyers. Professionals universally agreed that investors should spread their investment bets among different types of investments to reduce the overall volatility of their portfolio. If one investment sinks, the other may hold up or even take off.

While the concept of diversification revolutionized the investment world, it was driven by an amazing discovery which had two counterparts. First, it was established that the expected return of a portfolio is simply the *weighted average of each of the individual assets making up the portfolio*. Second, it was discovered that if the assets in a portfolio are not perfectly correlated, the risk of that portfolio will be *less than the weighted average of the risks of the individual assets* in the portfolio. So, by properly diversifying a portfolio with assets that do not move in tandem, an investor can *reduce the overall risk of the portfolio without sacrificing the average return*. This is the essence of the Modern Portfolio Theory.

CAPITAL ASSET PRICING MODEL

The Markowitz Model was theoretically sound. However, its serious limitation was that it related each security to every other security in the portfolio, demanding the sophistication and volume of work well beyond the capacity of all but a few analysts. Then came the *beta revolution*, launched by William Sharpe, who subsequently became the Nobel Laureate for his path breaking work. Sharpe assumed that the return on a security could be regarded as being related to a single index like the market index. This index should consist of all the securities trading on the market, and could be represented by a popular average like the S&P 500 Index. This new relationship was identified as the Market Model.

The Market Model provided the conceptual foundation for the Capital Asset Pricing Model (CAPM), which is at the heart of the Modern Portfolio Theory (MPT). Under the CAPM, the attention was shifted from variance between numerous securities in the market to beta, which measures nondiversifiable risk. Also, to complete the beta revolution, the relationship between risky and risk-free returns was carefully established around beta as the key variable of the model.

The finding of the CAPM with beta measuring the risk of risky securities, and the inclusion of risk-free securities in a portfolio is extremely powerful. It says that the expected return on a portfolio is equal to the risk-free rate plus a risk premium that is proportional to the risk measure, beta. Based on this relationship, three powerful conclusions were reached:

1. An astute investor expecting to beat the market without assuming additional risk must generate a rate of return that exceeds the expected return of this portfolio.
2. If an investor assumes a higher level of risk than is associated with this efficient portfolio, then a higher level of return must be realized to compensate for the additional risk assumed.
3. If the return of a portfolio with similar risk is less than the expected return of the efficient portfolio, then the investor failed to construct an efficient portfolio.

The basic assumptions of CAPM can now be summarized. (1) Investors are generally risk-averse. They expect to be rewarded for risk. (2) Investors behave in a rational manner. They choose only efficient portfolios, which maximize return for a given level of risk, or minimize risk for a given level of return. (3) Investors want to maximize their returns. They optimize their portfolio combinations by efficient diversification.

POWER OF DIVERSIFICATION

Basic Observations

By now, the importance of diverification has been amply stressed: Investors must make sure that their investment portfolios are suitably diversified, and that they are familiar with an array of mutual funds, because investing in funds is a good way to spread their risk and extend their opportunities.

Few of us have the time or the knowledge to diversify our holdings effectively. As a result, we wind up being either under-diversified or—its somewhat less evil twin—

over-diversified. Since both can result in an unfavorable outcome, it is important to understand the essence of proper diversification.

One of the key elements of the CAPM is that the market portfolio is the optimum portfolio. However, this portfolio consists of hundreds of securities, which makes it virtually impossible (except through an index fund) for anyone to invest in it. This difficulty must be viewed against the twin facts that diversification reduces diversifiable risk, and only the fully diversified market portfolio succeeds in completely eliminating this risk. Therefore, the critical question becomes: What is the minimum number of securities an investor must buy to reduce most of the diversifiable risk. Research studies have clearly demonstrated that, at the 15-stock level, almost 95 percent of the portfolio's diversifiable risk can be virtually eliminated.

Mutual fund investors enjoy a built-in head start on diversification, since most equity funds hold anywhere from several dozen to a few hundred stocks. However, that creates another interesting problem. Individual funds often concentrate on a narrow slice of the market, such as putting most of their money in technology companies, or focusing on just small-cap or large-cap issues. This means that investors are more vulnerable to price shifts than might be assumed, based on the number of stocks these funds own.

A different question now emerges: "How many mutual funds should an investor carry within a given investment class?" Or to put it differently, how many growth funds does an investor need before the benefits of diversification diminish? How many balanced or international funds? In short, how many funds is enough, and how much is too much?

A research study completed several years ago covered four equity categories—growth, growth and income, international, and balanced funds—and compared the results against the benchmark indexes. The study found that best results are obtained when for each category more than one, and no more than three, mutual funds are owned. By the time four funds are included, the category is highly correlated with the benchmark so little benefit is derived from the last addition. Also, in adding funds to mitigate risk and optimize performance, it is important to choose funds that are unrelated to one another. The story is much the same when overseas funds are considered. If one could select the single international fund with the smallest relationship to Morgan Stanley Capital International's EAFE stock index, the portfolio would still be at the 75 percent correlation mark. Adding a second fund would make the portfolio move in lockstep with the market.

Investors can consult Morningstar's *Value Line Mutual Fund Survey*, or a fund's annual report to see how various funds are correlated with each other, and with the relevant benchmark. In the final analysis, the best chance to beat the market is to invest in funds that bear little statistical relationship to a benchmark index.

In the end, it is important to add a caveat. In trying to figure out how many mutual funds should be selected for an efficient portfolio, investors should not lose sight of their investment objectives, their tolerance for risk, and their sense of whether the market is going to head up or down. After all, the objective of an efficient portfolio is not only to deliver the highest return for the level of risk acceptable to the investor, but also to provide the comfort level that every investor needs to stay the course.

Global Diversification

Thus far, the discussion has centered around the benefits of diversification without making a distinction between domestic and international funds. Academic studies have clearly demonstrated that foreign securities represent additional asset classes that can be blended with domestic stocks, bonds and cash to form a *balanced* portfolio. Even more important, the right combination of funds enables investors to earn higher returns over the long-term while actually reducing risk of the overall portfolio.

The reasons for focusing our attention on global investment should be spelled out. Two-thirds of the world's stock market values are outside the U.S. Also, investing outside the U.S. may reduce risk if overseas markets are not correlated with the U.S. market. For that reason, they are likely to hold up when we sink, smoothing out year-to-year returns for the overall portfolio. That is, markets do not move in lockstep, and blending international stocks with domestic issues can bring more stability to a portfolio.

THE EFFICIENT FRONTIER

The final step in building an *efficient* portfolio through diversification is to place this portfolio on the *efficient frontier*. This concept is discussed next.

The concept of diversification can be used to construct numerous portfolios with different combination of stocks, bonds, and cash. These portfolios will differ from each other not only with regard to the individual securities they contain, but with regard to the relative weights of individual securities as well. Assume that A, B, and C have been identified (see Figure 13-8) as model portfolios. Clearly, B is preferable to A, because both offer the same expected return, but B is less risky than the latter. Similarly, C is preferable to A, because it offers higher expected return, even though it is in the same risk class as A. However, portfolio B is *not* clearly preferable to portfolio C, because it offers lower expected return but also has smaller risk. An aggressive investor might prefer C, but a conservative investor would probably choose B.

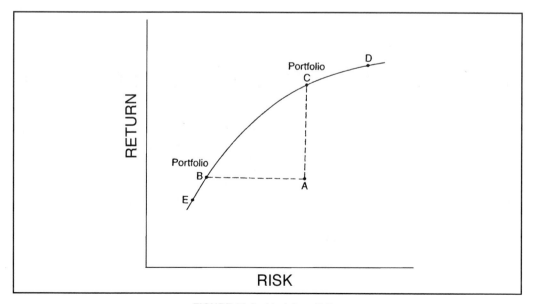

FIGURE 13-8 Model portfolios

From the foregoing discussion, a clear theme emerges. All portfolios below the EBCD curve are inefficient portfolios because, compared to the portfolios on the curve, they either offer lower returns or assume higher risks. More importantly, all portfolios *on the curve are efficient* in that each portfolio offers *the highest expected return for its risk class.* For this reason, the EBCD curve is known as the Efficient Frontier.

The power of the Efficient Frontier can be gleaned from the real world global portfolios presented in Figure 13-9(A and B). This chart underscores two important facts. First, once the risk level acceptable to an investor has been determined, it is important to create a portfolio that will lie on the efficient frontier for that level of risk. Second, diversification between stocks, bonds, and cash [Figure 13-9(A)], and between domestic and global diversification [Figure 13-9(B)] can increase return while reducing risk (a journey to the northwest).

The twin concepts of diversification and efficient frontier led to the establishment of asset allocation model as the foundation for diversifying a portfolio. This model is discussed next.

ASSET ALLOCATION MODEL

One of the hottest buzzwords in financial planning—the asset allocation model (AAM)—is no passing fad. Formally introduced into the finance literature more than three decades ago as modern portfolio theory, AAM provides the foundation for diversifying a portfolio.

Every investment portfolio can be plotted on Figure 13-10, which measures the returns obtained by various portfolios at different levels of risk. Each portfolio has a risk and a reward element. An investment counselor assembles a mix of assets to offer the highest return consistent with the client's risk level.

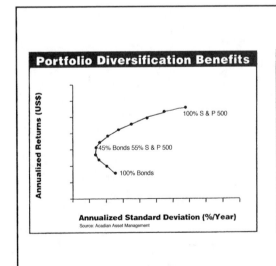

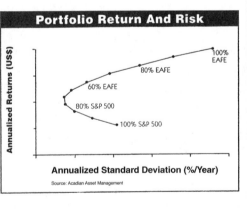

FIGURE 13-9 (A)   FIGURE 13-9 (B)

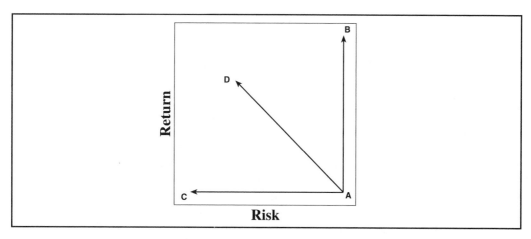

FIGURE 13-10 Risk-return relationship

Assume an investor currently owns a portfolio positioned at point A. The initial objective of the portfolio manager is to systematically alter the current mix so the portfolio will move from point A to point C which represents less risk without sacrificing return, or from A to B which represents higher return without assuming higher risk. The ultimate hope of using the AAM is to move portfolio A northwest and terminate the journey at, say, point D. if this could be achieved, the investor would realize a *higher return at a lower risk.*

Generally, investors diversify their holdings by spreading assets among companies, industries, and countries. However, the AAM suggests that investors should also diversify their securities across a minimum of three asset classes: stocks, bonds, and liquid instruments like Treasury bills or money market securities.

The logic behind the three-asset-class diversification strategy is simple: The stock and bond markets often do not move together. If the stock market is down, bonds could go up. Or if the long-term interest rates are falling, rates on short-term instruments could be increasing. So if an investor can diversify the holdings among various asset classes, the portfolio's exposure to any single investment arena is reduced. This tends to lower the risk without limiting the return.

The intuitive feelings investors have toward the benefits of diversification were first legitimized by a study published in the July/August 1986 issue of *The Financial Analyst Journal.* Using data on the investment strategies of 91 major pension funds over a ten-year period, the results showed that more than 90 percent of the variability in an individual portfolio's performance can be attributed to asset allocation policy, with market timing and the selection of securities playing only a minor role. Put differently, spreading assets across stocks, bonds, and short-term instruments can affect the variability in a portfolio's performance more than trying to pick the right stocks at the right time.

The Risk-Reward Connection

In order to fully understand the concept of AAM, we must establish the risk/reward connection, beginning by identifying the many types of risk that can influence a portfolio's returns. Market or systematic risk refers to that portion of total variability of stock's return caused by factors which simultaneously affect the average return of all marketable securities. That is, market risk refers to the possibility that individual investments could lose values because of a general weakness in the market.

Besides market risk there are other risks that affect the values of individual stocks and bonds in a portfolio. For instance, inflation risk is the probability that the value of the return on an investment would be eroded by inflation. Another risk particularly inherent in every investment in fixed-income securities is interest rate risk, which refers to the possibility that an increase in the interest rate would lower the value of interest-sensitive instruments such as bonds. However, the total impact of interest rate fluctuations on fixed-income securities may be confusing. For instance, higher interest rates may increase the interest rate of short-term instruments like money market accounts while lowering bond prices. In contrast, a decline in interest rates, which lowers the income from money market instruments, might increase the demand, and hence the value, of existing bonds carrying higher coupon rates.

Indeed, there are still more risks that can influence a portfolio's return. Nevertheless, when holdings are spread across various asset classes, the *decline* in value of one class due to these risk factors is likely to be accompanied by a simultaneous *gain* by another class. As a result, the portfolio's risk level would most likely be reduced when return increases.

In Figure 13-11, which presents the long-term historical return of various portfolios, two portfolios are of special interest. As expected, Portfolio A, which consists of only fixed-income securities, has the lowest return and a low level of risk. However, portfolio C, which combines equities and fixed-income securities, has a *higher* return and *lower* risk. This northwest journey is made possible by the application of the AAM.

Over a period of 20 years ending in 2004, a balanced, moderate-risk portfolio with 35 percent in stocks, 35 percent in ten-year Treasury bonds and 30 percent in Treasury bills gained substantially more than the investment in Treasury bills, but

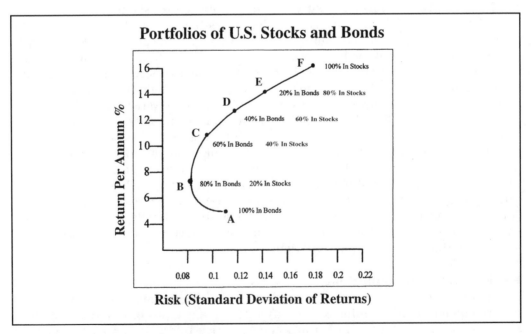

FIGURE 13-11 Return/risk tradeoff

it was worth much less than an all-stock portfolio. To earn the higher returns as compared to the Treasury bill investor, however, the diversified-portfolio investor encountered more volatility in annual returns. But these fluctuation were considerably less than those of the all-stock investor.

Interestingly, a diversified approach can mitigate the degree of loss in any one year. Even in 1974, when the S&P 500 stock index lost a whopping 26.5 percent, the diversified portfolio lost less than 5 percent.

An Essential Tool

In an AAM strategy, investments are typically distributed among three broad asset classes—stocks, bonds, and cash equivalents like money market securities. Each asset class offers specific advantages, as described below:

- *Stocks.* Historically, stocks have constituted the best performing asset class over the long term and also the best hedge against inflation.
- *Bonds.* Bonds can provide a regular stream of income and, historically, have offered greater stability than stocks.
- *Money Market Instruments.* Money market instruments like Treasury bills and high quality money market instruments provide liquidity and income and offer the surest means of preserving capital.

Allocating assets appropriately among stocks, bonds and cash equivalents can help investors achieve their long-term goals by managing risk. As demonstrated by several studies, individual investors often fail to match the long-term returns of the stock market, or even of the funds they own, because of a tendency to change strategies midstream. By attempting to provide a more stable, predictable return, the AAM may provide investors with the confidence they need to stay the course for the long term. Therefore, given the fact that most investors are expected to behave as though their time horizons were short, allocation of available funds among various asset classes may well represent the most important investment decision investors can make. In fact, as stated earlier, an important study concluded that 92 percent of the variability in the performance of a diversified portfolio was based upon the appropriate asset allocation policy, while security selection and market timing represented only six percent and two percent, respectively, of the variability in the portfolio's performance. Consequently, a realization of this power of the AAM to deliver attractive portfolio returns while minimizing risk may well be what investors need to stay the course and act as long-term investors.

To recapitulate, Asset Allocation works because of two important financial facts:

- Not all asset classes are adversely affected at the same time. For instance, in 1987 when the stock market started its free fall, the bond market, beaten down through much of the year, began a strong two-year rally. Subsequently, in 1990, the pattern repeated itself; a bond rally gathered steam as the stock market lost 16 percent.

- Assets rise and fall in value, but eventually the overall gains far exceed the losses. For example, despite the violent market fluctuations that were recorded between 1987 and 1991, bonds and stocks ended up with overall gains of 34 percent and 42 percent, respectively. Another important statistic:

between October 11, 1990 and August 10, 1997, there were 1,709 trading days. The days of up and down markets were, respectively, 923 and 777. And yet, during this time period, the market increased by a whopping 239.90 percent.

Asset Allocation Model Steps

The AAM involves a four-step process, which is presented in Table 13-8.

Step one. Determine the type of portfolio that matches the investor's risk tolerance level and can help the investor achieve his or her return objectives. Asset allocation portfolios are marketed as aggressive growth, growth, growth and income, balanced, and fixed income portfolios. Of these, aggressive growth portfolios offer the highest return but also have the highest risk. Both the return and the risk decline as we move from aggressive growth to growth, growth and income, balanced and fixed income portfolios.

Step two. Analyze the prevailing market and financial conditions. Results of this analysis form the basis for determining the percentage allocation of investable funds among the three major asset classes—namely, equity, fixed income, and money market instruments.

Step three. Select different types of investment products in each asset class. For the equity class, the following types of stocks may be selected: International large and small cap, domestic large, mid-cap and small-cap, value and growth stocks, aggressive and conservative stocks, and so on. The fixed income class may include: Government and corporate long-, intermediate-, and short-term bonds, international bonds, and municipal bonds.

Step four. Select the best mutual funds or individual securities that would match the selections made in step three. This is a major undertaking, and it requires both professional analytical skills and an extensive knowledge of the various investment products to complete this step.

A sample asset allocation portfolio format is presented in Figure 13-12 to demonstrate how the asset allocation process is pressed into action.

Risk Tolerance Guidelines

Asset allocation programs typically classify portfolio risk into three basic categories of investment portfolios that are unique because of their adherence to strict risk tolerance guidelines. These categories are popularly known as conservative, moderate and aggressive portfolios. Guidelines of these programs are designed with the objective of limiting the maximum decline in portfolio value under *adverse* market conditions to 0-10 percent, 10-20 percent and 20-40 percent, respectively. *Adverse* market conditions are defined as a substantial increase in interest rate accompanied by a similarly substantial decline in one or more commonly followed stock market indices over a 12-month period. The structured discipline helps protect the investor from exposure to unacceptable levels of market decline and allows the portfolio to seek the highest possible total return consistent with a tolerance level of risk tolerance.

It is important to recognize, however, that risk reduction is generally associated with a reduction in total return as well. That is, the more conservative the

TABLE 13-8 Asset Allocation Process

Asset allocation strategy involves the following four-step process. A sample four-step process is presented below.

Step one Determine the type of portfolio that meets the investor's needs and goals

Aggressive Growth
Growth
Fixed Income
Growth and Income
Balanced

Step two Determine percentage distribution of Asset Allocation classes
Based on portfolio type (Step one)

% Equity
% Fixed Income
% Money Market

Step three Select appropriate investment types

Stocks	Bonds	Money Market
Internationl	Government	Taxable
Domestic	Corporate	Tax Exempt
Large Cap	Domestic	
Small Cap	International	
Value	Municipal	
Growth	Long-term	
Income	Short-term	
Aggressive		
Conservative		

Step four Selection of apprpriate mutual funds/securities

Fund 1	Fund 4	Fund 7
Fund 2	Fund 5	Fund 8
Fund 3	Fund 6	Fund 9
Security #1	Security #2	Security #3

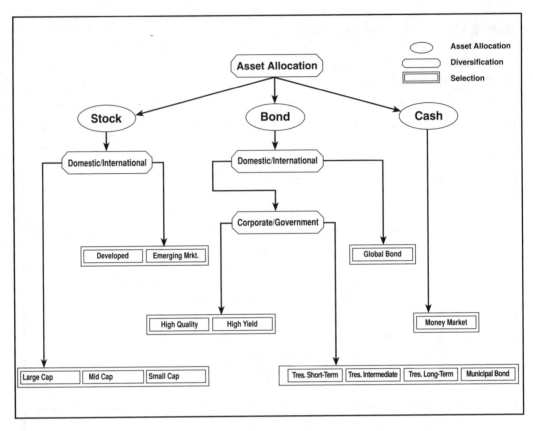

FIGURE 13-12 Dynamic asset allocation model

asset allocation strategy adopted, the greater the potential reduction in the expected return generated by that portfolio. However, a professional asset allocation strategist can succeed in significantly reducing the risk while sacrificing only a small amount in returns. That is, when an effective asset allocation strategy is used, the benefits associated with a reduction in risk can far outweigh its cost measured in terms of reduction in return.

In this context, it is important to establish a direct relationship between the three risk categories (conservative, moderate, and aggressive) and five categories under which Asset Allocation portfolios are typically marketed (Figure 13-13). Fixed income, growth and income, and aggressive growth categories are clearly considered, respectively, conservative, moderate, and aggressive portfolios, although these three types of categories frequently overlap. For instance, a growth portfolio could fall under both aggressive and moderate risk categories. Similarly, a growth and income portfolio could be classified under both moderate and conservative risk categories.

Summary

Based partly on the preceding discussions, and drawing upon the results of other studies, we can make the following statements:

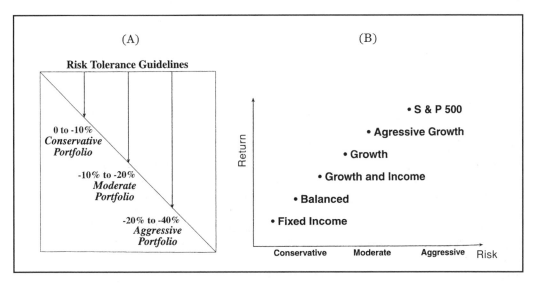

FIGURE 13-13 Asset allocation portfolios

- The majority of people, regardless of their time horizon, are risk-averse investors.
- Because of the many faces of stock market risk and the peculiarities of the market, even the long term investors are likely to behave as though they are short-term traders.
- Most investors do not stay the course and consequently fail to earn respectable returns on their investments.
- For short-term or uncertain time-frame risk-averse investors, which encompass the majority of investors, AAM provides an ideal strategy.
- The AAM can not only reduce the portfolio risk to a level acceptable to the investors, but also can achieve an increase in return.

SIZING UP A MUTUAL FUND PORTFOLIO

Mutual fund shares are easy to buy and sell. But it is infinitely more difficult to determine if the mutual fund portfolio is right for an investor. Part of the problem, of course, is that we are inundated with so much controversial material that it is difficult even for a sophisticated investor to sort out the wheat from the chaff. However, it does not have to be this way. Here are seven rules one can follow to build a mutual fund portfolio that is right for an investor.

Rule 1. Conduct an annual review. Frequently, we hear the celebrated phrase, *the past record does not guarantee future performance.* Since there is a lot of truth to it, one needs to make sure that the selected mutual funds' performance does not drastically lag the performance of their category as a whole.

For instance, in 2002 the equity market represented by S&P 500 registered a significant decline. If during that year an equity mutual fund lagged behind this rate of decline, it may pay to make a note of it. However, a word of caution is in order. One year does not establish a track record. The performance of every successful money manager occasionally lags behind the market or a relevant index, and it is inadvisable to fire a portfolio manager on the basis of one year's poor performance. However, it makes sense to call the manager of each under-performing fund in the portfolio and find out what has changed. If nothing has significantly changed, one should keep a close eye on it and determine in advance under what conditions it would be prudent to bail out of the fund.

Rule 2. Check the risk profile of the fund. Risk is one of the most misunderstood words in the investment world. The academicians measure it with beta, standard deviation and variance. The average investor classifies risk profiles as conservative, average and aggressive. A leading mutual fund classifies investor risk preferences as cautious control, balanced medium, and assertive dynamic.

Instead of getting mixed up with the perennial problem of defining risk, it might be desirable to adopt the following approach. First, it should be determined how the fund did during the bear markets of (1) January 1973-December 1974; (2) August 1987-October 1987; (3) July 1990-October 1990; (4) February 1994-April 1994; and (5) 2000-2002. If the fund did poorly during one or more of these market declines, the investor is likely to be exposed to serious risk in future down markets. If that is the case, then the investor may wish to reduce the holdings in such a fund to reduce the potential loss in a weak market.

Rule 3. Find out who is the boss. Most investors recognize their funds' names but are not concerned with the respective portfolio managers. This can be a costly mistake for two reasons. First, if the performance of the mutual fund is tied to a specific manager, and that manager leaves the fund, the investor may be surprised when the new manager's record card shows up. Second, if in the past a portfolio manager has been successful in following certain investment policy, but chooses to change that policy, that change may not even be recognized. This can prove to be troublesome in the long run.

It is, therefore, important that investors get to know their managers, their basic philosophies, and their track records. Fortunately, a growing number of mutual funds are recognizing the importance of exposing their fund managers directly to investors and, in fact, would like to expose them even more. Unfortunately, most shareholder representatives have limited training, and strict limitations are imposed on what they are allowed to say to callers. Therefore, to fill that information gap, some fund companies have inaugurated hot lines on which managers discuss their holdings and market outlook.

Rule 4. Tighten the portfolio. People are usually attracted to what is hot, and frequently wind up buying multiple funds with similar concentrations. For instance, until the fiasco with Mexico, Japan and Asia, millions of dollars were pouring into international funds. Similarly, because of the unmanageable flow of dollars, at one point many funds specializing in stocks of small companies stopped taking in new money. So, if an investor bought several top-performing funds at the same time, he or she may have ended up with several funds that invested in the same type of securities. It is therefore advisable to correct the situation and tighten the portfolio by weeding out funds that duplicate the types and investment philosophies the investor wishes to retain in the portfolio.

Rule 5. Eliminate unnecessary funds. Investors frequently make the mistake of owning several mutual funds to achieve similar objectives, such as retirement, financing college education or making large purchases. This is not only unnecessary but can be counterproductive, since it is both expensive and difficult to track a large number of mutual funds. Investors would, therefore, be better off streamlining their portfolios and having only a limited number of funds for each goal.

Rule 6. Beware of emerging markets. Financial magazines are replete with exciting stories about emerging markets. These markets, generally associated with Third World countries, are growing rapidly, often generating annual returns in excess of 30 to 40 percent, and sometimes even higher. It is therefore wise to allocate at least a portion of the portfolio to mutual funds specifically dealing with emerging markets. However, a word of caution is certainly in order. Investors who are risk averse or close to retirement should invest no more than five to ten percent of their portfolio in emerging markets.

Rule 7. Diversify the portfolio. Various types of investment can be included in a diversified portfolio. While one need not own every type of investment, the performance of the portfolio is likely to improve if it is broadly diversified between stocks, bonds, and money market securities, as well as between domestic and international markets.

Rebalancing a Portfolio

In the 1990's, and especially since the beginning of 1995 and until 2000, there was a surge in stock prices. Subsequently, during 2000 to 2002, all the market indexes suffered a significant decline but they rose again in 2003 and 2004. Because of the market's strong advance in the 1990's, and subsequent declines and advances since the beginning of 2000, it is likely that the equity portion of investors' portfolios has significantly changed, throwing off the original asset allocation distribution.

One effective way of guarding against *risk creep* and maintaining a consistent investment strategy is to regularly rebalance the portfolio. This simply means periodically shifting money among the various asset classes to keep the portfolio diversification in line with the desired asset allocation strategy.

The strategy of rebalancing a portfolio can not only protect investors from gradually taking on more risk than they realize, but it can also improve the portfolio's performance. This is because occasional rebalancing will force investors to shift money from an asset that has performed well (sell high) into one that has lagged (buy low). For example, if stocks have been in a slump, an investor using a rebalancing approach would shift money from bonds and money market securities into stocks, taking advantage of the lower stock prices. By the same token, if this strategy is followed, after a period of rising stock prices, funds would be shifted from stocks to bonds or money markets.

Let there be no misunderstanding, however. Asset rebalancing is not a market timing strategy, in which an investor attempts to *outguess* the vagaries of the financial markets. Rather, it is a systematic approach to maintaining a relatively consistent risk profile. The strategy is most appropriate for tax-deferred retirement plans, since gains realized on the sale of securities are not subject to taxation. It could also be used for regular accounts, but frequent rebalancing could cause complicated tax reporting headaches.

Rebalancing in Practice

The following example demonstrates the use of periodic rebalancing strategy. Consider the results of a $10,000 investment made in December, 1969 in two different tax-deferred plans with a diversified mix of 60 percent stocks, 30 percent bonds, and ten percent cash. One portfolio is rebalanced each quarter so that the original investment mix is maintained. In other words, if the percentage invested in stocks rise above the 60 percent guideline as a result of market appreciation, money is shifted from stocks to bonds and cash to bring the portfolio back in line with the investor's original strategy.

With the second portfolio, the investment mix is not rebalanced, so it changes over time reflecting the actual performance of stocks, bonds, and cash. In this case, the equity rose from 60 percent of assets at the beginning in December, 1969 to 74 percent by September, 1995, substantially raising the investor's risk exposure.

In this example, asset rebalancing helped mitigate losses during stock market downturns in 1980-1982, 1987, 1990 and 1994. Furthermore, the investor took advantage of the lower equity prices by shifting money into stocks during these periods.

It is also interesting to note that over the entire period the rebalanced portfolio modestly outperformed the unbalanced one, even though the latter took on a higher risk profile as its equity position increased over time. By September, 1995, the value of the more conservative, rebalanced portfolio was $145,000, compared with about $141,000 for the unbalanced one.

The results reflect the long-term impact of the 1973-74 bear market on the performance of these two portfolios. The steep decline in equity prices reduced the equity allocation of the unbalanced portfolio to 49 percent while the rebalanced portfolio maintained its 60 percent equity position by buying stocks at bargain prices. The rebalanced account benefitted from the market's recovery after the bear market, and it maintained its advantage every year after that.

While the unbalanced portfolio was able to close the gap during strong bull markets, its gains were not enough to overtake the rebalanced portfolio. In effect, the rebalanced portfolio reduced an investor's loss during severe market downturns, but over time provided a competitive return relative to a more aggressive portfolio.

Naturally, the relative performance of portfolios can vary, depending on the time period measured. Also, there is no guarantee that the story just presented will be repeated in the future or that a rebalancing strategy will always be effective. Still, periodically rebalancing a portfolio appears to be a conceptually sound strategy.

PORTFOLIO MANAGEMENT AND MONETARY POLICY

The basic rule of using the rebalancing strategy is that it be used at regular intervals, say, every quarter or every six months. However, another rule, which often supersedes the rebalancing rule, concerns a change in monetary policy, which may require immediate attention. Since these two rules appear to contradict each other, a brief explanation is necessary to clarify the issue.

The official goal of Federal Reserve System (FED) is to formulate monetary policy in order "to promote . . . maximum employment, stable prices to moderate long term interest rates." Since these can be, and often are, conflicting goals, the FED must try to simultaneously weigh several issues while striking a balance between the short-run and the long-run economic goals.

The FED's policy, known as monetary policy, works by affecting interest rates. Increases in interest rates raise the cost of borrowing and lead to reductions in business investment spending and household purchase of durable goods such as homes and autos. These declines in spending reduce the aggregate demand for the economy's output, leading firms to cut back on production and employment. On the other hand, interest rate declines stimulate aggregate spending and lead to increases in production and employment.

In recent years there has been a major shift in the way investors perceive the intent of the FED to pursue either a tight or an easy monetary policy. This shift has become so pervasive that today's market sharply reacts to every *anticipated move* by the FED, which exacerbates the volatility of the market experienced in normal times. This point requires elaboration.

Banks are legally required to hold a specified percentage of deposits in reserves, which they hold as vault cash or deposits with the FED. When banks need additional reserves in the short term, they can borrow directly from the FED at the discount rate. The discount rate is directly set by the FED in response to economic conditions, raising rates to slow borrowing and lowering rates to stimulate the economy. While banks can borrow directly from the FED, the FED frowns on excessive use of going to the discount window.

But the discount rate is virtually a defunct weapon. At present, member banks have only a relatively small amount (in millions) borrowed from the FED. And yet, total member bank reserves consisting of vault cash and deposits at the FED approach $100 billion. It can be seen that borrowed reserves at discount rate are miniscule.

Given FED's biases against excessive borrowing by banks, when short-term needs for cash arise, many banks borrow from other member banks with excess cash at a rate which is popularly known as the Federal funds rate. It is also called the FED's *target rate.*

And therein lies the problem. What does it mean when the FED says that it is going to target a rate that is determined in a market—interbank loans—in which the FED is not a participant? And yet, the stock market reacts sharply every time the FED changes its "target Federal funds rate." For instance, on November 6, 2001 it was widely reported in the financial press that the FED "lowered its key federal funds rate for overnight bank loans for the tenth time this year by 0.5 percent to two percent—the lowest level since during the Kennedy administration in 1961." Buoyed by this move, the Dow Jones jumped 1.59 percent and the NASDAQ rose by a whopping 2.31 percent.

This is the backdrop against which investment portfolios must be managed. While there is no question that, as a general rule, short-term fluctuations should not be allowed to unduly influence long-term objectives, due to the enormous effect that FED has on the stock market, it is important for every investor to watch the FED's moves closely and adjust their portfolios to protect these portfolios from being unduly influenced by short-term moves on the part of the Federal Reserve.

In this chapter, key concepts and strategies of investment management are presented. Investment planning strategies will be undertaken in the next chapter.

Everyone has the brain power to make money in stocks—not everyone has the stomach. If you are susceptible to selling everything in a panic, you ought to avoid stocks and stock mutual funds altogether.

Peter Lynch

APPENDIX TO CHAPTER 13:
FUNDAMENTAL AND TECHNICAL ANALYSIS

FUNDAMENTAL ANALYSIS

An Overview

A time-tested analytical method used by many financial planners is to identify, and eventually recommend, the purchase of undervalued securities. This strategy is based on the assumption that the price of an individual security always gravitates toward its intrinsic value, or in technical jargon, its present value. This method, called fundamental analysis, examines general economic conditions, such as economic growth, financial conditions, such as interest rates, and a host of related fundamental factors. This approach also requires the analysis of the industry conditions and projected industry growth. Finally, fundamental analysis involves the examination of a firm's economic performance and its potential earnings growth. Ratios, financial data, and analytical savvy are the cornerstones of fundamental analysis. As mentioned, the ultimate objective of fundamental analysis is to calculate the present value of a security so it could be compared with its current market price to determine whether or not it is an undervalued security and, therefore, offers an attractive investment opportunity.

Forecasting Earnings

Essentially, a dependable earnings forecast is the key to the calculation of the present value of a security. Consequently, forecasting earnings growth is at the heart of fundamental analysis. Accurate prediction of earnings growth, in turn, depends on a careful examination of the general economic conditions prevailing in the country, the industry conditions, and the overall growth of the company whose earnings are under analysis.

The economy. In a nutshell, earnings of a company largely depend on prevailing economic conditions. Similarly, forecasting of earnings depends upon the forecasting of economic conditions. A study of two groups of variables covering the economy and company earnings is helpful in predicting the future of the economy. Another measure of value is the dividend yield. Historically, a dividend yield of below three percent of all stocks taken as a group has signaled the end of a growing economy and a bull market.

A third measure of prevailing economic conditions is the existing liquidity situation. Stock prices increase to artificially high levels when an ever-expanding supply of money starts chasing a dwindling supply of stocks. For instance, mergers, leveraged buyouts, and stock buy-backs during the mid-80's resulted in a net decrease of $214 billion in publicly traded stocks, while the money supply initially rose by an equivalent amount. During the same period, $25 to $30 billion came from overseas investors, thereby aggravating the liquidity situation even further.

Analysis of the nation's general economic conditions is important because there is a direct relationship between the economy and the performance of an individual firm, of which earning power is a key measure. In general, growth in the real GDP, reflecting the nation's economic health, and changes in earning power, representing the performance of individual firms, are positively related.

The industry. Variations in earnings of individual companies are closely related to variations in earnings of related industries. This can be inferred from the fact that a significant portion of the price variations of an individual stock is the result of average price variations of all the companies within related industries.

The key industry fundamentals are presented in Table A13-1. Analysis of these fundamentals can help an investor identify those industries that are likely to record superior performance.

Published Reports. An investor need not depend totally on the annual report published by the company. Both Value Line and Standard & Poor's publish extensive data on approximately 1,700 stocks that are most actively traded. In addition, the publication entitled *Morning Star Mutual Funds* publishes extensive data on the more than 7,000 mutual funds.

TABLE A13-1 Key Industry Fundamentals

Indicator	Description
Historical Performance	
Industry Life Cycle	Three distinct phases
	Pioneering Stage—Rapid sales and earnings growth
	Investment Maturity Stage—Consolidate market positions and begin to encroach on competitors' market share by broadening capital base and establishing earnings and dividend policy.
	Stabilization—Unit costs become stable and market becomes saturated.
Performance During a Business Cycle	Cyclical or countercyclical performance of a company during an economic cycle.
Economic Structure	Degree of competition which prevails within the industry.
Capital Investment	Highly capital intensive industries usually make effective long-term plans for capital investment, are generally technologically more advanced than less capital intensive industries, and have a much larger growth potential than labor intensive industries.
Government Regulations	Some industries are subject to continual government intervention.
	Others may be subject to antitrust suits or attacks from environmental groups.
Labor Conditions	History of labor negotiations and impact of previous labor strikes can help determine the risks associated with certain industries.
Miscellaneous Factors	Price and income elasticities of demand for products, changes in consumer tastes, foreign competition, and the availability and cost of raw materials.

EPS Model. The annual report and the published reports just discussed provide a basis for predicting a company's future earnings. The techniques for estimating future earnings are based on a detailed examination, and eventual prediction, of several financial ratios.

The construction of the earnings per share model for XYZ company is presented in Figure A13-1. It shows that, for the EPS to increase, one or more of the key variables (production efficiency, coverage ratio, leverage ratio, and so on) must also increase. For instance, the company can increase its EPS from its current level of $13.35 by improving its production efficiency ratio of 14.4 percent, turnover ratio of 1.94, leverage ratio of 2.28, and so on.

P/E Ratio. The main purpose of undertaking fundamental analysis is to calculate the present value of a stock. It can then be compared with the current price to determine whether or not it is undervalued. A time-tested yet simple method is to estimate the present value by multiplying the projected future earnings by its P/E ratio.

Essentially, the P/E ratio is the multiple investors are willing to pay for each dollar of a company's earnings. Literally, it is the price of a company's stock divided by its annual earnings. If a stock sells for $50 a share and the company's next year's expected earnings are $5, it carries a P/E ratio of ten. It should be pointed out that the P/E ratio of a company with negative or negligible earnings is meaningless. However, the vast majority of stocks have meaningful P/E ratios as do most popular stock indexes.

The P/E ratio can be used to estimate the attractiveness of a stock. Consider first the big picture. The Standard & Poor's traditional P/E was 13 to 15 during a

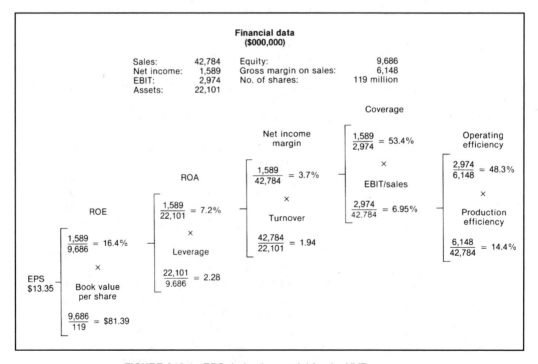

FIGURE A13-1   EPS derivation model for the XYZ company

bull market and eight to ten in a declining, or bear, market. So, when the Standard and Poor's P/E ratio shot up to 21.1, as was the case prior to the infamous Black Monday of October 19, 1987, there was definite cause for alarm. In the fall of 1988, the Standard and Poor's P/E ratio declined to around ten. It is worth nothing, however, that in 2001 the P/E ratio of S&P 500 was hovering around 30.97, but the fundamental factors supporting this P/E level were vastly different than they were in October 1987.

Two observations are apropos at this point. First, the case for stocks with low P/Es is compelling. Several studies have shown that stocks with P/Es below the market average have significantly out performed other stocks. Several years ago, one study showed that low P/E stocks return 16.8 percent annually, compared with 9.9 percent for the stocks included in the Standard & Poor's 500. Second, the P/E ratio is not a fixed number. Every company actually has several P/Es, which can significantly vary over time. Hence, care should be exercised when using this ratio to estimate the future value of a stock.

TECHNICAL ANALYSIS

An Overview

Up to this point, the discussion has centered around the selection of stocks by engaging in fundamental analysis. The techniques of technical analysis, however, are at odds with fundamental analysis. Proponents of technical analysis argue that, because the market price of a stock reflects *all* factors affecting it, a study involving only stock price movements is necessary. Technical analysts believe that the future expected price of a stock—the only variable that matters—can be predicted by carefully analyzing its past price behavior, because movements in past prices create discernible patterns that tend to repeat themselves in a predictable manner. Consequently, technicians concern themselves with predictions of short-term price movements in an effort to determine the best timing for purchases and sales of common stocks. For these reasons, it is sometimes claimed that the fundamental technique is generally best for selecting *what* stocks to buy or sell, whereas technical analysis primarily helps one decide *when* to trade in stocks. The factors used by technical analysts in making their buy and sell decisions are presented in Table A13-2.

Charting

Technical analysis of individual stocks involves the interpretation of important chart patterns known by such esoteric names as head and shoulders, necklines, triangles, double top, double bottom, wedges, flags, and saucers. Each pattern signals to technical analysts a major or minor upward or downward movement in the stock. Several popular chart patterns are discussed next.

Support and resistance levels. One of the most important aspects of chart analysis is the identification of support and resistance levels, as shown in Figure A13-2. A support level is a barrier to a price decline; a resistance level is a barrier to a price advancement. Although the barrier is an obstruction, it is by no means impassable. Stock prices do break support and resistance barriers.

TABLE A13-2   Factors Used in Technical Analysis

	Description	Claim by technical analysts
Activity factors		
High-Low Index	Average number of NYSE stocks making new highs (surpassing their previous highest price levels for preceding 52 weeks) minus the number making new lows.	During a rising market an increasing number of stocks reach new highs and a decreasing number reach new lows (market technically strong). The reverse is true in a declining market (market is technically weak).
Advances-Declines Index	Ratio of the number of issues that advanced to the number that declined.	Changes in the ratio predict short-term market trends.
Most Active Stocks	Wall Street Journal listing of most actively traded stocks, their high, low, and closing prices on the New York and American stock exchanges.	Because of degree of risk involved in holding low quality stocks, market is generally more vulnerable when low quality stocks become popular.
Lo/Price Activity Ratio	Compares activity in speculative stocks to that in quality issues. Represents the weekly ratio of volumes in Barron's Lo/Price Stock Index to volume in DJIA.	High speculative activity usually occurs at the top of the market, whereas low speculative activity occurs at the bottom.
Dow Jones Momentum Ratio	Measures spread between the DJIA and its 30-day moving average.	Assumed to pinpoint turning points in the market. In a bull market, difference of 30 to 40 points indicates the market has reached the top; −30 to −50 suggests the market has reached the bottom. In a bear market, a spread of 20 to 30 signals a market top, whereas −50 to −70 signals a market bottom.

TABLE A13-2 (continued)

Market strength factors

Breadth Index	Computed by subtracting the number of advances from the number of declines every week and dividing the result by the number of stocks that remain unchanged during that week. Index for the week is added to the previous week's figure.	When plotted on a graph, the trend in the market is determined from the direction of movement in the breadth index.
Relative Strength Index	Ratio of the price of a stock to the DJIA.	As long as the ratio continues to rise, that stock price is rising at a faster rate than the market and vice versa.
Volume of Trading	The volume of stocks changing hands daily.	Rise or decline in stock prices on high volume signals a continuation of the existing price trend; whereas a low volume points to an impending reversal of price trend.
Large Block Transactions	Financial journals regularly publish data concerning large transactions (25,000 shares or more) in specified stocks and prices at which these transactions were made.	Large blocks of shares traded on a downtick indicate a weak market. Conversely, large transactions on upticks suggest a strong bull market.

Directional factors

Daily Trading Barometer	A weighted composite of three oscillating factors: (1) Last 7 days of advances and declines on the NYSE; (2) Algebraic sum of the last 20 days of plus and minus volumes on the NYSE; and (3) Ratio of the closing value of the DJIA to the average closing price for the last 28 days.	Proponents argue that it is a reliable indicator of overbought and undersold market conditions.

Directional Moves	Directional moves of the various Dow Jones Indicators. While divergence is not unusual, it is assumed that this divergence is not likely to persist for long.	Movements in weaker segment of the market (transportation) precede movements in the stronger counterparts (industrials and utilities).

Contrary opinion factors

Short Interest	Measure of short sales. An investor is selling short when, without first owning a stock, he/she sells it at a certain price in the hope of later being able to buy it at a lower price and realizing a profit.	Two interpretations: (1) Large short interest indicates widespread expectation of a price decline and is bearish. (2) Indicates a strong potential demand for stock and is, therefore, bullish.
Odd-Lot Index and Odd-Lot Sales Index	Ratio of odd-lot sales to odd-lot purchases (less than 100 share units).	Small investors are ill-informed and can be counted on to make the wrong moves at critical moments. If odd-lotters are net-buyers, "smart money" will get out of the market.
NYSE Specialists Short Sales Ratios	Ratio of specialists short sales to total NYSE short sales.	Measures extremes of sentiment of NYSE specialists who sell short most heavily at market tops when nonmember enthusiasm for buying is greatest and less heavily at bottoms when public selling is accelerated.
Advisory Service Sentiment	Weekly index of the percentage of leading bearish advisory services.	When the advisory service becomes overly one-sided, technical analysts view it as a contrary indicator because services follow trends rather than anticipate changes.

Confidence factor

Barron's Confidence Index (CI)	Ratio of high grade to low grade bond yields. High quality bond yields are always lower than low quality bond yields because investors have more confidence in them.	In a rising market, the CI rises. When the CI slides downward, the market is believed to be getting ready for a downturn because investors are reluctant to place confidence in lower quality bonds.

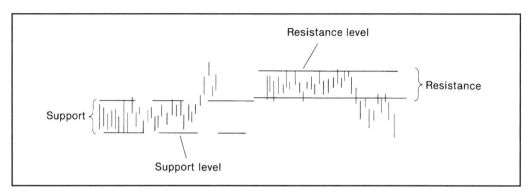

FIGURE A13-2 Support and resistance levels

Head and shoulders configurations. Basic reversal patterns help analysts identify the turning points so that they can decide when to buy or sell stock. The key reversal pattern is popularly known as the head and shoulders configuration. This configuration, shown in Figure A13-3, is merely another name for an uptrend or a downtrend in a stock; *neckline* is the familiar resistance or support level.

A head and shoulders formation should be analyzed against the background of volume trend. As the head and shoulders top is formed, resistance to further price increases dampens investor enthusiasm; therefore, the volume decreases on each of the rally phases within the top formation. The reverse is true when the head and shoulders bottom is under formation. It should be emphasized that the completion of a head and shoulders top or bottom is not considered final until the penetration of the neckline is apparent.

Five broad patterns. It is worth noting that of all the many chart patterns and techniques just discussed, five broadly classified patterns are claimed to best describe the price behavior of most stocks. These patterns, shown in Figure A13-4, should be self-explanatory.

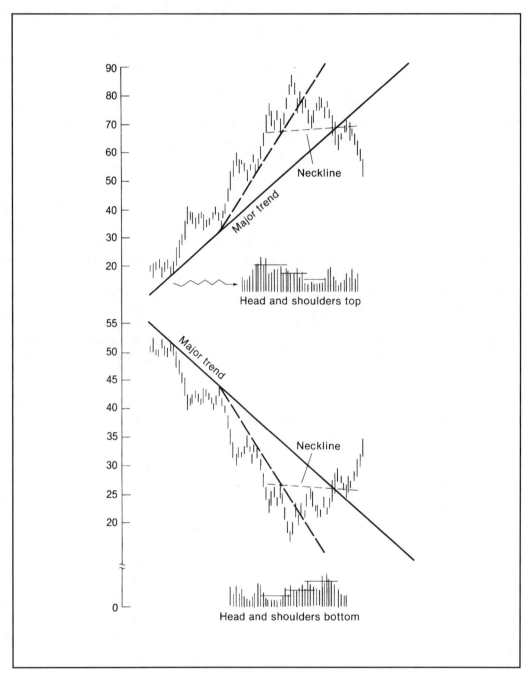

FIGURE A13-3   Head and shoulders configuration

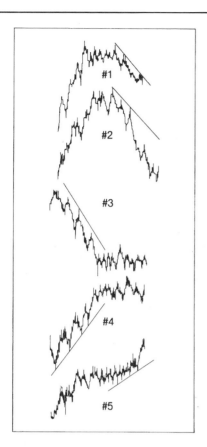

Chart Pattern #1

Stocks with vulnerable trends and/or possible downside potential.

Chart Pattern #2

Stocks with less vulnerability that appear to have reached possible lows, but need consolidation.

Chart Pattern #3

Stocks that have declined and experienced consolidation, and could do well in a favorable market.

Chart Pattern #4

Stocks that have performed relatively well but are currently in "neutral" trends.

Chart Pattern #5

Stocks in established uptrends and/or with possible upside potential.

FIGURE A13-4 Various chart patterns

CHAPTER 14

Investment Planning Strategies

INTRODUCTION

Investment planning can be a complex and often overwhelming task. However, the basic definition of investment planning is simple: the development and implementation of an investment portfolio designed to achieve the short- and long-run investment objectives articulated by an investor. This definition suggests that, for the investment planning process to be successful, a financial planner must not only understand the investor but also play a crucial role in achieving a delicate *balance* between risk and return, concentration and diversification, current income and growth, taxable and tax-advantaged investment, and liquid and nonliquid investments. An overview of the concept of investment planning is presented in Figure 14-1.

This chapter is divided into three parts. First we will analyze in detail the investment planning process. Second, the key investment planning strategies will be discussed. Finally, we will present a real world investment plan developed by using the investment planning process presented in the first part of this chapter.

INVESTMENT PLANNING PROCESS

INTRODUCTION

The investment planning process generally consists of five major steps: (1) Identification of client's goals. (2) Determination of the client's risk tolerance level. (3) Articulation of the client's investment preferences. (4) Analysis of current investment portfolio. (5) Reorganization of current investment portfolio. In discussing these steps, we will draw upon the investment models, theories, and concepts developed in the previous chapter. In our discussion we will also make extensive use of the basic investment alternatives presented in Chapter 12. A generous use of

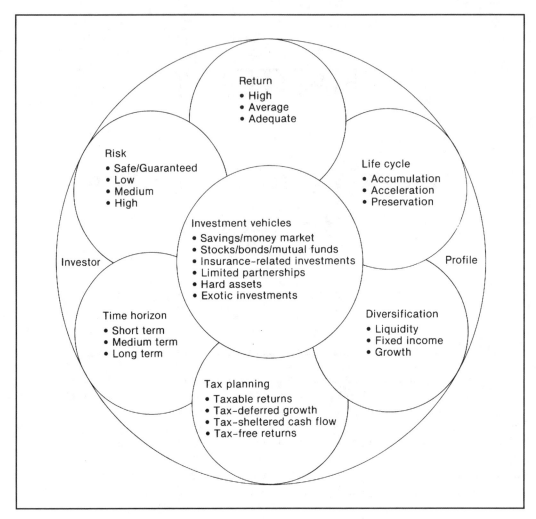

FIGURE 14-1   Concept of investment planning

forms and questionnaires will also be made to determine client's goals, risk tolerance level, and investment preferences.

GOAL SETTING

An Overview

The investment planning process is initiated with the identification of a client's
goals. This is easier said than done for several reasons: (1) Investment goals are
likely to change as the client passes through different stages of life cycle. (2) Investment planning objectives are harder to verbalize than other (education, risk
management, and so on) planning goals. For instance, it is difficult for many clients to state with any degree of certainty their needs for liquidity, current income,
and desired rate of growth of investable funds. (3) Few clients truly appreciate the
power of diversification and the value of using the Asset Allocation Model (AAM)

in constructing an investment portfolio. (4) Since the Tax Reform Act of 1986 removed most of the effects of tax considerations in investment planning, many clients naively assume that tax saving strategies no longer play an important role in investment goal setting. (5) Frequently, clients do not realize that sometimes the time horizon can determine the appropriateness of an investment product. For instance, the investment selected to fund a child's education may depend upon the number of years remaining before the withdrawal begins. (6) An unrealistic expectation of investment returns can frustrate the achievement of the desired goals. Development of strategies for dealing with these issues will provide the framework for a meaningful discussion of the process of setting investment goals.

Life Cycle

The starting point is the recognition of the stages of financial life cycle. Although an investor passes through many stages of life cycles, for simplicity, these stages will be classified into three broad categories, namely: accumulation, acceleration, and preservation.

The *accumulation* stage begins at the start of the investor's financial life. During this stage the investor's preoccupation is with: (1) protecting the growing family from a potential financial disaster due to death or disability; (2) providing for children's education; (3) accumulating basic assets like home and furnishings; and (4) building cash reserves and emergency funds to meet unexpected contingencies. An investment portfolio suited for this stage invariably consists of a large percentage of cash reserves and a variety of safe and low risk investments designed to help the investor's savings grow at a slow but steady rate.

The *acceleration* stage is ushered in when the investor enters the peak earning years and feels secure about having taken care of the family's basic needs and emergency situations. During this stage the investor may change from being risk averse to being a risk taker, since now the investor has the time and resources to recover from potential investment losses. So during the acceleration stage, the portfolio should be transformed into a risky portfolio by including higher risk investments with a potential for higher return.

The third stage, known as the *preservation* stage, begins when the investor starts preparing for retirement. Gone are the peak earning years. Also gone is the capacity to bounce back from significant investment losses resulting from taking high risks. During this stage the major objective is the preservation of capital accumulated during the previous stages so the maximum amount of capital would be available for generating current income when regular sources of earned income are exhausted. Once again, the portfolio is transformed into a relatively risk-free type appropriate for the accumulation stage, although the major emphasis shifts from low-risk, slow-growing, investments to income producing investments.

The concept of shifting investment goals as the investor passes through the three stages of life is presented in Figure 14-2.

Basic Investment Objectives

The second consideration in goal setting is the establishment of basic investment objectives which, in turn, leads to the determination of other, broad-based objectives like a proper balance between risk and investment return. The three basic investment objectives are liquidity, current income, and investment growth.

Liquidity. An essential component of a well-designed investment portfolio is the percentage allocated for cash reserves. The investor's liquidity needs can be classified into three categories: operating funds, emergency funds, and funds earmarked for capitalizing on future investment opportunities. The cash reserves portion of an investment portfolio satisfies all three liquidity needs of an investor.

Current income. The types and amounts of fixed income securities and annuities included in an investment portfolio are determined by two factors related to the investor's current income needs. First, the total of all the income sources—salary, pension, current investment income, bonus, and so on—should be compared with the current income needs to maintain the desired standard of living. The excess of income needs over total income sources, if any, is the amount of additional income which must be generated by new investments. Second, the investor should recognize the trade-off involved in this process: The higher the amount invested in securities generating current income, the lower the amount available for investing in growth securities, and the smaller the potential for future growth of the principal.

Investment growth. A key objective of investment planning is to maximize the growth of the total investment portfolio. Several major considerations determine the amount of investable funds to be allocated to growth investments and the types of investment products selected to achieve this objective. These considerations include the returns desired, the investor's risk tolerance level, and the investor's future income needs and time horizon.

Diversification and Asset Allocation Model (AAM)

The third element in the goal setting process is the realization of the benefits offered by the use of the AAM. One of the most celebrated bits of investment advice was given by Andrew Carnegie: "Put all your eggs in the same basket and watch it carefully." Unfortunately, this advice is impractical for most investors, for rarely

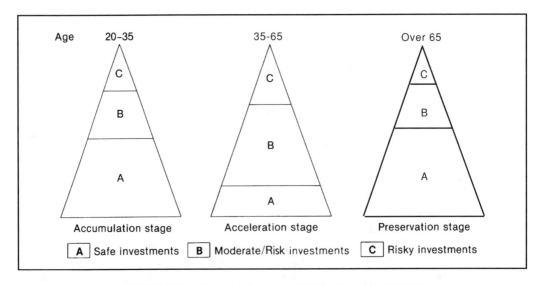

FIGURE 14-2 Life cycle stages and distribution of investment

do they have the time or the expertise to select the *right investments* and liquidate them at the *right time* when they are no longer attractive. Consequently, with rare exceptions, the use of the AAM becomes essential in investment planning.

It was explained in Chapter 13 that the AAM provides a system for diversifying a portfolio among three asset classes to optimize the portfolio return for a given level of risk. This diversification is the process of reducing risk within a particular asset class by spreading individual issues of stocks, bonds, or other investments within a broad range. While the value of diversification is generally appreciated, appreciation for the use of AAM depends upon the investor's level of sophistication. For instance, a sophisticated investor may use the AAM for (1) maximizing the portfolio return; (2) achieving a delicate balance between risk and return, and (3) finding the perfect mix between liquid, fixed, growth, and nonliquid funds. In contrast, a not-so-savvy investor may be content with a much more modest asset allocation objective of a safe portfolio with a relatively modest but reasonable return.

There is one aspect of diversification that deserves special mention; namely, the difference between growth and value investing in the area of large cap investments. A brief description of growth vs. value style investing is presented next.

Most investors have a common goal: The growth of investments over time. There are many ways of achieving this goal by investing in stocks, bonds, real estate, or any combination of these instruments. Mutual funds may provide the best answer for them.

Investment styles refer to the techniques used by fund managers to select securities and construct portfolios. It is possible for investors to have similar investment objectives of capital appreciation, but by using different criteria they may select totally different mutual funds to achieve this goal. Two major styles of stock selection consist of growth and value investing.

While investors can use both individual securities and mutual funds to achieve their goals, because of the complexity of dealing with single stocks and bonds, in most instances sticking with mutual funds may provide the most efficient results.

Even though the names may not directly reflect it, the primary focus of both styles is on capital appreciation—buying a stock today for less than it will be worth in the future. However, the two styles differ in defining a *good buy*. Growth stock managers look for companies with rapid and expanding growth, while value stock managers are attracted to the stocks of those companies whose prices appear to be cheap relative to their earnings, assets or dividends.

The growth-based investment style is generally concerned with selecting stocks that are expected to produce above-average and accelerated growth in earnings. Here the manager identifies the industries and companies that are in the aggressive growth stages of their life cycle—a period associated with rapid and increasing growth rates in sales and earnings associated with reasonable profit margins.

Minimally, growth companies maintain a growth rate above the rate of increase in GDP. Some experts consider the benchmark for classifying a growth stock as 20 percent annual growth rate in earnings per share (EPS). Growth rates of this magnitude generally require significant amounts of capital spending so the impressive growth pattern of the EPS could be maintained.

Value investing represents the selection of stocks that are priced low relative to their levels of earnings, sales, assets, and equity. Common measures of value include: low price-earnings ratios, low price-to-book ratios, and high dividend yields. Of course, that does not imply that all firms with low price-earnings ratios or high dividend yields offer good values. In fact, some stocks with low price-earnings ratios may have little future potential and deserve their low prices. Consequently, selecting good value stocks requires special skills and experience.

Markets often move on emotions and overreact to both good news and bad news. Value investing managers attempt to purchase stocks that are undervalued, because for psychological reasons they are neglected or are currently out of favor. That is why value managers are sometimes called contrarian investors.

It is important to understand some of the similarities and differences between growth and value investing. The diversification potential of holding investments representing both styles can be rewarding, because these two management styles are not at all alike in the short run.

Tax Considerations

At the heart of comprehensive investment planning is the tax ramification of managing an investment portfolio. The reason is that the meaningful return is the net after-tax return. The tax issues relating to various investments are discussed at length in Chapter 16 and need not be repeated here. Returns on various investment products can be classified as taxable, tax-deferred, tax-sheltered, and tax-free. Municipal bonds are tax-free. Many limited partnerships generate tax-sheltered cash flows. Insurance-related investments, such as annuities and single premium whole life, as well as all qualified plan investments, generate tax-deferred returns. Finally, returns on all other investments are fully taxable. Other things being equal, investors should attempt to maximize their after-tax investment returns.

Time Horizon

Time is of the essence in selecting the right investment. Product choices are frequently shaped by the amount of time remaining for the investor to reach financial goals. Classification of various investments into short-term, medium-term, and long-term, and the trade-offs associated with investments in different term categories, are presented in Table 14-1.

Investment Return

We have learned in Chapter 13 that risk and return are positively related. That is, the higher the return of an investment, the higher the risk it carries. This is the cornerstone of investment planning. In constructing a *target investment portfolio*, given the investor's risk tolerance, a financial planner selects those products that tends to optimize the portfolio's returns for the acceptable level of risk.

An important dimension of the problem of maximizing investment return is revealed by asking the question: What is the reasonable return an investor can expect from a given security or portfolio? This question is not easily answered, for a great deal of myth surrounds the topic of what constitutes a reasonable return from an investment.

Statistics on long-term returns on common stocks for the period 1926-2004 reveal several important facts. (1) On a year-to-year basis, at one extreme common stocks have yielded an annual return of as much as 54 percent, but they have also lost up to 43 percent during any given year. Put differently, an investor expecting to double the value of the common stock investment portfolio every two years could also suffer a massive loss of principal. (2) The longer an investor's time horizon, the smaller the risk of losing the principal; however, it also reduces the potential

TABLE 14-1 Terms of Investment

Investment examples	Advantages	Drawbacks
Short *(less than 2 years)*		
Money-market funds	Low volatility—price	Lower overall returns
Short-term CD's	changes slightly or not	Frequent reinvestment
Short-term bonds	at all	decisions
Treasury notes	Moderate yields	
	Regular income	
	Ready access to funds	
Medium *(3 to 5 years)*		
Intermediate-term bonds	Moderately high yields	Less safe than short-
Flexible-rate CD's	Price moves in narrow	term investments
High-income	range	Can be vulnerable to
conservative stocks	Regular income	inflation
GNMA's		Income can vary
Long *(more than 5 years)*		
Long-term bonds	Highest yields or capital-	Most volatility
Long-term CDs	growth potential	Less liquid
Real estate	Returns usually outpace	Principal can be
Growth stocks (if held)	inflation	vulnerable to inflation
Gold and silver		

for higher return. For instance, a five-year time horizon reduces the potential for an annual loss to 13 percent but it also reduces the potential for gain to 24 percent. (3) The average long-term annual return on common stock on a one-year basis is around 10 percent. This means that, following the Rule of 72, an investment earning a 10 percent annual return can be expected to double every 7.2 years (72/10 = 7.2).

Prioritizing of Goals

It is important for financial planners to learn about the priorities their clients place on various investment goals. The worksheet presented in Table 14-2 can be used to gather this information. This worksheet not only reveals how strongly investors feel about various investment goals but also helps them identify some of the goals which may be missed. Also, a rating of 1 or 2 selected for a specific goal would clearly suggest that the investor does not consider that goal to be significant.

Summing Up

The success of an investment planning process largely depends upon the ability of financial planners to help their clients clearly define their investment planning goals. Some investors prefer to state their investment goals in broad terms, such as diversification, a reasonable mix of liquid and nonliquid investments, and a balance between investment risk and return. Others may wish to achieve a specific investment goal like a net, after-tax, real rate of return of four percent. While both are acceptable forms of stated goals, a written set of clearly specified goals helps the planner appreciate more fully the client's risk and investing preferences, fears, and level of sophistication.

TABLE 14-2   Prioritizing Investment Goals

	Weak				Strong
Diversification	1	2	3	4	5
Liquidity	1	2	3	4	5
Safety of principal	1	2	3	4	5
Capital appreciation	1	2	3	4	5
Current income	1	2	3	4	5
Inflation protection	1	2	3	4	5
Future income	1	2	3	4	5
Tax reduction/deferral	1	2	3	4	5
Ease of management	1	2	3	4	5

RISK TOLERANCE LEVEL

Risk versus Return

In Chapter 13 it was explained that risk is associated with the variability of potential returns from the expected returns. It was also pointed out that risk and return are positively related; that is, investments offering higher returns generally carry higher degrees of risks.

Translating the concept of the positive risk-return relationship into the selection of various investment products, we can observe two important facts. (1) Debt securities generally carry lower risks and offer lower returns, whereas equity-type securities offer higher returns but also carry higher risks. (2) As the investor climbs the risk-return pyramid, both risk and return increase; the reverse is true when a move is made in the opposite direction.

It is necessary to reiterate that fixed income securities suffer a loss during inflationary periods when interest rates rise; however, they also offer an assurance of return of the principal upon maturity. In contrast, equity type investments offer a much greater potential for growth but have an increasing risk of losing the principal. Finally, the highly risky investments, such as tax shelters, commodities, and hard assets, may have the best potential for highest returns over time. However, they are illiquid and carry the maximum risk of losing the principal; in addition, some investments may also carry additional risk of the eventual loss of some of the tax benefits originally enjoyed by the investor if *phantom income* is received, or the IRS denies some of the previously realized tax benefits.

Risk Tolerance Level

Determining an investor's risk tolerance level is not a precise technique. Although in certain instances measuring risk tolerance *can* be objective, generally it is a *subjective* measure of the emotional and financial ability of an investor to withstand investment losses. Even more important, risk tolerance may rise with an increase in net worth, income, investment knowledge, and sophistication, and it could decline as the client approaches retirement. Nevertheless, as part of the investment planning process, it is essential for financial planners to make a concerted effort to determine the risk tolerance level for every client.

For simplicity, investors can be classified as high, medium, low, and zero risk takers. The most effective way of making this determination is to ask the investor to take a well-designed test. A *sample* test, presented in the box entitled "Do You Take Risks?" is designed to determine the investor's risk tolerance level. Another questionnaire, entitled "Measuring Attitude Toward Risk," helps record an investor's general attitude toward risk.

Summing Up

We have barely touched upon the many issues relating to the development of an investor's risk profile. Clearly, additional issues, such as the state of the investor's financial life, degree of affluence, and a host of other factors, should be analyzed

---

DO YOU TAKE RISKS? A QUIZ

1. An investment loses 15% of its value in a market correction a month after you buy it. Assuming none of the fundamentals have changed, do you:
   (a) Sit tight and wait for it to journey back up?
   (b) Sell it and rid yourself of further sleepless nights if it continues to decline?
   (c) Buy more—if it looked good at the original price, it looks even better now?

2. A month after you purchase it, the value of your investment suddenly skyrockets by 40%. Assuming you can't find any further information, what do you do?
   (a) Sell it.
   (b) Hold it on the expectation of further gain.
   (c) Buy more—it will probably go higher.

3. Which would you have rather done:
   (a) Invested in an aggressive-growth fund that appreciated very little in six months.
   (b) Invested in a money-market fund only to see the aggressive-growth fund you were thinking about double in value in six months.

4. Would you feel better if:
   (a) You doubled your money in an equity investment.
   (b) Your money-market fund investment saved you from losing half your money in a market slide.

5. Which would make you happiest?
   (a) You win $100,000 in a publisher's contest.
   (b) You inherit $100,000 from a rich relative.

   (c) You earn $100,000 by risking $2,000 in the options market.
   (d) Any of the above—you're happy with the $100,000, no matter how it ended up in your wallet.

6. The apartment building where you live is being converted to condominiums. You can either buy your unit for $80,000 or sell the option for $20,000. The market value of the condo is $120,000. You know that if you buy the condo it might take six months to sell, the monthly carrying cost is $1,200, and you'd have to borrow the down payment for a mortgage. You don't want to live in the building. What do you do?
   (a) Take the $20,000.
   (b) Buy the unit and then sell it.

7. You inherit your uncle's $100,000 house, free of any mortgage. Although the house is in a fashionable neighborhood and can be expected to appreciate at a rate faster than inflation, it has deteriorated badly. It would net $1,000 monthly if rented as is, or $1,500 per month if renovated. The renovations could be financed by a mortgage on the property. You would:
   (a) Sell the house.
   (b) Rent it as is.
   (c) Make the necessary renovations, and then rent it.

8. You work for a small but thriving privately held electronics company. The company is raising money by selling stock to its employees. Management plans to take the company public, but not for four or more years. If you buy stock, you will not be allowed to sell until shares are traded publicly. In the meantime, the stock will pay no divi-

dends. But when the company goes public, the shares could trade for ten to 20 times what you paid. How much of an investment would you make?
(a) None at all.
(b) One month's salary.
(c) Three months' salary.
(d) Six months' salary.

9. Your long-time neighbor, an experienced petroleum geologist, is assembling a group of investors (of which he is one) to fund an exploratory oil well, which could pay back 50 to 100 times its investment. If the well is dry, the entire investment is worthless. Your friend estimates the chances of success at only 20%. What would you invest?
(a) Nothing at all.
(b) One month's salary.
(c) Three months' salary.
(d) Six months' salary.

10. You learn that several commercial-building developers are seriously looking at undeveloped land in a certain location. You are offered an option to buy a choice parcel of that land. The cost is about two months' salary and you calculate the gain to be ten months' salary. Do you:
(a) Purchase the option.
(b) Let it slide—it's not for you.

11. You are on a TV game show and can choose one of the following. Which would you take?
(a) $1,000 in cash.
(b) A 50% chance at $4,000.
(c) A 20% chance at $10,000.
(d) A 5% chance at $100,000.

12. It's 1989, and inflation is returning. Hard assets such as precious metals, collectibles and real estate are expected to keep pace with inflation. Your assets are now all in long-term bonds. What would you do?
(a) Hold the bonds.
(b) Sell the bonds, put half the proceeds into money funds and the other half into hard assets.
(c) Sell the bonds and put the total proceeds into hard assets.

Source: Donoghue's *Moneyletter*—P.O. Box 6640 Holliston, MA, 01746.

(d) Sell the bonds, put all the money into hard assets and borrow additional money to buy more.

13. You've lost $500 at the blackjack table in Atlantic City. How much more are you prepared to lose to win the $500 back?
(a) Nothing. You quit now.
(b) $100.
(c) $250.
(d) $500.
(e) More than $500.

SCORING

Total your score, using the point system listed below for each answer you gave.

1. (a) 3 (b) 1 (c) 4
2. (a) 1 (b) 3 (c) 4
3. (a) 1 (b) 3
4. (a) 2 (b) 1
5. (a) 2 (b) 1 (c) 4 (d) 1
6. (a) 1 (b) 2
7. (a) 1 (b) 2 (c) 3
8. (a) 1 (b) 2 (c) 4 (d) 6
9. (a) 1 (b) 3 (c) 6 (d) 9
10. (a) 3 (b) 1
11. (a) 1 (b) 3 (c) 5 (d) 9
12. (a) 1 (b) 2 (c) 3 (d) 4
13. (a) 1 (b) 2 (c) 4 (d) 6 (e) 8

Below 21: You are a conservative investor who's allergic to risk. Stick with the sober, conservative investments until you develop the confidence or desire to take on more risk.

21–35: You are an active investor who's willing to take calculated, prudent risks to achieve greater financial gain. Your investment universe is more diverse.

36 and over: You're a venturesome, assertive investor. The choices that are available to you promise dynamic opportunities. Remember, though, the search for more return carries an extra measure of risk.

MEASURING ATTITUDE TOWARD RISK

For each statement, choose the answer that most resembles your attitudes toward investing over the next five years. Remember: There are no right or wrong answers.

	True	False	Not Applicable
1. I cannot afford any loss of principal regardless of potential return.	_____	_____	_____
2. I cannot afford any *significant loss* of principal but I want the best return I can get.	_____	_____	_____
3. Since I can get high yields from bonds, I don't wish to suffer through market ups and downs by investing in stocks.	_____	_____	_____
4. I want both income for current needs and reasonable growth of my portfolio.	_____	_____	_____
5. Since the economy changes rapidly, frequent rebalancing of my portfolio is essential to realize satisfactory results.	_____	_____	_____
6. Risk means major ups and downs in my portfolio even if the overall portfolio value continues to go up.	_____	_____	_____
7. I know investments generating higher returns have higher risks, but I must earn higher returns at any cost.	_____	_____	_____
8. I like to *play* the stock market, and long-term investment is not for me.	_____	_____	_____
9. There is no way to successfully compete with big investors, so I should concentrate on safe, guaranteed investment products.	_____	_____	_____
10. I like my portfolio to show superior results and I believe I need a professional to help me achieve my goal.	_____	_____	_____

before an accurate risk profile can be compiled. Because of space constraints, however, we present in the box entitled *Strategic Investment Planning Worksheet,* a simple worksheet which can assist a financial planner in developing a functional risk profile for the investor.

INVESTOR PREFERENCE

Investor preference refers to an investor's predisposition toward or away from specific investment products. As a result of past experiences, as well as previous training, most investors form opinions about various investments. The financial planner should learn not only about such opinions but also about the depth of these feelings. A simple questionnaire, presented in the box entitled "Attitudes Toward Investment Products," is designed to help the planner determine an investor's predisposition toward specific investments.

THE INVESTMENT PORTFOLIO

The objective of constructing a *Target Investment Portfolio* (TIP) is to bring about a synthesis between the various competing investment objectives just discussed. This goal is achieved by including the right combination of investments in the portfolio. In Chapter 12 we presented the basic investment alternatives. We will now discuss the place of these investments in a typical portfolio.

STRATEGIC INVESTMENT PLANNING WORKSHEET

A. TIME HORIZON

In order for historic rates of return and risk measurements to be a meaningful basis for investment planning, the investment time horizon ought to be at least five years. For most individuals and qualified plans this will be the case. While the plan will be reviewed and possibly revised on a regular basis, allocations should be based on long-term expectations.

1. Is your time horizon in fact five years or more? Yes_____ No_____

2. Do you foresee any specific need to withdraw principal during that time? Yes_____ No_____
   If so, what amount? $_____

3. What is a comfortable emergency reserve to meet unanticipated needs? $_____

B. RATE OF RETURN OBJECTIVES

Prior to considering rate of return, it is necessary to define the total amount of funds to be invested. Liquid investable assets refers to those assets which are earmarked for long-term investment in financial instruments (stocks, bonds, Treasury bills, and so on). For individuals, this means liquid net worth, less emergency cash reserve. Do not include illiquid funds targeted for real estate, metals, and other tangible assets. For qualified plans, liquid investable assets refers to total plan assets less any required reserve.

$_____ − $_____

Liquid net worth   Cash reserve

= $_____
    Total liquid investable assets

Following are three different ways to quantify return objectives (I–III). If only one is meaningful, fill out only the applicable section. If more than one, please prioritize. While hopefully a plan can be presented to meet all parameters, it may be necessary to make tradeoffs, and thus to know which set of objectives is most important to you.

I. Absolute Returns:

1. To what dollar amount would you like to see your assets grow in 5 years? $___ in 10 years? $_____

2. Alternatively, what compound annual rate of return would you like to achieve on your entire investment portfolio? _____%

3. Do you look for these assets to provide you an income at some point in the future? Yes_____ No_____
   If so, what amount (in today's dollars)? $_____ When_____?
   Some facts to help you answer the above:

Rates of return on the various asset classes have been as follows:

Equities	Historic (1926-2000)	13.0%	Current	?
Bonds		5.5%		8–9%
Cash Equivalents		3.6%		6–7%

$10,000 will grow to the following amounts at various rates of return:

	5 yrs.	10 yrs.
6% (approximate bond history)	$13,382	$17,908
8% (approximate current bond rate)	$14,693	$21,589
13% (approximate equity history)	$18,424	$33,946

II. Inflation Adjusted (Real Returns):

Would you prefer to confine the analysis to dollar returns or are goals more meaningful to you when restated to reflect purchasing power?

Dollar returns _____ Purchasing power _____ (If dollar returns, proceed to section III).

(a) In today's dollars, to what amount would you like to see your assets grow in 5 years?
$_____ in 10 years ? $_____

(b) What real rate of return (after inflation) would you like to realize over the long term?
_____%

III. Relative Return:

Most people like to set standards by which to measure the long-term performance of their equity managers. Which standard is most relevant to you?

_____ Outperform S&P 500.
_____ Outperform S&P 500
by _____%.

C. RISK

Most individuals and fiduciaries have a strong concern for "safety" or "preservation of capital." Yet most investments carry some risk of fluctuation in principal value. In fact it is *because* one assumes this risk that higher returns are expected. Risk can be quantified by the response to the following two questions concerning the overall portfolio.

1. Is a risk of loss once every three years tolerable to you? One in 10? 20? Never? Indicate one of the following:

    _____ one out of _____ years
    _____ never

2. Is a risk of extreme loss (greater than 15%) tolerable to you once every 10 years? 20? Never? Indicate one of the following:

    _____ one out of _____ years
    _____ never

To aid you in answering the above questions, the long-term rate of equity return mentioned earlier (11.8%) was achieved with approximately three loss years every ten. Moreover, extreme losses were suffered about one out of every 11 years while producing this return.

Source: Adapted from questionnaire developed by Investment Advisory Services (IAS), a division of Raymond James & Associates, Inc., St. Petersburg, Florida.

IAS utilizes the answers to this questionnaire to help clients allocate their assets in concert with their individual time horizon and risk tolerance.

ATTITUDES TOWARD INVESTMENT PRODUCTS

Please indicate the level of comfort with   the following criteria:
each of the following investments using

1	2	3	4	5	6	7
Can't Sleep at night	Jittery	No feeling either way	Comfortable	Extremely comfortable	Don't know	Don't Care

_____ Savings account		_____ Treasury bills
_____ Commodities futures		_____ AAA Corporate bonds
_____ Hedge funds		_____ Blue chip common stocks
_____ Private placement: real estate		_____ Utility stocks
_____ Zero coupon bonds		_____ Money market acct (uninsured)
_____ Growth mutual funds		_____ Municipal bond funds
_____ Gold coins		_____ High yield mutual funds
_____ Diamonds		_____ Call options
_____ Universal life insurance		_____ Variable life insurance
_____ High yield bond funds		_____ High grade bond funds
_____ Government bond funds		_____ Speculative stocks
_____ High quality stock funds		_____ International mutual funds
_____ Single prem. whole life		_____ Aggressive stocks funds
_____ GNMA		_____ Single prem. deferred annuity
_____ ETF shares		_____ Brokered CDs
_____ I shares		_____ Single prem. immediate annuity
_____ ADRs		_____ Equity indexed annuity
_____ Real estate investment trusts		_____ Variable annuity
_____ VUL		_____ ETFs

Cash Reserves and Emergency Funds

The starting point is to determine the percentage allocation for cash reserves and emergency funds. In a family's financial life there will occur unforeseen contingencies which must be successfully met if catastrophic consequences are to be avoided. In addition, cash reserves provide liquidity which can be used to capitalize on emerging investment opportunities. The primary considerations in selecting these assets are safety and liquidity with a clear understanding that the trade-off is a low investment return. Investments listed in Table 14-3 under "Cash Reserves and Emergency Funds" fall in this category.

Income Flow

Another investment planning consideration is the income a portfolio can generate to help maintain the desired lifestyle. Income-oriented investments emphasize current income but may sacrifice growth of the principal. Most, though not all, fixed income investments have a fixed maturity date. These securities appreciate in value during periods of falling interest rates but lose their value during periods of rising interest rates.

TABLE 14-3   Investment Vehicles and Their Objectives

Objective	Type	Investment vehicles
Cash Reserves and Emergency Funds	Cash Reserve	Cash Money Market Funds Savings and Loan Accounts Checking Accounts Short-term CDs Cash Value of Life Insurance Treasury Bills
Income Flow	Fixed Income	Corporate Bonds Government (Treasury) Bonds Municipal Bonds GNMA Bond Mutual Funds Fixed Annuities Convertible Bonds Real Estate Investment Trusts Utility Stocks Master Limited Partnerships
Growth	Equity	Common Stocks Variable Annuities Stock Mutual Funds Real Estate (Managed) Programs Option Income Programs Oil & Gas Income Funds
Long-term Growth and Tax Advantages	Real Estate Tax Shelters Hard Assets Miscellaneous	Real Estate Oil & Gas Drilling Programs Equipment Leasing Programs Hard Assets (Gold, Coins, Art) Commodities Series EE and HH Bonds

Let us add an important caveat here. The view that bonds are the primary vehicle for generating current income is too parochial. There are a number of other investments that are attractive as income generators. These include utility stocks, high-yield stocks, mortgage-backed securities, fixed annuities, master limited partnerships, and real estate investment trusts. Each has distinct investment characteristics and provides a valuable tool for income planning. A list of investments satisfying the income flow objective is listed in Table 14-3.

Growth

Equity investments offer a potential for appreciation in value but generate relatively limited amounts of cash flow. These investments are subject to market as well as industry- and company-related risks, and can result in sizeable losses if the investor is compelled to sell them under adverse market conditions. Investments listed in Table 14-3 under the category "Growth" are examples of products that satisfy the growth objective of an investor.

Long-Term Growth and Tax Advantages

The objectives of long-term growth and tax savings are achieved through investments in a variety of vehicles listed in Table 14-3. The main categories of these investments are discussed next.

Real estate investments. There are various ways in which an investor can participate in real estate investments. These include real estate partnerships, real estate investment trusts, investment in apartment complexes and shopping centers, and investment in undeveloped lands. Each has a different degree of risk associated with it, and great care should be exercised in making sure that the risk of a real estate investment is consistent with the risk tolerance level of the investor.

In general, real estate investments perform well during periods of economic growth and moderate inflation. However, history suggests that high interest rates are generally disastrous for these investments and real estate markets could be depressed for long periods. Also, real estate investments are illiquid and can rarely be converted quickly into liquid funds in an emergency.

Tax-sheltered investments. As a general rule, tax-sheltered investments generate cash flows which are sheltered from income taxes. This is accomplished by deducting depreciation, loan interest, and other deductible expenses against cash flow.

Although a number of tax shelters are still available on the marketplace, their number has greatly reduced following the passage of the Tax Reform Act of 1986. The reason is that this Act eliminated the benefits of many tax shelters and significantly reduced the tax benefits of others by requiring that the tax losses called passive losses be used to reduce only income from these limited partnerships called passive income. Consequently, only those tax shelters which are economically sound and offer attractive economic returns are worthy of consideration.

Hard assets. Generally, investments in gold, silver, rare coins, stamps, and precious metals, which are popularly known as hard assets, become attractive during periods of actual or anticipated high inflation and are therefore called inflation hedges. Investments in hard assets are good only for those risk takers who can sustain large losses and are not affected by their total illiquidity.

Miscellaneous investments. There are other investment products, such as commodities, exploratory oil and gas programs, and race horses, which have not yet been discussed. The list of these investments is long. It is, however, sufficient to say that these exotic investments are inappropriate for all but a chosen few who are highly sophisticated, affluent, and resourceful.

Target Investment Portfolio (TIP)

Let us analyze the current investment portfolio of the Brown family. The family consists of Ron, age 38, Sarah, 35, John, 10, and Susan, 7. The family's gross annual income is $85,000. The Brown family's investment portfolio is presented in Table 14-4 (Columns 1 and 2). The portfolio reveals that the Browns: (1) favor equity investments over fixed income investments (60 percent versus six percent); (2) have a low level of cash reserves (one percent); and (3) have invested disproportionately high percentages in real estate (14 percent) and tax shelters (16 percent). However, construction of a TIP by using the portfolio repositioning technique

TABLE 14-4 Ron and Sarah Brown, Investment Portfolio, December 31, 2001

Type (1)	Current amount (2)	Distribution (3)	Target distribution (4)	Recommended action (5)
Cash reserve	$ 2,500	1%	10%	+ $15,750
Fixed income	10,000	6	33	+ 50,225
Equity	110,000	60	33	− 49,775
Real estate	25,000	14	16	+ 4,200
Tax shelters	30,000	16	5	− 20,875
Hard assets	5,000	3	3	+ 475
Miscellaneous	0	0	0	0
Total	$182,500	100%	100%	$ 0

requires a great deal more *analysis* than just a superficial review of the current portfolio, as we shall now observe.

PORTFOLIO REORGANIZATION

The Basic Steps

An existing portfolio can be systematically reorganized by a financial planner by completing the following four steps:

Step 1. Reallocation of the percentage distribution of various classes of investments based on a change in economic conditions.

Step 2. Change in investment strategy because of a change in client's investment goals due to changes in life cycle, investment needs, time frame, and tax considerations.

Step 3. Change in product selection due to a change in client's risk tolerance level.

Step 4. Change in strategy to accommodate the client's special needs.

The Strategy

In order to make the discussion on the portfolio reorganization meaningful, we will assume that the Browns: (1) are risk averse; (2) must generate additional current income in order to maintain the standard of living with which they are most comfortable; and (3) realize that they should build up their cash reserve. On the basis of these considerations, and taking into account the desired percentage distribution of assets generated by the asset allocation model, a *target distribution* of investments is generated and presented in Table 14-4 (Column 4). We notice that recommended actions (Column 5) include: (1) building up the cash reserve by adding $15,750 to this category; (2) investing an additional $50,225 in fixed income securities to generate additional current income to meet their income needs; and (3) purchasing additional real estate ($4,200) and hard assets ($475). Funds for these investments are to be generated by liquidating $49,775 worth of equities and $20,875 currently invested in tax shelters.

The target distribution developed in the previous section represents the *conceptual* TIP for the Browns based on the AAM, their risk tolerance level, current income needs, and desire for growth. However, at this time this TIP may not be achievable for several reasons. (1) Because of their illiquidity, it may be impossible for the Browns to reduce their investment in tax shelters. (2) Due to the prevailing weak market conditions, at this time it might be undesirable to reduce the equity investment as recommended. (3) Investment recommendations may conflict with other financial goals. (4) Recommended investments may not be available at a reasonable price. (5) There might be unfavorable tax consequences of liquidating various investment products.

Despite the difficulties, however, the financial planner has the responsibility for acting upon the recommendations as best as possible. A financial planner, who is also a Registered Investment Advisor and feels qualified to do so, may perform this function. Alternatively, the responsibility for selecting specific products may be shifted to other investment professionals or advisors. Regardless of the strategy used, the financial planner should make sure that: (1) appropriate due diligence on each product is performed; (2) the recommended products fit the investor's portfolio; and (3) the client fully understands and accepts the advantages and drawbacks of each recommended product before investing in it.

A REAL WORLD INVESTMENT PLAN

INTRODUCTION

In the previous sections, we have presented the investment planning process and several key investment planning strategies. We are now ready to apply these concepts to a real world investment portfolio.

In this section we will present an efficiently constructed investment portfolio. The clients are John Klein, age 50, and Debby Klein, age 48. This couple has requested investment manager Ted Bower to construct an ideal investment portfolio for them. The portfolio presented next is directly addressed to John and Debby Klein.

PORTFOLIO PRESENTATION TO THE KLEINS

John and Debby Klein, several weeks ago you requested us to develop a plan for investing an economic windfall. John, during our initial interview you informed us that you are a 50-year-old Ph.D. with a degree in mechanical engineering, and you are employed as a senior manager with a very progressive engineering firm. Currently you participate in a defined benefit plan, which will provide you for life 70 percent of your salary, starting with your age 65. In addition, upon your death, this plan will pay your spouse during her lifetime an amount equivalent to 50 percent of your salary. It is our understanding that your wife is a homemaker, who receives no outside income and does not participate in a retirement plan.

The lump sum you have received is from the death of Debby's great aunt. This sum represents the net amount distributed to you after all the taxes have been paid.

GOAL SETTING

John, during our goals and objectives interview we discovered that you would like to retire at age 65. We also discovered that you want us to structure your investment portfolio so you would achieve several competing objectives. Here is a list of key objectives which you have identified for us:

- Your investments should generate sufficient income so you could maintain your desired lifestyle upon retirement.
- You want your investments to be fairly liquid so you could liquidate them in case of an emergency.
- For the reason just cited, you do not want us to invest your funds in tax-deferred, retirement vehicles.
- You liked the idea of our using the asset allocation strategy, so a proper balance between safety, liquidity and growth could be maintained.
- You showed a great deal of interest in learning about the products we intend to use in your investment portfolio.

RISK TOLERANCE LEVEL

A careful analysis of your risk tolerance questionnaire has clearly demonstrated that basically you are a risk averse person. However, we have also discovered that you did not recognize that risk has many faces, and that in the past the loss of principal is only one of many risks you have assumed. For instance, you had honestly believed that there was no market risk associated with investing in a *safe* government bond mutual fund when in reality only the reverse was true. However, after an extensive discussion we had with you on the topic of key stock and bond risks, and after studying a variety of published information we provided, we believe you have acquired a good working knowledge of the various faces of investment risk.

We are pleased to learn that even though you are basically a risk averse person, you do wish to assume *some* risk by investing a small portion of your funds in one or more relatively high-risk products. We will certainly take this fact into account in developing our recommendations.

TARGET INVESTMENT PORTFOLIO

We have made an extensive analysis of the Asset Allocation Model, your risk tolerance level, and your need for current income and growth. On the basis of this analysis we have developed for you a Target Investment Portfolio (TIP). However, before making a formal presentation of your TIP, let us specify the intermediate steps we completed as the basis for the construction of the TIP: (1) Initially we developed a *preliminary* TIP by applying our current Asset Allocation Model. In developing this model we analyzed the current business cycle, prevailing financial market conditions, inflationary expectations, interest rate predictions, and other ancillary factors. (2) On the basis of the goals and objectives interview we conducted several weeks ago, we developed a realistic risk profile for you. (3) We analyzed your current financial situation and seriously considered your special requests before finalizing your TIP.

John and Debby, your TIP (Target Investment Portfolio), which represents a 15-year capital growth portfolio, is presented in Figure 14-3. On the basis of this portfolio, we are making the following recommendations:

1. Since your TIP is a long-term growth-oriented portfolio, we recommend that the majority of the funds be invested in equity securities. History of long-term market performance has clearly demonstrated that, among all the various investment vehicles available, equity securities have provided by far the best returns.

2. Since the performance of various types of investments varies—sometimes greatly—over different economic cycles, in order to provide stability to the TIP, we recommend that a relatively small percentage of the portfolio be invested in fixed income securities and money market instruments.

3. In selecting bond mutual funds we will concentrate on funds which specialize in high quality corporate bonds and attempt to beat the performance of the Lehman Brothers Aggregate Bond Index. A small percentage of funds will also be invested in mutual funds investing in high yield corporate bonds and seeking to beat the CS First Boston High Yield Bond Index.

4. Not all the investment opportunities can be found within the U.S. In fact, since we live in a global economy, many excellent opportunities can be located beyond our borders. We recommend that a percentage of your funds earmarked for equities be invested in mutual funds investing in international developed markets. We will monitor the performance of these funds by comparing their returns with Morgan Stanley's EAFE Index.

5. We recommend that your U.S. investments in equity securities be allocated between large cap, mid cap and small cap mutual funds. Of these, 80 percent of the funds should be invested in large cap companies, equally dividing the funds between growth and value companies. Performance of these funds will be measured against S&P Barra Large Cap Growth and Large Cap Value Indexes.

6. The remaining 20 percent will be divided equally between the more aggressive mid-cap and small cap companies, with proportionate divisions between growth and value companies. The performance of mid cap funds will be judged against the Wilshire Mid Cap Index and for the small cap funds we will use the Russell 2000 Index.

Currently, we are in the process of finalizing your TIP. As soon as the portfolio has been properly structured, it will be presented to you for your consideration and approval. Once approved, it will be implemented.

One final point: We live in a dynamic world in which the market conditions continually change. It is therefore essential that we regularly monitor the performance of your portfolio vis-a-vis the changes that might be taking place in your financial life. Also, as part of our responsibility as your investment manager, periodically we will rebalance your portfolio so it would continue to reflect your goals, your desires, and your short- and long-term expectations.

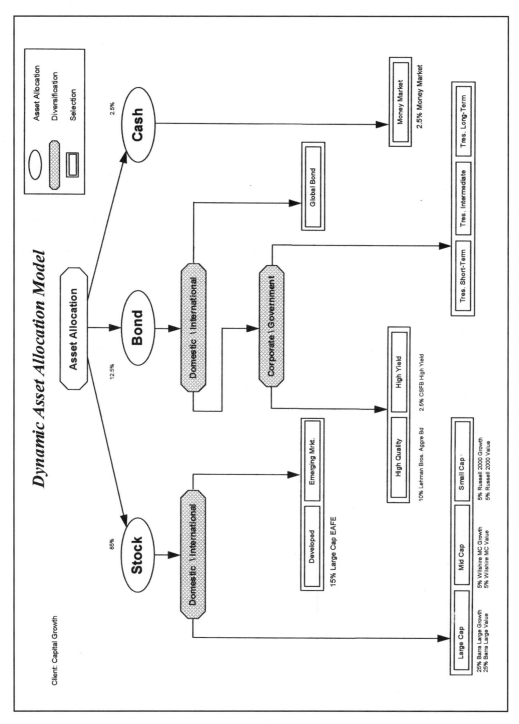

FIGURE 14-3 Dynamic Asset Allocation Model - Capital Growth

THE GOLDEN RETIREMENT YEARS

John and Debby, your main objective in engaging our investment management services is to make sure that your retirement years do in fact turn out to be the golden years. In order to give you a kaleidoscopic view of your retirement years, we are going to fast-forward the remaining 15 years of your working life. John, let us assume you just turned 65 and are reviewing with us your pre-retirement investment plan.

The 15-Year Record

As a direct result of our engaging superior fund managers, constantly monitoring the progress, and keeping you enlightened and informed about our activities, your portfolio has enjoyed a sustained, annual after-tax return of ten percent. Currently, the value of the portfolio is $1.2 million.

John, during the last five years, you were the senior vice president of engineering of Atlas Corp., and last year you earned an annual salary of $250,000. Upon retirement, your defined benefit plan will pay you an annual income of $175,000 for life.

John and Debby, you wish to receive a retirement income of $250,000 per year so you could maintain your lifestyle during retirement. This means that your investment portfolio must provide an annual cash flow of $75,000 (or a return of 6.5 percent) which, added to the defined benefit payment of $175,000 per year, should give you the retirement income you seek. While a 6.5 percent return can be realized, in the absence of a creative management strategy, the portfolio would not experience any growth. Therefore, our challenge is to develop a growing portfolio which will also provide the income you expect to receive upon retirement.

Investment Vehicles

Several investment products can be used to produce the desired results. Some of the more important ones are listed below.

Fixed annuity. At the currently prevailing interest rates, it is possible to select a fixed annuity that will guarantee an annual rate of 6.5 percent. However, annuities generally do not allow for growth of capital, and frequently the fixed rate is offered for a limited period.

Split annuity. In a split annuity, you invest a portion of the money in a fixed annuity which generates the pre-specified monthly income. The rest of the money can be invested in equities, so eventually it would equal the original amount.

Bond funds. Funds may be invested in a combination of high quality and high yield bond funds to generate the required income.

Jumbo CD. Another idea is to locate a *jumbo* CD that would pay the 6.5 percent interest you need.

Retirement Plan

John and Debby, you should be congratulated for reaching your golden years on schedule. We are also pleased to note that we have been quite successful in growing your initial investment of $300,000 into a tidy sum of $1.2 million. But it was not always an easy travel. Over the past 15 years we have seen the portfolio go up for a year or two only to fall down for some time. But because we used the time tested investment strategies and you stayed the course, you have successfully arrived at your destination on time.

And now it is time to once again present to you a retirement Target Investment Portfolio (Figure 14-4). Based on your risk tolerance and current expectations, we have concluded that for best results it would be wise to have four years of income available to you at all times. This money, which represents 25 percent of your portfolio, would be invested in money market instruments and short-term government bonds. The remaining 75 percent of the funds would be invested in equity securities, which would be designed to realize long-term growth.

We recognize that this portfolio must generate an annual return of 6.5 percent to meet with your demands for liquid funds. Our objective would be to let the funds grow at a rate higher than 6.5 percent, so both your income and growth objectives would be achieved in the long run.

In order to achieve our dual objective we have devised what we call the *moving money to the right strategy*. We do this by periodically liquidating a portion of equity and fixed income securities (located in the left and middle columns of Figure 14-4) and shifting the liquid funds to money market and short-term securities (located in the right column of Figure 14-4). We will also carefully monitor the performance of your portfolio and will rebalance it when warranted by changing conditions.

FINAL THOUGHTS

John and Debby Klein, the TIP we have presented to you is quite comprehensive. This is borne out by the fact that in developing it we have taken the following investment planning principles into account (A through F), some of which may not be evident to you:

A. *A*fter-tax return: Maximize, subject to income needs and risk tolerance level.
B. *B*alanced approach: Maintain a balance between liquidity, current income, and growth.
C. *C*lient's risk: Match investment diversification with investor's risk tolerance level.
D. *D*iversify: Diversify: (i) in terms of investment vehicles, (ii) within a class- or type of investment; and (iii) through different maturities and time horizons.
E. *E*liminate the tax of wealth: Use investment techniques to reduce or eliminate federal estate tax.
F. *F*ocus on growth over time: Use the time-honored time value of money concept to maximize growth of investable funds.

In addition, we have taken great pains in ensuring that the TIP is attuned to your attitudes toward risk, stability, investment return, liquidity, and ease of management.

John and Debby Klein, it is worth reemphasizing that since we do not live in a utopia, for reasons of practicality we have to assume that everything would not always run as smoothly as we would like. But in the end we are determined to

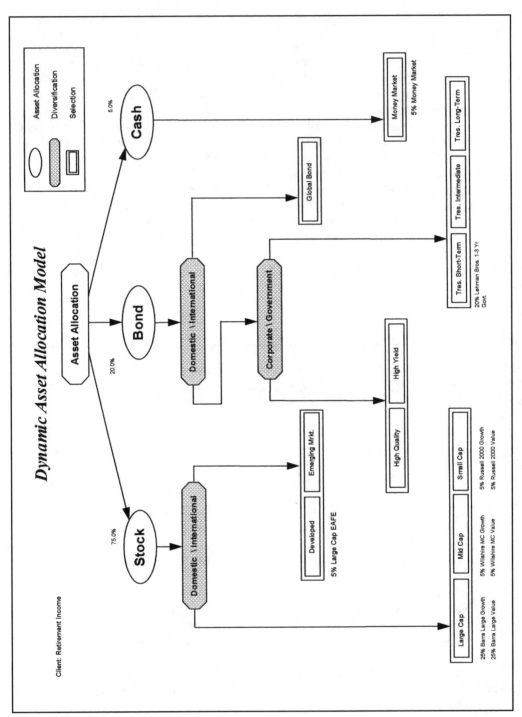

FIGURE 14-4   Dynamic Asset Allocation Model - Retirement Income

succeed. The trip tick we have developed for you is indeed a practical plan which can be implemented to maximize the benefits that can be derived from the realistic investment portfolio. We are ready to assist you in expeditiously completing the implementation process. In addition, we will constantly monitor your progress and hereby make a commitment to be of service to you for a long time.

In this chapter we have discussed investment planning concepts and strategies. The basic federal income tax structure will be presented in the next chapter.

The market is like a train sitting on the tracks. You can see the direction it's heading but you cannot dictate the time of departure. Those investors who put the market on a timetable not only become frustrated but end up making foolish moves. Instead, get on the train, sit back, and enjoy the scenery.

Roger Engermann

APPENDIX TO CHAPTER 14:
THE IMPACT OF TERRORISM ON THE ECONOMY
AND FINANCIAL MARKETS

NATURE OF THE PROBLEM

911

That's the number we normally dial when we face a crisis. It also represents the date of September 11 (2001) when a major disaster befell on our country, the attack of terrorists on the World Trade Center in New York and the Pentagon in Washington, D.C. Following that tragedy, we were told by many that the world would never be the same. We were also told that our lives as we once lived them would now be changed for the foreseeable future.

Currently, conventional wisdom dictates that we incorporate the possibility of terrorism into our daily decision-making processes. Much as we were never the same after Pearl Harbor, the events of mid-September, 2001, will undoubtedly scar us for generations.

Unfortunately, we find striking parallels to the early days of World War II, and in particular a poem by W.H. Auden, titled "September 1, 1939." The opening of this rather somber poem captures the despair of the country when Germany invaded Poland:

> *Waves of anger and fear*
> *Circulate over the bright*
> *And darkened lands of the earth,*
> *Obsessing our private lives.*
> *The unmentionable odour of death*
> *Offends the September night.*

Terrorism is an act of violence, and as in all acts of violence, there are no winners. To speak of the economic and financial consequences of the acts of terrorism committed on U.S. soil in no way lessens the enormous loss of human lives and property that is the physical cost of this act of terrorism. Yet to the extent that trading in goods, services and financial instruments is disrupted, the fallout from terrorism can be both pervasive and long lasting, affecting virtually every investor, every American.

FINANCIAL AND PSYCHOLOGICAL IMPACT

As a nation, following the September attack, we had the onerous task of rebuilding the country and combating global terrorism. Some economists argue that nations

---

This appendix was authored by Dr. Joseph Champagne, an industrial psychologist who is well experienced in the world of business and finance.

recover relatively quickly from such disasters as long as they retain their knowledge and skill levels. In the aftermath of the September 11 disaster we appear to have retained both; hence, using their argument, we should expect a full economic recovery. But what about how people will view their lives in the context of uncertainty for the months or even years ahead?

Financial Impact

The economic impact of the events of September 11, 2001, can be analyzed in at least two major ways: financial and psychological. The financial impact can be worrisome in the short run; but in the long run, after the immediate loss is absorbed, the process of rebuilding will get underway and hopefully, over the long term there will be only a negligible economic impact. In the past, that has been the ultimate outcome of every crisis, and despite the enormity of the September attack on our soil, the future may look very much like the past. The following is a sample of crises we have economically weathered during the last century:

President McKinley shot	September 6, 1901
U.S. enters World War I	April 6, 1917
Stock market crashes	October 24, 1929
Pearl Harbor is attacked	December 7, 1941
North Korea invades S. Korea	June 25, 1950
Eisenhower suffers heart attack	September 24, 1955
Cuban Missile crisis erupts	October 22, 1962
President Kennedy assassinated	November 22, 1963
OPEC oil embargo imposed	October 18, 1973
Market crashes in 1987	October 19, 1987
Iraq invades Kuwait	August 2, 1990

It is likely that the recessionary problems we were already facing in the latter part of 2001 were exacerbated by the September attack. Following the attack, our unemployment situation became worse. We lost a large portion of the budgetary surplus we had built up over several years. The stock market declined further, and the personal debt situation worsened. And most of the major financial publications and business commentators predicted that the economic slowdown, which began in 2000, would persist well into 2002.

But America became proactive. Before year-end 2001, the Administration and the Federal Reserve had already adopted a strategy of coupling their actions via interest rate and tax cuts. This was a strategy that had a good chance of working, because two large and powerful groups of people, American consumers and foreign investors, seemed willing to bet on America's growth prospects—especially when compared with the alternatives.

Psychological Impact

But we must now turn to an examination of the psychological impact of the terrorist attacks. It should be recognized at the outset that the September incident might not significantly change the investment behavior of the very rich or the very poor. But it is safe to conclude that due to the enormity of this incident, the September attack inexorably altered the financial psyche of millions of Americans, especially those who belong to the middle economic group.

Prior to the September incident, as a nation we were very self-confident and behaved as though a protective shield guarded us against unusual risks. Due to the longest expansion that had taken place in U.S. history in the 1990's, people viewed investment not as a risk taking activity, but as a normal and almost sure-fire way of making money fast. This belief impacted upon their willingness to live beyond their means in many cases by buying large homes, big cars, and expensive consumer items. We had become, in effect, almost indestructible. The result was extremely worrisome and as a nation we became too self-confident and overextended. This level of security and the associated carefree way of life it produced became an inherent weakness, with potentially grave consequences if not checked.

It is, of course, true that since the beginning of 2000, America had been experiencing an economic slowdown. Before the infamous September 11, the stock market in general, and the NASDAQ in particular, had suffered a significant decline. Unemployment levels were reaching an all-time high. Public and private debt had entered the danger zone. And consumer confidence was beginning to dwindle. Despite these ominous signs, however, many continued to believe, albeit naively, that the recession was a mere aberration from the norm, and that we were already headed back toward the magnificence of the 1990s.

The attack of September 11 brought us to a rude awakening in three ways. First, since this was the first time as an independent nation we were attacked in war on our soil, many were instantly convinced that the negative effects of this attack would linger on for a very long time. Second, this dastardly act threatened our symbols of hope, prosperity, freedom and world leadership. Third, we felt astonished that we were so seriously attacked not by a super power but by a bunch of renegades and terrorist fanatics who so disrupted our national pride and sense of confidence. When this event is viewed from the point of view of a philosophy of history, it might be recognized as the major turning point in reshaping the way we view ourselves as a nation and individually as persons living in an environment that is not immune to attack and disruption.

The inevitable question is this: What will be the long-term financial impact of the September 11 attack? Clearly, in the minds of individual Americans, following the attack the fear of vulnerability had reached a crisis point. People no longer believed that they could live in the protective custody of the government, or that the big brother would automatically be able to take care of them especially in retirement or in poor health. The nation was so shaken that the weakened self-confidence of citizens hit consumer and business confidence driving an already weakened economy into more serious problems. It was therefore possible to conclude that, with our sense of national security shaken, big-ticket purchases would be delayed, and long-range plans would be approached more cautiously. Many Americans would reconsider early retirement or sending their children to premier institutions of higher education. Above all, the dreams of a large home, an expensive car, and a trip around the world might well be put on a back burner, at least for the foreseeable future. Not only was the nation's financial confidence shaken, but regards for simple safety caused many to become regressive or to defer any immediate longer range personal plans. Behavior clearly changed after September 11, 2001.

CONCLUSION

With the events of September 11 etched in our consciousness and with the U.S. military response to global terrorism, most of us have started questioning in new ways the future. Is it better to liquidate all our investments and hoard them safely in bank accounts or CD's? Do we need to throw out all the time-tested investment principles and concepts in search of ultimate security? Should we buy life insurance in extraordinary high amounts? Should we set aside the entire cost of John's education right away? Has our world changed so much that we need to rethink everything? Are the plans we put into place viable or prudent any longer? Can we be confident in any future speculation? Can we any longer invest with confidence or if so, how should we invest?

Now more than ever the *traditional* well-established financial planning concepts are critically important tools. In fact, the old truths have endured precisely because they can help people cope with this kind of transformative event. But many will have to be shown anew that while their confidence may be shaken, life goes on and they must continue to plan for a future, even one less clear now than prior to September 11.

But the world-shifting events of September 11, 2001, did change our thinking. Up until that tragic day in September, many took their good fortune too much for granted, and indefinitely postponed taking those important actions which could have a major impact on their financial lives. These actions included buying reasonable life insurance, making appropriate investments, finalizing retirement plans, and arranging the assets to minimize the applicable taxes. Now it has become extremely important for financial planning professionals to help their clients recognize the urgency of putting their financial house in order so they could face such a calamity as September 11 with far less erosion of confidence in the future. Personal security must be established. Prudent investment strategies remain an important tool to maintain such security.

Financial planning professionals now have the added responsibility for helping people understand their fears, their anxiety, and their hesitation to take reasonable risks. If they succeed in achieving that objective, they would help valued clients modify their behavior, so the necessary steps can be taken right away to make their financial life safe, secure and enjoyable despite the uncertainty that the world faces in times such as these. One must never minimize the behavioral impact of a breach in personal security. But we can help people plan for a future that is prudently protected and reasonably managed. Such help will restore personal financial confidence and in so doing even affect the national economy in positive ways.

(Authors Note: Thoughts expressed by Dr. Champagne in this article are just as valid in 2005 as they were in 2001 when the article was written).

CHAPTER 15

The Basic Federal Income Tax Structure

THE BASIC TAX STRUCTURE

INTRODUCTION

The sweeping changes brought about by the tax laws enacted during the last several years, including the Taxpayer Relief Act of 1997 and the Economic Growth and Tax Relief Reconciliation Act of 2001, have successfully reduced income tax rates for many taxpayers. Yet, people still work from January through May each year just to pay their taxes. In fact, even though the highest income tax bracket is only 35 percent (2004), the federal, state, and city income taxes and the F.I.C.A. tax may combine to take nearly half of one's annual income, especially when the phaseouts for itemized deductions and personal exemptions are taken into account. Since problems facing federal and municipal governments today are increasing, and taxes are the major source of income for these governments, tax rates could increase some time in the future, taking an ever-increasing bite out of individual income. A basic understanding of tax law and the method of tax computation can help each taxpayer (1) utilize all allowable deductions to reduce taxes; (2) develop tax planning strategies to minimize long-term tax liability; (3) avoid violating tax limits or rules that could result in sizable tax penalties; and (4) make improved financial decisions, with full consideration of tax implications.

This chapter, and the one that follows, were critically reviewed for technical accuracy and enhancement by Mr. Robert Skubic, CPA, 445 S. Livernois, Suite 100, Rochester Hills, Mich. 48307. Tel: (248) 608-0197. The review was completed in 2004. However, the authors are solely responsible for the contents.

There are many types of taxes paid by individuals: federal, state, city, F.I.C.A., and so on. However, in this chapter we will concentrate only on federal income taxes because, for most individuals, this is the largest and most complex component of their tax liability.

2004 Standard Deductions

Single filers	$4,850
Joint returns and surviving spouses	9,700
Heads of household	7,150
Married individuals filing separate returns	4,850

Taxpayers who are age 65 or older, or who are blind, receive an additional standard deduction amount. For 2001, the additional amount for married taxpayers (filing jointly or separately) and surviving spouses is projected to be $900 and $1,100 for single individuals. If a taxpayer is both elderly and blind, two additional amounts are allowed.

2004 Personal and Dependency Exemptions

Individuals	$ 3,050

The deduction for personal exemptions is reduced by two percent for each $2,500 of adjusted gross income (AGI) in excess of the following threshold amounts:

	2004
Joint returns and qualifying widow(er)	$209,250
Heads of household	174,400
Single filers	139,500
Married individuals filing separate returns	99,725

2004 Phaseout of Itemized Deductions

Itemized deductions are reduced at a rate of three percent of AGI over the following threshold amounts:

Joint returns, surviving spouses, singles, and heads of household	$139,500
Married individuals filing separate returns	69,750

The maximum reduction is 80 percent of allowable itemized deductions. Medical expenses, investment interest, and casualty, theft or wagering losses are not subject to the phaseout.

COMPUTATION OF FEDERAL TAXABLE INCOME

Before embarking upon a discussion of the calculation of taxable income, it is useful to review the basic income tax structure, presented in Figure 15-1. This figure reveals that the first step toward arriving at the total box liability is the calculation of *gross income*. From this figure, standard or itemized deductions and exemptions are subtracted to arrive at the *taxable income*. This income is the basis for computing the tentative federal income tax. From this tentative figure, *tax credits* allowed by law for certain conditions are deducted.

Having briefly reviewed the basic income tax structure, we now proceed to a discussion of the procedures for calculating gross income.

Calculation of Gross Income

Calculation of tax liability begins with the computation of total gross income. Unless specifically excluded in the law, this income comprises all income received in the form of money, property, and services. For joint returns, incomes of both spouses must be reported. Also, based upon the source, income must be divided into several major categories. Each of these categories is discussed in detail in the following section.

Earned income. Earned income of employees, which is sometimes called active income, is reported annually on a W-2 form entitled "Wages and Tax Statement," or on Form 1099 for self-employed individuals. While salary, commissions, fees, and business profits are the most common forms of earned income, there are additional types of income directly related to gainful employment. An example of this type of income is self-employment income which is reported on Form 1099. Because earned or active income depends on some form of personal activity and remuneration for that activity, losses generally cannot be deducted against this form of income. The only exception is that ordinary and necessary business expenses may be deducted even if that results in a loss.

Portfolio income. Portfolio income, which is generated directly from investment activity, consists of interest, dividend income, and capital gains. The current tax law has very specific rules governing the reporting of portfolio income and deduction of losses against this income.

Interest. Interest income includes interest from accounts with banks, credit unions, savings and loan associations, money market funds, and mutual funds. Interest from the following sources must also be reported as income: (1) Personal notes; (2) loans and mortgages; (3) corporate bonds and debentures; (4) U.S. Treasury bills and bonds; (5) certain taxable municipal bonds; and (6) maturing or annual liquidation of U.S. savings bonds. Generally the payor sends each income recipient a Form 1099-INT for this income. If the total interest reported exceeds $400, the sources of interest must be reported on the tax return (Schedule B).

Dividends. Dividend income results from distribution of earnings and profits which corporations or mutual funds pay to shareholders. Generally, the payor sends the income recipient a Form 1099-DIV reporting dividend income. As with interest income, if the total dividend income exceeds $400, the sources of income must be detailed on the tax return (Schedule B).

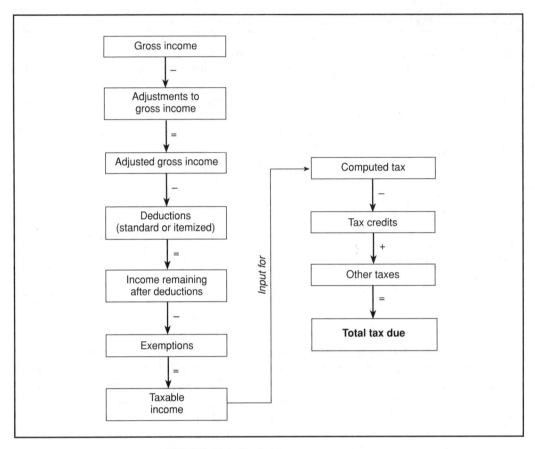

FIGURE 15-1 Basic income tax structure

All dividend income is subject to ordinary income tax. However, one notable exception is the dividend received from a mutual insurance company, which is treated as a nontaxable return of excess premium payment so long as it does not exceed accumulated premiums paid. However, if a mutual fund reports capital gains as dividend income, then this income would be included on 1040B; if it is long term, it would be reported on 1040D.

> *Going far beyond the call of duty, doing more than others expect...this is what excellence is all about. And it comes from striving, maintaining the highest standards, looking after the smallest detail, and going the extra mile. Excellence means doing your very best. In everything. In every way.*
>
> *Source: Great Quotations*

2004 Tax on a $20,000 profit from the sale of an investment		
Tax bracket:	*Short term*	*Long term*
10 percent	$2,000	$2,000
15 percent	$3,000	$4,000
25 percent	$5,000	$4,000
28 percent	$5,600	$4,000
33 percent	$6,600	$4,000
35 percent	$7,000	$4,000

Capital gains and losses: an overview. A capital gain is the profit realized from the sale of a capital asset, which refers to the property owned by an individual for investment purposes or for personal use. For example, stocks and bonds, real estate, furniture, automobiles, and household furnishings are all capital assets. Gains on property held for personal use must be reported as capital gains, but losses on these assets are not deductible. Gains on investment property, such as stocks and bonds, real estate, and so on, must also be reported as capital gains. However, capital losses on investments can be offset in full against capital gains. During any tax year, capital losses in excess of gains can be used to offset up to $3,000 of ordinary income on a dollar-for-dollar basis. Any excess losses realized during the tax year can be carried forward to offset capital gains and income in subsequent tax years. The major provisions of the current law affecting the treatment of capital gains are presented below.

Capital-Gains-Tax Rates. Regardless of income, everyone can qualify for a lower tax on profit from the sale of stock or other investments held for longer than 12 months. Currently, the long-term rate in the bottom tax bracket of 15 percent is ten percent; in other brackets it is 20 percent. But that ten percent rate may be illusory: A big capital gain during a given year can easily push someone in the bottom bracket into a higher one and cause part of the gain to be taxed at more than ten percent.

Long Term vs. Short Term. Assets held for one year or less are in the short-term category, while those held for more than one year are in the long-term category. The taxpayer should use Schedule D in Form 1040 to report the sales of assets and obtain the benefits of lower rates on qualifying long-term gains.

Selling and Buying. The lower tax on long-term gains makes the timing of sales quite important, since investors are required to offset capital gains with capital losses before figuring tax. If an investor has already taken long-term gains as the end of a year nears, for example, it may pay to put off selling shares until the next year that would create a loss. Since long-term gains are taxed at a lower rate, it is better to use losses to offset more highly taxed regular income. The maxim against letting taxes dictate investment decisions is as valid as ever. However, securities whose main appeal is fully taxed interest and dividends—such as corporate bonds or high-dividend stocks—are at a disadvantage compared with growth stocks, whose returns show up as capital gains. Art, antiques, stamps, gems, and similar items also bear a burden. Their top capital gains tax remains at 28 percent. Capital gains tax on collectibles is 15 percent for taxpayers in the 15 percent tax bracket.

Investing for the Long Haul. A new break offers incentives to patient investors who buy assets and hold them for a very long term. Assets purchased after the year 2000 and held for more than five years are taxed at a top rate of 18 percent. People in the bottom tax bracket will pay eight percent for assets held longer than five years.

Computation of capital gains and losses. Tax rules on capital gains and losses can best be understood by examining the following steps required for reporting gains and losses:

Step 1. Calculate the cost or tax *basis* of the capital asset. The basis is the purchase price of the asset, plus expenses incurred in improving the asset, minus depreciation (if applicable).

Step 2. Determine whether each transaction qualifies as a short- or long-term capital gain or loss by documenting the holding period. Then determine the net long-term or short-term capital gain or loss. The formula is:

Net Gain/Loss = Amount Realized – Adjusted Basis

Step 3. Calculate the net short-term capital gain or loss by subtracting short-term losses from short-term gains.

Step 4. Calculate the net long-term capital gain or loss by subtracting long-term losses from long-term gains.

Step 5. Determine the net capital gains amount by combining Steps 3 and 4.

The results of these computations are used to calculate the taxable income. The capital gain or loss reporting rules are summarized in Figure 15-2.

Wash sales. The wash sale provision applies to the sale of stocks and securities. This provision denies the deduction of a loss on the sale or exchange of securities if substantially identical securities are acquired within 30 days prior to, or subsequent to, the sale or exchange. The wash sale rules apply regardless of whether the individual voluntarily sells the stock to realize a loss for income tax purposes, is forced to sell, or sells to prevent an even greater loss. A repurchase of *substantially identical securities* within 30 days before or after the sale at a loss prohibits the deduction. These provisions also apply when the individual enters into an option to acquire substantially similar stocks or securities. The wash sale rules apply only to loss transactions and do not include transactions involving gains. The nondeductible loss is deferred and added to the purchase price of the reacquired shares to calculate the tax basis for that asset.

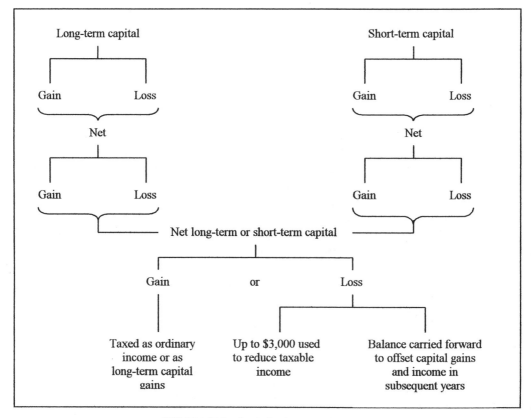

FIGURE 15-2   Capital gains tax calculation

Capital gains and sale of residence. If a homeowner is thinking of selling the principal residence, and the home appreciated in value since it was purchased, or the homeowner has accumulated a lot of deferred profit from previous sales, the tax law could be of significant value. But the law is still no more sympathetic than in previous years to homeowners who wind up selling at a loss. Here are the salient features of the relevant provisions of the current law.

House for Sale. Under the current law, up to $500,000 of current profit is tax free for joint filers ($250,000 for single filers). Even more important, a home-owner can claim a new $500,000 exemption every two years.

One requirement for tax-free profits generated by a home sale is that the home be the principal residence—but that could include a vacation home of the owner. Some sellers with large accumulated gains may find that $500,000 does not shelter all their profit. They may not be able to avoid paying taxes altogether by buying a new home as under prior law, but at least on the excess they can pay tax at the lower capital gains rate.

Selling at a Loss. Many people find it unfair that while they may have to pay tax when they sell a home at a profit, they are not able to deduct a loss generated by a home sale. Congress considered allowing a limited ability to deduct such losses but ultimately dropped the idea. Since so much home profit escapes taxes altogether, the rationale for deductible losses on home sales was considerably weakened.

Passive income. The tax law provides that losses from passive activities, such as tax shelters, in which an individual does not materially participate, may be used only to offset income from such activities. That is, *the passive activity losses may not be used to offset the income from compensation, interest, dividends, non-business capital gains, or active business income.*

Incidentally, passive activity losses can be carried forward and applied against income from passive activities in future years. These losses may also be deducted in the year in which the passive activity is entirely liquidated.

An exception to the passive loss rules applies to certain real estate activities with material participation. Individuals who own rental property, and whose adjusted gross income is less than $100,000, have the right to offset regular income with up to $25,000 of rental related losses provided they actively participated in the rental real estate activity. For individuals who are married but file separately, the amounts are $50,000 and $12,500, respectively. The maximum deduction is phased out between $100,000 and $150,000. Application of this exception to the passive income rule is demonstrated in Table 15-1.

Active or passive income. Not all incomes can be neatly categorized as either active or passive income. Examples of incomes which could be either active or passive include: (1) gains received on dealings in real estate and other property; (2) interest received on securities and loans; and (3) royalties. Expenses related to the generation of income under (1) and (3) may be deducted directly from income, rather than as itemized deductions subject to the two percent AGI floor.

Miscellaneous income. Individuals are taxed on certain types of incomes which do not fall into any of the categories just listed. These include: (1) annuities in excess of the original investment; (2) income from an interest in an estate or trust, excluding the principal of any gift or bequest received; (3) prizes and awards; (4) certain fringe benefits; and (5) up to 85 percent of Social Security benefits received.

TABLE 15-1   Allowable Deduction of Real Estate Losses

Assume Carl has annual wages of $70,000 and income from an equipment leasing limited partnership of $3,000.

Carl owns and operates a real estate investment property which generates the following tax loss.

Income	$35,000
Out-of-pocket operating expense	−$30,000
Net operating income	$ 5,000
Less depreciation expense	−$10,000
Net tax loss	−$ 5,000

Carl can use the $5,000 loss to offset his $3,000 income from a passive activity, and the remaining $2,000 to offset his ordinary income.

Tax-exempt income: municipal bonds. Municipal bonds are qualifying tax-free bonds issued by municipalities (such as states, cities, and school districts) to raise funds for financing local projects. Interest income from municipal bonds is completely exempt from federal income tax. The reason for this exemption is to make it easier for municipalities to sell bonds and obtain financing for community improvement by making the municipal bond interest rate more attractive than the interest rates on comparable corporate bonds, net of federal and state taxes. It should be mentioned, however, that municipal bond interest could be subject to the alternative minimum tax (discussed later).

Tax-exempt municipal bonds provide investors with an alternative to investing in taxable corporate bonds and U.S. Treasury instruments. The key question therefore becomes: Which of the three types of bonds offers a higher after-tax rate of return? The answer, of course, depends on the marginal tax bracket of the investor. Consider, for example, an investor in the 28 percent income tax bracket who wishes to purchase either a municipal bond paying eight percent or a corporate bond of equal riskiness, currently yielding ten percent. The municipal bond pays eight percent after-tax, whereas the corporate bond pays only 7.2 percent on an after-tax basis, as calculated here:

$$
\begin{bmatrix} \text{Before tax} \\ \text{interest rate,} \\ \text{e.g., } 10\% = .10 \end{bmatrix} \times \begin{bmatrix} 1 - \begin{bmatrix} \text{Investor's} \\ \text{income tax} \\ \text{rate, e.g.,} \\ 28\% = .28 \end{bmatrix} \end{bmatrix} = \begin{bmatrix} \text{After-tax} \\ \text{interest rate,} \\ \text{e.g.,} \\ 7.2\% = .072 \end{bmatrix}
$$

In this case, the investor in the 28 percent tax bracket will find the municipal bond to be more attractive than the corporate bond. A comparison of tax-exempt with taxable yields for several interest levels is presented in Table 15-2. It can be seen from this table that a taxpayer in the 35 percent tax bracket would prefer a fully taxable corporate bond over a municipal bond yielding eight percent only if the taxable bond yielded over 12.31 percent.

Social Security income. Many Social Security recipients pay higher rates than they expect because, once their incomes pass a certain level, as much as 85 percent of their Social Security benefits are taxed.

Under the current law, for single individuals with annual incomes of less than $25,000 and married couples filing a joint return with annual incomes of less than $32,000, no amount of Social Security income is taxable. For single individuals, *modified income* between $25,000 and $34,000 and married couples filing jointly with *modified income* between $32,000 and $44,000, no more than 50 percent of Social Security income is included in gross income. For single individuals with modified income in excess of $34,000 and married couples filing jointly with modified income in excess of $44,000, no more than 85 percent of Social Security is includable in gross income. For income above these limits, as much as 85 percent of Social Security income could be included in gross income. Thus, above the range, increases in the non-Social Security income have marginal effect on how much the benefit is taxed; below the range, none of the benefit is taxed.

TABLE 15-2   Tax-Exempt Yields and Equivalent Taxable Yields

Tax-exempt yields	*Tax brackets*		
(%)	*15%*	*28%*	*35%*
2.00	2.35	2.74	3.08
2.50	2.94	3.42	3.85
3.00	3.53	4.11	4.62
3.50	4.12	4.79	5.38
4.00	4.71	5.48	6.15
4.50	5.29	6.16	6.92
5.00	5.88	6.85	7.69
5.50	6.47	7.53	8.46
6.00	7.06	8.22	9.23
6.50	7.65	8.90	10.00
7.00	8.24	9.59	10.77
7.50	8.82	10.27	11.54
8.00	9.41	10.96	12.31
8.50	10.00	11.64	13.08
9.00	10.59	12.33	13.85
9.50	11.18	13.01	14.62
10.00	11.76	13.70	15.38
10.50	12.35	14.38	16.15
11.00	12.94	15.07	16.92
11.50	13.53	15.75	17.69
12.00	14.12	16.44	18.46
12.50	14.71	17.12	19.23
13.00	15.29	17.81	20.00
13.50	15.88	18.49	20.77
14.00	16.47	19.18	21.54
14.50	17.06	19.86	22.31
15.00	17.65	20.55	23.08

Nontaxable income. Several sources of income are treated as nontaxable income. These sources include: (1) gifts and inheritances; (2) interest on certain state and municipal bonds, and interest received from certain mutual funds that hold such bonds; (3) returns of capital; (4) reimbursements received from an employer for business expenses, if properly reported; (5) up to $500,000 of current profit from the sale of principal residence for joint filers every two years; (6) 15 percent of Social Security benefits up to the exempt amount; (7) compensation for injury or sickness, including Worker's Compensation and certain disability payments; (8) amounts received under insurance if the taxpayer paid the premium and did not deduct costs (e.g., medical) on prior returns; and (9) amounts contributed by the employer to an accident or health plan on behalf of the taxpayer and the family.

Adjustments to Gross Income

Once all forms of income (and appropriate losses) are totaled, a select group of expenditures can be deducted from gross income to help reduce the individual's final tax liability to its minimum legal amount. Currently, these deductions include business expenses for self-employed individuals reported on Schedule "C," interest penalties for early withdrawal of savings certificates of deposit, alimony payments, and contributions to qualified retirement programs, such as Keogh plans for the self-employed, and certain Individual Retirement Accounts (IRAs) for persons who are not self-employed. The IRAs require a brief explanation.

The 2001 Act made numerous changes to the tax rules affecting Individual Retirement Accounts and pension plans.

Maximum IRA Contributions

There are two types of IRAs: the traditional IRA, which provides for tax-deductible contributions (where the taxpayer qualifies) and taxable distributions; and the Roth IRA, which provides for after-tax contributions (again, where the taxpayer qualifies), but allows nontaxable distributions. In 2005, an individual may contribute up to a total of $4,000 a year to IRAs owned by that person.

The new law increased the maximum dollar limit for IRA contributions as follows:

Year	Maximum IRA Contribution
2002-2004	$3,000
2005-2007	$4,000
2008 and after	$5,000 (to be adjusted for inflation in $500 increments)

- The limit on annual additions (generally, employer and employee contributions and forfeitures) to defined contribution plans [such as 401(k) and profit sharing plans] is the lesser of 100 percent of compensation or $40,000 (2004). The new law also provides faster inflation-adjusting of the dollar limit by making the minimum adjustment $1,000 (down from $5,000), and $500 for 401(k) plans.
- The maximum annual benefit that can be funded under a defined-benefit pension plan for 2004 is the lesser of 100 percent of average compensation or $160,500.
- The amount of a participant's compensation that can be taken into account under a plan for 2004 is $200,000. The amount will be inflation-adjusted in minimum $5,000 increments.

Elective Deferrals as Roth Contributions

The new legislation allowed a 401(k) plan or 403(b) plan to include a "Roth contribution program," effective for tax years starting after 2005. This program permits a participant to elect to have all or a portion of the participant's elective deferrals to the plan treated like Roth IRA contributions. Thus, a designated Roth contribution will not be excludable from the participant's income when made, but, if all requirements are met, a distribution from the Roth contribution program will not be taxed. The annual dollar limit on designated Roth contributions is the annual limit on elective deferrals, reduced by elective deferrals that are not designated Roth contributions.

Catch-Up IRA Contributions

Individuals who have reached age 50 and meet the new tax law's AGI limits for regular contributions for the year may make additional "catch-up" IRA or Roth IRA contributions, to make up for possible missed retirement savings opportunities earlier in life. The otherwise maximum IRA contribution annual limit for a person who has reached age 50 by the end of the tax year (before application of the AGI phaseout limits) is increased by $500 for 2002 through 2005 and $1,000 for 2006 and after.

Deemed IRAs under Employer Plans

If an eligible retirement plan [such as a 401(k) or 403(b) plan] allows employees to make voluntary employee contributions to a separate account that is established within the plan and meets the requirements of either traditional IRA or Roth IRA, then the account is treated as a traditional IRA or Roth IRA. The contributions would be governed by the tax law rules for the type of IRA chosen.

Limits on Contributions to 401(k) and other Plans

The new law increased the amounts that may be contributed on a pretax basis to 401(k) salary deferral plans, 403 (b) tax-sheltered annuity plans, SIMPLE retirement plans, and 457 deferred compensation plans. The existing limits and new limits are as follows:

Year	401(k)/403(b) Plans	SIMPLE Plans	457 Plans
2004 (current)	$13,000	$9,000	$13,000
2005	$14,000	$10,000	$14,000
2006	$15,000	$10,000 (adjusted)	$15,000

All limits are adjusted for inflation after being fully phased in.

The new law also increased the percentage limit (currently 33-1/3 percent of compensation) for 457 deferred compensation plans to 100 percent for 2004.

Increase in Plan Contribution and Benefit Limits

The new law made changes relating to plan contributions and benefit limits, as presented below:

Catch-Up Contributions. The new law allowed older individuals to make special catch-up contributions. In the case of 401(k), 403 (b), SIMPLE, and 457 plans, an individual who has reached age 50 by the end of the year and who has already made the maximum allowable pretax elective deferral to the plan may make an additional pretax catch-up contribution. The maximum catch-up contribution is the lesser of (1) an applicable dollar amount (see table below) or (2) the participant's compensation less any other elective deferrals for the year.

Year	401(k)/403(b)/457	SIMPLE
2004 (current)	$3,000	$1,500
2005	$4,000	$2,000
2006 and after	$5,000	$2,500

Amounts adjusted for inflation in 2007 and after.

An employer is permitted—but not required—to make matching contributions with respect to catch-up contributions. Catch-up contributions are not subject to any other contribution limits or to the otherwise applicable nondiscrimination rules.

Credit for Elective Deferrals and IRA Contributions. For tax years before 2007, the new law provides a nonrefundable credit for contributions made by eligible taxpayers to qualifying retirement plans. In general, a tax credit of up to $1,000 (i.e., up to 50 percent of up to $2,000 of contributions) is available to single taxpayers (or married persons filing separately) with AGI of $25,000 or less, joint filers with AGI of $50,000 or less, and heads of households with AGI of $37,500 or less. The amount of the credit depends on the taxpayer's AGI and the amount of qualifying contributions. The credit is in addition to any deduction or exclusion allowed for the contributions. The credit is available for elective contributions to a 401(k), 403(b), 457, or SIMPLE plan, contributions to a traditional IRA or Roth IRA, and voluntary after-tax contributions to a tax-qualified retirement plan.

Deductions

The next step in the process of calculating tax liability is to subtract all allowable deductions from the adjusted gross income. There are two options permitted in this step: The taxpayer can take either the standard deduction or the itemized deductions.

Standard deduction. The standard deduction is the amount all taxpayers (except some dependents) are permitted to take when filing a tax return. The amount of the standard deduction is the dollar threshold for determining whether or not the individual may itemize deductions. The standard deductions for 2004 were listed earlier and are reproduced in Table 15-3. Incidentally, both the standard deduction and the additional allowances for the blind and the elderly are subject to inflation adjustments.

Itemized deductions. Individuals who have tax-deductible expenses in excess of the standard deduction amount may benefit from using the itemized deductions approach. These deductions represent those specific expenses that can be subtracted from adjusted gross income. Many categories of deductions can be utilized by taxpayers to minimize their tax liability. These include medical expenses, state and local taxes, interest, charitable contributions, business use of a home, casualty or theft losses, moving expenses (an adjustment), and miscellaneous expenses. Details of these deductions are discussed next.

TABLE 15-3 Standard Deductions

Filing status	*2004 Standard deduction*
Single	$4,850
Married, filing jointly	$9,700
(increased deductions exist for taxpayers age 65 or older or blind)	
Head of Household	$7,150
Married, filing separately	$4,850

In addition, the standard deduction is increased by $900 for an individual 65 years old or older or for a blind individual who is married (or $1,800 for a married individual who is both blind and 65 years old or older). An additional $1,100 is allowed for an unmarried individual who is 65 years old or older or blind ($2,200 if both). For a student or a dependent who may be claimed as a dependent by another person, the standard deduction is the greater of $750 or earned income plus $250, except that the deduction may not exceed the basic standard deduction.

Medical expenses. Medical expenses not reimbursed by insurance in excess of 7.5 percent of the adjusted gross income are deductible. These expenses include amounts paid for: (1) the diagnosis, treatment, or prevention of disease, including payments to health care professionals and facilities, plus prescription drugs; (2) transportation primarily for and essential to medical care; (3) insurance covering medical care; (4) lodging while away from home primarily for medical care; and (5) accommodating a home to fit the needs of a physically handicapped person.

One important note: Under the current law, for self-employed individuals, bigger adjustments for medical insurance coverage were being incrementally phased in over the next several years. The adjustment was completed in 2003.

State and local taxes. State, local and foreign property and income taxes, real estate taxes, and personal property taxes all qualify as itemized deductions. However, state and local sales taxes and employee payroll taxes (F.I.C.A.) are excluded from itemized deductions.

Interest expense. The tax rules applicable to the deductibility of various types of interest expenses are summarized in Table 15-4. A brief discussion of each of the five types of interest expense follows.

Qualified residence mortgage interest expense is deductible. Interest paid on first and second home mortgage loans is deductible if the amount of the acquisition indebtedness does not exceed $1 million. The term *acquisition indebtedness* is defined as debt that is incurred in acquiring, constructing, or substantially improving the taxpayer's principal residence, and is secured by such residence. Interest on home equity loans is also deductible, provided the

TABLE 15-4 Deductibility of Interest Expense

Interest category	*Its nature*	*Deductibility rules*
Qualified residence interest expense	Interest on indebtedness secured by any property that is a qualified residence of the taxpayer, plus one other residence.	Deductibility limits deductions of interest on acquisition loans of up to $1 million and home equity loans of up to $100,000.
Investment interest expense	Interest on debt incurred to carry property that is held for investment.	Investment interest is deductible to the extent of net investment income, which is equal to the amount of investment income over investment expenses. Interest paid on loans invested in tax-free investments like municipal bonds are not deductible.
Business interest expense	Interest on loans taken to operate a business.	All interest expenses are fully deductible.
Passive activity interest expense	Interest expenses generated in carrying out passive activity in which the person does not materially participate.	Deductible only to the extent of taxpayer's passive activity income. Nondeductible interest expenses during a tax year can be carried forward to future tax years.
Consumer interest expense	Interest on personal loans	Not deductible.

loan does not exceed the fair market value of the residence, reduced by the amount of mortgage on the residence. The aggregate amount of home equity debt may not exceed $100,000. Thus, the total amount of acquisition and home equity debt on a principal and second residence may not exceed $1,100,000 ($1 million plus $100,000). Interest represented by points paid to purchase a home or secure a home mortgage loan for home improvements is also deductible, but it must be pro-rated if instead of making an up-front payment it is added to the mortgage.

An example should make this provision clear. Suppose a homeowner paid $175,000 for a principal residence in early 2004. The original mortgage was $125,000, which was considered acquisition indebtedness. The current mortgage balance is $123,000. The homeowner takes out a second mortgage loan of $25,000 for home improvements. The acquisition indebtedness is now $148,000 ($123,000 plus $25,000). The interest on the acquisition debt, of course, is fully deductible.

An individual's deduction for investment interest expense is limited to the amount of net investment income. However, interest on loans to finance tax exempt investment, such as municipal bonds, is not deductible since the income generated is nontaxable. If an investor has a margin account with a stockbroker, in order to deduct the margin interest, the investor must have credits in the margin account sufficient to evidence payment of that interest. That is, the investor must have enough dividends, interest income, cash payments, or gains from security sales credited to the account during the year to cover the amount of interest charged to the investor. If need be, the investor should make a cash deposit to the margin account on or before December 31 to make the interest payment deductible for the year.

Another type of expense, namely, the business interest expense, incurred as a result of loans taken to operate a business, is fully deductible. However, passive activity interest expense, generated by carrying out a passive activity in which the taxpayer did not materially participate, is deductible only to the extent of the taxpayer's passive activity income.

In passing, it should be mentioned that consumer interest expense is not deductible.

Charitable contributions. Contributions to a qualified charity, which has been granted tax-exempt status by the IRS, are fully deductible only for itemizing taxpayers. Deductions for charitable cash contributions to churches, schools, and other qualifying nonprofit groups are limited to no more than 50 percent of AGI. There are additional limits on contributions to private foundations. Any *excess* deductions during a given tax year can be carried forward to the next five tax years.

The appreciation in gifts of tangible personal property, such as art, antiques, and collectibles, is disallowed entirely unless the gift is used for the charity's tax-exempt purposes. For instance, suppose a taxpayer donates to the local museum a painting that cost him $10,000 and is now worth $300,000. If the museum auctions off the painting instead of displaying it, the taxpayer will get a deduction of only $10,000. Incidentally, the 30 percent AGI limit on charitable contribution of appreciated ordinary income property is applicable. However, for gifts of capital gain property, the limit is 20 percent.

One final point: The deduction for using a car while helping a charity is 14 cents a mile.

Business use of a home. More and more Americans are working out of their homes. However, just because the home is used as a convenient place of business does not give the taxpayer an automatic right to deduct certain expenses. The office must be used exclusively on a regular basis as the principal place of any business operated by the taxpayer, or as a place to meet with patients, clients or customers of the business. Furthermore, if the taxpayer is an employee, for the expenses to be deductible, the use of a home office must also be for the convenience of the taxpayer's employer.

In recent years the IRS and the courts have chipped away at the definition of a home office, so that fewer and fewer self-employed people have qualified to deduct depreciation, utilities, and upkeep. One hurdle was that the home office generally had to be the place where the business people regularly met clients or where they spent most of their business hours and conducted their actual work, not just the paperwork. Now Congress has slightly eased the rules. Home-office deductions are allowed for space essential to the running of a venture, even if it is just for administration, provided that another such fixed location is not available.

At this point, a word of caution is in order. Deducting heat and electricity for one room, for example, may mean only a minor tax saving, and depreciation for the space must stretch over 39 years. Taking depreciation will also bar a tax exclusion for some of the profit if the house is sold. But someone who conducts business from home—whether or not a deductible office is set aside—can deduct telephone calls, supplies, and equipment as business expenses.

Casualty or theft losses. Casualty or theft losses relating to personal-use property net of reimbursement by the insurance company and in excess of ten percent of the AGI are deductible, and each loss is subject to a $100 floor. For them to be deductible, these must be personal losses attributable to theft or natural disasters, such as fire, storm, vandalism, flood, etc. Also, taxpayers may claim a deduction for decline in value of personal property stolen, damaged, or destroyed as a result of such occurrences. Finally, a different set of rules applies to disaster losses subsequently determined by the President of the United States to warrant federal assistance, and to bank deposit losses.

Moving Expenses. Qualifying unreimbursed moving expenses to a new job location are deductible as an above-the-line deduction.

To deduct moving expenses, the taxpayer must move at least 50 miles farther from the old residence than the old residence was from the old place of work, and, if self-employed, must work full time for at least 78 weeks during the 24 months immediately following the arrival, of which at least 39 weeks occur in the first 12 months.

Only certain types of expenses are fully deductible, such as the cost of moving household goods and related travel costs. Other expenses, such as the costs of pre-move house hunting trips, or temporary quarters at the new job location, are not deductible.

Miscellaneous expenses. Two general categories of miscellaneous expenses are deductible against AGI. The first category includes personal expenses incurred to generate employee business or investment income, or to preserve or protect income-producing assets. These expenses include: (1) union or professional association dues and membership fees; (2) a safe deposit box used to store papers related to income-producing investments; (3) purchase and maintenance of specialized clothing solely for on-the job use; (4) 50 percent of unreimbursed employee business meals, and entertainment expense; (5) tax counsel, tax preparation fees, and financial planning fees; and (6) tools used in a profession. These expenses are deductible only if they exceed two percent of the AGI.

The second general category of miscellaneous expenses includes: (1) gambling losses, but only to the extent of reported gambling income; and (2) business expenses for handicapped workers. Expenses in this category are not subject to the two percent floor in arriving at the adjusted gross income.

Summing up. Once the amount of the standard deduction or the itemized deduction has been determined, the greater of the two is subtracted from the AGI to arrive at the penultimate step in the process of taxable income calculations.

Exemptions

The final step necessary to determine taxable income is to compute exemptions, which represent the legally permitted deduction from the taxpayer's taxable income based on the number of persons supported by that income. The law permits a personal exemption of $3,050 (in 2004) with annual adjustments for inflation. The total value of exemptions is computed by multiplying each exemption by $3,050, that is, one for the taxpayer and each dependent. Once the value of exemptions is computed, the taxable income is determined by subtracting the exemptions from income remaining after deductions.

Number of Dependents

In order to meet the basic requirements, a dependent must: (1) have received less than $2,900 of gross income (tied to exemption amount); (2) have received from the taxpayer over half of the support in the tax year; (3) have been a citizen or resident alien of the U.S., a resident of Canada or Mexico, or an alien child adopted by and living the entire year with a U.S. citizen; and (4) have been related to the taxpayer or lived with the taxpayer the whole year. Incidentally, a person under 24 who is enrolled as a full-time student is exempted from complying with the first condition just listed, although the other three tests must be satisfied.

The tax law requires that a Social Security number be reported for all dependents. The law also requires that children (limit age 24) who can be claimed as dependents on parents' returns may not claim themselves on their own returns. Further changes in tax laws governing tax rates on the income of children under 14 will be discussed in Chapter 16 as they relate to the use of gifts as a form of tax planning.

EDUCATION PROVISIONS

The new law contains several provisions that add to the education incentives provided under current law.

Modification of Education IRAs

The tax law formerly allowed a taxpayer to make nondeductible contributions to an Education IRA for the purpose of paying the future higher education expenses (post-secondary tuition, fees, books, supplies, and equipment) of a designated beneficiary. Annual contributions to all Education IRAs for a beneficiary was limited to $500 and could not be made after that beneficiary reached age 18. The $500 contribution limit was phased out for taxpayers with AGI between $150,000 and $160,000 for joint filers. Taxpayers with AGI exceeding the higher amount were not allowed to contribute.

Education IRA distributions for qualified higher education expenses are excluded from income. If distributions are greater than expenses in a year, then a portion of the distribution is subject to income tax plus a ten percent additional tax penalty (some exceptions apply). Distributions generally must be made by the time the beneficiary reaches age 30.

Under the new Act, the Education IRA is called Coverdell Education Savings Accounts. The Act put into effect the following changes:

- Increased the annual limit on contributions to an Education IRA to $2,000 per designated beneficiary.
- Expanded the definition of qualified education expenses to include expenses for qualified elementary and secondary school (grades K-12; public, private, or religious) and to include certain room and board expenses, uniforms, computers, and extended day program costs.
- Increased the contribution phaseout range for joint filers to twice the range for single filers (i.e., to between $190,000 and $220,000 of AGI for joint filers).
- Eliminated the age 18 restriction on contributions for beneficiaries and the age 30 distribution rule in cases where a beneficiary has "special needs," to be defined in regulations.
- Clarified that corporations and other entities (including tax-exempt organizations) may contribute to Education IRAs.
- Coordinated the HOPE and Lifetime Learning Credits for education expenses with the exclusion for Education IRA distributions, so there is no dual tax benefit for the same expenses.
- Eliminated the six percent tax on Education IRA contributions made in the same year that contributions are made to a qualified state tuition program on behalf of the same beneficiary.

Qualified Tuition Programs

Also called college savings plans, or "Section 529 plans," these state-sponsored tuition programs offer parents and other taxpayers a tax-favored means of funding a child's future qualified higher education expenses. Under former law, earnings accumulated tax deferred and generally were taxable to the beneficiary (rather than the parent or other person who established the plan) when funds were distributed to pay expenses or education benefits were received. The beneficiary (or person allowed to claim the beneficiary as a dependent) could claim a HOPE or Lifetime Learning Credit for the tuition and related expenses paid with the distribution, if otherwise eligible.

For tax years starting in 2002, the new tax law:

- Allowed educational institutions (public or private) to sponsor prepaid tuition programs that satisfy the Section 529 requirements.
- Made distributions or education benefits received from qualified tuition programs excludable from income, starting in 2002 for state programs and in 2004 for qualified tuition programs maintained by an entity other than state.
- Coordinated this income exclusion with the HOPE and Lifetime Learning Credits so that the tax-free distribution cannot be used for the same expenses for which a credit is claimed.
- Set limits on the room and board allowance that may be paid with tax-free distributions.
- Imposed in 2002 a ten percent additional tax penalty on Section 529 program distributions included in income.

- Allowed tuition credits or other amounts to be transferred tax free from one qualified tuition program to another qualified program for the same beneficiary.
- Expanded the definition of "member of the family" for purposes of inter-family changes of designated beneficiaries to include first cousins of the original beneficiary.

Employer-Provided Educational Assistance

Employer-paid educational expenses are deductible by the employer and are excludable from the employee's income, up to $5,250 annually (if certain requirements are met). The new law extended the exclusion to graduate courses and made the exclusion for undergraduate and graduate courses permanent, effective for courses starting in 2002.

Student Loan Interest Deduction

Within limits, interest paid on qualified education loans is tax deductible. The deduction, which may be claimed whether the taxpayer itemizes or not, was allowed for up to $2,500 of interest paid each year during the first 60 months in which interest payments were required. Voluntary payments of interest did not qualify. Eligibility for the deduction was phased out for taxpayers with AGI of $40,000 to $55,000 for unmarried taxpayers and $60,000 to $75,000 for joint filers.

Starting in 2002, the new law repealed the 60-month limit on interest deduction as well as the restriction that voluntary interest payments are not deductible. The income phaseout ranges increase to $50,000 to $65,000 for unmarried taxpayers and to $100,000 to $130,000 for married couples filing jointly.

Deduction for Higher Education Expenses

In general, education expenses are not tax deductible, and while the HOPE and Lifetime Learning Credits are available for qualifying expenses, in some cases a deduction for the expenses would provide a greater tax benefit.

Recognizing this, Congress included in the new law a new deduction for qualified higher education expenses (defined in the same manner as for the HOPE Credit) that are paid during the year. The deduction may be claimed whether or not the taxpayer itemizes deductions. However, no education expense deduction may be claimed in a year in which a HOPE or Lifetime Learning Credit has been claimed for the same student. The maximum amount of the deduction—and the maximum income a taxpayer may have and still claim the deduction—is as follows:

Year	Maximum Deduction	Income Limit (AGI)
2004-2005	$4,000	Not exceeding $65,000 ($130,000 for joint filers)
	$2,000	Over $65,000 ($130,000 for joint filers) but not exceeding $80,000 ($160,000 for joint filers)

Those with AGI exceeding the maximums (and married-separate filers) may not claim any deduction. The deduction expires for tax years beginning after 2005.

COMPUTATION OF INCOME TAX

TAX COMPUTATION

Basic Computation

For 2004, there are six tax rates—10 percent, 15 percent, 25 percent, 28 percent, 33 percent and 35 percent as specified below for married filing jointly and surviving spouses:

For income of	The tax is
$0 - $7,000	10%
$7,000 - $28,400	$700 + 15% of the excess over $7,000
$28,400 - $68,800	$3,910.00 + 25% of the excess over $28,400
$68,800 - $143,500	$14,010.00 + 28% of the excess over $68,800
$143,500 - $311,950	$34,926.00 + 33% of the excess over $143,500
over $311,950	$90,514.50 + 25% of the excess over $311,950

Marginal Tax Rate

An understanding of the difference between *marginal* and *average* tax rates is crucial to the tax planning process. The average, or effective, tax rate is merely the total tax payable divided by taxable income. For instance, suppose in 2003 a married couple filing jointly had a taxable income of $68,799. This couple would pay a tax of $14,009 and the *average* tax rate would be 20.36 percent:

$$\frac{\text{Tax Payable}}{\text{Taxable Income}} = \frac{\$14,009}{\$68,799}$$

$$= 0.2036 \text{ or } 20.36\%$$

However, if the couple earned an additional $1, the *marginal* tax rate on this additional amount would be 28 percent.

The marginal tax rate is used to describe the rate at which a taxpayer pays tax on the last dollar of income earned. Taxable income that falls within certain *brackets* or ranges is taxed at a specified percentage as set forth in the Internal Revenue Code. In past years, determining a taxpayer's marginal tax bracket was done simply by looking up the taxable income on the IRS Tax Rate Schedules. It is the same in 2003 for low and middle income taxpayers. However, the method of tax computation is different for high bracket taxpayers.

If a taxpayer's income is above $100,000, one has to compute the tax using the worksheet presented in the boxed insert on page 15-22. We now present an example to illustrate the technique of a marginal tax bracket calculation.

2004-2006 FEDERAL TAX PLANNING WORKSHEET

GROSS INCOME:	Actual 2004	Projected 2005	2006
Salaries	$	$	$
Dividends			
Interest			
Business Income (Loss) *			
Net Long Term Capital Gains			
Other Capital Gains (Losses)			
Rents and Royalties			
Taxable Pensions and Annuities			
Partnerships, S Corporations and Estates and Trusts *			
Other Gross Income			
TOTAL GROSS INCOME:	$	$	$
LESS:			
Keogh or IRA Contributions	( )	( )	( )
1/2 Self- Employment Tax Deduction	( )	( )	( )
Alimony and other Deductions for AGI	( )	( )	( )
ADJUSTED GROSS INCOME:			
(AGI) (A)	$	$	$

* Passive limitation should not be ignored.

Let us assume John and Betty Smith file a joint return and have two dependents, which means that they can claim four exemptions. For 2004 John has a taxable income of $200,120. Since John's income is above the $100,000 limit, he must use the worksheet to figure his tax. In 2004, for a married taxpayer filing jointly with four exemptions, the marginal tax bracket is 35.5 percent for taxable income ranging between $166,450 and $297,300.

Tax Credits

After the tax liability is computed, tax credits may be used to reduce this liability dollar for dollar. Tax credits are available to persons for payment of foreign taxes and employment of special targeted groups in the form of job credits. Low

	Actual 2004	Projected 2005	2006
DEDUCTIONS AND EXEMPTIONS:			
Medical	$	$	$
(Less 7.5% AGI)	( )	( )	( )
State and Local Income,and Property Taxes			
Mortgage Interest			
Contributions			
Moving Expenses (Pre-AGI)			
Miscellaneous			
(Less: 2% of AGI)	( )	( )	( )
Exemptions ($2,900 in 2001)			
Total Deductions and Exemptions (B)	$	$	$
TAXABLE INCOME:			
(AGI Minus Total Deductions and Exemptions) (A) - (B)	$	$	$
Income Tax Before Credits	$	$	$
Less Tax Credits:			
Child Tax Credit	( )	( )	( )
Child Care Credit	( )	( )	( )
Other Credits	( )	( )	( )
Income Tax After Credits	$	$	$
Plus: Other Taxes (e.g., AMT, Self- Employment)			
TOTAL TAX	$	$	$
Withholding and Estimated Tax: To Date		$	
Expected for Remainder of Year		$	
Total Taxes Withheld and Paid		$	

income elderly taxpayers may be allowed a tax credit while receiving taxable disability benefits. Two other forms of tax credit, applicable to many taxpayers, are explained next.

Child and dependent care credit. A credit of anywhere from 25 to 35 percent of child or disabled dependent care expense is permitted under the law. The taxpayer is obliged to demonstrate that this expense, which may include home upkeep, cooking, and general care, such as a nursery, was necessary because the taxpayer was working, seeking work, or the spouse was attending school on a full-time basis. A maximum of $720 ($2,400 x .30) can be claimed as credit on expenses totalling $3,000. For taxpayers with two or more qualifying dependents, the credit is permitted on a maximum of $6,000 in expenses. In 2004 the tax credit is 35 percent if the AGI is $15,000 or less. The maximum credit could be $1,050 for one dependent and $2,100 for two or more dependents.

Income Tax Tables for 2005

Single Taxpayers

If Taxable Income Is: Over	But Not Over	The Tax Is	Plus	Of The Amount Over
$0	$7,300	$0	10%	$0
$7,300	$29,700	$730	15%	$7,300
$29,700	$71,950	$4,090	25%	$29,700
$71,950	$150,150	$14,652.50	28%	$71,950
$150,150	$326,450	$36,548.50	33%	$150,150
$326,450		$94,727.50	35%	$326,450

Married Taxpayers Filing Jointly

If Taxable Income Is: Over	But Not Over	The Tax Is	Plus	Of The Amount Over
$0	$14,600	$0	10%	$0
$14,600	$59,400	$1,460	15%	$14,600
$59,400	$119,950	$8,180	25%	$59,400
$119,950	$182,800	$23,317.50	28%	$119,950
$182,800	$326,450	$40,915.50	33%	$182,800
$326,450		$88,320	35%	$326,450

Head of Household

If Taxable Income Is: Over	But Not Over	The Tax Is	Plus	Of The Amount Over
$0	$10,450	$0	10%	$0
$10,450	$39,800	$1,045	15%	$10,450
$39,800	$102,800	$5,447.50	25%	$39,800
$102,800	$166,450	$21,197.50	28%	$102,800
$166,450	$326,450	$39,019.50	33%	$166,450
$326,450		$91,819.50	35%	$326,450

Married Filing Separately

If Taxable Income Is: Over	But Not Over	The Tax Is	Plus	Of The Amount Over
$0	$7,300	$0	10%	$0
$7,300	$29,700	$730	15%	$7,300
$29,700	$59,975	$4,140	25%	$29,700
$59,975	$91,400	$11,658.75	28%	$59,975
$91,400	$163,225	$20,457.75	33%	$91,400
$163,225		$44,160	35%	$163,225

Standard Deduction: Single = $5,000   Married/Joint = $10,000
Head of Household = $7,300   Married/Separate = $5,000
Personal Exemption: $3,200

Social Security Payroll Tax

	Maximum Taxable Wage Base	Tax Rate	Maximum Tax
Employee	$87,000	6.2%	$5,450
Self-Employed	$87,000	12.4%	$10,900

Medicare Part A Payroll Tax

	Maximum Taxable Wage Base	Tax Rate	Maximum Tax
Employee	Unlimited	1.45%	-
Self-Employed	Unlimited	2.90%	-

Personal Exemption

Amount. The personal exemption amount that a taxpayer may deduct for himself and each of his dependents is set at $3,100 for 2004. For example, a husband and wife with two dependent children filing a joint tax return would claim four personal exemptions, for a total of $12,400. A taxpayer (usually a child) cannot claim a personal exemption if he or she can be claimed as a dependent by another (usually a parent).

Reduction of Personal Exemption Amount. Personal exemptions claimed must be reduced by 2 percent for each $2,500 ($1,250 for married filing separately) or fraction thereof of adjusted gross income (AGI) in excess of the following amounts:

Taxpayer Status	AGI Level at which Reduction Begins
Single	$142,700
Married filing jointly	$214,050
Head of household	$178,350
Married filing separately	$107,025

For example, if a single taxpayer had an AGI of $179,500 and claimed three personal exemptions, her exemptions would be reduced by 32 percent ($40,000/$2,500 X 2%), or $2,880. Instead of getting the regular $9,150 (3 X $3,050) for three exemptions, she would only get $6,270 ($9,150 - $2,880).

The personal exemptions will be totally phased out if the taxpayer's AGI exceeds the pertinent AGI threshold level by more than $122,500 ($61,250 for married filing separately). Beginning in 2006, the reduction of personal exemptions for higher-income taxpayers will be gradually phased out and eliminated in 2010.

Standard Deduction

Amount. The standard deduction is a flat amount that a taxpayer may deduct in lieu of itemizing deductions. The 2004 standard deduction amount for each taxpayer category is:

Taxpayer Status	Standard Deduction
Single	$4,850
Married filing jointly	$9,700
Head of household	$7,150
Married filing separately	$4,850

Age 65 or Blind. Taxpayers who are age 65 or over, or who are blind, may take an additional standard deduction of $950 if married, or $1,150 if single, provided they do not itemize. If a husband and wife are both age 65 or over, they may claim an additional $1,900 (2 X $950) on their joint return. If a taxpayer is blind and at least 65 years old, he or she may also take $1,900 if married, or $2,300 if single.

Dependents. Taxpayers (usually children) who are claimed as dependents on another's (usually parents') tax return may only take a standard deduction of the greater of (1) $750 or (2) $250 plus earned income (up to the regular standard deduction amount).

Capital Gains and Dividends

Maximum Tax Rate on Long-term Capital Gains. The maximum tax rate on net long-term capital gains for individual taxpayers is 15 percent (5% for taxpayers in the 15% or lower regular income tax bracket). These rates apply to gain realized on the sale of capital assets held long-term on and after May 6, 2003. Long-term capital gains realized prior to that date generally are taxed at a top rate of 20 percent (10% for taxpayers in the 15% or lower regular income tax bracket).

Holding Period. The long-term rate generally applies to gains on the sale of capital assets held for "more than one year".

Short-Term Capital Gains. Net short-term capital gains are taxed at ordinary income rates.

Collectibles. Long-term capital gain from the sale of collectibles, antiques, artwork, and similar tangible property items is taxed at a top rate of 28%.

Depreciable Real Estate. Long-term capital gain attributable to recaptured depreciation on depreciable real estate is taxed at a top rate of 25 percent. The balance of such gain (over and above the recapture) is taxed at a top rate of 15 percent.

Sale of a Principal Residence. A seller of any age who has used real property as a principal residence for at least two of the last five years can exclude from gross income up to $250,000 ($500,000 if married filing jointly) of gain realized on a sale.

Maximum Tax Rate on Most corporate Dividends. The top federal income tax rate on most corporate dividends received by individual taxpayers is 15 percent. For individuals in the 15 percent or lower tax bracket, the tax rate on dividends is only 5 percent. Dividends eligible for the special tax rates are those received from domestic and foreign corporations whose stock is traded on a U.S. securities exchange or another established market. Mutual fund dividends that pass through to shareholders are taxable at the special rates to the extent they represent dividends the mutual fund earned on stock, and not other types of fund earnings such as interest.

Alternative Minimum Tax

Taxpayers are subject to an "alternative minimum tax" (AMT) instead of the regular income tax when they have substantial "preference income." This is income that is treated favorably under the regular income tax. Basically, the taxpayer must pay whichever tax is higher — the regular tax or the AMT.

Filing Status	2004 Exemption
Single or head of household	$40,250
Married filing jointly	$58,000
Married filing separately	$29,000

Caution: The exemption amounts above are phased out for certain taxpayers with higher AMT incomes.

AMT Income in Excess of Exemption	AMT Rate
First $175,000*	26%
Above $175,000*	28%

*$87,500 for married persons filing separately.

Itemized Deductions

Interest Expense. Most personal interest paid is not deductible, with certain important exceptions shown below:

Deductible	Not Deductible
1. Mortgage interest on up to two residences	1. Auto loan interest
2. Points on home mortgages	2. Credit card interest
3. Business interest	3. Most other consumer loan interest
4. Investment interest up to investment income	4. Prepaid interest other than points on home mortgages

State and Local Taxes. State and local income and property taxes are deductible by itemizers; state and local sales taxes are not. On 2004 federal income tax return, taxpayers can deduct the sum of:

- all state and local income taxes withheld from paycheck in 2004.
- all state and local estimated taxes paid in 2004, and
- state and local taxes paid with tax returns and extension requests filed in 2004.

Medical and Dental Expenses. Expenses paid for nearly all medical, dental and vision care during the year, and not reimbursed by insurance or other means, are deductible by itemizers to the extent that the total of such expenses exceeds 7.5 percent of AGI.

Losses. Individuals can deduct three basic types of losses: 1) business losses incurred in the taxpayer's unincorporated business, 2) investment losses if the investment was originally motivated by profit, and 3) casualty and theft losses, but each separate loss is reduced by $100, and the total of such losses is only deductible to the extent it exceeds 10 percent of AGI.

Reduction of Itemized Deductions by Higher Income Taxpayers. Itemized deductions must be reduced by 3 percent of AGI in excess of $139,500 ($69,750 for married filing separately). However, the maximum reduction is 80 percent. A few categories of itemized deductions are not subject to the reduction: medical expenses, casualty and theft losses, investment interest expense, and gambling losses.

Suppose a taxpayers AGI is $239,500 and there are $29,000 of itemized deductions subject to the reduction. The taxpayer's would lose $3,000 (3% of $239,500-$139,500) of itemized deductions, leaving $26,000 of itemized deductions.

Beginning in 2006, the reduction of itemized deductions by higher-income taxpayers will be gradually phased out and eliminated in 2010.

Never give up on what you really want to do. The person with big dreams is more powerful than one with all the facts.

H. Jackson Brown, Jr.

Calculating Taxable Income Using the Tax Rate Schedule

1. Enter taxable income　　　　　　　　　　　　　　　　　　　$200,120.00
2. A) Look under filing status
   B) Look for the tax rate schedule taxable income
   　　range taxable income falls under
   C) Enter the *lower number* from the tax range here　　　166,500.00
3. Put difference here　　　　　　　　　　　　　　　　　　$ 33,620.00
4. Enter *tax rate* from tax range line here　　　　　　　　　　x35.5%
5. Multiply lines 3 and 4　　　　　　　　　　　　　　　　$ 11,935.10
6. Enter the *tax amount* from tax range line here　　　　　+41,855.00
7. Add lines 5 and 6: This is total tax.　　　　　　　　　　$ 53,790.10

Earned income credit. This tax credit is available to those individuals whose earned income and AGI are each less than a prespecified amount. This earned income does not include workmen's compensation. An individual filing as head of household qualifies if there is a married child in the home who is a dependent. If qualified, an individual who might not have to file an income tax return could file for the earned income credit and receive an appropriate refund.

Credits

Even people with simple returns may want to opt for complexity—and more paperwork—if they have children going to college or are likely to do so in the future.

Overview. A tax credit of $1,500 a year adjusted for inflation beginning in the year 2001—President Clinton called it a *Hope Scholarship*—is available to defray the first two years of tuition and fees for students attending college or vocational school. Also, through the lifetime learning credit, third- and fourth-year students, graduate students, and others returning to school to improve their job skills get a yearly tax credit of up to $1,000 for 20 percent of their tuition and fees. The maximum credit now equals $2,000. Despite the publicity, lots of families will get no help from this tax break because their incomes are too high. The credits will start to phase out when adjusted gross income on a joint return tops $80,000 (40,000 on a single return). The credit drops to zero when income tops $100,000 (joint) and $50,000 (single). Adjustments for inflation began in the year 2002.

Child tax credit. The key break is a $1,000 tax credit per child for 2004. This is a valuable tax break: Credits, which can be written off directly against tax, are worth much more than deductions. A $600 credit wipes out $600 in tax, but a $600 deduction trims $600 from income subject to tax; in the 27 percent tax bracket, for example, it saves just $162 in tax. Taxpayers expecting to claim several credits can lower their withholding to enjoy the benefits of the break in each paycheck. Families with relatively high incomes are not able to take full advantage of the credits, and some well-to-do taxpayers do not benefit at all. Once modified adjusted gross income tops $110,000 on a joint return ($75,000 for a single filer), the amount of the credit gradually fades.

The credit applies to children and grandchildren age 16 and younger, unlike dependency exemptions, which can apply at any age. But to claim the credit, the child must qualify as the taxpayer's dependent. Divorced parents who argue about who gets to claim a child's exemption will find themselves arguing over the credit as well.

Alternative Minimum Tax

For some taxpayers, one final step remains in the calculation of tax liability: namely, calculation of the alternative minimum tax (AMT). This tax was conceived to prevent individuals from escaping taxation through investments that enjoy special tax treatment. The philosophy behind the rules for the AMT is to make it more difficult for affluent individuals to avoid taxes.

The basic concept of the AMT provision is that the taxpayer must pay the greater amount resulting from two different methods of calculating tax: first, by the regular method already described, and second, by the AMT method. This method of AMT calculation is illustrated in Figure 15-3.

The process of AMT calculation begins by adding back certain itemized deductions to the pre-exemption income already computed. These deductions include all state and local taxes, accelerated depreciation, and all miscellaneous expenses subject to the two percent threshold. Then a number of *preference items* are added back. These are items that receive preferential treatment under regular tax law.

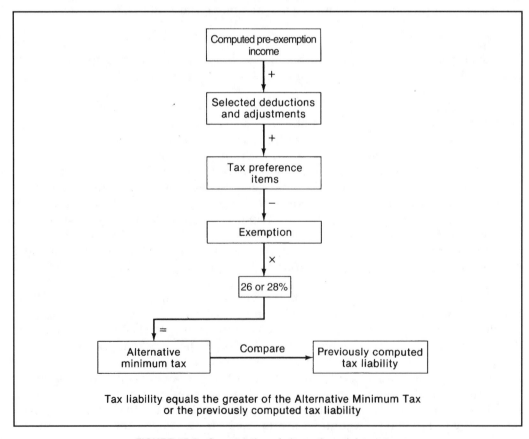

FIGURE 15-3 Computation of alternative minimum tax

Examples of preference items include incentive stock options and accelerated depreciation on depreciable real property. Once these additions are made, the taxpayer is allowed a flat exemption: In 2004 tax year, the exemption amounts as follows: (1) For married persons filing jointly, $49,000. (2) For heads of household and single filers, $35,750. These exemptions are phased out at high income levels. After this exemption is subtracted from the alternative minimum taxable income, the final figure is multiplied by 26 percent for the first $175,000 ($87,500 for married individuals filing separate returns), and by 28 percent of the excess for incomes exceeding $175,000. If this figure is greater than the tax liability computed by the regular method, the AMT becomes the individual's tax liability.

Below is a summary of AMT versus regular tax:

- Depreciation deductions for real and personal property may be less for AMT purposes.
- Interest deductions for refinanced property may be denied in certain instances.
- Certain excess intangible drilling costs are a tax preference item.
- The spread between the fair market value of an incentive stock option and the price paid for the option is a tax preference item.
- The interest on certain tax exempt private activity bonds is taxable for AMT purposes.
- No deduction for state and local taxes for AMT.
- No personal exemptions are allowed.

TAXATION OF CORPORATIONS

C Corporations

The Economic Growth and Tax Relief Reconciliation Act of 2001 left intact the current corporate tax rate schedule for the majority of C corporations. A marginal tax rate of 35 percent is imposed on corporate taxable income of $10 million to $15 million and above $18,333,333.

Corporate Tax Rates

$ 0 -	15% of taxable income.
$50,000 -	$7,500 plus 25% of excess over $50,000
$75,000 -	$13,750 plus 34% of excess over $75,000
$100,000 -	$22,250 plus 39% of excess over $100,000
$335,000 -	$113,900 plus 34% of excess over $335,000
$10,000,000 -	$3,400,000 plus 35% of excess over $10,000,000
$15,000,000 -	$5,150,000 plus 38% of excess over $15,000,000
$18,333,333 and over	$0 plus 35% of excess over $18,333,333

The lower corporate tax brackets are phased out for income subject to the 35 percent rate. This phaseout is achieved by imposing an additional three percent surcharge on taxable income between $15,000,000 and $18,333,333.

C Corporations with tax liabilities are required to make estimated tax payments if its tax liability is $500 or more. In order to avoid penalties, these estimated tax payments must be equal to 100 percent of the current year's tax liability or 100 percent of the prior year's tax liability, whichever is less (by assuming that the prior year return covered a period of 12 months and reflected a tax liability). Large corporations, those with taxable incomes of $1 million or more, must make estimated tax payments equal to 100 percent of their current year liability in order to avoid penalties. A large corporation may base its first required installment on the prior year's tax.

S Corporations

If a person owns a closely held business which is currently a C corporation or if forming a corporation is being considered, an S election should be investigated. S corporations still may be preferable for many closely-held business ventures because of the potential for a double tax on the ultimate sale by a C corporation of its assets with a resulting liquidation.

The following are some of the drawbacks inherent in the use of S elections:

- Losses from an S corporation in which the taxpayer/ shareholder does not materially participate on a regular, continuous and substantial basis may only be used against income from other passive activities.
- Losses from an S corporation, where deductible currently because of material participation or deductible later because of the lack of material participation, are limited to basis. A shareholder's basis is equal to the amount of money the shareholder has invested in the common stock of the corporation, plus loans directly made to the corporation from the shareholder plus prior year's income (or loss) less distributions made while the corporation is an S corporation.
- Certain tax-free fringe benefits, including medical reimbursement, cafeteria plans, group term life, health and disability insurance, if deducted by S Corporations are required to be included in the W-2 form of more than two percent shareholders.

C corporations that elect S status after December 31, 1986 are subject to a special tax on the pre- S corporation appreciation in their assets if these assets are disposed of within 10 years of making the election. Special rules are provided that are favorable to service businesses (such as incorporated medical or legal practices), so that proper planning can avoid what is called the "built- in gain tax."

In this chapter we have presented the basic federal income tax structure and have demonstrated the technique for computing federal income tax. In the next chapter we will explore in detail various tax planning strategies.

There can be no failure to a man who has not lost his courage, his character, his self-respect, or his self-confidence. He is still the king.
                                                        Orison L. Marken

APPENDIX TO CHAPTER 15:
JOBS AND GROWTH TAX RELIEF RECONCILIATION
ACT OF 2003

On May 28, 2003, the President signed into law the Jobs and Growth Tax Relief Reconciliation Act of 2003 (referred to as JGTRRA). The anticipated net cost of JGTRRA is $350 billion; but if the sunset provisions are eliminated, the ten-year cost of JGTRRA is estimated to be more than $800 billion. The key provisions of JGTRRA include:

1. *Acceleration of the Reduction of Other Regular Income Tax Rates for Individuals.* JGTTRA accelerates the reduction in the regular income tax rates in excess of the 15 percent regular income tax rates. The regular income tax rates in excess of 15 percent are 25 percent, 28 percent, 33 percent, and 35 percent. The provision does not modify the application of the pre-JGTRRA law sunset to the rate reductions as contained in the Economic Growth and Tax Relief Reconciliation Act of 2001 (EGTRRA).

2. *Reduction of Individual Capital Gains Rate.* JGTRRA reduces the 10 percent and 20 percent rates on net capital gains to 5 percent (zero, in 2008) and 15 percent respectively. These lower rates apply to both regular tax and the alternative minimum tax (AMT). The lower rates apply to assets held more than one year. The provision applies to sales and exchanges before January 1, 2009.

3. *Dividend Tax Relief for Individuals.* Under JGTRRA, dividends received by an individual shareholder from domestic and qualified foreign corporations are taxed at capital gains tax rates. This treatment applies for purposes of both the regular tax and the alternative minimum tax. Thus, under the provision, dividends are taxed at 5 percent (zero in 2008) and 15 percent. The provision applies to dividends received in tax years before 2009.

4. *Increased $179 Deduction.* JGTRRA provides that the maximum dollar amount that may be deducted under section $179 is increased to $100,000 for property placed in service in tax years beginning in 2003, 2004, and 2005. In addition, for purposes of the phaseout of the deductible amount, the $200,000 amount is increased to $400,000 for property placed in service in tax years beginning in 2003, 2004, and 2005. The dollar limitations are indexed annually for inflation for tax years beginning after 2003 and before 2006. The provision also includes off-the-shelf computer software placed in service in a tax year beginning in 2003, 2004, or 2005 as qualifying property. With respect to tax years beginning in 2003, 2004, and 2005, the provision permits taxpayers to make or revoke expensing elections on amended returns without the IRS's consent.

5. *Special Bonus Depreciation Allowance for Certain Property.* JGTRRA provides an additional first-year bonus depreciation deduction equal to 50 percent of the adjusted basis of qualified property. Qualified property is de-

fined in the same manner as for purposes of the 30 percent additional first-year depreciation deduction provided by the Jobs Creation and Workers' Assistance Act of 2002, except that the applicable timing period for acquisition (or self construction) of the property is modified. The additional first-year depreciation deduction of 50 percent is for all property placed in service of the same class life.

CHAPTER 16

Tax Planning:
Concepts and Strategies

INTRODUCTION

Tax planning is primarily concerned with the *timing* and *method* by which income is reported and deductions and credits are claimed. Tax law permits every taxpayer to select among various options in reporting income and claiming deductions and credits. Every taxpayer's obligation is to decide which of these options would minimize the overall tax burden. Interestingly, in 1945 the U.S. Supreme Court upheld the "legal right of a taxpayer to decrease the amount of what otherwise would have been his (or her) taxes or to avoid them altogether, by means which the law permits." Judge Learned Hand elaborated: "Nobody owes any public duty to pay more than the law demands; taxes are enforced extractions, not voluntary contributions. To demand more in the name of morals is mere cant."

A good place to identify financial planning needs is Form 1040. A planner can look at the various line items on the tax return and recognize potential financial risks the client faces and the tax planning strategies that could be adopted to reduce these risks and improve the financial well-being of the client.

In the first section we will discuss tax planning ideas for the individual taxpayer. Next, we will briefly review several key tax planning ideas for the business organization. Finally, we will discuss miscellaneous tax issues relating to the amendment of tax return and tax audit.

THE INDIVIDUAL TAXPAYER

There are many ways in which individual taxpayers can minimize their tax burden. These myriad tax reduction techniques can be conveniently grouped into five major categories, which we prefer to call the *five Ds*. These categories, presented in Table 16-1, will be discussed in the following pages.

DEDUCTION

In Chapter 15 we presented in detail the deductions allowed under current tax laws. In this section we will explore some of the important planning ideas pertaining to tax deductions.

The Forgotten Deductions

Many taxpayers assume, somewhat naively, that since there are 7.5 percent and two percent of the adjusted gross income (AGI) restrictions imposed on medical and miscellaneous expenses, respectively, they cannot possibly pass the threshold at which these expenses become deductible. This is usually not a valid assumption. For instance, medical expenses include not only doctor and hospital bills but also medically required home improvements, special schooling for a handicapped child, travel for medical care, eyeglasses, cosmetic surgery, and health insurance premiums. Even the difference in rental expenses if someone is forced to move to a larger home to accommodate a live-in nurse is deductible.

Another tax planning strategy is to group medical expenses in alternate years to make them deductible. For instance, the taxpayer may opt to have elective surgery or braces for the kids all in one year, so health care expenses will exceed the 7.5 percent of AGI limit. Here is a simple example to illustrate the point. Suppose John Case itemizes his deductions and has an AGI of $23,000, unreimbursed hospital and dental expenses of $600, and prescription drug expenses of $400. During the year he also paid $600 for medical insurance. The total medical expense deduction for 2004 is nil:

Hospital and dental expenses	$ 600
Payment for medical insurance	600
Medicine and drug expenses	400
Totals:	$1,600
Less 7.5% of adjusted gross income (.075 x $23,000)	1,725
Total medical expenses deduction for 2003	– $125
	= $0.

However, if during 2004 John would have spent an additional $400 for braces (dental expenses) for his daughter, he would have been able to take a deduction of $275 ($1,600 + $400 – $1,725).

Like medical deductions, miscellaneous deductions also offer a valuable opportunity for tax reduction. For instance, cost of membership dues, financial planning fees, investment-related expenses, accounting fees, and unreimbursed business expenses, are examples of often overlooked miscellaneous expenses. Although these are potentially important deductions, few individuals actually receive any tax benefit from them because of the two percent of the AGI threshold limitation.

Other itemized deductions often ignored by taxpayers involve charitable contributions and state and local income taxes. People who use their car in charity work can deduct $.14 per mile (2004) plus parking and tolls. Also deductible are expenses such as a scoutmaster's uniform, and phone calls and travel expenses for charity work. A ticket to a fund raiser is deductible to the extent that its price

TABLE 16-1 Five Ds of Tax Planning Techniques

Category	*Explanation*
Deduction	Acceleration of deductions allowed under the current law.
Diversion	Steps taken by a taxpayer to channel investment return into money which will be taxed at a lower rate, will escape taxation, or will reduce taxable gain.
Deferral	Actions taken to defer taxes to future years.
Deflection	Steps taken to shift taxable income to someone who would be taxed at a lower rate.
Diminution	Actions which will reduce taxes by adopting various strategies.

exceeds normal admission cost. By not accepting the ticket or returning it for re-sale, the taxpayer can in fact deduct the entire cost.

In the area of state income taxes, the taxpayer can count not only amounts withheld from the year's paychecks and any estimated payments made, but also the tax paid on the previous year's state tax return when filed. In some states, taxpayers can write off local taxes beyond income and real estate tax. Residents of several states, including California, New Jersey, New York, and Rhode Island, can deduct as state income tax the mandatory contribution they make to state disability funds. Auto license fees normally are not deductible, but some states like Colorado base part of the charge on the value of the car. That part of the fee is deductible as a personal property tax. Intangible taxes are also deductible.

Flexible Spending Arrangement

Flexible Spending Arrangement (FSA) has been available since 1978 and in recent years has become quite popular. Dollars deposited in a FSA come off the top of the salary through payroll deductions, from employer contributions, or from both. These contributions completely escape taxes, including Social Security and most state income taxes. Funds from a FSA may be used to reimburse taxpayers for the annual deductible under the employer's regular health plan, co-payments they must make to physicians, and any other expenses their health plan does not cover. These may include eye examinations, eye glasses, routine physicals, and orthodontia work. However, funds may not be used to pay for health insurance premiums. Annual limits for dependent care are $5,000; medical cost maximums are not set by law but by employers.

While FSA provides an excellent tax reduction strategy, it does have one important drawback: The money set aside in this account during a given year must be used during that year, or it will be forfeited.

Moving Expenses

The tax treatment of moving expenses is different from the treatment of most employee business expenses in that this deduction is not subject to the two percent floor that applies to other miscellaneous deductions. The moving expenses and company reimbursements must be accounted for separately on tax returns. All company reimbursements for personal moving expenses are considered taxable.

However, these expenses may be deductible, subject to limitations, as an above-the-line deduction if the move is related to beginning full-time employment in a new location beyond certain minimum distances from the previous place of residence. Deductible moving expenses include, with certain limitations, moving personal effects, traveling, lodging, and incidental expenses.

Tax-Deductible Interest

The deductibility of consumer interest was eliminated in 1991. Therefore, an interesting tax planning idea is to completely pay off all outstanding consumer loans. Money for paying off the consumer debt can be raised in several ways, each of which constitutes an important tax planning idea. Here is a partial list of tax-wise borrowing methods:

1. The taxpayer can take out a home equity loan. Interest on this loan is possibly fully tax-deductible.
2. If the taxpayer has accumulated cash value in a life insurance policy, it might be borrowed at a reasonable (say, six percent) interest. This interest cost on this loan would be much lower than the cost of a conventional consumer loan.
3. If circumstances permit, the taxpayer can sell an investment and use the proceeds to pay off a consumer debt. Later, the taxpayer could borrow on margin to make a similar investment. The interest on the second loan can be fully deducted against investment income.

A novel way to increase interest deductions is to shift debt on the vacation home (if it is also used as rental property) to the principal residence, thereby moving interest out of the lineup of expenses on the vacation home. For instance, if Judy Cuddy owes $50,000 on her vacation home, she can take out a $50,000 home equity loan on the primary residence and pay off the vacation home mortgage. Judy will get a tax deduction against regular income for interest she pays on the home equity loan. And she can continue to take deductions against rental income from the vacation home for taxes, maintenance, repairs, and depreciation.

One final point: Interest on loans taken out for investment purposes may be fully deductible. However, to take advantage of this situation, the taxpayer should be able to demonstrate that the loan was used for making investment.

Prepayment Strategy

When a taxpayer's itemized deductions are close to the standard deductions, prepaying certain expenses can not only lower overall tax liability, but it can also be useful if the tax rates were to decrease in the future. Some deductible items can be prepaid, such as charitable contributions, miscellaneous items, property taxes, and so on. This prepayment strategy will allow the taxpayer to claim an amount greater than the standard deduction in the current year, which will minimize current tax liability. Of course, if appropriate, in the following year the standard deduction can be used to minimize the tax burden.

For example, if in 2004 Bill Jones, a single taxpayer, had itemized deductions of $3,800, he could claim the standard deduction of $4,850. However, a more profitable method of managing deductions would be to prepay in 2004 as much of the 2004 deductions as possible, raising the total itemized deductions from $3,800 to, say, $4,800. This would allow Bill Jones to claim the excess itemized deductions of $250 in the first year, and still claim the standard deduction amount in the second year which, because of indexing, will be higher. This strategy would successfully reduce the overall tax liability for both years.

Marriage Penalty

Tax rates are structured in a way which make two single people with similar incomes usually pay more tax after marriage than they would have as singles. This is known as the marriage penalty. When both taxpayers earn about the same, they might save tax by postponing marriage. Conversely, a couple usually pays less combined tax after marriage when one spouse earns the bulk of the income. Such a couple could save on current taxes if they could get married during the current year instead of waiting until the following year.

Incidentally, changes in the tax structure have increased the advantages of using separate returns to get larger medical, casualty, and disaster loss deductions for high bracket taxpayers. This is due to the phaseout of the benefit of the 15 percent bracket and of personal and dependency exemptions for high income taxpayers.

The concept of marriage penalty applies to divorce as well. If both partners earn about the same, they may save on taxes by finalizing a divorce during the current year instead of postponing it until the following year. However, if one partner earns significantly more than the other, taxes will usually be saved if the divorce is postponed.

The Economic Growth and Tax Relief Reconciliation Act of 2001 revisited the Marriage Penalty Relief. As is normally the case, a married couple may file a joint tax return and be treated as one taxpayer, so that taxes are paid on the couple's total taxable income. While a married couple may file separate returns, this method usually results in higher taxes than filing jointly. A "marriage penalty" exists when the combined tax liability of a married couple filing jointly (MFJ) is greater than the sum of their tax liabilities computed as though they are two unmarried filers.

The new Act adds several measures to alleviate the marriage penalty. Beginning in 2005, the standard deduction amount for MFJ as a percentage of the amount allowed for single filers increases annually until it reaches 200 percent in 2009. In addition, beginning in 2005, the top of the 15 percent tax bracket for MFJ filers as a percentage of the dollar amount for single filers increases annually until it reaches 200 percent in 2009.

Other Deductions

Business expenses. Miscellaneous itemized deductions are ordinarily deductible only to the extent that they exceed two percent of the taxpayer's AGI. However, if the taxpayer reports self-employment income on Schedule C, many of the same expenses, which are then treated as business expenses, become fully deductible. Examples of these expenses include accounting fees, interest expense, professional licenses, subscriptions for publications, auto expense, rent, cost of resale products, and salaries to employees.

Real estate losses. An individual may deduct up to $25,000 for losses on rental property as long as the AGI does not exceed $100,000; between $100,000 and $150,000 of the modified AGI, the loss deduction is gradually phased out. Also, most real estate taxes and mortgage interest payments are deductible on a second personal residence.

Rental expense. The tax law states that if a home is used the greater of 14 days personally per year or ten percent of the number of days it is rented out at a fair rental price, then it can still be designated as a rental business. In such a situation the taxpayer is entitled to deducting a number of business expenses associated with this home on a limited basis.

In conclusion, it should be emphasized that every taxpayer should undertake as much tax planning as is necessary to take all the tax deductions allowed by law. A list of major allowable deductions is presented in Table 16-2.

DIVERSION

The second strategy of tax reduction is diversion, which refers to the steps a taxpayer can take to channel investment returns into money that will (1) be taxed at lower rates, (2) offer higher deductions, or (3) completely avoid taxation.

Home Ownership

The most widely used tax planning strategy of diversion is home ownership, because both mortgage interest and interest on home equity loans are tax deductible. Even mortgage interest on a vacation home used for rental income is deductible as rental expense as long as the home is used for personal use less than 14 days or ten percent of the number of days it is rented out, whichever is greater; otherwise this interest is possibly treated as an itemized deduction. Real estate taxes are deductible. Points paid on securing a mortgage on a primary residence are deductible.

TABLE 16-2   Deductions Allowed by Law

Fully deductible expenses:
- Property taxes
- State and local income taxes

Limited deductible expenses:
- Casualty and theft losses
- Charitable contributions (up to specified limits)
- Home mortgage interest (up to specified limits)
- Investment advisory fees
- Investment interest
- Medical expenses
- Moving expenses
- Safe deposit rental
- Tax return preparation fee
- Uniforms and protective clothing worn on the job
- Union dues
- Unreimbursed employee business expenses
- Work-related safety equipment and tools you supply
- Attorneys' fees for tax consultation

The most significant benefit to home ownership as a tax avoidance strategy, of course, is the ability to postpone almost indefinitely the recognition of gains on the sale of the principal residence. Under the current law, $500,000 of current and deferred profits is tax-free for joint filers ($250,000 for single filers). Also, the home-owner can claim a new profit exemption every two years.

Municipal Bonds

Interest on state and local obligations is not subject to federal income tax. It is also exempt from the tax of the state in which the obligations are issued. Tax law treats bonds issued after August 7, 1986, as follows:

1. Public-purpose bonds issued to meet essential government functions are tax-exempt.
2. Qualified private activity bonds issued to finance housing and student loans are tax-exempt for regular income tax purposes, but are subject to alternative minimum tax.
3. Taxable municipals are issued for nonqualifying private purposes, such as building a sports stadium. They are subject to federal income tax, but may be exempt from state and local taxes in the states in which they are issued.

Taxpayers can also save on taxes by investing in municipal bond funds. Interest on these bonds is exempt from federal income taxes. Of course, they could possibly be subject to individual state and local taxes. Also, capital gains distributions in municipal bond funds resulting from sales of municipal bonds are fully taxable.

Matching Incomes and Losses

The strategy of matching incomes and losses can also minimize the tax liability. The passive-loss limitation rule does not permanently disallow losses and credits from passive activities; rather, it specifies how and when the losses and credits can be claimed by the taxpayer. Losses from a passive activity are deductible only against income from that or another passive activity. Unused losses can be carried forward indefinitely and can be used to offset passive income realized by the taxpayer in subsequent years.

While the current law permits the postponement of current losses to future years, it is more beneficial for a taxpayer to be able to deduct the losses during the current year. For instance, if a taxpayer has significant capital gains from a passive activity in one tax year and has a potential loss on an investment, overall tax liability can be reduced by selling the losing investment and realizing the loss in the same tax year as the capital gain to offset the gain and reduce tax liability.

Tax Shelters

Because passive losses may only offset passive income, the use of tax shelters as a tax saving vehicle has been dramatically reduced. Historically, tax shelters represented investments designed to create *accounting losses* that could be used as deductions against taxable income from other sources. Investors did not materially participate in the management of these investments, hence the designation *passive activity*. Most shelters were set up to generate the largest deductions in the first few years so investors could get their money back quickly in the form of tax reductions. If the investment went well, eventually the tax shelter turned profitable. However, most tax shelters never turned profitable partly because relatively few economic benefits were expected from them. Under the current law, the writeoffs generated by tax shelters are deductible only against income from a passive activity.

The change in tax law shifted the emphasis in tax shelter investments from tax writeoffs to economic profit motive. As a planning strategy, taxpayers use tax shelters to help them appropriately time or offset their passive gains and losses. While investors who currently have significant passive income still seek passive losses, most investors with existing tax shelter investments and passive losses should seek to generate additional passive income.

Limited Partnerships

Most tax shelters are structured as limited partnerships, or master limited partnerships. Limited partnerships make an investor liable only for the amount of money invested in them by that investor. Many of the real estate limited partnerships intend to buy office buildings, shopping malls, apartments, or other real estate properties that can pay investors immediate rental income. Other major interests of limited partnerships include oil and gas, equipment leasing, and research and development. The losses from these partnerships are passed along in the form of writeoffs to the individual partners in proportion to their investment. Many partnerships require a minimum of $5,000 in investment, and currently promise to yield between four percent and 12 percent annually, which is partly shielded by depreciation and other writeoffs. However, investments in limited partnerships may have significant risk, and, in addition, promised income streams may not materialize. Despite these risks, however, limited partnerships frequently offer tax benefits which could reduce an individual's overall tax liability.

Master Limited Partnerships (MLPs) and Publicly Traded Partnerships (PTPs)

Many master limited partnerships (MLPs) and publicly traded partnerships (PTPs) are taxed as corporations so income or loss generated by the partnership business does not flow through to the partners. During 2004, any income allocated to a partner under these types of arrangements could not be offset against other passive activity losses. In these situations, losses could only be deducted against future income from that particular MLP or PTP. The taxable disposition of a PTP or MLP result in unlimited current deductibility of any suspended losses.

Personal Exemption

High-income taxpayers whose personal exemptions have been phased out might consider transferring cash or other income-producing assets to an older child or another dependent relative instead of continuing to support that person without getting any tax benefit. The recipient of these assets would possibly pay tax at the lowest rate on the income generated by these assets and, after taxes, will have more left to live on than they might have received from the taxpayer.

Like-Kind Exchanges

When property held for productive use in a trade, business, or for investment is exchanged for property of a "like-kind" used for a similar purpose, no tax-related gain or loss is recognized upon the exchange. Whether two properties are of a "like-kind" is generally determined on a case-by-case basis. For example, a swap of one real estate property for another is considered a like-kind exchange.

The tax law allows a lot of flexibility in this maneuver. The swapped properties do not have to be equal in value. In that case, tax rules allow cash, called "boot," to be paid to make up the difference in the property values, although the "boot" is taxable to the extent of the realized gain. Furthermore, properties do not have to fall into the same category. A vacant lot can be traded for a house, an office building can be exchanged for an apartment building, and a condominium is considered a like-kind exchange for a beach home, so long as each is an investment, and not a personal real estate property.

Often, the best time to consider a "like-kind" exchange is when a property has significantly increased in value. A swap lets a taxpayer secure the profit and plough back a larger untaxed fund into another underdeveloped property or a turnaround situation.

Charitable Donations

A novel charitable donation strategy, that lets the taxpayer receive both income and tax benefits, is called the Charitable Remainder Trust (CRT). These irrevocable trusts are set up to pay the noncharitable beneficiaries income for a certain period, or for life. When that period expires, the asset passes to the charity. There are two ways to accomplish this objective. In an *annuity trust*, the beneficiary receives a fixed dollar amount each year, which must be at least five percent of the initial principal. In a *unitrust*, the donor receives a percentage of the trust's assets each year; the income fluctuates with the value of the trust. Between the two, the annuity trust offers a bigger tax savings up front, as explained next.

The charitable tax deduction is based on the donor's age, income, and the gift's fair market value, which is derived from an IRS valuation table. The rates used in the table fluctuate monthly in response to fluctuations in the prevailing interest rates. When setting up an annuity trust, donors can choose the rate of the current month, the preceding month, or the month before that. The higher the rate, the higher the deduction. Of course, the contributions are subject to the normal deductibility rules (50 percent of adjusted gross income limit).

Tax-Free Social Security Benefits

As observed in Chapter 15, under the current law, for single individuals with annual incomes of less than $25,000 and married couples filing a joint return with annual incomes of less than $32,000, no amount of Social Security income is taxable. For single individuals with modified income between $25,000 and $34,000 and married couples filing jointly with modified income between $32,000 and $44,000, no more than 50 percent of Social Security income is included in gross income. For single individuals and married couples filing jointly with annual incomes in excess of these amounts, as much as 85 percent of Social Security could be included in total income.

A viable tax planning strategy for individuals with taxable Social Security benefits is to reduce modified income to the $25,000 (or $32,000 for married couples) level so that all Social Security benefits become nontaxable. This is accomplished by a thorough review of currently existing investments and, if appropriate, shifting part of the investments into assets that generate nonreportable income. An example of such an asset is a single premium deferred annuity. The income from this annuity is tax-deferred and therefore is not reported as current income for the purpose of Social Security tax calculation. Furthermore, when annuity payments are received, a portion of each payment is treated as a return of original principal and is not taxed. The remainder of the payment represents the prior deferred income and is fully taxed.

DEFERRAL

The third strategy of tax reduction is deferral, which refers to the action taken to defer taxes to future years. There are two main types of tax deferral: deferral with pre-tax dollars and deferral with after-tax dollars.

Deferral with Pre-Tax Dollars

Qualified pension and profit-sharing plans for business employees are essentially savings plans with two tax incentives for business contributions. First, money saved from current income and contributed to properly qualified plans is deductible from gross income as an expense and therefore reduces the business tax liability. Second, the interest income, dividends, and any capital gains earned in such plans are not taxable within the trust until the participant actually uses the retirement fund. The money is taxed as ordinary income when the funds are withdrawn.

Another choice relates to contributions to Keogh plans. Self-employed people with Keogh retirement plans can make tax-deductible contributions to several different kinds of plans. These people also have the right to deduct 60 percent of the cost of health insurance for themselves and their families as an adjustment to income for 2004. The deduction is also limited to the taxable income from the trade or business.

A further choice of tax-deferral is an IRA. An individual who is not covered by retirement plans at work as well as a married employee whose modified AGI on a joint return falls below $53,000 ($33,000 for single taxpayers) can deposit annually up to $4,000 (2005) each, or $8,000 for a couple, in IRAs. These contributions are fully tax deductible and related earnings are tax deferred. Furthermore, even those individuals who cannot make tax-deductible IRA contributions can make these contributions with after-tax dollars and are allowed to treat the IRA-related earnings as tax-deferred.

The Economic Growth and Tax Relief Reconciliation Act of 2001 made numerous changes to the tax rules affecting IRAs and pension plans. There are two types of individual retirement accounts: the traditional IRA, which provides for tax-deductible contributions (where the taxpayer qualifies) and taxable distributions; and the Roth IRA, which provides for after-tax contributions (again, where the taxpayer qualifies), but allows nontaxable distributions. An individual may contribute up to $4,000 a year in total to all IRAs owned by that person.

The new law increases the maximum dollar limit for IRA contributions as follows:

Year	Maximum IRA Contribution
2002-2004	$3,000
2005-2007	$4,000
2008 and after	$5,000 (to be adjusted for inflation in $500 increments)

Under the new Act, individuals who have reached age 50 and meet the tax law's AGI limits for regular contributions for the year may make additional "catch-up" IRA or Roth IRA contributions to make up for possible missed retirement savings opportunities earlier in life. The otherwise maximum IRA contribution annual limit for a person who has reached age 50 by the end of the tax year (before application of the AGI phaseout limits) is increased by $500 for 2002 through 2005 and $1,000 for 2006 and after.

If an eligible retirement plan [such as a 401(k) or 403(b) plan] allows employees to make voluntary contributions to a separate account established within the plan and meets the requirements of either a traditional IRA or Roth IRA, then the account will be deemed a traditional IRA or Roth IRA. The contributions would be governed by the tax law rules for the type of IRA selected.

The new Act increased the amounts that may be contributed on a pretax basis to 401(k) salary deferral plans, 403(b) tax-sheltered annuity plans, SIMPLE retirement plans, and 457 deferred compensation plans. The limits are shown below:

Year	401(k)/403(b) Plans	SIMPLE Plans	457 Plans
2004	$13,000	$9,000	$13,000
2005	$14,000	$10,000	$14,000
2006	$15,000	$10,000 (adjusted)	$15,000

All limits are adjusted for inflation after being fully phased in.

The new Act also increased the percentage limit for 457 deferred compensation plans to 100 percent for 2002 and after.

The new Act allowed older individuals to make special catch-up contributions. In the case of 401(k), 403(b), SIMPLE, and 457 plans, an individual who has reached age 50 by the end of the year and who has already made the maximum allowable pretax elective deferral to the plan may make an additional pretax catch-up contribution. The maximum catch-up contribution is the lesser of (1) an applicable dollar amount (see table below) or (2) the participant's compensation less any other elective deferrals for the year.

Year	401(k)/403(b)/457	SIMPLE
2004	$3,000	$1,500
2005	$4,000	$2,000
2006 and after	$5,000	$2,500

Amounts adjusted for inflation in 2007 and after.

An employer is permitted—but not required—to make matching contributions with respect to catch-up contributions. Catch-up contributions are not subject to any other contribution limits or to the otherwise applicable nondiscrimination rules.

For tax years starting in 2002, the new Act provided a nonrefundable credit for contributions made by eligible taxpayers to qualifying retirement plans. A tax credit of up to $1,000 (i.e., up to 50 percent of up to $2,000 of contributions) is available to single taxpayers with AGI of $25,000 or less, joint filers with AGI of $50,000 or less, and heads of households with AGI of $37,500 or less. The amount of the credit depends on the taxpayer's AGI and the amount of qualifying contributions. The credit is *in addition to* any deduction or exclusion allowed for the contributions. The credit is available for elective contributions to a 401(k), 403(b), 457, or SIMPLE plan, contributions to a traditional IRA or Roth IRA, and voluntary after-tax contributions to a tax-qualified retirement plan.

Deferral with After-Tax Dollars

Insurance contracts purchased with after-tax dollars provide an excellent vehicle for after-tax accumulation of earnings as long as these earnings accumulate within the policy contract. The types of insurance contracts which qualify for tax deferral include single premium deferred annuity, single premium whole life, single premium universal life, and variable life and annuities. These investments were discussed in Chapter 4. At the time of withdrawal, that part of the annuity payment which represents the cost of the initial investment is treated as a nontaxable return of principal; the balance of the withdrawal is taxed as ordinary income.

A second choice consists of nondeductible IRAs. These contributions can be made by those taxpayers with earned income who do not qualify for a deduction. The reason to make nondeductible IRA contributions is that earnings on such deposits, like earnings on deductible IRAs, accumulate without being immediately taxed. Incidentally, unlike deductible IRAs which cannot be withdrawn before age 59-1/2, without a penalty, nondeductible IRA deposits (but not the related earnings) can be withdrawn at any time without incurring a tax on principal or tax penalty for early withdrawal. For this reason, it is a good idea to segregate non-deductible IRAs from their deductible counterpart.

It should be mentioned here that taxpayers can also contribute to a Roth IRA with nondeductible dollars. From this account, tax-free withdrawals of contributions may be made at any time and earnings may be withdrawn tax-free after a five-year holding period by an individual who is 59-1/2 or older, or is disabled. Also, if the money is used to buy a first home, up to $10,000 may be distributed tax free. These deposits are limited when AGI exceeds $150,000 for couples or $95,000 for singles.

DEFLECTION

The fourth tax reduction strategy is deflection, which involves shifting taxable income to someone in a lower tax bracket. There are several ways of accomplishing this objective.

Kiddie Tax

The first deflection technique of reducing taxable income is to shift part of the income to a child. However, careful planning is required to take advantage of this technique. The reason is that there exists a "kiddie tax" for children under 14 with income in the form of interest, dividends, or capital gains. The salient features of this tax are presented next.

The kiddie tax is based on a parent's top rate if the child is: (1) under 14; and (2) has net investment income after reducing gross investment income by $1,500. This tax is not levied on earned income (like wages). Investment income is defined as any income other than earned income and may consist of interest, dividends, royalties, rents, and profits on the sale of property.

Only net investment income is subject to tax at the parent's top rate. For purposes of this rule, net investment income equals gross investment income minus $1,500 if the child does not itemize deductions. If itemized deductions are used, net investment income equals gross investment income reduced by the larger of: (1) $1,500; or (2) $750 plus itemized deductions that are directly connected with the generation of investment income.

Notwithstanding the existence of kiddie tax, a number of strategies can be used to beat the kiddie tax. For instance, a taxpayer can take advantage of the fact that the first $750 of an under-age-14 child's unearned income is tax-free. This is done by transferring assets that produce up to $750 of annual unearned income for the child. Another strategy is to switch the child's savings into investments that generate little or no current taxable income. These investments include U.S. Series EE bonds, municipal bonds, and tax-free zero coupon bonds. Also, minor's trusts, under which assets and earnings do not have to be turned over to the child until age 21, are hopefully taxed at a lower than parent's tax rate even though the child is under 14 and has unearned income of over $1,500. However, eventually this strategy does result in double taxation.

Gifts

An attractive way to shift income for an individual with a high marginal tax bracket is to give a gift to a child in a low tax bracket. A gift of cash would benefit the taxpayer if the after-tax return received by the child works out to be higher than the taxpayer's after-tax return. A gift of appreciated property, such as common stock or income producing property, can bring even higher tax benefits. For instance, the appreciated stock could be liquidated and reinvested to generate a greater after-tax return for the child than it would for the taxpayer. Although the gift is not deductible by the parent, it is not treated as income to the child.

The following example demonstrates the use of gifts as a way of reducing the tax liability. Assume John Smith wishes to create a college fund for his son Mike and has $10,000 in a money market fund earning four percent interest. Assuming a 27.5 percent tax bracket, John currently pays a tax of $110 per year (27.5 percent of $400). If he gives the fund to Mike, who has no other source of income, Mike immediately gains $110 because he would not owe this tax to the government.

Child Employment

A taxpayer can shelter income by putting a child on a summer payroll. A dependent child could earn as much as $4,850 in 2004 without paying tax on that income. Also, if the taxpayer's business is a proprietorship or a partnership with the spouse, the earnings of the child younger than 18 escape F.I.C.A. taxes as well.

DIMINUTION

In this concluding section we will briefly mention a potpourri of tax savings ideas which were not discussed in the previous sections.

Income Deferral

The deferral of income from current year to the following year will defer payment of income tax until April following the next tax year. Deferral of income may be accomplished by the following: (1) The timely negotiation of bonus or salary payment into the subsequent calendar year ("timely" in general, requires negotiation prior to rendition of services). (2) Accelerating the payment of business expenses, or delaying the mailing of bills or invoices, thus forestalling the collection of income. (3) Investment in Treasury bills, short-term certificates of deposit or similar investments where income will not be recognized until the following year. (4) Delaying retirement benefit payouts (in some cases including lump-sum distributions) until the following year or later. (5) Investment in U.S. Government Series EE savings bonds, since interest may be subject to Federal tax when the bond matures or is redeemed. (6) Deferring the exercise of stock options that result in the recognition of income as well as the sale of ordinary or capital gain assets.

Income Acceleration

Conversely, in order to reduce the tax burden taxpayers can switch next year's income into the current year. This may be accomplished by:

- Accelerating bonus payments.
- For cash basis taxpayer, accelerating mailing invoices and delaying the payment of business expenses.
- Investing in obligations which bear interest daily.
- Redeeming U.S. Government saving bonds.
- Taking IRA or qualified plan distributions.
- Selling appreciated securities.
- Taking the cash option rather than deferring a contribution to a 401(k) plan.

Itemized Deductions to Accelerate or Defer Income

The optimal year in which to reflect an itemized deduction is the year in which the taxpayer reaps the maximum tax benefit from that deduction. The payment in the current year, or deferral of payment to the following year, of certain deductions can minimize the overall tax liability. However, if the alternative minimum tax applies in the current year, accelerating the payment of itemized deductions may result in little or no tax benefit.

Bunching deductions for the current year should be considered if total itemized deductions are at or above the standard deduction amount. Acceleration of itemized deductions for taxpayers with AGI in excess of $132,950 may not reduce the tax liability.

State Income Tax

If a taxpayer projects a significant balance due with the annual state income tax return, he or she should consider increasing the current level of state tax withholding, or paying the fourth quarter installment (normally due January, of the following year by December 31, of the current year). In this manner, the payment of all state income tax will occur during the current calendar year and can be deducted on the annual Federal tax return. If payment of Alternative Minimum Tax is expected, the acceleration of the fourth quarter state payment may provide the taxpayer with little or no tax benefit. In addition to tax planning considerations, it is often advisable to pay state income tax currently to avoid penalties in the case of underpayment of estimated tax.

Charitable Contributions

Anyone planning additional charitable contributions should consider accelerating or deferring those payments. Prepayments of 2, 3, or more years of contributions to any charity could provide tax savings. Taxpayers should be aware that there are general limitations—50 percent, 30 percent, or 20 percent of AGI—which restrict the deduction for contributions based upon adjusted gross income and the type of donee organization.

Donations of used clothing, furniture, etc. to charitable organizations are deductible, in general, to the extent of their fair market value. The organization receiving the donation should provide the taxpayer with a receipt.

Contributions of Appreciated Property

In lieu of cash, a taxpayer should consider contributing property that has appreciated in value, and if sold, would have generated a capital gain. A deduction may be claimed for the full fair market value (within limitations based on the AGI), and, in most cases, no income is reportable for the increase in value. "Qualified" appraisals are required for many noncash contributions having a fair market value in excess of $5,000.

For purposes of calculating the AMT, contributions of appreciated property are not treated as a tax preference item. Accordingly, in many cases, in order to maximize the tax benefits it is preferable to contribute highly appreciated assets rather than cash to charity.

Medical Expenses

If the current medical expenses are expected to exceed 7.5 percent of the AGI, the taxpayer should pay by the end of the year all outstanding bills for doctor, dentist, hospital, lodging while away from home, medical care and pharmacy. For example, if in the current year the AGI is $30,000, the taxpayer can deduct medical expenses paid in excess of $2,250. If the taxpayer paid $2,100 in medical expenses to date, but could pre-pay another $500 this year, then this payment should be made to assure the deduction of $350. Conversely, if the 7.5 percent floor will not be approached during the current year, then further medical payments should be deferred until the following year.

The cost of unnecessary cosmetic surgery does not qualify as a medical expense.

Accelerating Interest Deductions

Generally, a deduction for prepayment of interest, including interest on home mortgages, is not permitted. However, it may be possible to accelerate one interest payment on outstanding loans. For example, if the taxpayer has a note or mortgage payment due on January 1, 2005, and makes the payment by December 31, 2004, then the extra month's interest on the 2004 tax return can be deducted.

Personal and Qualified Residence Interest

Consumer Loans. Interest paid on consumer loans, credit card loans, and other similar items, is not deductible. Consequently, the taxpayer should consider paying off all personal loans, where possible, since interest on these loans is no longer deductible.

Mortgage Interest. Interest paid on the mortgage securing the personal residence and one additional residence is deductible. The taxpayer may deduct qualifying mortgage interest provided the AGI does not exceed $139,500 ($69,750 if married filing separately). If the AGI exceeds this amount, the mortgage interest deduction is subject to the three percent reduction of itemized deductions. That is, the itemized deductions are reduced by three percent of the excess of the AGI over the $139,500 threshold. Acquisition indebtedness is debt incurred to acquire, construct, or substantially improve a principal or secondary residence. Mobile homes and some boats continue to qualify as a second residence. Acquisition indebtedness may not exceed $1 million.

The taxpayer may also deduct interest paid up to $100,000 on home equity indebtedness regardless of the way in which the proceeds are used. Home equity indebtedness may take the form of a home equity loan, a second mortgage or a refinancing of an existing mortgage.

The amount of home mortgage interest deductible for AMT purposes should be carefully examined when the original home mortgage loan has been refinanced. If a mortgage on a principal residence was refinanced after July 1, 1982, then only interest paid to buy, build, or improve the home would be deductible for purposes of the AMT computation.

To avoid the loss of deductible personal interest expense, the taxpayer should consider refinancing mortgages or home equity debts up to the $100,000 limitation and use the proceeds to reduce the consumer loans.

Points. Points paid in connection with the acquisition of a personal residence qualify as additional interest expense. The taxpayer may currently deduct the amount paid as points if the loan on which the points are paid is used to buy or improve the primary residence and the residence is secured by that loan. Points paid to secure a loan on a second home as well as points paid on refinancing an existing mortgage are deductible over the life of the mortgage.

Investment Interest

Investment interest deduction on Schedule A is limited to the taxpayer's net investment income. Investment interest in excess of net investment income may be carried forward and deducted from next year's net investment income.

Net investment income is defined as gross income from property held for investment plus net gains from the disposition of property held for investment and reduced by deductions which are directly connected with the production of investment income (other than interest). Therefore, using a margin account should be considered to acquire investments rather than investing cash and borrowing to acquire consumer goods. Note that interest paid on funds used to acquire or carry tax-exempt securities is not deductible.

The current law does permit the treatment of net capital gains as net investment income for purposes of the investment interest expense deduction limitation. Taxpayers can continue including net capital gains in the computation of investment income but only if it is elected not to apply the preferential capital gains rates to net capital gains.

Interest on loans used to invest in activities subject to the passive loss limitation rules is not classified as investment interest. Instead, it is treated as an additional passive activity deduction.

Employee Business Expenses

Home Office Expense. The cost of maintaining an office in a taxpayer's home is available as a deduction only if the home office is used exclusively on a regular basis as the principal place of business operated by the taxpayer or as a place to meet with patients, clients, or customers of the business. If the taxpayer is an employee, the use of a home office must be for the convenience of the taxpayer's employer. Thus, if an employer routinely provides adequate office space for its work force, an employee who chooses to work during evenings and on weekends at her or his personal residence is precluded from claiming a home office deduction.

Use of Personal Automobile for Business. An employee may deduct transportation expenses as a miscellaneous itemized deduction (subject to the two percent AFI floor) if the expenses are paid in connection with services performed as an employee and not reimbursed by the employer. Transportation expenses include the expenses of traveling from one place of business to another in the course of employment (and therefore not commuting) when the employee is not traveling away from home.

A limitation on the amount of annual depreciation expense applies to passenger vehicles. For passenger vehicles placed in service during 2004, the maximum deduction is $2,960. This amount is reduced if business use is less than 100 percent. Also, accelerated depreciation is allowed only for autos used more than 50 percent of the time for business driving.

Two Percent Floor - Miscellaneous Deductions. For 2004, employee business expenses are consolidated with miscellaneous itemized deductions, the total of which is deductible only to the extent it exceeds two percent of AGI.

Miscellaneous Deductions Subject to Two Percent Floor

Appraisal fees related to casualty losses
Education costs
Employee business expenses
Employee home office expenses
Employment related education
Investment expenses
IRA fees
Job hunting expenses
Job supplies
Legal fees
Professional and business association dues
Professional publications
Safe deposit box
Tax advice and preparation fees
Tools
Uniforms
Union dues
Unreimbursed employee business travel, meals, and entertainment expenses

---

Business Meals, Entertainment and Travel. Business meals, entertainment and travel expenses must be substantiated by the taxpayer in order to be deductible. Support for each expenditure that exceeds $75 must include the amount of the expense, date of the expense, the place, business purpose and business relationship between the parties.

The current law provides that deductions for meals and certain entertainment expenditures are limited to 50 percent of the amount paid.

Club Dues. Currently, no business expense deduction is allowed for club dues. All types of clubs are covered, including business, social, athletic, sporting, airline and hotel clubs. Specific business expenses, such as meals, green fees, etc., incurred at a club may still be deductible as long as such expenses meet the standard travel and entertainment deduction rules.

Deductibility of Entertainment, Meals and Travel

Entertainment	Percent Deductible
Tickets at sporting events associated with business discussion	50% limited to business use
Country club dues	-0-
Parking	100%
Meals	
Meals for employees working overtime where de minimis	100%
Meals ordered for staff meetings where de minimis	100%
Customer and employee meals when business is discussed	50%
Transportation to and from restaurants for business meals	100%
Travel	
Transportation and lodging expenses related to business	100%
Per diem reimbursements up to stated IRS limits	100%

Income Shifting

Because of scheduled future rate reductions there is more reason now to postpone income to lower the tax liability. Certain tax payments can be postponed by delaying some investments or other earnings. For instance, if a taxpayer defers non-wage income, which is not subject to withholding, the money could be received early in 2005 but taxes on this income will not be due until the 2005 tax return is filed in April 2006. Furthermore, delaying income can save a taxpayer on taxes if the future income is expected to fall into a lower tax bracket. Of course, the taxpayer still would have the obligation of prepaying 90 percent of all (wage and non-wage) income taxes to avoid underpayment penalties.

Expense Shifting

The reverse strategy works with respect to expenses. Since expenses reduce taxable income, accelerating deductions during the year may prove to be an attractive strategy. Prepayment of charitable contributions and professional dues, and realization of losses by selling property are examples of expense shifting.

Second Home

The IRS allows the taxpayer to deduct many of the costs associated with a second home as long as fair rental income is received from that home and annually it is not used for personal use for more than the greater of ten percent of the number of days it is rented or two weeks. Consequently, rental income and tax deductions generated by a second home can be an important part of a tax reduction strategy.

Alternative Minimum Tax

There is no relief from paying alternative minimum tax (AMT) if it exceeds the regular income tax. The purpose of AMT is to ensure that the wealthy taxpayer is prevented from avoiding a significant tax liability, so the tax burden on all taxpayers would be fairly distributed. In numerical terms, the AMT is equal to 26 percent of the *taxable excess* that does not exceed $175,000 after the AMT exemption, and 28 percent of the *taxable excess* above $175,000 after the AMT exemption. Beginning in the 2001 tax year through the 2004 tax year, the 2001 Act increased the exemption amounts for married persons filing jointly from $45,000 to $49,000.

Incidentally, while there is no way to avoid AMT, several carefully planned actions can reduce this tax. For instance, deferring deductible expenses to a later year, and deferring the exercise of an incentive stock option to a later year when income would not be subject to the AMT are examples of softening the impact of the AMT. Another strategy of lowering the AMT is to avoid investing in those municipal bonds whose interest is subject to AMT. For instance, the interest on private-purpose bonds issued after August 7,1986, is currently subject to AMT and should be avoided by taxpayers concerned with AMT taxes.

Social Security Benefits

Social Security benefits of someone under 65 are reduced if the earnings exceed a prescribed limit. For 2004, if the taxpayer is under the age of 65, that person will lose $1 of benefits for each $2 of earned income in excess of $11,640. This fact should be considered by all Social Security recipients.

Splitting Business Income

Tax on business income may be reduced if the taxpayer can shift part of the income to family members. This can be done by forming a family partnership or by making the family stockholders in a corporation. Generally, an S corporation in which stockholders elect to report income may be used more freely than a partnership to split income and reduce tax liability.

Mutual Fund Sales

A little-known tax savings strategy relates to the taxation of gains realized on the sale of a mutual fund or a stock. This strategy is best described by recounting the experience of a taxpayer named Bob Jones. To his dismay and utter disbelief, in May 2004 Bob was ordered by the Tax Court to pay $34,961 to the Internal Revenue Service. This situation was created in 2003 when Bob sold some of his shares in two mutual funds. To compute his capital gains and losses that year, Bob's return preparer subtracted from the sale price the cost of the fund's shares which were most recently purchased by Bob. The newer shares were purchased at much higher prices than those purchased seven years earlier. However, Bob never specified to his fund's transfer agent the particular shares that he wanted sold. The Tax Court therefore ruled that, in accordance with IRS regulations, Bob's return preparer should have assumed that Bob intended to sell the first shares. The result was devastating. Instead of a deductible $6,708 net long-term loss under the original calculation, Bob Jones was actually made liable for a $168,096 long-term gain.

A valuable lesson can indeed be learned from the harrowing experience of Bob Jones. When placing a sell order, a taxpayer must carefully instruct the broker or the mutual fund transfer agent to send a transaction confirmation that identifies the shares that were intended to be sold. This will allow the taxpayer to minimize the taxable gains or maximize the deductible losses for that year.

Early Withdrawal Penalty

Any withdrawal from an IRA account before age 59-1/2 is subject to an early withdrawal penalty. However, there is a little-known provision in the tax code that allows people who are younger than 59-1/2 to draw funds from their IRAs by receiving substantially equal periodic payments, at least annually, based on life expectancy. The following example is designed to illustrate this strategy.

Let us assume Bob Bloom, age 50, just rolled over $300,000 into his IRA. According to the mortality tables, Bob's life expectancy is 83.1 years. Bob could choose to annuitize his payments to avoid the early withdrawal penalty. For instance, an actuary using a standard mortality table and assuming eight percent interest would come up with an annuity factor of 11.109. Dividing the IRA balance of $300,000 by 11.109, the actuary would arrive at an annual payment value of $27,005.13. By annuitizing his distributions, Bob would be able to start drawing $27,005.13 a year starting at age 50, and he would not be subjected to the early withdrawal penalty. Of course, if Bob waits until he turns 59-1/2 before withdrawing the funds from the IRA investment, he would not be subject to the early withdrawal penalty even if he did not annuitize the investment for life.

S Corporation Strategy

One of the major attractions of S Corporations is that, with few exceptions, these entities are taxed like partnerships, thus eliminating corporate level taxation. In the past, when corporate rates were lower than individual rates, it made sense to retain earnings in the company. But now, depending on individual circumstances, it might lead to more tax savings if a regular corporation is restructured to an S corporation so earnings could be funneled straight through to the owner. This can be a passive activity if a shareholder is not an employee or officer and is therefore subject to passive loss rules. Also, note that the owner's pro rata share of earnings is taxable that year even if no cash distributions are made to the owner. Finally, it should be noted that this undistributed amount increases the basis for future tax considerations.

REAL WORLD FEDERAL INCOME TAX CALCULATIONS

Now that the techniques of individual federal income tax calculations have been discussed in detail, we will contrast the complexities of calculating federal income taxes of two families with differing income status.

ROGER AND CAROL KURT

Roger and Carol Kurt are, respectively, 40 and 35 years old. Roger is a GM employee and Carol is a bookkeeper at a local grocery store. In 2004 their gross wages and salaries were $107,500, and for that year they paid federal income tax of $14,900. A summary of federal tax calculations is presented in Table 16-3.

TABLE 16-3   Roger and Carol Kurt 2004 Federal Income Tax Analysis

---

Example I

	'04 Gross	2004
Total Gross Wages and Salaries	107,500	107,500
Total Contributions to Retirement Plans	(13,000)	(13,000)
Net Long Term Gain (Loss)	20,000	
Net Short Term Gain (Loss)	(3,000)	
Net Taxable Gain (Loss)		17,000
GROSS TAXABLE INCOME		**111,500**
ADJUSTED GROSS INCOME (AGI)		**111,500**
Itemized Deductions		
Medical Expenses	3,300	
State and Local Taxes	5,600	5,600
Mortgage Interest Paid	6,600	6,600
Charitable Contributions	600	600
Total Allowable Itemized Deductions		12,800
Total Deductions		12,800
Personal Exemptions		6,200
TAXABLE INCOME		**92,500**

TOTAL INCOME	**124,500**
Estimated Regular Federal Income Tax	14,900
Estimated Social Security	5,450
Estimated Medicare	1,559
Estimated State and Local Income Taxes	4,460
TOTAL TAXES ON INCOME	**26,369**
Federal Marginal Tax Bracket	25%
NET INCOME AFTER TAXES	**98,131**
Contributions to Employer Retirement Plans	13,000
NET SPENDABLE INCOME AFTER TAXES	**85,131**

SAM AND BETTY MASON

The situation of Sam and Betty Mason is vastly different from that of the Kurt family. Sam, age 58, is a highly successful financial consultant, and Betty, 56, was a Montessori school teacher. During 2004, their gross wages and salaries were $307,500, and their federal tax liability was $77,191. Because of the involved nature of this tax return, key sections of the Mason's federal tax return for 2004 are presented in Table 16-4.

The purpose for presenting the tax returns of the Kurts and the Masons is to underscore the point that federal tax preparation is serious business and, when warranted, the services of a professional CPA should be sought.

TABLE 16-4   Sam and Betty Mason 2004 Federal Income Tax Analysis

Example II

	'04 Gross	2004
Total Gross Wages and Salaries	307,500	307,500
Total Contributions to Retirement Plans	(13,000)	(13,000)
Net Long Term Gain (Loss)	20,000	
Net Short Term Gain (Loss)	(3,000)	
Net Taxable Gain (Loss)		17,000
GROSS TAXABLE INCOME		**311,500**
ADJUSTED GROSS INCOME (AGI)		**311,500**
Itemized Deductions		
Medical Expenses	3,300	
State and Local Taxes	5,600	5,600
Mortgage Interest Paid	6,600	6,600
Charitable Contributions	600	600
Phase out of Itemized Deductions		(5,160)
Total Allowable Itemized Deductions		7,640
Standard Deduction		9,700
Total Deductions (use standard deduction since it is higher)		9,700
Personal Exemptions		1,116
TAXABLE INCOME		**300,684**

TOTAL INCOME	**324,500**
Estimated Regular Federal Income Tax	77,191
Estimated Social Security Taxes	5,450
Estimated Medicare Tax	4,459
Estimated State and Local Income Taxes	12,460
TOTAL TAXES ON INCOME	**99,560**
Federal Marginal Tax Bracket	33%
NET INCOME AFTER TAXES	**224,940**
Contributions to Employer Retirement Plans	13,000
NET SPENDABLE INCOME AFTER TAXES	**211,940**

THE BUSINESS ORGANIZATION

INTRODUCTION

Once a decision has been made to establish a business, the entrepreneur must decide on the most appropriate form of that entity. There are tax considerations that will enter into this decision process. Normally, a business is conducted as a sole proprietorship, partnership, limited liability company or corporation.

For a sole proprietorship, partnership, or limited liability company, the business itself does not pay any income taxes. The sole proprietor, partners, or members include the profits or losses on their individual income tax returns. Except for an S corporation, profits of a corporation are taxed both to the corporation and to the shareholders when the profits are distributed as dividends. Also, except for an S corporation, losses sustained by the corporation usually cannot be included on shareholders' tax returns.

A sole proprietorship is the simplest form of business organization. The business has no existence apart from the owner. Its liabilities are the proprietor's personal liabilities, and the proprietary interest ends when the owner dies.

A partnership is a relationship existing between two or more persons who joined together to carry on a trade or business. Each person contributes money, property, labor, or skill and expects to share in the profits and losses of the business. A partnership is not a taxable entity, except for certain state taxes. However, it must compute its profit or loss and file a return.

A Limited Liability Company (LLC) is a form of unincorporated business organization allowed by statue in most states. An LLC is best viewed as a partnership or sole proprietorship surrounded by a limited liability shield. Properly structured, an LLC could be treated as a partnership or sole proprietorship for federal income tax purposes. It allows organizers to coordinate the benefits of taxation as a partnership or sole proprietorship with the limited liability profits of a corporation.

Corporations include associations, joint stock companies, insurance companies, and trusts that operate as corporations. Corporate profits normally are taxed to the corporation. When the profits are distributed as dividends, the dividends are taxed to the shareholders but are not deductible to the corporation.

A qualifying corporation, known as an S corporation, may choose to be exempt from federal income tax. Its shareholders, commonly known as partners, then include in their income their share of the corporation's separately stated items of income, deductions, losses (subject to passive loss rule if not active shareholders), and credit, and their share of other income or loss which is not separately stated. Although it is not generally liable for federal income tax, an S corporation may have to pay a tax on excess net passive investment income, a tax on capital gains, or the tax from recapturing a prior year's investment credit.

It is beyond the scope of this book to discuss in detail the tax considerations of the various types of business entities just presented. It may nevertheless be useful to briefly present some tax planning ideas relating to these business entities.

SOLE PROPRIETORS

As mentioned, a sole proprietorship is the simplest form of business organization. The business has no existence apart from the owner. Its liabilities are the owner's personal liabilities, and the proprietary interest ends when the owner dies. When the taxable income is calculated for the year, the owner must add in any profit, or subtract out any loss, from the sole proprietorship. Also, in this type of a business set up, the owner has an unlimited liability, which means that all the assets owned by the owner are *at risk.*

EXECUTIVES

The primary tax planning objective for most corporate executives is to reduce, defer, or eliminate the tax liability associated with salary income. There are pay benefits that are not taxable, such as certain fringe benefits, disability pensions, health and accidental death benefits, and certain housing costs while working abroad. Other tax savings plans may be instituted through pension and profit sharing plans, stock options, and deferred pay plans. The objective of these plans is to defer the receipt of salary income to a future time period when the income would hopefully be taxed at a lower tax rate.

Topics relating to pension and profit sharing plans are discussed in Chapter 11 and need not be repeated here. A brief review of several other related topics is undertaken here.

The major objective of a deferred pay plan is to postpone the tax on pay benefits to a year in which the executive would presumably be in a lower tax bracket. Another tax-free benefit for executives is to receive not only life insurance protection, but also accident and health benefits. A third benefit is a cash bonus associated with an increase in the price of employer stock. Each unit entitles an executive to cash an amount that is equal to the excess of the fair market value over the value on the date of the grant of the unit. The executive is taxed when the cash is received.

PROFESSIONALS

Many professionals prefer to form a limited liability corporation, or a corporation, both of which were covered in the previous section. For others who prefer to be sole proprietors, or partnerships, many of the planning ideas have been rendered obsolete under the current law. There is, however, an important strategy that is still applicable to doctors, lawyers, architects, professional financial planners, and other professionals who are in business for themselves.

Under the present law, passive losses can offset only passive income that is earned from passive activities. However, the law allows professionals who retain personal ownership of their offices and equipment to rent their office and equipment to their business. The rent they receive from the corporation is passive income. Then they shelter that income from taxes by offsetting it with passive losses from investments. The rent payments may leave the firm with less cash to compensate the professionals, but they can come out ahead, since the rental income offset by passive losses is not taxed as income but the compensation *is* taxed as ordinary income.

S CORPORATIONS

In order to qualify for S corporation status, a corporation must: (1) be a domestic corporation; (2) have only one class of stock; (3) have no more than 75 stockholders; (4) have only individuals, estates, certain eligible trusts or certain tax-exempt organizations as shareholders; and (5) have citizens or residents of the U.S. as shareholders. Basically, an S corporation is a hybrid business entity that combines the flexibility of the partnership format with the advantages of operation in the corporate form. The central fact about an S corporation is this: Unlike other corporations, S corporations generally pay no federal taxes. Instead, current net earnings or losses pass through to the stockholders, who will report them directly on their individual tax returns and get upward or downward adjustments in stock basis, depending upon the profit or loss realized by the corporation.

In addition to the key advantages just mentioned, S corporations enjoy the following advantages: (1) The corporate owner has limited legal liability, which sole proprietors and partnerships do not enjoy. (2) S corporation ownership can easily change hands, while sole proprietors and partnerships typically cannot. (3) Interest expense on debt to acquire or carry S corporation stock is deductible by the shareholders as investment interest, if there is material participation by the shareholders. (4) Nonsalary distributions by way of dividend distribution to shareholders avoid FICA taxes.

S corporations suffer from several drawbacks as well. (1) Fringe benefits to shareholders owning greater than two percent of company stock are nondeductible. These include medical insurance and reimbursement plans, disability income plans, and group term life insurance. (2) Any available investment tax credit or net operating loss carryovers under an existing C corporation are not available to the converted S corporation. (3) Passive losses are deductible inside C corporations, but only with limitations for S corporations.

An S corporation calculates its net income or loss, and allocates the net income or loss among its shareholders. If the S corporation has net income, each stockholder's share becomes part of his or her gross income. If the corporation has a net loss, when figuring gross income each stockholder's share is reduced, subject to the limits of basis and passive activity loss rules.

LIMITED LIABILITY COMPANIES

Limited Liability Companies (LLCs) are unincorporated entities that offer investors limited liability for debts incurred by the business. From an income tax standpoint, LLCs tend to resemble partnerships and proprietorships rather than corporations because income or loss generated from the LLC is taxed directly to investors based on their proportionate ownership. One danger inherent in using LLCs is that there have been relatively few litigations concerning the liability protection afforded by LLCs. While there is a large body of case law concerning the liability protection afforded by corporations and limited partnerships, it is still not clear under what circumstances the courts would permit a litigant to pierce the entity structure and reach individual members of an LLC.

AMENDMENT OF TAX RETURN

The tax law allows taxpayers to amend their previously filed tax returns, if they discovered that an error has been made in tax calculation.

Revising a tax return can boost the refund the taxpayer originally claimed or cut the taxes initially owed. It is also a way to correct an underpayment situation, thereby possibly reducing the payment of penalty and interest. Taxpayers should also bear in mind that amending a return will not, by itself, trigger an audit.

An overpayment of taxes can be rectified by filing a refund claim on Form 1040X. This would be the case if the taxpayer failed to take allowable deductions or credits, overstated income, or wished to take advantage of a retroactive change in the law.

The most important part of a refund claim is a statement of the reasons for a refund. A general claim simply noting an overpayment, without supporting facts and grounds, is not sufficient. A taxpayer must make a claim showing all the facts that support the claim, and the grounds for the claim.

TAX AUDIT

One of the most harrowing experiences for a taxpayer is to receive the following letter from the IRS: "Dear Taxpayer, we selected your federal income tax return for the years shown below to examine the items checked at the end of this letter. We have scheduled an appointment for you...."

"Prevention is better than the cure" is the maxim that best applies to all audit situations. Tax experts across the country point out that currently there are several areas that are carefully scrutinized by the IRS: (1) interest expense deductions; (2) mortgage points; (3) home-office deductions; (4) Schedule C (self-employed income); (5) passive income/losses, (6) alternative minimum tax, (7) itemized deductions, (8) tax shelter losses, and (9) suspicion that all income is not being reported.

If an audit letter is received from the IRS, it does not mean that the taxpayer must panic. It could be a routine query that is easily satisfied. In some easily resolved cases, the IRS merely conducts a mail audit. In other cases, however, a face to face meeting can be demanded.

In a personal audit, the best defense is consistency, cooperation, and confidence in handling the situation in a professional manner. In more complex cases, or in those cases where the taxpayer needs more support, it is often a good idea to take to the meeting a financial planner, a CPA, or an attorney licensed to practice before the IRS. Most issues are resolved satisfactorily by following these guidelines. If the impasse still persists, however, the taxpayer can take the IRS to court. However, the process can be complex, time-consuming, and possibly more costly than if it had never been initiated.

In this chapter various tax planning concepts and strategies have been presented. A discussion of financial independence planning will be undertaken in the next chapter.

Each problem has hidden in it an opportunity so powerful that it literally dwarfs the problem. The greatest success stories were created by people who recognized a problem and turned it into an opportunity.

Joseph Sugarman

CHAPTER 17

Financial Independence Planning

INTRODUCTION

In a strict sense, financial independence planning is a special case of retirement planning. The reason is not hard to find. In America, as a general rule, people retire at age 65, although there are many exceptions to this general rule. One such exception is to aspire to retire at a much younger age, say 40 or 50. Clearly, people can afford to retire at such a young age only if they become financially independent.

A comprehensive discussion of retirement planning issues was undertaken in Chapters 10 and 11. The same issues apply to financial independence planning, provided the retirement planning age is shifted from 65 to the desired financial independence age. Consequently, instead of repeating the already-familiar issues, we present here the golden rules of achieving financial independence, developed by James Stowers, President of Twentieth Century Mutual Funds.[1]

The biggest long-term financial risk that investors face is the shrinking value of a dollar. If every dollar today is worth only 50 cents ten years from now, then the consumer is in trouble. How can one afford to invest long-term money in money market accounts, bonds, cash-value life insurance or certificates of deposit? These are money *savers*, not money *makers*. Therefore, the solution is to have as little of the money tied to a dollar as possible.

STAY AHEAD OF THE SHRINKING DOLLAR

Money's value lies in what it can buy. To compensate for the decline in the value of the dollar, investors should put their money where it has a chance to grow significantly.

---

[1] James E. Stowers, *Golden Rules of Achieving Financial Independence*, <u>Bottom Line</u>, Volume 16, No. 5, March 1, 1995, pp. 1-2.

The only two investments that are likely to do that over time are real estate and stocks.

While real estate has its benefits, there are big drawbacks to its growth potential, especially if the money is invested in a home. For one thing, real estate requires a substantial investment—even if there is a large mortgage. For another, real estate is mostly illiquid—the homeowner may not be able to sell the property when money is needed. Finally, real estate that is owned and rented out must be managed. One can delegate responsibilities to a managing agent, but the homeowner must always make the important decisions.

THE CASE FOR STOCKS

People who fear stocks fear losing money. But if they are investing for the long-term value, that fear is unfounded. The value of the market historically goes up and down—but in the long term, it goes on to new highs.

When an investor buys stocks or stock mutual funds, the investment is not tied to the shrinking value of a dollar. It is tied to the value of growing companies. Therefore, there is an opportunity to more than compensate for the loss in a dollar's value.

SIX KEYS TO SUCCESS

Live within Means

In order to save money, consumers must fight to keep from spending what they have earned. Recognizing that there is a limit to the amount of money that can be spent is the first step to long-term financial planning. Everyone enjoys spending money, but tastes in restaurants, clothes, home furnishings and cars must be weighed against financial priorities.

Once money is saved, a different set of priorities can be placed on what is needed. Eventually, people who save will end up being able to do everything they truly want to do rather than just satisfying their impulses. Remember, the purpose in life is not just to save, but to be able to do what one wants to do when one wants to do it.

Build Up an Emergency Fund

The classic advice is to have six months' living expenses in investments that can be easily liquidated. But six months of living costs is a lot of money for most people, and setting this much aside may leave one with nothing to invest for the long term. Therefore, a rule of thumb is to keep not much more than one month's expenses in the bank. In addition, the long-term investments can be used as part of the reserve. When extra money is needed temporarily, these investments can be used as collateral for short-term bank loans—at low rates. Later, these loans should be paid off out of current income.

Start Saving Early

It takes much less money to reach the goal than one thinks, thanks to the extraordinary power of compounding. For instance, if from age 20 to age 65 an investor saves $50 a month and gets an average annual return of eight percent, at age 65 that investor can take out $1,658 every month until age 100. Put differently, the investor puts in a total of $27,000, but withdraws a total of $693,300. By comparison, to reach the same goal if the investor started saving at age 30, then $112 a month would have to be saved—more than twice as much.

Pay Yourself First

Investors should think of investing as their number-one financial obligation each month. It comes down to the personal priorities. How can investors become financially independent if they do not pay themselves first?

A simple rule of thumb is to save at least ten percent of gross income. As earnings rise, this percentage can be gradually increased. Money can always be found to meet this goal if the investor is absolutely determined to do so. In this connection, it is important not to overlook small—but constant—saving opportunities.

Reach for Higher Returns—Even at Some Risk

Smart people do not try to avoid risks but simply hold them within reasonable limits. In fact, those who stick to so-called safe investments face the greatest risk of all—the shrinking value of a dollar. The higher the rate of return, the less money investors have to save and the more they can eventually take out. For instance, at a ten percent return instead of eight percent, the 20-year-old saving $50 per month in the previous example would be able to withdraw $3,729 a month instead of $1,658, from age 65 to age 100. The extra benefit of two more percentage points comes to a total of $869,702.

Know the Limits of Your Knowledge

Before investing, it is important to ask whether the investor truly has the expertise to buy and sell individual stocks. Does the investor really know what stocks to buy and when to buy them? Also, is there enough time to keep an eye on the stocks throughout the week?

A professionally managed investment team such as a mutual fund could save valuable time and energy for the investing public. In the long run such a team could also make a lot more money for investors than they could for themselves, even when they have the technical competence to manage their own portfolios.

In this chapter, the golden rules of achieving financial independence have been presented. Once the goal is reached, retirement planning rules can be applied to manage the financial life of the financially independent family.

The world has the habit of making room for the man whose words and actions show that he knows where he is going.

Napoleon Hill

CHAPTER 18

A Comprehensive Financial Plan

INTRODUCTION

We have just completed a detailed study of the following eight key areas of financial planning:

- *S:* Safety through Risk Management Planning
- *E:* Educational Planning
- *C:* Cash Management, Savings, Credit, and Debt Planning
- *U:* Ultimate Disposition through Estate Planning
- *R:* Retirement Planning
- *I:* Investment Planning
- *T:* Tax Planning
- *Y:* Yearning for Financial Independence Planning

In this chapter, we will present excerpts from a professionally developed comprehensive financial plan. This plan is presented with the permission of Raymond James & Associates, Inc. in St. Petersburg, Florida.

Confidential Financial Analysis

Prepared especially for:

Mr. & Mrs. John Smith

January 2, 2005

Prepared as a service by John Q. Planner
Financial Advisor
Raymond James & Associates, Inc.
St. Petersburg, FL 813-573-3800

January 2, 2005

Dear John & Mary:

Thank you for allowing us to be of service by helping you meet your financial objectives. The financial planning process is a disciplined approach to making reasonable financial decisions. The attached is designed to help us in arriving at a reasonable decision based on your stated goals, the information you have supplied and the assumptions made. The attached may include hypothetical illustrations and assumed rates for investment returns, tax rates, inflation rates and the like. Of course, there can be no guarantee of the future performance of these assumptions.

These schedules were prepared based on information concerning your holdings and costs supplied by you. The values, except as noted, are based on current market values. The attached is intended to be used for financial planning purposes. We are not tax specialists and make no representations that the attached meets generally accepted accounting principles. It is not intended for tax, lending, legal or other non-financial planning purposes and should not be relied upon by third parties.

To the extent that general legal or tax strategies are discussed as part of the attached, we recommend that you consult with the appropriate professional advisor before implementing such a strategy.

Once again, thank you for the trust you have placed in us. We will endeavor to continue to earn that trust. Please contact me if you have any questions or concerns regarding this illustration.

Sincerely,

John Q. Planner
Financial Advisor

WHAT IS FINANCIAL PLANNING?

Simply stated, financial planning puts you in control of your financial life. Unquestionably, financial resources are a prime concern to all of us, regardless of sex, age, marital or career status. Managing these resources effectively is becoming increasingly important in an age when taxes, inflation, and inadequate financial management may lead to uncertain or unanticipated financial futures.

The relationship you establish with your financial planner is an important one. Financial planners have developed expertise in a number of areastaxes, investments, risk management, estate planning, income accumulationvital to your financial planning objectives, and thus can provide you with a balanced approach to your planning. As you may be aware, financial planners are not permitted to furnish tax or legal advice. We, therefore, encourage you to obtain independent tax and legal counsel as required.

Effective financial planning begins with a realistic assessment of your current financial situation.
This would entail gathering detailed background information covering all aspects of your financial life. Information such as income and expenditures as well as your individual and/or family financial position.

Once that has been done, financial objectives must be set and plans for meeting those objectives discussed. Stating your financial objectives in a concrete way is a difficult but essential part of the planning process. One reason many plans fail is that financial goals are not described in quantified terms but are vague and don't translate into action.

Finally, the plan best suited to help you reach those objectives must be established. This planning stage includes the budgeting of income and expenditures for the near term along with a forecast of future activity. This will give you an idea of future growth and the returns necessary to reach your overall net worth objective.

The next stage of the financial planning process calls for you to set the plan in motion. This may involve the purchase or sale of various assets, changes in your life insurance protection, additional liability coverage, and other possible changes. Keep in mind that, like any process, continual updating and review are necessary to keep you on course and aware of any needed adjustments.

Financial Advisor Net Worth/Balance Sheet

Report Date	....	**January 1, 2005**
Prepared for	....	**A Valued Client**
Financial Advisor's Name	....	**John Q. Planner**
Firm Name	....	**Raymond James & Associates, Inc.**
Firm Address & Phone	....	**St. Petersburg, FL Phone #813-573-3800**

ASSETS:	*See Comment!*	CURRENT VALUE
Cash	Cash (Checking,Savings)	15,000
	Cash (Other)	5,000
	Cash (Other)	4,000
	Money Market	2,000
	Life Insurance Cash Value	50,000
Investments	Certificates of Deposit	40,000
	Stocks	17,750
	Bonds -- Taxfree	9,700
	Bonds - Taxable	42,101
	Mutual funds-fixed	190,000
	Mutual funds-equity	
	Professional Money Manager	320,000
	Pension, Profit Sharing	164,000
	Individual Retirement Accts (IRAs)	25,000
	Annuities	
	Notes Receivable	
	Real Estate	
	Other	
Use	Home (Market Value)	250,000
	Personal Property	10,000
	Automobiles	35,000
	Collectibles	
	Other	
	Other	
	Other	
	Other	
LIABILITIES		
Long Term	Home Mortgage	175,000
"Secured"	Long Term Debt-Car Loans	20,000
	Real Estate Mortgages	5,000
	Loans Against Ins. Cash Value	
	Loans Against Investments	
Short Term	Credit Card Debts	3,000
"Unsecured"	Other Short Term Debts	
	Other Short Term Debts	
	Other Short Term Debts	
	Other Short Term Debts	
Life Insurance (Less Cash Value)		298,000

A Valued Client
Net Worth Statement - January 1, 2005

ASSETS

Cash and Cash Equivalents:

Cash (Checking,Savings)	15000	
Cash (Other)	5000	
Cash (Other)	4000	
Money Market	2000	
Life Insurance Cash Value	50000	
Subtotal:		$76,000

Invested Assets:

Certificates of Deposit	40000	
Stocks	17750	
Bonds -- Taxfree	9700	
Bonds - Taxable	42101	
Mutual funds-fixed	190000	
Professional Money Manager	320000	
Pension, Profit Sharing	164000	
Individual Retirement Accts (IRAs)	25000	
Subtotal:		$808,551

Use Assets:

Home (Market Value)	250000	
Personal Property	10000	
Automobiles	35000	
Subtotal:		$295,000
Total Assets:		**$1,179,551**

LIABILITIES:

Secured Liabilities:

Home Mortgage	175000	
Long Term Debt-Car Loans	20000	
Real Estate Mortgages	5000	
Subtotal:		$200,000

Unsecured Liabilities:

Credit Card Debts	3000	
Subtotal:		$3,000
Total Liabilities:		**$203,000**

Total Net Worth (Living Estate) $976,551

Life Insurance (Less Cash Value)	$298,000
Value of your death estate	$1,274,551

This report is based on information believed reliable. Future performance cannot be guaranteed.

Prepared as a service by John Q. Planner
Raymond James & Associates, Inc.
St. Petersburg, FL   Phone #813-573-3800

A Valued Client
Income and Expense Budget - January 1, 2005

Salary & Earned Income	9,500	93.0%	Payroll Deductions	150	60.0%
Child Support & Alimony	500	4.9%	Credit Union	0	0.0%
Pension & Social Security	0	0.0%	Mutual Funds	0	0.0%
Rental Income	20	0.2%	Stocks and Bonds	0	0.0%
Dividends, Interest, Cap Gain	200	2.0%	Real Estate	0	0.0%
Other	0	0.0%	Annuities	0	0.0%
Other	0	0.0%	Certificates of Deposit	0	0.0%
Other	0	0.0%	Qualified Retirement Plans	100	40.0%
Other	0	0.0%	Other	0	0.0%
Total Gross Income	**$10,220**	**100.0%**	Other	0	0.0%
			Other	0	0.0%
Mortgage Payment or Rent	1,200	100.0%	Other	0	0.0%
Residence Real Estate Taxes	0	0.0%	Other	0	0.0%
Vacation Home Mortgage	0	0.0%	**Total Savings & Investment**	**$250**	**100.0%**
Vacation Home Taxes	0	0.0%			
Automobile Loan(s)	0	0.0%	Religious Contributions	150	100.0%
Personal Loans/Charge Accts	0	0.0%	Charitable Contributions	0	0.0%
Child Support & Alimony	0	0.0%	**Total Contributions**	**$150**	**100.0%**
Other	0	0.0%			
Total Liabilities	**$1,200**	**100.0%**	Food	775	26.8%
			Clothing	200	6.9%
Federal Income Taxes	1,575	70.1%	Doctor & Dentist	50	1.7%
State & Intangible Taxes	473	21.0%	Prescription Drugs	75	2.6%
Local & Property Taxes	200	8.9%	Professional Fees	30	1.0%
Other	0	0.0%	Education Expenses	350	12.1%
Other	0	0.0%	Day Care	200	6.9%
Other	0	0.0%	Personal Care	50	1.7%
Total Taxes	**$2,249**	**100.0%**	Electricity, Gas, Fuel	230	8.0%
			Telephone	85	2.9%
FICA & Medicare - Client	671	77.0%	Water & Water Conditioners	15	0.5%
FICA & Medicare - Spouse	200	23.0%	Garbage and Pest Control	20	0.7%
Total FICA and Medicare	**$871**	**100.0%**	Home Maintenance & Repair	175	6.1%
			Pool Maintenance & Repair	0	0.0%
Life Insurance	45	10.7%	Security Systems	95	3.3%
Health Insurance	180	42.9%	Home Furnishings	200	6.9%
Disability Income Insurance	20	4.8%	Recreation, Entertain, Hobbies	125	4.3%
Auto Insurance	130	31.0%	Veterinarian & Pet Care	0	0.0%
Home Owners Insurance	45	10.7%	Books, Magazines	20	0.7%
Other	0	0.0%	Club Dues	0	0.0%
Total Insurance	**$420**	**100.0%**	Vacation and Travel	75	2.6%
			Children's Allowances	120	4.2%
Gas and Oil	50	66.7%	Gifts	0	0.0%
Maintenance and Repair	25	33.3%	Other	0	0.0%
License	0	0.0%	Other	0	0.0%
Public Transportation	0	0.0%	Other	0	0.0%
Parking	0	0.0%	Other	0	0.0%
Other	0	0.0%	Other	0	0.0%
Other	0	0.0%	Other	0	0.0%
Other	0	0.0%	Other	0	0.0%
Total Transportation	**$75**	**100.0%**	**Household Expenses**	**$2,890**	**100.0%**

Total Income	**$10,220**	**100.00%**
Total Expenses	**$8,105**	**79.30%**
Discretionary Income	**$2,115**	**20.70%**

This report is not indicative of any security's performance and is based on information believed reliable.
Future performance cannot be guaranteed and investment yields will fluctuate with market conditions.

Prepared as a service by John Q. Planner
Raymond James & Associates, Inc.
St. Petersburg, FL   Phone #813-573-3800

A Valued Client
Budget Summary - January 1, 2005

Total Income	$10,220	

Total Expenses	$8,105	
F.I.C.A.	$871	10.75%
Liabilities	$1,200	14.81%
Contributions	$150	1.85%
Income Taxes	$2,249	27.75%
Household Expenses	$2,890	35.66%
Transportation	$75	0.93%
Savings & Investment	$250	3.08%
Insurance	$420	5.18%

Discretionary Income	$2,115	

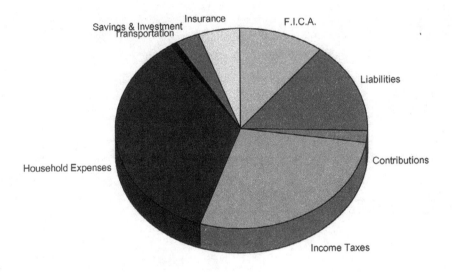

This report is not indicative of any security's performance and is based on information believed reliable.
Future performance cannot be guaranteed and investment yields will fluctuate with market conditions.

Prepared as a service by John Q. Planner
Raymond James & Associates, Inc.
St. Petersburg, FL   Phone #813-573-3800

COLLEGE PLANNING - THREE CRITICAL ISSUES

College costs are soaring. If college inflation rates continue, the cost of a college education will double every ten to twelve years. That means <u>one</u> year in college could cost the parents of a newborn the same amount as a <u>four</u> year college education costs the parents of an 18 year old today.

As society becomes more and more dependent upon high technology products and services, education will become increasingly more important. A generation or two ago, college-educated people were the exception. In the future, those without a college education may find themselves facing an insurmountable economic disadvantage in the work-place. The knowledge one needs to succeed is not only growing and changing, the rate of growth and change is accelerating.

Parents and grandparents are struggling to cope with the staggering cost of education. As the Baby Boom generation ages and its children start to approach college age, more and more families are establishing systematic savings programs to accumulate the funds they will need for their children's education.   Grandparents in increasing numbers are also adding needed funds for the next generation of college students.

The first question that must be answered by anyone saving for college is: "In whose name will the college funds be accumulated?" In the past, many people have placed college savings almost automatically in the name of the child. Up until 1986, the income tax laws encouraged this practice. Today, however, this question must be considered much more carefully and taxes are no longer the most important consideration. Today, there are three critical issues that must be examined before placing the college savings in the child's name.

The first issue is who will control the funds while the child is in college. The most common method of saving for college in a child's name is through a Uniform Transfer to Minors Act (or in some states the Uniform Gift to Minors Act) account. Under these accounts, an adult acts as "custodian" for the child's assets. The custodian makes all the investment decisions and controls how and when monies are paid out. In some states, the custodian's right to control the account ends when the child turns 18. Once the child has the right to control the account, there's no guarantee that the funds will be used for college.

College savings could add up to tens and even hundreds of thousands of dollars. Placing that amount of money in the hands of an 18 year old can be a dangerous combination. Parents hope that their parenting skills and the maturity levels of children will allow the child to make responsible decisions. However, if they are uncomfortable with the chance that college funds might be used for other purposes, parents should consider alternatives to custodial accounts.

The obvious alternative is to leave the funds in the parents' name. They will then control the distributions throughout the child's minority as well as during college. They might also want to use a "minor's trust." These irrevocable trusts allow the trustee to control the distribution of the funds after the child reaches 18 and they receive special gift tax treatment, provided they distribute all of the principal and accumulated income by the time the child turns 21.

Some individuals favor the 529 plan. The 529 plan allows the parents or grandparents to control the distributions indefinitely and receives special gift tax treatment. Distributions for qualified educational purposes are federal and, sometimes, state income tax free. Additionally, some states offer a state income tax deduction for contributions to their state's 529 plan.

The second critical issue to consider is college financial aid. There are many different grants, scholarships, work-study, and loan programs that are available to help college students and their families cope with the high cost of higher education. Many of these programs are based on financial need. With the ever-increasing cost of college, more and more middle and upper-middle class families are discovering that they can establish the financial need necessary to qualify for aid. For most financial aid purposes, the financial aid office will combine the income and assets of both the parents and the child when determining the family resources available.

Generally, for financial aid purposes about 5% of the parent's assets are considered available for college. However, 35% of the child's assets are considered available each year. Thus, if the parents have $10,000 in a mutual fund, $500 will be considered as a resource available for college. If the child has the same $10,000 mutual fund, $3,500 is considered as a resource. If college financial aid is a real possibility for a family, it may pay to save in the parent's name, rather than the child's.

The final critical issue is income taxes. The 1986 Tax Reform Act changed the rules for the taxation of college savings. The so-called "kiddie tax" discourages saving in a child's name if the child is under 14. For children under 14, the first $800 of unearned income is tax free. The next $800 is taxed at 10% (the child's rate). Any unearned income over $1,600 is taxed at the higher of the child's rate or his/her parent's rate. After the child turns 14, the amount over $800 is taxed at 10% up to the full extent of that bracket. For example, Jennifer is 10 and Jason is 15. They both have unearned taxable income of $5,000. Their parents are in the 25% tax bracket. The tax due on Jennifer's income is $930 ((10% x $800) + (25% x ($5,000 - $1,600). Jason's tax is $420 (10% x ($5,000 - $800). If a parent decides to invest for college in a young child's name, income taxes could be a significant drag on their return and should be considered when making investment decisions.

Financial Advisor Education Funding Analysis

Report Date...................................... **January 1, 2005**
Prepared for .... **A Valued Client**
Financial Advisor's Name .... **John Q. Planner**
Firm Name .... **Raymond James & Associates, Inc.**
Firm Address & Phone .... **St. Petersburg, FL   Phone #727-573-3800**

Child's name	Sally/Public	Sally/Private	Child3	Child4
Child's birthdate	5/16/1999	5/16/1999	1/0/1900	1/0/1900
Child's current age	5	5	0	0
Child starts college at what age?	18	18	0	0
Number of years in college	4	4	0	0
Annual college costs today**....................	$11,354	$27,516	$0	$0
Current value of education fund (if any)	$2,000	$2,000	$0	$0
Current after-tax return on investments	6.0%	6.0%	6.0%	6.0%
Assumed college cost inflation rate*	7.7%	5.0%	0.0%	0.0%
Deposits increase by what annual %?	0.0%	0.0%	0.0%	0.0%
Continue funding through college years?..	N	N	N	N

Comments .... Enter Misc. Comments Here

A Valued Client
Education Funding Summary - January 1, 2005

	Sally/Public	Sally/Private	-	-
Current age	5	5	0	0
Start school at age	18	18	0	0
Number of years in school	4	4	0	0
Annual college costs* today	$11,354	$27,516	$0	$0
Value of education fund	$2,000	$2,000	$0	$0
Current after-tax return	6.00%	6.00%	0.00%	0.00%
Assumed college cost inflation rate	7.70%	5.00%	0.00%	0.00%
Make deposits through college years	No	No		
Annual % increase in deposits	Level	Level		

Enter Misc. Comments Here

	Sally/Public	Sally/Private	-	-
Your child will enter College in	13 years	13 years		
Future first year cost	$29,782	$51,886	$0	$0
Future total cost of College	$133,607	$223,633	$0	$0

To reach your future education fund objectives, you must

Make a **one-time deposit** today of	$55,210	$93,936
OR begin making **annual** contributions of	$5,883	$10,010
OR begin making **monthly** contributions of	$497	$846

*2004-05 College Board Annual Survey of Colleges estimates annual
college costs (ie, tuition, fees and on-campus room and board) to be $27,516 for
private schools and $11,354 for public schools.

*This hypothetical report is not indicative of any security's performance and is based on
information believed reliable. Future performance cannot be guaranteed and investment
yields will fluctuate with market conditions.*

Prepared as a service by John Q. Planner
Raymond James & Associates, Inc.
St. Petersburg, FL   Phone #727-573-3800

A Valued Client
Annual Education Fund Schedule - January 1, 2005

	Sally/Public				Sally/Private		
Age	Annual Deposit	$11,354 Tuition at 7.7%	Year End Balance at 6.0%	Age	Annual Deposit	$27,516 Tuition at 5.0%	Year End Balance at 6.0%
			2,000				2,000
5	5,883	0	8,357	5	10,010	0	12,731
6	5,883	0	15,094	6	10,010	0	24,106
7	5,883	0	22,237	7	10,010	0	36,163
8	5,883	0	29,807	8	10,010	0	48,944
9	5,883	0	37,832	9	10,010	0	62,491
10	5,883	0	46,339	10	10,010	0	76,852
11	5,883	0	55,355	11	10,010	0	92,074
12	5,883	0	64,913	12	10,010	0	108,209
13	5,883	0	75,045	13	10,010	0	125,313
14	5,883	0	85,784	14	10,010	0	143,443
15	5,883	0	97,167	15	10,010	0	162,660
16	5,883	0	109,234	16	10,010	0	183,031
17	5,883	0	122,024	17	10,010	0	204,624
18	0	(29,782)	97,777	18	0	(51,886)	161,902
19	0	(32,075)	69,644	19	0	(54,480)	113,868
20	0	(34,545)	37,205	20	0	(57,204)	60,064
21	0	(37,205)	(0)	21	0	(60,064)	(0)
22	0	0	0	22	0	0	0
	0	0	0		0	0	0
	0	0	0		0	0	0
	0	0	0		0	0	0
	0	0	0		0	0	0
	0	0	0		0	0	0
	0	0	0		0	0	0
	0	0	0		0	0	0
	0	0	0		0	0	0
	0	0	0		0	0	0
	0	0	0		0	0	0
	$76,485	**($133,607)**			**$130,134**	**($223,633)**	

This hypothetical report is not indicative of any security's performance and is based on information believed reliable.
Future performance cannot be guaranteed and investment yields will fluctuate with market conditions.

Prepared as a service by John Q. Planner
Raymond James & Associates, Inc.
St. Petersburg, FL   Phone #727-573-3800

A Valued Client
Education Fund Analysis - January 1, 2005

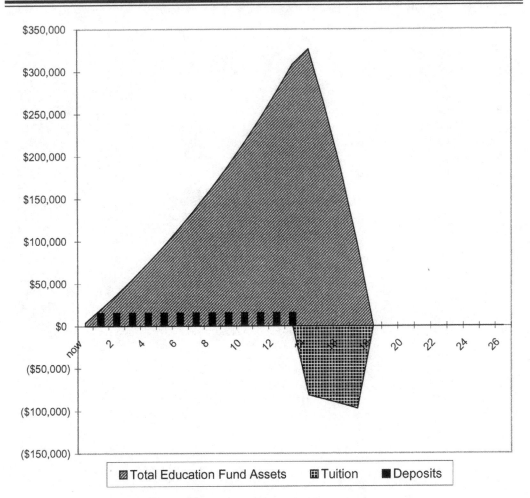

☒ Total Education Fund Assets   ⊞ Tuition   ■ Deposits

This hypothetical report is not indicative of any security's performance
and is based on information believed reliable.
Future performance cannot be guaranteed and investment yields will fluctuate with market conditions.

Prepared as a service by John Q. Planner
Raymond James & Associates, Inc.
St. Petersburg, FL   Phone #727-573-3800

THE IMPORTANCE OF INSURANCE

Financial planning represents an integrated approach to the development and implementation of plans for the achievement of individual or family financial objectives. Although financial objectives may differ in terms of individual circumstances, all integrated financial plans should include an analysis and recommendations that satisfy individual protection of wealth and income objectives.

While plans for the accumulation of wealth may be more exciting, the protection of that accumulated wealth cannot be overlooked. To find some method of protecting assets, or preserving the wealth represented by those assets, is the challenge people face, that is, the risk they face. Technically, a function of insurance is to reduce or replace uncertainty. However, insurance is more understandable if its function is stated as a reimbursement for the loss sustained. Loss is the undesirable end result of risk and is defined as the decrease or disappearance of value, usually in an unexpected or relatively unpredictable manner.

As you work toward formulating and implementing an integrated plan to meet your financial objectives, it may become apparent that the resources available to you are limited to the assets you own and your ability to produce income. In the event that either one of these resources are reduced (or disappear), your ability to meet your future financial objectives would be less than bright. However, by taking the appropriate steps to properly protect both of these "assets," you will ensure that your financial planning objectives will be met unhindered.

PROTECTING EXISTING ASSETS
It is essential that you have an adequate level of homeowner's insurance which takes into account the replacement value of your home, vacation property, furnishings, and other such assets. In addition, an adequate level of automobile insurance must be in place to protect you from a major property loss through accident or theft.

PROTECTING INCOME
A sufficient level of life insurance will allow for the replacement of a future income flow interrupted by death. Disability income insurance (most often overlooked) will provide income during a time period when the ability to earn income is not possible due to a disabling accident or illness.

PROTECTING BOTH
An acceptable level of liability insurance and health insurance prevent the eroding of your existing asset base and the potential use of earned income for unexpected emergencies.

Protecting the assets and income potential which you already possess is an essential step in preparing to meet your future financial objectives. The following pages reflect our analysis of your present insurance program, with our recommendations concerning its appropriateness.

Financial Advisor Insurance Needs Analysis

Report Date.......................................	**January 1, 2005**

Prepared for	**A Valued Client**
Financial Advisor's Name	**John Q. Planner**
Firm Name	**Raymond James & Associates, Inc.**
Firm Address & Phone	**St. Petersburg, FL Phone #813-573-3800**

Current Age of Survivor...	40
Survivor's assumed mortality age (or covered until age) .	85 Single Life Mortality=83
Years until youngest dependent is 18?	15

Monthly Living Expenses (in today's dollars)

Survivor's **monthly** living expenses-with dependents	$8,000
Survivor's **monthly** living expenses-no dependents........	$4,000
Survivor's **monthly** living expenses-in retirement	$3,000

Monthly Income Sources

Survivor's current **monthly** earned income	$3,000	
Survivor plans to retire at what age?	62	
Survivor's anticipated **monthly** pension income	$2,200	
Age at which pensions stops	70	
Monthly pension survivor benefit	$2,000	
Age at which pension survivor benefit stops	80	
Monthly Soc. Sec. benefit-with 2 dependents***	$1,865	(avg $1979)
Monthly Soc. Sec. benefit-no dependents***..................	$870	(avg $920)
Age at which normal Social Security benefits start	62	

Final Expenses

Final Expenses*	$5,000
Emergency Reserves-Usually two month's pay...............	$10,000
Lump sum needed today for education fund	$30,000
Enter Total Family Debts **...	$8,000
Estimated Estate Taxes and Probate Costs	

Current Liquid Assets

Current Liquid Assets Available	$200,000
Personally Owned Life Insurance on Deceased..............	
Existing Group Life Insurance on Deceased....................	$75,000
Retirement Plan Death Benefit	

Rates of Growth and Inflation

Estimated after-tax annual rate of return	6.0%
Estimated annual rate of inflation	3.0%
Estimated C.O.L.A. for Social Security benefits	1.6%

* Use $5,000 if your net worth, including real estate, is
  between $20-200,000, and $10,000 if it exceeds $200,000.

** If mortgage is included in total debt, do not include mortgage
   payment in estimated monthly living expense.

***The Social Security Online Website states that the 2005 Average Monthy SS Benefits
for a widowed mother and two children is $1979 and an aged widow(er) alone is $920.

A Valued Client
Insurance Needs Analysis - January 1, 2005

	With Children	Pre Retirement	Age 62 & After
Number of Years	15	7	23
Income Desired	8,000	4,000	3,000
Social Security	(1,865)	0	(870)
Earned Income or Pension	(3,000)	(3,000)	(2,200)
Pension Survivor Benefit	(2,000)	(2,000)	(2,000)
Monthly Shortage (Excess)	1,135	(1,000)	(2,070)
Capital Required (Excess)*	$241,035	($9,075)	$142,005

Total Capital Required for Income Shortage   **$373,966**

Plus Immediate Capital Requirements:

Final Expenses	5,000
Emergency Reserves	10,000
Education Fund	30,000
Debts	8,000
Taxes & Probate	0
Total	53,000

Total Death Capital Required   **$426,966**

Less:	Present Assets Available	200,000
	Existing Personal Life Insurance	0
	Group Life Insurance on Deceased	75,000
	Retirement Plan Death Benefit	0
	Total	275,000

Shortage to be Provided by Personal Life Insurance $151,966

* Assuming After Tax Return of 6.0% and Annual Inflation of 3.0%
Mortality age is assumed to be 85.
Social Security retirement benefits are assumed to begin at age 62.

This hypothetical report is not indicative of any security's performance and is based on information believed reliable.
Future performance cannot be guaranteed and investment yields will fluctuate with market conditions.

Prepared as a service by John Q. Planner
Raymond James & Associates, Inc.
St. Petersburg, FL   Phone #813-573-3800

A Valued Client
Insurance Needs Analysis - January 1, 2005

This hypothetical report is not indicative of any security's performance and is based on information believed reliable.
Future performance cannot be guaranteed and investment yields will fluctuate with market conditions.

Age	Social Security	Earned Income	Pension	Total Income	Living Expense	Excess (Need)	Capital Bal at 6.00% ret

Total Death Capital Required $426,966
Less immediate expenses at death .... (53,000)
Total capital required to provide future income stream 373,966

Age	Social Security	Earned Income	Pension	Total Income	Living Expense	Excess (Need)	Capital Bal at 6.00% ret
40	22,380	36,000	24,000	82,380	96,000	(13,620)	381,967
41	22,738	37,080	24,000	83,818	98,880	(15,062)	388,919
42	23,102	38,192	24,000	85,294	101,846	(16,552)	394,709
43	23,472	39,338	24,000	86,810	104,902	(18,092)	399,214
44	23,847	40,518	24,000	88,365	108,049	(19,683)	402,302
45	24,229	41,734	24,000	89,962	111,290	(21,328)	403,833
46	24,616	42,986	24,000	91,602	114,629	(23,027)	403,654
47	25,010	44,275	24,000	93,286	118,068	(24,782)	401,604
48	25,410	45,604	24,000	95,014	121,610	(26,596)	397,509
49	25,817	46,972	24,000	96,789	125,258	(28,470)	391,182
50	26,230	48,381	24,000	98,611	129,016	(30,405)	382,423
51	26,650	49,832	24,000	100,482	132,886	(32,404)	371,020
52	27,076	51,327	24,000	102,403	136,873	(34,470)	356,743
53	27,509	52,867	24,000	104,376	140,979	(36,603)	339,349
54	27,949	54,453	24,000	106,403	145,209	(38,806)	318,575
55	0	56,087	24,000	80,087	74,782	5,304	343,313
56	0	57,769	24,000	81,769	77,026	4,744	368,940
57	0	59,503	24,000	83,503	79,337	4,166	395,492
58	0	61,288	24,000	85,288	81,717	3,571	423,006
59	0	63,126	24,000	87,126	84,168	2,958	451,522
60	0	65,020	24,000	89,020	86,693	2,327	481,080
61	0	66,971	24,000	90,971	89,294	1,676	511,721
62	14,803	0	50,400	65,203	68,980	(3,776)	538,422
63	15,040	0	50,400	65,440	71,049	(5,609)	564,782
64	15,281	0	50,400	65,681	73,181	(7,500)	590,719
65	15,525	0	50,400	65,925	75,376	(9,451)	616,145
66	15,774	0	50,400	66,174	77,637	(11,463)	640,962
67	16,026	0	50,400	66,426	79,966	(13,540)	665,067
68	16,283	0	50,400	66,683	82,365	(15,683)	688,347
69	16,543	0	50,400	66,943	84,836	(17,893)	710,681
70	16,808	0	50,400	67,208	87,381	(20,174)	731,938
71	17,077	0	24,000	41,077	90,003	(48,926)	723,993
72	17,350	0	24,000	41,350	92,703	(51,353)	712,998
73	17,628	0	24,000	41,628	95,484	(53,856)	698,690
74	17,910	0	24,000	41,910	98,349	(56,439)	680,786
75	18,196	0	24,000	42,196	101,299	(59,103)	658,985
76	18,487	0	24,000	42,487	104,338	(61,851)	632,962
77	18,783	0	24,000	42,783	107,468	(64,685)	602,373

A Valued Client
Insurance Needs Analysis - January 1, 2005

This hypothetical report is not indicative of any security's performance and is based on information believed reliable.
Future performance cannot be guaranteed and investment yields will fluctuate with market conditions.

Age	Social Security	Earned Income	Pension	Total Income	Living Expense	Excess (Need)	Capital Bal at 6.00% ret
78	19,084	0	24,000	43,084	110,692	(67,609)	566,851
79	19,389	0	24,000	43,389	114,013	(70,624)	526,000
80	19,699	0	24,000	43,699	117,433	(73,734)	479,402
81	20,014	0	0	20,014	120,956	(100,942)	401,168
82	20,335	0	0	20,335	124,585	(104,250)	314,732
83	20,660	0	0	20,660	128,323	(107,663)	219,494
84	20,991	0	0	20,991	132,172	(111,182)	114,811
85	21,326	0	0	21,326	136,137	(114,811)	(0)
0	0	0	0	0	0	0	(0)
0	0	0	0	0	0	0	(0)
0	0	0	0	0	0	0	(0)
0	0	0	0	0	0	0	(0)
0	0	0	0	0	0	0	(0)
0	0	0	0	0	0	0	(0)
0	0	0	0	0	0	0	(0)
0	0	0	0	0	0	0	(0)
0	0	0	0	0	0	0	(0)
0	0	0	0	0	0	0	(0)
0	0	0	0	0	0	0	(0)
0	0	0	0	0	0	0	(0)
0	0	0	0	0	0	0	(0)
0	0	0	0	0	0	0	(0)
0	0	0	0	0	0	0	(0)
0	0	0	0	0	0	0	(0)
0	0	0	0	0	0	0	(0)
0	0	0	0	0	0	0	(0)
0	0	0	0	0	0	0	(0)
0	0	0	0	0	0	0	(0)
0	0	0	0	0	0	0	(0)
0	0	0	0	0	0	0	(0)
0	0	0	0	0	0	0	(0)
0	0	0	0	0	0	0	(0)
0	0	0	0	0	0	0	(0)
0	0	0	0	0	0	0	(0)
0	0	0	0	0	0	0	(0)
0	0	0	0	0	0	0	(0)

MONTHLY DISABILITY ANALYSIS

What is your most valuable asset? For most people, it is not their home, car, business, or retirement plan. Their most valuable asset is their ability to earn a living. In spite of the enormous value of your ability to get up every morning and go to work and in spite of the fact that you are far more likely to be disabled than die during your peak working years, most people are not adequately protected for this risk. The disability risk can be simply stated. It is the risk that your ability to earn a living will stop, but your bills and other financial obligations will not.

To quantify this risk, begin with the income you will require in the event of a total disability. Start your calculation by examining your current living expenses. Exclude from living expenses income taxes, debt payments, and regular savings for retirement or some other financial goal. Add to your current monthly income an amount that approximates the additional expenses you believe you might have to pay if you were disabled. Consider items such as additional medical expenses, rehabilitation therapy, and the like.

Next, deduct those expenses that would be eliminated by a disability. For example, if you become totally disabled your commuting expenses, work clothing expenses, and vacation expenses would probably go down. Next, add in your monthly debt payments for your mortgage loan, car loan, consumer loans, existing credit card balances, etc. Finally, you may wish to consider including an additional amount for the savings that will be needed to fund your retirement and/or your children's education. The net result of these calculations is the income you will need during a period of disability.

Next, calculate the income sources you will have during disability. Consider employer-provided benefits such as salary continuation payments, disability insurance benefits, and/or other benefits provided to their employees. You may also already own a policy of disability insurance that should be factored into your calculation. You should also consider the earnings of your spouse. If your spouse does not currently work outside of the home, estimate the likelihood of the being able to work, the time it will take for them to secure employment, and the earnings they might expect when employed.

You may also be entitled to government sponsored disability payments. You may be entitled to payments under a state sponsored worker's compensation program. However, these benefits are available only if your disability is work-related and the amount of the benefit varies greatly from state to state. Social security disability benefits may also be available. Unfortunately, the criteria to qualify for these benefits is extremely restrictive. In fact, about 70% of all claims for benefits are denied. The final potential resource to consider in the event of disability is your investment income from interest, dividends, rents, and similar sources.

The difference between your income need and the resources available to you in the event of disability is the financial risk that you face in the event of a disabling illness or injury.

Financial Advisor Disability Needs Calculator

Report Date... **January 1, 2005**
Prepared for .... **A Valued Client**
Financial Advisor's Name .... **John Q. Planner**
Firm Name .... **Raymond James & Associates, Inc.**
Firm Address & Phone .... **St. Petersburg, FL   Phone #813-573-3800**

Client's Current Age...	42
Estimated **ANNUAL** Return on Investments	7.0%
Estimated **ANNUAL** Rate of Inflation	3.0%
Effective Tax Rate	25.0%
Assume Disability occurs in what Mo/Year..............	9/2004
Current **MONTHLY** Living Expenses if disabled	
(other than taxes & debt service).........................	2,700
MONTHLY Debt Service	925
MONTHLY College Funding	325
MONTHLY Retirement Savings	275
TOTAL INCOME NEEDED	**$4,225**
Anticipated **MONTHLY** Employee Benefits	
(Salary Cont, Sick Pay, Accrued Vacation, etc).......	$3,500 /mo
Month/ Year Payments Begin 10/2004	
Month/ Year Payments End 3/2005	
Anticipated **MONTHLY** Group Disability Benefit	$2,350 /mo
Month/ Year Payments Begin 4/2005	
Month/ Year Payments End 4/2008	
MONTHLY Individual Disability Income	$0 /mo
Month/ Year Payments Begin 1/1900	
Month/ Year Payments End 1/1900	
Taxable? Y/N N	
Other **MONTHLY** Income (Spouse's Salary, etc)....	$2,200 /mo
Month/ Year Payments Begin 10/2004	
Month/ Year Payments End 10/2029	
MONTHLY Investment Income	$100 /mo
Taxable? Y/N Y	
Anticipated **MONTHLY** Social Security Disability....	$0 /mo
Taxable? Y/N Y	

A Valued Client

Disability Needs Analysis Summary- January 1, 2005

	0-6 Mos.	6-12 Mos	Year 2	Year 3	Year 4	Year 5
From	Sep-04	Mar-05	Sep-05	Sep-06	Sep-07	Sep-08
Until	Mar-05	Sep-05	Sep-06	Sep-07	Sep-08	Sep-09
Income Needed	**$25,509**	**$25,894**	**$52,966**	**$54,577**	**$56,237**	**$57,948**
Employee Ben.	13,125	0	0	0	0	0
Grp Disability	0	8,813	21,150	21,150	12,338	0
Individual DI	0	0	0	0	0	0
Other Income	8,333	10,138	20,737	21,368	22,017	22,687
Investment Inc.	459	476	1,002	1,075	1,153	1,236
SS Disab Income	0	0	0	0	0	0
Total Cash Flow	**$21,917**	**$19,426**	**$42,889**	**$43,592**	**$35,508**	**$23,923**
Disability Income Surplus (Need)	**($3,592)**	**($6,468)**	**($10,077)**	**($10,985)**	**($20,730)**	**($34,025)**

ASSUMPTIONS:
- Disability is assumed to occur in September 2004
- Employee benefits are assumed to be taxable.
- Disability benefits are assumed to be tax exempt.
- Other Income is adjusted for inflation and assumed to be taxable.
- Social Security Disability Income projected COLA adjusted at 85% of current inflation rate. Payments are assumed to begin after five months.

This hypothetical report is not indicative of any security's performance and is based on information believed reliable. Future performance cannot be guaranteed and investment yields will fluctuate with market conditions.

Prepared as a service by John Q. Planner
Raymond James & Associates, Inc.
St. Petersburg, FL   Phone #813-573-3800

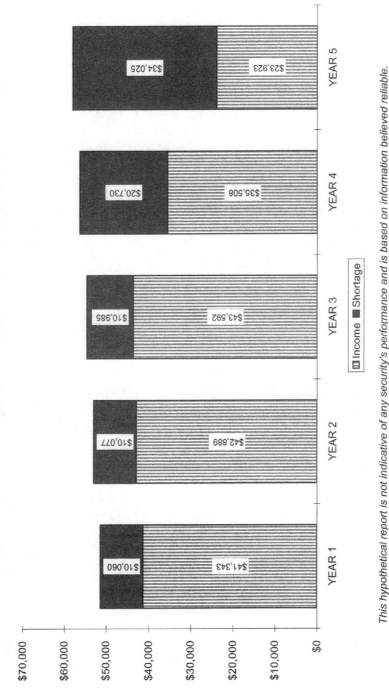

A Valued Client
Disability Needs Analysis - January 1, 2005

Income ▤　Shortage ■

	YEAR 1	YEAR 2	YEAR 3	YEAR 4	YEAR 5
Shortage	$10,060	$10,077	$10,985	$20,730	$34,025
Income	$41,343	$42,889	$43,592	$35,508	$23,923

This hypothetical report is not indicative of any security's performance and is based on information believed reliable.
Future performance cannot be guaranteed and investment yields will fluctuate with market conditions.

Prepared as a service by John Q. Planner
Raymond James & Associates, Inc.
St. Petersburg, FL   Phone #813-573-3800

ASSET ALLOCATION - HOW AND WHY

A close examination of the vast majority of extraordinarily wealthy people reveals that they have violated one of the basic rules of good investing: diversification. Would Sam Walton have been as wealthy as he was if he diversified out of Wal-Mart? A great many wealthy people became wealthy because they owned one stock or piece of real estate that skyrocketed in value. Often, they were among the people that built the company. Other times, they had heredity on their side. In any case, they are wealthy, in part, because they did not diversify. However, lack of diversification may also be the quickest way to the poor house. Betting the ranch on one company or one anything gives about the same chance of success as the average lottery player - not very good odds.

Warren Buffet, billionaire investor and prairie wit, has two rules of investing:

Rule #1	Never lose
Rule #2	Never forget Rule #1

Mr. Buffet made his billions by diversifying his investments. Diversification means more than just owning more than one stock or more than one bond. It also means owning more than one type of asset. The diversification among different types of assets - stocks, bonds, cash, real estate, etc. - is the essence of asset allocation.

There are many different ways to approach the asset allocation process. Tactical asset allocation involves quickly moving significant portions of your portfolio rapidly between asset classes in an effort to capitalize on short-term differences in relative valuation or in response to expected short-term economic trends. The tactical asset allocator relies almost exclusively on being in the right asset at the right time in order to profit. Tactical asset allocators don't really care, for example, what stocks they own as long as they are invested in stocks when they think the stock market will rise. Tactical asset allocators tend to invest in a broad "basket" of stocks or bonds, often assembling a basket to resemble a widely followed index like the S&P 500. Tactical asset allocation is most effectively practiced by a few large professional money managers with sophisticated knowledge and computer equipment. It is not an asset allocation method suited for most individual investors acting on their own. Of course, if an individual believes in the benefits of tactical asset allocation, and some of the professionals have been quite successful, he or she can hire one of the well-known professionals to manage their account.

Another method of asset allocation might be termed strategic asset allocation. Under this methodology, the original asset allocation is made based on some combination of investor goals, investor "time horizon" (or how long it will be before they need the money they are investing) and the current long-term economic outlook. The asset allocation "model" may change from time to time based on changes in the investor's financial situation and /or changes in economic conditions. In any case, the changes to the model tend to be gradual and relatively small. The investor should review his or her portfolio periodically and adjust as needed. These reviews are generally done quarterly, but should be done, at a minimum, annually. For example, consider a hypothetical strategic asset allocation that places 50% of assets in stocks, 40% in bonds and 10% in cash. Upon review of current economic conditions, the investor decides conditions are right for a bull market in stocks. Therefore, the investor shifts his allocation to 60% stocks by reducing the commitment to bonds and cash by 5% each. Strategic asset allocation allows the investor to respond to changing economic conditions and changes in his or her own situation without making a big bet on timing the market.

The final general method of asset allocation is to use a "fixed allocation." Using this method, the investor makes the initial asset allocation and stays with it. Using a fixed allocation does not mean, however, that you merely allocate and then forget. On the contrary, a fixed allocation also requires periodic fine-tuning. Investors who use a fixed asset allocation review their portfolio and then adjust their holdings to return the portfolio to the original balance. For example, assume another very simple, hypothetical asset allocation of 50% stocks and 50% bonds. At the end of the period, say one year, the stock portion represents 60% of the portfolio and bonds total 40%. The fixed asset allocator sells enough stocks to reduce the stock component to 50% and uses the sales proceeds to buy bonds. The fixed asset allocation method forces an investor to sell assets that have performed well (taking profits) while simultaneously buying assets that are relatively "cheap" (lowering the average cost of each investment). Fixed asset allocators will never hit investment "home runs." On the other hand, they attempt to avoid strike outs and hope to hit lots of doubles and singles and over time get into the Hall of Fame. Fixed allocations might also change as the investor's goals and life circumstances change.

Deciding on the initial asset allocation can be a tricky proposition. Having professional help to make the decision is important. The decision-making process begins by stating a goal or objective for the investment. For example, are you investing this money because you are going to retire in twenty years or because you have just retired and need inflation-resistant income? Your time horizon will be a critical factor in deciding your asset allocation. The longer you have to invest, the more you can invest in assets, like stocks, that have historically provided the best long-term returns, but may suffer more short-term volatility. Most people, particularly retired people underestimate their time horizon. Retired people in their sixties will probably live well into their eighties and beyond. Over such long periods of time, inflation is far more insidious than the short-term swings in the stock market.

Your "risk tolerance" is another factor to consider when allocating assets. Theoretically, risk tolerance is basically a function of your time horizon. In other words, the longer you have to invest the more risk you can tolerate. Nice theory, but theories don't own stocks and bonds, people do. And people sometimes don't feel comfortable being exposed to as much short-term up and (particularly) down swings in the market. Investor psychology is an important component in allocating assets. You should take your emotional as well as theoretical risk tolerance into account when allocating assets.

The final component in the asset allocation process is to decide which types of assets will be included. Basically, there are only two ways to make an investment:

loan it or own it. "Loanership" assets are generally thought of to be less risky than "ownership" assets. Loan assets tend to pay a fixed rate of return and provide a promise that your investment will be returned at some point in the future. They provide certain returns if held to maturity but little or no hedge against inflation. Loanership assets include U.S. Treasury securities, corporate bonds, municipal bonds, certificates of deposit, foreign bonds and fixed annuities. Obviously, some types of loan assets have more risk than others. Low grade corporate bonds (so-called junk bonds) generally have more risk than a high quality municipal. Even within an asset type, for example U.S. government bonds, some loan assets have more risk than others. Long-term government bonds are subject to much more volatility due to interest rate changes than are short-term government bonds.

Ownership assets give you the right to share in the growth of the value of the asset whether it is a corporation or piece of real estate. Ownership assets do not provide a certain return, although past performance does not guarantee future results, over time investors have been generally rewarded for the additional risk they take with a higher return. Having at least some ownership assets in your portfolio is an alternative to potentially beat inflation over the long run. Typical examples of ownership assets include U.S. common stocks, foreign stocks (please note that international investing involves special risks, including currency fluctuations, different financial accounting standards, and possible political and economic volatility), real estate and tangibles. Like loan assets, the different types of ownership assets have different levels of risk. For example, common stock of a large "blue chip" U.S. company is generally considered less risky than a stock in a small company from Chile.

Just as "man does not live by bread alone," investors cannot prosper in one type of investment. Balance is an essential component of a healthy lifestyle. It is also an essential component of a healthy investment portfolio. Asset allocation is the road to achieve that balance.

ALTERNATIVE MINIMUM TAX

The Alternative Minimum Tax (AMT) was created by Congress to help insure that taxpayers, both individual and corporate, who enjoy economic income do not escape taxation through "over-use" of tax benefits provided under the regular tax system. The AMT is actually a separate, parallel tax system. The apparent complexity of the AMT may concern many taxpayers. Fortunately, the AMT applies to only a tiny fraction of all taxpayers.

The basic formula for the AMT is fairly straight-forward. The computation begins with "taxable income" as it is computed under the regular tax system. This figure is then either increased or decreased, depending on circumstances, by AMT "adjustments". Next, AMT "preferences" are added. Then, the AMT "exemption" is subtracted. The result of these computations is Alternative Minimum Taxable Income or AMTI. Now, multiply AMTI by 26% if your AMTI is under $175,000 and 28% for AMTI over $175,000 to arrive at the AMT. Finally, after deducting certain credits, compare the AMT to the tax computed under the regular tax system. The taxpayer is liable for the larger of the two taxes.

One of the confusing areas of the AMT is the exemption amount. If you are married filing joint returns, or are a surviving spouse, your exemption amount will be $58,000 for 2004 ($45,000 after 2004). When your alternative minimum taxable income (AMTI) exceeds $150,000, however, your exemption amount will begin to phase out 25 cents on the dollar of AMTI in excess of $150,000. Thus, you will be entitled to no exemption for the taxable year if your AMTI equals or exceeds $346,000. For single taxpayers and unmarried heads-of-household, the annual exemption amount is $40,250 for 2004 ($33,750 after 2004). Again, a phase-out of 25 cents on the dollar applies. In this case, the phase-out begins at $112,500 of AMTI, resulting in the exemption being fully phased out at $255,500. Thus, taxpayers with large amounts of taxable income may not be shielded from AMT by an exemption amount.

Adjustments can either increase or decrease AMTI. Some of the more common adjustments that individuals have to deal with include the absence of a standard deduction and state income tax refunds are not taxable. There are no itemized deductions for state and local taxes, personal interest and miscellaneous deductions subject to the 2% floor. Also, the medical expense deduction floor is raised to 10% of AGI from 7.5%. Unlike adjustments, tax preference items can only increase AMTI. The more common preference items that effect individuals include the spread between the option price and the exercise price for "incentive stock options" which is called the bargain element. Also, interest on "private activity" municipal bonds are included in AMTI but are normally exempt from regular tax. This type of bond is often referred to as an "AMT" bond for this reason.

A feature added to the AMT by the 1986 Tax Reform Act is the "alternative minimum tax credit." Under the provision, a taxpayer will be entitled in a future year to a credit for any AMT paid in a previous year. The credit, which is available against regular tax, can only be used to the extent that the regular tax for the taxable year exceeds the taxpayer's AMT for that year.

Other complex special rules apply and various elections may prove helpful in minimizing your potential exposure to AMT. If you think that you might be subject to the AMT and wish to explore ways in which this liability can be minimized or avoided, your financial planner is ready to help.

	% of Portfolio	% of Total	Historical Total* Return%	Total* Return$	Amount to Invest
Hypothetical Portfolio Size:		**$750,000**			
Cash Reserves	**10.0%**		**5.00%**	**$3,750**	**$75,000**
0					
Fixed Income /Debt	**30.0%**		**8.05%**	**$18,113**	**$225,000**
Government Bonds		25.0%	9.00%	5,063	56,250
Corporate Bonds		25.0%	9.45%	5,316	56,250
Municipal Bonds		25.0%	6.50%	3,656	56,250
Annuities		25.0%	7.25%	4,078	56,250
		0.0%	0.00%	0	0
		0.0%	0.00%	0	0
Equity/Growth	**50.0%**		**10.00%**	**$37,500**	**$375,000**
Capital Growth		30.0%	12.00%	13,500	112,500
Growth/Income		40.0%	10.00%	15,000	150,000
Hedged/Defensive		30.0%	8.00%	9,000	112,500
		0.0%	0.00%	0	0
		0.0%	0.00%	0	0
		0.0%	0.00%	0	0
Real Estate & Tangibles	**10.0%**		**6.50%**	**$4,875**	**$75,000**
Real Estate		50.0%	7.00%	2,625	37,500
Leasing		50.0%	6.00%	2,250	37,500
Precious Metals		0.0%	0.00%	0	0
Misc (Oil & Gas, CATV, Etc)		0.0%	0.00%	0	0
		0.0%	0.00%	0	0
Hypothetical Totals			**8.57%**	**$64,238**	**$750,000**

*Total Return includes all income, dividends & capital appreciation.

This hypothetical report is not indicative of any security's performance.
Future performance cannot be guaranteed and investment yields will fluctuate with market conditions.

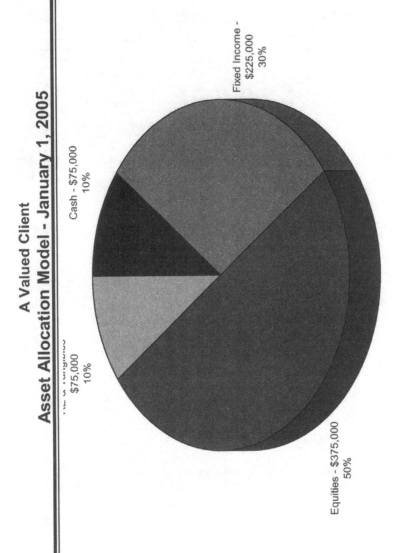

A Valued Client
Asset Allocation Model - January 1, 2005

Cash - $75,000
10%

Fixed Income -
$225,000
30%

$75,000
10%

Equities - $375,000
50%

This hypothetical report is not indicative of any security's performance and is based on information believed reliable. Future performance cannot be guaranteed and investment yields will fluctuate with market conditions.

**Prepared as a service by John Q. Planner
Raymond James & Associates, Inc.
St. Petersburg, FL   Phone #813-573-3800**

Financial Advisor Asset Diversification Analysis - Input Data

Report Date.. **January 1, 2005**
Prepared for .... **A Valued Client**
Financial Advisor's Name .... **John Q. Planner**
Firm Name .... **Raymond James & Associates, Inc.**
Firm Address & Phone .... **St. Petersburg, FL   Phone #813-573-3800**
Marginal Tax Bracket **28%**

Asset Category	Liquid	Codes AA	Tax	CURRENT Present Value	CURRENT Total Return*	TARGET Present Value	TARGET Hypothetical Return*
Cash	Y	C	Y	5,000	3.50%	5,000	3.50%
Money Mkt-Taxable	Y	C	Y		6.40%		6.40%
Money Mkt-Taxfree	Y	C	N		4.50%	52,900	4.50%
Savings	Y	C	Y		5.00%		5.00%
Cert. of Deposit	Y	C	Y	30,000	7.00%	30,000	7.00%
Ins. Cash Value	Y	C	N				
Annuities	S	D	D	25,000	8.00%	50,000	8.00%
Stocks, growth	Y	E	Y	100,000	17.00%	100,000	12.00%
Stocks, income	Y	E	Y		7.00%		7.00%
Bonds -- Taxable	Y	D	Y		10.00%		10.00%
Bonds -- Taxfree	Y	D	N		8.40%		8.40%
Mut Funds-growth	Y	E	Y		15.75%	20,000	12.00%
Mut Funds, income	Y	D	Y	20,000	8.90%	30,000	10.69%
Collectibles	N	R	Y		5.00%		5.00%
IRA-Debt	S	D	Q	325,000	8.50%	100,000	8.50%
IRA Equity	S	E	Q	150,000	10.00%	400,000	10.00%
Tax Shelters/Credit	N	R	N				
Real Estate	N	R	N	400,000	5.00%	87,100	12.00%
Personal Property	Y	X	N	87,500		87,500	
Residence-Net	Y	X	N	184,800		184,800	
Prof $$ Mgr-Equity	Y	E	Y			90,000	12.00%
Prof $$ Mgr-Debt	Y	D	Y			90,000	12.00%
Other	Y	E	Y				
Other	Y	E	Y				
Other	Y	E	Y				
Other	Y	E	Y				
Other	Y	E	Y				
Other	Y	E	Y				
Other	Y	E	Y				
Other	Y	E	Y				
Other	Y	E	Y				
Other	Y	E	Y				
Other	Y	E	Y				
Other	Y	E	Y				
Other	Y	E	Y				
TOTALS				**$1,327,301**		**$1,327,300**	

A Valued Client
Asset Diversification Analysis - January 1, 2005

Liquidity:

	Current		Target/Hypothetical	
Liquid	$427,300	32.2%	$690,200	52.0%
Semi Liquid	$500,000	37.7%	$550,000	41.4%
Non Liquid	$400,000	30.1%	$87,100	6.6%

Diversification:

	Current		Target/Hypothetical	
Cash	$35,000	3.3%	$87,900	8.3%
Debt	$370,000	35.1%	$270,000	25.6%
Equities	$250,000	23.7%	$610,000	57.8%
RE & Tangibles	$400,000	37.9%	$87,100	8.3%
Misc.	$272,300	NA	$272,300	NA

Tax Status:

	Current		Target/Hypothetical	
Taxable	$155,000	11.7%	$365,000	27.5%
Taxfree	$672,300	50.7%	$412,300	31.1%
Non-Qual Deferred	$25,000	1.9%	$50,000	3.8%
Qualified Deferred	$475,000	35.8%	$500,000	37.7%

This hypothetical report is not indicative of any security's performance and is based on information believed reliable.
Future performance cannot be guaranteed and investment yields will fluctuate with market conditions.

Prepared as a service by John Q. Planner
Raymond James & Associates, Inc.
St. Petersburg, FL   Phone #813-573-3800

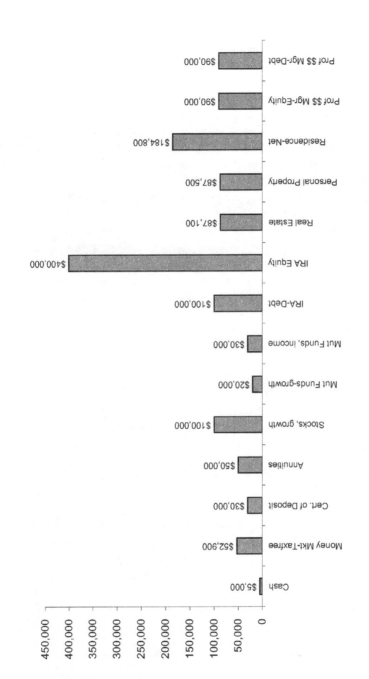

A Valued Client

Target Portfolio Allocation - January 1, 2005

Cash	$5,000
Money Mkt-Taxfree	$52,900
Cert. of Deposit	$30,000
Annuities	$50,000
Stocks, growth	$100,000
Mut Funds-growth	$20,000
Mut Funds, income	$30,000
IRA-Debt	$100,000
IRA Equity	$400,000
Real Estate	$87,100
Personal Property	$87,500
Residence-Net	$184,800
Prof $$ Mgr-Equity	$90,000
Prof $$ Mgr-Debt	$90,000

This hypothetical report is not indicative of any security's performance and is based on information believed reliable. Future performance cannot be guaranteed and investment yields will fluctuate with market conditions.

**Prepared as a service by John Q. Planner
Raymond James & Associates, Inc.
St. Petersburg, FL   Phone #813-573-3800**

Financial Advisor 2004 Federal Income Tax Analysis

Report Date...................................... **January 1, 2005**
Prepared for .... **A Valued Client**
Financial Advisor's Name .... **John Q. Planner**
Firm Name .... **Raymond James & Associates, Inc.**
Firm Address & Phone .... **St. Petersburg, FL   Phone #727-573-3800**
Same Year Planning (**Y/N)..............   Y

0.0%

**Input Same Year Tax Planning Report Labels Here....................	2004	Label 1	Label 2
Personal Information	2004	2004	2004
Filing Stat (**S**=Single, **J**=Jt, **H**=HOH)	J	J	J
# of Personal Exemptions	2	2	2
# of Deduc. for Over 65, Blind,Etc.	0	0	0
Gross Taxable Income	2004	2004	2004
Client's Total Gross Wages & Salaries	100,000	100,000	100,000
Client's contributions to employer retirement plans	10,500	10,500	10,500
Spouse's Total Gross Wages & Salaries	45,000	45,000	45,000
Spouse's contributions to employer retirement plans	4,000	4,000	4,000
Client's Self Employment Income	0	0	0
Spouse's Self Employment Income	0	0	0
Taxable Interest & Non-Qualified Dividend Income	3,000	3,000	3,000
Qualified Dividend Income	2,500	2,500	2,500
Net Long Term Capital Gain (Loss)	5,000	5,000	5,000
Net Short Term Capital Gain (Loss)	(5,000)	(5,000)	(5,000)
Taxable IRA, Pension or Annuity Distributions	0	,0	0
Total Social Security Benefits	0	0	0
Miscellaneous Income	0	0	0
Tax Free Income	2004	2004	2004
Tax Exempt Interest Income	0	0	0
Tax Free Insurance CSV Borrowings	0	0	0
Annuity Return of Principal	0	0	0
Tax Sheltered Cash Flow	0	0	0
Other Tax Free Income	0	0	0
Adjustments to Income	2004	2004	2004
Total AMT Adjustments & Pref. Items	0	0	0
Deductible IRA, Keogh & SEP Contrib.	3,000	3,000	3,000
Other	0	0	0
Deductions	2004	2004	2004
Medical Expenses **	0	0	0
State & Local Property Taxes	4,500	4,500	4,500
State & Local Income Taxes or State Sales Tax	3,000	3,000	3,000
Mortgage Interest Paid	12,400	12,400	12,400
Investment Interest **	0	0	0
Charitable Contributions	2,000	2,000	2,000
Business/Misc. 2% Deductions**	0	0	0
** Allowable amount will be calculated based on limitation rules, etc.			
Credits	2004	2004	2004
Miscellaneous Tax Credits	0	0	0

A Valued Client

2004 Federal Income Tax - January 1, 2005

Taxable Income	**$104,900**

Total Income to 15.0% bracket	$102,400
Less Income in 25.0% bracket	$58,100
Less Net Capital Gains & Qualified Dividend Income	$2,500
Non Capital Gain or Qualified Dividend Income	$102,400

25.0% Bracket base tax		$8,000	
Plus 25.0% tax on amount over threshold:			
	$102,400		
Threshold	($58,100)		
	$44,300 * 25.0%	$11,075	
Tax on Non Capital Gain or Qualified Dividend Income			**$19,075**

Taxable Long Term Capital Gains & Qualified Dividend Income	$2,500	
Long Term Capital Gains & Qualified Dividend Income subjected to 5% tax	0	0
Long Term Capital Gains & Qualified Dividend Income subjected to 15% tax	2,500	375
Tax on Long Term Capital Gains & Qualified Dividend Income		**$375**

Total 2004 Regular Federal Income Tax	**$19,450**

2004 Joint Tax Table				
	Threshold		Base	Bracket
	$0		$0	10.0%
	$14,300		$1,430	15.0%
	$58,100		$8,000	25.0%
	$117,250		$22,788	28.0%
	$178,650		$39,980	33.0%
	$319,100		$86,328	35.0%

This schedule is an approximation intended for planning purposes only.
It is not a substitute for your tax return. Please review with your tax advisor.

Prepared as a service by John Q. Planner
Raymond James & Associates, Inc.
St. Petersburg, FL   Phone #727-573-3800

A Valued Client
2004 Federal Income Tax Analysis - January 1, 2005

	'04 Gross	2004	Label 1	Label 2
Total Gross Wages and Salaries	145,000	145,000	145,000	145,000
Total Contributions to Retirement Plans	(14,500)	(14,500)	(14,500)	(14,500)
Taxable Interest and Non-Qualified Dividend Income	3,000	3,000	3,000	3,000
Qualified Dividend Income	2,500	2,500	2,500	2,500
Net Long Term Capital Gain (Loss)	5,000	0	0	0
Net Short Term Gain (Loss)	(5,000)	0	0	0
GROSS TAXABLE INCOME		**$136,000**	**$136,000**	**$136,000**
Adjustments to Income:				
Deductible IRA, Keogh & SEP Contribs.		(3,000)	(3,000)	(3,000)
ADJUSTED GROSS INCOME (AGI)		**$133,000**	**$133,000**	**$133,000**
Itemized Deductions:				
State and Local Taxes	7,500	7,500	7,500	7,500
Mortgage Interest Paid	12,400	12,400	12,400	12,400
Charitable Contributions	2,000	2,000	2,000	2,000
Total Allowable Itemized Deductions		21,900	21,900	21,900
Total Deductions		21,900	21,900	21,900
Personal Exemptions		6,200	6,200	6,200
TAXABLE INCOME		**$104,900**	**$104,900**	**$104,900**
		0	0	0
TOTAL INCOME		**$150,500**	**$150,500**	**$150,500**
Estimated Regular Federal Income Tax		19,450	19,450	19,450
Estimated FICA Taxes		10,342	10,342	10,342
Estimated State and Local Income Taxes or State Sales Tax		3,000	3,000	3,000
TOTAL TAXES ON INCOME		**$32,792**	**$32,792**	**$32,792**
Federal Marginal Tax Bracket		25.0%	25.0%	25.0%
Combined State & Federal Effective Tax Rate		22.0%	22.0%	22.0%
NET INCOME AFTER TAXES		**$117,708**	**$117,708**	**$117,708**
Contributions to Retirement Plans		17,500	17,500	17,500
NET SPENDABLE INCOME AFTER TAXES		**$100,208**	**$100,208**	**$100,208**

This schedule is an approximation intended for planning purposes only.
It is not a substitute for your tax return. Please review with your tax advisor.
Prepared as a service by John Q. Planner
Raymond James & Associates, Inc.
St. Petersburg, FL   Phone #727-573-3800

A Valued Client

2004 Federal Income Tax Analysis - January 1, 2005

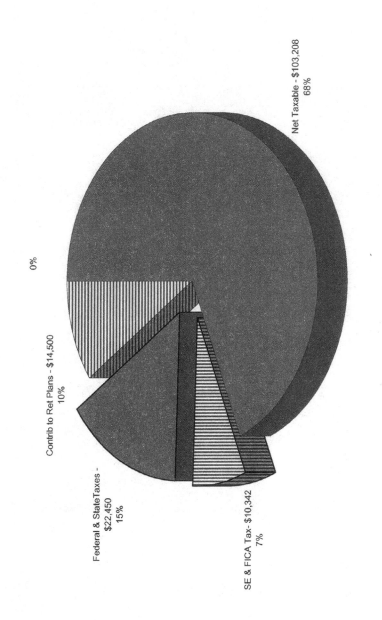

Net Taxable - $103,208
68%

0%

Contrib to Ret Plans - $14,500
10%

Federal & State Taxes -
$22,450
15%

SE & FICA Tax - $10,342
7%

Prepared as a service by John Q. Planner
Raymond James & Associates, Inc.
St. Petersburg, FL   Phone #727-573-3800

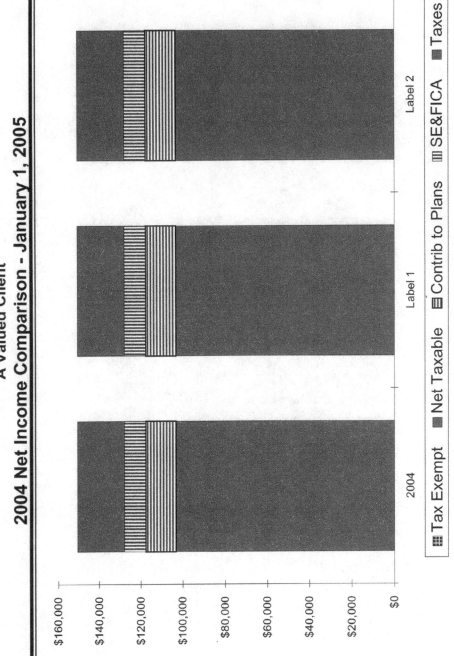

A Valued Client
2004 Net Income Comparison - January 1, 2005

Prepared as a service by John Q. Planner
Raymond James & Associates, Inc.
St. Petersburg, FL   Phone #727-573-3800

Financial Advisor Retirement Required Savings

Report Date..	**January 1, 2005**	
Prepared for	**A Valued Client**	
Financial Advisor's Name	**John Q. Planner**	
Firm Name	**Raymond James & Associates, Inc.**	
Firm Address & Phone	**St. Petersburg, FL Phone #813-573-3800**	
Client's Current Age	48	
At what age would you like to retire?	60	
Social Security Begins at what age? (min 62, widow 60) .	62	
Mortality age	90	Single life table=83
Annual living expenses in today's dollars	$45,000	
Anticipated Future **Annual** Social Security Benefit	$13,255	
How much **Annual** income can you count on at		
retirement from other sources (pension) net of taxes?...	$0	
Is this income stream adjusted for inflation? (Y/N)	N	
Estimated annual growth of income............................	0.00%	
What is the total amount of assets you have		
set aside and earmarked for retirement?	$250,000	
Current **Annual** savings amount	$5,000	
What is the total future value of assets you would		
like to preserve for your heirs	$0	
Hypothetical investment return, net of taxes	6.00%	
Estimated annual living expense rate of inflation	3.00%	
Estimated Social Security C.O.L.A. rate (C.P.I.)...............	1.60%	
Savings (deposits) to retirement assets increase		
by what annual rate? (Enter zero for level deposits)	5.00%	

A Valued Client
Retirement Savings Analysis Summary - January 1, 2005

Assumptions:

Current Age	48
A Valued Client would like to retire at age:	60
Social Security assumed to begin at age:	62
Assumed mortality age:	90.0
ANNUAL living expenses in today's dollars	$45,000
Anticipated ANNUAL Social Security Benefit	$13,255
ANNUAL retirement income from other sources:	
Is other income adjusted for inflation?	No
Annual Rate of other Income Growth	
Total current value of retirement assets:	$250,000
Total current annual savings amount:	$5,000
Total future value to preserve for heirs:	
Hypothetical investment return, net of taxes	6.00%
Estimated annual living expense rate of inflation	3.00%
Estimated Social Security C.O.L.A. rate (C.P.I.)	1.60%
Savings (deposits) to retirement assets	
increase by this percentage each year:	5.00%

You will be retiring in 12 years at age 60.

To maintain your current standard of living in
   future retirement years, you will need: $5,347 monthly
                                                       $64,159 annually

To ensure that you reach your retirement
   objectives, you must:

Make an additional contribution today of:	$314,034	for a total of	$564,034 lump sum
or make additional annual contributions of:	$22,555	for a total of	$27,555 per year
or make additional monthly contributions of:	$1,875	for a total of	$2,291 per month

Or limit your annual standard of living to $23,717 (today's dollars)

This report is not indicative of any security's performance and is based on information believed reliable.
Future performance cannot be guaranteed and investment yields will fluctuate with market conditions.

Prepared as a service by John Q. Planner
Raymond James & Associates, Inc.
St. Petersburg, FL   Phone #813-573-3800

A Valued Client
Retirement Required Savings Schedule - January 1, 2005

This hypothetical report is not indicative of any security's performance and is based on information believed reliable. Future performance cannot be guaranteed and investment yields will fluctuate with market conditions.

Age	Retirement Fund Balance	Annual Deposit	Hypothetical Return on Investment	Social Security Income	Other Income	Living Expenses	Year-End Balance
48	250,000	27,555	16,653	0	0	0	294,209
49		28,933	19,388	0	0	0	342,530
50		30,380	22,375	0	0	0	395,284
51		31,899	25,631	0	0	0	452,814
52		33,494	29,178	0	0	0	515,486
53		35,168	33,039	0	0	0	583,693
54		36,927	37,237	0	0	0	657,857
55		38,773	41,798	0	0	0	738,428
56		40,712	46,748	0	0	0	825,888
57		42,747	52,118	0	0	0	920,753
58		44,885	57,938	0	0	0	1,023,576
59		47,129	64,242	0	0	0	1,134,947
60	*RETIREMENT*	0	64,247	0	0	(64,159)	1,135,035
61		0	64,137	0	0	(66,084)	1,133,088
62		0	64,697	13,255	0	(68,067)	1,142,973
63		0	65,180	13,467	0	(70,109)	1,151,511
64		0	65,579	13,683	0	(72,212)	1,158,561
65		0	65,885	13,901	0	(74,378)	1,163,970
66		0	66,089	14,124	0	(76,609)	1,167,573
67		0	66,181	14,350	0	(78,908)	1,169,196
68		0	66,150	14,579	0	(81,275)	1,168,651
69		0	65,985	14,813	0	(83,713)	1,165,735
70		0	65,674	15,050	0	(86,225)	1,160,234
71		0	65,203	15,291	0	(88,811)	1,151,916
72		0	64,559	15,535	0	(91,476)	1,140,534
73		0	63,726	15,784	0	(94,220)	1,125,823
74		0	62,689	16,036	0	(97,047)	1,107,502
75		0	61,430	16,293	0	(99,958)	1,085,267
76		0	59,932	16,554	0	(102,957)	1,058,795
77		0	58,174	16,818	0	(106,045)	1,027,743
78		0	56,136	17,088	0	(109,227)	991,739
79		0	53,796	17,361	0	(112,504)	950,393
80		0	51,129	17,639	0	(115,879)	903,282
81		0	48,111	17,921	0	(119,355)	849,958
82		0	44,714	18,208	0	(122,936)	789,944
83		0	40,909	18,499	0	(126,624)	722,728
84		0	36,666	18,795	0	(130,423)	647,767
85		0	31,952	19,096	0	(134,335)	564,479
86		0	26,731	19,401	0	(138,365)	472,246
87		0	20,966	19,712	0	(142,516)	370,408
88		0	14,619	20,027	0	(146,792)	258,262
89		0	7,645	20,347	0	(151,195)	135,058
90		0	0	20,673	0	(155,731)	0

A Valued Client
Retirement Required Savings Schedule - January 1, 2005

This hypothetical report is not indicative of any security's performance and is based on information believed reliable.
Future performance cannot be guaranteed and investment yields will fluctuate with market conditions.

Age	Retirement Fund Balance	Annual Deposit	Hypothetical Return on Investment	Social Security Income	Other Income	Living Expenses	Year-End Balance
91	To Heirs	0	0	0	0	0	0
92		0	0	0	0	0	0
93		0	0	0	0	0	0
94		0	0	0	0	0	0
95		0	0	0	0	0	0
96		0	0	0	0	0	0
97		0	0	0	0	0	0
98		0	0	0	0	0	0
99		0	0	0	0	0	0
100		0	0	0	0	0	0
101		0	0	0	0	0	0

A Valued Client
Retirement Alternatives - January 1, 2005

Initial savings needed to reach goal of early retirement at age 55, target retirement age 60, and postponed retirement at age 65 assuming deposits increase at a rate of 5.0% per year:

	Earlier Retirement Age 55	Target Retirement Age 60	Postponed Retirement Age 65
Years until retirement	7	12	17
Future monthly living expenses	$4,612	$5,347	$6,198
Future annual living expenses	$55,344	$64,159	$74,378
To ensure that you reach your retirement objectives, you must:			
Make a lump sum contribution now of:	$487,943	$314,034	$163,380
Begin making annual contributions of:	$71,704	$27,555	$10,357
Begin making monthly contributions of:	$5,979	$2,291	$859
Or limit your annual standard of living to:	$18,794	$23,717	$30,677

Net return on investment is assumed to be 6.00%
Annual living expenses are assumed to increase by 3.00%
Annual Social Security cost of living adjustments are assumed to be 1.60%

This hypothetical report is not indicative of any security's performance and is based on information believed reliable. Future performance cannot be guaranteed and investment yields will fluctuate with market conditions.

Prepared as a service by John Q. Planner
Raymond James & Associates, Inc.
St. Petersburg, FL   Phone #813-573-3800

A Valued Client
Retirement Matrix - January 1, 2005

Initial savings needed to reach goal of retirement at age 60, assuming various annual rates of inflation, returns on investment and increasing at a rate of 5.0% per year:

		Annual Inflation Rate		
		2.0%	**3.0%**	**4.0%**
Annual Return	**8.0%**	$2,459 *per year* $206 *per month*	$10,704 *per year* $898 *per month*	$21,258 *per year* $1,783 *per month*
	6.0%	$15,231 *per year* $1,267 *per month*	**$27,555** *per year* **$2,291** *per month*	$43,550 *per year* $3,621 *per month*
	4.0%	$33,595 *per year* $2,769 *per month*	$52,589 *per year* $4,334 *per month*	$77,583 *per year* $6,394 *per month*

This hypothetical report is not indicative of any security's performance and is based on information believed reliable. Future performance cannot be guaranteed and investment yields will fluctuate with market conditions.

Prepared as a service by John Q. Planner
Raymond James & Associates, Inc.
St. Petersburg, FL   Phone #813-573-3800

Financial Advisor Review of Current Portfolio

Report Date: January 1, 2005
Prepared for: A Valued Client
Financial Advisor's Name: John Q. Planner
Firm Name: Raymond James & Associates, Inc.
Firm Address & Phone: St. Petersburg, FL   Phone #813-573-3800
Marginal Tax Rate: 31%   Auto Price? (Y=ADP,R=Reuters,N)   N

Description	# of Units or Shares	Date of Purchase	Cost PerShare	Current Price PerShare	Annual Income PerShare	AA	Tax	Symbol	Fund?	Total Cost	Current Mkt Value	Profit (Loss)	Gross Income	Gross Yield	Net Income After-tax*	Net Yield	% of Port
Cash Accounts	0	1/0/1900	0.00	0.00	0.00	C	Y			0	0	0	0	0.0%	0	0.0%	0%
CMA Account	29,543	1/1/1990	1.00	1.00	0.04	C	Y			29,543	29,543	0	1,182	4.0%	815	2.8%	1%
Heritage Ltd Govt	110,000	1/1/1991	1.00	1.00	0.04	U	Y			110,000	110,000	0	4,400	4.0%	3,036	2.8%	4%
Muni Bond Portfolio	225,000	3/6/1992	0.80	1.00	0.07	M	N			180,000	225,000	45,000	16,110	7.2%	11,116	4.9%	8%
XYZ Agressive Stock	150	11/16/1994	950.00	1020.00	75.00	A	Y			142,500	153,000	10,500	11,250	7.4%	11,250	7.4%	5%
Heritage CapApp Trust	3,500	11/16/1994	11.00	35.50	0.36	B	Y			38,500	124,250	85,750	1,260	1.0%	869	0.7%	4%
Phnx Big Edge Annuity	2,675	8/3/1995	11.35	11.68	0.23	D	D			30,361	31,244	883	625	2.0%	431	1.4%	1%
Swaheli Co PSPlan	12,600	10/14/1992	1.00	1.00	0.09	D	Q			12,600	12,600	0	1,134	9.0%	1,134	9.0%	0%
WW- IRA	972,500	1/8/1975	1.00	1.00	0.08	E	Q			972,500	972,500	0	77,800	8.0%	77,800	8.0%	35%
	228,000	1/1/1966	1.00	1.00	0.08					228,000	228,000	0	17,100	7.5%	17,100	7.5%	8%
CW-IRA-Templeton Fore	3,800	2/3/1990	9.10	9.13	0.43	F	Q			34,580	34,694	114	1,631	4.7%	1,631	4.7%	1%
Seligman Growth	4,500	3/16/1994	5.28	3.13	0.10	B	Y			23,760	14,085	(9,675)	428	3.0%	295	2.1%	1%
VKM US Govt	7,357	3/16/1994	15.32	15.32	1.35	U	Y			112,709	112,709	0	9,932	8.8%	6,853	6.1%	4%
Residence	1	1/18/1990	135000.00	225000.00	0.00	X	N			135,000	225,000	90,000	0	0.0%	0	0.0%	8%
Note Payable	50,000	7/9/1993	-1.00	-1.00	0.00	X	N			(50,000)	(50,000)	0	0	0.0%	0	0.0%	-2%
Merrill Stock Portfolio	445,000	2/28/1994	1.00	1.00	0.04	E	Y			445,000	445,000	0	17,800	4.0%	12,282	2.8%	16%
Merrill Muni Bond Portfol	122,000	2/28/1994	1.00	1.00	0.07	D	Y			122,000	122,000	0	7,930	6.5%	5,472	4.5%	4%
	0	1/0/1900	0.00	0.00	0.00					0	0	0	0	0.0%	0	0.0%	0%
	0	1/0/1900	0.00	0.00	0.00					0	0	0	0	0.0%	0	0.0%	0%
	0	1/0/1900	0.00	0.00	0.00					0	0	0	0	0.0%	0	0.0%	0%
	0	1/0/1900	0.00	0.00	0.00					0	0	0	0	0.0%	0	0.0%	0%
	0	1/0/1900	0.00	0.00	0.00					0	0	0	0	0.0%	0	0.0%	0%
	0	1/0/1900	0.00	0.00	0.00					0	0	0	0	0.0%	0	0.0%	0%
	0	1/0/1900	0.00	0.00	0.00					0	0	0	0	0.0%	0	0.0%	0%
	0	1/0/1900	0.00	0.00	0.00					0	0	0	0	0.0%	0	0.0%	0%
	0	1/0/1900	0.00	0.00	0.00					0	0	0	0	0.0%	0	0.0%	0%
	0	1/0/1900	0.00	0.00	0.00					0	0	0	0	0.0%	0	0.0%	0%
TOTALS										2,567,053	2,789,625	222,572	168,581	6.0%	150,084	5.4%	100%

* Assuming a 31% marginal tax rate.

This report is not indicative of any security's performance and is based on information believed reliable. Future performance cannot be guaranteed and investment yields will fluctuate with market conditions.

Prepared as a service by John Q. Planner
Raymond James & Associates, Inc.
St. Petersburg, FL   Phone #813-573-3800

A Valued Client
Review of Current Portfolio Summary – January 1, 2005

Portfolio Allocation		% of Port
	$2,789,625	
Personal/Use	$175,000	N/A
Cash	$139,543	5.3%
Debt & Fixed Inc	$1,597,809	61.1%
Equities	$877,273	33.6%
Real Est & Tang		

Cash 5%
Equities 34%
Debt/Fixed 61%

Debt/Fixed Income Detail		% of Fixed
	$1,597,809	
General Debt/Fixed Inc	1,107,100	69.3%
U.S. Govt	337,709	21.1%
Munis	153,000	9.6%

Equity Detail		% of Eq
	$877,273	
General Equities	673,000	76.7%
Agg Growth	124,250	14.2%
Growth Fund	45,329	5.2%
Foreign	34,694	4.0%

Non Qual Defd 0%
Qualified Defd 47%
Taxable 46%
Taxfree 6%

Tax Status Detail		Income	Yield
	$2,789,625		
Non Investment Assets	$175,000		
Taxable Investments	$1,213,831	$59,666	4.9%
Tax Free Investments	$153,000	$11,250	7.4%
Non Qual Tax Deferred	$12,600	$1,134	9.0%
Qualified Tax Deferred	$1,235,194	$96,531	7.8%

This report is not indicative of any security's performance and is based on information believed reliable. Future performance cannot be guaranteed and investment yields will fluctuate with market conditions.

Prepared as a service by John Q. Planner
Raymond James & Associates, Inc.
St. Petersburg, FL   Phone #813-573-3800

A Valued Client

Current Portfolio Detail Allocation – January 1, 2005

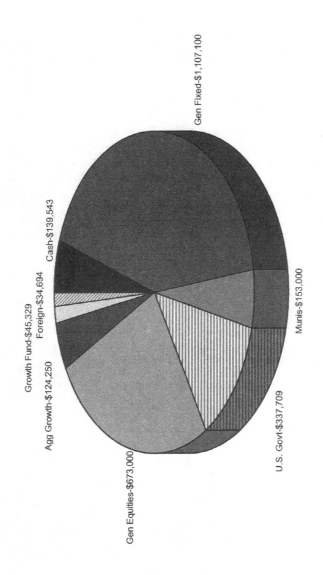

Growth Fund-$45,329

Foreign-$34,694

Cash-$139,543

Agg Growth-$124,250

Gen Fixed-$1,107,100

Munis-$153,000

Gen Equities-$673,000

U.S. Govt-$337,709

This report is not indicative of any security's performance and is based on information believed reliable. Future performance cannot be guaranteed and investment yields will fluctuate with market conditions.

Prepared as a service by John Q. Planner
Raymond James & Associates, Inc.
St. Petersburg, FL   Phone #813-573-3800

MODERN ESTATE PLANNING

One of the most often neglected areas of the financial planning process is the estate planning. Estate planning concepts and techniques have undergone radical transformations over the last 10 years. If you haven't updated your estate plan recently, you might be surprised what a modern estate plan is able to accomplish.

Estate planning is no longer just a matter of distributing assets at your death with a will. Modern estate planning can also help you have tough medical decisions made for you and help you manage your financial affairs. Without the proper application of these techniques an expensive legal guardianship proceeding might be required. Your family might also be forced to pay thousands, even hundreds of thousands, of dollars in unnecessary estate administration and tax expenses.

One of the cornerstones of modern estate planning is the revocable living trust (hereafter referred to simply as a living trust). A living trust is a very powerful legal device that allows you to create a mechanism for the efficient management of your financial affairs if you become disabled. A living trust also provides a way for you to transfer assets to your family at death outside of the probate system. By-passing probate will save your family the publicity involved in a public probate proceeding and can save your family from much of the delay and expense associated with probate. A living trust can also provide tax saving provisions to help reduce the federal estate tax. This tax can take up to 60 percent of an estate.

The living trust is not a complete substitute for a will. Nor is it always appropriate in every case. Most people who have a living trust also have a will to cover any assets they have not transferred into the trust. A living trust is a very viable and flexible tool used to accomplish many goals. It should be considered as a part of any modern estate plan.

Another modern estate planning device to manage one's financial affairs is the durable power of attorney. This legal document allows you to appoint another to act on your behalf in the management of your financial affairs. The individual you appoint is permitted to act on your behalf even if you become incapacitated. Some practical and legal limitations often make the durable power of attorney a less than perfect substitute for a living trust. However, these devices are useful to supplement living trusts.

Dealing with health care decisions can be difficult even under the best of circumstances. Coping with these problems when a loved one is unable to make decisions for him/herself can be devastating. Two modern estate planning tools are available to help address these problems. The living will is a document by which you leave instructions regarding your care in the event you are faced with a life threatening illness or injury and are unable to make your own decisions about your care. Without a living will, families must sometimes agonize and even go to court over a decision to stop using heroic efforts to keep a loved one on life support systems. The living will can be used to provide the help they need at this most difficult time.

The other device is the durable power of attorney for health care. This modern estate planning tool allows you to authorize another to make all medical decisions for you in the event you become unable to make them for yourself. This form of the durable power of attorney shares much in common with the durable power used to facilitate financial decision making. Health care durable powers are sometimes called "health care proxies" or "designation of health care surrogate." Although the terminology may vary from state to state, the concept is the same.

Modern estate planning is a "team sport" not a "do-it-yourself" project. To actually draft the legal documents necessary to put your modern estate plan into action, you will need to see a lawyer experienced in estate planning matters.

UNDERSTANDING THE FEDERAL ESTATE TAX

The Internal Revenue Code imposes a transfer tax on voluntary transfers. If made during your lifetime, the transfer tax is a gift tax. If the transfer is made upon your death, the transfer tax is an estate tax.

The federal estate tax is imposed on the privilege of transferring property at death. The amount of tax (imposed at progressive rates) depends on the value of the property transferred. The tax is imposed not just on property transferred through the probate process (that is, property controlled by your will or by operation of the locally applicable laws of inheritance and descent), but also extends to all transfers taking place at your death outside the scope of the probate system. This would include transfers of joint tenancies, transfers resulting from beneficiary designations on life insurance policies and other similar properties, and certain transfers in trust. Thus, the concept of the "taxable estate" for federal estate purposes is broader than the probate estate of most decedents.

Your federal "gross estate" consists of the fair market value of all your property interest before reduction for the various deductions allowed in arriving at the "taxable estate." The Internal Revenue Code defines the gross estate broadly. The following property interests may be part of your gross estate:

A. All property owned directly by you. These property interests are broadly defined and include all property subject to probate administration.

B. Property transferred by you during your lifetime with certain "strings attached" (usually in the form of trusts but not always). Transfers subject to these provisions include the following:

    (1) Transfers under which you retained the use and enjoyment of the property during your lifetime (including the standard revocable living trust).

    (2) Transfers under which you retained the power to alter the time and manner of enjoyment or the identities of the beneficiaries (including, for example, an irrevocable trust for the benefit of your children if you retained the power to alter the respective share in the trust to be enjoyed by each child).

    (3) Transfers under which the right to enjoy property is conditioned upon the beneficiary surviving you if you retained a right to take the property back if the beneficiary died first and the actuarial value of that reversionary interest exceeds 5% of the value of the trust.

C. Annuities (or other payments) receivable by any beneficiary by reason of surviving you   under any agreement by which an annuity was payable to you (or for any period which does not in fact end before your death).

D. Joint property (i.e. with a right of survivorship, and not as tenants in common), and tenancies by the entirety, except to the extent it can be shown that your surviving cotenant contributed to the acquisition or improvement of the property and except for certain joint interest between husbands and wives.

E.   All property over which you have, at the time of your death, a "general power of appointment." General powers of appointment must be distinguished from "special" or "limited" powers of appointment, which are not included in your gross estate.

F.   Life insurance proceeds if the proceeds are
      (i)   receivable by your executor or
      (ii)   receivable by any other beneficiaries where you possessed at your death any "incident of ownership."

G.   Under some circumstances, interests given away within three years of death are included in your gross estate. This three year rule now applies only for the following transfers:
      (i)   transfers "with respect to" life insurance
      (ii)   releases or exercises of general powers of appointment and
      (iii) releases of the "strings" previously retained in the intervivos transfers described above.

Deductions from your gross estate allowable in determining the amount of your federal taxable estate include the following:

A.   Certain expenses and indebtedness, such as:
      (1)   Funeral expenses
      (2)   Expenses of last illness
      (3)   Expenses of administration
      (4)   Claims against the estate
      (5)   Mortgages and the indebtedness with respect to property included in the gross estate

B.   Certain losses experienced during administration of the estate

C.   Transfers for public, charitable and religious uses

D.   Transfers to a surviving spouse

COMPUTING THE TRANSFER TAX

A "unified" rate schedule is applicable to both taxable gifts and estate transfers. The unified rate schedule consists of progressively higher rates which are applied to lifetime transfers (cumulative) and transfers at death. The unified credit operates to protect small transfers and estates from taxation. The estate value needed to produce a tax equal to the credit is protected from tax. The protective value of the credit is referred to as the "exemption equivalent" of the credit. The unified credit is currently $555,800 which is the amount of tax on the first $1,500,000 of a taxable estate.

In addition to the unified credit against the tax, other credits are allowed. However, some of these other credits are only available if equal offsetting obligations are paid (for example, the credit for state death taxes paid). The state death tax credit will be gradually phased out beginning in 2003, until full repeal in 2005. Upon repeal, this credit will be replaced with a deduction for state death taxes paid. Other credits are only available if unusual events occur (such as a rapid series of deaths triggering the credit for tax on prior transfers). These additional credits are normally important for planning purposes.

It appears that the unified credit shelters the majority of transfers and estates from federal transfer taxes. It also appears that many estates will not be subject to tax because the necessary planning steps have been taken to reduce or eliminate the tax. However, if a transfer or estate is subject to tax, the tax quickly becomes a hefty one. If you think your estate may be subject to a federal transfer tax, you should consult with your financial advisor along with a qualified estate planning attorney.

Financial Advisor Estate Analysis - Personal Data Input Sheet

Report Date................... **January 1, 2005**
Prepared for .... **A Valued Client**
Financial Advisor's Name **John Q. Planner**
Firm Name .... **Raymond James & Associates, Inc.**
Firm Address & Phone ..... **St. Petersburg, FL   Phone #727-573-3800**

Is this estate plan for a married Couple (C) or Single (S)? ...	C	Married Couple
Client's first name	Sam	
Spouse's first name	Sally	
Type of Will (C=Credit Shelter, S=Simple)...........................	C	Credit Shelter in place
Max Dollar Amount to CST at 1st Death........................	$3,500,000	
First to Die (C=Client, S=Spouse)	C	Client dies first
Sam dies in what year?	2005	
Sally outlives Sam by how many years?	5	
Current value of assets that pass to someone other		Grow?
than Sally at Sam's death (excluding TOD assets)		N
Current value of assets to charity at Sam's death		N
Current value of assets to charity at Sally's death		N
Sam's Prior Taxable Gifts		
Sally's Prior Taxable Gifts		
Considering firesale, estimated % of CMV	100.0%	
Annual NET Estate Growth Factor	3.00%	
Estimated Probate Expense %	1.0%	
Estimated Administration Expense % (min 0.5%)	0.5%	
Does Marital Trust exist at first death? (Y or N)	Y	
Post 2009 Exclusion Amount...	$3,500,000	
Post 2009 Maximum Estate Tax Rate (Max is 60%)...........	45.0%	

Comments ....
Comments ....
Comments ....
Comments ....

A Valued Client
Estate Analysis Assumptions - January 1, 2005

Sam's death in year 2005, 0 years from now
Sally's death in year 2010, 5 years from now

(1) Total Liquid Assets defines combined liquid assets, including insurance proceeds, which are available to satisfy transfer expenses at death.

(2) Administration expenses may include court costs, professional fees, fiduciary costs, estate tax preparation and similar expenses.

(3) Assuming heirs had to sell non-liquid assets at "fire sale" to raise cash to satisfy estate, probate and administrative expenses, this is client's estimate of real market value that the heirs would be able to realize.

Assumes a Credit Shelter agreement exists when first death occurs in 0 years
with marital trust at first death.

Net Estate Growth Factor -- Refers to the annual growth rate of total estate assets (including investments and personal property) taking into account assets removed through consumption, expenditures or gifts.

Estate Shrinkage -- Refers to total dollars lost to administrative expenses, taxes and forced liquidation discounts, offset by dollars replaced through wealth replacement insurance.

Prepared as a service by John Q. Planner
Raymond James & Associates, Inc.
St. Petersburg, FL   Phone #727-573-3800

Financial Advisor Assets Input Sheet - A Valued Client

Asset Description	Current Value	Owner or Insured (J,M,C or S)	Liquid (Y or N)	Estate Code*
CASH ********************				
CD-5 1/4% due 9/97	40,000		Y	R
Elite #1234567	15,000		Y	R
INHERITED *****************				
Home Depot Stock	1,000,000		Y	L
Broward Swr 5.6% '3/17	1,000,000		Y	L
RETIREMENT *************				
IRA-Dean Witt USG	150,000		Y	X
IRA-Alliance HiYld	250,000		Y	X
Qual Plan-Fixed	500,000		Y	X
Qual Plan-Cash	22,000		Y	X
JT. ACCOUNT*************				
GT Global High Inc A	39,627		Y	R
Steadman Ocanogra	4,350		Y	R
ANNUITIES ***************				
American Skandia SPDA	25,000		Y	X
REAL ESTATE **********				
Residence	375,000		N	R
Farm Proceeds	750,000		N	R
OTHER *****************				
Coin Collection	10,000		Y	R
Jewelry	8,000		Y	R
Automobiles	20,000		Y	R
Note Receivable	50,000		Y	R
Mortgage	(112,718)		Y	R
Automobile Loans	(10,500)		Y	R
Life Ins on Sam	500,000		Y	I
Life Ins on Sally	10,000		Y	I
TOTAL:	**4,645,759**			

* R=Regular, X=Pension or Annuity, L=Living Trust, I=Insurance, T=WRT, D=Transfer-on-Death

A Valued Client
Current Asset Inventory - January 1, 2005

	Total Estate	Sam's Assets	Sally's Assets	Joint Assets	Outside the Estate
CASH *******************					
CD-5 1/4% due 9/97	40,000	40,000			
Elite #1234567	15,000	15,000			
INHERITED *****************					
Home Depot Stock	1,000,000	1,000,000			
Broward Swr 5.6% '3/17	1,000,000	1,000,000			
RETIREMENT **************					
IRA-Dean Witt USG	150,000	150,000			
IRA-Alliance HiYld	250,000	250,000			
Qual Plan-Fixed	500,000	500,000			
Qual Plan-Cash	22,000	22,000			
JT. ACCOUNT*************					
GT Global High Inc A	39,627	39,627			
Steadman Ocanogra	4,350	4,350			
ANNUITIES ***************					
American Skandia SPDA	25,000	25,000			
REAL ESTATE **********					
Residence	375,000	375,000			
Farm Proceeds	750,000	750,000			
OTHER ******************					
Coin Collection	10,000	10,000			
Jewelry	8,000	8,000			
Automobiles	20,000	20,000			
Note Receivable	50,000	50,000			
Mortgage	(112,718)	(112,718)			
Automobile Loans	(10,500)	(10,500)			
Life Ins on Sam	500,000	500,000			
Life Ins on Sally	10,000	10,000			
TOTALS:	**$4,135,759**	**$4,645,759**			
Total Life Insurance:	**$510,000**				
Total Death Estate:	**$4,645,759**				

This report is not indicative of any security's performance and is based on information believed reliable.
Future performance cannot be guaranteed and investment yields will fluctuate with market conditions.

Prepared as a service by John Q. Planner
Raymond James & Associates, Inc.
St. Petersburg, FL   Phone #727-573-3800

A Valued Client
Estate Flow Chart - January 1, 2005

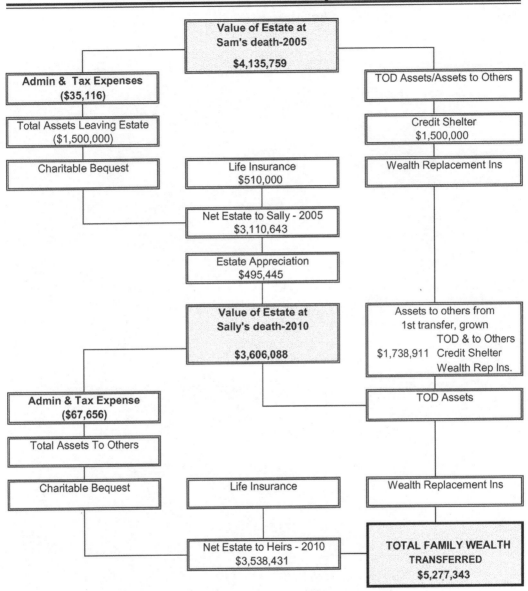

This report is not indicative of any security's performance and is based on information believed reliable.
Future performance cannot be guaranteed and investment yields will fluctuate with market conditions.

Prepared as a service by John Q. Planner
Raymond James & Associates, Inc.
St. Petersburg, FL   Phone #727-573-3800

A Valued Client
Basic Estate Tax Calculation - January 1, 2005

Sam's death in year 2005, 0 years from now

Gross Estate of Decedent			$4,645,759
Less Expenses and Fees		(35,116)	
Less Charitable Gifts		0	
Less Marital Deduction		(3,110,643)	
	Total	(3,145,759)	
Taxable Estate			$1,500,000
Plus Prior Taxable Gifts		0	
Tentative Taxable Estate			$1,500,000
Gross Estate Tax			555,800
Less Unified Credit			(555,800)
Total Estate Taxes at Sam's Death			**$0**

Sally's death in year 2010, 5 years from now

Gross Estate of Decedent		$3,606,088
Less Expenses and Fees	(18,030)	
Less Charitable Gifts	0	
	(18,030)	
Taxable Estate		$3,588,057
Plus Prior Taxable Gifts	0	
Tentative Taxable Estate		$3,588,057
Gross Estate Tax		1,535,426
Less Unified Credit		(1,485,800)
TOTAL ESTATE TAXES AT SECOND DEATH		**$49,626**

This report is not indicative of any security's performance and is based on information believed reliable.
Future performance cannot be guaranteed and investment yields will fluctuate with market conditions.

Prepared as a service by John Q. Planner
Raymond James & Associates, Inc.
St. Petersburg, FL   Phone #727-573-3800

A Valued Client
Estate Liquidity Analysis - January 1, 2005

	Within Estate	Outside Estate
Sam's death in year 2005, 0 years from now		
Value of Estate, grown at 3%	$4,135,759	
Plus Wealth Replacement Insurance		
Plus Life Insurance	510,000	
Total liquid assets available (1)	3,520,759	
Administration and/or Probate Expense (2)	(35,116)	
Estate Tax Expense (43% marginal rate)		
SURPLUS (DEFICIT)	3,485,643	
Less total liquid & non liquid assets spent	(35,116)	
Less TOD assets not passing to Sally at Sam's death		
Less other assets not passing to Sally at Sam's death		
Less Credit Shelter Assets	(1,500,000)	1,500,000
Net Value of Survivor's Estate at First Transfer	**$3,110,643**	
Total assets outside the estate		$1,500,000

	Within Estate	Outside Estate
Sally's death in year 2010, 5 years from now		
Value of Estate at second transfer, grown at 3%	$3,606,088	
Assets outside estate, grown at 3%, 5 years.		$1,738,911
Plus Wealth Replacement Insurance		
Plus Life Insurance		
Total liquid assets available (1)	2,301,904	
Administration and/or Probate Expense	(18,030)	
Estate Tax Expense (45% marginal rate)	(49,626)	
SURPLUS (DEFICIT)	2,234,248	
Less total liquid & non liquid assets spent	(67,656)	
Net Value of Estate at Second Transfer	**$3,538,431**	
Total assets outside the estate at second transfer		$1,738,911
Total Family Wealth Transferred	**$5,277,343**	
ESTATE SHRINKAGE	**($102,772)**	

This report is not indicative of any security's performance and is based on information believed reliable.
Future performance cannot be guaranteed and investment yields will fluctuate with market conditions.

Prepared as a service by John Q. Planner
Raymond James & Associates, Inc.
St. Petersburg, FL   Phone #727-573-3800

A Valued Client
Estate Analysis Executive Summary - January 1, 2005

First transfer 0 years from now	Within Estate	Outside Estate
Total estate at Sam's death in 2005	**$4,135,759**	
Plus Life Insurance	510,000	
Less administration and/or probate expenses	(35,116)	
Less assets going to credit shelter	(1,500,000)	1,500,000
Net estate to Sally at first transfer	**$3,110,643**	
Total assets outside the estate		$1,500,000

Second transfer 5 years from now	Within Estate	Outside Estate
Total estate at Sally's death in 2010	**$3,606,088**	
Assets outside the estate, grown		$1,738,911
Less administration and/or probate expenses	(18,030)	
Less estate taxes at 45%	(49,626)	
Net estate to heirs at second transfer	**$3,538,431**	
Total assets outside the estate at second transfer		$1,738,911

Total Family Wealth Transferred	**$5,277,343**	
ESTATE SHRINKAGE	**($102,772)**	

Assumes annual net estate growth of 3%.

This report is not indicative of any security's performance and is based on information believed reliable.
Future performance cannot be guaranteed and investment yields will fluctuate with market conditions.

Prepared as a service by John Q. Planner
Raymond James & Associates, Inc.
St. Petersburg, FL   Phone #727-573-3800

A Valued Client
Estate Distribution - January 1, 2005

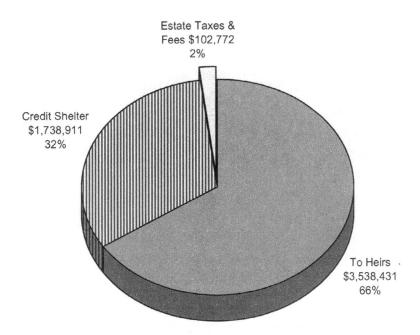

Sam's death in year 2005, 0 years from now
Sally's death in year 2010, 5 years from now

This report is not indicative of any security's performance and is based on information believed reliable.
Future performance cannot be guaranteed and investment yields will fluctuate with market conditions.

Prepared as a service by John Q. Planner
Raymond James & Associates, Inc.
St. Petersburg, FL   Phone #727-573-3800

A Valued Client

A Valued Client
Estate Ownership - January 1, 2005

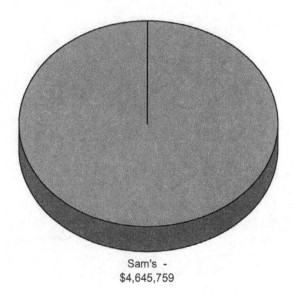

Sam's -
$4,645,759

This report is not indicative of any security's performance and is based on information believed reliable.
Future performance cannot be guaranteed and investment yields will fluctuate with market conditions.

Prepared as a service by John Q. Planner
Raymond James & Associates, Inc.
St. Petersburg, FL   Phone #727-573-3800

Remember you will not always win. Some days, the most resourceful in-
dividual will taste defeat. But there is, in this case, always tomorrow—
after you have done your best to achieve success today.

Maxwell Maltz

PART III

Special Topics in Financial Planning

In Part I we described the emerging role of the professional financial planner in a highly complex economic and financial environment. In addition, we discussed how the financial planner begins the planning process by selecting and intereacting with clients. Finally, we demonstrated the use of time value of money as an effective tool for solving financial problems.

Part II was devoted to a detailed analysis of the eight key financial planning areas; namely, safety through risk management planning; educational planning; cash management, savings, credit, and debt planning; ultimate disposition through estate planning, retirement planning; investment planning; tax planning and yearning for financial independence planning. In our presentation, the structure and concept of each area (except financial independence) was first developed, followed by a detailed discussion of the planning strategies associated with that area.

In Part III we discuss two special topics in financial planning: life after divorce, and planning for widows. In this part, we also discuss the essentials of running a financial planning practice and the technique of valuing a planning practice for purposes of negotiating a sale of the practice.

CHAPTER 19

Life After Divorce

ROLE OF FINANCIAL ADVISOR

There are about 1.4 million divorces every year in the U.S. That is at least 2.8 million people who are affected by the emotional and financial trauma of divorce-not counting their children, in-laws, relatives, and friends. This has created a real market niche for professionals who are needed in all phases of the divorce process to help create equitable settlements.

When people think about getting divorced, the first professional that comes to mind is an attorney. Unfortunately, the assistance of a CPA, financial planner, or Financial Divorce Specialist, is not generally sought until it is too late.

Couples getting divorced are overwhelmed by a myriad of complicated financial questions. These include, but are not limited to, the following: (1) How do we value our property? (2) Who gets each property? (3) What are the tax issues? (4) How should retirement funds and future pensions be divided? (5) How will the lower-earning spouse survive? (6) What kind of additional help or support does each person need? (7) Who gets the house? (8) Will either person have to pay capital gains tax? (9) Who gets the children? (10) Who will pay for college, summer camp, and orthodontia for the children? (11) What happens if a paying ex-spouse dies? Clearly, a financial planner can provide answers to these and related questions, thereby making the divorce process smooth and efficient.

There are many titles for a financial expert; namely, CPA, financial planner, Certified Financial Planner and Chartered Financial Consultants. In addition, on the financial scene there is a new type of professional, known as Financial Divorce Specialist. This divorce specialist is generally a financial planner who has been trained to work with people in the process of getting a divorce. Typically, they

This chapter was written by Carol Ann Wilson, CFP, FDS, president of Financial Divorce Association, Inc., Box 11276, Boulder, Co 80301. Tel: 888-332-3342. E-mail: HYPERLINK "mailto:carolann@carolannwilson.com" carolann@carolannwilson.com. It is excerpted from The Financial Guide to Divorce Settlement by Carol Ann Wilson, published by Marketplace Books, copyright 2000.

team up with attorneys, dealing with all the financial issues in each case, and appearing as expert witness in court, if needed.

In divorce, many important financial questions need to be resolved. It is beyond the scope of this book to undertake a comprehensive discussion of all of these questions. Consequently, the discussion that follows is limited to the five key topics: (1) Property Valuation and Settlement; (2) Career Assets; (3) Dividing the House; (4) Qualified Plans; and (5) Alimony Payments.

PROPERTY VALUATIONS AND SETTLEMENT

In the case of a divorce, when looking at the property issues a couple must always ask the following three questions: (1) What constitutes property? (2) What is the property worth? (3) How will this property be divided? In the words of Lenore Weitzman, "most divorcing couples have household furnishings (89%), cars (71%), and some savings in the form of money in bank accounts, stocks, or bonds (61%). Almost half (46%) of the couples own or are buying a family home, which is likely to be a couple's most valuable asset. Only a small percentage of divorcing couples has pension (24%), a business (11%), or other real estate (11%)." [1]

As a general rule, there is virtually no limit to what items can be identified as property. Typically, property includes family home, rental property, cars, art and antique collections. It can also include bank accounts, mutual funds, stocks, bonds, life insurance cash value, IRAs, and retirement plans. However, for purposes of analysis, property can be broadly divided into two major categories: separate property and marital property. The former includes what a person brings into the marriage, inherits during the marriage, and receives as a gift during marriage. In contrast, marital property is everything acquired during the marriage, no matter who owns the title to it. In some (but not all) states, marital property also includes the increase in the value of separate property.

Incidentally, there are two types of states; namely, community property and equitable distribution. Each type treats property ownership differently. Consequently, it is important to know what rules of property division are followed by the state of residence of the divorcing couple.

Property Valuation

Although there exists no mechanical guidelines for valuing property, the following examples can be used to demonstrate the rules that can be applied to value property associated with a divorce case.

---

[1] *The Divorce Revolution* by Lenore Weitzman, Chapter 3: "The Nature of Marital Property," *The Free Press* (A Division of Macmillan, Inc.), 1985.

Case 1. Assume Beth and her husband are getting a divorce. When they got married, Beth had $1,000 in a savings account. During the marriage, her $1,000 earned $100 in interest, so the account is now worth $1,100. Since Beth did not add her husband's name to the account, her property is $1,000, although in some states, the interest of $100 will be treated as a marital asset. Had Beth put her husband's name on the account, she would have definitely turned the entire account into a marital asset.

Case 2. In second or third marriages, both spouses may bring a house into the marriage. Suppose after her marriage Beth retained the title to the house she owned at the time of marriage. At that time, the house was worth $100,000, and it had a mortgage of $70,000, so the equity in the house was $30,000.

All that is changed now. Today Beth is getting divorced, the house is worth $150,000, the mortgage is down to $50,000, and the equity in the house has increased to $100,000. These facts are summarized below:

	At the time of marriage	*At the time of divorce*
Market Value	$100,000	$150,000
Mortgage	– 70,000	– 50,000
Equity	$ 30,000	$100,000

If at the time of marriage Beth had put her husband's name on the deed to the house, technically she would have given what is called a "presumptive gift" to the marriage, thereby turning the house into a marital asset.

Case 3. Beth's aunt died and left her a $10,000 inheritance. If she had put it into an account with her name on it, then at the time of divorce, that inheritance would be treated as her property (except for the increase in value). It is the same with a gift. However, if she had put it into a joint account, then she would have turned the inheritance into marital property.

Case 4. Every month Beth deposits $100 into her savings account. The current balance of her account is $2,600. At the time of her divorce, this money would be treated as marital property, because it is acquired during her marriage.

Case 5. Beth owned stock worth $10,000 when she got married. Today she is getting a divorce, and the stock is worth $9,000. This would constitute a $1,000 marital loss. And if there is a marital gain in one asset, it can be offset with a marital loss in her stock investment.

Division of Property

Martha and Tom have been married for 35 years. She stayed home and took care of the four children. Tom earns $150,000 per year and has started a business in the basement of their home, which he expects will generate spendable income after he retires. He has a pension fund, which is valued at $90,000. They have a savings account with a balance of $28,000, and he values the business at $75,000. Their joint assets total $328,000:

House	$135,000
Pension	90,000
Savings	28,000
Business	75,000
Total	$328,000

Assuming a 50/50 property split, $328,000 will be split equally between Martha and Tom, and each will receive $164,000. However, in this case, splitting the property and assets down the middle may not be the most equitable division. The following split may be more equitable, since it represents individual preferences of both spouses:

	Total	*Martha*	*Tom*
House	$135,000	$135,000	
Pension	90,000		$90,000
Savings	28,000		28,000
Business	75,000		75,000
Total	$328,000	$135,000	$193,000

If this split is accepted, Martha would receive $135,000, whereas Tom would receive $193,000. If a 50/50 property split is desired, then Tom would owe Martha $29,000. This unequal distribution can be evened out with a Property Settlement Note, which is a note from the payer to the payee for an agreed-upon length of time using a reasonable rate of interest. If the above settlement is unacceptable, the following alternative split might be more palatable, since it splits the pension between the two spouses:

	Total	*Martha*	*Tom*
House	$135,000	$135,000	
Pension	90,000	45,000	$45,000
Savings	28,000	14,000	14,000
Business	75,000		75,000
Total	$328,000	$194,000	$134,000

At first blush it appears that this settlement is grossly unfair to Tom. However, for several reasons that may not necessarily be the case. For one thing, Martha is not in good health and it is unlikely that she would be able to get a job that pays above the minimum wage. For another, her largest asset is the house, which is an illiquid asset. Therefore, considering her age, her health, and her lack of work experience, this settlement may be more equitable than it appears.

Equal versus Equitable Concept

Property divisions can be likened to trading. Generally, assets are traded back and forth until the couple agrees on the division. However, in an equitable property division state, it means splitting the property equitably. It should be understood that "equitable" does not mean "equal;" it only means "fair."

A second problem of "equality" is that a 50/50 division of property may not produce equal results—or equal standards of living after the divorce—if the two spouses are unequally situated at the time of divorce. This is most evident in situations where older homemakers are involved. After a marital life devoted to homemaking, typically the wife is left with little marketable skills. Consequently, the wife is likely to require a greater share of the property to cushion the income loss she would undoubtedly suffer after divorce.

Generally, a 50/50 division is preferred when the property ownership is in a state of equitable division. However, an uncritical application of this rule may not always be desirable. For instance, let us assume that the husband owns $2 million worth of separate property, while the marital estate totals $200,000. If the judge knows that the husband is walking away with $2 million of separate property, then he may not offer the husband 50 percent of the marital property.

Financial Divorce Specialists handle this type of problem with software designed to show the long-term result of any given settlement in divorce. The program illustrates both graphically and numerically how each party will fare financially when certain assumptions are used in dividing the marital property. For instance, if the analysis shows that the wife will exhaust her assets within eight years while the husband's assets will continue to grow, then appropriate adjustments may have to be made in the divorce settlement agreement.

CAREER ASSETS

With many couples, one spouse has significant assets tied to his or her career. These career assets include life, health, disability, and long-term health care insurance, vacation and sick pay, Social Security, unemployment benefits, stock options, and pension and retirement plans. In addition, such items as future promotions, job experience, seniority, professional contacts, and education are also considered career assets.

As a general rule, career assets should be considered in arriving at an equitable settlement. For example, take a family where the husband is the sole wage earner. The wife put the husband through school and helped him become established. Simultaneously, she abandoned her own educational aspirations and also quit her job so she could keep the family together as the husband moved from one place to another. Together they made the decision to spend the time and energy to build his career with the expectation that she will share in the fruits of her investment through her husband's enhanced earning power. Over time, the husband has built up a significant amount of career assets.

In the case presented above, it is reasonable to assume that the career assets are jointly owned by both spouses. And even in two-income families where one spouse's (usually the husband's) career assets take priority, both spouses should expect to share the rewards of that decision.

The Family Business

In divorce, where one of the marital assets is a business, the task of dividing this asset becomes even more challenging. The business can be formal like dentistry, medicine, or law, or it can be as informal as a home-based business. Additionally, a business can be a sole proprietorship, a partnership, or a corporation.

Valuing the Business

Let us begin with a simple illustration. Becky and James are getting divorced after 35 years of marriage. James owns a heavy construction business. He has agreed to split the assets 50/50, and says that the CPA at work values the business at $300,000. Not surprisingly, Becky informs her attorney that she used to keep the company's books and knows for sure that the business generates an annual income of more than $1 million. She is convinced that the value of the business is much greater than $300,000.

Convinced that Becky 's observation was sound, her attorney insisted to have the business appraised. The appraisal did cost Becky $4,300, but it was worth the cost. The appraiser valued the company at $850,000, which laid the foundation for a much more equitable settlement.

In a divorce situation, it is almost mandatory to have the business appraised. This task is best performed by Certified Business Appraisers (CBAs) who value both small and large businesses. To earn this designation, appraisers must pass a rigorous written exam and submit appraisals for review by a committee of experienced peers.

Dividing the Business

There are three options when deciding how to divide the business: (1) One of the spouses keeps the business. (2) Both spouses continue to own the business. (3) The couple sells the business outright and divides the proceeds between the two spouses. Each option is discussed next.

One Spouse Keeps the Business. In the case of Becky and James, it was clear that since the business was run by James, he would buy out Becky's interest and either pay for her share or give her other assets of equal value. If appropriate assets were not available, a Property Settlement Note could be signed which would obligate James to pay Becky over time.

It should be mentioned in this connection that the situation would become more complicated if James decided to buy back the company's shares owned by Becky. For one thing, if there had been an increase in the value of the stock, then Becky could be liable for capital gains tax. For another, if James bought her shares directly, then such an action would be considered a transfer of property "incident to divorce." In that case, the basis would go with the stocks and would not be recognized until the stocks are sold by Becky.

Joint Ownership of Business. It is extremely difficult to divide a family-owned business. This is because spouses generally have emotional ties with the business. Additionally, any attempt to divide the business may deal a mortal blow to its day-to-day operation. Therefore, in situations where the couples are better business partners than marriage partners, and are capable of working together in the business even after the divorce is final, they should continue to jointly operate the business. In most instances, however, such an arrangement would be impractical.

Sell the Business. The third viable option is to sell the business and divide the profits. That way, both parties can find another business they like to operate or simply decide to retire. The problem, of course, is to find a suitable buyer for a jointly-owned business. Consequently, since decisions need to be made to run the business until it is sold, it might become problematic as revealed by the following illustration.

> Stella and Dan owned a national franchise fast-food business. They also owned the land and the building where the business was located. The couple had worked hard on this business together to make it a success. When they were divorced, Dan took the business and Stella took ownership of the land and the building. This decision make Stella the landlord which allowed her to not only control the rent that the business paid her but also to give her the authority to decide how repairs and maintenance on the building would be handled. Soon Stella and Dan realized that they had made a bad decision. Hence, to correct the situation, their attorneys hammered out a new buy-out agreement which allowed Dan to keep the business and the property, and gave Stella sufficient funds to move out of the area and start a new business.

DIVIDING THE HOUSE

In many divorces, who should get the house constitutes one of the key issues. For instance, should the wife or the husband get the house, or should they sell it and split the profit? Oftentimes, the answer is not as easy or clear as it may first appear. In most instances, because of her emotional attachment to it, the wife wants to keep the house. Unfortunately, she may not consider all the financial ramifications of managing that asset. For instance, if it has a lot of equity in it, then she will receive an illiquid asset that does not generate current income.

Three Basic Options

There are three basic options to approaching the issue of who gets the house: to sell the house, to have one spouse buy out the other spouse's half, or to have both ex-spouses continue to own the property jointly.

Sell the House. Selling the house and dividing the profits that remain after sales costs and the mortgage is paid off is the easiest and most "clean" way of dividing equity. Concerns that will need to be addressed include: the basis and possible capital gains (addressed later in this chapter), buying another house vs. renting, and being able to qualify for a new loan.

Buy Out the Other Spouse. Buying out the other spouse's half works if one person wants to remain in the house or wants to own the house, but there are difficulties with this option that need to be considered.

First of all, a value of the property needs to be agreed to. This is the equity in the house. Next, decide on the dollar amount of the buyout. Will the dollar amount be subtracted from it selling costs and capital gains taxes (in case the owner needs to sell it sooner than expected)?

Own the House Jointly. The other option—continuing to own the property jointly—is one used by some couples when they want the children to stay in the house until they finish school, reach a certain age, or the resident ex-spouse remarries, or cohabits. The couple may agree to sell the house after the children have graduated from school and split the proceeds evenly. The one who stays in the house in the meantime can pay the mortgage payment while all other costs of maintaining the house plus taxes and repairs can be split evenly. Again, this creates a tie between the ex-spouses that may create stress.

Tax Issues for Sale of a Residence

There are two special rules relating to divorce.

Ownership Period. If one spouse, pursuant to a divorce decree or separation agreement, is required to grant the other spouse the right to temporary possession of the home, but retains title to the home, and the home is later sold, the non-occupying spouse will be treated as having owned the home for the period of time that the occupying spouse owned the home as principal residence.

Use Period (new law). In the event one spouse transfers a residence to the other pursuant to a divorce decree, the "transferring spouse" shall be able to include the receiving spouse's use period in computing his own use period.

It should be noted that if one or the other remarries prior to sale of a jointly owned home, the remarried spouse can use the new spouse's time in the home to meet residency requirements to use the "married filing jointly" exclusion amount.

Example 1. John and Mary are getting divorced. John is awarded the family home jointly owned for four years. At the end of four years, John sells the home, and 50 percent of the proceeds are sent to Mary. John sells the home for $400,000. Mary will receive $200,000 and be entitled to use her $250,000 exclusion even though she has not lived in the home for the previous four years.

Example 2. John sells the home for $750,000. Mary will receive $375,000. If the basis in the property was $100,000, Mary's portion of the basis would be $50,000 leaving her with $325,000 gain. Even though she uses her $250,000 exclusion, she will be taxed on $75,000 of gain.

One good thing that the new tax law gave us is that this is not a one-time exclusion. We can use it over again every two years. So each time we buy a house and sell it after two years, we can use the exclusion.

PENSION PLANS

Pensions—also referred to as retirement plans—are recognized as part of the joint property acquired during the marriage and are treated as part of the assets to be divided upon divorce. Pension and retirement benefits that are earned during the marriage are potentially of great value. In a lasting marriage, they are generally the most valuable asset owned by a couple.

Method of Dividing Plans

There are two primary methods for dividing pension benefits. The first is the "buy-out" or "cash-out" method, which awards the non-employee spouse a lump sum settlement—or a marital asset of equal value—at the time of divorce in return for the employee's right to keep the pension. The second method is the "deferred division" or "future share" method where no present value needs to be determined. Each spouse is awarded an equal share of the benefits if and when they are paid.

There are two main types of retirement or pension plans: defined-contribution and defined-benefit. Basic explanation of how each plan works is presented next.

Defined Contribution Plan

One type of defined-contribution retirement plan is the 401(k) plan. However, even in the overall group of 401(k)s, there are different types with different rules. Each company can set its own rules for its retirement plans.

Three Types of Defined Contribution Plans. Marco Associates has three employees. John Jones is married and works for a company that has a 401(k) plan. John puts all of his retirement money into the 401(k) plan, and the company does not match his contributions. Any money that an employee puts into a 401(k) is considered to be fully vested by the company. John has worked for this company for three years and has accumulated $1,500 in his plan. This amount is assigned to the marital pot of assets.

Next, we present the case of Jim who works for a company where only the employer contributes to the 401(k) plan. Jim has worked there for three years and the value of his 401(k) plan is $1,500. The company uses a vesting schedule, which regulates what percentage of the plan's value belongs to Jim. In a typical vesting schedule, an employee is 30 percent vested in three years, 60 percent in five years, and 100 percent in seven years. According to this schedule currently, Jim is 30 percent vested. Therefore, his portion of 401(k) is $450 (30% of $1,500). This amount is assigned to the marital pot of assets.

Finally, we present the case of Sam. The policy of Sam's company is that, for every dollar Sam puts in his 401(k) plan, the company matches it with 50 cents. Sam has worked for the company for three years and currently has $1,500 in his 401(k) plan. Out of $1,500, Sam's contribution is $1,000 and the company has put in $500 with its matching program. In this case, although Sam is 30 percent vested, he is 100 percent vested insofar as his own contribution ($1,000) is concerned. Therefore, Sam's marital portion of the 401(k) plan is $1,150 ($1,000 + 30% of $500). The following table contrasts the three qualified plans presented above.

	John	*Jim*	*Sam*
Employee/Employer contribution	None	None	$1/50 cents
Length of employment	3 years	3 years	3 years
Value of 401(k) at divorce	$1,500	$1,500	$1,500
Percent vested	100%	30%	30%
Marital portion	$1,500	$450	$1,150

Clearly, each of the three different defined contribution plans valued the marital portion of 401(k) in a different way, depending on the company's policy. Therefore, in order to divide this asset in a divorce, a Qualified Domestic Relations Order (QDRO) must be used.

Qualified Domestic Relations Order (QDRO). In 1986 an amendment to the Retirement Equity Act empowered state courts to determine the division of certain pension and retirement plans that are covered by ERISA. QDRO[3] is an order from the court to the employer's pension plan administrator to spell out how the plan's benefits are to be assigned to each party in a divorce. QDROs must be prepared by professionals like an attorney or someone who specializes in QDROs. This Order determines what portion (from 0 percent to 100 percent) of the money in the plan is to be assigned to the employee's spouse.

Transferring Assets from a Defined Contribution Plan. When the ex-spouse receives the 401(k) asset, a set of specific rules apply, as can be seen from the following illustrations.

> Esther was married to an airline pilot named John who was nearing retirement. At the time they were both age 55. There was $640,000 in John's 401(k) plan, and in the event of a divorce the retirement plan was prepared to transfer $320,000 to Esther. In such a contingency the law allowed Esther to transfer the money into an IRA and defer taxes on this amount. However, because of the divorce, her legal fees were $60,000, and she needed another $20,000 to fix the roof of her house. Therefore, she held back $80,000 and transferred the remaining amount into her IRA. She was able to spend the $80,000 without incurring a 10 percent penalty.

> Because the 401k withholds 20 percent to apply toward taxes on a withdrawal, Esther should have asked for $100,000. After the 20 percent withholding, she would have $80,000 in cash and $220,000 to transfer to her IRA.

> The reason as to why this strategy worked is that an IRS rule specifies that any money received from a qualified plan in a divorce settlement can be withdrawn without penalty (even if the recipient is under age 59-1/2), although income taxes would be due on the funds withdrawn from the IRA. [Tax code (72)(t)(2)(C)].

Incidentally, it is important to differentiate between rolling over and transferring money from a qualified plan. The Unemployment Compensation Amendment Act (UCA) specifies that funds withdrawn from a qualified plan or tax-sheltered annuity would be subject to 20 percent withholding. However, that rule does not apply to IRAs or SEPs.

Defined Benefit Plan

A defined-benefit retirement plan promises to pay the employee upon retirement a predetermined amount of monthly income. Frequently, pension plans specify whether the income will be paid for life, during the life of both spouses, or for a certain period of time. The value of a defined-benefit plan is determined by the company's guarantee to honor a predetermined plan formula, and not by the account balance of the plan.

---

[3] Informational Guide on "QDROs" Under the IBM Retirement Plan, Prepared for Counsel in Domestic Relations Matters. June 1, 1991.

In a defined-benefit plan, the determination of the monthly income could be based on either a simple or a complex formula. For instance, the amount of monthly income could be determined by a complex calculation which could include the following: (1) the employee's final average salary; (2) an annuity factor based on the employee's age at retirement; (3) annual average Social Security tax base; (4) total number of years of employment; (5) age at retirement; (6) method chosen by the employee to receive payment of voluntary and required contributions; and (7) single life annuity or joint life annuity. The following is an example of how a complex defined-benefit plan might work.

Let us assume that based on today's earnings and length of time with the company, starting with age 65 Henry will receive $1,200 per month from his pension plan. Currently, Henry is 56 years old, and he has to wait nine more years before he can start receiving his pension. However, at the present time it is possible to calculate the *present value* of this future stream of income, or "future benefit," which can be included in the list of assets for purposes of dividing the property in a divorce settlement.

Incidentally, in the case of a divorce settlement it is possible to divide the defined-benefit plan according to a QDRO by stating that Ginny will receive $600 when Henry retires. However, the problem with that strategy is that, when he retires nine years later, Henry's monthly pension will undoubtedly be larger than the $1,200 amount. Nevertheless, if the QDRO states that, at Henry's age 65, Ginny would start receiving $600 per month, then she will not be allowed to participate in the growth of the pension.

Another factor which may complicate this matter is the assumption on which the company calculates the size of the pension. It is therefore important to find out whether the $1,200 pension is based on *today*'s earnings and time with the company, or on the assumption that he will stay with the company until age 65 with projected growth in earnings built into the calculation. If the pension document does not clarify this issue, then the assistance of the plan administrator should be sought to clarify the matter.

The above discussion makes one important point: It may not be in Ginny's best interest to accept the $600 per month settlement. Consequently, assuming that they have been married for 32 years and Henry's retirement is nine years away, it might be more prudent to use the following method:

Number of years married while working	32 years
Total number of years until retirement	41 years
Henry's expected monthly pension upon retirement	$1,800
Ginny's share of monthly income	Half of [32/41 x $1,800], or $702

The pension benefit of $702 might represent a more equitable division of the pension plan based on the premise that Ginny was married to Henry during the period when the majority of the build-up in the plan occurred.

Incidentally, it is important to ascertain if the plan will start making monthly payments to Ginny even if Henry chooses not to retire at age 65. Some companies do allow the ex-spouse to start receiving benefits at retirement age even if the employee chooses to postpone retirement.

Case studies demonstrating three different parameters of defined benefit plans

Case 1. Based on the employee's termination of employment
Richard, who is 52, will receive $2,600 per month ($31,200/year) at age 65 from his defined benefit plan. This calculation is based on his years of service and current earnings. Richard's life expectancy is 78.9 years. Using a financial calculator:

$$Payment = \$31,200$$
$$n = 13.9 \text{ (Life expectancy of 78.9 less retirement age of 65)}$$
$$I = 5.5$$
$$PV = \$278,758$$

That is, a lump sum of $278,758 would be needed to pay Richard $31,200 per year for 13.9 years, starting with his age 65.

Next, we calculate the present value of $278,758, which works out to $148,450:

$$FV = \$278,758$$
$$n = 13$$
$$I = 5.5$$
$$PV = \$148,450$$

Thus, if $148,450 is invested today at 5.5 percent, then in 13 years the money would grow to $287,758. That amount would be sufficient to pay Richard $31,200 per year for 13.9 years. Based on this calculation at the time of divorce, Richard's wife will be awarded one half of $148,450, or $74,225.

Case 2. Based on the employee working until age 65
Henry and Sara have been married for 25 years. Henry has been working for his company for 20 years. Henry is going to continue to work there *at his current level* after they have been divorced. His defined-benefit pension plan will pay him $2,600 per month at age 65. He is now age 52 and his life expectancy is 78.9 years.

The present value in this case is exactly the same as the first one—$148,450. However, since Richard has worked for one company for 20 years and intends to work for the same company for a total of 33 years, the marital portion of his pension will be 20/33rds of the present value:

$$(20/33) \text{ x } \$148,450 = \$89,970$$

That is, the present value of the marital portion of Henry's pension is $89,970.

Case 3. Variation of Case 1
Larry and Sue have been married for 15 years. Larry has worked for his company for 20 years, but no longer wishes to work for that company. Larry is now age 52, and his life expectancy is 78.9 years. Here, again, the present value is $148,450—the same as in the two previous cases. However, in this case, the marital portion of the pension is $111,337:

$$(15/20) \text{ x } \$148,450 = \$111,337$$

That is, the present value of the marital portion of Larry's pension is $111,337.

Let us assume that in this case a QDRO was drafted which would allow Sue to receive a portion of the monthly payment when Larry retires. Under that arrangement, when Larry retires, Sue will receive 75 percent (15/20) of the marital portion of the monthly payment. That is, upon Larry's retirement, Sue would start receiving half of 75 percent, or 37-1/2 percent, of $2,600. In other words, Sue would receive a monthly income of $975 (37-1/2 % of $2,600).

Public Employees Pension Plan

Another type of defined benefit plan is available to public employees, such as school teachers, principals, librarians, firemen, policemen and state troopers. In a divorce, typically this type of plan will not allow any division by order of a QDRO.

In a defined benefit plan covering public employees, each year employees get a statement showing their contributions to this plan. This sum of money plus interest is available if the employee quits or is fired. However, if the job continues for a minimum number of years (usually 20 or 25), the employee will receive an annuity retirement payout which is equal to a percentage of the final pay. The following example illustrates this point.

Janice and Frank had been married for 23 years. Frank started out as a school teacher, and at the time of their divorce he was the Principal of the high school in a small city. The statement of his retirement account showed that he had paid in $82,050 which Frank used as the value of his retirement. His attorney accepted this number. However, Janice's attorney hired a financial expert who determined that, upon retirement, Frank will receive 60 percent of his final average salary, or $32,050 per year. The expert testified in court that the present value of the marital portion of that future stream of income was $373,060, and not $82,050 as determined by Frank. The judge agreed with Janice's position and determined that via a Property Settlement Note Frank would have to make a prespecified monthly payment to Janice for 20 years.

MAINTENANCE

For all practical purposes, alimony and maintenance payments are synonymous terms. Alimony is a series of payments from one spouse to another, or to a third party on behalf of the receiving spouse. Alimony is treated as taxable income to the recipient and, with few exceptions, it is a tax-deductible expense to the payer. The term "maintenance" implies virtually everything that alimony does.

Issues Relating to Maintenance

It used to be that "fault" determined alimony. Today, alimony is awarded based on any one of the following criteria: (1) need; (2) ability-to-pay; (3) length of marriage; (4) previous lifestyle; and (5) age and health of both parties.

Rehabilitative Maintenance

Maintenance stops upon the death of the payor, or upon the remarriage of the recipient. In the 70s courts began to recognize the need for a transition period, because it was unrealistic to expect that the non-working spouse would instantly

reach her earning potential. For this reason, the concept of rehabilitative maintenance was introduced. For example if the wife needs three years of school to finish
her degree, or requires special training to update old skills, then she may be given
"rehabilitative" maintenance for that period. Such a provision will give her the much-
needed temporary financial help, so ultimately she would be able to earn an amount
sufficient to support herself.

Modifiable versus Non-modifiable Maintenance

The one constant in life is change. Consequently, it is safe to assume that the
final settlement decided in court will not apply to all possible future scenarios. To
allow some flexibility to accommodate the unexpected changes, frequently the court
maintains "jurisdiction" over a divorce case by adopting the modifiable maintenance
provision. This allows the court to modify the terms of support if warranted by a
significant change of circumstances. Incidentally, non-modifiable maintenance provision is rarely used because it is largely impractical.

Guaranteed Maintenance

The divorce decree clearly stipulates that for a specified time a certain amount
of maintenance will be paid. However, there are several ways in which an ex-spouse
can avoid making the mandated payments. To safeguard against such a contingency,
courts have devised certain actions which are discussed next.

Life Insurance. Alimony payments stop upon the death of the payor. Therefore, frequently it is stipulated in the divorce decree that life insurance will be
carried on the life of the payor to replace the alimony payments in the event of the
payor's death. Incidentally, if a new policy is to be purchased, it should be done
before the divorce is final, so the uninsurability of the payor would not be an issue.
Also, for two important reasons, the recipient spouse should either own the life
insurance or be an irrevocable beneficiary. First, such an arrangement would guarantee that premiums will be paid when due. Second, if the beneficiary spouse either owns the policy or is an irrevocable beneficiary, and the premium payments
are made under a legal obligation imposed by the divorce decree, then the premiums are considered to be alimony and hence can be treated as tax deductible by
the payor. A second way to guarantee the stream of maintenance income in the
case of payor's disability is to have the payor purchase a disability insurance. The
ex-wife cannot own the disability policy, but she should make the payments to ensure that the policy would remain in force.

Annuity. A third way to guarantee maintenance is to have the payor buy an
immediate annuity that will pay for a specified period a guaranteed fixed monthly
payment equal to the maintenance payment.

CHILD SUPPORT

In a divorce situation, the non-custodial parent is usually ordered to pay a predetermined amount of child support to the custodial parent. The remainder of the
child's expenses are paid by the custodial parent.

All states have established guidelines that help the courts decide the amount of child support to be paid. The support obligation of each parent is often based on the ratio of each parent's income, the percentage of time the child spends with each parent, and the amount of alimony payments made to the custodial parent. An example should make this clear.

Paul's gross income is $4,300 a month and Becky's gross income is $900 a month; together they earn $5,200, as shown below:

	Amount	*Ratio*
Paul	$4,300	83%
Becky	900	17%
	$5,200	100%

The table shows that Paul is earning 83 percent of the total income and Becky is earning the remaining 17 percent. The couple has two children. The Child Support Guidelines for two children is $983. Using the Guidelines, 83 percent of the suggested monthly payment of $983, or $813, is what Paul owes Becky for monthly child support *if he pays no maintenance.*

Now let us assume that Paul is going to pay Becky a maintenance of $1,000 a month. In that case $1,000 would be transferred from Paul's income to Becky's income, as shown below:

	Amount	*Ratio*
Paul	$4,300 – $1,000 = $3,300	63%
Becky	$900 + $1,000 = $1,900	37%
	$5,200	100%

The total income stays the same but the relative percentages significantly change. So, using the same Guidelines formula, Paul will pay $624 per month ($983 x 63%) to Becky instead of the $813 amount which was determined in the previous case. It can therefore be stated that, as a rule, child support decreases with an increase in maintenance payments.

Modifying Child Support

A critical question in divorce planning is: What happens when circumstances change after the divorce becomes final? This would be the case if the husband or the wife loses the job, one person becomes disabled, a settlement or judgment is awarded against one spouse that was started when they were still married, or when one of them wins the lottery.

Unfortunately, the property settlement is considered final and cannot be changed, unless of course it can be demonstrated that fraud was involved. However, the child support and maintenance can be modified when there is a significant change in circumstances.

INCOME TAX CONSIDERATIONS

Child support payments cannot be deducted by the payor and are not includable in the income of the recipient. If the divorcing parents have only one child, during any taxable year that child can be counted as an exemption by only one parent.

Unless otherwise specified, the exemption usually goes to the parent who has the physical custody of the child for the greater portion of the calendar year.

Incidentally, the tax exemption for a child can be traded back and forth from year to another between the parents with a written waiver or IRS Form 8332. Once the custodial parent has executed the waiver, the noncustodial parent must attach the form to his or her income tax return. If the waiver is for more than one year, a copy of the form must be attached to the noncustodial parent's return for each year.

If the family has more than one child, the parents may divide up the exemptions. The children's Social Security numbers must be listed on each parent's tax return. That rule is designed to ensure that if both parents claim the same child or children on their individual tax returns, then they will inevitably invite an IRS audit.

Incidentally, for either parent to claim the exemption, the child must be in custody of at least one parent for more than one-half of the calendar year. If the child lives with a grandparent or someone other than a parent for more than one-half of the calendar year, neither parent can claim the exemption.

Child Care Credit

A custodial parent who pays child care expenses so that he or she can be gainfully employed may be eligible for tax credit for up to $2,400 ($4,800 for two or more children). To claim this credit, the parent must maintain a household that is the home of at least one child, and the day care expenses must be paid to someone who is not claimed as a dependent. Only the custodial parent is entitled to claim both the child and the dependent care credit. This is true even if the custodial parent does not claim the dependency exemption for the child. A noncustodial parent may not claim a child care credit for expenses incurred even if that parent is entitled to claim the exemption for the child.

Head of Household

A head-of-household filing status is available for those who are divorced (single), who provide more than one-half the cost of maintaining the household, and whose household is the principal home of at least one qualifying person for more than one-half of the year. A "qualifying person" is their child or any other person who qualifies as their dependent.

In determining whether the home is the principal home of the child for more than one-half of the year, absences for vacation, sickness, school, or military service cannot be counted as time spent away from home if it was reasonable to assume that the child would return to the home.

It takes courage to push yourself to places that you have never been before . . . to test your limits . . . to break through barriers.

Daniel Webster

CHAPTER 20

Planning for Widows

INTRODUCTION

Psychologists say that the loss of a husband is the single most stressful event in the life of a wife. Recently, it was estimated that in the U.S. about 12 percent of some 100 million adult women are widows. Statistics also reveal that widows out-live their husbands by approximately seven years.

In the financial planning profession there are many advisors who *target market* to women. It is highly likely that even those who do not specialize in working with widows sometimes will wind up working with them. These widows could be the surviving spouses or the mothers of current clients, or they could be the advisor's own mother or mother-in-law. For these reasons, this chapter is devoted to a brief discussion of the issues relating to planning for widows. However, advisors who are more serious about pursuing this line of work are strongly advised to study Alexandra Armstrong and Mary Donahue's book, *On Your Own, A Widow's Passage to Emotional and Financial Well-being*, published by Dearborn, a Kaplan Professional Company, Third Edition 2000.

DIFFERENCES AMONG WIDOWS

Levels of Differences

Let us discuss the *widow* market. It is a comparatively large market. Women are still outliving men. In the U.S., 73 percent of women die as single individuals.

Ms. Alexandra Armstrong, CFP, is nationally recognized as an expert in planning for widows. This is borne out by the fact that the book, *On Your Own* (Dearborn Publishing Company), which she co-authored, quickly sold 25,000 copies, and is already in its third edition. Because of the complexity and the sophisticated nature of the subject matter, as the leading authority, Ms. Armstrong was invited to write this chapter. We are certain that the reader will greatly benefit from her experiences in planning for widows.

However, all widows are not alike. Just as we would not place all retirees into one group, we should not also do the same with widows. For instance, widows differ with respect to age, causes of the spouse's death, ages and number of dependents, depth of their financial knowledge, and the amount of financial resources they own. It is important for advisors to know what the differences are, and how best to work with individual widows with specific characteristics.

The Age Issue

Most of us have a visual picture of widows as being little-old, blue-haired, ladies in their seventies. Actually 26 percent of widows are under the age of 65 and ten percent are under the age of 55. Therefore, we should recognize that the reactions to widowhood of the older widows will be different from those who are their younger counterparts.

Cause of Husband's Death

It is important to quickly determine the cause of the husband's death. If, for instance, the husband had been ill for some time, then it would not be a great shock to the widow when he dies. In contrast, when the husband's death is sudden, the widow will take more time to recover emotionally, and hence it would initially be harder to effectively work with her.

Responsibilities for Dependents

Next, it is important to learn about the ages and educational needs of the dependent children. Also, if the children are entitled to receive Social Security income, it is important to know how long they would be eligible to receive these payments.

Interestingly, widows with dependent children tend to recover emotionally faster than widows who have only themselves to worry about. This is because the widows pull themselves out of their own mourning in order to help their children. In fact, in the long run, the fact that these people work together as a family unit benefits both the widow and the children.

An integral part of planning for widows is the determination of economic conditions of each of the children and grandchildren. This is because the widow may consider it desirable to contribute to their financial well being either on a regular or on a when-needed basis.

Before leaving this topic, it should be mentioned that sometimes an adult child would like to accompany the mother to the office of the advisor for the initial interview. This is because the adult child wants to make sure that the advisor will serve the interests of the mother. In such a situation, the advisor should ask the widowed mother if she would like copies of all correspondence sent to various family members. Even if the adult children don't accompany the mother to visit with the advisor, the advisor should still ask if she would like others copied on your correspondence to them. This is the best way to make the children permanent allies rather than adversaries of the advisor.

Amount of Financial Knowledge

During the initial interview, it is critical to determine the depth of financial knowledge and experience of the widow. Although women are constantly learning about finances and investments, many are financially ignorant either because they are not interested, suffer from math anxiety, or their husbands did not involve them in the financial decision-making process. They may have handled the checkbook and paid household expenses but have not been involved in the investment process.

A frequent mistake advisors make is in assuming that the widow who has a career outside the home is better able to handle her own financial affairs. Often this is not true. This woman has been taking care of her husband, her home, her family and her job. Handling the financial matters as well is often delegated to her husband with a sigh of relief.

Regardless of how financially ignorant a widow appears to be, one should not make the mistake of confusing a lack of knowledge with a lack of ability to learn. Often, all that the widow needs is the reassurance that, over time, she can acquire the knowledge with the assistance of the advisor. It is important to emphasize that learning about financial matters is at best a gradual process, and at worst it can appear to be at an extremely slow and time consuming activity.

Amount of Financial Resources

As expected, there are significant differences in the amount of wealth inherited by a widow. Many advisors naively assume that widows who inherit substantial sums of money are in better shape than those who inherit less or none. While this is financially true, psychologically the widow is often overwhelmed by the enormity of the responsibility.

In some cases what seems to be a large amount of money to the widow may give her a false sense of security which sometimes leads to extravagant spending behavior, especially in the initial stages. That is, urge to spend has psychological roots. The widow is in a situation which she did not cause nor could she prevent from happening—widowhood. Consequently, to prove to herself and others that she is in control, she spends money lavishly on such items as redecorating her house, taking the family on trips, and/or buying a new car. It is therefore wise to impress upon her that this money has to support her for the rest of her life. Thus she needs to watch what she spends, particularly in the initial stage.

SIMILARITIES AMONG WIDOWS

Experience teaches us that while all widows are not the same, they do have certain things in common. For instance, even if the husband dies of a lingering illness and one might assume that there would only be a minimal effect on the widow, there is still the initial psychological shock of his absence from her life, especially if they had enjoyed a long and happy married life. If the death is sudden or unexpected the shock prolongs the healing process. Recognition of this is important, because the appearance of outward calm on the part of the widow might be highly deceptive—at least during the initial months after the death of the husband. Consequently, it is highly desirable to put any advice given to the widow in writing so she can refer back to it at a later date. Following such a practice would have the added advantage of creating a permanent record which could be referred to by the advisor or by anyone else who may have an interest in this matter.

Another factor which is common among most widows is that they are afraid of the future—handling financial affairs as well as their personal lives. Moreover, this fear is intensified by those who lack experience in handling financial affairs. This is borne out by the fact that even relatively wealthy widows fear outliving their wealth.

WINNING WIDOWS AMONG CLIENTS

For those interested in *target marketing* to widows, the best source of prospecting is through other professional advisors like estate planning lawyers, CPAs, grief counselors, psychologists, spiritual advisors, and funeral directors. This method of marketing provides the all-too-valuable third party endorsement.

Attorneys

One of the best sources of referrals is the estate planning attorneys. However, the process of establishing a workable relationship with an attorney is not easily accomplished.

There is, of course, no single formula that can be adopted to assure success in working with attorneys. Some advisors prefer to establish a two-way relationship with them, while others are more comfortable taking a longer view of the task. One strategy, which proved to be highly effective for Alexandra Armstrong, consisted of having business lunches with estate planning attorneys one-on-one on a systematic basis. During these meetings, she would ask about the kind of client they preferred and would also tell them how she could help their clients budget and invest. Once Mrs. Armstrong was comfortable with the personality and the competence of the estate planning attorneys, she kept in touch with them by mailing them letters and articles of interest. Although results were not immediate, eventually these efforts handsomely paid off for her as well as for the participating attorneys.

Accountants

Accountants and CPAs who prepare tax returns for widows can also act as a good referral source. Here again, it is desirable to establish a two-way street for referrals. It also pays to apprise the accountants of the services the advisor performs for widows and indicate that the advisor intends to send them clients who need tax preparation services.

Estate Planning Council

An effective strategy for getting referrals is to become active in the local estate planning council. The membership, which is possible only through the nomination by existing members, is comprised of the estate planning lawyers, accountants, insurance agents, trust officers, and financial planners. Typically, these groups discuss the estate planning topics in their quarterly meetings. In many instances council members are looking for referrals, which provides the advisors the opportunity for establishing a long-term relationship with these members.

Emotional/Spiritual Advisors

As mentioned, the death of a husband is a traumatic experience. Consequently, most widows could benefit from assistance of established professionals like grief counselors, psychologists, spiritual advisors, and widow support groups. Not all financial advisors have either the expertise or the desire to act as emotional or spiritual advisors. However, those who want to work with these advisors should consult a minister or a rabbi, so they could be included in the *approved* list of financial advisors.

Funeral Directors

Like other business professionals, funeral directors are very much interested in attracting referral business. Consequently, advisors willing to work with widows could give funeral directors gifts like Armstrong's book, *On Your Own*, with his or her business card attached.

Widow Support Groups

An effective way of getting referrals is to speak to the widow support groups. Such a forum allows the advisor to persuade the attendees that they understand, and are sensitive to, the special needs of widows.

Other Widows

Clearly, the best source of referral is a widow who is also a client. When a widow is appreciative of the advisor's performance, and learns that the advisor is looking for referral business, quite often she is happy to refer friends and acquaintances.

WORKING WITH WIDOWS

Widows of Clients

Advisors interested in working with widows of their own clients should establish an initial contact soon after the notice appears in the obituary columns. It is therefore necessary for the advisors to scan this column on a daily basis. The simplest way of making contact with a widow is to attend the funeral services (or at least visit the funeral parlor) and contribute to the favorite charity of the deceased person. In addition, it is advisable to write the widow a note expressing sorrow and saying that he/she is available to meet with the widow and/or her other advisors as soon as she is up to it. These activities clearly demonstrate to the widow that the advisor cares for her and shares in her grief.

An efficient way of establishing credibility with the widow's accountant and attorney is to send them an investment portfolio priced as of the date of death and a current cash flow statement (if available). In all probability they will need these statements in the near future, and providing these statements to the professionals before they ask for them could result in the advisor's receiving new business from them.

Initial Office Visit

As soon as possible after the death of the husband, the advisor should arrange for the widow to have an initial visit in the office. Since this visit is crucial to the future relationship, it is imperative that the meeting be conducted with utmost care.

More specifically, in arranging this meeting the advisor should treat the widow as if she was a prospective client, even though the widow was a client when the husband was alive. Additionally, the advisor should suggest that the widow bring with her a family member, a close friend or a relative to the meeting. This is because the widow is not likely to remember everything that was discussed at the first meeting. Another person not directly suffering from the loss could review some of the important topics later with her in the privacy of her home.

Incidentally, if the widow feels up to the task, prior to the meeting it is desirable to send her a financial planning questionnaire. The widow could bring the finished questionnaire to the meeting which would undoubtedly assist the advisor in providing timely assistance. However, realistically speaking, in her mental condition a new widow may not be in a position to provide all the information needed to complete the questionnaire. In that case, the advisor must show sufficient flexibility to allow her to take additional time to complete the task after the initial meeting or during the meeting.

In addition to being flexible, it is important for the advisor to immediately express concern and sympathy for the loss of the husband. This is because during this period of grief nothing upsets a widow more than the perception that the advisor *does not seem to care* about her personally, and is only interested in her money. In the final analysis, expressing concern about her situation could very well be the key to keeping the widow as a long-term client.

One final point: At the initial meeting the critical question on the mind of every widow is: "Will I have enough money to live on?" The advisor can alleviate a great deal of her fear and anxiety by answering that question at the earliest possible opportunity.

Avoiding Irrevocable Decisions

It is often said that a widow should avoid making irrevocable decisions during the first year of her husband's death. This is a sound advice and it should be repeated often by the advisor.

In keeping with the advice just presented, it is highly desirable for the advisor to suggest that the widow stay in her present home for at least one year. This will not only provide the continuity that she desperately needs, but it will also solve the problems associated with selling a home and moving to a new environment. Of course, selling the home and moving to another city where the relatives reside might constitute a viable alternative. However, this alternative should be explored only if the widow knows other people living in the new town and is comfortable joining social and civic organizations to keep her occupied and entertained.

At a more mundane level, the widow should be cautioned against spending large sums of money on big ticket items like a car, an extended trip around the world, or expensive jewelry. This is because, at the initial stage, it is difficult to determine how much money she will need in the future to maintain her desired standard of living.

Another area of major concern is the compulsion the widow may feel to convert the husband's life insurance funds into a lifetime annuity so she would be assured of receiving steady income for life. As appealing as that might initially appear, such an irrevocable decision should not be made until after the advisor has had the opportunity to analyze the total picture.

To recapitulate, during the first year after the death of the husband, it is preferable that the widow not make any irrevocable decisions. The reason is that death brings trauma to one's life, and even those widows who appear to be operating normally are affected by it. Therefore, initially the advisor should concentrate on short-term decisions and leave the other ones to be tackled at a later date.

Follow-Up Meetings

Once the formalities of the initial meeting are completed, it will be necessary to collect from the widow all the relevant information. It is certainly more convenient and efficient if the widow could be persuaded to bring all the information to the office. However, that may not be practical if the widow is feeling totally lost and helpless in handling the administrative details. In that case the advisor may not have any choice but to arrange for someone to visit the widow in her home. In either case, it would be highly desirable for the advisor to help the widow get organized by suggesting she buy a filing cabinet and providing her with folders with the appropriate labels for convenient use.

EXPLAINING THE FINANCIAL PLANNING APPROACH

In most instances, the greatest value added service provided by an advisor is in the area of financial planning. Here the advisor must be both creative and technically proficient in order to provide the quality of service the widow richly deserves. How financial advisors should handle this task is best explained by Alexandra Armstrong herself in the boxed insert.

EXPLAINING THE FINANCIAL PLANNING APPROACH

Alexandra Armstrong, CFP™, CMFC

After I have listened to the widow explain her situation, I tell her how I think I can be of assistance. First, I tell her it is essential that she has a financial plan prepared for her so I can objectively look at her current situation as well as her future prognosis. I explain to her that it is not sufficient just to focus on her current expenses and income, but to do some long term planning as well. In fact, even though she is concentrating on getting through each day, our job is to plan for the rest of her life.

I have found that the widow may resist going through the financial planning process. She is worried as to whether she will have sufficient income and is thus impatient to get the money to work for her as soon as possible. However, I end up convincing her that the selection of the investments is part of the big picture and that I could give her better advice if I could look at the total picture first. In addition, I inform her that once the information is in a computer, I would be in a better position to assist her with future decisions.

Next, I explain that the first step toward preparing a financial plan is to determine her financial goals, one of which undoubtedly is to have sufficient income to live on. Of course, I must also examine her secondary goals, such as educating her children/grandchildren. In other words, I not only review her financial goals with her, but also help her prioritize them. Incidentally, this is not the time to tell her that she may not be able to achieve all her goals even if that appears to be a certainty. At this point I just obtain her *wish* list.

Then I discuss her attitude toward risk which is generally risk averse, at least initially until she is more comfortable with her financial situation. Finally, I review her investment objective, which most widows say is *high current income.*

After reviewing the *soft* parts of the financial plan, I help the widow determine her assets and liabilities. To make it easier I suggest she divide her assets between personal and retirement assets. Then we discuss her current and future liabilities.

But as I said above, her primary concern is: "Do I have enough to live on?" I explain to her that we will *run the numbers*, reflecting her current investments and expected income. Then we will balance that income against her estimated future expenses. Incidentally, some widows know exactly what they spend and can project what they will spend in the future because they paid all the household bills, while others feel helpless because they did not participate in the budgeting process.

In both cases I ask the widow to review their checkbook over the past six months, keeping in mind that these expenses have to be adjusted downward. Based on this information I suggest that she estimate her expenses. I recommend that she make two columns of expenses—one with the required expenses (such as mortgage payments) and the other one for her *wish* list.

Incidentally, one of the most common questions asked me at this point is, "Should I pay off the mortgage so I don't have that high monthly expense?" I respond by saying that might be a good idea except that by doing so she will lose the tax deductions. This is an example of the type of question that will be much easier to answer once we have looked at the total picture of projected cash flow and taxable income.

At this point I do caution the widow against spending substantial amounts of money on items like a new car, redecorating the house, or taking a family vacation. I suggest her to go slow on this type of expenditure so she will not spend the money she might need in the future. I also tell her that at the other extreme are those widows who are so worried about running out of money that they spend nothing. Here again, I tell her that once we have the financial plan in place, it will be relatively easy to determine how much discretionary income she will have.

A similar issue surrounds loaning money to family members or friends. Often, a widow is approached for loaning money, or making new investments. On this point I suggest that she should turn down the request for a loan until she fully understands her total financial situation. I tell her that she can even use me as an excuse for such a refusal.

An important issue to discuss with the widow is that when we prepare her financial plan we make the assumption that she will not remarry. This is because there is no guarantee that her new husband will be able to support her. By accepting this assumption, she will accept the fact that the funds she has might be all that she is going to have for the rest of her life.

I tell her that the *first cash flow statement* I will include in her financial plan will be an estimate of her expenses. Then after six months we will see if these estimates are still realistic. That's why I tell her that, starting immediately, she should start keeping a record of her expenses starting now. Actually, giving the widow these tasks makes her feel that she is getting back control of her life.

I tell the widow that subsequent to this meeting I will send her a letter summarizing what I understood her situation to be, what services I thought I could provide her and what it would cost. I ask that the widow sign and return to us this *letter of understanding* so we can start working on her financial plan.

In this letter we give the widow an estimated cost for the plan. We further explain that the price we quote is the most she would have to pay. However, if it takes less time than what we estimated, then we will charge less than the estimated cost. Again I think it is important that there is a clear *paper trail* of what I plan to do for the client.

We also enclose a contract which we ask her to sign and return to us which gives that fee quote. When we receive that back from her, we send her a copy for her files, as well as a letter introducing her to the members of my staff she may be talking to at our firm.

THE FINANCIAL PLAN

Collection of financial data is a prerequisite for the development of the comprehensive financial plan. However, creativity as well as sensitivity on the part of the advisor can go a long way toward developing a financial plan that will be deeply appreciated by the widow. This is easier said than done, because people differ both with respect to the details they can comprehend and the level of sophistication with which they are comfortable. In addition, if the widow has difficulty reading the fine print, then she might have difficulty reading the plan unless the print was enlarged to suit her needs.

Once the financial plan is completed, it should be mailed to the widow with the request that she take the time to study it, and develop a list of items that are either unclear to her or require additional explanation. Simultaneously, the plan should be mailed to other professionals or family members who have been identified by the widow.

As a general rule, the financial plan should include taxable income and cash flow projections for the current year as well as for the following two years. In addition, it should have the current balance sheet so the widow will have a complete picture of where she is now and where she is headed.

More specifically, the cash flow statement should include the projected expenses provided by the widow. These include both regular expenses as well as the one-time expenses. Also, the balance sheet should provide details of various asset and liabilities, and the current net worth.

After the widow has had the opportunity to review the financial plan, the advisor should adopt a strategy that best suits the situation. For instance, if the plan predicts that the widow will experience cash flow problems, then it would be desirable for the advisor to suggest ways of cutting down on expenses, or increasing the income. And even when problems are not anticipated, the advisor may be able to improve the financial picture by rearranging the investments or cutting down those expenses that the widow considers to be excessive or of marginal benefit. It is important to add here that, as an integral part of the overall strategy, the advisor should also review the current estate plan, the insurance coverage, and the tax status of the widow.

EDUCATING THE WIDOW

As mentioned, the presentation of the financial plan is almost always followed by a set of recommendations for remedial action. This occasion also creates an opportunity for explaining to the widow the pertinent financial concepts. These concepts can include, but are not limited to, the following:

- Reasons for prioritizing short- and long-term goals
- Techniques of educational planning if children are involved
- Tax planning
- Impact of inflation on future income
- Investment planning vis-à-vis diversification and reduction of risk

It is apropos to point out here that the discussion of financial concepts should be simple and straightforward, and it should always be undertaken in the context of the widow's current financial situation. Furthermore, even when the widow comprehends the financial concepts fairly well, recommendations for immediate actions should be kept at a bare minimum. The reason for this cautionary approach should now be obvious. As already stated, almost in all instances, during the initial period widows find it difficult to cope with the permanent loss of their husbands; hence it is not the time for recommending radical changes in their financial life, particularly if it was an investment selected by her husband.

BEYOND IMPLEMENTATION

The planning process does not end after the advisor's initial recommendations have been implemented. In fact, depending upon individual circumstances, it is advisable to continue for several years the review process on a regular basis. More specifically, for the first two or three years, it is highly desirable to have periodic face-to-face meetings with the widow. After that, if all goes well, annual meetings will probably be all that is necessary to help the widow achieve her long-term financial goals.

NON-FINANCIAL ADVICE

There is a widely-held belief that widows need about a year to recover from the loss of their husbands. This belief is somewhat misleading because widows never quite recover from the permanent loss of their partners. Nevertheless, it is safe to assume that, after the first year or so, most widows learn fairly well how to cope with the situation and get on with their lives.

In our opinion, it is not the place of the financial advisor to provide non-financial emotional support for the widow. However, if the advisor perceives that the widow is having difficulty recovering emotionally, the advisor can encourage the widow to seek the assistance of a grief counseling professional.

SPECIAL AREAS OF CONCERN

Advisors dealing with widows must recognize that they need more hand holding particularly initially than the average clients. This is borne out by the fact that widows tend to be deeply concerned with some issues that to other people appear to be trivial. For this reason, advisors should be sensitive to the special needs of their widow clients and respond to them promptly.

At this point, a word of caution might be in order. While it is desirable to be receptive to the needs of the widow no matter how trivial they may appear to be, it is equally important to ensure that the widow does not become too emotionally dependent on the advisor. This is especially important since it is in her best interest to become both financially and emotionally independent at the earliest possible opportunity.

CONCLUSION

Working with widows can be both challenging and rewarding. It requires special sensitivity, patience, and unique planning skills. Perhaps the best way to conclude this chapter is to present the advice of Alexandra Armstrong in her own words: "I like working with widows. I find them a good group to work with but I also recognize that not every planner is temperamentally suited to working with them. You need to genuinely care about helping the widow recover—both financially and emotionally. This may require more patience than you need in dealing with other clients. They do not always hear or understand what you say to them so you may find yourself repeating the same concepts with them over and over. That is, working with widows requires that you be a good listener. Also, it is not an exaggeration to say that oftentimes you spend as much time discussing family relationships as you do in dealing with her financial affairs.

I find it rewarding to be able to use my experience to help widows who really need and value my help. We really can make a difference in the quality of their lives. However, we cannot lose sight of the fact that with the trust they give us comes a responsibility. As advisors, it is our responsibility not to take advantage of their trust but to help them achieve financial stability *for the long term.*"

Quality is never an accident; it is always the result of high intention, sincere effort, intelligent direction and skillful execution; it represents the wise choice of many alternatives.

Willa Foster

CHAPTER 21

Managing a Financial Planning Practice

INTRODUCTION

The greatest challenge financial professionals face is the establishment and marketing of a successful financial planning service. This is easier said than done. For one thing, running a successful business requires the effective use of many talents and qualities. For another, even if a planner could possess all of these qualities—which is highly unlikely—it still would not be a good use of time to perform the myriad functions all by himself or herself. That is why it is extremely important for a financial planning business to reach the required minimum size as soon as possible so it could afford to engage the services of all the people necessary to efficiently market a successful practice.

This chapter is divided into three sections. Section I provides a conceptual framework for establishing and managing a successful financial planning practice. Clearly, some of the information included in this section will be either too advanced for small planning businesses or too basic for the large ones. However, as a compromise, we will present our approach to developing a *typical financial planning practice*. But the framework for the practice we selected is flexible, so it could be easily modified to suit the needs of a financial planning practice of any size.

At this point, an important caveat should be added. We believe that practice management is as much an art as it is a science, and a conceptual framework will not provide sufficient information for the serious planner. Therefore, we have invited Deena Katz, a nationally recognized expert in practice management, to share with us both the conceptual and practical aspects of managing a financial planning practice. Ms. Katz has gained years of experience as the President of Evensky, Brown & Katz, a highly successful financial planning practice based in Coral Gables, Florida, and has published two outstanding books on this subject.

Deena Katz on Practice Management for Financial Advisors, Planners, and Wealth Managers (Bloomberg Press, 1999)[1] provides a practical hands-on approach to the management of a financial planning practice. The book breaks down the management into core components, making it easier for the reader to focus on those areas that need attention. It provides practical and tested approaches to the every day problems that a modern financial planning practice faces.

Deena Katz's Tools and Templates for your Practice for Financial Advisors, Planners, and Wealth Managers (Bloomberg Press, 2001)[1] is the perfect complement to her first book. This book is a treasure chest. Ms. Katz has opened up her private files and given you all the forms her firm uses on a daily basis. These forms are available on the CD-ROM, included with the book. She also provides the logic, insight and use of each of the forms. For a new practitioner or a seasoned veteran, this book can make a practice become more efficient.

Since Ms. Katz's communication style is significantly different from our style, for obtaining best results, in Section II we will reproduce excerpts from her practice management book. Financial planners, who are serious about this subject, however, should be forewarned that these excerpts only scratch the surface, and they should read both of Katz's books on practice management.

Finally, in Section III issues relating to the sale of a practice are presented. This section concludes with the presentation of a real world case study.

SECTION I
CONCEPTUAL FRAMEWORK
FOR PRACTICE MANAGEMENT

GETTNG STARTED

Like most other professional service businesses, financial planning is labor intensive. This feature of the planning business causes problems in a profession subject to ever-increasing labor costs, intense price competition, shortage of qualified personnel, and restricted client budgets for professional planning services. In such an environment, efficient management of available resources is especially important. In a financial planning business these are comprised of human (professional and support), physical (equipment, office, furniture), and capital resources. Management of these resources requires the development of a business plan which determines the goals of the business, and actions that should be taken to meet these goals.

The cornerstones of a financial planning business plan are organization, operation, finance, and marketing. Each area must be developed fully and coordinated with the rest in order to make the business plan truly functional.

---

[1] From *Deena Katz on Practice Management for Financial Advisors, Planners, and Wealth Managers.* ©1999 by Deena B. Katz. *Deena Katz's Tools and Templates for Your Practice for Financial Advisors, Planners and Wealth Managers.* ©2001 by Deena B. Katz. Excerpts from the book are reproduced with permission of Bloomberg Press, Princeton, New Jersey.

A detailed blueprint of a financial planning written business plan is presented in Figure 21-1. The business plan is divided into two broad segments: The external environment and the corporate structure.

EXTERNAL ENVIRONMENT

The best business plans are developed in the context of a thorough analysis of the external factors which have an impact upon the business, such as the economics of the planning business, the nature of the marketplace, the scope of the target market, and the regulatory and social environment.

Economics of Planning Business

As mentioned, the financial planning business is labor intensive. That is, the primary factor in production is people, as opposed to capital resources, such as land, factories, and equipment. Since labor—or more specifically labor with high technical competence and marketable skills—is expensive, a financial planning firm is often faced with costs which rise faster than the ability of the firm to increase earnings, resulting in a perennial income squeeze.

The problem of income squeeze often leads to ancillary problems which can best be described as "growing pains." Eventually, many successful financial planning practices are faced with the decision to either expand the business or let the

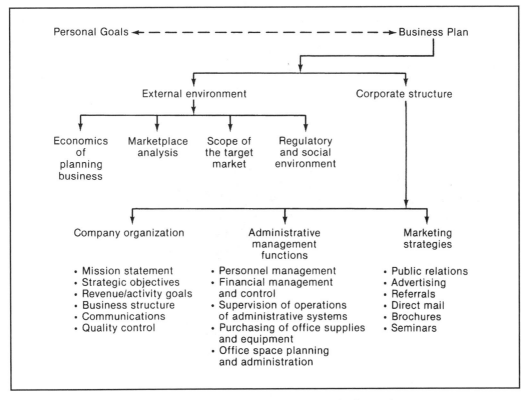

FIGURE 21-1 Financial planning: a written business plan.

work suffer in both quality and efficiency. If the former is selected and professional staff is added, support services must simultaneously be increased, thereby reinforcing the increasing labor cost aspect of the business.

There are three key alternatives to expanding the business: (1) The firm can raise fees, but market competition and the existing fee structure set at limits clients are willing to pay often make this alternative unacceptable. (2)The financial planner can work longer hours. This, too, may be unacceptable, for it may interfere with the planner's personal goals in addition to affecting the quality and timeliness of the work the planner produces. (3) The financial planner can *manage* the practice with greater efficiency. Professionals who can successfully manage their practice are able to grow gracefully and economically, ultimately succeeding in building a practice which will support them for life.

In general, practice management is the efficient use of available human, physical, and capital resources to achieve the business goals established by the professional financial planner. Practice management requires planning which establishes the organization's goals and the steps to meet them. These steps consist of: (1) efficient positioning of resources; (2) implementation of each of the activities designed to achieve the goals; and (3) control, which must be exercised on a regular basis.[2]

Marketplace Analysis

The state of the competition must be evaluated when a business plan is developed. The key questions pertinent to marketplace analysis are as follows: (1) What are other financial planners and advisers doing to market themselves? (2) What services and products are they providing? (3) What are their fee structure? (4) What are their relative sizes that make them competitive in the marketplace? (5) Are bankers, brokers, insurance agents, attorneys, CPAs, and financial consultants providing financial planning services?

Several generalizations can be made about the marketplace analysis. First, the general public may be ignorant about the nature of a comprehensive financial plan. Planners and financial products sales organizations could take advantage of such a situation by offering products or substandard plans as state-of-the-art comprehensive financial plans. Second, because of their size and financial strength, large brokerage and insurance firms could become formidable competition, since they can inundate the marketplace with commercials, bulk mailings, seminars, and other large-scale promotional schemes. Third, planning services performed by many competitors might be influenced by commission structures rather than client need. Knowledge of what the competition is doing in each of these areas can help a planner design a superior business plan.

Scope of the Target Market

A market can be defined in terms of income, age, sex, education, occupation, religion, and a host of other criteria. While the most commonly used criteria for

---

[2] Ward Bower, "Effective Management Helps Planners Realize their Own Financial Goals." *The Financial Planner*, March 1983, p. 97.

selecting financial planning clients are income and net worth, they are by no means the only criteria for defining a financial planning target market.

Regulatory and Social Environment

An effective business plan must take into account the existing regulatory and social environment. An individual offering comprehensive financial planning services for compensation must be a registered investment adviser under the Investment Advisers Act of 1940. In addition, a planner marketing investment products must be a registered representative of a broker-dealer who is a member of the NASD and SIPC. However, the problems of dealing with the prevailing regulatory environment go far beyond getting properly licensed. In view of numerous abuses by unethical, self-designated financial planners, the SEC, NASD, and individual states are not only establishing tougher standards against unscrupulous practices, but are also raising the regulatory standards. The overall trend toward more regulation and more control continues unabated.

The tougher regulatory environment is not the only challenge financial planners face. Often, a negative attitude is shown by the media and some of the general public toward the financial services industry. A business plan must include ways of marketing legitimate, comprehensive, respectable financial planning services to a highly suspicious and nervous public.

CORPORATE STRUCTURE

Next, we will focus on that part of a business plan which deals with corporate structure. This topic can be discussed in terms of company organization, administrative management functions, and marketing strategies.

Company Organization[3]

Mission statement. A financial planning firm's mission statement should contain at least the following:

1. Definition of the purpose of the business, including identification of the target market.
2. Strategy for organizing the entire business into divisions, the responsibility assigned to each, and the general authority under which each division operates.
3. Definition of relationships between company entities.
4. Specific goals to be achieved for profitability, development of new business, sales, motivation, and management skills.
5. Company principles to be implemented throughout all company entities.
6. Company commitment to human resource development.
7. Statement of how the mission will be regularly reviewed to assure that it is current.

In smaller companies, it is often sufficient for a mission statement to include a definition of the general marketplace in which the company operates, a general

---

[3] This discussion is adapted from John H. Melchinger, *Marketing Your Financial Planning Services.* Handout material distributed at the workshop conducted at the IAFP, Detroit, February 15, 1989.

BLUEPRINT FOR PRACTICE MANAGEMENT SUCCESS: THE BIG NINE ELEMENTS

In "working through" the big nine components that are essential to sound practice management, it is important to also consider each step in light of the following questions: Does this make good business sense? How will this affect the synergy and "personality" of the organization?

Goal identification.
- Know who you are.
- Know what you want to accomplish.
- Know who will have an effect on your decisions.

Strategic Planning.
- Long-term goals—more than one year.
- Short-term goals—less than one year.
- Business planning.
- Budgeting.

Associate Staff.
- How involved will other planners be in the running of the business?
- How many now—and in the future?
- What are their special talents?
- What is the psychological profile of the associate staff?

Client Administration.
- Who works with them and what are the functions performed for them?
- How effectively do you serve their needs?
- What is the division of the client work load?
- Is there continuity of attitude toward clients?

Structure of the Business.
- In deciding on a company name, consider: community identity, avoiding confusion with the competition
- Will the business be a sole proprietorship, partnership, regular corporation, sub-S corporation?

- What are the implications of becoming a Registered Investment Adviser?
- Will there be officers and directors? Consider length of service as a criterion if there are; consider also the advantage you may gain in having a "devil's advocate" viewpoint.
- What type of insurance do you need for the business?
- Where will you locate? Remember, plan for growth.

Support Staff.
- Remember, you *do* get what you pay for.
- Remember also, they are a valuable asset.
- When prospecting and screening for support staff, don't forget: know what you want, interview carefully, have others interview the applicants, prepare written job descriptions, be prepared to train, provide a career path.

The Work Environment.
- Is it stress-free (relatively!) and conducive to everyone's being productive?
- Does it provide for good physical interaction of people?
- What do your employees think about the workplace? Ask them!
- How's the lighting, heating/cooling, phone system, furniture?
- Aim for a first class image—professional, clean, productive.

Administration and Operations.
There's no getting around it. You *must* consider all of the following:
- Staffing.
- Policies and procedures.
- Filing systems.
- Bookkeeping systems.
- Computer needs.
- Stationery/business cards.

- Compliance, compliance, compliance!
- Library development.
- Banking relationships.
- Business meetings.
- Design of forms and contracts, interoffice and for clients.
- Office equipment.
- Incentives and awards.

Source: Ruth N. Goldstein, "The Business of a Practice," *Financial Strategies*, Summer 1987, p. 13.

Image.
- How's your office location? What's the parking like?
- Is the decor warm and inviting?
- Get a good conference table—don't deal with clients across your desk.
- The little things *do* count—have coffee cups and ashtrays on hand.
- Consider translating your image to something tangible—a good, well designed corporate brochure or an audio-visual presentation.

explanation of the products and services the company provides, and a broad statement of the philosophical framework within which these particular products and services will be provided.

Strategic objectives. These long-term objectives are hard to achieve within specific time frames. For example, a company may aspire to grow to a certain size, but it cannot reach this target in one workable time frame such as one year. As a result, the strategic objective may be to *ultimately* gross $1 million a year, but the goal for the *current* year might be to generate only $150,000 of gross revenue.

Revenue/Activity Goals. Revenue goals need to be measured within very specific time frames. It is equally important to specify the monitoring and adjustment of these activities so the achievement of goals within workable time frames is assured. For example, an annual goal of $240,000 gross revenue for a firm is important, but it is equally important to understand how much progress has been made at any time during the course of the year. For instance, the planner should know where the firm stands at the end of each month on a pro rata basis against the annual goals.

In addition to revenue goals, activity goals are especially important, especially for a small organization. To this end, departments with sales producers who also have marketing responsibilities should be monitored for the amount of activity they have in the marketplace in addition to their sales results. The achievement of aggressive revenue goals will certainly come more from aggressive activity levels than from simply focusing on the goals. It is the responsibility of the financial planner with management responsibilities to assure that high activity levels are sustained.

Business Structure. The most effective way to develop an efficient business structure is to chart the organization, which may be complicated or relatively simple. Furthermore, the basic structure of an organization should clearly indicate the lines of accountability and communication.

Communications. There is a wide variety of ways in which communication links could be established. With the nature and form of most important communications in a company— including meetings and forums—the lines of communication and significant styles of communication should be clearly indicated. Also, as lines of communication are developed, special attention should be paid to improve their effectiveness.

Quality control. In a financial planning practice it is easy to become absorbed in the large scale production of financial plans at the expense of quality. Unfortunately, in a financial planning business long-term success cannot be achieved if the quality of the planning process is compromised. A mechanism for maintaining quality control should therefore be an integral part of the company organization.

Administrative Management Functions[4]

Administrative management functions in a medium- or large-size financial planning office should include the following:

Personnel management. This function includes hiring, disciplining, and discharging staff employees; performance evaluation and review and salary administration of those employees; maintenance of personnel records; and promulgation and enforcement of personnel policies.

Financial management and control. Financial planning firms should: (1) develop budgets for income, expense, and capital items; (2) control cash flow and disbursements; (3) invest excess cash prudently; (4) supervise bookkeeping personnel; and (5) work with the firm's accountant to ensure timely preparation of financial statements and tax returns.

Supervision of operation of administrative systems. This function includes the supervision of systems for handling new clients and matters, indexing, reminder systems, time keeping and/or billing systems, and the like.

Purchasing of office supplies and equipment. Purchasing requires extensive research and establishment of systems for replenishing supplies.

Office space planning and administration. This category consists of landlord relationships, space planning and design, and leasehold improvements. These activities are necessary, and become increasingly time-consuming, with the growth of a professional service firm. Ultimately, retention of a professional business manager can be justified by the incremental income that would be generated by the planner's spending additional time on client-related activities, rather than on internal administration.

---

[4] Ward Bower, op. cit., p. 100.

Marketing Strategies[5]

After completing an in-depth analysis and committing to the decisions made regarding the company organization and administrative management functions, an effective marketing plan can be constructed. The basic marketing devices include the following:

1. Public relations
2. Advertising
3. Referrals
4. Direct mail
5. Brochures
6. Seminars

Determining the right combination of all these elements is critical so the implementation of the marketing plan will be both successful and rewarding.

Public Relations. Public Relations (PR) activities are among the most cost-effective means of placing and keeping the planner's story in front of the public. Essentially, PR involves: (1) articles written by or about the planning professional; (2) press releases; (3) public speaking; (4) statements made by the planner that appear in consumer-related publications; and (5) television and radio appearances. These activities cost relatively little in hard dollars, but their effective use requires a great deal of time and preparation.

The first step in starting a PR campaign is to determine what contacts and sources are available and which ones are necessary. The list should include television and radio stations and names of key people in magazines, newspapers, civic groups, and professional associations. Also, the organizations within the marketing area that use speakers should be listed.

Press Releases. Steps in using press releases effectively include: (1) getting to know the key editors and writers and having something to offer them; and (2) announcing office relocation, personnel changes, seminars, awards received, civic recognition, or new services offered. In all cases, the format the publication prefers should be used. Planners should be as accessible and cooperative as possible to make it easy for the media to work with them. This strategy can be used primarily to develop and maintain name recognition.

Writing Articles. Articles can be used to position the planner as an authority, in addition to developing and maintaining name recognition. Articles should be submitted to trade journals, consumer magazines, or local newspapers. A recent photograph and a brief biography should be included with the article. If possible, relationships should be developed with the financial editors in each publication. A professional planner who can consistently produce timely and informative copy may even gain the opportunity to become a regular columnist. A sample of a newspaper column by a financial planner is reproduced in the following boxed insert.

---

[5] Adapted from John C. Sweet, "Precision Marketing: Choosing and Using the Right Medium." Reprinted with permission from *Personal Financial Planning:* Volume I, Number 1, November/December 1988, pp. 18-22. Copyright Warren, Gorham and Lamont, Inc., 210 South St., Boston, MA, 02111. All rights reserved.

SID MITTRA
Don't base retirement on recent abnormal return

There used to be only two types of animals — bull and bear — that roamed the stock market jungle. Now there is a third — the bloodhound — and it is creating havoc in the market. But this must be a temporary phenomenon, because you are used to double-digit returns. Right?

First, let's put the market into proper perspective. As the accompanying chart shows, the 1990s, with 25 percent to 40 percent returns, were not normal. And even if you take the 15-year period ending in 2000, you still notice that stocks had a gain of 16 percent a year, while bonds clocked in at 8.6 percent.

So why are these returns abnormal? Ibbotson Associates has divided the past 75 years into 61 rolling 15-calendar-year stretches, starting with the 15 years through year-end 1940. It found that out of these 61 rolling periods, there were just 13 occasions (one out of five) when stocks generated 16 percent a year or more (and none even approached the 30-percent mark). Most of these abnormal 15-year periods were in

the late 1950s and early 1960s block, and they reappeared in the late 1990s.

Let's create three "what if" scenarios for purposes of long-term planning.

Suppose you create a portfolio of 80 percent stocks and 20 percent bonds, and invest $5,000 a year for 15 years. If, during this period, the market delivers the returns of the past 15 years, you'd end up with a portfolio worth $262,000, according to T. Rowe Price.

Now, let's say the returns matched those of the past 50 years, when stocks earned 12.8 percent annually and bonds gained 6.5 percent. In that case, you'd have only $200,000 in your portfolio.

Finally, let's assume stocks generate only a conservative 9 percent a year, which is a safe bet, given the way the market is behaving these days. Then you'd have only $109,000 to $153,000, or 41.6 percent less than you'd have if the market behaved as it did during the past 15 years.

So what does all this mean? It

means that in making projections for retirement planning, it is wise not to use the abnormal returns of the past 15 years. In fact, it is better to be conservative in making these projections.

But what if that torpedoes your retirement dreamboat? In that case, play it safe by planning to save more, save longer, or postpone the day when you can begin playing at Pebble Beach (they do have a public golf course, you know).

(Ideas and suggestions for local investment adviser, educator and author Sid Mittra should be sent to Sid Mittra, c/o Business Editor, The Oakland Press, P.O. Box 436009, Pontiac MI 48343.)

Source: Oakland Press, July 8, 2001

Public Speaking. In public speaking, targeting the audience and developing a presentation that is of special interest to the group being addressed are critical. Practicing the speech beforehand is a necessity and may include taping and listening to the written speech and rehearsing the material in front of office staff or family. Being comfortable in front of an audience will make for a more effective presentation. The first moments of the introduction are critical and should be smooth. If handout materials and visual aids are necessary, they should have a professional appearance.

If at all possible, handouts with information about the financial planning firm should be made available at the presentation. Also, the planner should keep in mind that each attendee is a prospective client and should be treated with care.

Broadcast Appearances. If a suitable radio or television forum exists in the geographical marketplace, the planner should contact the program director to discuss his or her qualifications for an appearance on a financial program. If the director is amenable to the idea, the topics that may be of interest to the audience and that would fit the station's format should be discussed in detail. Since financial issues and concerns are always of interest to some people and sometimes interesting to everyone, a regular appearance might be possible.

This device works to establish a visual image of the planner as an authority on financial planning within a geographical area. It should be noted, however, that broadcast appearances are very time intensive, and if poorly produced, the planner's image could suffer.

Advertising. Advertising the practice and its activities should help create a demand for the firm's services and differentiate it and the planner from other firms in the marketplace. Unlike PR, advertising is time intensive and costs hard dollars. Therefore, before embarking on an advertising campaign and committing money to advertising, the planner must be very knowledgeable about the media that will influence the target clients and prospects. What do they read? What do they listen to? What sources of advice do they generally pay attention to? These questions must be answered in order to receive the greatest return on the investment of advertising dollars.

Radio and Television Ads. Radio can be effective if used selectively. The message should point out one or more consumer needs and suggest that the advertiser is the one who can meet those needs. Radio ads are generally wasteful if used only to create awareness. When using this medium the planner should:

- Select a station that reaches the target audience.
- Use repetition: ten 30-second ads work better than five 60-second ads.
- Buy a "block of time" that will be heard before an interesting program.
- Always use a professional voice.
- Always use a professional script.

The use of television advertising for the vast majority of financial planners is questionable due to production and air time costs. It is therefore rarely recommended unless the planner has deep pockets, is in a smaller marketplace, and can place the ads before or after a popular stock market or business program.

Publications. As with any advertising, knowing the target market is critical when selecting the proper print media. The planner's and the firm's image should be matched to the publication's image and target market for both magazines and newspapers.

The ad's design, copy, size, and location, both on the page and in the publication, all contribute to the creation and development of the planner's image. From a design standpoint, the ad should command attention, be pleasant and easy to read, and generously use white space and margins. Copy should attract attention, help create a need in the reader's mind, show how the planner can meet that need, and project the difference between the planner and other planning professionals. A provocative headline can help to attract attention and spark interest.

The size of the ad will depend on the planner's budget. The cost and the required budget allotment depend, of course, on the publication's circulation, the day or days the ad will run, the cost of the design, and the section of the publication that will work best to fulfill the planner's purpose. In a newspaper, the ad should be placed near the sports section, business section, or lifestyle pages to attract different targeted audiences. Even the best designed and most costly ads will fail if improperly placed.

Yellow Pages. Another advertising option is to buy a yellow pages ad that provides more information than the standard listing. What follows are some basic yellow page guidelines:

- Design a display ad that describes the planner's credentials, and use "sell" copy.
- Use a headline that shows some specialization, such as "Small Business Tax Adviser" or "Preretirement Specialist."
- Place the display ad in the financial planning or adviser section.

Referrals. Referrals are a cost-effective means of identifying prospective clients. Many people are willing to help planners by suggesting names if the referral process is made easy for them, they are not embarrassed by what is done with the referral, and they are kept informed on how things are going. Referrals can come from a variety of sources, including current clients and local allied professionals.

To use referrals effectively, the planner should create a story about the business. This task should not be too difficult, considering the amount of time that was spent and the information that was summarized in the formal business planning process. The planner should then tell the story to individual clients, small groups of clients, accountants, and attorneys, and ask if they will endorse the planner either directly or indirectly in a presentation of their referral. They might be willing to write a letter or recommendation on their letterhead, or they might allow the planner to write it for them. They also might be willing personally to introduce the planner to the interested individual.

Most accountants and attorneys are concerned about client control. This concern should be addressed up front, and the planner should indicate how he or she will attempt to make them the "hero" throughout the relationship. From a cost/return standpoint, this referral device can be the most effective tool in finding new clients.

Direct mail. As with other strategies, direct marketing will only be effective if meaningful targets have been chosen. General mailings with general information will only produce a smaller bottom line profit. The purpose of client segmenting is to attract the best potential clients while spending as little as possible.

Developing the mailing list is the first step. This list may be bought, rented, or created by the planner. In renting, the planner should be selective in terms of demographics, and take the time to find the most appropriate list broker. The list can include as many or as few names as the planner chooses, and mailing activity can begin in only a few weeks' time.

Creating a list is time-consuming but worth the effort because it can be used repeatedly. To build the list, the planner can refer to reverse telephone directories and member rosters of important clubs, civic groups, churches or synagogues, chambers of commerce, trade associations, or professional organizations.

Cost control is important. The budget must provide for the list purchase, postage (first class or bulk rate), artwork (unless the mailing is a simple letter), typesetting and printing or copying, and the cost of folding the enclosures and stuffing the envelopes.

For best results, the mailing should not coincide with a holiday or prime vacation times. To determine the effectiveness of the mailing, the results should be analyzed. Great care should be taken to compare the resultant income against expenses to determine the project's profitability.

Brochures. Although considered only a part of direct marketing activities, brochures are actually appropriate for the firm's use in other ways. For example, brochures can be used in handouts at seminars, speaking engagements, and small group presentations as well as for clients, prospects, and allied professionals.

An attractive, well-written brochure can be a valuable marketing tool. It can be a waste of money, however, if it is developed without specific attention to the target audience, brochure content and copy, or the piece's general purpose. The company brochure should include:

- An introduction to the benefits of a financial plan.
- The planner's background, credentials, and philosophy.
- The planning process according to the planner.
- An explanation of how people can engage and pay for the planner's services.

Professionals can be hired to complete the design, copy, and production phases. The design should be simple, the copy direct and informative, and the paper stock somewhat heavy. The brochure's size should allow for easy mailing and storage in a standard file folder.

Not every financial planning organization needs an expensive brochure. Any attractive and informative written piece that tells the story and presents the services in a fashion consistent with the desired image should achieve the planner's objective.

Seminars. Seminar presentations can be an excellent source of financial planning engagements. A successful seminar benefits everyone—the planner, the attendees, and the clients. Seminars provide the planner with visibility, an opportunity to demonstrate expertise, and a vehicle with which to build rapport while conveying professionalism to the audience. Seminars also present an opportunity for the planner to convey his or her message to a group in a nonthreatening, low pressure atmosphere.

The key to conducting a successful seminar is advance planning. The following is a typical advance planning schedule for conducting a financial planning seminar.

Six Weeks Before the Seminar. Six weeks prior to the seminar the following decisions/actions should be completed:

1. Decide on the subject and speaker.
2. Determine the seminar objective and attendee profile.
3. Develop a theme for the presentation and marketing materials.
4. Decide on program style.
5. Contact the speaker.
6. Line up those NASD registered personnel who will staff the seminar.
7. Determine the order of seminar presentation.

8. Select and contract for a location.
9. Determine the seating configuration.
10. Select the marketing plan for the seminar.
11. Prepare and clear through broker/dealer's compliance department all advertising, invitations, and sales materials.

Two to Four Weeks Prior to Seminar. Two to four weeks prior to the seminar, the following actions/decisions should be completed:

1. Write the script and finalize it.
2. Address invitations.
3. Mail seminar invitations.
4. Place advertisements.
5. Make name badges.

Day of the Seminar. If all of the preceding steps have been successfully completed, the seminar will also be a success. The seminar speaker must never forget that the main purpose of conducting a financial planning seminar is to convert a potential client into a long-term client. However, it is also important to remember that the speaker should also educate the audience so the attendees will receive true value from attending the seminar.

Follow-up. Follow-up is extremely important both with attendees and those who registered for the seminar but did not show up. Studies show that less than 25 percent of what is seen and heard is retained after 48 hours without reinforcement and reiteration. For this reason all seminar attendees should be contacted within two days to assure high receptivity. The no-shows should also be contacted because often they are as receptive as the attendees. In the end, the key to any successful seminar is preparation and follow-up.

SECTION II
DEENA KATZ ON PRACTICE MANAGEMENT

In this section, we reproduce from Deena Katz on Practice Management two topics of special interest to all financial planning practices. Deena Katz is a nationally recognized expert on practice management and has a distinct style for communicating her ideas. It should be reiterated here that everyone serious about practice management would be well advised to read both of her books listed in the introduction.

PEOPLE MAKE IT HAPPEN[6]

It is virtually impossible for you to meet all of your clients' needs without the help of good support staff. As your practice grows, delegating to key people is crucial to

---

[6] Deena Katz on Practice Management, op. cit., pp. 89-109.

your growth and success. Yet, nearly every adviser I know has experienced difficulty finding the right people, hiring them and keeping them. The larger the practice, the more difficult that job gets.

There are many proven ways to attract good personnel, but the only way to keep them is through quality training, good compensation and benefits, and a nurturing, stimulating, challenging work environment. The success of your practice depends on the people who interact with your clients every day. In fact, long-term clients are comfortable and secure with long-term employees.

You've probably spent significant time figuring out how to manage your clients' expectations. It's worth the effort to figure out how to manage your staff's expectations as well. Just remember, where clients are concerned, there is no way to compensate for lousy support staff.

Hiring, Mentoring, and Internships

We've devoted a great deal of time in our practice to finding the most effective approach to hiring and retaining good people. We prefer the mentor-apprenticeship method of staffing. We search for people with good education and good personalities who demonstrate the most flexibility in terms of their work style. When someone meets these requirements, we can generally integrate him into our workplace by training him in our philosophy and methods. One of our favorite sources for new staff is through internships. However, this requires a two- to three-year training period, and a considerable corporate investment of time and money.

We nearly always promote from within and seldom hire someone who will "hit the ground running." This gives us ample familiarity of an employee's work style and capabilities, as well as how he or she will integrate with other staff members.

Currently, there are over 100 educational programs at colleges and universities nationwide who offer financial planning programs registered with the CFP Board of Standards. Their graduates may sit for the comprehensive CFP exam. The University of Miami offers the CFP program as part of its master's in accounting and personal finance. We approached the director of the program and expressed an interest in working with the school to provide business experience for interns. As a result, we've had some great intern relationships that have blossomed into permanent employment.

Texas Tech in Lubbock, Texas, has a very impressive internship program, designed by Dr. Jerry Mason, who heads their financial planning curriculum. His students are bright, capable, and well trained. The students volunteer as support staff for the IAFP Success Forum each year. This is a good opportunity to connect with possible candidates for your office.

Virginia Tech in Blacksburg, Virginia, has a new financial planning internship program as well, run by Dr. Bruce Brunson. Dr. Brunson's program is similar to Texas Tech's, and his students often attend the IAFP Success Forum to meet planners. I have provided contact information in the Resource chapter.

Cindy Conger of Arkansas Financial Group feels that technology has replaced lower-level positions in their practice. Nowadays, even assembling their files requires some financial knowledge. They use interns to help in all aspects of the business, particularly in assisting the planners. "It's a matter of attitude," says Cindy. "I can ask a file clerk to prepare our client files in a certain way, but that file clerk sees that job as menial. When our intern prepares those files, he knows it is vital to the operation of the practice. His attitude toward the job is different, so his end work product is different." Interns are young, eager to learn, enthusiastic, grateful for the work, and they can always teach you something.

In the early years of our practice, we called our professional support staff para-planners, then associate advisers. We discovered that clients tend to identify the term "associate adviser" with junior people. Since we are attempting to encourage closer relationships between our clients and these professionals, we need to make sure that they are professionally elevated and presented as seasoned staff. Therefore, these days, we use the term "adviser" to describe the professional staff who work directly with clients. All our advisers are Certified Financial Planner licensees or are working toward that designation. To differentiate, we now refer to the firm's principals as the "partners," rather than the "advisers."

Currently, we have three partners, four advisers, four executive assistants, a comptroller/office manager, a director of operations, a director of concierge services and an intern.

Naturally, as soon as you bring other advisers into your practice, you will want to have a formalized agreement about whether clients are considered to be company or personal contacts and how situations will be handled if you agree to part company with the advisers. We request that our advisers sign non-compete agreements. I've included a simple sample on the following page.

This document states that clients are clients of the firm. In essence, this precludes advisers from soliciting clients for business if they leave the firm. As your practice becomes less dependent upon you and more dependent upon others on your team, a non-compete document is vital. Additionally, if you are planning for the transfer of your practice sometime in the future, you will want these agreements to ensure that key personnel will remain with the firm, even if you don't.

Rick Adkins of Arkansas Financial Advisory told me that his decision to require a non-compete was a difficult hurdle. "Our biggest concern was letting ambitious junior staff interact with our clients, yet this was essential if we were going to grow into a viable business." Rick and his partner Cindy Conger explained that in exchange for signing the non-compete agreement, staff would have full access to clients and become instrumental in a shift in client control. "Once everyone signed," confided Rick, "we all felt a certain relief and freedom."

Taking Care of Your Most Valuable Asset: Your Staff

Your staff members are the people who make the very first impression on your prospects and can enhance or destroy relationships with existing clients. If you want to attract great clients, hire great staff, train them, and then empower them. You must give them a sense of self-worth beyond their value as an employee, and then compensate them accordingly. Just as you would with your best clients, find out what they expect from this relationship and manage their expectations. We want our staff to know how important they are to our business, so we spend significant time demonstrating how much we value them.

Money Plus

In 1998, Princeton Research found that workers aged eighteen to twenty-nine felt that advancement, opportunity, and benefits (health coverage, vacations, flextime) were more important than money or number of working hours. Seventy percent of our employees are under age thirty. It is very clear that our staff wants flexibility, benefit choices, respect, personal and professional challenge, plus money. Money is essential, yet money by itself is not enough.

The Following Is an Agreement
Between Joe Adviser and Planning Firm

1. In recognition of the costs incurred by the Firm for training and education, Joe Adviser agrees that if Planning Firm severs the relationship with him for cause, he will not form or join a competing investment advisory firm in Our Town for a period of twelve (12) months after leaving the Firm.

2. Joe Adviser acknowledges that all clients are clients of the Firm and he agrees, should he leave the Firm, not to contact any clients or prospects he has served or which were being served by the Firm during his relationship with the Firm. He acknowledges that the files and records of client accounts are records of the Firm and shall not be copied or used for any purpose other than that approved, in writing, by the Firm. Joe Adviser acknowledges that he recognizes that the Firm considers its material and process proprietary and that he will keep this confidential. Should Joe Adviser leave the Firm he will neither remove any material nor use the material for his own use.

3. Joe Adviser agrees to follow the policies of the Firm. Joe Adviser without the prior approval, in writing, of the partners will provide no correspondence or other printed material, other than strictly operational, to the public (including media). Examples would include market commentary, "interim reports," plans, and policies.

4. This agreement supersedes all previous agreements.

Signed_____   Signed_____
          (Joe Adviser)   (President (For the Firm))

Date_____   Date_____

Jerry Neill of Neill & Associates in Kansas City told me that not long ago several of his employees abruptly quit. He conducted exit interviews to ask what some of the problems were. Among other things, they all said it wasn't "a fun place to work." "I just didn't understand that," Jerry told me. "This is not the kind of business I grew up in. Work is work." So Jerry hired a business consultant who made some simple suggestions to keep the troops happy. "These people would have killed for a casual-dress Friday. How did I know?" Jerry's consultant suggested they have more family-centered activities such as a company picnic and holiday party. Of course, now casual Fridays in his office are a must. Jerry and his partners hired an office manager who, along with other key personnel, has completely rewritten the employee manual. The office manager is closer in age to their under-thirty employees, and the change in the office has been remarkable.

Not everyone can afford to hire a business consultant like Jerry did, so you might want to check out Jane Applegate's *201 Great Ideas for Your Small Business* (Princeton, New Jersey: Bloomberg Press, 1998) for some great tips on taking care of employees and creating a better workplace.

Ross Levin explains that he and his staff go out together about once a quarter, usually to celebrate something, like tax day or some bogus event that requires a celebration. "Everyone loves this. We have a good time and enjoy each other's company." Karen Spero, of Spero, Smith Investment Advisers, Inc. in Cleveland, Ohio, also arranges company luncheons and outside-office activities. There is a trend among established advisers toward creating office-family activities with opportunities for employee bonding. We've seen our staff develop such strong relationships over the years that they create and plan activities on their own now.

Eleanor Blayney and I have had numerous discussions about managing and compensating staff. I suspect this is a hot topic among planners who started their careers as sole practitioners and wound up growing into larger firms with numerous personnel. Eleanor considers her staff members not only valuable assets, she has compared them to capitalizing a business. "If you wanted to capitalize a new business," she says, "you would probably have some bondholders and some stockholders. In staffing, the bondholders are the steady, loyal employees who are not particularly looking for advancement, but enjoy what they do and fully intend to do it as long as they work. They would like to be well paid for their efforts but are not generally motivated by entrepreneurial career path incentives. Bondholder staff wants security and income. Conversely, the stockholders, on a career path, want incentives, challenges, and opportunity." Eleanor believes that these two "asset classes" should be treated differently and offered different remuneration and benefit packages.

Compensation

We have designed our staff compensation based upon the career path the individual has chosen. Once a year, my partners and I take each employee to a private lunch and we review his or her personal goals. We want to ensure that they remain successful, satisfied members of the staff. Career paths are not written in stone. One of our advisers began working in back-office operations. Each year for several years we met and discussed his plans for the future. Each year, he told us he was happy in operations and had no plans to do anything else. Then one year, because of personnel changes, we asked him to sit in on some client meetings until we hired someone new. Within the month he declared an intention to take CFP courses and accept the responsibilities of an adviser. He has made it quite clear that his future plans involve entrepreneurial risks. He wants to become a rainmaker, developing his own client base, and eventually working independently. Because of his new career path, our requirements for him changed. He tells me that now he averages a sixty-hour workweek.

Bonuses

I never really believed in giving bonuses. Bonuses always felt so unpredictable. I also believed they were not necessarily the best incentives for everyone. I preferred ensuring a reasonably good salary. Then I discussed the issue with Dick Thaler, who is a behavioral finance professor at the University of Chicago. He reminded me that classical finance theory maintains that the rational investor makes decisions based on rational thought. Behavioral finance theory maintains that investors are not rational, but are predictable, basing their decisions on mental shortcuts or rules of thumb to solve complex problems. These mental shortcuts are known as heuristics. One of these heuristics Thaler refers to as "mental accounting." This is the human, non-rational approach to tracking and evaluating transactions. Thaler related the issue of bonuses to the mental accounting heuristic he calls "separate pockets." Applying this heuristic to your employees' behavior may elicit some interesting insights.

In his book, *The Winners Curse* (Princeton, New Jersey: Princeton University Press, 1992, pp. 112–16), Thaler discusses bonuses and windfalls. If you pay your employee $50,000 per year, he will live a $50,000 lifestyle. If, alternatively, you pay him $40,000 with a predictable $10,000 bonus annually, he will live a $40,000 lifestyle, using the extra $10,000 for something special, possibly even investing it. In other words, bonuses encourage savings. Thaler was persuasive. This, for me was a powerful argument for paying a bonus, and more compelling to me than just a calculation of how to get the most out of a worker. I consider it one of my responsibilities as an employer to encourage my staff to save and invest.

Peggy Ruhlin of Budros & Ruhlin explains that they have a "growth sharing" arrangement for providing bonuses for their advisers. Each year a percentage of the firm's gross is deposited into an account to be shared by the employees based on a point system. Peggy said they elected to base these bonuses on the gross, rather than the net profits so that the advisers will be assured of some extra compensation even if the company has no profit for the year. The staff is given points for longevity, client retention, support for new business, achieving a new professional designation, or completing continuing education courses. They are bonused annually based on the number of points acquired during the year.

Because of my discussions with Dick Thaler, we have two bonus programs. One is designed for the benefit of all employees and is calculated purely upon the number of years of service. It is not based on profits—gross or net. The bonus is paid on the first of December so I refer to it as the Christmas Club. The second one, the merit bonus, is much more subjective. My partners and I set aside a bonus amount, based upon our profits for the year. We assign one point for every $250, and each partner is allocated one-third of the points. We then cast our points for the employees we think have done the best job overall during the past year. For example, if we have $9,000 for bonuses, each partner would have twelve points to give away.

Bonuses do not necessarily have to be in the form of cash. One year Bugen Stuart Korn & Cordaro gave their staff gift certificates for a cruise. David Bugen made arrangements with the local travel agent so that each employee had a budget to design his or her own cruise. The company picked up the tab.

Empowerment

I've required our adviser employees to investigate benefit options to help us structure them for the benefit of all of us. I have discussed the dollars we have available for benefits and I let them decide how to put this package together. They present their findings to all of us at a weekly staff meeting. A staff committee also designed our investment policy and manages our profit sharing plan.

We have devised a staffing philosophy, much the same as we designed a business and investment policy. There are several components that are key to this philosophy: worker empowerment, warm working environment, non-accusatory attitudes toward errors, and continuing education. We use cross training and team building to help facilitate our philosophy. Last year, for example, our employees divided themselves into teams, addressing our prospect and client delivery systems, such as brochures, data gathering questionnaires, and review documents. At a company staff meeting, each team presented recommendations for improving or redesigning our systems. We are still in the process of implementing their recommendations.

Our employees are given titles, commensurate with their responsibilities. Further, they are empowered with the authority to make a situation right for the client. Staff is trained to accept responsibility for errors, even if they are not ours. We never argue with a client or make him feel uncomfortable about a situation. We call this empowerment Nordstrom Authority.

If you've ever been to San Francisco, you may have been to Nordstrom's department store. They are nationally known for their superior service. During my first visit, I bought a suit that needed a minor alteration. When I went to pick it up later that day, it was not ready. I reminded the clerk that I was going home early the following day. After a profuse apology, the saleswoman reassured me, "Don't worry, the suit will be ready at 7:00 this evening. I will have it delivered to your hotel by 7:30 p.m." It was. She did not have to obtain permission from anyone else.

The first time one of our advisers used his Nordstrom Authority, a new client had just complained that during a transfer of funds, one security was liquidated when it should have been transferred in kind. The result was a loss of about $650 to the client. Although the transferring firm caused the error, our advisers told the client, "You are absolutely right. I will immediately call to have it rectified. Don't worry," he went on to say, "I will make your position whole as though the transfer had been made correctly." Later that afternoon the new client called once again, this time concerned that the adviser would be "eating the mistake himself." The adviser told the client he appreciated his calling but that he need not be concerned. It is the policy of the firm to stand behind the client and the adviser.

Aside from the usual benefits, we have also instituted a Personal and Professional Development Fund in our firm. Employees may spend up to $1,000 per year for courses or seminars to further their professional or personal development. In past years, staff has taken courses from Dale Carnegie Institute, Evelyn Wood speed-reading classes, advanced computer courses, neurolinguistic programming classes, and seminars for executive assistants and middle managers.

Naturally, we subsidize anyone who wants to pursue the Certified Financial Planner designation, and it is a requirement for those who will work directly with clients. Interested employees are required to pay for the first course. If they decide to continue, we pay for the remaining courses and examinations, and reimburse them for the first one upon successful completion of the program.

Because of Karen Spero we have formalized a program for staff to attend professional conferences and conventions. Karen and I were preparing for a practice management conference presentation two years ago and she told me, "This would really be great for my associates to hear. One of these days we're going to have to start sending our junior staff to these meetings. They would really benefit from the experiences." So one year, as an experiment, we sent six of our staff members to a Schwab conference in Orlando. Our comptroller and my partner Harold's assistant also chose to go. They expressed some trepidation, figuring that the sessions might be over their heads. They were wrong. They came away from the sessions, and the networking, with new acquaintances and great ideas. More importantly, they developed a different perspective about their knowledge and level of expertise.

Titles and Business Cards

When I was fourteen, I took a job working for an interior designer after school. She had a two-year-old daughter. Although my primary responsibility was looking after her daughter, I was also required to dust the store displays several times a week while Suzie took a nap. I figured this was busy work because my new boss did not want to pay me just for sitting around while Suzie napped, but I wanted the job, so I dusted well. After several weeks my boss presented me with a box of business cards with "Deena Lynn Boone, Assistant" printed on them under her store name. "You've done a great job," she said, "and you deserve a promotion." There was no actual change in salary or job responsibilities, but I was invited to place some of my precious cards in a small silver tray near the door. I didn't just have a job, I had a career. Now I not only dusted the displays, I rearranged them with care and creativity. Especially in smaller organizations, titles ignite pride, contribute greatly to self-esteem, and, of course, impress mothers. In our office, everyone has a title; everyone has a card. Everyone has a career.

Realizing Potential

Karen spero feels that it is her responsibility to help her staff realize their own potential. To that end, she has devised a self-assessment form that all staff members are required to complete at the beginning of each year. Karen says that she and her partner, Robert Smith, gain much insight into their staff and the growth potential of each one. They use the self-assessments to help guide the upcoming year's activities. From an analysis of these responses, you may discover that your people have interests in areas of which you were unaware.

For example, Karen's first two questions focus on goal setting and reviewing accomplishments in light of those goals.

1. What do you regard as your most significant accomplishment last year and why?
2. What do you most want to accomplish this year? Describe at least three goals and how you plan to achieve them. Please be as specific as possible.

Karen confided to me that from responses to these two questions she learned that one of her employees had a strong interest in spending more time with clients rather than in the back office. "Frankly," said Karen, "she was hired for her analytic expertise. I never really thought she was interested in client communications. Naturally, we were delighted to shift responsibilities to give her new opportunities."

The next three questions invite employees to offer perspectives on their current positions, the resources and support they want, and how Karen and her partner should evaluate the employees' work.

Thanks to Karen, I've used these questions not only in our practice, but as part of consulting for other firms. One response I received from a particular employee surprised me. The respondent prefaced his remarks by thanking me for asking. It seems that he had been given a work responsibility because the last employee to handle it left the practice. He was told that he would have this responsibility until a new employee was hired. New employees were hired, but no one ever revisited this work responsibility, and by default, after two years, he still had it. "I was not trained to do this and I really feel I am not doing the best job. I am certain that someone else would handle it better." When I asked him why he did not bring this up with his boss, he said, "He's not interested in how the work gets done, he just wants us to 'Make It So.'" By not encouraging his employee to provide feedback, the employer guaranteed that his staff would "Make It So-So" inefficiently.

It is vitally important to ask staff what resources or support systems they need to work more effectively. You might be surprised at some of the answers you receive to the next two questions.

3. What resources/support would make you more efficient in your job?
4. How much and what type of supervisory input do you feel you require to accomplish your job?

My comptroller presented me with a list of answers to the resources question. "Our director of concierge services needs her own credit card to purchase gifts and make arrangements for special events for clients. She should need authorization only for purchases in excess of $500. You should get our intern permission to use the law library at the University of Miami so he can have more flexibility in his research. He should be allowed to set his own schedule. He can just check in to see that we don't have anything more pressing for him here at the office. And," she added, with authority, "put a waterfall in the conference room. It will be very soothing to clients and will be a good retreat for us when we feel overwhelmed." She does, he does, I did, and we do.

The next four questions were helpful in creating our work teams. We were able to encourage people who complemented each other to work together on projects.

5. What three skills/abilities do you see as your strengths? What three skills/abilities do you see as weaknesses?
6. How would you further develop your strengths?
7. What aspects of your job are most appealing?
8. What aspects are least appealing?

Several of Karen Spero's employees answered number 5 stating that they felt they lacked skills necessary to communicate well with clients. As a result, Karen arranged for her staff to attend seminars on improving communication abilities.

The last three questions will help get a sense of the vision and goals each person has in the workplace.

9. Please write a description of your job as it now exists. (Be as brief as possible; bullet points are okay.)
10. Please write a job description of what you would like your job to be. (Be as brief as possible; bullet points are okay.)
11. Now describe your job in five years.

I particularly like this last question. On a consulting job, one employee told me that she pictured herself retired in two to three years. From this, I fully understood her demonstrable lack of energy and enthusiasm for her job. She was coasting until retirement. With an understanding of her personal goal, I was able to arrange for her early retirement over the next year, during which time she enthusiastically trained her replacement.

My sister owned her own business for twenty years. On the wall in her office hung a poster with the following line: "If you aim at nothing, you're sure to hit it." Karen's self-assessment survey encourages everyone to set goals and measure progress.

Food, Comfort, and Other Care

My partner Peter Brown remarked that we have one of the few cafeteria benefits programs in this country that actually involve food. Our office kitchen, fondly known as the "great room," has become the center of our office activities and our home hearth, so to speak. I hadn't thought much about the impact this lunchroom has had on everyone until I sauntered in one day for my own coffee and found a couple of clients sitting at our lunch table, sharing sodas and jokes with two of our advisers. Everyone feels at home. It's what we had in mind.

Our food fetish started with an Alpha Group visit to Advent Software in San Francisco. As we were shown around the programmer floors, I noticed trays of fresh fruit and baked goods at various locations around the work areas. Advent's president, Stephanie DeMarco, told me that the trays are delivered each morning for staff to nosh on all day. She also has fresh flowers delivered once a week. The programmers told me it makes a comfortable environment, facilitating thought and creativity.

We grabbed the idea and expanded it. Rather than the same fruit and pastry plate every day, staff decides what they will order on a weekly basis. Mornings we all meet around the big table for morning coffee, breakfast treats, and vitamins. Yes, vitamins. A few years ago our office manager, Mena Bielow, decided that we were passing around colds and flu too frequently. She brought in a bottle of vitamin C and insisted that everyone take one 1000 mg tablet each morning. After a few weeks, we all felt better and had fewer illnesses among us. Now, the company provides a selection of multi-vitamins, and Mena monitors our intake. Mena also ensures that everyone has a company-paid annual physical and flu shot.

Often our morning coffee moments turn into brief, informal coordinating sessions with everyone discussing his or her planned activities for the day. Lunches are usually enjoyed together at the big table in our great room. At any time during the day there are pastries, fruit, cookies, and hot and cold drinks. For the staff meetings each week, the company provides a full breakfast, and Fridays are generally company-catered pizza lunches. This environment facilitates personal as well as business discussions.

Birthdays and anniversaries with the company are excuses to get together for conversation and cake. Our comptroller always assigns someone to choose a small gift and card that everyone personally signs. Often if clients are visiting, they join in the festivities. Everyone loves the special attention.

Owning Up to Mistakes

Back in the 1970s I read a book on transactional analysis, *I'm OK, You're OK*, by Thomas A. Harris. One silly vignette stayed with me. Since then, I've used the concept numerous times in working with staff. Your spouse is fixing breakfast and inadvertently burns the toast. You know it's inadvertent because nobody gets up one morning and says, "I think I will burn the toast this morning so it's inedible." You come down to breakfast and see the burnt toast. You could say, "How could you be so stupid to burn this toast?" or, "This toast is burnt; I won't eat it." Now, you know that your spouse already knows the toast is burnt, and that mentioning something he or she already knows is unproductive. Your spouse probably already feels bad about the toast. A transactionally aware person says, "You must be having a bad morning. What can I do to help?"

When staff makes a mistake, it is rarely intentional. It is usually for one of three reasons: our system isn't working, someone made a bad judgment call, or someone inadvertently did something stupid. Since staff is empowered to make judgment calls, there will be times when they will be wrong. If the mistake recurs, it's probably the system. If it's just plain stupidity, even the best of us does something stupid from time to time that's forgivable. If it's terminal stupidity, that's probably an indication that it's time to free up someone's future.

I believe in fixing the problem, not the blame. To encourage people to admit mistakes, I devised the Turkey Award. The Turkey is a goofy-looking stuffed animal suspended from a gold cord. At each Friday meeting, we discuss our mistakes for the week. The person who made the stupidest, craziest, most unbelievable mistake gets the turkey for the week. He or she is saluted with the Turkey "gobble" and the stuffed turkey sits on his or her desk for the week. We have given the Turkey for cutting off a tie in the shredder, trying to send a fax to our own fax number, confusing two clients with similar last names, and preparing a rebalancing proposal using the wrong portfolio policy. Despite the array of available scenarios, these days we are hard pressed to give the Turkey away. For all mistakes, I always ask, "Did this happen because the system is bad?" If that's the case, we revise the system.

I've noted earlier, each staff member has the power to do what must be done to make it right for the client. That means eating transaction charges when we've made a trading error, sending an apology gift to a client for a mistake, or accepting the blame for a situation even though we know we weren't responsible for it. I support my staff and any of their decisions to make a situation right for the client. I only ask to be informed as soon as the problem arises. Most of the time, staff tells me the problem and their solution simultaneously.

Ross Levin tells the story of a huge trading mistake made in his office last year. One of his staff members thought he was buying one fund, when he actually purchased another. By the time the trader discovered the error two months later, the fund they actually bought was down $13,000. "We believe in owning up to mistakes immediately. This is a client who would probably have never known we'd made this mistake. Of course, we brought it to his attention and we made it right, which means we ate the $13,000. We were honest, no matter how painful. Now, we have a client for life."

Appreciation

I have been talking about appreciation that we as employers have for our staff and the ways we demonstrate it. We also provide opportunities for staff to show their appreciation for each other. The companion to our Turkey is the Star, a stuffed gold star with multi-colored streamers hanging from a long ribbon. The Star of the Week is nominated at our weekly staff meetings, right after we declare the Turkey. We have awarded a star for chasing down the mail carrier when we inadvertently mailed 100 letters without postage. We've given stars for fixing the stapler, volunteering to stay late and help an associate get out an important mailing, and for discovering an error on a client's death certificate that saved us and his attorney a great deal of aggravation. The Platypus Award is given to a deserving employee who has received both a star and a turkey during the same week. It is rare, but it has happened.

I particularly like Greg Sullivan's (Sullivan, Bruyette, Speros & Blayney) appreciation strategy. He buys a batch of lunch coupons at the local deli in his building. He gives everyone ten $5 coupons to give away to thank a co-worker for appreciation for something special. The only requirement is that if you give one away, you must inform a principal and report why.

Employee Reviews

Jeffrey Pfeffer, the Thomas D. Dee professor of organizational behavior at the Stanford Graduate School of Administration, said that many business people compare annual employee reviews with "filling out your income tax form. It's not a process that anybody likes, but you've got to do it." (Michael Barrier, "Reviewing the Annual Review," *Nations Business*, September 1998, pp. 32–34.) It does have to be done, but it doesn't have to be painful. Before my reviews, I talk with my partners and my office manager. Together we compare notes about each staff member. Using these discussions and my own observations, I formulate a list of strengths and weaknesses for each person. That list becomes the basis for my reviews. I used to use Employee Appraiser software (Austin-Hoyne), which I thought was fairly good. But I found the framework only made my discussions stilted since they were not formulated by me or directed by the self-assessments.

I also use this review time to elicit their recommendations; in essence, they are judging me as a leader. This has been helpful to me personally and I welcome their thoughts. From time to time when I have fallen behind in giving out my reviews, staff has asked me for them.

I usually conduct my reviews based on the self-assessment document that staff members complete. There are a few items to keep in mind when you conduct a review.

- Keep the review private.
- Focus on the employee. Do not make comparisons to others.
- Ask them how they think they are doing. You'll be surprised at how candid people can be about their own work.
- If you have tough criticisms, cover that first. Always end with something positive, encouraging, and upbeat.
- Give them an opportunity to make open and honest observations about anything, with no recriminations. Be sure to tell them that the comments will not leave the room, and mean it.
- Ask them how they think you can be a better leader.
- Take notes on what you have discussed and file them in a permanent employee file.

Little Things

The bottom line is that we treat our staff the way we would like them to treat our clients: Intensive Customer Care. We surprise them from time to time with an impromptu party after a particularly grueling week. When we travel, we always bring them small mementos of the places we've visited, so they know we're thinking about them, and they return the favor. We have arranged to have the local dry cleaners pick up their laundry at the office each week. We have an annual company picnic to which families and friends are invited. We have even sent interested staff to a local nutritionist for counseling and menus. (With our food fetishes, is it any wonder?)

Our holiday party includes spouses and significant others. We choose a fine restaurant for dinner then retreat to my house for "The Rookie Show." For the past five years, we were hiring new people so fast that each time we got together for the annual holiday party, there were so many new faces, we practically had to wear nametags. My partner Peter decided we needed some sort of ice breaker and initiation rite, so he created the Rookie Show. At each holiday party, anyone who is new to the firm in the past year must perform for the rest of us. They can sing, dance, tell a joke—whatever they want to do. It's a great deal of fun and a wonderful bonding mechanism.

All of these little things demonstrate our support and interest in them as individuals, not just our employees. They show their support and interest in us by taking very good care of our clients.

If It Ain't Fixable, Break It Off, ASAP

Thus far, I have discussed getting and keeping good staff and promoting good teamwork. However, I must also discuss the topic of terminating staff. This is not an easy task. Most of us have never been trained as human resource professionals. Advisers don't like confrontation, we want everyone to like us. If the salesman's curse is to close the sale, then the planner's curse is the need for everyone to like us.

During the ten years that Murphy Brown was on television, she fired no fewer than ninety-two secretaries. They ran the gamut from bizarre, unskilled, or bossy, to timid, overqualified, or certifiably insane. This was great comedy, but it's not so funny when it sits outside your office. My partner Peter loves to tell the story of the time he had to fire Harold's secretary because Harold stopped coming to work in order to avoid her. He couldn't work well with her, but he just couldn't let her go. Peter didn't want to fire her either, but it was that, or let Harold work from home for the rest of his life.

Over the past twenty-three years in business, I have formed several hard and fast rules about hiring and firing employees.

- *Have a written job description and a salary range with an absolute maximum in mind before you start interviewing.* Always ask what their salary requirements are. If your offer and their requirements are too far apart, one of you has unrealistic expectations.
- *Don't hire on impulse.* Take time to evaluate the candidates thoroughly. Check references and ask them to visit more than once. Let staff interview them too. Good people are going to evaluate their job opportunities carefully. Be sure they are a good fit.
- *If it's not working out, fire sooner rather than later.* Don't wait for things to get better. They won't. "We had a very toxic person in our office once," Ross Levin told me. "It really affected morale. We should have terminated that relationship six months before we did. Today, we're happier and more efficient."
- *Keep copious notes on employees,* including personal discussions and your observations, as well as observations from others. You never know if you may need them later.

- *If someone quits, then later asks you to rehire, don't.* Office environments are dynamic. Although he may have been the right person for the job before he left, it does not necessarily follow that he will be the right person now.
- *Allow a limited time for two employees to solve their own conflicts.* Allow a limited time for you to mediate. When all else fails, terminate one or both of them. Forcing warring employees to work together can threaten the success of your company.

People Management Is the Key

Happy, efficient, hard-working staff is critical to your business. Learn how to manage them or immediately pass the responsibility to a partner who can. If you don't have a partner, or neither of you have the skills to successfully manage people, hire someone to do it for you.

You may be able to solve your management problems by hiring an office manager, someone who is capable of directing the daily activities of the practice. Your office manager can hire and fire, supervise personnel, and manage daily work responsibilities. Decisions of marketing, budgeting, and long-range planning still fall to you.

If you feel you need a higher level of expertise, it is unlikely that you will be able to hire someone with the skills necessary to take over the management of the entire business. Most people with chief operating officer level skills will be working for a large company, commanding a hefty salary, or they will be running their own smaller business. Consider taking on a partner who has administrative skills who will complement your own skill set.

CONSISTENCY AND SUCCESSION[7]

It's the shoemaker's children, they say, who go barefoot. Most advisers avoid thinking about retirement death, or the chance that they or their partner will become disabled. Struggling to acquire and retain clients always seems to take precedence. I am not going to cover business succession planning techniques and mechanics in this chapter. You're a planner; I assume you know the basics. I want to explore the effect of a traumatic personal event on your practice and clients and to suggest how to make some practice contingency plans to be implemented in times of crisis. I also want to discuss some of the issues you must address when considering the transfer of your business. First, I'd like to share with you the experience of a few friends who have actually faced these issues.

Crisis Planning for Death

I met Andrew Wray about ten years ago at an ICFP retreat. At the time, Andrew was a planner in Memphis with a small, successful practice and one partner, Bill Howard. Andrew and Bill met when they were taking courses for the CFP exam and had practiced together since 1985. They were best friends. The clients were all considered clients of the firm, but they primarily had a relationship with either

---

[7] Deena Katz, op. cit., pp. 57-67.

Andrew or Bill. One Saturday evening, while working late, Andrew, then only forty-nine, suffered a heart attack and died at his desk. Andrew's son discovered his body when he went to the office because his dad had not returned home or responded to his worried family's phone calls. By Sunday morning, Andrew's death had affected not only his family, but Bill's life, and the lives of all their clients.

All of us in the planning community were stunned. Andrew was young. Andrew was presumably in good health. Andrew was gone. My partner Harold and I, along with many other advisers, offered help to Bill. Unfortunately, we did not know how we could be of assistance.

Bill, shocked and grieving, recognized immediately that the clients would also feel the tremendous loss. He began to make phone calls to each of them. He felt it was imperative to inform them of Andrew's death before they heard it anywhere else. So while Andrew's family was making preparations for the funeral, Bill was talking with the clients, assuring them of the business continuity and ongoing professional support. In the subsequent weeks, Bill met with each of Andrew's clients. He was pleased to find that for the most part, they were not concerned about the company's stability. Naturally, they were upset. In many cases, the grief for the loss of Andrew helped forge stronger relationships with Bill.

As Bill provided care for his clients, he was personally grieving for his friend and partner. He was also personally worried about his responsibilities to the staff. He and Andrew had just signed a new five-year lease and hired four additional staff people. Andrew had carried the primary responsibility for running the office. Bill had never been interested in that aspect of the practice. Now he had to take over under the worst circumstances. Bill had to keep the staff together, make the clients feel comfortable and confident, and finally, try to take care of himself.

The firm's staff was also suffering from grief and shock. Within one year, three left, compounding the chaos. Bill confides that systemization, coupled with his own tenacity, kept the business going. Two years after Andrew's death, Bill changed the name of the company. He felt this was necessary in order to focus on the future and keep the business growing. In hindsight, Bill said he probably should have done that sooner, but didn't want to seem disrespectful to Andrew's memory.

Disability Crisis

It's prudent to consider the possibilities of a partner dying. It is also important to consider the possibility of a partner suffering a disability or illness that might keep him or her from working for many months or years. This requires an entirely different type of contingency planning, because at some point you expect the partner to return. Consequently, it is necessary to also consider what that re-entry might be like.

A few years ago, John Ueleke of Legacy Wealth Management in Memphis, Tennessee, was diagnosed with a rare cancer. As part of his treatment plan, he had to move to Houston for several months. John told me, "When your practice gets large enough, and your staff consists of more than just you and a couple of support people, you have to think not only of your clients, but also of the employees who rely upon you for their livelihood. I realized that I had to make plans not just for my clients, but for the management of the business, too. I needed to do this so I could focus on myself, and getting better."

In the few days before John had to leave for Houston, he and his partners Bob Winfield, Dick Vosburg, and Sarah Haizlip worked out a new business plan. They used this as an opportunity to restructure their practice, making some changes they'd been thinking about in the past few months anyway. They began by developing a client strategy delivery worksheet, listing who was currently responsible for delivery of services to each client. They also reviewed the nature of their relationship with all of their clients. They listed client personality traits and familiarized each other with the nature of the engagement and client's personal circumstances. Based on this information and knowledge of their own personality style, they then assigned a primary partner, a primary assistant, and a backup partner.

They also felt it was important to be upfront with the clients about John's illness. Together they wrote a letter, explaining what they knew about John's condition and how they planned to redistribute the workload. John explains, "This brought an additional benefit. I was able to elicit support from my clients. Through this experience I have learned that we rely on our clients not only for financial sustenance, but for personal and spiritual support as well."

In preparation for this book, I discussed contingency plans with many successful planners, including Bill Howard, John Ueleke, and Bob Winfield. I've divided their suggestions into three parts: an action plan for now, a contingency plan for during a crisis, and one for after a crisis.

An Action Plan for Now

- *Draft a buy-sell agreement and fund it if required.* Many planners told me that in the early years, there seemed no reason to have a buy-sell agreement. The company wasn't worth much and was often burdened with debt from the start-up costs. Unfortunately, those same planners told me that by the time the company was making a nice profit, the partners were so preoccupied with growth, they never got around to revisiting the need for that agreement.

- *Get your business insurance planning in order.* Maintain and continually update all pertinent information including types and amounts of coverage, beneficiary designations, deductibles and exclusions, premium payments, renewal dates and contact phone numbers (including pager numbers), plus mail and e-mail addresses.

- *Get your personal risk management planning in order.* This includes disability and life insurance as well as property and casualty coverage. For example, when hurricane Andrew devastated much of South Florida in 1992, my partners and I were able to concentrate on the problems caused to our business (e.g., property damage and long-term power disruptions) and the problems faced by our clients, because our own personal insurance was adequate to cover the costs of quickly rectifying the damage to our own property. There were a few less-prepared planners who suffered significant business disruption because they had to spend so much time resolving their personal recovery problems.

- *Get your personal estate planning documents in order.* The quality of your personal estate planning will have a significant impact on your partner(s) and staff should you die while still active in the business.

- *You may be emotionally at risk to the family of a deceased partner.* If the family does not understand the business arrangements you and your partner have devised, they may have unrealistic expectations about the amount due them. You and your partner should consider discussing the rationale of your arrangement with those who may be beneficiaries. If you are not comfortable having the discussions prior to a crisis, consider writing a letter or making a videotape explaining your decisions, so that it will be available when needed.

- *Develop and document a contingency plan* for keeping your staff, clients, and partner's family informed of important activities and practice changes during the period of crisis.
- *Systematize your office activities and, based on this, prepare a crisis action plan.* No matter what the crisis, certain activities must be completed. If your contingency planning indicates that you will be required to bring in outside help (e.g., accounting support, computer consultation, personal counseling), determine and document in advance the type and sources of this assistance. Maintain a list of time-sensitive activities and a list of who will handle these activities during a crisis.
- *Maintain a comprehensive inventory of important documents* (e.g., property and casualty insurance policies, corporate records) and where to find them.
- *Establish a comprehensive computer backup system.* List where backups are stored and who has responsibility for the archiving system.
- *In addition to your client list, maintain a comprehensive and continually updated list of other important contacts,* such as your attorneys, bankers, accountants, property, casualty and health insurers, etc. Include a notation of when and how they should be contacted (phone, letter, or e-mail) and who will be responsible for the contact.
- *Clearly define the managing partner's responsibilities and plan for short-term coverage* of these responsibilities in the event of his absence.
- *Prepare a "re-entry plan"* in cases where a partner may return after a prolonged absence. Include how responsibilities will be redistributed and how long this assimilation will take.

During a Crisis

- *Implement the action plan.* This is *not* the time to rethink your strategies. Follow the plan.
- I*mmediately contact clients personally* and assure them that you and your partner(s) had developed a comprehensive contingency plan and it is being implemented.
- *Take care of yourself emotionally.* Do not assume that you are Superman or Wonderwoman. You are human. Get a counselor or therapist to help you work through the emotional trauma you are experiencing.
- *Take care of your employees.* Consider counseling for your key employees.
- *Implement the contingency plan strategy* for keeping staff, clients, and your partner's family informed.

After the Crisis

- *Review with your staff, clients, and personal advisers* how well your crisis plan worked. Make adjustments and document them.
- *If the crisis was due to the death of a key person or partner,* review the business plan to establish new goals and objectives for the business.
- *Revisit all legal documents* to ensure that they reflect the nature and intention of the current owners or partners.

John Ueleke summed up your responsibilities to your company best: "When your business gets to a certain size, you realize that many people are depending upon its continuance. Never forget that you are not in this alone. You owe it to your clients, your staff, and your partners to see that your company will survive."

Business Succession

As planning practices mature, the decision of whether you want your business to outlive you becomes more pressing. To me, this decision differentiates a practice from a business. A practice is based on a personality. If that personality leaves, the practice dissolves. A business is dependent on structure, philosophy, and continuity; it does not rely upon any one personality.

The Loyola University American Family business survey of 1995 on small business succession revealed that 50 percent of all CEOs are within five years of retirement. Furthermore, over 70 percent had not yet identified a successor.

Greg Sullivan, of Sullivan, Bruyette, Speros & Blayney, and his partners have prepared for their succession by grooming younger people to move into key positions. This takes considerable time and training, but ensures continuity with clients. The partners and planners at SBSB work as a team to meet the clients' needs. Jim Bruyette explained that their decision to become somewhat dispensable within the client relationships is bittersweet. "One of my favorite clients called not long ago and I picked up the call. After a few moments of small talk, the client explained that he had actually asked for my associate, Mark. 'I need some advice,' he said, 'I can just talk it over with Mark.' Although that's the idea, I didn't feel particularly wanted or needed."

Eleanor Blayney confided that she likes the idea that her practice will survive her. "I envision one day, fifty years from now, two SBSB planners will walk through our office, looking at the picture of our founding partners. One will ask the other, 'Who was this Eleanor Blayney, anyway?'"

It's a good idea to consider your own plans for retirement before you commit to an exit strategy. Judy Lau, CFP, of Lau & Associates in Wilmington, Delaware, is a sole practitioner. Judy always thought that she'd sell her company to another planner one day and just retire. Recently she began to reconsider the ultimate disposition of her business. "If I retired, I would only want to play 50 percent of the time. I would need something else to do, so I probably would do volunteer work. The more I thought about this, the crazier it seemed. Let's see, I am going to stop doing something that I really love and for which I am very well paid, so that I can play half the time. In my spare time, I will work for a volunteer organization where I will have no control, no respect, no pay, and no appreciation. What's wrong with this picture?" Judy finally decided that she would hire someone with a high level of skills to work with her now to share the workload. This will allow her to take more time away from her office. Eventually her younger partner will assume ownership.

Outright Sale

If you are not planning to groom a successor, you may be thinking of an outright sale to someone already in the business. Loyola University's business survey found that only 40 percent of owners had determined the value of their businesses. If your business were a major asset, wouldn't you want to be aware of its worth so you could know how it would fit with your future plans?

In preparation for this book, I spoke with Mark Tibergien, of Moss Adams LLP in Seattle, Washington. Mark's expertise is valuing and facilitating the transfer of financial service companies. I asked Mark for some hints for financial advisers planning a sale as their exit strategy. Here is his "Dos and Don'ts" list:

- *Don't overestimate the value of your practice.* It's a buyer's market. You know what that can do to the price.
- *Do consider other issues besides price.* Mark reports that in his experience, only 30 percent of the deals are consummated. The failure of the rest is due to terms, contrary cultures, or differences in philosophy.
- *Do get a professional valuation.* If you are counting on the sale of your business for retirement, you definitely need a valuation to incorporate into your capital needs calculation. "Ask yourself, 'Can I afford to retire without including the value of my business?' You must perform the same analysis for yourself that you'd do for any financial planning client. As a rule, you shouldn't count on your business as a retirement bailout; merely your bonus," says Mark.
- *Don't overestimate the goodwill aspect of your business.* There is no correlation between goodwill and the number of years you have been in this business. Goodwill is that intangible that keeps clients coming to you. Your participation (or lack of it) in the new business may have a significant impact on the goodwill factor.
- *Do start your planning early.* Know the elements of valuation and manage your practice with that in mind.
- *Don't compare your business to others and anticipate the same terms.* Businesses are unique; valuations are unique; transfers are unique.
- *Don't confuse your business with asset managers.* When Michael Price sold Heine Securities to Franklin Templeton in 1996 for $800 million, we were all extraordinarily impressed with the purchase price. But remember, there is a great difference between asset managers and asset gatherers.

It is important to remember that the value of your business is realized every day in the form of high income. The more your practice is dependent upon you, the less attractive it is to a buyer. The more closely your company resembles a commercial enterprise, the more likely you will have something to transfer. A prospective buyer will be interested in your client demographics, your philosophy with regard to investments, and the nature of the income (e.g., if the income is largely dependent upon investment performance and market performance). He will also be interested in the level of service, operations, and the standardization you've instituted in your business.

Valuation

Naturally, it is possible that you might consider the sale of your practice to someone who is not in this profession. This may be a much more difficult hurdle. During my interview with Mark, he walked me through an important reality check that I want to share with you.

There are two popular methods for valuing a company. One uses a multiple of the gross; the other uses a multiple of the net profit. The problem with using the gross figure is that the cost of realizing that income is not factored in. Mark suggests

---

Consider planner Shari's practice. . .

She has a good thing going and grosses annually	$500,000
Based on conversations with friends she expects 4x gross or	$2,000,000
Now, in order to generate net profit, the firm has some expenses.	
I'd calculate the firm's net income as follows:	
Revenue	$500,000
Less:	
Direct expenses (including fair compensation for Shari)	
Operating expenses	
Taxes	
In a well-run practice these run about 80% of gross	($400,000)
Net Profit	$100,000

Comparing the net profit of $100,000 to the projected sales price of $2,000,000 suggests a 5 percent capitalization rate. Mark concludes "that's about the return on a U.S. Treasury bond. Why on earth would anyone want to invest in a planner's business for a return that's about the same as a Treasury?"

---

that planners thinking in terms of gross numbers may be living in a world of unrealistic expectations. He explained it this way:

Bottom line—to increase the value of your business, follow these four tenets from Mark Tibergien:

1. Maximize cash flow. Pay yourself a reasonable salary and watch your expenses.
2. Minimize risk. Ensure the operation of your business is not entirely dependent upon you.
3. Manage growth. Prepare for growth; don't let it surprise you.
4. Enhance transferability. Systematize your operations.

Don't Wait—Plan Now

Stan Corey of Great Falls Financial Services in Great Falls, Virginia, has been concerned with succession planning for some time now. "I am a sole practitioner. I have long dialogues with my clients about their own future plans, but I haven't had much to say to them about mine. Recently, I have discussed this with other planners in my area. We have agreed to formulate some succession plans among us. We will agree in advance on who is willing to pay for our clients if we retire or die."

Warren Mackensen of Hampton, New Hampshire, has the same idea. In his relationship manager software, ProTracker, he has built a field for an adviser to track relationships with other advisers who can take over during a crisis, or retirement. "We provide a description of our clients online. If someone is interested, we agree on terms and that's it. It's a good idea for small firms."

It is clear that no matter what size of business it is, you must think about its future, and yours. When you review a client's financial activities, you don't hesitate to discuss gaps in his risk exposures, e.g., no disability, no life insurance, no estate plan. Yet, many of the advisers I've interviewed in the past months have neglected to follow their own advice. Don't procrastinate. As your business grows, you will have less time to devote to your own planning. Do it now.

SECTION III
SALE OF PRACTICE[8]

INTRODUCTION

One of the greatest excitements in the life of a financial planner comes from the idea of establishing a financial planning practice. After spending a lifetime making the practice blossom and mature, there comes a time when the planner might wish to sell the practice and transfer the business to a buyer. Clearly, the most difficult challenge the planner will ever face is in preparing for the sale of the company.

Any financial planner considering a sale of a financial planning practice should take the following key steps:

- Strategically position the practice for sale
- Ensure that the practice has the appropriate personnel in place to manage the business in the absence of the principal
- Develop the systems to ensure that the practice is operated efficiently
- Take the necessary steps to enhance relationships with clients and strengthen their ties to the practice
- Organize records and financial data

These are at best difficult chores, and at worst, can become nightmares if not properly conducted. This is because it is often difficult to assess exactly what intrinsic value is associated with the practice. Also, the risk factor associated with a transaction is always hard to determine. Finally, since each practice is unique, and the parties involved in a sale transaction come in all shapes and sizes, no standard transaction structure has been developed that lends itself to an uncritical use in all situations.

A comprehensive discussion of each of the topics identified above is beyond the scope of the book. However, for practical reasons, some basic issues concerning the sale of a practice will be explored in the following pages.

BEST TIME TO SELL A PRACTICE

The best time to sell a practice is when the seller is ready to move on. This is easier said than done. For one thing, selling a practice is often associated with losing control over the most valuable asset a planner owns. For another, arriving at a value for a financial-advisory firm is an extremely difficult exercise, and the buyer and the seller have very different ideas of what the business is worth. Regardless of the difficulties involved, once the seller believes that it is time to "smell the roses," it is important to start the process of selling the practice.

---

[8] This section was authored by Jack DiFranco, Managing Director of Stout Risius Ross (SRR). The company provides a full range of financial advisory services to help companies increase shareholder value through effective financing, acquisition, and divestiture transactions. Tel: 248 208.8800.

THE PROCESS OF SALE

The sale process includes four key phases: *preparation, initiation, narrowing the field,* and *closing the transaction.* In the preparation phase, potential buyers are first identified. There are three types of buyers including *financial buyers, strategic buyers* and *insiders.* Financial buyers are parties who purchase companies principally for a financial return. These buyers are often private equity funds or other investment firms. Strategic buyers are parties within the same or similar industry as the company being sold. These buyers have some connection that enables the acquisition to have a strategic fit. Transactions with strategic buyers typically create some synergistic benefit through cost savings or revenue enhancement opportunities. Finally, the spectrum of potential buyers also includes insiders. Insiders are generally other business partners (perhaps minority shareholders), key employees, or the current management of the practice. The preparation phase also includes the preparation of a Confidential Memorandum, a comprehensive document that describes the practice and summarizes its financial performance.

In the initiation phase, potential buyers are contacted to determine their preliminary interest in the practice. Before any information is provided, the buyer must typically sign a Confidentiality Agreement that provides that the information will be kept in strict confidence and not used in any way other than to assess the acquisition opportunity. Generally, before any additional information is provided or meetings with management are held, the buyer is asked to submit a non-binding Letter of Interest. The Letter of Interest sets forth the preliminary transaction outline including the buyer's first offer as it relates to the value of the business.

The next phase is narrowing the field. In this phase, the buyers are provided the opportunity to meet with the owners and management to better understand the business and assess the opportunity. With these meetings and certain additional information, the buyer is then asked to submit a Letter of Intent. Although still generally non-binding, this document is a much more detailed expression of interest with most (if not all) of the economic and structural terms of the deal specified. The culmination of this phase is to narrow the list of buyers to one party with whom a Letter of Intent is executed.

The final phase is closing the transaction. The two principal activities of this phase are due diligence and the negotiation and drafting of the definitive purchase agreements. It is very typical for numerous issues to emerge during this phase. If all issues can be resolved and appropriately reflected in the definitive agreements, then the transaction can close.

VALUATION OF PRACTICE

One of the most challenging aspects of selling a practice relates to the task of calculating its fair market value that is agreeable to both buyer and the seller. This is due to the fact valuing a practice is as much an art as it is a science. Valuation is also very much a function of negotiation.

Announcements by a handful of industry experts indicate that advisers should be valued at some multiple of cash flow or revenue. However, multiples have little practical value, because no outsider knows the real numbers behind the transactions used to determine the multiples. The discounted cash flow method is often used to capture the value of future cash flows the practice is expected to generate. However, the method of using discounted cash flow analysis is fraught with dangers, because often a lot of negotiation is required to come up with a cash flow figure both buyer and seller can agree on. This is due to the fact that the practice will change operationally after the sale is completed. Since the discounted cash flow method is widely used in valuing financial planning practices, it will be discussed in detail in the next section.

Conceptual Framework

The discounted cash flow (DCF) analysis rests upon forecasting free cash flows for a period of three to five years and discounting these flows back to the present by using an appropriate discount rate. The equation for the DCF analysis is as follows:

$$\text{Current Value} = \frac{\text{FCF (1)}}{(1+d)^1} + \frac{\text{FCF (2)}}{(1+d)^2} + \frac{\text{FCF (3)}}{(1+d)^3} + \dots \frac{\text{FCF (5)}}{(1+d)^5} + \frac{\text{FCF (n)}}{(1+d)^n}$$

where FCF = Free Cash Flow
      d = Discount Rate or Required Rate of Return

An example should make this clear. Assume the following information pertains to ABC practice:

Year 1: Free Cash Flow = $200,000
Year 2: Free Cash Flow = $300,000
Year 3: Free Cash Flow = $400,000
Year n: Free Cash Flow = $500,000
Discount Rate for Years 1 through 3: 22 percent
Capitalization Rate = 20 percent

In this example, the cash flows for the first three years are $200,000, $300,000 and $400,000, and the cash flows from year then on until perpetuity are fixed at $500,000. The discount rate is 22 percent for the first three years, and the capitalization rate (for cash flows until perpetuity) is 20 percent. The value of this practice is $874,073:

$$\$874,073 = \frac{\$200,000}{(1+.22)^1} + \frac{\$300,000}{(1+.22)^2} + \frac{\$400,000}{(1+.22)^3} + \frac{\$500,000}{(1.20)^3}$$

Estimating Cash Flow

What makes calculating cash flow so difficult is that the proprietors usually mix their personal finances with those of the business and present the numbers in a way that reduces their over tax burden. A potential buyer, however, wants to know the practice's true bottom line.

Another potential problem relates to the accurate determination of fair compensation for labor and fair reward for ownership. There are two ways in which financial planners get compensated for their participation in the practice. The most common method is to take home whatever is left after all the overhead expenses have been paid, so for income tax purposes it could be declared that the practice did not make any profit. For instance, suppose John Jones Planners have four planners who manage $500 million, generating $3 million in gross revenues. A third of that $3 million goes to running the business, leaving the four partners with $2 million. Each partner receives $500,000 a piece, and the firm declares zero profits.

The second method is a variant of the first and is much more realistic. In this case, as employees, each of the planners takes $250,000 as a fair compensation for labor. That leaves $1 million as free cash flow, which also represents a fair reward for ownership. Here the buyer and the seller could more readily accept the cash flow number as the basis for a fair evaluation of the value of the practice.

The Discount/Capitalization Rate

Determining the accurate discount rate is a difficult chore. This is because a number of factors must be carefully analyzed before a final decision can be made. Some of the key factors include: (1) Size of the practice; (2) prevailing economic conditions; (3) nature of the book of business; (4) stability of future cash flow; and (5) expected return on alternative investments. Experts claim that financial planning practices should use discount rates ranging from 20 percent to 40 percent. Whatever the rate is selected for valuing a practice, it should reflect not only the normal rate of return but also the attendant risks associated with the expected cash flow of the firm.

A REAL WORLD CASE STUDY

In this final section, the discounted cash flow analysis is applied to the valuation of Morton Dean & Associates (MDA), a hypothetical financial consulting firm operating in the Midwest.

Income projections for MDA for Year 1 through Year 6 are presented in Table 21-1. The techniques for making these projections are discussed next.

Assets Generating Highest Fees

These assets (line A-1) represent the accounts that do not exceed $500,000 per account. Owners of these portfolios pay higher management fees because the size of each account is not sufficiently large to qualify for preferred management fees. This category of assets is valued by taking the following three steps.

First, a ten percent annual rate of growth is applied to the existing assets during the entire period (line A-2).

Second, after a thorough review of the past history, and taking into account the future growth potential, it is assumed that new assets will come under management as indicated on line A-3. Average assets under management during the six-year period are presented on line A-5.

Third, management fees earned by MDA on these accounts, net of broker-dealer fees, are estimated to be 0.915 percent, and total management fees earned on this type of assets are presented on line A-6.

Assets from Affluent Clients

Assets per account of $1 million or more managed at the average preferred management fees of 0.60 percent (net of broker-dealer fee) are included in this category (B). Using the same method of extrapolation, the average assets under management are determined and presented on line B-5 for the six-year period.

Assets in Qualified Plans

Because of the policy of offering special discounts to these institutions, these assets

TABLE 21-1 Income Projections

		For the Year Ending				
		Year 1	Year 2	Year 3	Year 4	Year 5	Year 6

		Year 1	Year 2	Year 3	Year 4	Year 5	Year 6
A. Client Category 1	*10.0%*						
1 Beginning assets under management		25,600,000	32,160,000	39,376,000	46,313,600	52,944,960	59,239,456
2 Growth in existing assets		2,560,000	3,216,000	3,937,600	4,631,360	5,294,496	5,923,946
3 New assets		4,000,000	4,000,000	3,000,000	2,000,000	1,000,000	0
4 Ending assets under management		32,160,000	39,376,000	46,313,600	52,944,960	59,239,456	65,163,402
	0.915%						
5 Average assets under management		28,880,000	35,768,000	42,844,800	49,629,280	56,092,208	62,201,429
6 Management fees		264,252	327,277	392,030	454,108	513,244	569,143
B. Client Category 2	*10.0%*						
1 Beginning assets under management		14,200,000	15,620,000	17,182,000	18,900,200	20,790,220	22,869,242
2 Growth in existing assets		1,420,000	1,562,000	1,718,200	1,890,020	2,079,022	2,286,924
3 New assets		0	0	0	0	0	0
4 Ending assets under management		15,620,000	17,182,000	18,900,200	20,790,220	22,869,242	25,156,166
	0.600%						
5 Average assets under management		14,910,000	16,401,000	18,041,100	19,845,210	21,829,731	24,012,704
6 Management fees		89,460	98,406	108,247	119,071	130,978	144,076
C. Annuities and 401(k)	*10.0%*						
1 Beginning assets under management		5,000,000	5,500,000	6,050,000	6,655,000	7,320,500	8,052,550
2 Growth in existing assets		500,000	550,000	605,000	665,500	732,050	805,255
3 New assets		0	0	0	0	0	0
4 Ending assets under management		5,500,000	6,050,000	6,655,000	7,320,500	8,052,550	8,857,805
	0.500%						
5 Average assets under management		5,250,000	5,775,000	6,352,500	6,987,750	7,686,525	8,455,178
6 Management fees		26,250	28,875	31,763	34,939	38,433	42,276
D. Insurance Commissions							
1 2nd to die policies		40,000	40,000	40,000	40,000	40,000	40,000
2 Annual increases		0	0	0	0	0	0
3 Insurance commission income		40,000	40,000	40,000	40,000	40,000	40,000
E. Other Income							
1 Beginning assets under management		44,800,000	53,280,000	62,608,000	71,868,800	81,055,680	90,161,248
2 Ending assets under management		53,280,000	62,608,000	71,868,800	81,055,680	90,161,248	99,177,373
3 Average assets under management		49,040,000	57,944,000	67,238,400	76,462,240	85,608,464	94,669,310
	0.200%						
4 Other income as a % of assets under mgt.		98,080	115,888	134,477	152,924	171,217	189,339
F. Total income		518,042	610,446	706,516	801,042	893,872	984,834
Implied growth			17.8%	15.7%	13.4%	11.6%	10.2%

are assumed to generate average management fees of 0.50 percent (line C-6), and the ending assets under management for the six-year period under review are presented on line C-4.

Other Income

Although MDA is primarily an investment management company, it does provide other services, chief among them being insurance, financial planning, and consulting services. After considerable discussions it was decided that the simplest way of estimating this source of income is to assume that "other income" will equal 20 percent of assets under management (E-4).

Total Income

Total assets under management (average) are presented on line E-3 and total projected annual incomes during the six-year period are presented on line F.

Discounted Cash Flow Analysis

The next step in the valuation process is the application of the discounted cash flow analysis to the estimated free cash flow of the practice. This analysis is presented in Table 21-2 entitled, *Discounted Cash Flow Method*. The salient features of this analysis are presented next.

First, estimated income figures calculated in Table 21-1 are presented on line 1. Second, subtracting normal expenses (lines 2-8), and interest and taxes (lines 11 and 13), we arrive at net income estimates (line 14). Then, after various adjustments we arrive at distributable cash flow for the six-year period (line 18).

Third, a discount rate of 22 percent is selected for discounting the cash flow, because the assumed risk premium included in this rate appears to reflect the risk associated with operating this practice. Using this rate, the present values of distributable cash flows for five years are presented on line 20.

For the sixth year a capitalization rate of 19 percent is used by subtracting a residual growth rate of 3 percent from the 22 percent rate used as the present value factor. The present value of the residual flow is presented on line 29.

Finally, adding the two present values together, the total operating value, which also equals the business enterprise value, is presented on line 32. Given that there is no interest-bearing debt, the fair market value of MDA is calculated at $800,000 (rounded) and presented on line 35.

Transaction Structure

There are several ways of structuring a transaction between the buyer and the seller. The buyer may choose to make a cash payment to the seller to consummate the sale. The sale can also be structured with the consideration paid on an earn-out basis. In this case, the buyer would pay the seller some proportion of revenues or profits over a specific period of time. Another method would involve the seller financing all or a portion of the purchase price with a note to be paid over an appropriate amortization period.

It is not uncommon for a transaction to be structured with one or more of the features discussed above (e.g., a cash down payment, with a seller note and a contingent earn-out for some up-side). Because of their unique nature as a service business, sales of financial planning practices often require a certain degree of creativity and flexibility. To illustrate, our hypothetical example involves a sale to management.

TABLE 21-2 Discounted Cash Flow Method

		For the Year Ending				
		Year 1	Year 2	Year 3	Year 4	Year 5	Residual
1	Income	$ 518,042	$ 610,446	$ 706,516	$ 801,042	$ 893,872	$ 984,834
	Expenses						
2	Salaries and related benefits	119,726	125,713	131,998	138,598	145,528	149,894
3	Executive compensation	181,315	213,656	247,281	280,365	312,855	344,692
4	Occupancy costs	40,067	41,269	42,507	43,782	45,096	46,449
5	Professional fees	23,783	24,972	26,220	27,531	28,908	29,775
6	Fixed expenses	60,197	63,206	66,367	69,685	73,169	75,364
7	Variable expenses	13,961	16,451	19,040	21,587	24,089	26,541
8	Depreciation	0	0	0	0	0	0
9	Total expenses	439,048	485,267	533,413	581,549	629,645	672,714
10	Earnings before interest and taxes	78,994	125,179	173,103	219,493	264,227	312,120
11	Interest expense	0	0	0	0	0	0
12	Earnings before income taxes	78,994	125,179	173,103	219,493	264,227	312,120
13	Income taxes	(15,108)	(32,070)	(50,760)	(68,852)	(86,298)	(104,977)
14	Net income	63,886	93,109	122,343	150,641	177,928	207,143
	Adjustments						
15	Add: depreciation	0	0	0	0	0	0
16	Less: capital expenditures	0	0	0	0	0	0
17	Less: additional working capital	0	0	0	0	0	0
18	Distributable cash flow	63,886	93,109	122,343	150,641	177,928	207,143
19	Present value factor (22.0%)	0.9054	0.7421	0.6083	0.4986	0.4087	
20	Present value of distributable cash flow	$ 57,840	$ 69,096	$ 74,418	$ 75,108	$ 72,715	

21	Total present value of cash flows (years 1 to 5)	349,177
29	Present value of residual cash flow	445,551
30	Total operating value	794,728

22	Residual cash flow	$ 207,143	
	Residual capitalization rate		
23	Discount rate	22.0%	
24	Less: residual growth rate	-3.0%	
25	Capitalization rate	19.0%	
26	Residual cash flow value	1,090,226	
27	Present value factor	0.4087	
28	Present value of residual cash flow	$ 445,551	

31	Plus: nonoperating assets	0
32	Business enterprise value	794,728
33	Less: interest-bearing debt	0
34	Marketable, controlling-interest value of equity	794,728
35	Rounded	$ 800,000

Under this scenario, the sale will involve 100 percent seller financing. The payment terms of the note will be tailored to track the cash flow being generated by the business.

Structural Example

Step 1. The analysis begins by repeating in Table 21-3, line 1, earnings before interest and taxes (see line 10 in Table 21-2). These amounts are adjusted as follows:

1. Estimated compensation for Executive 1 (line 2) and Executive 2 (line 3) are added back to arrive at the adjusted EBITDA (earnings before interest, taxes, depreciation and amortization).
2. Interest expense (line 5) and intangible amortization (line 6) are deducted to arrive at earnings before taxes (line 7).
3. From the figures calculated in #2 above, taxes are deducted (line 8), and amortization is added back (line 10), thus arriving at the total cash flow after tax figures (line 11).

Step 2. The agreed upon value for the transaction is $800,000. The payment schedule is presented on lines 17 through 22. The principal payments are presented on line 18, whereas interest payments on the unpaid balance, calculated at 9 percent, are presented on line 20. Annual payments to the seller, spread out over a six-year period by mutual consent, are presented on line 22. These payments were selected to provide a degree of cushion going forward.

The total payment by the buyer to the seller, which includes the sale price of $800,000 plus interest, equals $1,016,000 (line 23).

True Net Cash Flow

The two critical questions for the buyer of a financial planning practice are: "What is the *true* bottom line?" and "After meeting all the overhead obligations, can the practice make the payments associated with the sale and generate a reasonable profit?" While these questions are answered in Table 21-3, the results of this analysis are demonstrated more clearly in Table 21-4 for the first year of the projection. A brief discussion of the items included in this table for the first year now follows.

The analysis begins by restating the total income for Year 1, taken from Table 21-1, line F. From this amount office expenses of $202,733 are deducted to arrive at the cash flow after expenses. Office expenses are calculated as follows (see Table 21-2):

Total Expenses (line 9)	$439,048
Less Executive # 1 Compensation (line 3)	$181,315
Less Executive # 2 Compensation	$ 55,000
Total Expenses	$202,733

The compensation of $55,000 for Executive # 2 is included in the salaries and benefits figure of $119,726 (line 2). This is what is called the adjusted EBITDA.

From adjusted EBITDA, the following items are deducted: a) Interest on the unpaid balance of the sale price, $67,500; b) Payment of Principal, $100,000; and c) Tax payment on the profit of the practice, $72,457. This amount equals the cash available before distributions to Executive No. 2. Distributions of $55,000 to this executive results in a net cash flow of $25,352 (Table 21-3, line 15). This is the net profit for running the practice, or it can be called the cushion available for meeting an unexpected contingency.

TABLE 21-3 Proforma Cash Flow Analysis

		For the Year Ending						
		Year 1	Year 2	Year 3	Year 4	Year 5	Year 6	Year 7
1	Earnings before interest and taxes	$78,994	$125,179	$173,103	$219,493	$264,227	$312,120	$321,483
2	Executive 1 compensation	181,315	213,656	247,281	280,365	312,855	344,692	355,033
3	Executive 2 compensation	55,000	57,750	60,638	63,662	66,853	70,195	73,705
4	Adjusted EBITDA	315,309	396,586	481,021	563,528	643,935	727,007	750,221
5	Less: interest expense	(67,500)	(57,375)	(45,000)	(30,375)	(13,500)	(2,250)	0
6	Less: intangible amortization	(66,667)	(66,667)	(66,667)	(66,667)	(66,667)	(66,667)	(66,667)
7	Earnings before taxes	181,142	272,544	369,354	466,486	563,768	658,090	683,554
8	Distribution for taxes 40%	(72,457)	(109,018)	(147,742)	(186,594)	(225,507)	(263,236)	(273,422)
9	After tax earnings	108,685	163,526	221,613	279,892	338,261	394,854	410,133
10	Add back amortization	66,667	66,667	66,667	66,667	66,667	66,667	66,667
11	Total cash flow after taxes	175,352	230,193	288,279	346,558	404,927	461,521	476,799
12	Less: min. executive distributions 10%	(50,000)	(55,000)	(60,500)	(66,550)	(73,205)	(80,526)	(88,578)
13	Net available cash	125,352	175,193	227,779	280,008	331,722	380,995	388,221
14	Less: principal amortization	(100,000)	(125,000)	(150,000)	(175,000)	(200,000)	(50,000)	0
15	Net cash flow (cushion)	25,352	50,193	77,779	105,008	131,722	330,995	388,221
16	Debt Amortization:							
17	Beginning balance	800,000	700,000	575,000	425,000	250,000	50,000	0
18	Less: principal amortization	(100,000)	(125,000)	(150,000)	(175,000)	(200,000)	(50,000)	0
19	Ending balance	700,000	575,000	425,000	250,000	50,000	0	0
20	Interest expense 9%	67,500	57,375	45,000	30,375	13,500	2,250	0
21	Principal amortization	100,000	125,000	150,000	175,000	200,000	50,000	0
22	Total payments to Seller	167,500	182,375	195,000	205,375	213,500	52,250	0
23	Aggregate payments to Seller	$1,016,000						

TABLE 21-4 Free Cash Flow

Income	$518,042 (Table 21-1, line F)
Less office expenses before executive comp.	$202,733
Income after office expenses	$315,309 (Table 21-3, line 4)
Less interest expense	$ 67,500 (Line 5)
Less principal amortization	$100,000 (Line 18)
Less tax payments	$ 72,457 (Line 8)
Cash flow before executive distributions	$75,352
Less min. executive distributions	$50,000 (Line 12)
Net cash flow (cushion)	$25,352 (Line 15)

Incidentally, starting with year seven, after the debt relating to the sale of the practice is completely liquidated, the buyer will have the potential for making a very decent profit on the investment. Of course, over the first six years, a lot would depend upon how the business is run and the ingenuity of the buyer to take this practice to a much higher level profitability and excellence.

Concluding Remarks

As stated earlier, the sale of a practice is as much an art as it is a science. There is no one established structure which is applicable to all situations. The real world case study presented above clearly justifies the claim that special skills, good judgment, and an appreciation of the biases and idiosyncrasies of both the buyer and the seller are required for the successful sale of a financial planning practice.

CONCLUSION

In this concluding chapter we have provided a conceptual framework for establishing and managing a successful financial planning practice. We have also provided views on practice management and succession planning by Deena Katz, who is one of the leading experts on this subject. Finally, in the concluding section, a detailed analytical framework of the sale of a financial planning practice is presented by Jack DiFranco, who is recognized as an expert in the field.

In conclusion, we can say with confidence that, in the final analysis, long-term success of a financial planning practice will depend upon efficiently providing the highest level of service with ethics, codes of conduct, integrity, sincerity, and professionalism.

Freedom to fail is vital if you're going to succeed. Most successful people fail time and time again, and it is a measure of their strength that failure merely propels them into some new attempt at success.

Michael Korda

Appendix

Today every planner must have Internet access. As the Financial Calculator was to yesterday's planner, today the Internet has become an indispensable tool. With markets and information moving at lightening speed, the Internet allows planners access to data within minutes that would have taken weeks to find, if it was available at all.

There are hundreds of web sites devoted to the financial planning and investment industry. You will have to do some searching to find out which sites will benefit your practice and which ones only take up your time.

Listed below are some useful sites that you might want to use to get started. Remember, the Internet is a tool. While it cannot replace a financial planner, it *can* enhance your value to your clients.

1. Start with a good search engine. Several sites, like Yahoo, AOL and Lycos— all provide some form of search engines. www.refdesk.com is one of the most complete search sites currently available.

2. www.cfp-board.org is a must. This observation comes from the CFP Board in Colorado. They have lots of resources, including training programs all across the country, on-line publications for prospective advisors, and many useful links.

3. Sites associated with major exchanges are very good. They provide information about exchanges, rules and regulations, as well as stock research, quotes and links to other useful resources. Included here are www.nasdaq.com, www.nyse.com, and www.amex.com. NYSE site is very good and even has a virtual tour of the floor.

4. All major publications and news services have their own sites. Egs: www.barrons.com, www.dowjones.com (for The Wall Street Journal), www.money.com, www.fortune.com, www.cbs.marketwatch.com and www.bloomberg.com. They all offer research, market watch, and market news.

5. In addition to the media having sites, there are other Internet only sites, like Yahoo Finance and Lycos Finance, which are accessible via direct link through the Yahoo and Lycos websites. These sources have all the tools for research, as well as quotes and news. Zacks provides good research http://my.zacks.com. Charting can be done using any possible indicator at Big Charts http://bigcharts.marketwatch.com.

6. Let us not forget www.sec.gov, which is SEC's official site, and NASD Regulation's site, www.nasdr.org with all the news on compliance. This is a must for advisors.

7. Information on mutual funds can be found at www.standardpoor.com, www.morningstar.com, and www.brill.com. They have ratings, analysis of performance, charts, holdings, etc. All major fund companies have sites as well.

The Internet should be used only as a tool. It should not, in fact cannot, replace the personal interaction between the planner and the client.

Index

A

Academic degrees 1-15
Accelerating interest deductions 16-15
Accountant 1-13
Adjustable life insurance 4-23
Adjustments to gross income 15-10
ADV Part II 2-7
Advantages of fund investment 12-9
Advertising 21-11
Age-weighted profit sharing plans 10-26
Agency issues 12-2
Aggressive growth funds 12-9
AICPA 2-2
Aid
    financial 6-18
Alpha 13-11
Alternative minimum tax 15-27, 16-19
Alzheimer's coverage 5-31
Amendment of tax return 16-26
Analysis
    capital needs 4-39
Analyzing
    client information 2-31
    financial data 1-11, 2-29
Annual compounding
    multiple years 3-2
Annual exclusion 9-7

Annuity
    disposition of proceeds 11-16
    distribution 11-12
    equity-indexed 12-27
    future value of 3-12
    lump sum distribution of 11-18
    options, fixed and variable 4-46
        fixed income option 4-46
        fixed period option 4-46
        life-income option 4-46
    present value 3-17
    present value of 3-15
    principle 11-14
    private 9-36
    tax treatment of 11-17
    variable 4-47, 11-17
Annuity due 3-16
    future value of 3-16
    present value of 3-15, 3-17
Applicable exclusion amounts 8-20
Asset allocation
    diversification and 14-4
    funds 12-11
    model 13-30, 13-34, 14-4
    model steps 13-34
    strategy 6-14
Asset Replacement Trust 9-23
Attorney 1-13

Auto dealers 7-25
Automatic savings plans 7-16
Automobile insurance
  basic coverages of personal 5-49
  bodily injury liability in 5-50
  cost of 5-52
  coverage for damage to insured's auto
    5-50
  liability coverage 5-49
  loopholes in 5-52
  medical payments 5-50
  no-fault 5-53
  planning strategy 5-54
  policy 5-47
  property damage liability in 5-50
  uninsured motorists in 5-50
  worksheet 5-54

B

Balanced
  equity income funds 12-10
Bank
  checking accounts 7-18
  savings accounts 7-18
Bankruptcy 7-30
Benefits
  Social Security 16-19
Best time to sell practice 21-34
Best's Insurance Report 5-31
Beta 13-9
BLDRS 12-35
Blended insurance policy 4-21
Blue chip stock 12-7
Blue Cross Blue Shield 5-16
Bodily injury liability 5-50
Bond ratings 12-5
Bond risk reduction strategies 13-4
  adopting dollar cost averaging strategy
    13-5
  diversifying with international bonds
    13-5
  investing in tax-exempt bonds 13-5
  laddering bond investments 13-4
Bonds
  buying 13-5
  callable 12-5
  corporate 12-4

  municipal 16-7
  selling 13-6
Brochure Rule 2-7
Budgeting 7-6
Burden of debt 7-29
Business
  dividing the 19-6
  valuing the 19-6
Business expenses 16-5
Business income
  splitting 16-19
Business organization 16-23
Business owners
  estate planning of 9-42
Business purchase agreement 9-43
Business structure 21-7
Business use of a home 15-16
Buy-Sell agreement 4-50
Bypass trust 9-10

C

C Corporations 15-31
Cafeteria plans 4-29
  advantages of 4-30
Calculation of net worth 7-2
Call option with stock sale 13-21
Callability risk 13-4
Callable bonds 12-5
Capital Asset Pricing Model 13-27
Capital gains
  and losses 15-5
  from sale of residence 15-7
  or losses on fund sales 13-24
Capital maximization strategy 4-60
Capital needs analysis 4-39
Career assets 19-5
Cash flow analysis
  steps in 7-7
Cash management planning 7-3
  budgeting 7-6
  cash flow 7-7
  cash flow analysis 7-6
  cash flow planning 7-9
Cash value insurance 4-12
  cash value 4-12
  death protection 4-12
  dividend option 4-13

emergency fund 4-14
equal-payment plan (level premiums) 4-12
essential features 4-12
flexibility 4-12
lifetime protection 4-14
permanence 4-12
Casualty or theft losses 15-17
Catch-up on IRA contributions 15-12
Categories of credit 7-26
Certificates of deposit 7-20, 12-2
Certificates of indebtedness 12-2
Certified Financial Planner 1-3
Board of Standards 1-3
five Cs of 1-4
professionalism of 1-4
Charitable contributions 15-16, 16-15
Charitable deductions 8-23
Charitable donations 16-9
Charitable Lead Trust 9-20
Charitable Remainder Annuity Trust 9-18
Charitable Remainder Unitrust 9-18
Charitable Trust 9-18
Child employment 16-13
Child support 19-14
Claims against estate 8-23
Client 1-4
common denominators 1-5
becoming disabled 1-7
dying too young 1-7
living too long 1-6
emerging 1-4
information 2-28
qualifying a potential 2-3
Closed-end versus open-end funds 12-8
COBRA 5-15
Code of Ethics and Professional Responsibility 1-3, 1-17
Codicil 8-8
Coinsurance clause 5-40
College costs 6-1
compounding, magic of 6-2
deduction for higher education expenses 6-10
employer-provided educational assistance 6-10
estimated family contributions 6-5
family's expected contribution 6-5, 6-17

Federal Stafford Loans 6-15
financial aid 6-18
financial assistance 6-14
grants and scholarships 6-14
reduction of debts 6-18
repayment of student loans 6-17
student loan interest deduction 6-10
Tax Relief Reconciliation Act of 2001 6-10
tuition vs. savings plan 6-8
UGMA and UTMA 6-4
work study programs 6-16
College savings
bonds for education 6-11
TIPS 6-12
College savings plans 6-4
education IRAs 6-5
Section 2503 (c) Minor's Trust 6-13
Section 529 Plans 6-7
UGMA and UTMA 6-4
zero coupon option 6-11
CollegeSure CD 6-13
Combo strategy 11-28
Commercial banks 7-24
Commercial insurance companies 5-18
Common law states 8-13
Common stock 12-7
Communication 1-8
with planning client 1-8
with potential client 1-8
Community property and the transitory couple 8-14
Community property states 8-13
Company organization 21-5
Company-sponsored qualified plan and Keogh plan 11-14
Compensation
deferred 4-52
Competence 1-15
academic degrees 1-15
continuing education 1-16
credentials 1-15
experience 1-16
Compound interest 3-2, 6-2
Compounding
annual, multiple years 3-2
Comprehensive health insurance 5-6
Comprehensive plan 1-3, 1-12

Computation of
  capital gains and losses 15-6
  estate taxes 8-19
Constant ratio plan 13-19
Consumer credit
  categories of 7-26
  installment purchases 7-28
  revolving and optional charge accounts
    7-28
  thirty-day or regular charge accounts
    7-28
Consumer finance companies 7-24
Continuing education 1-16
Contract
  life insurance 4-15
  signing a formal 2-6
Contributions
  charitable 16-15
  of appreciated property 16-15
Convertible bonds 12-5
Convertible term 4-10
Convertible trust 9-40
Coordination with 1-12
  accountant 1-13
  attorney 1-13
  insurance counselor 1-14
  other professionals 1-14
  portfolio manager 1-14
Corporate bonds 12-4
  types of 12-4
    callable bonds 12-5
    convertible bonds 12-5
    debentures 12-5
    guaranteed bonds 12-5
    junk bonds 12-5
    mortgage bonds 12-5
    zero coupon bonds 12-5
Corporate retirement plans 10-9
  coverage requirements 10-11
  funding requirements 10-14
  participation requirements 10-11
  plan investment rules 10-14
  specific requirements 10-11
  types of plans 10-15
  vesting requirements 10-14
Corporate structure 21-5
Corporations
  taxation of 15-31
Cost of auto insurance 5-52

Cost of life insurance 4-40
  benchmark method 4-43
  interest-adjusted cost index 4-42
  net-cost method 4-41
Covered calls
  strategy of 13-20
Credentials 1-15
Credit
  and debt planning 7-22
  basic issue of 7-26
  categories of 7-26
    installment purchases or time-
    payment plans 7-28
    revolving and optional charge ac-
    counts 7-28
    thirty-day or regular charge accounts
    7-28
  history 7-25
  protection of 7-26
  types of 7-26
Credit unions 7-24
Crime insurance 5-42
Crisis planning for death 21-27
Criteria for savings media selection 7-17
  liquidity 7-18
  return on savings 7-18
    bank checking accounts 7-18
    bank savings accounts 7-18
  safety 7-17
Crummey Trust 9-25
Cyclical company stocks 12-7

D

Data gathering 1-10, 2-7
Data refinement 2-30
Dealing with death 8-3
  psychological implications of 8-3
Debentures 12-5
Debt
  burden of 7-29
  credit or 7-23
Decreasing term 4-10
Deductibility of IRA 10-34
Deductibles
  potential savings from 5-3
Deduction 16-2
Deduction for higher education expenses
  6-10, 15-20

Deemed IRAs under employer plans 15-12

Deena Katz on practice management
    21-14

Default risk 13-3

Defensive stocks 12-7

Deferment 6-17

Deferral 16-10
    of income 16-13
    with after-tax dollars 16-12
    with pre-tax dollars 16-10

Deferred compensation 4-52

Deferred variable annuity 12-24

Defined benefit plans 10-23

Defined contribution plans 10-15, 11-10
    401(k) plan 10-22
    employee stock ownership plan 10-23
    money purchase pension plan 10-20
    profit sharing plan 10-21
    simple retirement plan 10-20
    simplified employee pension plan 10-21
    stock bonus plan 10-22
    thrift plan 10-23

Definition
    of financial planning 1-3

Deflection 16-12

Dental expense insurance 5-7

Determination of life insurance needs
    4-2, 4-38

Diamonds (DIA) 12-33

Differences among widows 20-1

Diminution 16-13

Direct mail 21-12

Direct rollovers 10-28

Direct transfer 10-29

Director's liability insurance 5-57

Disability
    definition of 5-9

Disability income insurance 5-8
    coordination of benefits 5-12
    cost of a disability policy 5-11
    definition of disability 5-9
    determining the income need 5-10
    features of a good policy 5-10
    integration with social security 5-9
    types of disability insurance 5-8
    waiting period 5-8

Disability-to-LTC "conversion" policies
    5-12

Disadvantages of gifts 9-8

Distribution from qualified plans 11-8
    other qualified plans 11-8
    pension plans 11-8
    profit sharing plans 11-8
    required distributions 11-9
    taxation of IRAs 11-12
    taxation of Keogh plans 11-12
    taxation of plan benefits 11-11

Distribution rules 10-28

Distributions to beneficiaries 11-10

Diversification 12-9, 14-4
    and asset allocation model 14-4
    power of 13-27

Diversion 16-6

Dividing the business 19-6

Dividing the house 19-7

Divorce
    and pension plans 19-8
    career assets 19-5
    child support 19-14
    equal versus equitable concept 19-4
    income tax considerations 19-15
    maintenance in 19-13
    property valuation and settlement in
        19-2

Dollar cost averaging 13-17

Donations
    charitable 16-9

Durable power of attorney 8-10

Dynasty Trust leveraging GSTT exemption
    9-28

E

Early retirement 11-25

Early withdrawal penalty 16-20

Economic Growth and Tax Relief Recon-
    ciliation Act 8-20, 15-3

Economics of planning business 21-3

Educating widow 20-9

Education
    college costs of 6-1
    college savings plans for 6-4
    deduction for higher expenses 15-20

Education IRAs 6-5
    modification of 15-18

Educational investment alternatives 6-11
    CollegeSure CD 6-13

low-load insurance 6-12
savings bonds for education 6-11
Section 2503 (c) minor's trust 6-13
Treasury Inflation Indexed Securities
6-12
zero coupon option 6-11
Educational planning 6-19
Effective interest rate 7-29
Effective savings strategies 7-16
automatic savings plans 7-16
goal setting 7-16
savings-first approach 7-16
self-rewarding plan 7-16
Efficient Frontier 13-29
EGPRIM 1-9, 2-2, 2-7
Elective deferrals as Roth contributions
15-11
Emerging trends 1-1
American dream realities 1-2
retirement realities 1-2
Employee business expenses 16-17
Employee stock ownership plan 10-23
Employer-provided educational assistance
15-20
Equal-payment plan 4-12
Equity
return 13-6
risk 13-9, 13-15
securities 13-6
Equity-Indexed Annuity 12-29
Establish client objectives 1-9, 2-30
Estate
gross 8-22
inter vivos trust 8-15
liquidity 9-40
living trust 8-15
preservation and distribution strategies
9-37
Estate and gift tax rates 8-27
Estate distribution 8-2
Estate planning 8-1, 9-1
advanced strategies 9-45
Charitable Lead Trust 9-20
Charitable Remainder Annuity Trust
9-18
Charitable Remainder Unitrust 9-18
concepts and strategies 9-1
convertible trust 9-40
Crummey Trust 9-25

durable power of attorney 8-10
family limited partnerships 9-21
federal income tax considerations 9-41
for business owners 9-42
generation skipping transfer tax 9-26
gift tax calculation 9-7
irrevocable gift trust 9-20
life insurance trust 9-16
lifetime gifts 9-6
objectives and tools 8-4
overview 8-4
pooled income fund 9-20
power of appointment 9-32
power of attorney 8-10
Qualified Personal Residence Trust
(QPRT) 9-33, 9-34
recapitalization 9-35
revocable living trust 9-38, 9-39
sophisticated estate tax reduction
strategies 9-21
split dollar arrangement 9-28
sprinkling trusts 9-24
stepped-up basis rule 9-41
strategies 9-5
survivorship life insurance 9-42
trust 9-16
will 8-5
codicil 8-8
holographic 8-8
mutual 8-8
reciprocal 8-7
simple 8-7
Estate tax
and life insurance 4-17, 4-33
and trusts 9-10
computation of 8-19
covering 9-24, 9-29
history of 8-2
marital deduction 9-2
reduction strategies 9-2
Estate tax calculation 8-21
Estate taxes
life insurance 4-33
Estate trust 9-16
Ethics 1-17
commitment to 1-17
Ethics code 1-3
Eurodollar futures 12-31

Exchange-traded index funds 12-23,
    12-38
Exchange-traded index investing 12-35
Executives 16-24
Expense
    needs vs sources of income 4-39
    ratio 12-13
    reduction 7-14
    reduction worksheet 7-15
    shifting 16-19
Expenses
    business 16-5
    employee business 16-17
    medical 16-15
    moving 16-3
    rental 16-6
Experience 1-16
Explaining financial planning approach
    20-7
External environment 21-3
Eye care insurance 5-7

F

Family income policy 4-11
Family limited partnerships 9-21
Family's expected contribution 6-17
Federal estate taxes 8-19
Federal income tax considerations 9-41
Federal Stafford Loans 6-15
Federal stafford loans 6-15
Federal taxable income
    basic structure 15-1
    calculation of gross income 15-3
    computation of 15-3
    considerations 9-41
    credits 15-29
        child tax credit 15-29
        overview 15-29
    standard deductions 15-2
Fee reduction strategies 12-13
Flexible spending arrangement 16-3
Filling disability benefit gaps 5-13
Financial aid 6-18
Financial assistance 6-14
    federal stafford loans 6-15
    grants and scholarships 6-14
    student loans 6-15
    work study programs 6-16

Financial independence planning
    overview 17-1
    six keys to success 17-2
Financial plan 20-9
Financial planning 1-3
    approach 20-7
    concept of 1-3
    definition of 1-3
    five Cs of 1-4
    key areas of 1-3
    process 2-2
    questionnaire 1-10
    subject areas 2-2
Financial planning process 2-4
    implementation of 2-33
    monitoring and review 2-33
Fixed annuity
    fixed income option 4-46
    life-income option 4-46
    period option 4-46
Fixed income
    funds 12-10
    investments 12-1
    security return 13-2
    security risk 13-2
        callability risk 13-4
        default risk 13-3
        inflation risk 13-3
        interest rate risk 13-2
        liquidity risk 13-4
        maturity risk 13-3
    security, risk of 13-2
Floater policies 5-41
Flood and earthquake insurance 5-42
FOLIOfn 12-31
Forbearance 6-18
Four Cs of credit 7-25
Fund investment
    advantages of 12-9
Fundamental analysis 13-42
Funds left with insurance company 4-48
Future value
    annuity due 3-16
Future value: annuity 3-12
Future value: fixed sum 3-2
Futures 12-31

G

Gaps in homeowners' policies 5-44
Gaps in medicare 5-19
Gathering data 1-10, 2-7
General obligation bonds 12-4
Generation skipping transfer tax 9-26
Gift tax
  calculation 9-7
  rate schedule 8-27
Gifts 16-13
  annual exclusion 9-7
  disadvantages of 9-8
  lifetime 8-19, 9-6
  special property 9-8
  to charity 9-8
  via a trust 9-8
Goal setting 7-11
  worksheet 7-12
Government health care insurance
    5-15, 5-18
Government sponsored plans 10-4
Graduated payment 6-18
Grantor Retained Annuity Trust 9-29,
    9-46
Grantor Retained Unitrust 9-29
Grants and scholarships 6-14
Gross estate 8-22
Gross income
  adjustments to 15-10
Group health insurance 5-13
Group life insurance 4-28
Growth and income funds 12-10
Growth company stocks 12-7
Growth funds 12-10
  aggressive 12-9
Guaranteed
  bonds 12-5
  funds 4-35
Guardian for minor children 8-12

H

Hard assets 14-16
Head of household 19-16
Health insurance
  group 5-13
  worksheets 5-29

Health insurance, sources of 5-15
  health maintenance organizations 5-16
  preferred provider organizations or
    PPOs 5-16
  traditional or major medical care 5-16
Health insurance, types of 5-5
  comprehensive health insurance 5-6
  dental expense insurance 5-7
  eye care insurance 5-7
  hospital insurance 5-5
    hospital indemnity insurance 5-5
    hospital-service-incurred plans 5-5
    hospitalization insurance 5-5
  major medical expense insurance 5-6
  medical expense insurance 5-6
  supplemental health insurance 5-8
  surgical insurance 5-5
Health Maintenance Organizations
    (HMOs) 5-16
High valued dwelling 5-43
HIPAA 5-15
Hiring, mentoring, and internships 21-15
Holographic will 8-8
Home office protection 5-44
Home ownership 16-6
Homeowner's policies
  cost issues of 5-41
  coverages 5-33
  covering unscheduled personal prop-
    erty 5-40
  details 5-43
  forms 5-29, 5-31
  gaps in 5-44
  major provisions 5-40
  worksheet 5-45
Hospital insurance 5-5

I

i Shares 12-22, 12-34
i Shares MSCI index funds 12-34
Ideal health insurance
  company 5-31
  plan 5-32
Implementation 1-11
Income
  acceleration 16-14
  deferral 16-13
  flow 14-14

shifting 16-18
tax considerations 19-15
Income stocks 12-8
Income tax considerations in divorce
    19-15
Index funds 12-11, 12-19
    fewer capital gains of 12-20
    lower cost of 12-20
    pitfalls of 12-21
Indexed Annuity 4-48
Individual Retirement Account (IRA)
    10-31
    before vs after-tax contribution 10-37
    deductibility of 10-34
    deductible vs nondeductible contribu-
        tions 10-35
    direct rollovers 10-28
    distribution 11-21
    distribution rules 10-28
    education 6-5
    excess contributions 11-13
    long-term accumulation 10-35
    mandatory withholding rules 10-28
    premature distributions 11-13
    rollover vs transfer 10-37
    Roth 10-34
    systematic withdrawal 11-21
    taxation 11-12
    types of 10-36
Individual retirement annuity plan 10-37
Individual retirement plan 10-36
Inflation
    guard policies 5-40
    in financial calculation 3-20
    risk 13-3
Installment
    sale 9-42
    sales and SCINs 9-31
Insurance
    automobile 5-47
    cash value 4-12
    counselor 1-14
    disability insurance 5-8
    floater policies 5-41
    health 5-4
    key man 4-52
    life 4-1
    shopping for 5-2
    umbrella liability 5-56

Insurance against significant risks 5-2
Insurance counselor 1-14
Insurance for professional 4-55
Insurance in qualified plans 4-51
Insurance policies
    blended 4-21
    switching 4-33
Insurance report
    Best's 5-31
Inter vivos trust 8-5
Interest
    adjusted cost index 4-42
    compounding 3-2
    investment 16-16
    simple 3-1
    tax-deductible 16-4
Interest deductions
    accelerating 16-15
Interest rate
    effective 7-29
    normal vs. effective 3-20
Interest-sensitive whole life 4-23
Internal rate of return 3-21
International Index Investing with i Shares
    MSCI funds 12-23
International/global funds 12-10
Investment interest 16-16
Investment planning 14-1
    goal setting 14-2
    long-term growth 14-16
    objectives 14-3
    process 14-1
    risk vs return 14-8
    tax advantages 14-16
    tax considerations 14-6
Investment portfolio 14-12
Investment return 14-6
Investment vehicles
    bond funds 14-22
    fixed annuity 14-22
    jumbo CD 14-22
    split annuity 14-22
Investor preference 14-11
IRA distribution 11-21
    systematic withdrawal: insurance plan
        11-22
    systematic withdrawal: personal
        investment 11-21

IRAs
   catch-up contributions 15-12
   deemed under employer plans 15-12
   distribution 11-21
   rollover versus transfer 10-37
   taxation of 11-12
   types of 10-36
      individual retirement plan 10-36
Irrevocable gift trust 9-20
Irrevocable life insurance trust 9-46
Itemized deductions to accelerate or defer
      income 16-14

J

Joint ownership 8-13, 9-3
   common law states 8-13
   community property and the transitory
      couple 8-14
   community property states 8-13
   joint tenancy with rights of survivorship
      8-14
   key advantages 9-3
   key disadvantages 9-4
   planning strategies 9-5
Joint tenancy with rights of survivorship
      8-14
Junk bonds 12-5

K

Keogh plan 10-39
   defined benefit 10-39
   defined contribution 10-39
   overview 10-38
   profit sharing 10-39
   taxation of 11-12
   types of 10-39
Key man insurance 4-52
Key planning areas 1-4
Kiddie tax 16-12

L

Letter of last instructions 8-9
Level term 4-10
Life insurance
   adjustable 4-23

and estate taxes 4-33
basic types of 4-4
cash value 4-12
companies, rating of 4-35
contract 4-15
determination of needs 4-38
distribution during life 4-32
distribution upon death 4-31
exchange 4-33
for individual family members 4-27
   insurance for children 4-27
   spousal insurance 4-27
for the professional 4-55
group 4-28
in irrevocable trust 4-49
in qualified plans 4-51
interest on policy loans 4-32
key reasons for purchasing 4-1
loans from 4-44
MECs 4-33
need, determination of 4-38
overview 4-1
   of policies 4-8
planning 4-38
policies, types of 4-4
policy dividends 4-32
policy withdrawals/loans 4-32
riders 4-29
sale or disposition, surrender, maturity
   4-33
settlement options 4-45
single-premium whole life 4-17
split-dollar 4-53, 9-28
survivorship variable life 4-27
switching of policies 4-33
taxation of 4-31
term 4-7
trust 9-16
types of policies 4-4, 4-18
universal life 4-18
variable life 4-22
variable universal life 4-22
Life insurance companies 7-24
Life settlement options 4-61
Lifetime gifts 8-19, 9-6
   annual exclusion 9-7
   disadvantages of gifts 9-8
   estate with and without lifetime gifts
      9-9

gift tax calculation 9-7
gifting via a trust 9-8
gifts to charity 9-8
planning ideas involving gifts 9-7
special property 9-8
Like-kind exchanges 16-8
Limited liability companies 16-25
Limited partnerships 16-8
Limited-payment life 4-16
Limits on contributions to 401(k) and
other plans 15-12
Lipper 12-18
Living benefit provision 4-63
Living trust 8-15
Loans from a life insurance policy 4-44
Loans from qualified plans 11-22
Long-term health care 5-27
Loopholes in auto insurance 5-52
Loss control through preventive measures
5-3
Low-load insurance 6-12
Lump sum distribution 11-18
Lump sum payment
tax-free 4-46
Lump sum versus IRA 11-19

M

Magic of compounding 6-2
Maintenance 19-13
Major medical expense insurance 5-6
Managing a financial planning practice
21-1
Mandatory withholding rules 10-28
Marital deduction 9-2
Marital trust 9-12
Market benchmarks 12-41
Marketable government issues 12-2
agency issues 12-2
certificates of indebtedness 12-2
treasury bills 12-2
treasury notes and bonds 12-2
Marketing strategies 21-9
Marketplace analysis 21-4
Marriage penalty 16-5
Master Limited Partnerships 16-8
Matching incomes and losses 16-7
Maturity risk 13-3

Maximum IRA contributions 15-11
Medical expense insurance 5-6
Medical expenses 16-15
Medicare 5-23, 10-8
gaps in 5-19
health savings accounts 5-24
recent improvements 5-23
Medicare prescription drug improvement
& modernization 5-26
Medicare supplement policies 5-27
Mid-cap SPDRs (MDY) 12-33
Minimum distribution rules 11-9
Minimum monthly balance requirement
7-19
Minor's Trust, Section 2503 (c) 6-13
Minor's trust, Section 2503(c)
power in 9-40
Miscellaneous investments 14-16
Modified Endowment Contract 4-19, 4-33
material changes test for 4-18
seven-pay test for 4-18
Monetary policy 13-40
Money market funds 12-11
Money market mutual funds 7-20
Money purchase pension plan 10-20
Monitoring and review in financial
planning 1-11
Morningstar 12-18
Morningstar Risk-Adjusted Rating 13-14
Mortgage bonds 12-5
Mortgage interest 16-16
Moving expenses 16-3
Multiple compound periods per year 3-6
Multiple year annual compounding 3-2
Municipal bonds 12-4, 16-7
general obligation bonds 12-4
revenue bonds 12-4
Mutual fund alphabet 12-15
Mutual fund investment
advantages of 12-9
Mutual fund portfolio
sizing up a 13-37
Mutual fund prospectus
reading a 12-15
Mutual fund rating services 12-18
lipper 12-18
morningstar 12-18
standard & poor's 12-19
Thomson financial 12-19

Mutual fund sales 16-19
Mutual funds 12-8
    12b-1 Fee 12-12
    alphabet 12-15
    average cost method 13-24
    closed-end vs open-end 12-8
    expense ratio 12-13
    fees and expenses 12-11
    first-in, first-out method 13-24
    load or sales charges 12-11
    management fees and operating ex-
        penses 12-12
    objectives and policies 12-15
    portfolio 13-37
    prospectus 12-15
    rating services 12-18
    redemption fees 12-12
    sale of 13-21
    specific identification method 13-24
    supermarket charges 12-13
    taxes 13-24
    traditional index funds 12-19
    trustee fees 12-13
    types of 12-9
Mutual funds fees and expenses 12-11
Mutual will 8-8

N

Nasdaq-100 index tracking stock (QQQ)
    12-34
Net worth 7-2
    and cash management planning 7-2
    basic concept 7-2
    calculation of 7-2
    planning 7-2
    planning strategy 7-3
Net-cost method 4-41
NMHPA 5-15
No-fault insurance 5-53
No-lapse guaranteed option 4-67
Nominal interest rate vs effective interest
    rate 3-20
Non-blue chip stocks 12-7
Non-financial advice 20-10
Non-marketable government issues 12-3
    series EE bonds 12-3
    series HH bonds 12-3
    series I bonds 12-3

Nonqualified deferred compensation plan
    11-26

O

Option spreads 12-30
Options 12-30
Organization
    company 21-5
    of personal records 5-3
Organizations
    Health Maintenance (HMOs) 5-16
    preferred provider (PPOs) 5-17
Other professionals 1-14
Other tax considerations 11-13

P

Partnerships
    family limited 9-21
Pell grants 6-14
Penalty tax 4-18
Pension enhancement strategy 11-23
Pension plans 11-8, 19-8
    defined benefit plan 19-10
    defined contribution plan 19-9
    method of dividing plans 19-8
Personal and qualified residence interest
    16-15
Personal exemption 16-8
Personal financial planning 1-3
    concept of 1-3
    five Cs of 1-4
    key areas of 1-3
    process of 2-2
    subject areas of 2-2
Personal records
    organization 5-3
Personal representative 8-10
Personal retirement plans 10-31
Plan
    comprehensive 1-12
    government-sponsored 10-4
    presentation 2-32
Planning
    cash management 3-26, 7-3
    credit and debt 3-26
    educational 3-24

life insurance 4-38
risk management 3-23
savings 3-26
systematic savings 7-11
Planning ideas involving gifts 9-7
Pooled income fund 9-20
Portfolio
income 14-1
management and monetary policy 13-40
manager 1-14
reorganization 14-17
Power of appointment 9-32
Power of appointment trust 9-12
Power of attorney 8-10
Power of diversification 13-27
Practice
best time to sell 21-34
sale of 21-34
valuation of 21-35
Preferred Provider Organizations (PPOs)
5-5, 5-17
Preferred stock 12-6
convertible 12-6
participating 12-6
Premature distributions 11-13
Preparing the family 9-43
Prepayment strategy 16-4
Present value
annuity 3-15
annuity due 3-17
fixed sum 3-7
of perpetuity 3-17
of uneven payment series 3-18
Preventive measures
loss control through 5-3
Private annuity 9-36, 9-42
Private foundation 9-46
Private long-term care coverage 5-30
alzheimer's coverage 5-31
custodial care coverage 5-30
deductible period 5-30
guaranteed renewability 5-30
home care 5-31
inflation protection 5-31
pre-hospitalization 5-31
Private mortgage insurance 5-42
Probate 8-12, 9-38
Process of sale 21-35
Processing financial data 1-11, 2-29

analyzing client information 2-31
data refinement 2-30
establish client objectives 2-30
preliminary analysis 2-29
Professional liability insurance 5-57
Professional portfolio management 12-9
Professionals 16-24
Profit sharing plan 10-21, 11-8
age-weighted 10-26
Property damage liability 5-50
Property valuations and settlement 19-2
Protection of credit history 7-26
Public relations 21-9
Public speaking 21-10
Publicly Traded Partnerships (PTPs) 16-8
Purpose of a trust 8-18

Q

QTIP trust 9-13
Qualified Personal Residence Trust 9-33
Qualified plans
direct rollovers 10-28
distribution from 11-8
distribution rules 10-28
mandatory withholding rules 10-28
Qualified tuition programs 15-19
Qualifying potential client 2-3
Qualitative data 2-29
Quantitative data 2-28

R

R-squared 13-12
Rate of return
internal 3-21
Ratings of insurance companies 4-35
rating agencies 4-36
role of guaranteed funds 4-35
Real Estate Investment Trusts (REITs)
12-29
Real estate investments 14-16
Real estate losses 16-5
Recapitalization 9-35
Reciprocal will 8-7
Recommendations for action 1-11, 2-32
basic recommendations 2-32
plan presentation 2-32

Redemption fees 12-12
Reduction of college debts 6-18
   financial aid 6-18
   lower tuition rate 6-19
   teaching position 6-19
   tuition at freshman rate 6-18
Referrals 21-12
Regulatory and social environment 21-5
Renewable term 4-10
Rental expense 16-6
Repayment of student loans 6-17
   consolidation 6-18
   deferment 6-17
   forbearance 6-18
   graduated payment 6-18
Replacement cost 5-41
Required distributions 11-9
   minimum distribution rules 11-9
      defined benefit plans 11-10
      defined contribution plans 11-10
      distributions to beneficiaries 11-10
Retirement
   benefits, Social Security 10-7
   early 11-25
   estimate 11-5
   withdrawals and loans from qualified
      plans 11-25
Retirement budget 11-3
   retirement expenditure analysis 11-3
   retirement income 11-3
Retirement distribution choices 11-21
Retirement income
   needs analysis 11-3
   planning for 10-3
Retirement planning
   concepts and strategies 11-1
   defined benefit plans 11-10
   defined contribution plans 11-10
   distribution from qualified plans 11-8
   distributions to beneficiaries 11-10
   loans from qualified plans 11-22
   pension plans 11-8
   profit sharing plans 11-8
   strategies 11-22
Retirement plans
   401(k) plan 10-22
   corporate 10-9
   defined benefit 10-23
   defined contribution 10-15

Individual Retirement Account (IRA)
   10-31
   qualified plans and key features 10-32
   Roth IRA 10-34
   Social Security 10-4
   target benefit 10-29
   tax-sheltered annuity 10-30
Return on Savings 7-18
Revenue bonds 12-4
Revocable living trust 9-38
Rights 12-6
Risk
   avoidance 4-2
   callability 13-4
   default 13-3
   equity 13-9
   maturity 13-3
   reduction 4-3
   retention 4-3
   sharing 4-3
   tolerance guidelines 13-34
   tolerance level 14-8
   transfer 4-3
   versus return 14-8
Rollovers
   direct 10-28
Roth IRA 10-34
Rule of 72 3-5
Runmoney, Foliofn, etc. 12-31

S

S Corporation strategy 16-20
S Corporations 15-32, 16-25
Sale
   process of 21-35
Sale of practice 21-34
Sale/Gift leaseback 9-35
Saving for college cost 6-4
Saving in child's name 6-4
Savings
   bonds for education 6-11
   for college 6-4
   safety in 7-17
   self-rewarding plan for 7-16
Savings accounts 12-1
Savings and loan associations 7-24
Savings media selection criteria for 7-17

Savings planning
   tax considerations 7-21
Savings strategies 7-16
Savings-first approach 7-16
Scope of the target market 21-4
Second home 16-19
Second-to-die insurance 9-42
Section 2503 (c) minor's trust 6-13
Section 303 stock redemption 9-36
Section 419 plan 4-51
Section 529 plans 6-7
   vs. UGMA/UTMA 6-8
Securities and Exchange Commission
   (SEC) 2-7
Security 1-4, 2-3
Select sector SPDRs 12-33
Selection of a trustee 8-18
Self-funded employee health benefits 5-18
Self-rewarding plan 7-16
Seminars 21-13
Series EE bonds 12-3
Series HH bonds 12-3
Series I bonds 12-3
Seven-pay test 4-18
Sharpe ratio 13-14
Shopping
   for insurance 5-2
   for term policies 4-11
Short sellings 12-31
Signing formal contract 2-6
Similarities among widows 20-3
Simple interest 3-1
Simple retirement plan 10-20
Simple will 8-7
Simplicity and minimum balance require-
   ments 7-21
Simplified employee pension plan 10-21
Single-premium whole life 4-17
Social Security 10-4
   Act of 1935 10-4
   benefits for spouse and children 10-6
   benefits of 5-12, 11-22, 16-19
   disability benefits 10-8
   eligibility issue 10-5
   income estimate 10-9
   medicare 10-8
   taxation of benefits 10-8
   taxes 11-25
   types of benefits 10-6

Sole proprietors 16-24
Sources of consumer credit 7-24
   auto dealers 7-25
   commercial banks 7-24
   consumer finance companies 7-24
   credit unions 7-24
   life insurance companies 7-24
   savings and loan associations 7-24
SPDRs (SPY) 12-33
Special areas of concern 20-10
Special insurance 5-42
   crime insurance 5-42
   flood and earthquake insurance 5-42
   replacement cost 5-42
Special service features 7-21
Special spousal benefit 11-26
Special use valuation 9-36
Specialty/sector funds 12-10
Speculative stocks 12-8
Split-dollar arrangement 9-28
Split-dollar life insurance 4-53
split-dollar regulations
   new 4-65
Splitting business income 16-19
Sprinkling trusts 9-24
Standard & poor's 12-19
Standard & poor's depositary receipts
   12-23
Standard deviation 13-12
Standby or convertible trust 9-40
State income tax 16-14
State inheritance tax 8-26
Stepped-up basis rules 9-41
Stock
   buying a 13-15
   common 12-7
   preferred 12-6
   selling a 13-16
   types of 12-7
      blue chips 12-7
      non-blue chip 12-7
Stock bonus plan 10-22
Stock risk
   limiting the 13-17
Stocks
   types of
      cyclical company 12-7
      defensive 12-7
      growth company 12-7

income 12-8
   speculative 12-8
Straddle, strip, strap and strangle 12-31
Strategy of covered calls 13-20
streetTRACKS 12-34
Student loan interest deduction 15-20
Student loans 6-15
  consolidation 6-18
  deferment 6-17
  forbearance 6-18
  graduated payment 6-18
  repayment of 6-17
Supplemental health insurance 5-8
Surgical insurance 5-5
Survivorship life (second-to-die) policy
   4-24
  accelerated death benefits 4-25
  charity 4-25
  children 4-25
  first-to-die policies 4-24
  irrevocable trust 4-25
  living death benefits 4-26
  second-to-die policies 4-25
Survivorship life insurance 9-42
Survivorship variable life 4-27
Swaps 12-31
Switching insurance policies 4-33
Systematic savings planning 7-11

T

TAMRA of 1988 4-17
  material changes test 4-18
  seven-pay test 4-18
Target benefit plans 10-29
Target Investment Portfolio (TIP)
   14-12, 14-16
Tax
  alternative minimum 15-27, 16-19
  computation 15-21
  federal estate 8-19
  gift 9-7
  gift tax rate 8-27
  state income 16-14
Tax audit 16-26
Tax computation 15-21
Tax considerations
  excess contributions 11-13

insufficient distributions 11-14
  other 11-13
  premature distributions 11-13
Tax credits 15-22
Tax deductions 15-13, 16-2
Tax planning
  concepts and strategies of 16-1
  deductions in 16-2
  deferral 16-10
  deflection in 16-12
  diminution in 16-13
  gifts in 16-13
Tax Relief Reconciliation Act of 2001 6-10
Tax return
  amendment of 16-26
Tax shelters 16-7
Tax treatment of annuity payments 11-17
Tax-deductible interest 16-4
Tax-free social security benefits 16-9
Tax-sheltered annuity 10-30
Tax-Sheltered Annuity (TSA) 10-30
Tax-sheltered investments 14-16
Taxation of corporations 15-31
Taxation of IRAs 11-12
Taxation of keogh plans 11-12
Taxation of life insurance 4-31
  distribution during life 4-32
    exchange 4-33
    interest on policy loans 4-32
    policy dividends 4-32
    policy withdrawals/loans 4-32
    sale or disposition, surrender, matu-
     rity 4-33
  distribution upon death 4-31
Taxation of plan benefits 11-11
  annuity distribution 11-12
  lump sum distribution 11-11
  rollovers 11-12
Taxation of social security benefits 10-8
Taxes
  alternative minimum 15-27
  federal income considerations 9-41
  social security 11-25
Taxes of
  mutual funds 13-24
Technical analysis 13-45
Tenancy by the entirety 8-14
Tenancy in common 8-14
Term insurance 4-7

dividends in 4-7
essential features 4-7
level 4-10
nonparticipating 4-7
participating 4-7
renewable 4-10
types of 4-10
Term insurance features
   convertibility 4-11
   flexibility 4-11
   shopping for term policies 4-11
The 1981 Economic Recovery Tax Act
      (ERTA) 9-2
Theory of efficient portfolio 13-26
Theory of portfolio construction 13-25
Theory of risk transfer 4-2
   risk avoidance 4-2
   risk reduction 4-3
   risk retention 4-3
   risk sharing 4-3
   risk transfer 4-3
Thomson financial 12-19
Thrift plan 10-23
Time value of money 3-1
Treasury bills 7-20, 12-2
Treasury FITRS 12-35
Treasury Inflation Indexed Securities 6-12
Treasury Inflation-Protection Securities
      12-3
Treasury notes and bonds 12-2
Trusts 8-14, 9-10
   asset replacement 9-23
   bypass 9-10
   charitable 9-18
   charitable lead 9-20
   Charitable Remainder Annuity 9-18
   Charitable Remainder Unitrust 9-18
   convertible 9-40
   crummey 9-25
   estate 9-16
   estate taxes and 9-10
   grantor retained annuity 9-29, 9-46
   grantor retained unit 9-29
   irrevocable gift 9-20
   irrevocable life insurance 9-46
   life insurance 9-16
   pooled income fund 9-20
   power of appointment 9-12
   purpose of 8-18

QTIP 9-13
   qualified personal residence 9-33
   revocable living 9-38
   selection of a trustee 8-18
   sprinkling 9-24
   testamentary 8-15
   wealth replacement 9-23
Tuition programs
   qualified 15-19
Tuition vs. savings plan 6-8
Types of credit 7-26
   categories of credit 7-26
      installment purchases or time-
         payment plans 7-28
      revolving and optional charge ac-
         counts 7-28
      thirty-day or regular charge accounts
         7-28
Types of funds 12-9
   aggressive growth 12-9
   asset allocation 12-11
   balanced/equity income 12-10
   fixed income 12-10
   growth 12-10
   growth and income 12-10
   index funds 12-11
   international/global 12-10
   money market 12-11
   specialty/sector 12-10
Types of IRAs 10-36
   individual retirement annuity plan
      10-37
   individual retirement plan 10-36
Types of plans 10-15
   401(k) 10-22
   age-weighted profit sharing 10-26
   defined benefit 10-23
   defined contribution 10-15
   employee stock ownership 10-23
   money purchase pension 10-20
   profit sharing 10-21
   simple retirement 10-20
   simplified employee pension 10-21
   stock bonus 10-22
   target benefit 10-29
   tax-sheltered annuity 10-30
   thrift 10-23
Types of stock 12-7
   blue chips 12-7

cyclical company 12-7
defensive 12-7
growth company 12-7
income 12-8
non-blue chip 12-7
speculative 12-8
Types of stocks
income 12-8
Types of term insurance 4-10
convertible term 4-10
decreasing term 4-10
family income policy 4-11
level term 4-10
renewable term 4-10
variations in renewal and conversion
privileges 4-10

U

UGMA and UTMA 6-4
Umbrella liability insurance 5-56
Uninsured motorists 5-50
Universal life 4-18
Unscheduled personal property 5-40

V

Valuation of practice 21-35
Valuing the business 19-6
Valuing the estate 8-22
Vanguard VIPER shares 12-35
Variable annuity 4-47, 11-17, 12-24
benefits of 12-25
deferred 12-24
drawbacks of 12-25
new features of 12-26
Variable immediate annuity 12-26
Variable installment plan 13-20
Variable life 4-22
Variable life insurance 12-28
Variable universal life 4-22, 12-29
Variations in renewal and conversion
privileges 4-10

W

Warrants 12-6
Wash sales 15-6

Wealth replacement trust 9-23
WHCRA 5-15
Whole life 4-14
single-premium 4-17
Widows
differences among 20-1
educating 20-9
planning for 20-1
similarities among 20-3
special areas of concern of 20-10
winning among clients 20-4
working with 20-5
Will 8-5, 9-37
absence of 8-5
basic structure 8-8
codicil 8-8
drafting of 8-7
durable power of attorney 8-10
guardian for minor children 8-12
holographic 8-8
importance of 8-5
letter of last instructions 8-9
mutual 8-8
personal representative 8-10
power of attorney 8-10
probate 8-12
reciprocal 8-7
simple 8-7
Winning widows among clients 20-4
Work study programs 6-16
Working with widows 20-5

Z

Zero coupon
bonds 12-5
option 6-11